# The
# United States Congress
## Second Edition

# The
# United States
# Congress
## Second Edition

**E. Scott Adler**
UNIVERSITY OF COLORADO–BOULDER

**Jeffery A. Jenkins**
UNIVERSITY OF SOUTHERN CALIFORNIA

**Charles R. Shipan**
UNIVERSITY OF MICHIGAN

**W. W. NORTON & COMPANY**
*Independent Publishers Since 1923*

Copyright © 2021, 2019 by W. W. Norton & Company
All rights reserved
Printed in the United States

Editor: Peter Lesser
Project Editor: Taylere Peterson
Associate Editor: Anna Olcott
Managing Editor, College: Marian Johnson
Managing Editor, College Digital Media: Kim Yi
Production Manager, College: Sean Mintus
Media Editor: Spencer Richardson-Jones
Media Editorial Assistant: Lena Nowak-Laird
Media Project Editor: Marcus Van Harpen
Marketing Manager, Political Science: Ashley Sherwood
Design Director: Rubina Yeh
Designer: Juan Paolo Francisco
Photo Editor: Ted Szczepanski
Director of College Permissions: Megan Schindel
Permissions Assistant: Patricia Wong
Composition: Westchester Publishing Services
Manufacturing: Maple Press

Permission to use copyrighted material is included on page C-1.

ISBN: **978-0-393-42825-4** (pbk.)

W. W. Norton & Company, Inc., 500 Fifth Avenue, New York, NY 10110-0017
wwnorton.com
W. W. Norton & Company Ltd., Castle House, 15 Carlisle Street, London W1D 3BS

1  2  3  4  5  6  7  8  9  0

*For our families:*
*Pam, Anna, and Rose*
*Lisa*
*Kathy, Jeff, and Becca*

*We thank them for their support, love, and encouragement, and for reminding us that as important and interesting as Congress is, there are other things that are far more important and interesting.*

# Brief Contents

# Contents

# 3 Elections

# 4 Representation

# 5 Committees

# 6 Parties

# 7 Policy Making in the House and Senate

# 10 Congress and the Bureaucracy

# 11 Congress and the Courts

# 12  Congress and Interest Groups

# About the Authors

**E. SCOTT ADLER** is Professor of Political Science at the University of Colorado, Boulder. His current research uses theoretical models of legislative organization to examine congressional agenda setting and committee power. He is the author of *Why Congressional Reforms Fail: Reelection and the House Committee System* (University of Chicago Press, 2002), which was awarded the Alan Rosenthal Prize from the Legislative Studies Section of the American Political Science Association, and *Congress and the Politics of Problem* Solving (Cambridge University Press, 2012, co-authored with John Wilkerson). He is also co-editor of *The Macropolitics of Congress* (Princeton University Press, 2006). He has published articles in the *American Journal of Political Science*, *Legislative Studies Quarterly*, and *Urban Affairs Review*. Adler is co-PI of the Congressional Bills Project, which has compiled and coded data on all bills introduced in Congress since World War II. From 2006 to 2007, Adler was a Visiting Professor at the Center for the Study of American Politics and Department of Political Science, Yale University. He received a BA from the University of Michigan in 1988 and a PhD from Columbia University in 1996.

**JEFFERY A. JENKINS** is Provost Professor of Public Policy, Political Science, and Law, Judith & John Bedrosian Chair of Governance and the Public Enterprise, Director of the Bedrosian Center, and Director of the Political Institutions and Political Economy (PIPE) Collaborative at the University of Southern California. He previously held tenure-stream positions at the University of Virginia, Northwestern University, and Michigan State University. His research interests include American political institutions and development (with a special emphasis on Congress and political parties), lawmaking, separation of powers, and political economy. Much of his work takes a positive political theory (or rational choice) approach and examines how political actors pursue their interests while being constrained by formal and informal institutional arrangements. His current work involves papers on the ideological content of federal lawmaking in the postwar era, and book projects on how civil rights policy has been dealt with in Congress over time and how the Republican Party evolved in the South after the Civil War. Jenkins holds a PhD in political science from the University of Illinois at Urbana-Champaign and an MS in mathematical methods for the social sciences from Northwestern University. He has been a postdoctoral fellow at Princeton University and Michigan State University. He currently serves as the Editor-in-Chief of *The Journal of Politics*.

**CHARLES R. SHIPAN** is the J. Ira and Nicki Harris Professor of Social Sciences at the University of Michigan, where he holds appointments in the Department of Political Science and the Ford School of Public Policy. Prior to joining the faculty at Michigan, Shipan served on the faculty at the University of Iowa, and he has also held positions as a research fellow at the Brookings Institution and as a visiting scholar at Trinity College in Dublin, the U.S. Studies Centre at the University of Sydney, the London School of Economics, and Australian National University. He is the author of *Designing Judicial Review*, is the co-author of *Deliberate Discretion?*, and has written numerous articles and book chapters on political institutions and public policy. He is conducting research on presidential discretion over policymaking, congressional delegation to the courts and the bureaucracy, the effects of bipartisanship on public policy, and why bad policies are more likely to spread than good policies. Shipan received a BA in chemistry from Carleton College and an MA and PhD in political science from Stanford University.

# Preface

Congress is *always* in the news. Not a day goes by without the House, the Senate, or individual members of Congress, doing something—taking action (or not), making statements, holding hearings—that attracts the attention of both traditional and social media. The focus of this attention might be the attempt (and failure) to address thorny issues related to immigration. It might be about responding to the coronavirus pandemic and providing relief for people who are out of work. Or perhaps it might be the insurrection that occurred in January 2021, when supporters of then-President Donald Trump stormed the Capitol and threatened the health and safety of our representatives and senators. It might be about changing tax or health policy. Or perhaps it might be reactions to the latest tweets from President Trump on issues like tariffs, Russian interference in the 2016 election, or the latest appointments to the federal courts. For close observers of politics, there is never a dull moment on Capitol Hill.

The three of us would characterize ourselves as close observers of politics. But although we avidly consume the latest news and social media reports about Congress, we do so from a particular perspective. Yes, we read newspapers and online magazines, listen to podcasts, and follow politicians and journalists on Twitter—but our focus goes well beyond these activities. We have also devoted our careers to conducting and publishing research about this central institution of American government. It is the combination of these two perspectives—observing what is happening in Congress, while also engaging in and producing new analyses of Congress—that led us to realize that the time is ripe for a fresh look at the "first branch" of American national government. Why does Congress so often fail to pass new policies? Why does it sometimes succeed? Why are there endless internal squabbles and machinations between Democrats and Republicans on Capitol Hill? How should we understand the role of parties and congressional committees? Why does Congress sometimes seek to rein in the other branches, but at other times defer to them? What role do elections and interest groups have on the internal operations and output of Congress?

These are questions that we regularly think about, ones that we have studied in our own research. But more than that, they are also the sorts of questions that we regularly get from students. We constantly touch on these issues when we teach our own courses. Yet existing books on Congress do not consistently approach these questions in a way that we and our students are looking for. It is this gap that led us to write this book.

To be able to answer these important questions, as well as countless others, requires a comprehensive understanding of how Congress works. Some of this understanding can come from knowing the basic functions and institutions of Congress—how members get elected, what parties and committees do, what tools exist for dealing with the other branches, and so on. In this book, we provide this essential information, the nuts and bolts about how the institution works, which serves as a good start for understanding Congress. But it's only a start. We also want students to be critical thinkers, to be able to analytically assess, understand, and evaluate Congress (and politics more generally) for a lifetime.

In our view, for students to acquire this analytical ability they need to gain an appreciation of the rich and exciting research on Congress. This body of research goes well beyond studies that we have conducted ourselves and includes work done by an exceptionally talented and diverse group of scholars. It is this broad set of exciting studies that we engage with, explain in an accessible way, and sometimes critique, throughout this book. Our goal is to use and communicate this research to address a deceptively simple overarching question: How do we know what we know about Congress? That is, while we want to convey facts about Congress, we also want to disseminate to a broad audience the arguments, theories, and evidence that congressional scholars regularly produce. In doing so, we talk about Congress not just in descriptive terms, but in the analytical way that political scientists do.

Of course, the accumulated research on Congress is vast, at times unwieldy, and sometimes internally inconsistent. Thus, to effectively communicate this material, we emphasize three main themes that provide a fundamental underpinning for an evaluation of any particular aspect of Congress: *governing*, *representation*, and *separation of powers*. We save detailed discussions of these themes for the substantive chapters of this book, but here it's worth setting out a brief description of what we mean by each theme.

- *Governing*: Citizens see Congress as the nation's primary institution for democracy and governing. The Framers also saw it that way, which is why the Constitution identifies Congress as the first branch of government. Much of the recent hand-wringing regarding gridlock and lack of legislative productivity is predicated on the notion that the House and Senate should be more effective in their governing responsibilities. Governing is, in large part, lawmaking, but also includes bureaucratic oversight, influencing public opinion, and establishing policy priorities as an agenda for the nation. Governing in Congress requires collective decision making and a certain level of cooperation. Throughout this book, we examine the aspects of congressional organization, bicameral structure, and the electoral system that both help and hinder collective choice.

- *Representation*: Governing is predicated on the notion of representation, which is the fundamental link between lawmakers and their constituents. But representation is not merely a bilateral relationship between voters and their member of Congress. There are many constituencies that lawmakers must respond to—stakeholders within their districts or states, such as businesses and organized groups; ideological and policy-interested groups outside their districts or states; potential reelection supporters; party leaders; the president; and more. For members of Congress, having to satisfy multiple constituencies often makes collective action and collective choice a challenge. Put simply, representation and governing can sometimes be at odds.

- *Separation of powers*: Although Congress is the first branch of the federal government, it is not the only branch. Lawmakers on Capitol Hill must negotiate the broader institutional labyrinth created by the Framers—including the president, the bureaucracy, and the courts, and their shifting powers over time. How do shifts in these relationships alter the strategies of individual lawmakers and the collective activities of the legislative body? Governing further entails interaction outside these branches. Most notably, bureaucrats and interest groups have multiple venues for access to the governing process, which can add to the difficulty of passing laws and influencing policy.

These three themes, which appear in nearly every chapter in this book, help both to organize our approach to any particular topic and to provide continuity across topics.

Again, in exploring these themes and in covering the topics found in each chapter, we go well beyond description and examples—although we freely acknowledge their importance—and present an explicitly *political science* view of Congress, one that involves asking questions, developing theories, creating arguments, collecting data, and assessing evidence. Too often, there is a gulf between how Congress is taught, or presented, in textbooks, and how political scientists analyze it. We aim to bridge this gulf. We do this in part by including, in each chapter, a section called **How We Study**, which delves deeply into a specific course of study and explains how it has added to our knowledge of Congress. But more generally, this approach of focusing on, and introducing students to, political science underpins every page of this text.

Our unique approach allows us to provide students with the current state of knowledge on standard topics, such as congressional elections or the relationship between Congress and interest groups. But it also allows us to delve more deeply into topics that scholars have devoted increased attention to in recent years, such as legislative effectiveness, policy making, and the relationship between Congress and government agencies. In addition, we stress that in order to understand the House and Senate now, we have to understand how they operated in the past. We do this in part through a chapter that focuses on congressional development. But we also include in each chapter a specific section called **Then and Now**, which takes a key aspect of that chapter—for example, how the filibuster has been used in the Senate—and examines how that congressional activity, process, or structure has changed over time.

In all of this, we strive for balance. In part, this means that we balance description and examples with analysis and presentations of research. It also means that we balance a focus on the current Congress with a focus on the past, and that we balance discussions of our three themes. But it also means that we strive for balance in our overall assessment of Congress. Finding aspects of Congress to criticize is not difficult—and we don't shy away from such criticisms. At the same time, there are things the institution does well, and we note these too. Furthermore, sometimes when Congress is criticized along one of the dimensions that we explore—say, governing—it is because that aspect of its job has come into conflict with another, like representation. This is not to excuse failures; rather, it is to indicate, and to appreciate, why they might occur.

Ultimately, we hope this book will pique the interest of students to further pursue questions regarding Congress, representation, or even governing in general. Perhaps even better, it could serve as a useful resource for the next generation of scholars, practitioners, and voters. We know that many factors affect whether students become interested in politics. Sometimes that interest eventually translates into going to graduate school and making the study of politics a vocation or pursuing a career in the world of politics or policy making, or simply being a politically informed citizen. We believe our book—which combines facts and social science—will serve as a good introduction to both the world of congressional politics and the important insights gained from the academic study of Congress.

At this point, one task remains for us in this preface—acknowledging the enormous and invaluable help we received during the writing of this book. In part, this book is the product of the many conversations and interactions the three of us have had over the years. But more than that, it is a product of the more general scholarly conversation that we have been fortunate to be part of over the years—a conversation that has taken place with the generous community of scholars who study Congress. This conversation has occurred at conferences, at research presentations, through journals and reading each other's papers, via email and social media, and—most recently, and most directly, for this book—through the exceptionally insightful set of reviews that an outstanding set of scholars provided on each chapter in this book. These reviews improved the manuscript in countless ways—correcting errors, providing new insights, alerting us to studies we had neglected or hadn't known about, suggesting different emphases, and often filling holes we didn't even know existed. In many ways all the scholars (and students) who contributed to this endeavor can lay some claim to this sizable collective effort and achievement. For these and other contributions, we are extremely grateful and offer our thanks to the following reviewers:

Sarah Anderson, University of California Santa Barbara
David Bateman, Cornell University
Jim Battista, SUNY Buffalo
William Bianco, Indiana University
Sarah Binder, George Washington University
Bethany Blackstone, University of North Texas
Barry Burden, University of Wisconsin–Madison
David Canon, University of Wisconsin–Madison
Jamie L. Carson, University of Georgia
Jason Casellas, University of Houston
Jennifer Hayes Clark, University of Houston
Meredith Conroy, California State University, San Bernardino
Michael Crespin, University of Oklahoma
James M. Curry, University of Utah
Charles J. Finocchiaro, University of Oklahoma
Jeremy Gelman, University of Nevada, Reno
Thomas Gray, University of Texas at Dallas
Matthew Green, Catholic University of America
Jeff Grynaviski, Wayne State
Lisa Hager, South Dakota State University
Peter Hanson, Grinnell College
Laurel Harbridge-Yong, Northwestern University
Douglas B. Harris, Loyola University Maryland
Thomas Hayes, University of Connecticut
Rebekah Herrick, Oklahoma State University
Gary E. Hollibaugh Jr., University of Pittsburgh

Jennifer Hopper, Southern Connecticut State University
Jack Johannes, Villanova University
Kristin Kanthak, University of Pittsburgh
Stephanie Dean Kerce, Georgia State University
Jaclyn J. Kettler, Boise State University
Aaron S. King, University of North Carolina at Wilmington
Gregory Koger, University of Miami
Christina Kulich-Vamvakas, Suffolk University
John Lapinski, University of Pennsylvania
Tim LaPira, James Madison University
Jennifer Lawless, American University
Jeffrey Lazarus, Georgia State University
Beth Leech, Rutgers University
Jason MacDonald, West Virginia University
Bryan Marshall, Miami University
Robert McGrath, George Mason University
Natasha Altema McNeely, University of Texas, Rio Grande Valley
Scott Meinke, Bucknell University
Thessalia Merivaki, Mississippi State University
Kenneth W. Moffett, Southern Illinois University Edwardsville
Nathan Monroe, University of California, Merced
Timothy Nokken, Texas Tech University
Sarah Oliver, Towson University
Ian Ostrander, Michigan State University
Hong Min Park, University of Wisconsin-Milwaukee
Jeffrey Peake, Clemson University
Kathryn Pearson, University of Minnesota
Justin Peck, Wesleyan University
Brittany N. Perry, Texas A&M University
Daniel Ponder, Drury University
Eleanor Powell, University of Wisconsin–Madison
Molly Reynolds, The Brookings Institution
Josh Ryan, Utah State University
Lisa M. Sanchez, University of Arizona
Eleanor L. Schiff, Bucknell University
Emily Schilling, University of Tennessee, Knoxville
Scot Schraufnagel, Northern Illinois University
Joel Sievert, Texas Tech University
Gisela Sin, University of Illinois, Urbana-Champaign
Peverill Squire, University of Missouri
Andrew J. Taylor, North Carolina State

Richard Waterman, University of Kentucky
Gregory Wawro, Columbia University
Alan Wiseman, Vanderbilt University
Jennifer Victor, George Mason University
José D. Villalobos, University of Texas at El Paso

In addition to these reviewers, we are also deeply appreciative to the following scholars, who provided a helpful mixture of suggestions, insights, and data: Leticia Arroyo Abad, Dan Auble, Mike Bailey, Michael Berry, Alex Bolton, Jamie Carson, Jeff Cohen, Lee Drutman, Matthew Eshbaugh-Soha, Mike Fix, Dan Franklin, Sara Hagedorn, Peter Hanson, Jennifer Lawless, Josh Kennedy, Christina Kinane, Gregory Koger, Barbara Koremenos, Tim LaPira, Kenny Lowande, Jason MacDonald, Bryan Marshall, Alyx Mark, Noel Maurer, Rob McGrath, Nolan McCarty, Anthony Madonna, Scott Meinke, Ian Ostrander, Max Palmer, Dan Ponder, Andy Rudalevige, Josh Ryan, Judy Schneider, Geoffrey Skelley, Sean Theriault, and Mike Zilis. And we are particularly grateful for the useful feedback we received on early drafts of chapters from students in the following classes on Congress: Scott Minkoff's class at SUNY New Paltz, Adam Cayton's class at the University of West Florida, and Tim Nokken's class at Texas Tech University.

We benefited from outstanding research assistance and feedback from a number of students, including Adam Cayton, Jared Cory, Ryan Dawkins, Stefani Langehennig, Ben Lempert, Eugenia Quintanilla, Sinead Redmond, Rebecca Shipan, and James Strickland. We also thank the Hoover Institution, which provided several weeks over the years for collaborative work on Stanford University's beautiful campus.

Finally, we have been fortunate to work with an incredible team at Norton, starting with Peter Lesser, whom we thank for his excellent insights, positive attitude, general encouragement, and—not least—his amazing patience (accompanied, when necessary, by subtle—or not-so-subtle—nudges). The book is also much better due to the careful and cheerful editorial efforts of Anna Olcott and Samantha Held. Our project editor Taylere Peterson went above and beyond to ensure the high quality of the book, and production manager Sean Mintus kept us on schedule. We thank media editor Spencer Richardson-Jones and media editorial assistant Lena Nowak-Laird for coordinating the media components, and media project editor Marcus Van Harpen for all his hard work on the ebook.

E. Scott Adler
Jeffery A. Jenkins
Charles R. Shipan

# The
# United States
# Congress
## Second Edition

# 1

# Representation and Governing in a Separated System

In 2020, the United States faced its greatest national crisis since the Second World War. The crisis began in December 2019, when a virus that the World Health Organization declared a "public health emergency of international concern" suddenly appeared in Wuhan, China. COVID-19, a severe acute respiratory syndrome coronavirus, quickly spread beyond China's borders and reached the United States in January 2020. By the end of March 2020, COVID-19 was in all 50 U.S. states and had officially been declared a pandemic. By mid-May, nearly all states had adopted "shelter in place" orders, over 1.5 million COVID-19 cases were reported nationally, and more than 90,000 Americans had died as a result of the virus.

As political leaders in the United States—including President Donald Trump, Treasury Secretary Steven Mnuchin, numerous federal agency heads, and all 50 state governors—scrambled to react to the health and economic havoc the virus had wreaked, the U.S. Congress played a central role in organizing a national response to the crisis. In early March, Congress passed a law to provide $8.3 billion in emergency funding for federal agencies to respond to the COVID-19 outbreak, including funds to support the development of a vaccine and to provide loans to

**★ FAMILIES FIRST ★**

In March of 2020, Congress passed the CARES Act to provide economic relief to families and businesses across the nation. Here, Speaker of the House Nancy Pelosi is joined by House Minority Leader Kevin McCarthy (R-Calif., left) and House Majority Leader Steny Hoyer (D-Md., right).

small businesses. Two weeks later, Congress passed a second law guaranteeing free COVID-19 testing, establishing paid leave from employment, enhancing unemployment insurance, and expanding Medicaid funding. Toward the end of March, Congress passed the Coronavirus Aid, Relief, and Economic Security (CARES) Act, which provided $2 trillion in COVID-19 relief. The CARES Act included a stimulus payment of $1,200 to every American making $75,000 or less, added $600 a week to unemployment benefits for four months, provided $100 billion to hospitals and health care providers, and authorized $500 billion in loans for small business, states, and municipalities. Finally, at the end of April, Congress provided an additional $484 billion for small business loans and $75 billion for hospitals.

This set of bills that Congress passed was the federal government's main initial response to the pandemic. (Congress then passed an additional $900 billion in relief in late December 2020, after some CARES Act programs had expired.) But the passage of these laws also provides a window into how Congress works. Most simply, the laws demonstrate that—counter to popular perceptions—Congress can rise to a challenge and act. Congress may show signs of dysfunction, as we will see throughout this book, but it also continues to pass major legislation.

A closer look at how Congress passed these laws reveals other important insights. Although members of both parties came together to enact this legislation, there was partisan conflict along the way, with the Democratic majority in the House and the Republican majority in the Senate butting heads on how the legislation should be structured. Democrats routinely sought more cash payments to individuals—some wanted payments to be monthly and in larger amounts—while Republicans focused more on providing aid to businesses. Democrats also sought to include economic aid to state governments, while Republicans balked. Senate Majority Leader Mitch McConnell (R-Ky.) even suggested that states facing severe financial difficulties should simply declare bankruptcy.

Congress also drafted the crisis legislation within a broader political environment where many leaders and institutions were taking action. In March, the Federal Reserve lowered target interest rates significantly—the largest emergency rate cut since the 2008 global financial crisis—in an attempt to counteract COVID-19's effect on the American economy. President Trump directed the Department of Housing and Urban Development (HUD) to suspend foreclosures and evictions until the end of April. He also ordered the Federal Emergency Management Agency (FEMA) to build emergency medical stations containing thousands of beds in New York, California, and Washington. Perhaps most importantly, Treasury Secretary Mnuchin—at President Trump's request—worked to settle disagreements between the Democratic House and the Republican Senate by negotiating the structure of legislation with key congressional leaders, including Speaker of the House Nancy Pelosi (D-Calif.) and Senate Minority Leader Chuck Schumer (D-N.Y.). In other words, Congress acted, but it didn't act alone. Instead, it was responsive to the actions and wishes of other institutional actors, especially the executive branch.

The laws that Congress passed in response to the pandemic illustrate another key feature of how Congress operates: the role of procedures in shaping the outcomes of legislation. Rather than sending these bills to congressional committees with expertise in, say, the workings of small businesses or the financial system, Congress centralized the writing of these bills in the offices of party leaders. And instead of going through standard procedures for appropriating money, Congress treated several laws as "supplemental appropriations." Arguably, both of these procedures—letting congressional leaders write the laws, and treating them as supplemental appropriations—were necessary, if Congress was to respond rapidly. Yet these decisions meant that most members of Congress played little role in designing the laws, and the amount of funding was not tied to the congressional budget process and the amount of money that Congress decides to spend each year through that process.

The CARES Act thus illustrates a range of important aspects of Congress. When Congress passes laws, it is executing its governing function, but members of Congress never completely agree on what these laws should contain. Instead different members push for different benefits to be included—as we saw with Republican support for business and Democratic support for payments to individuals, especially those who earn lower incomes. And ultimately, Congress does not act alone. Instead, it acts within a separation-of-powers system. For the CARES Act, it was in close communication with the executive branch; in other policy areas it also interacts with the courts.

In this chapter and throughout this book, we explore each of these topics. As with any in-depth social-scientific analysis, knowing the historical context and using the best available information and most advanced analytical techniques available to assess Congress's performance are critical to a proper understanding of this complex and fascinating lawmaking body. We start by examining the core democratic principles that define Congress, all of which we highlighted in Congress's response to the COVID-19 outbreak: representation, separation of powers, and governing.

## CONGRESS AND THE CORE DEMOCRATIC PRINCIPLES: REPRESENTATION, SEPARATION OF POWERS, AND GOVERNING

The primary imperative of Congress—the goal that it must achieve collectively as an institution, as well as the objective of individual lawmakers—is *representing* various constituents within a complicated web of *separated institutional powers* to *govern* the nation. This is the goal the Framers set for themselves after their rebellion against the tyranny of the British Empire; however, they soon discovered that designing such a system would be complicated, controversial, and fraught with pitfalls. Understanding representation, separation of powers, and governing is central to understanding Congress today and throughout history.

### Representation

There is no principle more central to our democracy than **representation**, which is the link between citizens (constituents) and their political agents (lawmakers) they elect to act on their behalf. Representation is critical in any consideration of U.S. politics, and it can take different forms. When thinking about how lawmakers translate what their constituents want into policy actions, we might perceive a representation spectrum. On one end, lawmakers follow their constituents' preferences, faithfully doing what their constituents would want them to do. When lawmakers behave in this way, we say that they act as *delegates*. At the other end of the representation spectrum, lawmakers pursue their constituents' interests but not necessarily their preferences. In some cases, constituents' preferences are not fully formed or even discernible. Thus lawmakers must rely on their own judgment and make independent decisions. When lawmakers behave in this way, we say that they act as *trustees*.[1]

If representation is the link between constituents and lawmakers, what constitutes a constituent? Each member of Congress is elected from a specific geographic unit, either a state or a district. We consider the citizens of those units to be the geographic constituency that members of Congress represent. Yet there are other constituencies to keep in mind. Sometimes, members of Congress focus on particular subgroups within their larger geographic constituency. They might also respond to groups of individuals with shared interests—perhaps racial or religious groups—who may not necessarily reside in their districts or states. And they might sometimes represent the interests of the nation as a whole.

The nature of congressional representation was central to the Framers' debates during the Philadelphia Convention (see Chapter 2). *The Federalist Papers*, a collection of 85 essays written by Alexander Hamilton, James Madison, and John Jay in 1787 and 1788 to persuade the states to support the ratification of the Constitution, reveal the logic of the Constitution's proponents.[2] In *Federalist 10*, Madison makes the case for a large and diverse republic that sends a sizable set of delegates to Congress. He contends that in a republic with varied and often narrow interests, a representative democracy (rather than a direct democracy) is essential, as representatives chosen by the people are likely to be "more consonant of the public good." Within the republic they were creating, Madison writes, Congress was intended "to refine and enlarge the public views, by passing them through the medium of a chosen body of citizens, whose wisdom may best discern the true interest of their country, and whose patriotism and love of justice will be least likely to sacrifice it to temporary or partial considerations."[3] In other words, according to Madison, the interests and voice of the people need to be filtered through and clarified by elected representatives.

Throughout U.S. history, debates about representation emerge again and again. In this book, we investigate the topic of representation from many angles. For example, how do constituents' opinions or interests translate into the actions of those who govern and make laws? In our democracy, elections are the principal way of controlling public officials.[4] But do elections work as intended? That is, do elections—and the threat of being voted out of office—lead members of Congress to better represent their constituents? Once the Seventeenth Amendment allowed citizens to vote directly for senators, did this affect the behavior of senators? What are the challenges and advantages of representing the interests of those who have sometimes been shut out of our political system—people of color, women, and others?

Congress is empowered by the Constitution to create laws that respond to constituents' policy goals. When suffragists fought for the right to vote in the early 1900s, they lobbied Congress to advocate for their enfranchisement.

## Separation of Powers

The consent of the governed motivated the Framers to craft sufficient representation of varied interests. But perhaps equally important were the Framers' fears about the power of an unchecked central authority. After all, the colonies were breaking away from a British monarchy they believed to be tyrannical because of its concentration of power in one person and one office.[5] To avoid this concentration and the subsequent tyranny it might produce, they instead advocated for a system in which power was separated across institutions.

Not surprisingly, the Framers steadfastly incorporated this **separation of powers**, along with its associated system of **checks and balances**, into the Constitution. As the Framers saw it, institutions should have the ability to counteract one another, thereby preventing any one branch of government from becoming too powerful and eventually subsuming the others. Madison writes, "The great security against a gradual concentration of the several powers in the same [branch], consists in giving to those who administer each [branch], the necessary constitutional means, and personal motives, to resist encroachments of the others. . . . Ambition must be made to counteract ambition. The interest of the man must be connected with the constitutional rights of the place."[6]

Congress is at the center of a government where powers are divided and interconnected. The authority to make law is a responsibility shared between Congress and the president, often with validation or input by the courts. Congress and the president also share a responsibility for ensuring the day-to-day operations of a vast government bureaucracy that is charged with carrying out the law. As we explore in Chapter 9, the two branches often exercise their powers of governance in union, but sometimes conflicts emerge.

Another way in which the Framers checked the powers of the different branches was by embedding fundamentally different perspectives and motivations into their designs. Each branch's authority is derived and constituted in a completely different way, with each relying on a different constituency. Members of Congress are beholden primarily to their geographic constituency; presidents usually see the entire nation as their constituency; and federal judges, given that they are not elected, are not directly beholden to any constituency (although they are nominated by the president, approved by the Senate, and depend on Congress and the president for their budgets and structure and to enforce decisions). Different powers and motivations help each branch maintain distance from, and influence over, other branches.

## Governing

When designing the Constitution, the Framers focused much more on Congress than on the executive and judicial branches because they intended to make Congress the linchpin of a new **governing** structure. As such, the section of the Constitution that enumerates the structure and powers of Congress (Article I) is the first, and by far the longest, portion of the Constitution. Among the extensive powers and authority expressly granted to Congress in the Constitution are the responsibilities for taxing and spending, borrowing money and taking on government debt, regulating interstate and foreign commerce, constructing a federal court system, declaring war and supporting a standing military, impeaching and trying presidents, overriding presidential vetoes on legislation, confirming high-level executive and judicial appointments, and ratifying treaties with other nations.

However, it is the Constitution's **necessary and proper clause** (sometimes called the elastic clause) that gives Congress its preeminent governing authority:

> *To make all Laws which shall be necessary and proper for carrying into Execu-*
> *tion the foregoing Powers, and all other Powers vested by this Constitution in*
> *the Government of the United States, or in any Department or Officer thereof.*

Congress's exercise of this power over more than two centuries has helped it to maintain power in the federal policy-making process.

Interestingly, Congress's governing responsibilities are where its representation imperative collides with the powers of the other branches. Congress struggles to govern at times because its members must also respond to district constituents, while the president, with a diverse electorate and a national mandate, is in a better position to define and carry out a policy agenda.

## CONGRESS AND AMERICAN POLITICS THROUGHOUT HISTORY

Throughout American history, power has shifted among the presidency, Congress, and the judiciary. But over time Congress has led most major changes in federal policy. Throughout this book, we discuss the history of Congress and how it informs our analysis and understanding of Congress today.

When we look at congressional history, some key ideas emerge. A central goal of the American Revolution was to create a democratic system with a represen- tative legislature at its core. Decades of rule by the British Crown and a lack of citizen participation in colonial governing led to a groundswell of support for revolution in the early 1770s. Although the first Continental Congress was composed of an unelected group of intellectual and business elites, state conven- tions eventually selected delegates to represent the colonies. It took time and a faltering economy for the post–Revolutionary War Continental Congress (with only state-level representation) to be replaced by a federal Congress with both state-level and population-based representation. Throughout this book, we explain the logic and implications of Congress's organization and representa- tional structure, which has existed now for over 230 years.

Congress has been the principal actor in policy making since the Founding of the United States. Consider, for example, the primary issue of debate during the nation's first century: slavery. In many ways, the structure of Congress specified in the Constitution—a bicameral legislature with different forms of representation (states for the Senate versus congressional districts for the House)—can be attributed to disagreements among the states on the matter of slavery. And only a few years after the Constitution was ratified, Congress acted to foster and per- petuate slavery. First, it reinforced the slave clause of the Constitution with the Fugitive Slave Act of 1793 (guaranteeing the return of an escaped enslaved person to their owner), and then it revised and strengthened that act in 1850. As the country expanded west, Congress extended the reach of slavery via the Missouri Compromise (1820), the Compromise of 1850, and the Kansas–Nebraska Act (1854), which provided for the admission of new slave states into the Union.

Congress's role changed dramatically after the Civil War broke out. First, Congress ended slavery via legislation that would become the Thirteenth Amendment (1865). Then, following the war, Congress worked to build a post-slavery society, first by granting explicit legal rights to formerly enslaved people in the Civil Rights Act of 1866 (enacted over President Andrew Johnson's veto). Later that year, Congress passed legislation that would become the Fourteenth Amendment (ratified in 1868), providing citizenship and equal protection of the laws to all citizens. And through the Reconstruction Acts (1867 and 1868), Congress defined the terms by which southern states would be readmitted to the Union—including the requirement that they ratify the Fourteenth Amendment and adopt new state constitutions granting voting rights to Black men.

We also see Congress at the center of many other federal policy decisions over the course of the nation's history (although, as we will see in the next section and in Chapter 9, Congress has lost much policy-making power to the president). During the Great Depression of the 1930s, the monumental expansion of federal authority in managing the economy and assisting in the lives of struggling Americans was in many respects driven by lawmakers on Capitol Hill.[7] As we saw earlier, Congress passed several major laws in response to the COVID-19 pandemic. And Congress has been at the core of landmark changes to our electoral system through the expansion of constitutional voting rights[8] and improved ballot access,[9] regulation of election administration,[10] and restrictions on candidate and party campaigns.[11] Stated simply, if something important is happening in U.S. political life, Congress is usually deeply involved.

## THIS IS NOT YOUR GRANDPARENTS' CONGRESS

There is a conventional wisdom regarding how Congress works—which is really an idealized version of how it *should* work. In this view, sometimes referred to as the **textbook Congress** and depicted in the wonderful (if corny) Schoolhouse Rock cartoon "I'm Just a Bill," Congress is an orderly, proper organization. That is, it is an institution where lawmakers engage in high-minded debate about key issues of the day, they search for the best policies, and laws are enacted through standardized processes—for example, allowing expert committees to develop policy options that members then openly debate on the floor, all in pursuit of the best outcome.

The Congress of today is notably different from this textbook Congress and from the Congress of a generation or two ago (when it was decidedly more like the textbook ideal). As we saw in the example of the CARES Act, Congress often strays far from standard practices, even when it reaches a successful outcome. More generally, Congress—and its relationship to other political actors—is constantly changing.

Take, for example, the separation of powers between Congress and the executive branch. The foundational idea is that Congress legislates policy that the executive branch then carries out. In reality, Congress over time has relinquished significant power and influence to the office of the president. Some of this has occurred deliberately; as the nation's political economy expanded greatly over the centuries, Congress has needed to offload some governing authority to the executive branch. In addition, Congress has often ceded responsibility to the executive branch during times of crisis, such as during the aftermath of the 9/11 attacks. But Congress's recent inability to perform some of its most basic duties—enacting budgets, reauthorizing expiring federal programs and agencies, and ensuring that the Treasury may continue to borrow money to keep the government solvent—has further transferred power away from Congress and toward the president.

For example, the president's Office of Management and Budget and even federal departments themselves (such as the Department of Agriculture and the State Department) set the spending agenda when they request funding, often with minimal input from congressional leaders and committees. Moreover, dysfunction on Capitol Hill has accelerated congressional staff turnover and decreased institutional memory of how programs are reauthorized. This gives the White House the upper hand in policy negotiations and passing the government's yearly budget. Congressional dysfunction and how it alters the balance of power will be a topic to which we return throughout this book.

The story of today's Congress is also the story of extraordinary partisanship. Indeed, even when there is broad agreement that Congress needs to act, such as in response to the COVID-19 pandemic, the two parties might push for very different sorts of policy solutions. Throughout congressional history, parties have influenced our core democratic principles. In terms of representation, parties provide a way for voters to understand where politicians stand on particular issues and support those politicians' campaigns. Parties also focus candidates' efforts during elections. In a separation-of-powers system, parties often coordinate goals across branches and act as a mechanism for negotiating and bargaining. With respect to governing, parties define agendas, organize the process of lawmaking on Capitol Hill, and assemble the majorities necessary for congressional action.

Yet parties' roles in Congress have evolved in recent years to fundamentally redefine lawmaking and lawmakers. Both in Congress and in public, parties are now more polarized than at any other point in the modern era. Partisanship has become more tribal as support for partisan teams has often outweighed commitments to values and ideology. For example, when Congress enacted a sweeping overhaul of tax policy at the end of 2017, the measure was passed without a single Democratic lawmaker in either chamber supporting it.[12] In contrast, the

Gridlock over a second bill to expand funding for unemployment insurance, state and local governments, COVID-19 testing, and stimulus checks exemplified the dysfunction of the contemporary
Congress. Democrats like then-Senate Minority Leader Chuck Schumer, pictured here holding a sign
indicating when COVID-19 benefits would end without further relief, blamed Senate Republicans for
the delay in passing the bill, and Republicans blamed Democrats for being unwilling to compromise.

last major tax reform, which took place during the Reagan presidency in 1986,
was the result of bipartisan negotiations and passed with the support of Republican and Democratic majorities.

## HOW DO WE KNOW WHAT WE KNOW ABOUT CONGRESS?

As the academic discipline of political science emerged in the late nineteenth
and early twentieth centuries, it focused mainly on Congress—the primary governing and representative institution in the United States. Over time, political
science research has produced countless insights about Congress, the policy-
making process, and American politics more generally. For example, as we will
explain throughout this book, studies have examined how members of Congress
interact with and represent their constituents. They have shown how and when
Congress is able to change policy, along with the role that committees and
parties play in the policy-making process. They have examined the racist and
misogynist barriers that have prevented people of color and women from

participating fully in the political process, and then how congressional actions and outcomes shifted as more (if still not a proportional number of) legislators came from these groups. They have explored the conditions under which Congress can (or cannot) influence the courts, the president, and government agencies, as well as the extent to which interest groups influence Congress. And they have shown how reelection motivates legislators, explaining how members vote (on mundane issues like roads or controversial issues like the impeachments and conviction trials of President Trump), when and why they vote with other members of their party, and even the institutional structure of Congress itself.

We will address these and a wide range of other notable questions of politics throughout this book. But the findings of these studies are the outcomes of research processes that should be considered in detail. In our view, to appreciate the insights that generations of congressional scholars have produced, and to think critically about those insights, we must understand how scholars approach their work. Rather than taking the knowledge generated by congressional scholars as a matter of fact, we believe it is important to examine how these experts came to know what they know.

Woodrow Wilson was one of the first political scientists to systematically analyze Congress. Before becoming president of the United States (or even president of Princeton University), Wilson wrote his PhD dissertation on the importance of Congress in a separation-of-powers system and the need to reconsider its institutional advantages. That study, titled *Congressional Government* (published in 1885),[13] remains one of the most widely cited books on Congress today.

As the social sciences began to embrace data, the earliest applications of statistical techniques to the study of politics were quantitative analyses of congressional roll call votes.[14] One particularly influential study, conducted by sociologist Stuart Rice in 1924, created a way to measure *voting bloc unity* (that is, which members tend to vote with which other members in Congress). Contemporary scholars continue to use Rice's measure in a wide variety of legislative studies.[15] In the 1950s, as the field of political science expanded, studies of public opinion and voting behavior became the fastest-growing areas of political science research.

Also in the 1950s, the groundbreaking American National Election Study—still the leading survey of political opinion today—began gathering a wealth of data from presidential and congressional races. Beginning in the early 1960s, scholars interested in understanding representation matched data on voters' opinions with policy activities, specifically congressional roll call votes.[16] Around the same time, scholars began studying Congress members' attitudes on the functioning of the institution and potential reforms in Congress itself.[17] Today the field of public opinion research is massive, and understanding how opinions translate into action is now ubiquitous in nearly every aspect of modern society, from commerce to politics.

In the 1950s and 1960s, scholars interested in studying the factors influencing election outcomes gravitated to congressional races because they offered an enormous number of cases (435 House races and 33 or more Senate races every two-year election cycle) to test the effects of constituency conditions, lawmaker behavior, and incumbency.[18] They collected massive amounts of data at the congressional district level over numerous decades and across a wide variety of conditions. A parallel line of research that began around the same time focuses on the role that parties play in organizing lawmakers and directing the work of Congress.[19]

The mid-twentieth century also saw the creation of game theory, which explores the incentives of, and strategic interactions between, individuals. Not surprisingly, the study of Congress was fertile ground for its development. In the mid-1950s, scholars seeking insights into the notion of power—a critical concept in the study of politics—based their conclusions on the process of voting in the U.S. Senate.[20] Eventually, as students of Congress grew increasingly interested in the importance of institutions—or how rules, structures, and processes affect political outcomes—they began to apply game theory and other related theories (including spatial voting theory, which holds that members of Congress can be arrayed ideologically on a line from left to right) to examine the committee system and the role that parties play in legislative politics.[21]

To test these theoretical concepts, researchers needed to estimate lawmakers' ideological positions. Congress, with its thousands of roll call votes, was an ideal venue. The preferences of every member could be derived from how they voted, which meant that researchers could situate each lawmaker's ideology relative to the ideology of every other lawmaker.[22] The techniques developed for estimating ideology in Congress eventually extended to other political venues where voting occurs, such as the courts, state legislatures, and foreign lawmaking assemblies.[23]

Not all research advances have come from statistical studies of large congressional data sets. In the 1950s and 1960s, political science began introducing sociological and anthropological techniques, broadening its methodology to examine politics by using in-depth case studies and participant observation. Congress was one of the many venues used for this kind of qualitative research. In the mid-1950s the American Political Science Association (APSA) began placing scholars, called congressional fellows, in the offices of Congress members to work as regular staff. Researchers were thus able to observe lawmakers first-hand, which led to the collection of novel data and the creation of hundreds of unique studies from an insider's perspective.[24] An extraordinary amount of the research cited in this book was produced by scholars who early in their careers served as congressional fellows.[25] Perhaps the most gifted observer of the behavior of Congress members, Richard Fenno followed lawmakers around their districts and constructed what is still considered the most important study of representatives' interactions with constituents.[26]

In groundbreaking work beginning in the 1960s, political scientist Richard Fenno (left) followed lawmakers in and out of Washington to study how they interact with, and represent, constituents. Here, Fenno is pictured with Representative Barber Conable (R-N.Y.).

Not long after developing the congressional fellowship, APSA sponsored the Study of Congress Project, which produced many detailed case studies illuminating aspects of congressional organization and operations, ranging from party leadership to the culture of specific House and Senate committees.[27] Many of the scholars who had spent so much time observing on the Hill became key players in the congressional reform movements of the 1970s and 1990s.[28]

In recent years emerging data and information now available on the Internet have opened up new avenues of research. These new data hold the potential to answer long-standing questions in new ways and address questions never before considered. Detailed coding of roll call votes has allowed us to investigate how much congressional behavior is truly ideological and how much is simply parties staking out positions on policies and organizing their members as teams.[29] Innovations in computational social science and text analysis have led to pathbreaking studies of lawmaker press releases that reveal differing styles of representation.[30] Scholars have used the plethora of data about lawmaker behavior, such as cosponsorship of bills or membership on internal policy caucuses, to examine how members of Congress form networks and how the existence of these networks influences lawmaking.[31] Similarly, by combining advanced statistical techniques with extensive data on congressional campaign contributions, scholars have mapped the ideological positions of incumbents and challengers for congressional seats.[32] And researchers have also begun to draw conclusions from the mass of information available through new online activities. For example, members of Congress reinforce polarizing viewpoints by sharing ideologically divisive news on their social media feeds.[33]

Each year, dozens of books by political journalists and historians recount the travails of lawmaking on Capitol Hill. Add to these books the nightly reflections—and the noise generated by nightly shouting matches about politics and policy from some pundits on cable news—and you have a media landscape filled with opinion, prediction, and partisan rancor. What is usually missing from this landscape are analyses and insights gleaned from sustained social scientific inquiry. Knowing how the political scientists cited in this book do their work can help us better understand their findings and cut through the exaggerated political noise in the United States today.[34]

Furthermore, in order to effect change—whether in the form of a new policy, better representation of women and people of color, more congressional control over the policy-making efforts of other branches, or greater participation in elections—one must first have a systematic and deep understanding of how that particular aspect of politics works. Only with that understanding, which comes from the research studies we cover, can one begin to know how to appropriately pursue change.

The scholars cited in this book identify critical questions. They then pose hypotheses to guide their research into these questions. With hypotheses in hand, scholars then consider the best ways to measure causes and effects. Testing these hypotheses can take years and involve extensive data collection and sophisticated analysis. And while there is often debate about the best way to conduct a study, the insights are often unique and can be meaningful for understanding both how Congress works and what change is possible. We build on these scholarly works to explain the politics on Capitol Hill and beyond.

## THE PLAN OF THIS BOOK

What should you expect from this book? First and foremost, each chapter centers on what we believe to be the most important topics in studying Congress: how members of Congress run their campaigns and get elected, what committees do, the nature of the interactions between the president and

Congress, interest groups' ability to influence the lawmaking process, and whether individual lawmakers and Congress as a whole are effective. In each chapter, three overarching themes guide our exploration of Congress.

First, the core democratic principles of *representation, separation of powers,* and *governing* serve as each chapter's point of departure. These principles are the backbone of American democracy. When Congress does not meet its responsibilities with regard to these core democratic principles, there is cause for concern.

Each chapter in this book is therefore structured around explaining aspects of one or more of these principles. For example, when we study parties in Congress, we describe how parties facilitate the representation process, how parties facilitate (or hinder) cooperation and oversight between the branches of government, and how parties articulate a governing agenda for lawmakers and the public. When we study congressional committees, we explore how these panels of policy specialists oversee executive branch agencies and formulate laws. As you read, the core principles of representation, separation of powers, and governing will help you organize and make connections between key concepts.

One caveat is that each chapter does not necessarily focus on all of the core principles in the same depth. For example, when we study the interactions between Congress and the president, we are by definition focusing on separation of powers and governing. Although representation plays a part in the priorities and actions of lawmakers and the president, it takes a back seat to the other two democratic principles.

Second, throughout this book, we place today's Congress, which seems so different from conventional views of Congress, in its historical context. Accordingly, in each chapter, we offer a section titled "Then and Now." These sections explore how Congress has changed over the course of years, decades, or even centuries. Sometimes, these changes have occurred quickly. Sometimes, they are slow-moving transformations that are perceptible only with many years of hindsight. Our goal in underscoring the evolution of Congress is to understand why Congress has changed and what that means for Congress today and in the future.

Third, to be fully conversant in the actions and accomplishments of the contemporary Congress, it is not enough merely to know the facts about the institution. It is also important, as we discussed, to understand how political scientists know what they know. Each chapter thus includes a "How We Study" section that delves into a specific question relevant to the subject of that chapter, how social scientists approach that question, and the resources and tools they use to search for answers. We hope these sections will help you develop a deep understanding of cutting-edge research and the newest and most important findings by congressional scholars.

Let's begin.

# 2

# The Historical Development of Congress

Congress is significantly polarized by party. Democrats and Republicans in Congress rarely see eye to eye on important policy matters and regularly disagree about the right direction for the country. Partisanship has also affected how Congress relates to the other two branches of the federal system. For example, a Republican House spent four years investigating whether Democratic president Barack Obama's State Department, led by Hillary Clinton, was responsible for security lapses surrounding the terrorist attack on the U.S. Consulate in Benghazi, Libya, in 2012. Yet the Republican House and Senate in 2017 were slow to investigate charges of Russian tampering in the 2016 U.S. presidential election and that country's ties to Republican president Donald Trump and members of his administration. Moreover, filling vacancies on the Supreme Court has emerged as one of the most partisan issues of the twenty-first century. In early 2016, the Republican Senate refused to consider Obama's choice of Merrick Garland to replace deceased (Republican-appointed) Antonin Scalia. The following year, however, the Republican Senate seated Trump's nominee, Neil Gorsuch, changing the Senate rules prohibiting a filibuster on Supreme Court nominees to do so. And in late September 2020, President Trump nominated Amy Coney

SOUTHERN CHIVALRY — ARGUMENT versus CLUB'S.

Congressional partisan politics are not unique to the modern era. Several years before the start of the Civil War, animosity between the parties turned violent when proslavery Democrat Preston Brooks (S.C.) attacked antislavery Republican Charles Sumner (Mass.) on the floor of the Senate.

Barrett to replace Ruth Bader Ginsburg, who died earlier that month. Despite being so close to the November elections and the GOP's previous claim that a Supreme Court vacancy so late in the election cycle shouldn't be filled before citizens went to the polls, Republican Majority Leader Mitch McConnell pushed the nomination through the Senate in late October, and Barrett was seated.

While these events underscore how Congress today is deeply divided by party, it would be wrong to characterize contemporary American politics as unique. American politics at other points in history has been similarly polarized, and Congress has seen its share of heated (and sometimes overheated) partisanship. Prior to the Civil War, members of Congress, deeply divided over slavery, often carried pistols into the chamber in anticipation of personal challenges. And in 1857, violence erupted when Democratic representative Preston Brooks (S.C.) beat Republican senator Charles Sumner (Mass.) nearly to death on the Senate floor over a speech that Sumner made sharply criticizing slaveowners, including Brooks's cousin, Democratic senator Andrew Butler (S.C.). These divisions became insurmountable three years later. After Republican Abraham Lincoln was elected president, Democrats from the Deep South resigned from Congress after their states—which were unwilling to be governed by an antislavery president—seceded from the United States.

In addition, changing chamber rules to achieve partisan ends has been a strategy of party leaders in Congress across time. Toward the end of the nineteenth century, for example, House Speaker Thomas Reed (R-Maine) believed "the best system is to have one party govern and the other party watch," and he used strong-arm tactics to ensure that his Republican majority would get their way. Reed reinterpreted House rules to limit the rights of Democrats, after which the Republicans steamrolled them on a number of policy issues. The Democrats cried foul over Reed's tactics but could do nothing about it. And when the Democrats regained the majority, they adopted the same strategies that Reed had used.

Thus, if we are to understand contemporary politics in Congress, we must understand the past. This is true for two reasons. First, it is common for commentators to believe that what happens in Congress today is unprecedented. Often it is not. To properly evaluate the distinctiveness of contemporary congressional action requires a long view and a detailed understanding of congressional history. Second, the contemporary Congress and how it relates to the executive and the judiciary has changed over time. While Congress was designed to be the nation's leading institution, and operated as such for much of our history, its relative position has declined in recent years as the executive and judiciary have grown in prominence and power. The contemporary Congress also reflects changes in the social and political fabric of the United States—changes that affect whom members represent and how they are elected. Studying the contemporary Congress without a solid understanding of how the institution has developed over time runs the risk of misinterpreting contemporary actions and events.

## CONSTITUTIONAL FOUNDATIONS

In the fall of 1774, leaders from the thirteen American colonies gathered in Philadelphia to discuss and coordinate their resistance to rule by the British Crown. Their primary point of contention was that the colonies had been governed by a foreign monarch (King George III) without any direct representation of the people being governed.

In what became known as the first Continental Congress, these colonial leaders—unelected members of the intellectual and business elite—devised a plan for boycotting British products and resisting the king's decrees. These plans also created what would develop into statewide conventions acting in place of the colonial assemblies that the British had disbanded. Eventually, those conventions selected delegates to the second Continental Congress, also in Philadelphia, in the spring of 1775. That legislative body, now with a full-on insurrection to manage, created more formal governing bodies in the colonies, constructed a coordinated military, and raised funds to finance the war effort.

The members of the second Congress would sign the Declaration of Independence in 1776 and draft the Articles of Confederation. In contrast to the governing authority that existed in most other places in the Western world, the Articles sanctioned a legislative body composed of representatives of the various states assembled into a confederation. The Congress created under the Articles was the sole instrument of a national government; however, after the colonists emerged victorious from the Revolutionary War, the new confederation government faced massive public debt, a struggling economy, and widespread discontent with its performance. The congressional institutions under the Articles proved too weak to allow for effective governing: all important decisions required supermajorities, laws passed by Congress were not binding on the states, and limited rules of procedure meant that legislating was nearly impossible.[1]

Consequently, 55 delegates from the 13 states met again in Philadelphia in 1787 to consider an initial revision of the Articles.[2] While the delegates had no mandate to redraft the governing document for the new nation, after much deliberation, this is exactly what they decided to do. Organizing themselves into a Constitutional Convention, the delegates all agreed that the national government needed to be strengthened and that Congress needed stronger internal institutions. But there were disagreements between delegates from large (more populous) and small (less populous) states about how representation in the new national legislature would be designed. Delegates from the large states wanted representation to be based exclusively on population, while delegates from the small states desired equal representation for each state regardless of population. Ultimately, they reached a compromise wherein they would split the difference: Congress would be bicameral, with representation in the lower chamber (the House of Representatives) based on population and in the upper chamber (the Senate) based on equality. Members of the House would be elected directly by the people, while members of the Senate would be chosen by state legislatures.

In drafting what would become the U.S. Constitution, the delegates—often called the Framers—established a federal system in which the national government would be supreme over state governments. And while they saw the need for both a national executive and a national judiciary, the Framers also clearly established the national legislature as the most important institution within the new federal system. Even so, to protect against the possibility of majority tyranny, they separated institutional powers and created checks and balances among the three branches. The Congress was the chief lawmaker, with the power to lay and collect taxes, to borrow and coin money, and to regulate commerce (Article I, Section 8). The president was given the power to veto acts of Congress (Article I, Section 7), which Congress could override by a two-thirds vote in each chamber. The president and Senate would share authority on treaty making, ambassador appointments, cabinet-level executive appointments, and judicial appointments (Article II, Section 2). The courts, by comparison, were woefully underdeveloped: only a Supreme Court was specified (Article III, Section 1), and no power of "judicial review"—the ability to declare a law unconstitutional—was created. Only later, in *Marbury v. Madison* (1803), did Chief Justice John Marshall "discover" judicial review.

Thus within this new constitutional order, the Framers clearly considered Congress to be supreme. The president was a significantly weaker number two, and the Supreme Court was a distant third. This was the constellation of forces when the first federal Congress assembled in the spring of 1789.

## THE ANTEBELLUM ERA (1789–1861)

The years from the constitutional founding through the Civil War mark the first period of U.S. congressional history. Congress, at this time, was the preeminent power in the federal government. The nation's political-economic growth and development during these decades was accomplished largely, but not exclusively, by congressional statute. Congress as an institution changed considerably during this time from a body that was built on norms and temporary structures to one that was guided by rules and where permanent structures conducted business.[3]

Political parties in Congress also emerged during this time, created by ambitious politicians to help expedite governing, and three different party systems spanned the era. Partisans in Congress routinely battled over the federal government's role in the economy, with Federalists, and later Whigs, advocating for a more active federal government to help develop the nation and Jeffersonian Republicans supporting a weaker federal government that would leave more decision-making power to the states. In time, an issue that both parties sought to keep off the legislative agenda emerged to threaten the continued existence of the new nation: slavery. Congressional deals postponed the inevitable for several decades, but eventually slavery tore the nation apart.

### The Early Years

On March 4, 1789, the first federal Congress convened. Over the next four decades, Congress would develop into the foundation for the institution we see today. In its earliest years, Congress was not overly complex. The number of representatives and senators was relatively small, decisions were deliberative, and political parties were nonexistent. The House was considered the unruly body, while the Senate was viewed as the more high-minded and dispassionate body.

Very quickly, however, congressional leaders realized that discussing and debating each bill or issue as a body (or a "committee of the whole") was extremely time consuming. Leaders in both the House and Senate quickly moved to create committees to handle legislative business. For much of Congress's first 30 years, "select" committees dominated. These committees were temporary, often created to perform a single task, such as drafting a piece of legislation, and expired at the end of a Congress's two-year cycle. By the mid-1810s, "standing" committees became common. Standing committees were permanent bodies that existed beyond a given Congress. Their permanent nature would allow them to serve as repositories of information and expertise, both of which (congressional leaders learned) were important for policy making. By the late 1820s, standing committees dominated both chambers.

Parties in Congress also emerged quickly. In the first Congress, legislative activities were organized around leading figures in the new nation: Alexander Hamilton, Thomas Jefferson, and James Madison. Despite possessing a majority in Congress, Hamilton's proponents, who sought a strong national government, often found themselves stymied on the floor by Jefferson and Madison's supporters, who preferred stronger states' rights. The core problem was that Hamilton's followers struggled to stick together on key votes, while Jefferson and Madison's followers were able to raise issues strategically to split the Hamiltonian coalition.

As a result, Hamilton and his lieutenants began to develop the institutional machinery that would constitute the nation's first political parties: informal whip systems to share information, informal caucuses to communicate the importance of remaining unified on major issues, and informal floor leader positions to align member behavior during congressional proceedings and votes. Stated differently, a bond of partisanship was created, whereby members were educated on how they would be better off in the long run if they coordinated their actions and voted together. Soon thereafter, Hamilton's proponents began winning consistently on key policy votes and thereby became a formidable legislative coalition. Jefferson and Madison's forces responded to the Hamiltonians' newfound governing success by adopting the same institutional techniques.[4]

By the mid-1790s, an institutional party system was in full swing, and parties became the means by which Congress governed. Hamilton's proponents began calling themselves Federalists, while Jefferson and Madison's followers referred to themselves as Jeffersonian Republicans. The two parties reflected different groups in society and had different visions for the nation's future. The Federalists, based in the Northeast, were more elitist and represented financial and commercial interests, while the Jeffersonian Republicans, based in the South, were the party of the common people and represented agrarian and worker interests. This period in which Federalists and Jeffersonian Republicans vied for political control would be known as the first party system. For the first decade of the new nation, the Federalists were the majority party in Congress. With Thomas Jefferson's election as president in 1800, the Jeffersonians took control of Congress, and the Federalists were relegated to a permanent minority.

This era also saw the emergence of the first strong Speaker of the House of Representatives, Henry Clay of Kentucky. Before Clay, Speakers hesitated to use the authority of the office in a strict partisan or individualistic way and often demurred to the wishes of strong presidents (such as Thomas Jefferson) on matters of policy. Clay made the speakership a partisan office and showcased its independence by creating new standing committees, granting new rights to committees, and strategically allocating committee assignments. For example, Clay created a new set of "oversight" committees to monitor expenditures in the executive Departments of State, Treasury, and War, thus elevating the position of Congress (especially the House) in the constitutional order.[5]

## The Second Party System and Slavery

From the 1830s through the mid-1850s, a new party system operated in Congress and in the nation: the second party system, in which Whigs faced off against Democrats on the national stage. The Whigs replaced the Federalists and were similar philosophically. They were the big-government party of the time and sought to use the power of the federal government in an activist way. To help develop the nation's economy, they proposed protecting the country's infant industries through a high tariff, linking population centers and markets through the federal funding of internal improvements (such as national roads and canals), and providing financial stability for the nation by creating a national bank. The Democrats, as the descendants of the Jeffersonians, were the small-government party. They preferred lower tariffs to help expedite trade and the sale of agricultural products overseas, internal improvements to be the exclusive jurisdiction of the states, and banking to be decentralized and thus locally controlled. The Democrats were led by President Andrew Jackson from Tennessee and his successor, Martin Van Buren, from New York, while the Whigs were led by (now Senator) Henry Clay, former president and now Representative John Quincy Adams (Mass.), and Senator Daniel Webster (Mass.).

Suffrage rights broadened considerably during this era, as wealth and property restrictions were largely erased. This made participatory democracy considerably less elite. Unlike during the first party system, when the Federalists and Jeffersonians were mostly institutional parties (or "parties in Congress"), both the Democrats and Whigs had mass followings, with extensive connections at the state and local levels. Finally, the Democrats and Whigs were both interregional parties, with wings in both the North (the free states) and the South (the slave states).

To maintain interregional harmony, leaders in both parties sought to focus political conflict on issues that divided them from each other—tariff rates, internal improvements, banking—rather than on issues that divided along regional lines. However, a regional issue—slavery—was always bubbling under the surface and threatening to tear both parties apart.[6] By the time of the second party system, slavery was governed by the Missouri Compromise (1820). This law admitted Missouri into the Union as a slave state, admitted Maine into the Union as a free state, and established Missouri's southern border as the dividing line for slavery rights (prohibited above the line, allowed below) in the remainder of the western territory acquired via the Louisiana Purchase (1803). The Missouri Compromise, and subsequent statehood decisions, established a rough parity in free versus slave states. This provided southern (slave) states with an implicit policy veto in the Senate: as long as southern senators controlled half the seats in the chamber, they could join together to block any proposals that might attempt to restrict slavery.

By the early 1840s, southerners looked west for more land to populate and extend slavery.[7] Led by Democratic president James Polk, the Democratic majority in Congress—over the objections of the Whigs—sought to annex the Independent Republic of Texas, which Mexico still considered part of its nation. As a result, Mexico and the United States went to war. And after several years of hostilities, the United States extracted huge tracts of Mexican land by treaty: California and the territory that would become New Mexico, Arizona, Utah, Nevada, and parts of other states. Eventually, Congress adopted a series of laws to decide the slavery status of these newly acquired western territories. Known together as the Compromise of 1850, these laws established the right of "popular sovereignty," allowing the people of the territories to decide for themselves whether slavery would be allowed or prohibited.

The Compromise of 1850 would put significant pressure on the interregional dynamics of the two parties. Slavery had become a lightning rod in mass politics, and pro- and antislavery forces fought to extend or abolish slavery in the West. Members of Congress were often torn between following their parties—and establishing a coherent governing strategy—and representing the wishes of their constituents back home. Most members eventually voted with their region (free or slave) rather than with their party, but Democratic leaders were able to convince enough northern Democrats to support the Compromise of 1850 to get the deal done.

Four years later, proslavery forces continued their search for new land. This time, congressional Democrats sought to undo the basis of the Missouri Compromise by making the free territory within the remaining Louisiana Purchase land open to slavery via popular sovereignty. Once again, Democratic leaders coerced a small number of northern Democrats in the House to support the deal (known as the Kansas-Nebraska Act), while the Whigs were split perfectly by region (northerners against, southerners for). While the Democrats would be hurt (in the North) by their support of slavery extension, the Whigs would not survive at all. Slavery had exposed the Whigs as too fractured to be a viable governing coalition. As a result, the Whigs' national organization collapsed, and northern and southern party members sought new partisan homes.

## The Rise of the Republicans and the Third Party System

As the Whig Party collapsed, a new major party emerged to take its place. The growth of antislavery popular politics in the North, helped along by the Democrats' continued push to extend slavery, eventually led members of various antislavery parties and groups (such as the Liberty Party, the Free Soil Party, and the Northern Whigs) to combine their efforts under one banner.[8] This new party—the Republican Party—was a wholly northern party, organized explicitly around antislavery principles.[9] The Republicans achieved their first major victory in the House speakership election of 1855–56, when antislavery candidate Nathaniel Banks of Massachusetts was elected after two months and 133 ballots. In 1857, in the *Dred Scott* case, the Supreme Court ruled that slavery was a constitutional right that Congress could not legislate, which created an uproar in the North and helped the Republican Party grow. The following year, the Democrats suffered their first slavery-extension defeat, when their attempts to convert the Kansas Territory into a proslavery state failed. Finally, in 1860, Republican Abraham Lincoln of Illinois was elected to the presidency.

Lincoln's election was too much for the proslavery forces, and 11 southern states seceded from the Union and formed their own government: the Confederate States of America.[10] Yet Lincoln and the Republicans tried to reunify the country before it was too late. In early 1861, both the House and Senate, now controlled by the Republicans, passed (by the necessary two-thirds vote required to change the Constitution) legislation for a proposed Thirteenth Amendment that would have preserved slavery rights for all time in states where it already existed. Lincoln supported this proposed amendment after he ascended to the presidency later that year.[11] The amendment was never ratified, however, and the southern states were determined to strike out on their own.[12] President Lincoln was equally determined to keep the Union together. As a result, the American Civil War began.

# THE CIVIL WAR THROUGH THE EARLY 1930s

The years spanning 1861 (the beginning of the Civil War) and 1932 (the election of President Franklin Delano Roosevelt) represent the middle period of congressional history. During this time, great changes occurred throughout the country. After a bloody Civil War, the United States needed to rebuild, and a period of Reconstruction ensued. New citizenship and voting rights were granted to the formerly enslaved people, and the southern states, which had seceded, were formally brought back into the Union. At the same time, the nation was industrializing at a rapid pace, which created a host of new political and economic issues involving the regulation of business and the rights and obligations of citizens in the new, modern economy. By the early years of the twentieth century, the United States was well on its way to becoming a world power, and governmental infrastructure began expanding to meet those needs. At the heart of all these changes was Congress.

## The Civil War

During the Civil War, Congress often found itself in a secondary role to the president in matters of governance. As discussed earlier, despite clear subservience to Congress, the president occasionally played a meaningful role in national policy making. Sometimes, this occurred via direct presidential action, as when Thomas Jefferson purchased the Louisiana Territory from France in 1803. But often, this occurred because of congressional deference to the occupant of the White House (as during the Jefferson, Jackson, and Polk presidencies). But once the southern states had seceded and war was declared to keep the Union together, the president—Abraham Lincoln—as commander in chief took center stage. At the same time, Congress, led by Republican majorities in both chambers, was determined to remain relevant.[13]

Much of Lincoln's authority stemmed from pressing political realities. Because the Civil War began when Congress was not in session, Lincoln was forced to make a series of important policy decisions by executive decree. For example, after the Confederates captured Fort Sumter (off the coast of Charleston, South Carolina) in April 1861, Lincoln immediately called up 75,000 volunteers to quell the rebellion and declared martial law between Washington, D.C., and Philadelphia. In July 1861, Lincoln called Congress into an emergency session, wherein lawmakers ratified his executive actions as war powers necessary to preserve the Union. Congress then produced a revenue act to finance the war effort and a conscription act—the first draft in American history—to build an army.

Thus early in the war, the president was the guiding force in national policy making, with Congress occupying a secondary role. Yet Republican majorities in the House and Senate were not content to relinquish all power to the president. They oversaw Lincoln's handling of the war effort by creating the Joint Committee on the Conduct of the War. Made up of strongly antislavery Republicans (who became known as Radicals) from both chambers of Congress, the Joint Committee investigated all aspects of major battles and frequently second-guessed military strategy.[14]

During the war, congressional Republicans continued to pursue their prime policy goal: eliminating slavery. In the first year of the war, the Republican-led Congress set the course for abolition by passing two confiscation laws (freeing enslaved people via the seizure of Confederate "property") and a compensated emancipation law specific to the District of Columbia, which partially compensated slaveowners for releasing enslaved people. These congressional acts helped establish abolition as the ultimate goal of the Union war effort and set the groundwork for Lincoln's Emancipation Proclamation (issued in September 1862, to take effect on January 1, 1863), which freed all enslaved people in Confederate territory. Congress then moved to abolish slavery entirely via legislation that would become the **Thirteenth Amendment**, which was passed and ratified in 1865.

## Reconstruction and Its Aftermath

In time, the Union emerged victorious from the Civil War, and national political leaders turned their attention to the next major challenge: North–South reconciliation. Thanks to war demands and commander-in-chief responsibilities, the presidency had risen in the nation's constitutional order; whether such an activist presidency would carry over into peacetime was the question. The early postwar years would provide the answer, as the president and Congress clashed over how the conquered Confederate South should be "reconstructed" and reintegrated into the Union. In the end, Congress established complete control over Reconstruction policy, reversing early presidential efforts and overturning subsequent presidential vetoes. This early postwar period was Congress's high-water mark in terms of authority in the nineteenth-century constitutional order and returned the presidency to its relatively weak position of the prewar era (where it would remain until the early twentieth century).

Shortly before the war ended, John Wilkes Booth, a Confederate sympathizer, assassinated Lincoln. Vice President Andrew Johnson, a former "War Democrat" from Tennessee, ascended to the presidency. Johnson's plan for reuniting North and South was amicable (and likely would have mirrored Lincoln's plan): if the states that had seceded were prepared to pledge their allegiance to the United States and recognize the legality of the Thirteenth Amendment, he was prepared to welcome them back. Radical Republicans in Congress had a much different idea, seeking instead a fundamental rebuilding of southern society that would elevate Black men to political equality with Whites and prevent former slaveowners from regaining power.

Johnson and Congress battled over these different visions. Thanks to Johnson's inept leadership and reports that former Confederates were attempting to create new institutions (Black Codes) that would economically subjugate newly freed Black people, the Radical Republicans emerged victorious. With supermajorities in both the House and Senate following the elections of 1866, the Republicans passed legislation that would become the **Fourteenth Amendment** (guaranteeing federal citizenship to formerly enslaved people along with due process and equal protection under the law) and the **Fifteenth Amendment** (prohibiting the use of race, color, or previous condition of servitude as criteria for denying voting rights). And in four Reconstruction Acts, they carved up the South into military zones and established martial law in order to compel southern Whites to accept Black citizenship and voting rights. Moreover, the Radicals directed the military to be proactive in registering African Americans to vote, thereby creating a viable southern wing of the Republican Party.

With this Radical Reconstruction, the Republican-led Congress steamrolled Johnson. All four of the Reconstruction Acts were adopted over a Johnson veto, and several southern states, reconstructed per the Radicals' wishes, were readmitted by overriding Johnson. In all, Johnson issued 21 regular vetoes during his presidency, and the Republican-led Congress overrode 15 of them. Eventually, the Radicals grew tired of Johnson's intransigence and in early 1868 sought to impeach him.[15] In the end, they fell one vote short of the two-thirds vote necessary for conviction in the Senate, and Johnson survived.[16] But he was rendered impotent for the remainder of his term, and the presidency itself was minimized.

Thanks to enfranchisement and aggressive registration efforts, African Americans in the South quickly remade the region. Freedmen voted in large numbers and helped establish strong Republican governments throughout the former Confederate states. Many southern Republican politicians were White, but African Americans were also elected to a substantial number of offices. Between 1870 and 1876, 632 African Americans served in southern state legislatures, 14 in the U.S. House, and two in the U.S. Senate.[17] Thus African American suffrage also led to significant descriptive representation—with African American constituencies electing politicians who "looked like them" and could relate to and understand their experience in a deeper way.

Radical Reconstruction would not last, however. Southern Whites and the Democratic Party worked hard to challenge the new Republican governments, using violence and intimidation to dampen African American voting power. Congress actively investigated such illegal activities, delegating power to the president to protect African Americans and preserve their voting rights. These congressional efforts helped, but White southerners continued to press for White supremacy and northern support for Reconstruction declined amid an economic depression that began in 1874. As a result, Democrats began winning elections and taking back state governments in the South. By 1877, the transition was complete: in exchange for the Democrats conceding the disputed presidential election of 1876 to Republican Rutherford Hayes, Republicans stopped stationing the army at southern polling places. Shortly thereafter, Democrats took over the last three Republican-controlled state governments in the South.[18]

While Reconstruction ended officially in 1877, African American rights did not disappear overnight. Although White southerners continued to use violence and intimidation to suppress African American voting, Republicans had some electoral success in portions of North Carolina, Tennessee, and Virginia. Indeed, from 1877 to 1900, five additional African Americans from the South were elected to the U.S. House. That said, White southern Democrats were ever watchful for a Republican resurgence. So when Republicans in the 51st Congress (1889–91) nearly passed a new Federal Election Law to enforce African American voting rights in the South, the Democrats moved away from violence and intimidation and toward legal remedies. Starting in 1890 in Mississippi, Democrats made statutory and constitutional changes at the state level to disenfranchise African Americans. These changes, which included poll taxes, literacy tests, and residency requirements, became known as Jim Crow laws, and by 1908, all states in the South had adopted some form of them.[19] They did not discriminate explicitly by race—and thus sidestepped the Fifteenth Amendment— but they were extremely effective at eliminating African American participation in the South and, by extension, Republican representation in Congress.[20]

In the end, Jim Crow laws essentially eliminated African American voting in the South for generations, and the region became dominated by the Democratic party for the first half of the twentieth century.[21] As African American voters in the South were disenfranchised, African American members of Congress also disappeared. Republican George H. White (N.C.), who left the House in 1901, would be the last African American member of Congress from the South to serve during this era. An African American would not represent a southern state in Congress again until 1973, when Democrats Barbara Jordan (Tex.) and Andrew Young (Ga.) were seated in the House.

## The Gilded Age and Progressive Era

The half-century spanning 1870 to 1920 saw the end of Reconstruction and the period of White "redemption" in the South. But in other parts of the country, different trends were underway. One was a surge in industrialization and national economic development, which created a period of significant income inequality referred to as the Gilded Age. A second trend was, in many ways, a response to the first: the economic expansion and development of the Gilded Age concentrated wealth in the hands of a few and bred rampant political and economic corruption. As a result, reformers sought social, economic, and political change in the country. This period of changing societal priorities and democratizing political processes is known as the Progressive Era.

With the Civil War over and the institutions of Reconstruction in place, Republicans in Congress turned their attention to economic policy. Republicans, like the Whigs before them, believed the federal government should promote economic development. Thus federal spending on infrastructure—railroads, canals, and rivers and harbors—grew considerably in the 1870s and 1880s. While new federal spending expanded, interest-group lobbying also grew as businesses sought out politicians in Washington to "grease the wheels" for their favored projects.[22] This lobbying bred corruption, both in President Ulysses S. Grant's administration and in Congress.[23]

As the federal government expanded in the national political economy and interest groups emerged (along with opportunities for corruption), congressional career patterns changed as well. As government power and influence began to shift from the states to the federal government, politicians began to adjust their aspirations accordingly. Prior to the Civil War, ambitious politicians normally sought a career in the party rather than in Congress, and politicians moved back and forth among local, state, and federal elective (and appointed) positions. As federal policy making grew and Congress's role in major economic decisions expanded, ambitious politicians began to view Congress as a final destination. By the end of the nineteenth century, a "congressional career" had become the norm for most members of Congress.[24]

Along with the rise of careerism, the electoral process changed in ways that provided members of Congress with more direct control over their political lives. Prior to the 1880s, during the party-ballot era, the two parties created and distributed ballots, which gave them considerable control over the electoral process. Such ballots were often color coded and listed only one party's candidates for each office, which limited voters' choices and revealed their party preferences to all who might be watching (thus incentivizing vote buying and intimidation). In the 1880s, party ballots gave way to state-sponsored (or Australian) ballots, which made voting secret and gave electoral authority to state governments.[25] Voters were now provided with "official" ballots that listed multiple party candidates for each office, and they could split their tickets (by selecting different party candidates for various offices) if they so desired—all without anyone observing their voting choices.

The Australian ballot directly linked House members and their constituents. Voters could now reward or punish individual representatives for their behavior in office. In the party-ballot days, voters were largely restricted to casting votes for an entire party ticket; state-sponsored ballots incentivized House members to respond to their constituents' preferences and find ways to signal their efforts and achievements. As a result, congressional seniority on standing committees increased substantially around the turn of the twentieth century, as members viewed committees as a mechanism to build policy expertise and claim credit for policy achievements.[26]

While the Australian ballot affected elections, an additional reform took hold in the first two decades of the twentieth century that affected nominations: party primaries began to replace party nominating conventions. Primaries allowed citizens to determine directly who would represent the party for elective offices, such as the House of Representatives. This move to direct representation *within* the party had two main effects: (1) it reduced the power of party leaders to screen candidates and influence the substantive direction of the party, and (2) it helped reduce internal party conflict, as factional groups were more likely to accept democratic decisions by the people rather than nondemocratic decisions by a select group of party actors.[27]

At the same time parties were losing power in elections, they were gaining power in Congress. In the 1870s and 1880s, the minority party often used House and Senate rules to prevent the majority party from pursuing its policy agenda. This ended in 1890, when Speaker Thomas Reed (R-Maine) reinterpreted the House rules to limit the power of the minority. Republicans then adopted a series of changes to the House rules—over Democrats' strenuous objections—that codified and enhanced Reed's rulings. These "Reed Rules" allowed the majority party to govern effectively, pushing the minority aside and establishing a two-decade period of strong party government in the House.[28] In the Senate, a Reed-style revolution did not occur, as a single leader did not emerge to promote efficient governing. Instead, a four-person Republican team—known as the Senate Four— was created to mimic the strong party leadership in the House.[29]

Republicans' strong rule in the House and Senate between 1890 and 1910 often promoted the conservative interests of eastern bankers and financial elites, and thus was increasingly challenged by Republicans with more progressive leanings, both in Congress and in the figure of President Theodore Roosevelt.[30] After being stymied for years by Speaker Joe Cannon (Ill.), who followed Reed in governing the House with an iron fist, progressive Republicans in the House joined with Democrats to strip Cannon of most of his power—including the ability to make committee assignments—and shift authority in the chamber away from majority party leadership and toward the standing committees.[31] This shift would typify politics for most of the remaining twentieth century, as **committee government** characterized how power was structured in the House and seniority became the new way of attaining chairs and achieving influence within the committee system.[32]

The revolt against Cannon ushered in a decade of significant progressive changes, some internal to Congress and some resulting from Congress's actions.

A progressive–conservative split in the Republican Party led to progressive Democrat Woodrow Wilson's election to the presidency in 1912. Republican factionalism also carried over into Congress, as narrow Democratic majorities in both chambers rode in on Wilson's coattails. As a result, Democrats in Congress looked to Wilson to create a broad agenda that would allow them to survive and thrive, even if Republicans got their house in order.

Wilson met regularly with House and Senate party leaders and directed their policy efforts. As a result, the Democrats tried to create a binding party caucus on some policy issues during the Wilson years, wherein Democratic lawmakers were formally expected (or bound) to support the party's decisions on the floor.[33] This brief period represents the closest America ever came to a system of parliamentary government. And while this experiment did not work as intended and was abandoned quickly, the Democrat-led Congress enacted a set of progressive reforms during the Wilson years, including a new federal banking system, new antitrust legislation, and the first child labor laws.[34] Moreover, Wilson's role as national policy leader would become (after a brief retrenchment in the 1920s) the standard for presidents thereafter and help define the modern political era.

In the Progressive Era, Congress also addressed major governing and representational issues. The **Sixteenth Amendment** provided for a federal income tax, which gave the federal government a new and important revenue stream and helped eliminate a prime source of governing difficulty in Congress.[35] The **Seventeenth Amendment** democratized the Senate by replacing indirect elections (wherein state legislatures elected senators) with direct elections. Senators, like House members, would now be chosen directly by voters, and would consequently behave more in keeping with a constituency-based electoral connection.[36] The **Nineteenth Amendment** provided voting rights for women, thereby doubling the number of voters in federal elections (although a majority of states had provided women with some voting rights by then, often these were limited to local or school elections). Jeannette Rankin (R-Mont.) was the first woman elected to Congress—as a member of the House—in 1916. Rankin led the House debate on legislation that would become the basis of the Nineteenth Amendment. Finally, the **Twentieth Amendment** adjusted the congressional calendar and resolved some important representational and governing problems that had existed since the nation's founding (more on this below).

## Conservative Revival

By the start of the 1920s, the progressive movement had lost steam. Theodore Roosevelt had died, and the conservative and progressive wings of the Republican Party had begun to cooperate again. As a result, the Republicans were able to dominate elections, and they enjoyed unified control of government for the entire decade. Moreover, the conservative wing of the party called the shots, buoyed by an economic boom across all sectors of the economy.

The last vestiges of progressivism in the Republican Party were effectively eliminated during this time. A number of midwestern Republicans fought against the conservative party leadership in the House, opposing the speakership election of Republican William Gillette (Mass.) in 1923 and backing Progressive Robert La Follette's (Wis.) presidential campaign instead of Republican nominee Calvin Coolidge in 1924. Conservative Republican leaders quickly asserted their authority, however, and punished the progressive defectors. Speaker Nicholas Longworth—Gillette's successor—stripped them of their committee seniority and banished them from the party conference until they pledged their loyalty.[37] These sanctions eventually brought House Republican progressives in line, while Republican progressives in the Senate held out a while longer.[38] The Republican Party would thereafter be a conservative governing authority. Progressivism, which had been part of both parties since the nineteenth century, would exist in a meaningful way in only the Democratic Party going forward.

Two statutory changes affecting Congress's governing and representational roles also occurred during the 1920s. First, in 1921, Congress passed the Budget and Accounting Act, which required the president to submit an annual budget for the entire federal government to Congress. The act also created the Bureau of the Budget, which later became the Office of Management and Budget, to help the president assemble budgetary requests from executive agencies. This act is generally viewed as the starting point for the institutional presidency (or the modern presidency), which possesses independent sources of expertise and information. While individual presidents like Theodore Roosevelt and Woodrow Wilson had wielded influence in the early twentieth century, the 1921 act began empowering the office of the presidency with substantial capacity and authority, which increasingly made it a governing rival to Congress. Second, in 1929, a new Apportionment Act was passed, capping the size of the House of Representatives at 435 members. Prior to that, House size had increased in a near-continuous fashion after every decennial census, threatening the chamber's ability to govern effectively. House size, with one exception, has been permanently capped at 435 ever since.[39] As the U.S. population continues to grow, this "435 cap" means that House members have come to represent more people over time.

While economic prosperity defined most of the Roaring Twenties, a stock market panic and crash in October 1929—driven by excess stock speculation, lax banking and financial regulation, risky corporate mergers, and plummeting consumer confidence—led to personal and corporate bankruptcies and bank failures. The economy sank into a full-scale depression, with double-digit unemployment, housing foreclosures, and additional business collapses. The Herbert Hoover administration and the Republican Congress were slow to respond, and the depression deepened. Eventually, the Republicans lost the House in 1930, and the Democrats, behind the presidential candidacy of Franklin Delano Roosevelt (FDR), swept the 1932 elections and gained unified control of the federal government. The Democrats enjoyed sizable majorities in both the House and Senate— and two years later, supermajorities. FDR and the Democrat-led Congress would have a profound effect on American society, and their New Deal for the American People would usher in a new era in American national governance.

---

## THEN AND NOW
## LAME-DUCK SESSIONS OF CONGRESS

Before 1933, Congress had a timing problem. Article I, Section 4, of the Constitution stipulated that Congress would assemble at least once per year and established the first Monday in December as the date of convening. This led to the adoption of a two-session format, with a first ("long") session extending from December through late spring or early summer and a second ("short") session extending from December through noon on March 4, the official end date of the given Congress.[40]

The December convening decision resulted in an odd institutional arrangement, as the short session of a given Congress met after many states held their elections to the next Congress.[41] As a result, the short session had three different member types: (1) those who had won reelection, (2) those who had lost their reelection or higher-office bids, and (3) those who had decided to retire. The short session thus became known as the **lame-duck session**, because it was populated in part by members who would be exiting the chamber in a few months. These exiting members (or lame ducks) were no longer formally tied to their constituents via an electoral connection, but they still enjoyed all the privileges of reelected members, including the ability to cast roll call votes. This created a clear **agency problem** in representation. That is, without the threat of being voted out of office, lame ducks had no incentive to be accountable to constituents and might decide instead to pursue other interests.[42]

The number of lame ducks in short sessions was often considerable. For example, in the period between 1877 and 1933 (after Reconstruction but before the New Deal era), lame ducks constituted around 30 percent of the House on average. In some Congresses, lame ducks even represented a majority of the chamber. Given the size of this group and the aforementioned agency problem, lame-duck sessions were often unpredictable affairs, frequently characterized by spotty attendance and procedural-delaying tactics used to string business along until the Congress's expiration. A more serious concern was fraud, as lame ducks

**FIGURE 2.1**    Sequence of Congressional Sessions and Elections, Pre– and Post–Twentieth Amendment

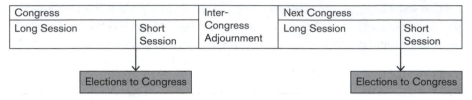

Pre–Twentieth Amendment

| Congress | | Inter-Congress Adjournment | Next Congress | |
|---|---|---|---|---|
| Long Session | Short Session | | Long Session | Short Session |

Elections to Congress                    Elections to Congress

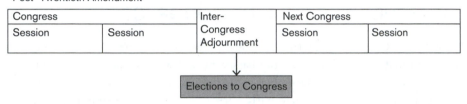

Post–Twentieth Amendment

| Congress | | Inter-Congress Adjournment | Next Congress | |
|---|---|---|---|---|
| Session | Session | | Session | Session |

Elections to Congress

were sometimes accused of selling their votes, most notably to the president in exchange for executive appointments.

In 1922, the issue came to a head with the passage of a controversial ship subsidy bill supported by President Warren Harding and passed with votes from numerous Republican lame ducks—votes that Harding was accused of buying with promises of executive appointments.[43] Angered by these accusations, Senator George W. Norris (R-Neb.), a strong proponent of reform, introduced a resolution to move the starting date of Congress forward and eliminate the lame-duck session. Thanks to growing public support, Norris pushed his resolution through the Senate, but he was blocked by the conservative Republican leadership in the House. Finally, in 1932, on his sixth attempt, Norris succeeded, and his resolution passed in both the Senate and the (now Democrat-controlled) House. Within a year, the Twentieth Amendment was ratified by three-quarters of the states and officially took effect in 1933.

The Twentieth Amendment significantly reconfigured the congressional calendar.[44] Congress would now open in early January, and the lame-duck (short) session would be replaced by a second long session that also convened in January. This meant that elections to the next Congress would take place during the adjournment between Congresses, instead of during the adjournment between sessions of a given Congress (see Figure 2.1). This addressed the agency problem by solidifying the representative-constituency relationship and strengthening electoral accountability, with all members of Congress serving only during periods between elections. Threats of vote buying and low attendance were thereby reduced, increasing the likelihood of good governance.

While the Twentieth Amendment eliminated the regularly occurring lame-duck session, a different kind of lame-duck session was still possible. That is, the Twentieth Amendment did not expressly prevent Congress from reconvening in the time between the November elections and the seating of new members the following January.

This new form of lame-duck session has been held 23 times between 1935 and 2020; these sessions convened sporadically during much of the twentieth century. In the 29 Congresses between the 74th (1935–36) and 102nd (1991–92), only 10 included a lame-duck session. Recently, however, lame-duck sessions have been more regular. In the last 14 Congresses—the 103rd (1993–94) through the 116th (2019–21)—13 have included a lame-duck session. More specifically, each of the last 12 Congresses has included a lame-duck session. In other words, a postelection lame-duck session has become institutionalized.

Lawmakers have convened contemporary lame-duck sessions for a variety of reasons. Three of the first four lame-duck sessions following the Twentieth Amendment met for reasons related to World War II. Others have been held to deal with specific issues that have arisen, such as the censure of Senator Joseph McCarthy (R-Wis.) in the 83rd Congress (1953–55), passage of a new General Agreement on Tariffs and Trade in the 103rd Congress (1993–95), and impeachment proceedings against President Bill Clinton in the 105th Congress (1997–99). Still others have been convened to complete important business that was cut short by external events, such as dealing with President Nixon's domestic agenda in the 91st Congress (1969–71), which was stalled by the Vietnam War, and completing important trade and energy bills in the 93rd Congress (1973–75), which were delayed by the Watergate scandal.

Increasingly, however, party leaders have viewed contemporary lame-duck sessions as a means to provide political cover for fellow partisans. Leaders will delay consideration of some issues (and, more important, votes on those issues) until after the November elections so that their members will not have to take unpopular positions before voters go to the polls. These issues usually involve spending-related legislation, specifically appropriations bills. Other difficult issues have included a gasoline tax (which provoked a lame-duck session filibuster in the 97th Congress, 1981–83), a congressional pay raise, immigration reform, and bankruptcy reform. In recent years, Congress has also used the lame-duck session to create a Department of Homeland Security (107th Congress, 2001–03), bail out General Motors and Chrysler (110th Congress, 2007–09), and approve sweeping criminal justice reform (115th Congress, 2017–19), and adopt a supplementary COVID-19 relief package (116th Congress, 2019–21).

As contemporary lame-duck sessions have become regular events over the past two decades, it is important to remember why the Twentieth Amendment was passed: Senator Norris made a strong case that the agency problem in lame-duck sessions could (and did) lead to representational breakdowns and the passage of policy outcomes that were contrary to the wishes of the people. More generally, Norris and his reform colleagues believed that the very existence of a lame-duck session, with a set of representatives no longer electorally tied to their constituents, was a recipe for governing disaster.

Norris's concerns are valid again today. Are the benefits of a given Congress meeting between the November elections and the January convening of a new Congress worth the costs of policy making with an agency problem in representation? Scholars of Congress and the general citizenry must understand the representational and policy consequences of contemporary lame-duck sessions—and must ask these questions.

### Critical Thinking

1. Why might we be less concerned about an agency problem in lame-duck sessions today relative to the pre–Twentieth Amendment era?
2. If we were to search for evidence that lame ducks are behaving contrary to their constituents' wishes in the modern Congress, where would we look? What data might we collect, and how would we analyze them to determine if problems exist?
3. Why might we think that party leaders in the nineteenth century—either congressional leaders or presidents—had more influence on the behavior of lame ducks than party leaders do today?

## THE NEW DEAL THROUGH THE PRESENT

The years spanning 1933 (the beginning of the New Deal era) through the present represent the third period of congressional history. During this time, the nation—and the federal government's role in it—has changed profoundly. Congress has been a major force in contemporary policy achievements, but the constitutional order has shifted. The executive branch has grown in size and power since FDR's presidency, with the federal bureaucracy playing a greater role in policy decisions and implementation. In addition, an activist Supreme Court emerged in the 1950s and 1960s to usher in new social change. The Court's liberal tendencies shifted in a more conservative direction in the ensuing decades, but its position at the forefront of policy change remained. In recent decades, Congress has become more divided by party and more polarized ideologically, which has hampered its ability to govern, and the executive and judiciary have stepped in to fill the void.

## The New Deal

Once inaugurated, Roosevelt wasted little time in responding to the many problems that the nation faced: more than 12 million people out of work, a 50 percent drop in farm prices, and state banking near collapse. Over his first 100 days in office, FDR worked with the Democrat-controlled 73rd Congress (1933–35) during an emergency session to produce a number of landmark laws that he promised would represent a "New Deal for the American People." This 100-day burst represented a new era in activist federal government, as laws were adopted to stabilize the banking system, alleviate low farm prices, provide relief to needy families, offer jobs to unemployed men in conservation-related projects, and otherwise mitigate the effects of the Great Depression across the country. By the end of FDR's first two years in office, Congress had passed additional legislation to prop up the home mortgage industry, regulate the securities industry, and provide easier farm credit. The work of the 73rd Congress is often referred to as the First New Deal.

The following Congress, the 74th (1935–37), was more ambitious and more liberal in its scope, and its policies came to be known as the Second New Deal. Whereas the First New Deal sought to manage the underlying emergencies of the depression head on, the Second New Deal aimed to create significant social change. FDR believed the depression was caused, in part, by an underlying system of inequality, and he pushed Congress for legislation that would level the playing field. Congress responded with (1) the Social Security Act, which provided a system of old-age and survivors' pensions and unemployment compensation; (2) the National Labor Relations Act, which guaranteed organized labor's right to bargain collectively; and (3) the Revenue Act, which increased surtax, estate, and progressive tax rates on high-earning Americans. The 75th Congress (1937–39) continued with legislation in this same vein, passing the Federal Food, Drug, and Cosmetic Act, which required accurate labeling of ingredients and proof in advertising in the areas of food, drugs, and cosmetics, and the Federal Fair Labor Standards Act, which provided a federal minimum wage and maximum workday and prohibited child labor.

The 75th Congress also saw conflict between the branches of government, as FDR grew frustrated with a Supreme Court that declared portions of his New Deal agenda unconstitutional. FDR proposed packing the Court with as many as six new Supreme Court justices, a move opposed by southern Democrats and Republicans in Congress. FDR responded by lobbying the country (via radio-based fireside chats) in an attempt to move public opinion toward his position. Ultimately, Congress refused to produce the legislation necessary to increase the size of the Supreme Court, but the justices—perhaps concerned that their power would diminish if they didn't support the president more consistently—became more accepting of various New Deal programs. While this achieved Roosevelt's initial goal of protecting and furthering the New Deal agenda, the Court-packing overreach helped create a conservative coalition in Congress composed of southern Democrats and Republicans that would prevent further liberal policy initiatives, especially those in the area of labor policy. The conservative coalition would be an impediment to liberal policies in Congress for the next several decades, as the seniority system in Congress often provided southern Democrats with powerful committee chairs, which they used to block legislation that might liberalize civil rights policy.

In the following Congress, the 76th (1939–41), a new law—the Administrative Reorganization Act—would significantly change the nation's constitutional order. In adopting the act, which FDR strongly supported, Congress provided the president with the ability to hire additional senior staff and reorganize the executive branch (including federal agencies and the federal bureaucracy) for efficiency reasons. FDR used this authority to create the Executive Office of the President, which included a variety of important support staff that expanded greatly over time. Overall, the Administrative Reorganization Act—building on the earlier Budget and Accounting Act—helped expand the institutional presidency and formed the basis of an increasingly powerful, better staffed, and more efficient executive branch that could compete with, and often rival, Congress in national policy making.

## World War II and Its Aftermath

In early December 1941, the United States entered World War II. Over the next several years, Congress passed a number of laws to support the war effort.[45] Among them were the First and Second War Powers Acts, which provided the president with additional power to organize the executive branch to effectively manage commander-in-chief duties.

By the end of the war, the presidency had become a powerful force in domestic and international politics. But once peace was at hand, Congress quickly sought to rein in the executive branch and reorganize and strengthen its own institutions. In the 79th Congress (1945–47), the Democratic majority enacted the Administrative Procedure Act, which created and codified standards for executive agency behaviors and operations and provided for judicial review of agency decisions. They also passed the Legislative Reorganization Act of 1946, which streamlined the committee systems in the House and Senate and strengthened professional staff and information services.

The following Congress, the 80th (1947–49), was the first Republican-controlled Congress since the late 1920s, and Republicans continued (with the help of southern Democrats) to rein in the executive branch. They also tried to undo

THE GALLOPING SNAIL

The Great Depression inspired President Roosevelt to push the often slow-moving Congress to enact sweeping domestic policy legislation. This era saw a dramatic increase in the power of the executive branch at the expense of Congress.

some aspects of the New Deal. The **Twenty-Second Amendment** limited the number of times an individual can be elected president to two, thereby preventing another FDR from emerging (he was elected four times). The Presidential Succession Act established the Speaker of the House and the president pro tempore of the Senate as the next two individuals in line for the presidency after the vice president. Finally, the Taft-Hartley Act weakened the national position of organized labor by allowing states to pass laws preventing unions from requiring employee membership and prohibiting unions from contributing to political campaigns.

## Civil Rights and the Great Society

The 1950s were mostly a period of divided government, and compared to the New Deal era, domestic legislative achievements were modest. The Federal-Aid Highway Act of 1956, which helped construct the modern interstate system, was the most lasting and important enactment. But change was coming on another policy front: in 1954, the Supreme Court ruled in *Brown v. Board of Education of Topeka* that public school facilities segregated by race were inherently unequal and thus unconstitutional (overturning the 1896 *Plessy v. Ferguson* ruling). This was a major victory for the civil rights movement, and it paved the way toward eliminating Jim Crow–based segregation in the South. It also put pressure on Congress to produce new civil rights legislation. In 1957, Republicans, seeing potential electoral gains among African American voters in the North, joined with northern Democrats to push through a new Civil Rights Act, the first of its kind since 1875. While it was mostly symbolic—creating a new Commission on Civil Rights, placing a Civil Rights Division in the Justice Department, and giving the attorney general injunction power in the face of state-level voting-rights abuses—the new act set the stage for further, and more substantive, action.

The 1960s saw a new liberal moment in American society. All branches of government—the presidency, led by John F. Kennedy and Lyndon B. Johnson (LBJ); the Supreme Court under Chief Justice Earl Warren; and Congress— would work both separately and together to craft liberal policy. In Congress, where the liberal wing of the Democratic Party grew substantially after the 1958 midterm elections, the chief battleground was civil rights. In 1960, Congress adopted a new Civil Rights Act that slightly strengthened the voting-rights provisions in the 1957 act. The Kennedy administration and liberal Democratic leaders in Congress then began work on creating a more landmark set of civil rights policies. Their first success was the **Twenty-Fourth Amendment** (passed in 1962 and ratified in 1964), which eliminated the poll tax, a chief means of disenfranchisement in southern elections. Kennedy's assassination in 1963 left LBJ to continue to press for civil rights. Backed by large numbers of northern Democrats and assisted by a substantial group of Republicans, he threw his full weight behind the next set of congressional achievements: (1) the **Civil Rights Act of 1964**, which outlawed discrimination based on race, color, religion, sex, or national origin and prohibited unequal application of voter registration requirements, and (2) the **Voting Rights Act of 1965**, which eliminated any further deterrents to voting, including literacy tests and voter qualifications.[46] Southern Democrats fought these legislative initiatives aggressively, but they no longer possessed the numbers or power in Congress to prevent change. Three years later, in 1968, Congress passed a final Civil Rights Act that eliminated discrimination in the sale, rental, or financing of housing.

In the 1960s, Democratic leaders in Congress collaborated on a number of significant civil rights reforms with Presidents Kennedy and Johnson. Johnson signed the Civil Rights Act of 1964 surrounded by the bill's congressional sponsors and civil rights leaders, including Martin Luther King, Jr.

The push for civil rights was only one element of LBJ's policy agenda.[47] After his election in 1964, and with large Democratic majorities in both the House and Senate, Johnson sought new social welfare policies that would augment, and perhaps rival, New Deal programs. LBJ's policy agenda, called the Great Society, focused on alleviating poverty. The 89th Congress (1965–67) advanced the president's agenda by passing a number of landmark laws, including (1) legislation that established Medicare (health coverage for the elderly) and Medicaid (health coverage for the needy and disabled), (2) the Elementary and Secondary Education Act and the Higher Education Act to help students from needy families get better public education all the way through college, and (3) the Child Nutrition Act, which provided breakfast to children in poor areas.

Despite controlling the presidency and large majorities in Congress, however, the Democrats never quite achieved all that they might have. The liberal moment eventually passed, thanks to LBJ's support of the military conflict in

Vietnam and continuing racial unrest at home. The escalating costs of the Vietnam conflict led Congress to rein in domestic spending, and racial discord reflected by urban riots throughout the North soured the public on further Great Society initiatives.

## Watergate and Congressional Reassertion

Republican Richard Nixon was elected president in 1968, and divided government would characterize the first half of the 1970s. The Democrats held majorities in both chambers of Congress for the entire decade, giving them more than a quarter century of continuous control. Initially, Nixon and the Democratic Congress worked together on several policy areas, including the environment, transportation, and nuclear arms limitation.[48] Voting rights were also extended via the **Twenty-Sixth Amendment**, which lowered the voting age to 18 in all federal, state, and local elections.

During his second term, Nixon was involved in a scandal dubbed Watergate after a break-in (and subsequent cover-up) at the Democratic National Committee headquarters in the Watergate Hotel in Washington, D.C. The president and many of his White House associates were implicated in the conspiracy, and Nixon was eventually forced to resign. He was replaced by Vice President Gerald Ford. In response to the scandal, the 93rd Congress (1973–75) took steps to reclaim authority from the executive branch, through (1) the War Powers Resolution, which required the president to consult Congress before committing troops in a military action (adopted over Nixon's veto); (2) the Budget and Impoundment Control Act, which created committees in both chambers to analyze the president's budget, established a Congressional Budget Office to help compile budgetary information, and prevented the president from indefinitely rejecting congressionally approved spending; and (3) an expansion of the Freedom of Information Act (adopted over President Ford's veto), which increased transparency in federal agencies and imposed deadlines for them to meet public information requests.

As Congress responded to presidential scandal, the Supreme Court continued to assert itself. Following the *Brown v. Board of Education* decision in 1954, the Court issued a series of decisions in the 1960s expanding civil liberties and civil rights.[49] And in 1973, with *Roe v. Wade*, the Court moved into social policy by striking down state laws that criminalized or restricted access to abortion, declaring that a right to privacy existed in the Constitution. This decision signaled that the Court was willing to "legislate" on important policy topics.

At the same time, Congress continued to reorganize itself. A new Legislative Reorganization Act in the 1970s made all roll call votes public, reduced the power of committee chairs, enhanced information technology, increased congressional staff, and expanded the Congressional Research Service. Liberal members within the Democratic Party worked to expand their authority by weakening the seniority system (as the automatic method for achieving committee chairs) and decentralizing committee power while expanding the authority of subcommittees.

Congress's demographic makeup also began to change during this time. Social dynamics in American society started to shift in the 1960s, and women and people of color began to challenge preexisting power structures dominated by White men, ultimately affecting the composition of Congress. During the 1970s, the number of women and African Americans elected to the House grew. Congress remained an overwhelmingly White, male institution, but the change was significant, and since then the number of female, African American, Latino, and Asian American representatives has grown gradually but consistently.

With the election of Jimmy Carter as president, the late 1970s witnessed unified Democratic government. Carter had a stormy relationship with his fellow Democrats in Congress—often relying on his own advisors instead for advice and counsel—but several important laws were passed during these years: Congress created a Department of Energy, began deregulating the airline industry, expanded environmental protections, and prevented the spread of nuclear weapons.

## The Reagan Revolution

After Carter, Republicans won the next three presidential elections (1980, 1984, and 1988), with former California governor Ronald Reagan leading a Republican resurgence. Reagan's landslide victories in 1980 and 1984 also produced a Republican Senate, ending more than a generation of Democratic rule. The House remained Democratic, however, and divided government characterized all of Reagan's presidency and the four years under his successor, George H. W. Bush. President Reagan worked with the Democrats in the House to, among other things, increase defense spending and reform the personal and corporate tax systems.[50]

The 1980s also marked the beginning of the **polarization** in Congress—or ideological difference between the parties—that we observe today. Over the decade, the two parties became more internally homogenous and more ideologically different from each other. The full effects of the Voting Rights Act, along with Reagan's election, pushed conservative southerners into the Republican Party and made southern Democrats in Congress—now composed mostly of moderate Whites and liberal African Americans—look more like northern Democrats. Liberal Republicans in the North also largely disappeared during this time. In effect, the two parties were better able to sort themselves ideologically. Since the late 1950s, the Democrats in Congress had been mostly a liberal party, and the Republicans had been mostly a conservative party, but each had members along the full ideological spectrum. During the Reagan era, the Democrats became a strongly liberal party and the Republicans a strongly conservative party (this ideological separation has only increased since then). Because party members now largely shared the same policy goals, they were more willing to cede power to party leaders to set the legislative agenda to help the party achieve those goals.[51]

In addition, the Republican takeover of the Senate led Democrats to organize and coordinate their messaging activities to better frame for the public the differences between the two parties. And in the House, younger Republicans, tired of being the "permanent minority party" in the institution, clashed with more-senior Republicans over strategy, with the younger members seeking a more confrontational approach. Eventually, the younger members would win out, electing Newt Gingrich (Ga.), a well-known partisan instigator, as Republican minority whip in 1989. The Republicans' confrontational approach in the House would be mimicked by Republicans in the Senate. Back in the minority after the 1986 elections, Senate Republicans increasingly pursued a strategy of obstruction in which they were more willing to use the filibuster to slow down or stymie Democratic measures.[52] These activities in both chambers epitomized the growing polarization that was occurring in Congress.

## Bill Clinton and the Contract with America

Divided government—and increasing acrimony between Republicans and Democrats—would underscore the 1990s. Early in the decade, the United States entered a military conflict in the Middle East. Responding to Iraq invading Kuwait, President George H. W. Bush sought Congress's approval to mobilize U.S. troops to drive Iraqi forces out of the region. Congress passed the Persian Gulf Resolution, providing the president with this authority, along with appropriations to fund Operation Desert Shield and Operation Desert Storm, covering the costs of the war. Overall, military operations in the Persian Gulf were successful, thanks in part to their limited scope, and public support for the military was quite high (unlike Vietnam a generation earlier).

While Bush's popularity was very high after the Persian Gulf War, it eroded quickly because of an economic recession at home. As a result, former Arkansas governor Bill Clinton defeated Bush in the 1992 presidential election, and Clinton enjoyed unified Democratic control of government during his first two years in office. While the 103rd Congress (1993–95) did not produce the comprehensive national health care law that Clinton sought, it did respond with major legislation that reduced the budget deficit, established background checks on handgun

The Republicans swept the House and Senate in 1994 on the political strength of their Contract with America, a proposed conservative policy agenda spearheaded by Speaker of the House Newt Gingrich (Ga.). Future Speaker John Boehner (Ohio) stands just to Gingrich's right.

purchases, initiated a "don't ask, don't tell" policy regarding gay people in the U.S. military, and provided significant funds to states to fight crime.[53]

Despite these considerable Democratic policy achievements, the Republicans enjoyed great success in the 1994 midterm elections—so much so that they won majority control of both the House and Senate for the first time since the early 1950s. Republicans attributed their electoral success to the Contract with America, a set of conservative policy reforms the party introduced during the congressional campaign that they promised to enact should they become the majority.[54] Led by new Speaker of the House Newt Gingrich, the Republicans set out to implement various Contract provisions. Some were successful, such as the Congressional Accountability Act, which required that all federal laws apply equally to Congress, and the Line-Item Veto Act, which provided the president with the power to eliminate specific provisions of spending bills (until it was struck down by the Supreme Court in 1998). Other Contract priorities were not successful, however, such as imposing term limits on members of Congress. Republicans also made a number of internal changes to Congress, reducing the number of committees, eliminating some committee staff, and imposing term limits on committee chairs. These internal changes reduced committee (and subcommittee) power and concentrated more authority in the hands of party leaders.

From a policy perspective, the Republican Congress often had an adversarial relationship with President Clinton. Yet they managed to work together to produce some truly important legislation during the last six years of Clinton's presidency. This included reforming the federal welfare system, helping to reduce the federal deficit, and providing matching funds to states for health coverage of low-income children. But Congress and the president also clashed repeatedly.[55] Disputes over spending in the 1996 federal budget negotiation led to two government shutdowns in late 1995, and public opinion polls suggested that Americans largely blamed congressional Republicans for these shutdowns.[56]

Conflict between congressional Republicans and the president peaked in Clinton's second term in office. As interparty relations in Congress became increasingly strained, with filibustering in the Senate continuing to rise, information emerged about an extramarital affair between Clinton and Monica Lewinsky, a White House intern. Republicans sought to impeach Clinton on the basis of perjury (stemming from his false testimony under oath about the affair) and obstruction of justice. The House succeeded in impeaching him on the two counts, but the Senate failed to muster the required two-thirds vote to convict, and Clinton remained in office.[57] The Republican Party had overreached, and House Republicans were increasingly fed up with Speaker Gingrich's leadership. Amid rumors of a potential ouster, Gingrich stepped down from the speakership, in part because the Republicans lost five House seats in the 1998 midterms—after internal polls suggested they would gain more than 20 seats.

## Deeply Divided in the Twenty-First Century

The partisan acrimony of the 1990s only increased during the first two decades of the twenty-first century. Republicans and Democrats in Congress have become even more polarized, with no end in sight. The new century began with the closest presidential election in American history, a virtual tie between Texas governor George W. Bush and vice president Al Gore. The outcome came down to a handful of votes in Florida and how those votes would be tallied in a recount. Eventually, the Supreme Court stopped the recount and decided the election for Bush in a 5–4 vote.[58]

President Bush enjoyed unified Republican government during much of his first six years in office.[59] The biggest challenge that Bush and the Republican-led Congress faced was the terrorist attacks that destroyed the World Trade Center, damaged the Pentagon, and left thousands of Americans dead on September 11, 2001. Very quickly, Osama bin Laden and Al Qaeda were implicated, and Congress authorized the use of force against them and their allies (the Taliban in Afghanistan). A year later, as part of the Global War on Terror, Congress authorized the president to take military action to remove Iraqi president Saddam

Hussein and eliminate the country's nuclear capability.[60] The Global War on Terror effort also helped produce important legislation at home. Congress passed the USA PATRIOT Act, which provided American law enforcement and intelligence agencies with more power and discretion to prevent incidents of domestic terrorism (at the cost of individual civil liberties). Congress also passed the Homeland Security Act, which created a new cabinet-level department that absorbed major portions of 22 existing agencies to prevent domestic terrorist attacks.

The Global War on Terror influenced Bush's domestic agenda, but he and Congress still managed to pass a number of major initiatives, including a considerable personal tax cut adopted before September 11.[61] Shortly thereafter, Congress passed a major education bill, the No Child Left Behind Act, which established standards for states in reading and math for students in grades 3 through 8. Congress also passed a campaign reform bill, the Bipartisan Campaign Reform Act, which limited the amount of money that corporations, unions, and individuals could contribute to political parties. Later in Bush's first term, Congress adopted legislation that limited abortion rights and added a voluntary prescription drug benefit for Medicare beneficiaries.[62]

The Democrats retook the House and Senate in 2006, and Senate Republicans in the 110th Congress (2007–08) responded by filibustering more than twice as often as the previous Congress—an all-time high (by a considerable amount) at that time.[63] The Democrats then swept the Republicans out of government in 2008 behind the presidential candidacy of Democratic senator Barack Obama (Ill.). Initially the Democrats held a major advantage in the 111th Congress (2009–10), as they controlled 60 seats in the Senate (before Senator Ted Kennedy's death) and thus could overcome any Republican filibusters. Their signature achievement during this time was the Patient Protection and Affordable Care Act (or Obamacare), a comprehensive federal health insurance law.[64] Other major legislative achievements included an economic stimulus to combat the effects of the post–September 11 Great Recession, an overhaul of financial regulation in the country, and the repeal of the Clinton-era "Don't Ask, Don't Tell" policy.[65]

The Republicans won back the House in 2010, and the last six years of Obama's presidency were characterized by divided government and high levels of partisan polarization. Governing was more difficult, as Republicans were determined to limit Obama and the Democrats' legislative achievements. In this way, the congressional Republicans during the Obama years were different from the congressional Republicans during the Clinton years. While Gingrich and the Republicans clashed with Clinton on numerous occasions, they were willing to make deals with him when it was in their interest. The post–2008 Republicans had no interest in working with Obama and actively sought (but failed) to prevent his reelection.[66]

Once in office, House Republicans sought deficit reduction, especially the younger Tea Party–affiliated members, who were elected on an anti-government agenda, and the two parties worked on a "grand bargain" to reduce spending and the deficit by more than $3 trillion. Congress passed and Obama signed the Budget Control Act of 2011, but delayed implementation of its terms threatened to take the federal government over the fiscal cliff, risking governmental default. As a result, Congress passed a stopgap measure, permanently extended the Bush-era tax cuts, and modestly raised taxes on the wealthy. Around the same time, the Supreme Court in *Citizens United v. FEC* (2010) overturned key provisions of the Bipartisan Campaign Reform Act of 2002—specifically, those that prohibited corporations and unions from funding "electioneering communications" (broadcast ads that mention a candidate in any context) within 30 days before a primary or 60 days before a general election. While some believe the Court decision was a victory for free expression (by equating political speech with First Amendment rights), one consequence was that election spending by corporations was no longer limited, thus increasing political tensions in an already highly polarized environment.

The remainder of the Obama presidency saw additional conflict. After Obama's reelection in 2012, the Senate Republicans in the 113th Congress (2013–15) tripled the number of filibusters from the preceding Congress—nearly doubling the previous all-time high.[67] In October 2013, the government shut down for more than two weeks, again over appropriations and spending levels. Constant Republican filibustering of Obama's executive branch nominees led Democratic Majority Leader Harry Reid (Nev.) to invoke the "nuclear option" and eliminate filibuster rights on all executive-branch nominations and federal judicial appointments below the level of Supreme Court. House Republicans, in an attempt to curry favor with their constituents back home, staged dozens of fruitless roll call votes to repeal Obamacare. And in perhaps the most blatant application of partisanship yet, after the Republicans took back the Senate in 2016, they refused to consider Obama's nominee for the Supreme Court—Merrick Garland—after the death of Justice Antonin Scalia. Such a refusal was unprecedented in president–Senate relations on Supreme Court nominations.

In 2016, Donald Trump was elected president, and the Republicans maintained majority control of both the House and Senate. Throughout the first year of the Trump administration, the Republicans in the 115th Congress (2017–19) continued their attacks on the signature achievement of the Obama administration—the Affordable Care Act. While the Republicans in the House managed to pass a bill that would have repealed and replaced Obamacare, the Republicans in the Senate came up just short.[68] Nonetheless, the Republicans produced some successes. The Republican Senate confirmed a slate of Trump's conservative cabinet-level appointments, over the near-unanimous objections of Democrats. (Thanks to the Democrats' "going nuclear" in 2013, they could not block any of these nominees by filibuster.) Majority Leader Mitch McConnell (Ky.) later invoked the nuclear option on Supreme Court nominations in order to sidestep a Democratic filibuster

Democrats in Congress were vocal in their opposition to Donald Trump and congressional Republicans' legislative initiatives, including the Tax Cuts and Jobs Act, various immigration policies, and attempts to repeal the Affordable Care Act. Here, Senator Elizabeth Warren (D-Mass.) speaks to demonstrators outside the Capitol to protest the Tax Cuts and Jobs Act, which included lowering the tax rate for the wealthiest Americans.

and confirm Neil Gorsuch, a Trump nominee. The Republicans also passed a major tax reform bill, reducing tax rates for both businesses and individuals, and the bill included a provision repealing the individual mandate—a crucial component of the Affordable Care Act.[69] Thus while the Republicans were unable to roll back Obamacare directly, they may have found a way to kill it indirectly.[70] As of now, the fate of the Affordable Care Act remains to be seen. Finally, in October 2018, after a bruising partisan battle that transfixed the nation, Senate Republicans confirmed Brett Kavanaugh to the Supreme Court—amid accusations of sexual assault against him—to replace the retiring Anthony Kennedy.

The Republicans lost the House in the 2018 midterms, and partisan polarization in the 116th Congress (2019–21) was at an all-time high. Early on, the conflict between the Democratic House and President Trump reached a fever pitch, with House Democrats seeking to impeach him on two charges—abuse of power and obstruction of Congress—related to his alleged attempt to influence the government of Ukraine to look into the financial dealings of his Democratic rival, former Senator Joe Biden (Del.), and Biden's son. On December 18, 2019, the House voted to impeach President Trump on both counts.[71] The case then moved to the Republican-controlled Senate, which, on February 6, 2020, voted to acquit President Trump on both counts.[72]

As the full impeachment process was winding down, the nation began to face a monumental challenge—the pandemic associated with COVID-19, the novel coronavirus (see the opening of Chapter 1). Despite the impeachment's lingering partisan animosity, the Democratic House and the Republican Senate managed to work together to provide important relief measures for the country. But after the passage of the initial relief measures in March 2020, partisan divisions reemerged. In May, the Democratic House passed another bill to provide $3 billion in relief, but the Republican Senate would not bring it to a vote. After months of partisan bickering, in December 2020 during the lame-duck session, a new $900 billion relief package was adopted.[73]

Finally, the November 2020 presidential election saw former-Vice President Joe Biden defeat President Trump by a final 306–232 electoral vote tally. Rather than concede, President Trump charged—without evidence—that the election had been stolen through massive vote fraud and proceeded to launch a series of lawsuits to challenge the outcome. All of the lawsuits were rejected in court as baseless. When the 117th Congress convened to count and certify the Electoral College vote on January 6, 2021, President Trump encouraged a massive protest in the District of Columbia and told his supporters to "walk down to the Capitol."[74] The result was tens of thousands of protestors overrunning security at the Capitol building, knocking over barricades, charging into the Senate chamber, and breaking into congressional offices (including Speaker Pelosi's).[75] Members of the House and Senate were rushed out to a secure location and kept there for hours. Finally, Congress reconvened later that evening and by early morning certified the election results and affirmed Joe Biden as the next president of the United States.[76] How the 117th Congress and new Biden administration handle the next couple of years will help determine whether partisan rancor abates, COVID-19 is defeated once and for all, and American society returns to a degree of normalcy.

## HOW WE STUDY
## IDEOLOGY IN CONGRESS

To study Congress at different points in time and across time, political scientists have sought ways to understand how representatives and senators make decisions. One way is to argue that legislators have preferences on policy and, more generally, preferences *across* policy areas—which we call **ideologies**. We typically think of ideology in terms of left-right positions on a line. A representative with a liberal ideology would be on the left; a representative with a conservative ideology would be on the right. A liberal ideology would be consistent with positions such as being pro-choice on abortion and supportive of more-restrictive gun laws. A conservative ideology would be consistent with the opposite positions: being pro-life on abortion and opposed to restrictions on gun ownership.

Figure 2.2 illustrates how we might think of these concepts. Here we consider ideological positions on a line, where the underlying issue is gun control. The leftmost (or liberal) point is consistent with the position of no access: no one is allowed to have a gun. The rightmost (or conservative) point is consistent with the position of no restrictions: anyone who wants any kind of gun can have one with no governmental interference. The median position is the middle (or center) of the space and is the midpoint between these two extreme positions. On most policy issues in the United States, people—and parties—typically have left-of-center or right-of-center positions, but rarely does anyone hold the most extreme positions. For example, on the question of guns, most people believe some restrictions are necessary, but they disagree as to whether there should be more restrictions (the left-of-center position) or fewer restrictions (the right-of-center position). In this book, we refer to such preference and policy comparisons along a line as **spatial models**.

Systematic study of ideology requires some way of measuring it. One could ask legislators questions, perhaps in a survey, to get a sense of their preferences on a range of issues. But that method is problematic. First, legislators may answer questions strategically (or not at all), based on how they think the survey analysts, or their constituents, believe they should respond. For example, on sensitive topics such as race or gender, legislators might provide more liberal answers than they would otherwise give.[77] Second, survey-based ideology measures are relatively new and thus give us a picture of only the contemporary Congress. If we wanted to compare legislators' ideologies in earlier eras to those today, survey-based measures would not be helpful.

An alternate way to measure legislators' ideologies is to use roll call voting data. That is, we can track how legislators vote in Congress and use those votes to draw conclusions about their ideologies. Roll calls on the floor of Congress are public—they can be observed by constituents, interest groups, and the media—and often have direct policy consequences. As such, a vote is a clear signal about how a legislator views an issue. Individual roll call votes have been a staple of legislative proceedings going back to the first Congress in the late eighteenth century, making them extremely useful for measuring ideology across time.

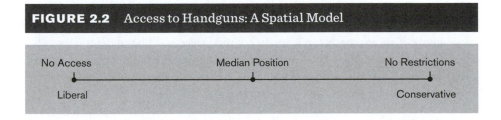

**FIGURE 2.2    Access to Handguns: A Spatial Model**

The simplest measure of ideology that can be created from roll call votes is a basic rating that shows, for some number of votes, how often a legislator voted with the liberal or conservative position. For example, assume that we are analyzing how legislators voted on 10 roll call votes, and we establish whether the "yea" or "nay" position on each corresponds to the liberal position. We would then calculate how many times, over these 10 votes, each legislator voted for the liberal position. If a legislator voted for the liberal position on 7 of the 10 votes, then he would receive a rating of 70. By contrast, if a legislator voted for the liberal position on only 2 of the 10 votes, then she would receive a rating of 20. The range of ideological positions would span from 0 to 100, with 0 being a perfect conservative ideology and 100 being a perfect liberal ideology.

Interest groups often create ratings (or scores), based on a set of carefully chosen roll calls, as a way to assess how members of Congress vote on issues that they care about. Examples of interest groups that produce regular legislative ratings include the Americans for Democratic Action (ADA), the American Conservative Union (ACU), the League of Conservation Voters, and the National Taxpayers Union. Interest-group scores, then, correspond to how often members of Congress supported positions in line with that group's stated preferences on specific issues.

ADA and ACU scores, which are based on a range of roll call–based issues, are often used as measures of basic left-right (liberal-conservative) ideology. They have been important in a number of political science studies across time. But these scores, and really any interest-group scores, are susceptible to **artificial extremism**. That is, interest-group scores, by their nature, are based on roll call votes that are selected because they draw stark differences between liberal and conservative positions. In other words, the vote positions themselves—the "yea" and "nay" positions—represent ideologically distinct alternatives, often very liberal and very conservative positions. This type of roll call selection is useful for identifying those legislators who are truly liberal or conservative. But moderate legislators are not given moderate policy positions to vote for; instead, they must vote for the liberal or conservative positions. This setup tends to make moderates appear to be more extreme—either more liberal or more conservative—than they really are.[78]

Concerns about artificial extremism have led scholars to search for other roll call–based ways of measuring legislator preferences. One solution is to develop ideology measures that use all (or nearly all) roll call votes in a given Congress, not just votes on a handful of ideologically divisive issues. A large sample of roll call votes records a variety of policy positions taken by members of Congress, including moderate positions, and thus allows scholars to differentiate legislators more finely. This approach can identify conservatives and liberals, but it can also identify true moderates, right-leaning and left-leaning moderates, and so on. In other words, more, different data will yield a truer distribution of ideological types than just two groups (one conservative and one liberal).

The gold standard for broad roll call–based ideology is the NOMINATE score, created by political scientists Keith Poole and Howard Rosenthal.[79] NOMINATE scores, which range from −1 (most liberal) to +1 (most conservative), are based on a statistical technique from psychology and incorporate all non-unanimous roll call votes in a given Congress. The statistical technique is more complicated than a simple rating, but the output is similar in that legislators who vote more alike are placed nearer to one another on the left-right scale.

Figures 2.3 and 2.4 illustrate two phenomena: (1) the artificial extremism of interest-group scores and (2) how NOMINATE scores can differentiate members more precisely across the ideological spectrum. Figure 2.3 shows ACU scores for House members. These scores are meant to showcase conservative tendencies—in keeping with the goals of the ACU. Based on the handful of roll call votes comprising the ACU's scoring, most members possess near-perfect ratings—either at or near zero or at or close to 100 percent. There are very few members in the middle of the space. Figure 2.4, by comparison, shows NOMINATE scores for House members. While the NOMINATE scores also yield two "humps," the scores are not nearly as bunched together, and the medians (or midpoints) of the two distributions are located far from the most extreme values. In short, there are far more members with NOMINATE scores near the middle of the space. Thus NOMINATE, by using nearly all roll call votes in a given Congress, differentiates members on a range of issues and avoids presenting a distribution of members' preferences that is artificially extreme.

Several types of NOMINATE scores exist. The most common NOMINATE score is a dynamic one that allows scholars to compare legislators from the same chamber (House or Senate) across time. Dynamic scores also allow individual legislators to move to the left or right based on changes in their voting behavior across time. Static scores, which provide a single ideological position for each legislator across time, allow for comparison of individual legislators across chambers and across time.

Poole and Rosenthal have found that a single left-right (or liberal-conservative) NOMINATE dimension—often characterized as representing conflict over the role of government in the economy—correctly predicts most individual-level votes in Congress across time.[80] Sometimes, however, issues do not fall neatly on the basic liberal-conservative spectrum—issues, for example, that divide each party. In these cases, a second NOMINATE dimension is needed, and its addition improves predictive power. Across congressional history, such second-dimension issues have included slavery early in the nineteenth century, currency (gold versus silver) later in the nineteenth century, and civil rights during the mid-twentieth century. However, in recent decades, no new second dimensions have emerged. Instead, a single liberal-conservative dimension appears to encapsulate most political conflict in Congress.

**FIGURE 2.3**   ACU Scores, 115th House (2017–19)

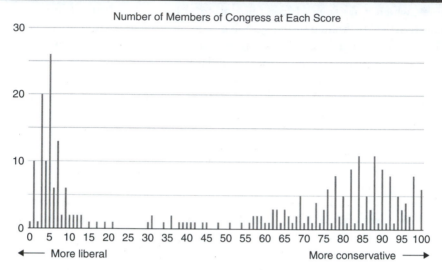

American Conservative Union, http://acuratings.conservative.org (accessed 1/6/20).

**FIGURE 2.4**   NOMINATE Scores, 115th House (2017–19)

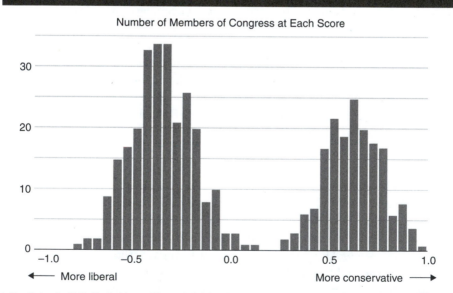

Jeffrey B. Lewis, Keith Poole, Howard Rosenthal, Adam Boche, Aaron Rudkin, and Luke Sonnet. 2019. *Voteview: Congressional Roll-Call Votes Database*, https://voteview.com/ (accessed 1/6/20).

In addition to providing individual-level data on members of Congress, NOMINATE scores can also be used to examine more macro-level congressional phenomena. For example, the median members of the Democratic and Republican parties can be identified by chamber in each Congress. This provides a way to assess the relationship between ideology and partisanship over time. And the difference between the median Democrat and the median Republican can be used as a measure of polarization in each congressional chamber.

We will use NOMINATE throughout this book to examine how Congress behaves—so bookmark this explanation, as you will likely need to return to it.

## Critical Thinking

1. Imagine that three members of Congress—Mr. Smith, Ms. Jones, and Mr. King—vote on 10 roll calls that an interest group deems important for its mission. The 10 roll calls, members' votes, and the interest group's position on each roll call appear in the table below. A "yea" vote is cast in support of a legislative measure (encapsulated in a roll call, labeled RC), while a "nay" vote is cast in opposition.

| | RC1 | RC2 | RC3 | RC4 | RC5 | RC6 | RC7 | RC8 | RC9 | RC10 |
|---|---|---|---|---|---|---|---|---|---|---|
| Mr. Smith | Yea | Yea | Nay | Yea | Nay | Yea | Nay | Nay | Yea | Nay |
| Ms. Jones | Nay | Yea | Nay | Nay | Yea | Yea | Nay | Yea | Nay | Yea |
| Mr. King | Yea | Nay | Yea | Yea | Nay | Nay | Yea | Nay | Yea | Yea |
| Interest-Group Position | Yea | Nay | Nay | Yea | Yea | Yea | Nay | Nay | Nay | Nay |

Calculate a pro-interest group rating for each of the three members of Congress.

2. Imagine that a committee in Congress is made of 10 members: five Democrats and five Republicans. The first-dimension NOMINATE scores for the 10 members of Congress (labeled MC1 through MC10), along with their party affiliations (D = Democrat, R = Republican), appear in the table below.

| | MC1 | MC2 | MC3 | MC4 | MC5 | MC6 | MC7 | MC8 | MC9 | MC10 |
|---|---|---|---|---|---|---|---|---|---|---|
| Party Affiliation | D | D | R | D | R | D | R | R | R | D |
| NOMINATE Score | −0.7 | −0.1 | 0.6 | −0.5 | 0.2 | −0.2 | 0.8 | 0.5 | 0.4 | −0.3 |

Line up the members from left to right along a single dimension and identify:

   a. which member of Congress is the Democratic median on the committee,

   b. which member of Congress is the Republican median on the committee, and

   c. the degree (or amount) of partisan polarization that exists on the committee.

3. While roll call votes help us study legislators' preferences systematically across chambers and across time, what might be some of their limitations? How might these limitations potentially affect our analyses?

# CONCLUSION

The role that Congress plays in governing and representation in our separated system has changed over time. When the Constitution was drafted, the Framers viewed Congress as the chief institution in the federal system. Congress was the representative body of the people and would govern based on representatives' and senators' decisions. The other institutions in our federal system—the president and the courts—would provide some checks and balances, thereby allowing a system of separate powers to exist. But Congress was intended to be the engine that drove the republic.

The first period of American congressional history reflected the Founders' aspirations. Congress largely determined the major policies of the day, as the presidency was underdeveloped and the federal courts were only beginning to evolve. The second period of American congressional history, from the Civil War through the early 1930s, saw a slight shift: Congress was still paramount, but the presidency and courts were beginning to develop as rivals. By the third period of congressional history, the "institutional presidency" had emerged and a more activist Supreme Court became more willing to decide policy matters that Congress was not able or willing to address.

As we turn our attention to contemporary American politics, we see Congress hampered by polarization and the accompanying policy gridlock, which has only incentivized the president and the courts to look for ways to expand their authority. This status quo entered a new phase with the election of President Trump, who has been unwilling to be constrained by the prevailing norms and institutional roles of our federal system. Should collective action and collective will fail to rein in a more aggressive president, Congress's authority will be further reduced in the constitutional order.

## Discussion Questions

1. In designing the Constitution, the Framers considered Congress to be the most important institution in the new federal government. And, indeed, Congress dominated the federal government throughout much of American history. But today, that is not the case. Should we be troubled by this change? Or have other considerations emerged over time that require the president and courts to play a more meaningful role?

2. The number of citizens that House members (in their districts) and senators (in their states) represent has increased over time. What does this change imply about the quality of representation today? Is it necessarily worse than in the past, or have other conditions changed to make it easier for members of Congress to connect with constituents?

3. Congress has become more polarized by party over the last few decades. While this complicates Congress's ability to govern—and creates opportunities for the president and the courts to exert policy-making authority—how should we think about polarization in the context of representation? Is it possible that greater polarization reflects successful representation of constituency interests? Why or why not?

4. As the "Then and Now" section describes, postelection lame-duck sessions have become common in contemporary politics, in part because party leaders have come to view these sessions as the best time to hold necessary but politically difficult votes. But is it worth sacrificing representation for better governing? Or are the dangers of undemocratic and possibly even corrupt policy outcomes too great?

5. In recent years, the Senate has eliminated the use of the filibuster in the consideration of executive appointments, including on Supreme Court nominees. Should the Senate do away with the filibuster on standard policy matters? Why or why not? How would completely eliminating the filibuster affect how Congress governs?

# 3

## Elections

The 2018 midterm elections took place two years into the Trump administration. Both parties campaigned hard, with Democrats emphasizing the
Republicans' attempts to repeal Obamacare (see the opening of Chapter 4),
while Republicans trumpeted the recently enacted Tax Cuts and Jobs Act
(see the opening of Chapter 5) and stoked fears about illegal immigration.[1]
In the end, the Democrats scored a huge victory, gaining 40 seats in the
House and winning majority control of the chamber in advance of the
116th Congress.

The 2018 midterms were historic for a number of reasons. Alarmed by
the high stakes, more voters turned out than in any midterm election in more
than 100 years.[2] And the Congress they elected would be the most racially and
ethnically diverse in history, with the most women ever. For the Democrats,
the face of the 2018 midterms was Alexandria Ocasio-Cortez (or AOC), a
woman of Puerto Rican descent who had not previously held elected office.
AOC defeated Democratic Caucus chair Joe Crowley of New York (a 10-term
incumbent) in the primaries, and once in Congress, she would headline a group
of young progressive women of color known as The Squad, including Ilhan
Omar (Minn.), Ayanna Pressley (Mass.), and Rashida Tlaib (Mich.), who cham-

Representatives Alexandria Ocasio-Cortez (D-N.Y.), Ayanna Pressley (D-Mass.), Rashida Tlaib (D-Mich.), and Ilhan Omar (D-Minn., not pictured) were among the historic number of women elected to Congress in 2018. As progressive Democrats, they hoped to move the Democratic Party to the left, and earned the nickname "The Squad" for their unified efforts to do so.

pioned progressive policy (like the Green New Deal) and sought to move the Democratic Party to the left.[3]

Though the 2018 midterms were historic in demographic terms and in the defeat of a powerful congressional incumbent in a primary, they were also very much in keeping with established trends. For example, as we will discuss later, the party of the president almost always loses House seats in the congressional midterms, so Democrats gaining seats in 2018 was not unexpected.

In this chapter, we cover the institutional foundations of congressional elections, the rise of congressional careerism, and the role of ambition in the decision to seek election to Congress. We also examine why reelection rates for members of Congress have been so high and why incumbents sometimes (but rarely) lose. We also learn that most congressional seats turn over due to retirement (rather than lost reelection). We conclude by noting some data trends that suggest that the value of incumbency might be eroding as politics becomes more nationalized in the early twenty-first century.

## SOME BASICS OF CONGRESSIONAL ELECTIONS

Elections are at the heart of our representative democracy. An **electoral connection** links citizens and their representatives in Congress. Citizens use elections to choose who will serve their interests in Congress and to evaluate their representatives' performance. Citizens either reward members of Congress for doing a good job by granting them another term in office, or they punish them for not performing well enough by replacing them with someone else. Elections thus serve as an accountability mechanism, a way for citizens every two years (or six years in the case of senators) to ensure that their representatives are behaving as faithful agents.

Congressional elections occur on Federal Election Day, the first Tuesday after the first Monday in November in even-numbered years. Sometimes congressional elections overlap with presidential elections (during presidential election years), and sometimes they do not (during midterm election years). All House seats and about one-third of Senate seats are up for election every two years, with senators composed of three classes (with elections staggered across six years).

The contemporary Congress is a professional legislature, composed mostly of individuals who desire a lengthy congressional career. Most incumbent members of Congress seek reelection—on average, over 80 percent in the Senate and over 90 percent in the House in the post–World War II era—and most of them win their races. There are differences between the House and Senate, however (see Figure 3.1). House incumbents who seek reelection usually win at a higher rate than similar Senate incumbents, and there is much less year-to-year variation in the House than in the Senate.

But differences aside, the bottom line is: once elected, congressional incumbents typically seek another term in office, and they usually succeed. As a result, Congress members in both chambers have built substantial congressional careers, serving an average of 10 years since the early 1950s. At the beginning of the 117th Congress, the average for representatives and senators was 8.9 and 11 years, respectively.[4] Initial electoral success breeds considerably more electoral success.

## THE INSTITUTIONAL FOUNDATIONS OF CONGRESSIONAL ELECTIONS

The modern electoral environment—wherein careerism is a goal and incumbency is a powerful factor in achieving that goal—developed around factors both internal and external to Congress. One important factor is the institutional context—the constitutional foundation for congressional elections and the relevant federal and state laws and processes.

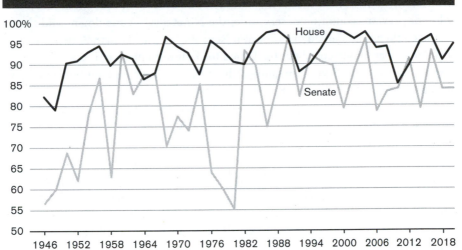

**FIGURE 3.1**    Percentage of Incumbents Seeking Reelection to the House and Senate Who Win, 1946–2020

Brookings Institution, www.brookings.edu/multi-chapter-report/vital-statistics-on-congress "Congressional Careers: Service Tenure and Patterns of Member Service, 1789–2021," EveryCRSReport, January 5, 2021, https://www.everycrsreport.com/reports/R41545.html (accessed 1/21/21); 2020 Senate elections updated by the author.

## The Constitution

While the Framers said almost nothing in the Constitution about who may vote in congressional elections, they did specify age, citizenship, and residency requirements for congressional candidates. The Constitution also establishes that Senate representation is based on equality, with each state having two senators, and House representation is based on population, with more-populous states receiving more representatives.[5]

In terms of elections, the Constitution stipulates, "The Times, Places, and Manner of holding Elections of Senators and Representatives, shall be prescribed in each State by the Legislature thereof; but the Congress may at any time by Law make or alter such Regulations" (Article I, Section 4, Clause 1). And while states have largely determined when, where, and how to hold congressional elections, Congress has stepped in occasionally to make regulations (as we discuss next). The Constitution also stipulates, "Each House shall be the Judge of the Elections, Returns and Qualifications of its own Members" (Article I, Section 5, Clause 1). Thus if the results of a House or Senate election are disputed, the members of the relevant chamber decide who is duly elected and has a right to the seat. Stated differently, the Constitution establishes the House and Senate as the final arbiters of the election of their own members (see "Then and Now," on the next page).

Since the Founding, additional amendments liberalized suffrage requirements and increased the number of eligible voters in congressional elections. The Fifteenth Amendment held that voting could not be denied on account of race, color, or previous condition of servitude; the Nineteenth Amendment said that voting could not be denied on account of sex; the Twenty-Fourth Amendment stipulated that voting could not be denied for failure to pay a poll tax or other tax; and the Twenty-Sixth Amendment held that voting could not be denied on account of age, if citizens are 18 years or older.

The Seventeenth Amendment directly affected the congressional election process: it altered the method by which senators were elected. Before the Seventeenth Amendment, the people elected House members directly, while state legislatures elected senators (and thus senators were elected indirectly by the people). The Framers considered this to be a compromise, whereby popular democracy and high responsiveness to the people would characterize the House, while deliberate and dispassionate decision making by professional politicians insulated from momentary (and potentially radical) shifts in public opinion would characterize the Senate.

By the late nineteenth century, progressive reformers sought to make the Senate more directly reflect the popular will. But the immediate motivation for the Seventeenth Amendment, which was ratified in 1913 and established the direct election of senators by the state citizenry,[6] was to limit corruption in the electoral process.[7] Progressives contended that wealthy interests had effectively bought control of the Senate by buying a key group of state legislators. Direct election would make such vote buying considerably less efficient, as buying pivotal groups of voters in an entire state would be incredibly expensive. In addition, states sometimes went without Senate representation because of deadlocked state legislative elections (which happened at least fourteen times around the turn of the twentieth century). Direct election would eliminate these deadlocks and the resulting seat vacancies.[8]

---

## THEN AND NOW
## DISPUTED ELECTIONS IN THE HOUSE
## OF REPRESENTATIVES

How often has the Article I, Section 5, power been invoked? That is, how often has a chamber of Congress decided the rightful occupant of a congressional seat in a disputed election case?[9] In the case of the House of Representatives, there have been 613 disputed election cases across history, or an average of over 5 per Congress.[10]

Disputed election cases have been concentrated in particular periods. Most disputed election cases occurred in the latter part of the nineteenth century—after the Civil War and during Reconstruction and the Gilded Age. The high of 38 cases occurred in the 54th Congress (1895–97).

As the number of House seats in a given Congress has fluctuated over time, a more meaningful way to assess the importance of the disputed election procedure is to calculate the percentage of House seats disputed in each Congress (Figure 3.2).

In three different Congresses, more than 10 percent of House seats were disputed, with a high of 11.5 percent in the 41st Congress (1869–71). In recent years, this percentage has dropped off considerably. In the last century, the per-Congress average has been less than 1 percent, and many Congresses have seen no disputed election cases at all.

Why were so many House seats disputed in the late nineteenth century? Many of these cases stemmed from the loser of an election accusing the winners or their campaigns of criminal behavior, like bribery of voters or election officials, illegal alteration and counting of ballots, and fraudulent certification of election

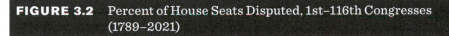

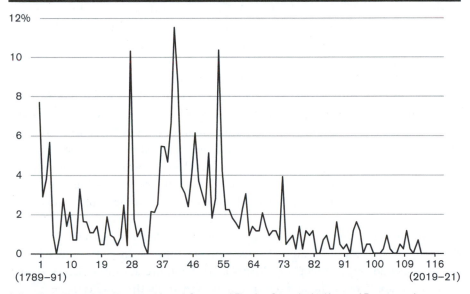

**FIGURE 3.2**  Percent of House Seats Disputed, 1st–116th Congresses (1789–2021)

Jeffery A. Jenkins. 2004. "Partisanship and Contested Election Cases in the House of Representatives, 1789–2002." *Studies in American Political Development* 18: 112–35; data updated by authors through 2021.

results. Many cases also involved insufficient provision of polling places, voting by persons not properly registered, and improper treatment of ballot boxes.

In the late nineteenth century, the major parties were evenly matched at the national level, so a swing of a few seats could decide majority control of the House. Republicans brought most of the disputed election cases, stemming from elections mostly in the South. Republicans held that Democrats were using whatever means necessary to prevent African Americans—who had been granted citizenship and voting rights after the Civil War—from voting and selecting representatives who would serve their interests in Congress. With control of the House hanging in the balance, Republican leaders actively encouraged disputed election cases as a way to maintain a partisan foothold in the South and to fight back against Democrats' electoral shenanigans.

Table 3.1 documents seat changes resulting from disputed election cases in the House from Reconstruction through the early twentieth century. The Republicans were the majority party during most of this period, but with slim margins toward the end of the nineteenth century. The "additions" in the table represent flips in the partisan control of seats. That is, via Article I, Section 5, the House decided to unseat the ostensible winner of the election (the individual with the most votes based on the count) and award the seat to the loser instead, based on evidence of fraud or other irregularities. In most of the cases, the majority party awarded seats to their members and unseated members of the other party. The Republicans were aggressive in these efforts, adding as many as 10 seats in a given Congress (the 41st). While some of these seat additions came from outside of the South, most were in former Confederate states or other former slave states.

By the turn of the twentieth century, Republican efforts to flip seats had largely come to an end. The 1894–96 elections had created a partisan realignment in the country, making the Grand Old Party (GOP) competitive or dominant in every region outside of the South. As a result, the Republicans no longer needed representation in the South to maintain majority control of the House. Moreover, beginning in the 1890s, Democratic state governments in the South began to make legal changes to disenfranchise African Americans, which severely limited Republican representation. Thus, the southern wing of the GOP largely disintegrated, and it would not reemerge in a meaningful way until the 1960s.

In the twentieth century, disputed election cases faded away, and the last time the House flipped a seat because of a disputed election was in 1985. Why have disputed election cases effectively disappeared? First, literacy rates increased, and media coverage (from radio and television) expanded. By the early twentieth century, the populace was better informed, which required party leaders to better justify their reasons for disputing elections and thereby attempting to over-

**TABLE 3.1**  Seat Changes Resulting from Disputed Election Cases, 40th–61st Congresses (1867–1911)

| Congress (Years) | Majority Party | MAJORITY PARTY ADDITIONS | | | MINORITY PARTY ADDITIONS | | |
|---|---|---|---|---|---|---|---|
| | | Former Confederacy | Other Former Slave States | Non-South | Former Confederacy | Other Former Slave States | Non-South |
| 40th (1867–69) | Republicans | 0 | 1 | 1 | 0 | 0 | 0 |
| 41st (1869–71) | Republicans | 5 | 0 | 5 | 0 | 0 | 0 |
| 42nd (1871–73) | Republicans | 1 | 0 | 0 | 2 | 0 | 0 |
| 43rd (1873–75) | Republicans | 1 | 1 | 0 | 3 | 1 | 0 |
| 44th (1875–77) | Democrats | 2 | 0 | 2 | 0 | 0 | 0 |
| 45th (1877–79) | Democrats | 2 | 0 | 3 | 0 | 0 | 0 |
| 46th (1879–81) | Democrats | 1 | 0 | 0 | 1 | 0 | 0 |
| 47th (1881–83) | Republicans | 5 | 1 | 0 | 0 | 0 | 1 |
| 48th (1883–85) | Democrats | 2 | 0 | 4 | 2 | 0 | 0 |
| 49th (1885–87) | Democrats | 0 | 0 | 1 | 0 | 0 | 0 |
| 50th (1887–89) | Democrats | 0 | 0 | 0 | 0 | 0 | 0 |
| 51st (1889–91) | Republicans | 5 | 3 | 0 | 0 | 0 | 0 |
| 52nd (1891–93) | Democrats | 0 | 0 | 1 | 0 | 0 | 0 |
| 53rd (1893–95) | Democrats | 0 | 1 | 2 | 0 | 0 | 0 |
| 54th (1895–97) | Republicans | 4 | 2 | 3 | 0 | 0 | 0 |
| 55th (1897–99) | Republicans | 3 | 0 | 0 | 0 | 0 | 0 |
| 56th (1899–1901) | Republicans | 3 | 0 | 0 | 0 | 0 | 0 |
| 57th (1901–03) | Republicans | 0 | 2 | 0 | 0 | 0 | 0 |
| 58th (1903–05) | Republicans | 0 | 0 | 2 | 0 | 0 | 0 |
| 59th (1905–07) | Republicans | 0 | 1 | 0 | 0 | 0 | 0 |
| 60th (1907–09) | Republicans | 0 | 0 | 0 | 0 | 0 | 0 |
| 61st (1909–11) | Republicans | 0 | 0 | 0 | 0 | 0 | 0 |

rule the voters' will. Second, the South, where most disputed elections occurred, was no longer a partisan battleground. Once their disenfranchisement provisions were in place, the Democrats controlled the South through the late twentieth century as effectively a one-party region. Third, voting became secret with the advent of the Australian ballot, and voting technology improved, making it more difficult for outright fraud to enter congressional elections.

A question arises: Could the majority party in a highly polarized Congress with narrow seat margins use claims of illegal voting to revive the use of disputed elections? Many states have pursued voter identification laws based (ostensibly) on this concern, with the goal of preventing noncitizens from corrupting the electoral process. But, so far, Congress has not attempted to revive the disputed election procedure. However, given the hyperpartisanship that exists in Congress today, disputed elections—used for raw partisan benefit—could return. For example, if the Republicans are unwilling to allow a Democratic president to fill a vacancy on the Supreme Court, as happened when President Obama nominated Merrick Garland in 2016 following Antonin Scalia's death (see Chapter 11), just about any strategy seems to be in play.[11]

### Critical Thinking

1. If the Democrats were using fraud and intimidation to restrict African American voting in the South during and after Reconstruction, were the Republicans in the House justified in flipping seats via disputed election cases? Why or why not?
2. Although the Constitution states, "Each House shall be the Judge of the Elections, Returns and Qualifications of its own Members," if an election dispute for a House or Senate seat were to occur today, do you think the relevant chamber should have the power to decide the outcome? Or would you rather that a federal court handle the case?
3. If a serious election dispute were to occur today and require the House or Senate to sit in judgment and decide the outcome, what issues do you think would be in play? Why might the ostensible loser of the election call the result illegitimate or tainted?

## Federal Law

Federal law affects the congressional election process in various ways. We discuss three such ways here: the regulation of elections, apportionment, and campaign finance.

**REGULATION OF ELECTIONS**    As noted previously, the Constitution grants to the states the primary responsibility for deciding when, where, and how to hold congressional elections but allows Congress to intervene in the process via federal law. Congress has intervened sparingly over time, but such efforts have significantly influenced congressional elections.

For example, federal law has affected how states elect their representatives.[12] The Constitution specifies that House members "shall be apportioned among the several States . . . according to their respective Numbers" and that "the number of Representatives shall not exceed one for every thirty Thousand" (Article I, Section 2, Clause 3).[13] But the Constitution does not specify how that **apportionment** should occur or which geographic unit to use. From the first Congress, the typical unit was a district: a group of whole counties that add up to the minimum population necessary for a representative.[14] And while most districts were **single-member districts**, in which citizens elected one representative, others were multi-member districts, in which citizens elected more than one representative. In addition, some states elected their House members by general ticket, with the entire state acting as a single district. If a state was entitled to six House members, for example, all citizens in the state would get to vote for six candidates, and the six individuals with the highest vote totals would be elected. In 1967, Congress passed a law that prohibited anything other than single-member districts, because it was afraid that the southern states might adopt general ticket systems in the wake of the Voting Rights Act of 1965, with the goal of diluting the voting power of newly enfranchised African Americans.

Federal law has also affected elections by specifying when states elect their representatives. While the Constitution stipulated that "the House of Representatives shall be composed of Members chosen every second year by the People of the several states" (Article I, Section 2, Clause 1), exactly *when* during the year was never stated. Initially each state chose its own Election Day, and over the course of an election cycle for a given Congress, 18 months could separate the first state election and the last state election. Congress rectified these timing discrepancies in stages. In 1845, Congress established the first Tuesday after the first Monday in November as the date for voting in presidential elections.[15] In 1872, as part of a new apportionment act, Congress mandated that congressional elections match up with presidential elections. And while the various states did not fully align their elections for another decade, the 1872 act established a single Federal Election Day.[16] After the adoption of the Seventeenth Amendment, Senate elections were also held on this date.

A final example of federal involvement in congressional elections concerns the method of electing representatives.[17] Because of high illiteracy rates in the nation's early years, voting was often conducted by voice in public. Over time, most states adopted some form of written or printed ballot, which the political parties handled themselves. In 1871, Congress codified this trend by mandating that all votes in House elections use written or printed ballots, with any voice votes being thrown out.[18] In 1899, Congress acknowledged advances in vote-counting technology and allowed voting machines to be used in House elections. Congress would not legislate on voting technology again until the Help America Vote Act (HAVA) in 2002, which it adopted in the wake of the disputed and controversial Bush–Gore presidential election in 2000. HAVA sought to establish minimum standards for election administration across the states, mandating that all states and localities upgrade their election procedures, including their voting machines, registration processes, and training of poll workers.

**APPORTIONMENT**    As noted earlier, the Constitution specified that apportionment of the House among the states was to be based on population. The Framers made an initial enumeration of 65 seats distributed across 13 states, with the "actual Enumeration" to be made "within three Years after the first Meeting of the Congress of the United States, and within every subsequent Term of ten Years, in such Manner as they shall by Law Direct" (Article I, Section 2, Clause 3). A national census would be conducted every 10 years (decennially) to determine the population for the individual states—"the whole Number of free Persons, including those bound to Service for a Term of Years, and excluding Indians not taxed, three fifths of all other persons."[19] The "three-fifths clause," a compromise made at the Constitutional Convention, allowed slaveowners to count three-fifths of enslaved people as "other persons" for purposes of representation in the House and the electoral college.

Over time, a congressional apportionment has followed every national census (except after the 1920 census, when urban and rural representatives could not agree on an apportionment plan).[20] As Table 3.2 indicates, the size of the House increased substantially across the first 13 apportionments (and censuses) until it was capped at 435 members in 1911.

Underlying these enumerations was the question of what method of apportionment to use.[21] The simplest way to determine how many representatives a state will receive is first to divide the U.S. population by the number of House seats. This yields the "divisor." Each state population is then divided by the divisor. The result is a whole number and a fractional remainder (a decimal). But different apportionment methods—developed by political luminaries like Thomas Jefferson, Daniel Webster, and Alexander Hamilton—handle those fractional remainders differently,[22] and fierce battles were waged in Congress over which method would be used. Members of the political party in power often selected the method that would yield the largest number of House seats for their party. Eventually, at the urging of Congress, a committee of mathematicians studied the question to determine which method was mathematically fairest. They settled on a method developed by Edward Huntington (a mathematician at Harvard) and Joseph Hill (a statistician for the Bureau of the Census). Congress quickly adopted it in 1940, and the following year made

## TABLE 3.2    Congressional Apportionment over Time

| Act of | House Size | Method Used | Population of United States | Based on Census of |
|--------|-----------|-------------|-----------------------------|--------------------|
| 1792 | 105 | Jefferson | 3,929,326 | 1790 |
| 1802 | 142 | Jefferson | 5,308,483 | 1800 |
| 1812 | 182 | Jefferson | 7,239,881 | 1810 |
| 1822 | 213 | Jefferson | 9,638,453 | 1820 |
| 1832 | 240 | Jefferson | 12,866,020 | 1830 |
| 1842 | 223 | Webster | 17,069,453 | 1840 |
| 1852 | 234 | Hamilton | 23,191,876 | 1850 |
| 1862 | 241 | Hamilton | 31,443,321 | 1860 |
| 1872 | 292 | Hamilton | 39,818,449 | 1870 |
| 1882 | 325 | Hamilton | 50,189,209 | 1880 |
| 1891 | 356 | Hamilton | 62,947,714 | 1890 |
| 1901 | 386 | Webster | 76,212,168 | 1900 |
| 1911 | 435 | Webster | 92,228,496 | 1910 |
| — | — | — | 106,021,537 | 1920 |
| 1929 | 435 | Webster | 122,775,046 | 1930 |
| 1940/41 | 435 | Huntington-Hill | 132,164,569 | 1940 |
| — | 435 | Huntington-Hill | 150,697,361 | 1950 |
| — | 435 | Huntington-Hill | 179,323,175 | 1960 |
| — | 435 | Huntington-Hill | 203,302,031 | 1970 |
| — | 435 | Huntington-Hill | 226,545,805 | 1980 |
| — | 435 | Huntington-Hill | 248,709,873 | 1990 |
| — | 435 | Huntington-Hill | 281,421,906 | 2000 |
| — | 435 | Huntington-Hill | 308,745,538 | 2010 |

reapportionment of the House's 435 seats automatic following each census according to the Huntington-Hill method.

**CAMPAIGN FINANCE**    Congressional election campaign financing has been a hot button issue since the early 1970s. The issue itself is far older, however. Throughout the nineteenth century, congressional candidates and their parties relied on those who held patronage appointments—government jobs based on partisan loyalty—for money. Patronage appointees were expected to contribute a portion of their salaries to the party to support its electoral candidates. As progressives attacked the patronage system after the Civil War, and as civil service reforms were eventually passed in the 1880s, the parties looked to bankers and wealthy industrialists for donations. Progressives continued their assaults and eventually Congress passed several campaign finance laws in the early twentieth century, but without enforcement mechanisms to regulate the reporting of contributions and force compliance. Hence, these laws were mostly ignored.

This lack of enforcement changed with a 1974 amendment to 1971's Federal Election Campaign Act (FECA). Passed in the aftermath of the Watergate scandal and significant campaign finance violations in the presidential election of 1972, the FECA Amendment of 1974 limited campaign contributions by individuals, political parties, and political action committees (PACs—corporations had set up the first PACs earlier in the century to channel contributions and sidestep earlier laws). The amendment also established spending limits, and, perhaps most important, created the Federal Election Commission (FEC) to enforce the law. FECA was quickly challenged in the federal courts, leading to the Supreme Court's decision in *Buckley v. Valeo* (1976), which affirmed the contribution restrictions under FECA but struck down spending limits in general.

Because FECA did not prohibit corporations, labor unions, and membership organizations from creating PACs, and because PACs were allowed to contribute more to campaigns than individuals, the number of PACs nearly tripled between 1978 and 2016, and total contributions from PACs to congressional candidates more than tripled (adjusted for inflation) over the same time span.[23] In addition, a 1979 amendment to FECA allowed political parties to receive unlimited soft-money contributions—donations that could be used to further a party's electoral goals but not directed to specific candidates. The 1979 amendment led to an explosion in contributions; the amount of soft money contributed to the parties more than quadrupled between 1992 and 2002.[24] Because FECA did not regulate how soft-money contributions could be used, wealthy donors, PACs, and the parties themselves set the terms.

After several election cycles, many observers came to realize that the misuse of soft money was undermining FECA's effectiveness, and they sought new reforms. Eventually, in 2002, a coalition of Republicans and Democrats in Congress passed the Bipartisan Campaign Reform Act (BCRA). The BCRA, otherwise known as McCain–Feingold after the act's two legislative sponsors, Senator John McCain (R-Ariz.) and Representative Russell Feingold (D-Wis.), eliminated soft-money contributions to political parties, raised individual contribution (hard-money) limits, and restricted "electioneering communications" broadcast ads (especially by corporations and unions).

Reformers initially saw the BCRA as a victory, especially after it largely withstood a special-interest challenge before the Supreme Court in *McConnell v. Federal Election Commission* (2003). However, big-money interests quickly devised a workaround, establishing issue advocacy groups known as 527 organizations, named for their position in the federal tax code, that do not expressly support or oppose specific candidates. The BCRA did not regulate 527 organizations, which meant there were no limits on who could contribute, no caps on overall contributions, and no spending limits. Attempts after 2003 to bring 527 organizations under the BCRA umbrella failed. More recently, in *Citizens United v. Federal Election Commission* (2010), the Supreme Court (in a 5–4 decision) held that, based on the free speech clause of the First Amendment, the government could not prohibit corporations, labor unions, and other membership organizations from contributing to electioneering communications. Two months later, in *SpeechNOW.org v. Federal Election Commission*, the U.S. Court of Appeals for the D.C. Circuit used the *Citizens United* decision to deny Congress the ability to restrict organizations' independent expenditures. This decision led to the creation of independent expenditure PACs, also called super PACs.

The two 2010 court decisions had a major effect on campaign finance. While super PACs cannot contribute directly to candidates or coordinate with them, they do facilitate corporations, labor unions, and other membership organizations unlimited spending in congressional elections. The amount of money in politics is thus at an all-time high and increasing. And, for now, Congress has few options to prevent further growth.

## State Law

State law has perhaps the most pervasive influence on congressional elections. Its effects are felt in numerous ways at different points in the process.

**ELECTION AND BALLOT LAWS**    For much of American history, states were given free rein to determine when, where, and how to hold congressional elections. For example, during the Jim Crow era, southern states used a variety of techniques, including poll taxes and literacy tests, to disenfranchise African Americans. Many of these state-level restrictions on voting were swept away with time. The most significant remaining restriction involves the disenfranchisement of people convicted of felonies. Only two states, Maine and Vermont, provide unrestricted voting rights for people with criminal convictions. Most states lift felon-voting restrictions after parole, probation, or release, although some states require felons to submit a formal petition to the court for the restoration of voting rights or a pardon from the governor, either of which might be denied. One state—Iowa—never restores voting rights to people with felony convictions.[25]

In recent years, a new form of voter disenfranchisement has emerged: voter identification laws. Voter ID laws request or require voters to show a form of identification at the polls. Some of the laws require a photo ID (such as a driver's license), while others allow an ID that indicates a formal residence (for example, a bank statement). If a voter does not have the required identification, states handle the next step differently. Some states are not strict; they allow the voter to sign an affidavit of identity or allow a poll worker to vouch for the individual. Other states are strict and permit voting only on a provisional ballot. For the vote to be counted, the voter must take additional action (such as presenting required ID at an election office) after Election Day.

In 2000, only 14 states had voter ID laws. In 2020, there were 34 states that had voter ID laws in place (see Figure 3.3).[26] Why the increase? Democrats contend that Republican state governments have passed the new laws to decrease voting by low-income people and people of color, who are most likely to be affected by such ID requirements and who would likely vote Democratic. Republicans have countered that such laws maintain election integrity and help eliminate illegal voting. Most experts, however, believe that there is little evidence to suggest that illegal voting—principally voting by noncitizens—is large or widespread.[27] These arguments aside, battles over voter ID laws and voter fraud have moved to the courts, and Pennsylvania and North Carolina have struck down these laws as unconstitutional. In other cases, states have been forced to weaken their existing laws. More court cases

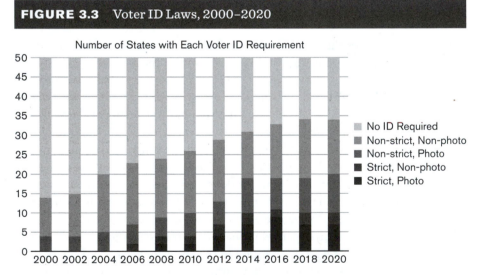

**FIGURE 3.3**   Voter ID Laws, 2000–2020

Number of States with Each Voter ID Requirement

Legend:
- No ID Required
- Non-strict, Non-photo
- Non-strict, Photo
- Strict, Non-photo
- Strict, Photo

(x-axis: 2000 2002 2004 2006 2008 2010 2012 2014 2016 2018 2020)

National Conference of State Legislatures, www.ncsl.org/research/elections-and-campaigns/voter-id-history .aspx; www.ncsl.org/research/elections-and-campaigns/voter-id.aspx (accessed 3/1/20).

are on the horizon, and partisan battles over voter identification are likely to continue.

Meanwhile, 39 states have made voting easier by allowing citizens to cast their votes early.[28] Early voting periods vary by state, ranging from 4 to 45 days before an election, with the average around 19 days. And 24 states currently allow early voting on weekends. In addition, all states allow absentee voting and will mail absentee ballots to voters who request them. Five states—California, Colorado, Hawaii, Oregon, and Washington—automatically send mail-in ballots to voters. And, in 2020 during the COVID-19 outbreak, 40 states temporarily modified their mail-in voting procedures in a variety of ways (such as extending deadlines or automatically mailing ballots or ballot applications).[29] These pre-Election Day state laws have increased voter turnout; in 2020, more than 101 million votes were cast before the official Federal Election Day.[30]

Finally, states control the format of the ballots and the technology (voting machines) used. This was not always the case. During much of the nineteenth century, parties managed the balloting process. Party workers stood outside the polls with stacks of party ballots and handed them out to voters. The party ballots listed only that party's candidates, and the ballots were often color coded. Voting was therefore public (not secret), as voters placed their color-coded ballots in a clearly observable ballot box, which jeopardized the integrity of the entire voting process. In the late nineteenth century, progressives sought to clean up the process, and ballot management slowly shifted to state governments. Between 1888 and 1910, nearly every state adopted the Australian ballot (see Chapter 2).[31] The Australian ballot itself can be organized in different ways; with a party-bloc ballot, candidates are listed by party, and with an office-bloc ballot, candidates are listed by office. Ballots can also take different forms. The infamous "butterfly ballot," which was at the heart of the voting controversy in Palm Beach County, Florida, in the 2000 presidential election, is one example of an office-bloc ballot.

**REDISTRICTING**   While the Constitution and federal law apportion congressional districts, states draw congressional district lines. And, in most states, the state legislatures manage the line-drawing (or **redistricting**) process. That said, federal guidelines and court rulings over the years have constrained states by requiring congressional districts to have certain features or identifying desirable qualities. These include:

1. Compactness (minimize, to the extent possible, the geographic space or volume within a district, to allow better and more efficient constituent-representative relations)
2. Contiguity (ensure that the geographic space within a district is connected)

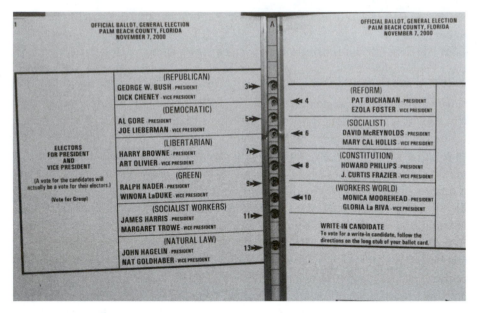

Florida's ballot from the 2000 presidential election is an example of an office-bloc ballot. This ballot reportedly confused some voters, causing them to inadvertently vote for Pat Buchanan instead of Al Gore.

3. Equal population (conform to the "one person, one vote" principle; ensure that votes are worth the same amount across districts)
4. Preservation of existing political communities (attempt to keep together existing political boundaries such as cities and counties; attempt to keep together demographic communities based on race, ethnicity, or religion)
5. Partisan fairness (percentage of votes for a party in a state should translate roughly into the same percentage of seats in Congress)
6. Racial fairness (prevent the dilution of minority voting power)

The *Wesberry v. Sanders* (1964) Supreme Court case established the equal population criterion. Prior to that time, **malapportionment** was a problem. That is, some districts in a state were considerably uneven in terms of population. As a result, the votes of citizens in a low-population district were worth more than the votes of citizens in a high-population district. Malapportionment typically favored rural districts and voters over urban districts and voters.

The compactness criterion is often violated when line drawing produces a greatly misshapen district, or **gerrymander**. (These districts are named after Elbridge Gerry, the early nineteenth-century governor of Massachusetts, who drew a state senate district that looked like a salamander as a way to connect distant groups of Federalist voters.) Gerrymanders are created for specific political purposes. The earliest, like Gerry's, were constructed to create as many majority-party-controlled districts as possible (conflicting with the partisan fairness criterion). Partisan gerrymandering has been common ever since. Often it means packing as many voters of the other party as possible into a small number of districts to dilute their voting power. Sometimes, it means breaking apart (or "cracking") an existing district controlled by the other party and forcing the incumbent to compete in a tougher electoral environment.

One of the most controversial cases of partisan redistricting occurred in Texas, when the Republicans in 2002 won majority control of the state legislature for the first time since Reconstruction. Encouraged by U.S. House Majority Leader Tom DeLay (R-Tex.), instead of waiting for the next decennial census (which is customary), the Republican state legislative majority in 2003 attempted to redraw district lines a year after the former Democratic majority did the same thing. Despite considerable political spectacle and media attention, the Texas Republicans were successful, and their efforts largely held up when challenged in court. As a result, the Texas delegation in the U.S. House flipped—from 17–15 Democrat after the 2002 elections to 21–11 Republican after the 2004 elections.

While the Republicans scored a victory, they did not emerge unscathed. Because of his fundraising efforts in support of the redistricting, DeLay was eventually charged with felony campaign finance violations and later convicted—a turn of events that discouraged other party leaders from similar pursuits.[32]

But gerrymandering can be bipartisan as well. A bipartisan gerrymander is a compromise between the parties. It limits competitiveness (and thereby uncertainty) in the electoral process, with the goal of maintaining the status quo (and thus protecting incumbents of both parties) in a state. Bipartisan gerrymanders increased after the 2000 redistricting process, occurring in Illinois, Mississippi, and Wisconsin; however, only New Jersey engaged in bipartisan gerrymandering after the 2010 redistricting.[33]

Gerrymandering has also been used to produce more African American and Latino members of Congress. Following the 1990 federal census, the Justice Department used Section 4 of the Voting Rights Act to require states to maximize their number of **majority-minority districts**, in which a majority of constituents are non-White. Many oddly shaped districts resulted. Perhaps the most famous is that of Representative Jesús G. "Chuy" García (D-Ill.) in the Chicagoland area.[34] In the 4th District in Illinois, two largely Latino communities were connected in a winding way, leading some to call the district "earmuffs" because of its appearance.[35]

Oddly shaped districts notwithstanding, the efforts paid off: after the 1992 elections, the number of African American representatives in Congress increased from 28 to 38, and the number of Latino representatives increased from 10 to 17.[36] But there was an unexpected consequence: creating majority-minority districts

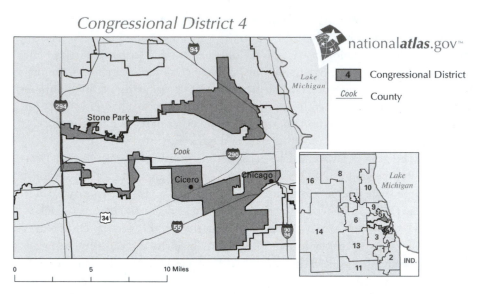

## Congressional District 4

Illinois's 4th Congressional District unites two predominantly Latino communities along a highway, giving it its "earmuff" shape.

in the South led to other districts becoming Whiter, resulting in Republican victories in those districts. According to political scientist David Lublin, "for many of the moderate to conservative politicians who traditionally dominated southern politics, racial redistricting provided a real incentive to seek office as a Republican instead of a Democrat."[37] As a result, the GOP made significant gains throughout the South, helping the Republicans become the majority party in the House in 1994. An effort to provide more descriptive representation for minorities thus led unexpectedly to a situation in which they received less substantive representation (as the Democrats lost control of the House and thus the ability to shape the legislative agenda).

Not long after the 1992 elections, racial gerrymandering was challenged in a series of Supreme Court cases—pursuant to the equal protection clause of the Fourteenth Amendment—and the process was greatly restricted. Race could still be considered in a redistricting effort, but it could not be the predominant factor.[38]

While racial gerrymanders have been challenged successfully in the courts, partisan gerrymanders have not. In 1986, the Supreme Court ruled that a partisan gerrymander could in theory violate the equal protection clause, but the Court could not agree on a standard to follow.[39] In June 2018 the Court considered the issue once again, based on the Federal District Court decision in

*Gill v. Whitford* (2016), which held that a partisan gerrymander in Wisconsin violated aspects of the First and Fourteenth Amendments.[40] In the end, the Court made no ruling on the question of partisan gerrymandering, sending the case back to the Federal District Court on a technical matter.[41] Finally, in June 2019, the Court ruled definitively on the constitutionality of partisan gerrymandering. Considering a case of partisan redistricting in North Carolina, the Court ruled in *Rucho v. Common Cause* (2019) that partisan gerrymandering claims were not justiciable, because according to Chief Justice John Roberts, "they present political questions beyond the reach of the federal courts."[42] With the *Rucho* verdict, future legal challenges to partisan gerrymandering were forbidden.

**PRIMARY ELECTIONS**    All states allow voters to select the party nominees for congressional office in primary elections, but this was not always the case. And different states have adopted very different forms of primary elections, which affect the types of party nominees chosen.

Like the Australian (secret) ballot, primary elections were a progressive reform adopted in the early twentieth century. Before then, the parties controlled the congressional nominating system, and party nominations were indirect; voters would choose delegates to local and state party conventions, and those delegates would choose the party's congressional nominees. Progressive reformers sought to eliminate the party convention system and replace it with one in which voters selected party nominees directly. They were successful, and the direct primary was created. An election would be held wholly within a party, only partisan candidates would be considered, and voters would choose directly among them. The winner of a party's primary election would be the party's candidate in the subsequent general election to Congress. This reform weakened party power generally, as party leaders lost control of the candidate-selection process. But the reform also helped heal divisions within the parties. Party factions that lost out under the indirect nominating system—and sometimes accused party leaders of playing favorites and rigging the system against them—were more willing to accept the voters' decisions in primary elections.[43]

Over time, primary elections have evolved, and some clear types now exist (Figure 3.4).[44] The main distinguishing criterion involves who is allowed to vote in a party's primary. **Closed primaries** restrict participation to only those voters who affiliate (register) with that party prior to the election. They are used in 10 states. **Semiclosed primaries** allow affiliated voters and independents (or unaffiliated voters) to participate. They are used in 12 states. **Open primaries** have no party registration requirement and thus allow voters of any

**FIGURE 3.4**   Primary Types by Party

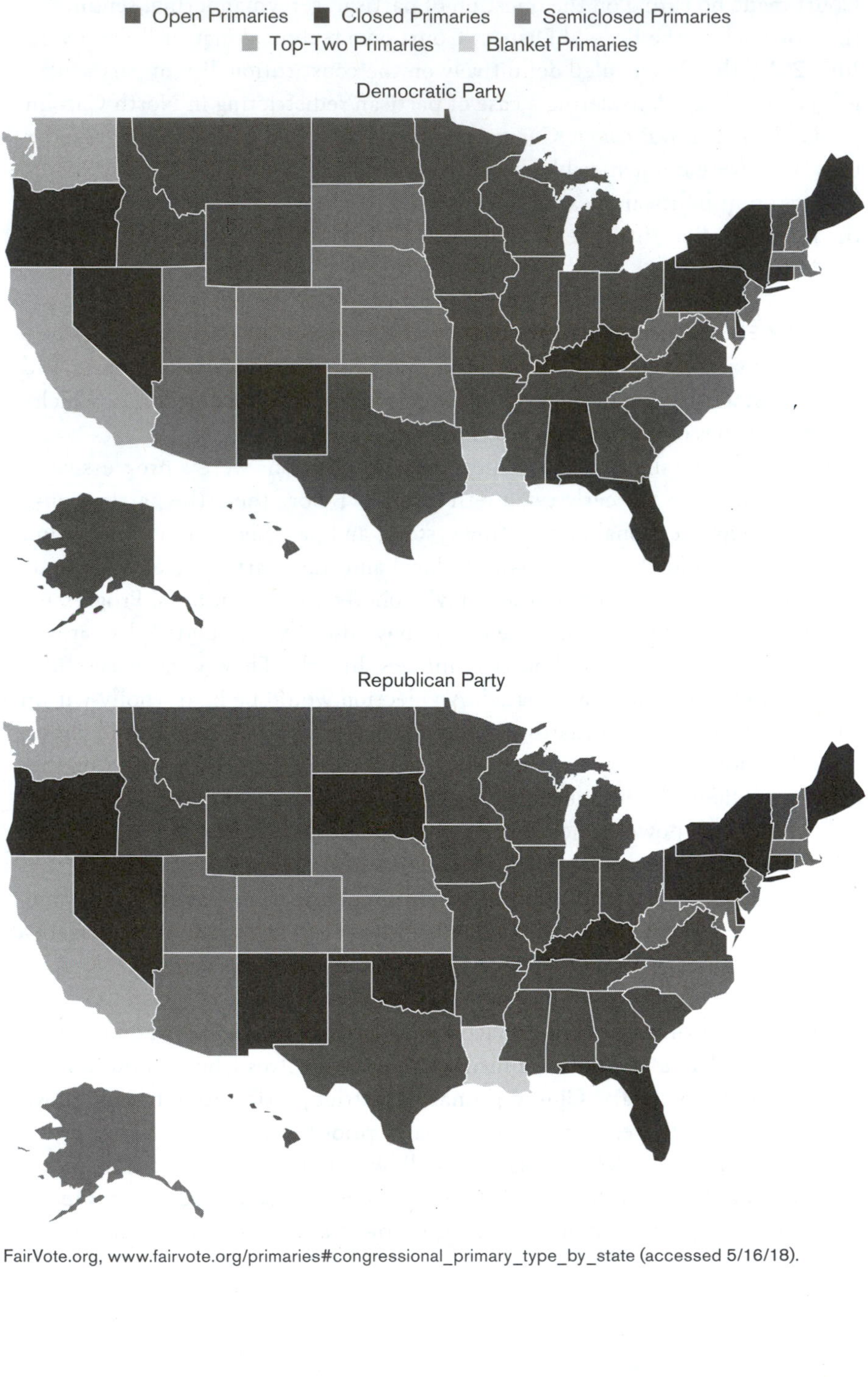

■ Open Primaries   ■ Closed Primaries   ■ Semiclosed Primaries
■ Top-Two Primaries   ■ Blanket Primaries

Democratic Party

Republican Party

FairVote.org, www.fairvote.org/primaries#congressional_primary_type_by_state (accessed 5/16/18).

partisan affiliation (as well as independents) to vote in any party's primary (but only one primary). They are found in 21 states. Alaska, Alabama, Oklahoma, and South Dakota have dual systems, with one party using one primary system and the other party using a different primary system. California and Washington state have a **top-two primary**, in which, regardless of party affiliation, all candidates are placed on the same primary ballot, all voters get to participate, and the top two finishers are then placed on the general election ballot. Finally, Louisiana has a **blanket primary**, where voters participate in both primaries (Republican and Democrat), and the top finisher from each party is placed on the general election ballot. These different types of primaries influence nominee selection in different ways.

The closed primary gives party leaders the strongest hand in controlling the context and process. Thus the eventual party nominees are more likely to be members of the party establishment. The open primary, by comparison, leaves party leaders much weaker, and mavericks and individuals with cross-party appeal have a better chance of being nominated. And in terms of the nomination itself, 40 of 50 states determine a winner based on plurality rule—where the candidate with the largest number of votes receives the nomination. But in 10 states, eight of which are in the South, a majority is required. Thus if the top vote-getter in the initial primary election receives only a plurality of votes, a runoff is triggered, and the process continues until a majority winner emerges.

Finally, primary elections differ from general elections in two important ways. First, turnout in primaries is considerably lower than turnout in general elections. In recent years, primary election turnout has been one-half to one-third of turnout in general elections. Second, the voters in primary elections tend to be more partisan, more ideological, more politically aware, better educated, and wealthier. As a result, voter distributions are skewed to the left in Democratic primaries and to the right in Republican primaries, which incentivizes each party's candidates to appeal to more extreme interests in that party.

How often are incumbents defeated in primaries relative to general elections? Figure 3.5 provides the answer. There is a lot of variation in both the House data and the Senate data, but the House data fluctuate less, and there is always at least one case in every election year of a House incumbent losing in a primary. The Senate data show seven cases in which half or more of defeated incumbents lost in the primaries, but also 18 cases in which no defeated incumbents lost in the primaries. Overall, though, data on the House and the Senate tell a similar story. From 1946 to 2020, on average, around 21.6 percent of defeated incumbents in the House and 21 percent in the Senate lost in the primaries.[45]

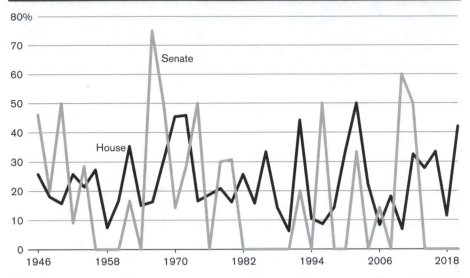

**FIGURE 3.5**    Percentage of Defeated Incumbents Who Lose in the Primaries

Brookings Institution, www.brookings.edu/multi-chapter-report/vital-statistics-on-congress (accessed 1/21/21).

# WHO SEEKS ELECTION TO CONGRESS?

Now that we know the basic rules and procedures of congressional elections, we can examine who runs, who wins, and how voters decide. To begin, we ask a basic question: Who seeks election to Congress?

## The Rise of Congressional Careerism and the Electoral Connection

In the nation's first 100 years, individuals who served in Congress did not expect to stay for an extended period of time.[46] During this period, the parties controlled the electoral process. They determined the design and distribution of the ballots and largely chose the nominees. As a result, a political aspirant's career track was different than it is today. A career in politics meant a career in the party, not a career in any one political institution (such as Congress). Often, political aspirants in the nineteenth century pursued a leapfrog strategy in building a political career, with a seat in Congress representing just one stop along the way. An individual often moved from a state legislature to Congress and then back again, sometimes also seeking a governorship or judgeship. Access to these latter positions often hinged on how he or she performed in Congress, as party leaders back home kept a close eye on Washington politics. Moreover, the parties cared about keeping congressional seats under their control and often formally prohibited careers in Congress. Some state parties adopted strict rules of rotation in office, whereby individuals were allowed to serve only a single term in Congress. Rotation in office provided congressional experience to a wider set of party politicians and allowed party leaders to use a congressional seat as a reward for those who served the party especially well. To choose one notable example, Abraham Lincoln was affected by rotation in office, as Whig rules in Illinois restricted him to a single term in the House of Representatives.[47]

Progressive-Era democratization of the electoral process—the Australian ballot, primary elections, and overall loss of party control over the process—affected politicians' career decisions. By the end of the nineteenth century, voters were able to punish or reward candidates individually. And if members of Congress wanted to stay in office, they now had a greater incentive to respond to voters' needs. The Australian ballot and the party primary firmed up the constituency-representative linkage by increasing accountability. The electoral connection as we know it in contemporary politics had emerged.

After the Civil War, the federal government expanded considerably as national-level governmental activity grew. With the political action increasingly in Washington, salaries for members of Congress improved. And as the nation's political economy expanded, outside financial opportunities for members of Congress also multiplied.[48] By the turn of the twentieth century, members of Congress increasingly wanted to build their careers there.

Most scholars agree that congressional careerism—as opposed to party-focused careerism—can be traced back to the Progressive Era. As David Brady and his coauthors note, "After 1900, the number of freshman House members sharply declined and the average years of incumbent service grew dramatically. . . . [B]y 1920 the House had been transformed from a body of amateur members to a modern legislature of professional politicians with established careers in Washington."[49]

## Ambition and Strategic Choice

At the heart of the contemporary electoral connection is the assumption that members of Congress are ambitious and strongly desire to be reelected.[50] In fact, in his famous book, *Congress: The Electoral Connection*, political scientist David Mayhew calls members of Congress "single-minded seekers of reelection."[51] This statement is too strong; Mayhew intended it as a simplification. Members of Congress care about other things, including career advancement within the institution and good public policy.[52] But it is fair to say that all other goals require them to get (re)elected first.

Ambition is also at the heart of challengers' decisions to seek election to Congress. Like congressional incumbents, challengers value the office for a host of reasons, but as the reelection-rate figures indicate (see Figure 3.1 on page 63), unseating an incumbent is very difficult. A challenger must be highly ambitious, willing to assess the costs and rigor of a serious congressional campaign and devote a huge amount of time to the endeavor.

The decision to run for a seat in Congress is a strategic calculation for incumbents, for would-be challengers facing an incumbent, or for individuals considering an open seat. A simple "calculus of election" equation captures all the relevant considerations:

$E(U) = (P \cdot U) - C$, where

> $E(U) =$ the expected utility (the satisfaction or benefit) of choosing to run for an office
>
> $P =$ the probability of winning in a race for an office
>
> $U =$ the utility associated with holding an office
>
> $C =$ the cost of running for an office

The decision to run, then, comes down to the value of $E(U)$. If the expected utility is positive, the person should choose to run. If the expected utility is negative, the person should choose not to run.

The variables in the equation (P, U, and C) depend on the individual candidate and the strategic context. For example, for the typical incumbent seeking reelection, P will be very large. Incumbent members of Congress possess a host of advantages in any election. (We discuss this incumbency advantage, and its various sources, in the next section.) The typical challenger, facing the typical incumbent, will have little chance; hence, P for the typical challenger will be small.

The utility associated with holding a seat in Congress (U) is a subjective assessment. By definition, an ambitious person will value the seat highly. Typical incumbents have already experienced a stream of benefits by holding the office, so their assessment will be very high. The cost of running for the office (C) will also be a subjective assessment. Individuals running in their first election will incur a variety of costs, including opportunity costs (foregone benefits from other activities or opportunities), campaign costs (including not only the funds themselves but also the efforts necessary to raise them), and personal costs (health costs associated with conducting a serious campaign and costs to family members for making all aspects of their lives public). Arguably, an incumbent faces lower costs for future races: with experience, campaigning becomes more efficient, personal costs can be better assessed and managed, and so on. In other words, start-up costs are extremely high, but if an individual is elected, subsequent costs are lower.

We can classify the individuals who run for Congress in two basic groups: amateurs and professionals. Amateurs are political novices, having never served in an elected office. They sometimes emerge, or are recruited, around an issue-based cause, and they often contest a seat held by a strong incumbent. Many amateurs are long-shot candidates who secure a nomination because other (more experienced or connected) candidates don't want to waste time taking on an entrenched incumbent. Because of their inexperience or naïveté, amateurs often seriously overestimate their likelihood of winning and greatly underestimate the costs associated with running a congressional campaign. And while long-shot amateurs occasionally beat the odds and win—as AOC did in defeating Joe Crowley—some amateurs possess attributes that make them formidable candidates. These amateurs are highly visible or highly wealthy. They might be astronauts, actors, entertainers, athletes, war heroes, or business leaders.[53] Their star qualities appeal to donors and voters, which increases their likelihood of making a successful electoral challenge.

Unlike amateurs, professionals are seasoned politicians. They have held political office before, and they understand the rigors of organizing and running a campaign and the odds of beating an incumbent. They are significantly more strategic than amateurs, carefully studying the political climate and dispassionately calculating the costs and benefits of making a serious run for office.[54] Professionals avoid long-shot campaigns and consider entering a race only when the odds of winning are better: when an incumbent is vulnerable (because of a scandal, a shift in public mood, or a redrawn congressional district) or if a seat is open (no incumbent is running). When they do choose to run against an incumbent, media and campaign watchers will cover the race closely in anticipation of a highly competitive election.

Professional politicians may choose not to enter a congressional race (either against an incumbent or for an open seat) because they currently hold an elected office and do not want to give it up for the chance of winning election to a higher office. To study this issue of progressive ambition more formally, we can rewrite the simple calculus of election equation as follows:

$$E(U_L) = (P_L \cdot U_L) - C_L$$
$$E(U_H) = (P_H \cdot U_H) - C_H$$

Here two sets of offices are considered: a lower office (designated by subscript $L$) and a higher office (designated by subscript $H$). A professional then considers the expected utility associated with running for each office and selects the one that is larger. In other words, if $E(U_L) > E(U_H)$, then the individual should run for the lower office, and vice versa.

Amateur candidates who run for congressional office are sometimes successful if they have preexisting name recognition. John Glenn, one of the United States' first astronauts, won election to the Senate in 1974. Al Franken, a comedian known for his appearances on *Saturday Night Live*, won election to the Senate in 2008. Glenn retired after serving 24 years. Franken announced his retirement in 2017 upon allegations of sexual harassment.

We might think of these equations in terms of seats in the House (lower office) and Senate (higher office). Usually, the safe bet for a House incumbent is to seek reelection rather than to make a run for a Senate seat. Having been elected (at least once), House incumbents understand their district, have built a campaign and fundraising network, and (probably) will not face a strong challenger. By comparison, a bid for the Senate is considerably less certain. Even if the Senate incumbent is vulnerable, House incumbents have to weigh a variety of considerations. Can they raise funds across the state as they do in their district? Would they be able to build a larger and broader campaign staff in time? Do their ideological positions, which fit their district well, also have statewide appeal? Who else from the party might choose to run? At the same time, a Senate seat brings several benefits: more perks, greater media attention, a larger say in policy matters (as one of 100, rather than one of 435), and more stability (with a six-year term instead of a two-year term). A Senate seat also makes further progressive ambition—a run for the presidency—more likely.

Keep in mind that these equations are based on rational calculation. Would-be candidates weigh the subjective costs and benefits of running for office, or two different offices, and make a purely analytic decision. They will run for a particular office if the expected utility is positive, or they will choose the higher expected utility between two offices. These models assume that all potential candidates consider running for office. But structural issues in American society may not align with that assumption.

For example, political scientist Jennifer Lawless finds that women are significantly less likely than men to consider running for office and then choose to run. She attributes this gender gap in political ambition to recruitment patterns (party leaders are less likely to seek out women as potential candidates) and gender differences in self-perception (women are less likely than men to see themselves as qualified to run). Lawless finds this gender gap not only when comparing men and women generally but also when comparing men and women *within* racial categories, uncovering significant differences between White men and White women, African American men and African American women, and Latino men and Latina women. Interestingly, Lawless does not find evidence of a similar racial gap in ambition among men: there are no significant differences in the political ambitions of White, African American, and Latino men.[55]

An additional structural factor that influences who considers running for office is the ideological environment. Political scientist Danielle Thomsen finds that as the political world has become more polarized, with the Democratic Party becoming more liberal and the Republican Party becoming more conservative, the types of candidates who choose to run have changed. Specifically, moderates in both parties—Republicans who are more liberal than the norm and Democrats who are more conservative—have opted out of the candidate pool, because they view themselves as outsiders with little chance of winning nominations. And with fewer moderate candidates vying for party nominations, Thomsen argues that the ideological gulf between the parties in Congress has widened further.[56]

# THE INCUMBENCY ADVANTAGE

We've seen that incumbent members of Congress possess an advantage in elections (Figure 3.1). Why? What advantages do members of Congress have when they seek reelection?

## Institutional Advantages

Incumbent members of Congress receive a personal allowance that they can use in a variety of ways to meet the needs of their districts or states (more on this in Chapter 4). They can hire personal staff to service the needs of their constituents and to help draft legislation. They can travel to their districts or states to meet with constituents, give speeches, and conduct fundraisers. Given their position as sitting lawmakers, they are routinely in the news, and they can also use the wealth of communications technology in Congress to stay in touch with local media back home. Finally, the legislative structure and process in Congress allows incumbents to claim credit for their achievements (often through committee work) and take positions on a range of issues (through bill introduction, roll call voting, and floor speeches).

These institutional advantages render members of Congress highly visible, with significant name recognition in their districts or states. This visibility has been an important factor in explaining citizens' voting behavior in the post–World War II era.[57] Most challengers do not possess these institutional luxuries and thus struggle for recognition.

## Money

When it comes to fundraising, incumbents have a huge advantage over challengers. Donors understand that, all else equal, incumbents who seek reelection are very likely to win. They want their campaign contributions to be meaningful, and they want to buy access to the person who holds the seat. The incumbent is simply a much better bet.

The cost of winning an election to the House or Senate has increased considerably over the last three decades. It was over twice as expensive to win a House or Senate seat in 2018 as it was in 1986 (controlling for inflation). Today, candidates spend over $2 million (on average) to win a House seat and

**FIGURE 3.6**    Average House Campaign Expenditures: Major Party General Election Candidates, 1974–2018 (in 2018 Dollars)

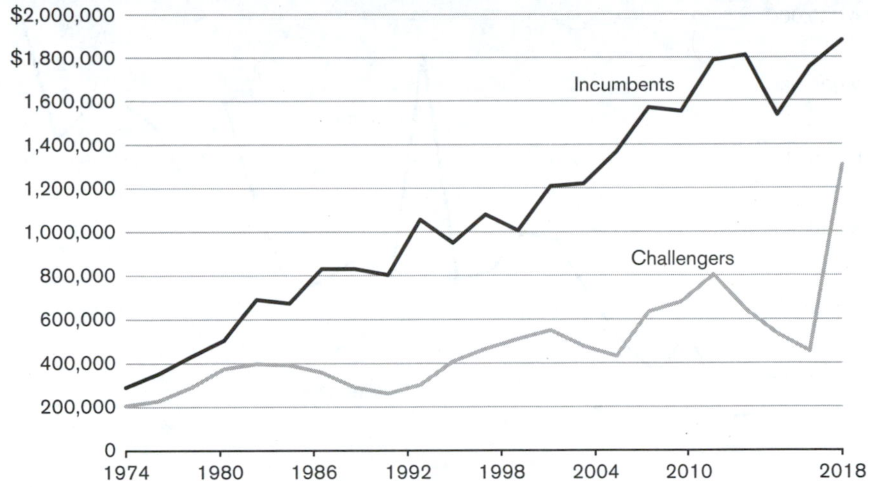

Brookings Institution, www.brookings.edu/multi-chapter-report/vital-statistics-on-congress (accessed 1/21/2021).

over $14 million to win a Senate seat. Money is crucial, and those who can raise it for their campaigns have the best shot at winning.

How does campaign spending differ between incumbents and challengers? In 2018, average spending by House incumbents was nearly 1.5 times as large as average spending by challengers. But this wasn't always so. As Figure 3.6 shows, a significant widening first occurred in the mid-1980s and continued until recent years when House incumbents sometimes spent more than three times as much as challengers. In 2018, however, money flowed into the campaign coffers of Democratic challengers, as a rebuke of the Trump administration (and in an attempt to defeat Republican incumbents).[58]

Spending in Senate elections has fluctuated more than spending in House elections. As Figure 3.7 shows, average spending in the Senate in the mid- to late 1970s followed a pattern similar to that of spending in the House. Incumbents outspent challengers on average, but the gap was relatively small. After some fluctuation, the gap widened briefly in 2014, but has shrunk since then.

Today, the price of competing meaningfully with, and perhaps defeating, an incumbent is exorbitant. To have a reasonable chance, a challenger must close the fundraising gap considerably. For example, in the 13 House races in 2014 in which a challenger defeated an incumbent, the gap was much smaller ($3 million on average spent by incumbents; $2.13 million by challengers). The same was true for the five Senate races in 2014 in which a challenger defeated an

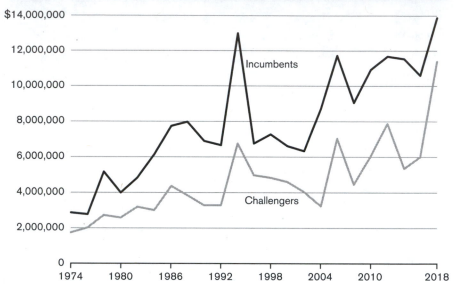

**FIGURE 3.7** Average Senate Campaign Expenditures: Major Party General Election Candidates, 1974–2018 (in 2018 dollars)

Brookings Institution, www.brookings.edu/multi-chapter-report/vital-statistics-on-congress (accessed 1/21/21).

incumbent ($17.07 million on average spent by incumbents; $12.05 million by challengers).[59]

Overall, given the wealth of advantages that comes from incumbency, matching an incumbent's fundraising is difficult, and few challengers try. Many would-be challengers are scared off by the financial hurdles they would face if they attempted a serious run.

## Legislative Redistricting

Following the *Wesberry v. Sanders* (1962) Supreme Court decision, legislative redistricting has also been tied to the power of incumbency. Many scholars have argued that the Court-ordered redistricting in the 1960s presented opportunities for political gain. Political scientists Gary Cox and Jonathan Katz have shown that Democratic legislatures (and federal courts dominated by Democratic judges) in the 1960s reduced competition in congressional elections significantly by packing Republicans into a small number of districts, which gave Democrats a meaningful electoral advantage in the remaining districts.[60] This redistricting solidified the Democrats' hold on the House, even as the civil rights movement was changing the political world around them.

Politically motivated redistricting has continued into the present day. In a recent study, political scientists Jamie Carson, Michael Crespin, and Ryan Williamson examined the effects of redistricting on electoral competition in the House from 1972 to 2012.[61] They compared the effects of redistricting efforts made by three different decision makers: state legislatures, courts, and commissions. Like Cox and Katz, Carson and coauthors found that congressional districts that are redrawn by state legislatures (politicians) produce significantly less competitive elections (and are biased toward the interests of the parties in power) when compared to congressional districts that are redrawn by courts and commissions (more independent actors). This difference is most pronounced since the early 1990s, as the parties have increasingly become polarized and line drawing (via computer software) has become more technologically advanced.[62]

## HOW WE STUDY
## THE INCUMBENCY ADVANTAGE

Identifying the factors that give congressional incumbents an advantage when they seek reelection is valuable, but we also want to assess the importance of that advantage over time. Stated differently, we want to measure the incumbency advantage. We want to assess how much of an incumbent's vote total can be attributed to being an incumbent.

Political scientists have developed many advanced statistical techniques to calculate the incumbency advantage,[63] all building on two simple measures:

1. The Sophomore Surge: the electoral gain an incumbent achieves when running for reelection for the first time
2. The Retirement Slump: the electoral loss for a party when an incumbent member of Congress retires

Both the Sophomore Surge and the Retirement Slump are calculated relative to a partisan baseline, which is the "normal" partisanship in the district plus trends over time. The partisan baseline is estimated using open-seat elections, in which no incumbents run. The Sophomore Surge and Retirement Slump represent deviations from that partisan baseline. The Sophomore Surge is the change in the vote from an incumbent's initial election to his or her first reelection. The Retirement Slump is the change in the vote from an incumbent's final reelection to his or her party's vote in the next election when it contests an open seat. The size of the Surge and Slump can then be considered the value of incumbency,

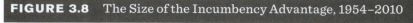

**FIGURE 3.8**    The Size of the Incumbency Advantage, 1954–2010

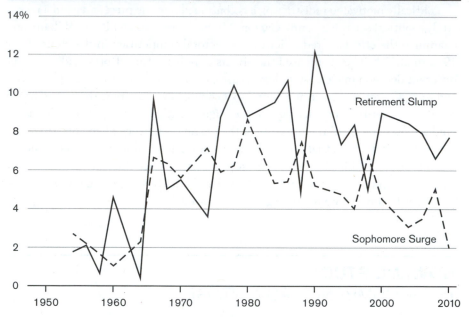

Robert S. Erikson. 2017. "The Congressional Incumbency Advantage over Sixty Years: Measurement, Trends, and Implications," in *Governing in a Polarized Era: Elections, Parties, and Political Representation in America*, ed. by Alan S. Gerber and Eric Schickler, 80. New York: Cambridge University Press.

where the Surge represents the bonus of incumbency and the Slump represents the loss of incumbency.

As Figure 3.8 illustrates, for the three decades spanning the 1970s through the 1990s, the Sophomore Surge and Retirement Slump measures tell a similar story, suggesting that that the incumbency advantage averaged between 7 and 8 percentage points. In other words, the value of being an incumbent during those three decades—all the institutional advantages, the money-raising advantage, and the redistricting advantage—was worth 7 or 8 percentage points of the two-party vote. Viewed from the perspective of a challenger during that time, a 7 to 8 percentage-point advantage meant that incumbents had a large head start toward getting reelected, even before the race began and votes were cast. The incumbency advantage was a huge hurdle for a challenger to overcome.

The 2000s saw a drop in the incumbency advantage, down to roughly 3 percentage points (based mostly on the Sophomore Surge measure).[64] The estimate for 2010 is even smaller—only 2 percentage points (similar to the estimates from the 1950s and early 1960s). Why the drop? The best evidence suggests that the 1970s through 1990s might have been an unusual period; partisan identification was weak, and voters used other information (including name recognition, which helps incumbents) to make their choices. Partisanship has become much more important in recent years, and thus voters increasingly use it, rather than other information, when making their vote choices. We discuss this nationalization of politics in more detail below.

### Critical Thinking

1. How is the incumbency advantage related to the Australian ballot? Do you think an incumbency advantage existed when the parties controlled the balloting process? Why or why not?
2. If a House incumbent decides to run for a Senate seat, will the incumbency advantage that she enjoyed in her district help in her Senate election campaign? Why or why not?
3. Do you consider the Sophomore Surge or the Retirement Slump to be a better measure of the incumbency advantage? Why?

---

# WHEN AND WHY DO INCUMBENTS LOSE?

Given the many advantages that incumbents possess, why do they sometimes lose? As we have noted, quality challengers, who generally represent the best hope against an entrenched incumbent, understand the structural challenges of taking on a sitting member of Congress. Thus there must be compelling reasons why experienced, quality challengers choose to oppose an incumbent.

## National Tides

Sometimes the party in power is blamed for poor economic conditions or failure to govern effectively. In such cases, voters respond by disproportionately punishing members of Congress from that party who are running for reelection. If some incumbents are marginal—having narrowly won one or more recent elections—a partisan tide puts them at risk of being voted out of office.

Historically, and as mentioned at the start of this chapter, House members from the president's party suffer losses in midterm elections. Generally, these midterm results are considered corrections, as winning presidential candidates generally improve the election performance of all party members down the ticket in the year that the president is elected (a phenomenon we call **presidential coattails**). Two years into a presidential administration, however, any honeymoon period has long passed, and presidential popularity usually declines as a result of presidents having to make any number of decisions, at least some of

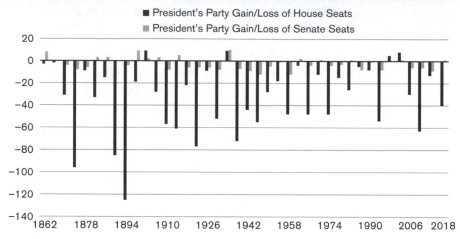

**FIGURE 3.9**    Gains and Losses by the President's Party in Midterm Elections, 1862–2018

- President's Party Gain/Loss of House Seats
- President's Party Gain/Loss of Senate Seats

Data collected by authors.

which will be unpopular. As a result, incumbent members of the president's party lose any presidential bump that they may have received two years earlier.

Figure 3.9 documents the midterm performance of the president's party in both the House and Senate since the Civil War. The negative effect is more pronounced in the House than in the Senate, in part because of the scale of potential loss; all House seats are up for reelection every two years, whereas only about one-third of Senate seats are. The negative effect in the House has spanned different eras in American history, with only four cases of a positive result for the president's party: 1902 (shortly after Theodore Roosevelt replaced William McKinley, following the latter's assassination), 1934 (the first election after Franklin Delano Roosevelt and the Democrats' realigning election victory of 1932), 1998 (following the government shutdown battles between congressional Republicans and President Clinton, for which the GOP was largely blamed), and 2002 (the first election after the 9/11 terror attacks, when the country rallied around President George W. Bush).

## Scandals

Incumbents who are involved in a scandal take an electoral hit if they try to seek reelection. The average scandal-ridden incumbent who tries to remain in office can expect to see his or her vote total drop by 5 to 11 percentage points in the next election.[65] For incumbents who are somewhat marginal, this decline could be enough to cost them reelection. Political scientist Rodrigo Praino and his coauthors found that over a 30-year period, 25 percent of House incumbents who were involved in an ethics investigation were defeated in a primary or general election, compared to only 5 percent of those not being investigated.[66]

## Redistricting

Elections following a significant redistricting can sometimes put an incumbent at risk. A redistricting could protect all incumbents, as we discussed previously. But if the redistricting is an aggressive partisan gerrymander, then it might split another party's incumbent's district. The incumbent may then face a new and uncertain electorate, with many of the new district's voters coming from the other party. A partisan gerrymander could also attempt to split two existing other-party districts and combine them into one, which could result in two other-party incumbents facing off against each other. For example, in 2012, Republicans redrew district lines in Pennsylvania and put two Democratic incumbents, Jason Altmire and Mark Critz, into the same House district.[67] Critz defeated Altmire in the Democratic primary and then lost the general election to Republican Keith Rothfus, allowing the GOP to pick up a seat.[68]

## Internal Party Changes and Conflicts

Sometimes, the nature of an incumbent's party may change, leaving incumbents out of step with their primary constituency. Often, change in a district or state will be gradual, but sometimes an abrupt change occurs. For example, primary elections in the South in the middle of the twentieth century were typically conservative affairs. To win a Democratic primary, a candidate had to be reliably conservative, especially on issues of race and labor. However, the Voting Rights Act of 1965, which enfranchised African Americans and thereby diversified the southern Democratic electorate, forced a number of conservative southern Democrats from office. Many retired, some became Republicans, but some were defeated in primary elections by more moderate Democratic candidates.[69] More recently, the Tea Party movement developed quickly after Barack Obama's presidential election in 2008 and has challenged many establishment Republican incumbents. While Tea Party–backed candidates have done best in open-seat elections (races in which no incumbents were running), they have scored some significant primary victories against GOP incumbents, with David Brat's defeat of Republican House Majority Leader Eric Cantor in 2014 being the most significant.

## Retirements: The Hidden Story

While the previously mentioned factors help to explain why incumbents sometimes lose in their reelection bids, they also reveal why some incumbents decide
not to seek reelection.[70] Not all retirements are strategic, of course. Some members retire for age or health reasons, or simply because they would like to pursue
another line of work. And some retire because they intend to seek a higher
office. But many who anticipate a tough reelection battle, or a likely defeat,
refrain from making the attempt. For example, in 2017, Senators Jeff Flake
(R-Ariz.) and Bob Corker (R-Tenn.), who both ran afoul of President Trump and
were looking at serious primary challenges, retired.[71] Prior to the 2018 elections,
34 Republicans in the House—including Speaker Paul Ryan—announced that
they would not seek reelection, likely fearing a Democratic tidal wave in
November in response to the unpopularity of the Trump administration.[72]

Figure 3.10 illustrates the percentage of exiting incumbents who leave Congress
by choice (retirement), rather than by law (having been defeated in a primary or
general election). Both the House and Senate data display some variability, but the
general trends show that, over time, a greater percentage of incumbents have left
office via retirement. The only significant deviations have occurred in recent years,
especially in 2010 and 2012, when a number of House incumbents who sought
reelection were defeated.

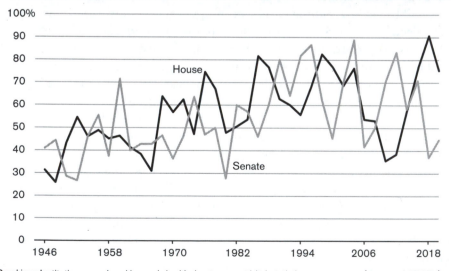

**FIGURE 3.10**    Percentage of Exiting Incumbents Who Leave Office by
Retirement, 1946–2020

Brookings Institution, www.brookings.edu/multi-chapter-report/vital-statistics-on-congress (accessed 1/21/21).

# THE NATIONALIZATION OF POLITICS

As noted earlier, most scholars find a large incumbency advantage in the last three decades of the twentieth century but a much smaller (and declining) advantage in the early twenty-first century. Why has the incumbency advantage shrunk, and what does this shrinkage tell us about the dynamics of today's electoral politics?

Most scholars believe that a **nationalization** of electoral politics has occurred in recent years.[73] In other words, voters are relying more and more on simple party cues to make their vote choices. They increasingly associate with a given party, and they vote for members of that party instead of voting based on other factors, such as incumbency. Political scientist Morris Fiorina sums up this process of nationalization succinctly: "When elections are nationalized, people vote for the party, not the person. Candidates of the party at different levels of government win and lose together. Their fate is collective."[74]

As a result of nationalization, **split-ticket voting**—voting for one party's candidate for one office and the other party's candidate for another office in the same election cycle—has decreased. Figure 3.11 reveals the percentage of congressional districts carried by a presidential candidate of one party and won by a House candidate of the other party. Since the 1980s, the percentage of split districts has plummeted.

In the early 1950s, a relatively low percentage of congressional districts were split. Over time, partisan identification weakened and ticket splitting increased. This trend led scholars in the 1970s and 1980s (and even in the early 1990s) to talk about party decline and even the demise of parties as we knew them. During this period, partisanship was a much weaker predictor of vote choice in national elections, and voters relied on other information, including the name recognition that comes with incumbency. Correspondingly, incumbency advantage was strongest in the 1970s and 1980s. Beginning in the 1990s, party became a much stronger predictor of vote choice in national elections, and it has grown to the point that today it overrides every other consideration.[75] District electorates now overwhelmingly vote straight party tickets, and the incumbency advantage has shrunk as a result.

What causes nationalization? Scholars disagree. Some believe it is due mostly to shifts in the mass electorate: citizens have become more loyal to a given party. Ideology and party have become better aligned—"conservative" with Republican and "liberal" with Democrat. This alignment allows citizens to simply pull a party lever in the voting booth rather than spend time choosing candidates office by office.[76] Others argue that nationalization is mostly elite driven: party leaders in Congress have increasingly emphasized party loyalty as a requirement for members to advance in the chamber and to receive rewards. And leaders now devote significant resources to creating a single party message in advance of the

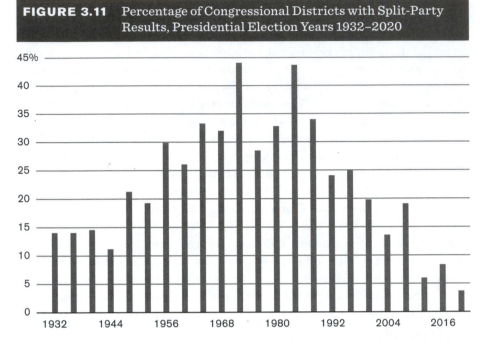

**FIGURE 3.11**   Percentage of Congressional Districts with Split-Party Results, Presidential Election Years 1932–2020

Brookings Institution, www.brookings.edu/multi-chapter-report/vital-statistics-on-congress/ and author's updates.

next electoral cycle. As a result, elites have made party the overriding factor in the congressional environment, which includes elections.[77]

Which argument is correct? More research is needed to determine a definitive answer, but both are likely correct to some degree. Elite and mass politics are usually interdependent. An important and related question is: Will nationalization continue? Are there factors that might lead party and ideology to diverge once again? Or will incumbent politicians begin to reassert authority to create their own messages? Some believe that the rise of the House Freedom Caucus, a group of very conservative House Republicans who have organized around issue positions and messages that diverge from the Republican leadership, signals an anti-partisan reassertion of authority. A similar splinter group within the Democratic Party has not yet formed, although populist tensions—associated with Bernie Sanders's failed bids for the Democratic presidential nomination in 2016 and 2020—could eventually produce a Freedom Caucus–like group on the left. "The Squad," as noted in the opening of this chapter, could indicate things to come for the Democratic Party, if more progressive members are elected to the House. .

Finally, apart from eroding the incumbency advantage, what has the recent trend toward nationalized elections meant? Because politicians' fates are now intertwined, we have seen more wave elections, where governing coalitions are swept in and out of power, as in 2006, 2010, 2014, and 2018. How should we evaluate these wave elections? On the one hand, waves can be viewed as good things, as greater nationalization forces parties to take collective responsibility for translating election promises—many of which are broad in scale and affect the nation as a whole—into policy. On the other hand, regular elections and the ever-present possibility of new waves give parties little time to develop and implement their policy agenda fully. The policy-making process takes time, especially if well-thought-out and comprehensive policies are to be adopted. The continual possibility of wave elections makes it difficult to produce good policies.[78]

## Conclusion

This chapter introduces the notion of the congressional electoral connection. Members of the House and Senate care about building a career in Congress. To show that they've been good representatives, incumbents use a variety of institutional advantages to service their constituents' needs. In doing so, they hope to be reelected. Elections promote accountability in the constituency-representative linkage. Every two years (House) or every six years (Senate), constituents can evaluate how their representatives have performed and punish or reward them by voting them out of office or granting them another term.

And the evidence shows that constituents overwhelmingly reward incumbents. Reelection rates for incumbents in both the House and Senate are extremely high. It is very difficult for a challenger to unseat an incumbent. Challengers do not have incumbents' institutional advantages, and they struggle to raise campaign funds to keep up with incumbents. When an incumbent does lose an election, it is usually to a quality challenger—someone who has held political office before and who enters a race strategically when the national or local conditions are favorable. Often, vulnerable incumbents will retire strategically rather than put themselves in a position to lose a reelection bid.

In recent years, however, there is some evidence that the electoral power of incumbency is waning. Various data point to increasing nationalization in politics as voters rely more heavily on party to guide their voting behavior. As a result, other sources of potential voting information, including candidate name recognition (which goes hand in hand with incumbency), have become less important. Thus more straight party voting is occurring, and the incumbency advantage is declining. Nationalization has led to more wave elections, in which governing coalitions come in and out of government in single swoops, enhancing partisan collective responsibility but also putting great pressure on the policy-making process.

Scholars and pundits will be watching these trends to see if they are temporary or more permanent. Whichever the case, it is clear that the current electoral environment is both dynamic and fluid, and upcoming elections will undoubt-edly be both interesting and unpredictable.

## Discussion Questions

1. Is it a good thing that, once elected to Congress, individuals in the modern era typically seek a long congressional career? What are the pros and cons of a Congress made up of many members who have served for a long time?
2. Of the various primary election systems used in the United States—open, closed, semiclosed, top-two, and blanket—which one is the best? Why?
3. Has the increasing nationalization of congressional elections in recent years been—on the whole—a good thing or a bad thing? Explain.
4. Three potential candidates—Mr. Pink, Ms. Green, and Mr. Black—are consid-ering a run for the House of Representatives in 2020. Based on the candidate-by-candidate data that follow, determine whether each of the potential candi-dates should run for a House seat. (Hint: refer to the discussion on page 84.)

   (a) *Mr. Pink*: probability of winning=0.45, benefit of holding office=60 utils, cost of running=30 utils
   (b) *Ms. Green*: probability of winning=0.3, benefit of holding office=100 utils, cost of running=25 utils
   (c) *Mr. Black*: probability of winning=0.4, benefit of holding office=50 utils, cost of running=20 utils

5. Three House members—Rep. Wolf, Rep. Bird, and Rep. Deer—are consid-ering a run for the Senate in 2020. Based on the candidate-by-candidate data that follow, determine whether each of these House members should run for election to the Senate or run for reelection to the House. (Hint: refer to the discussion on page 85.)

   (a) *Rep. Wolf*: probability of winning reelection to the House=0.7, benefit of holding House seat=20 utils, cost of running for reelection to the House=10 utils; probability of winning election to the Senate=0.5, benefit of holding Senate seat=60 utils, cost of running for election to the Senate=25 utils
   (b) *Rep. Bird*: probability of winning reelection to the House=0.8, benefit of holding House seat=10 utils, cost of running for reelection to the House=6 utils; probability of winning election to the Senate=0.4, benefit of holding Senate seat=70 utils, cost of running for election to the Senate=25 utils
   (c) *Rep. Deer*: probability of winning reelection to the House=0.55, benefit of holding House seat=20 utils, cost of running for reelection to the House=5 utils; probability of winning election to the Senate=0.5, benefit of holding Senate seat=40 utils, cost of running for election to the Senate=15 utils

# 4

## Representation

After the Affordable Care Act (Obamacare) was adopted in 2010, Republican Party leaders promised their constituents—especially party activists and important campaign donors—that they would repeal it. During the later years of the Obama administration, this promise led to numerous repeal efforts, though all proved fruitless because the Democrats controlled the presidency and, for several years, the Senate. Nonetheless, these efforts signaled that Republican Party leaders were listening to their constituents and that they were determined to succeed.

The elections of 2016 changed the game. When the electoral dust had settled, Republicans found themselves in control of the House, the Senate, and the presidency. President-elect Trump actively supported repealing Obamacare, so Republican leaders in Congress were suddenly on the spot: future fundraising and electoral success for the party would mean delivering on past promises. This pressure filtered down to the Republican membership in both chambers. Taking anti-Obamacare positions on roll calls that were not going to change policy was a thing of the past; a real opportunity to repeal the law was at hand.

But Republican lawmakers were in for a rude awakening as the 115th Congress (2017–19) convened. Repeal efforts stalled as public pressure to preserve

Amid the congressional push to repeal Obamacare in early 2017, many constituents gathered outside their representatives' district offices, and inside town hall meetings, to voice their support for the existing law and their opposition to the repeal efforts.

Obamacare mounted. In town halls (events that allow citizens to gather and engage directly with public officials), Republican members of Congress were excoriated for their attempts (and continued plans) to roll back Obamacare. In Chico, California, one constituent told Representative Doug LaMalfa, "I hope you suffer the same painful fate as those millions that you have voted to remove health care from. May you die in pain."[1] In Idaho, constituents angrily denounced Representative Raúl Labrador after he claimed, "Nobody dies because they don't have access to health care."[2] And in Plattsburgh, New York, chants of "shame, shame, shame" greeted Representative Elise Stefanik for her support of GOP repeal attempts.[3]

As Republican leaders persisted in their attempts to roll back Obamacare during the spring and summer of 2017, some GOP lawmakers avoided town halls altogether.[4] Those who continued to hold town halls tried to control them; some Republican lawmakers claimed that "paid liberal protesters" from out of town were descending on their town halls to cause trouble. While there was little evidence to support these claims, some legislators responded by holding lotteries for seat assignments or checking IDs to validate home addresses.[5] After many fits and starts, Republican House leaders in July 2017 were able to coordinate enough of the party's rank and file to repeal Obamacare; however, Republican Senate leaders fell one vote short in a dramatic late-night session.[6]

The GOP's repeal attempts would go on to cost them in the 2018 midterm elections. Voters in close House races named health care as one of their most important considerations,[7] and Democrats made it a major campaign theme, picking up 40 seats and regaining control of the House. The attempt to repeal Obamacare shows that for many members of Congress, representing constituent interests and governing are not always easy or compatible, especially on important and controversial policies. Rolling back Obamacare was important for the Republican Party in general, which needed to keep its collective promises over the previous years and show that it could govern when given the opportunity. But the effort was detrimental to GOP members whose constituents were not in favor of its repeal.

This chapter addresses some of the fundamental questions about the role that members of Congress play in American life. For example, what does it mean to represent someone? Do members of Congress always do what their constituents want? Or do they sometimes use their own expertise and experience to make decisions? Do members of Congress think about everyone in their district or state? Or do they focus more on those individuals who will be important for their reelection efforts? And what if other political actors—party leaders or interest groups, for example—pressure members of Congress to act against the interests of some in their district or state? How do members of Congress balance these pressures while remaining electorally accountable to constituents back home?

# THE BASICS OF REPRESENTATION

In a **direct democracy**, citizens make political decisions directly—but this kind of system is ill-suited to solving the many complex problems that a large and diverse republic often faces. As we learned in Chapter 1, the Framers established a **representative democracy** at the federal level, in which citizens in the United States choose political agents in regular elections to act on their behalf—that is, to represent them. These political agents are thus known as representatives. They are selected from geographic units—states for senators and districts for House members—and assemble in Congress to perform their legislative roles.

The size of Congress has increased substantially over time. The first federal Congress was composed of only 90 members—26 senators (two from each of 13 states) and 64 House members (distributed based on population across the states). As new states were added to the nation, the Senate and House grew. Today, Congress is made up of 535 representatives from 50 states: 100 senators and 435 House members.

Article I of the Constitution established the requirements for being a federal representative. To serve in the House, an individual must be at least 25 years of age and a citizen of the United States for at least seven years at the time of election. To serve in the Senate, an individual must be at least 30 years of age and a citizen of the United States for at least nine years at the time of election. In both cases, an individual must live in the state in which he or she is chosen.

Each Congress assembles for two years, in between the November elections that occur in every even-numbered year. The first Congress convened in 1789, and the opening of each subsequent Congress has taken place in every odd-numbered year. The 117th Congress, following the 2020 elections, convened in January 2021. All House seats and one-third of Senate seats are up for election every two years.

## IS CONGRESS REPRESENTATIVE OF THE NATION?

Do members of Congress resemble their constituents? In other words, does Congress reflect the rich diversity that exists in the United States? The answer is essentially "no." Table 4.1 provides a breakdown of some important demographic characteristics, comparing members of the 117th Congress to the U.S. population as a whole (based on most recent U.S. Population data).

**TABLE 4.1**  Does Today's Congress "Look Like America"?

|  | House | Senate | U.S. Population |
|---|---|---|---|
| Age (average) | 58 | 64 | 38 |
| Women (%) | 27 | 26 | 51 |
| Bachelor's degree (%) | 95 | 100 | 36 |
| Protestant (%) | 54 | 58 | 43 |
| Catholic (%) | 31 | 24 | 20 |
| Jewish (%) | 6 | 8 | 2 |
| African American (%) | 13 | 3 | 13 |
| Latino American (%) | 9 | 5 | 19 |
| Asian American (%) | 3 | 3 | 6 |

Pew Research Center, "Faith on the Hill," January 4, 2021, https://www.pewforum.org/2021/01/04/faith-on-the -hill-2021/; U.S. Census Bureau, "United States Population Estimates," https://www.census.gov/quickfacts /fact/table/US/LFE046219; U.S. Census Bureau, "U.S. Census Bureau Releases New Educational Attainment Data," March 30, 2020, https://www.census.gov/newsroom/press-releases/2020/educational-attainment.html; GovPredict and Phone2Action, "The Members of the 117th Congress," GovPredict, December 4, 2020, https://www.govpredict.com/blog/the-members-of-the-117th-congress (accessed 1/12/21).

First, members of Congress are more than a generation older than the average American. Second, nearly all members of Congress possess a bachelor's (four-year college) degree, as opposed to just over a third of the U.S. population.[8] Third, members of both the House and Senate are more religious generally—and more Protestant, Catholic, and Jewish specifically—than the U.S. population.[9] Fourth, Congress is considerably more male and more White than the nation as a whole. Women make up slightly more than half of the U.S. population, but they comprise just over a quarter of Congress. And the percentages of African Americans, Latinos, and Asian Americans in both chambers lag the respective national percentages. In sum, if we believe that Congress should mirror the important demographics in society—in order to ensure those demographics are truly represented—then these numbers are concerning. (We'll have more to say on this point shortly.)

While the membership of the current Congress may not reflect the U.S. population, it *is* more reflective than past Congresses have been. Diversity has been on the rise, especially over the last 25 years (see Figures 4.1 and 4.2). Since the 102nd Congress (1991–93), the number of women in Congress has more than quadrupled. During the same time, the number of African American members has more than doubled, the number of Asian American members has more than tripled, and the number of Latino members has nearly quadrupled. Thus while

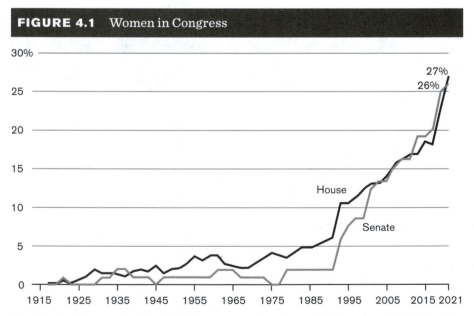

**FIGURE 4.1**   Women in Congress

Data do not include nonvoting delegates. Figure represents the makeup of the Congress on the first day of the session.
Pew Research Center, www.pewresearch.org/fact-tank/2019/02/15/the-changing-face-of-congress/; Center for American Women and Politics, "Women in the 117th Congress," January 1, 2021, https://cawp.rutgers.edu/sites/default/files/resources/press-release-women-in-the-117th-congress_0.pdf (accessed 1/12/21).

the 116th Congress ranks 76th out of 193 countries in terms of women's parliamentary representation and underrepresents people of color, the trends are positive toward a national legislature that more closely resembles the nation, at least on these dimensions.[10] The 117th Congress, in fact, counts the most women members and is the most racially diverse in the nation's history.[11]

At the same time, trends are not guarantees. For example, after a big jump in the number of African Americans in Congress following the 1992 elections, the overall count has risen only slightly since, with some intermittent declines (most recently in 2008). In addition, the diversity gains in Congress are very lopsided in terms of party, with Democrats disproportionately leading the way. In the 117th Congress, 74 percent of women, 95 percent of African Americans, 75 percent of Latinos and Latinas, and 89 percent of Asian Americans were Democrats.

**FIGURE 4.2** Growing Racial and Ethnic Diversity in Congress

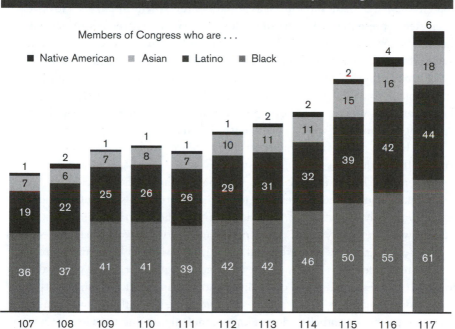

Note: Data do not include nonvoting delegates. Figure represents the makeup of the Congress on the first day of the session. The category of "Asian" includes Pacific Islanders. Members who have more than one racial or ethnic identity are counted in each applicable group.

Pew Research Center, www.pewresearch.org/fact-tank/2019/02/15/the-changing-face-of-congress; Ethan Cohen, Liz Stark, and Adam Levy, "117th Congress: Breaking Down the Historic Numbers," CNN Politics, January 3, 2021, https://www.cnn.com/2021/01/03/politics/117th-congress-historic-numbers/index.html; Amy Lieu, "A Record Number of Asian American Lawmakers Are Headed to Congress," The American Independent, January 2, 2021, https://americanindependent.com/asian-americans-pacific-islanders-congress-2020-election-senate-house/; Levi Rickert, "How Native Americans in Congress Voted on Electoral College Objections," Native New Online, January 7, 2021, https://nativenewsonline.net/currents/how-native-americans-in-congress-voted-on-electoral-college-objections (accessed 1/12/21).

## CHARACTERIZING REPRESENTATION

As we noted in Chapter 1, representation is fundamental to our system of government. Citizens (or constituents) select agents (or representatives) to act on their behalf in Congress. Constituents evaluate their representatives' performance in office and hold them accountable in regular elections.[12] Representatives are either rewarded for their performance and given another term, or they are punished and replaced by someone else.

But what does it mean to act on citizens' behalf? In short, what does it mean for a member of Congress to represent her constituents?[13] Recall from Chapter 1 that representation has often been characterized in two ways: (1) delegate-based or (2) trustee-based. In a **delegate** role, an elected representative assesses where her constituents stand on issues and supports those preferences through votes, speeches, and the introduction of legislation. A representative as delegate, therefore, channels the wishes of her constituents. This was the mode of representation envisioned by James Madison, as argued in the *Federalist Papers*. However, an elected representative in a **trustee** role acts very differently, taking actions that she believes are in the best interests of her constituents, even if such actions are at odds with their stated preferences. For example, a representative as trustee may believe that her expertise and experience require her to support legislation or vote in a way that runs counter to what her constituents say that they want. This was the mode of representation envisioned by Edmund Burke, a conservative thinker of the late eighteenth century.

In reality, no member of Congress acts as a perfect delegate or a perfect trustee. If constituents—or *some* constituents—care deeply about an issue, a representative has an incentive to satisfy their wishes. Political scientist R. Douglas Arnold famously referred to such constituents as "attentive publics."[14] On highly salient issues, such as gun rights and abortion rights, groups of citizens will care deeply about public policy and follow congressional proceedings very closely. Legislators often respond to such attentive publics—and represent their stated preferences—because they are more likely to organize politically, contribute time and money to campaigns, and vote in elections. On the other hand, Congress deals with many issues that are not especially controversial, or that constituents by and large do not know much about, and thus legislators are freer to act as trustees. Indeed, if constituents lack information on a complex issue that is on the legislative agenda, and thus do not necessarily possess true preferences, members of Congress must represent them by relying on their own expertise or experience or by turning to others for advice.[15]

# HOW DO MEMBERS OF CONGRESS REPRESENT CONSTITUENTS?

Members of Congress represent their constituents by voting on and crafting legislation, performing acts of constituency service, and making speeches and interacting personally with constituents.

## Legislating

Perhaps the clearest way that members of Congress represent their constituents is through day-to-day activities in the legislative process. Each Congress adopts hundreds of new laws, and constituents judge legislators on how they voted on bills that went on to become law. This is especially true of bills on highly salient issues, such as the adoption of and attempts to repeal Obamacare.

Yet a vote by a member of Congress often involves more than simply following constituents' interests. For example, party leaders in Congress may pressure lawmakers to vote a certain way in order to expedite the party agenda. And such pressure may take the form of rewards or punishments. For example, when Tom DeLay (Tex.) was the Republican majority leader in the House, he got Republican members to vote for the party's policies by promising money for their reelection campaigns (a reward) or threatening to run a primary challenger against them (a punishment).[16]

The president may also try to influence a lawmaker's vote, in combination with or separate from congressional party leaders. President Lyndon Johnson was famous for meeting with members of Congress in person and browbeating them into supporting his position—a persuasive technique that became known as the "Johnson treatment." Often, when it looks like a vote will be close, the president will pick up the phone and call wavering members to persuade them. For example, in March 2010, prior to the final vote on the Affordable Care Act in the House, when the outcome was far from certain, President Obama called undecided Democrats and asked why they "were not being part of the team."[17] More than seven years later, in July 2017, President Trump eschewed the phone in favor of his preferred means of communication—Twitter—to pressure Republicans to vote to repeal Obamacare: "After 7 years of talking," he tweeted, "we will soon see whether or not Republicans are willing to step up to the plate!"[18]

Interest groups, which may or may not include constituents, will also often pressure members on votes that they care about, with implicit promises of more campaign donations down the line or threats of future donations being cut off or distributed to election challengers. The National Rifle Association, for example,

President Lyndon Johnson was known for his aggressive, intimidating efforts to persuade members of Congress to support his issue positions.

lobbies members to preserve gun rights, and it distributes considerable sums of money—over $28 million during the 2020 general election cycle—to influence congressional legislation and election outcomes.[19] Finally, other members of Congress sometimes lobby their fellow lawmakers on issues that they care about, providing information in hopes of influencing their votes.

For all of these reasons, a lawmaker's vote often involves more than the simple constituency-representative link would imply. Many forces are in play, with some more powerful or relevant than others.

Constituents may also judge a member of Congress on her role in crafting legislation that goes on to become law (and sometimes a "landmark law"). Constituents may look at the committee that she sits on—and the work the committee did in navigating the bill through the legislative process—or the effort that she expended to craft and sponsor new legislation. A member of Congress who has a more active role in the production of legislation via committee work and bill sponsorship will often have a stronger claim to being an effective representative.[20] An individual vote, after all, rarely determines whether a bill succeeds in becoming a law.

Of course, while working to produce new legislation is a typical way that members of Congress fulfill their roles as representatives, *preventing* new policy from being adopted is also important. Sometimes, the choice between producing and preventing comes down to whether a member is in the majority or the minority. Majority parties are much better positioned to pass new legislation. Minority parties, on the other hand, work mostly to block policies that run contrary to their constituents' wishes. Thus how a member of Congress spends his legislative time will be a function, at least in part, of whether his party is in power or not. But there are exceptions. In the House, the Freedom Caucus (associated with the Tea Party) emerged in 2015 to encapsulate conservative efforts to reduce the size of the federal government. This group of conservative Republicans represented their constituents by refusing to go along with Speaker John Boehner on what many considered to be routine aspects of governing—such as funding the Department of Homeland Security, raising the debt ceiling, and granting the president the authority to negotiate international trade deals.

## Constituency Service

Another common way a member of Congress serves as a representative is through constituency service, also known as **casework**.[21] This refers to the various tasks that a member of Congress can perform to fix problems for constituents and otherwise satisfy their requests, often by contacting the appropriate federal agency. These tasks may seem minor—helping to locate a lost Social Security check, identifying the right forms to fill out to receive certain federal benefits, or writing a letter of recommendation for a child's college admission, for example—but they are important to constituents. And by dutifully providing such assistance, a member of Congress can build a reputation as a responsive representative, which can go a long way toward helping him be successful and get reelected. During his time in Congress, former three-term senator Al D'Amato (R-N.Y.) was known as "Senator Pothole" for his intense focus on constituency service. And he took great pride in the nickname: "It means you're attentive and you're there and available. And that pothole may be a matter of life or death for the person whose needs you are addressing. To them, that's not a pothole; that is making a difference in their lives."[22]

Members of Congress typically rely on their office staff to perform casework. This is a relatively recent phenomenon. Until the early twentieth century, most members of Congress did their jobs without official help. Only committee chairs had an office and a staff person. If a certain task was required, the average member did it himself, and if he needed assistance, he generally paid for it out of pocket. But beginning in the twentieth century, and formalized and expanded in the Legislative Reorganization Act of 1946, members of Congress were provided with personal allowances, known as general expense accounts, to help them do their jobs.[23]

In the House, a member's allowance account can be used for all official expenses, from hiring personnel, renting office space, and purchasing equipment to covering travel and mail costs. The average allowance for a House member in 2019 was just over $1.38 million. From this account, House members can hire no more than 18 full-time and 4 part-time personal staff members. In the Senate, the average allowance in 2019 was just under $3.74 million. A senator faces no restrictions on the number of personnel she may employ, and Senate allowances vary more than House allowances, as the size of the staff-assistance and office-expense components are based on the population of each state. So, in 2019, Senate allowances ranged from just under $3.44 million to more than $5.42 million.

Constituency service has become increasingly important to members of Congress over time. Part of this is demand-driven: constituents' needs and requests are ever increasing, and congressional representatives are much more accessible in the Internet age. But part is also supply-driven. As party machines have disappeared and parties as organizations have grown weaker, more casework has fallen to individual members of Congress and thus more of their personal allowances have been devoted to performing constituency service.

Lawmakers have both a Washington, D.C., office and a set of district or state offices. Personnel employed in the D.C. office include chiefs of staff, legislative assistants, and press aides. They perform the day-to-day legislative functions in support of lawmakers: providing advice, drafting legislation, researching policy, writing speeches, and communicating with the media and other member offices. Personnel employed in district or state offices are closer to constituents and thus better able to perform constituency service. As Figure 4.3 illustrates, the percentage of congressional staff located outside of D.C. has grown over time. In 1978, only a quarter of Senate staff worked in state offices; by 2016, this figure had grown to over 43 percent. While the House has not shifted quite as dramatically, it has followed a similar pattern. In 1978, one-third of House staff was located in district offices. By 2016, that figure was over 47 percent (and in fact exceeded 50 percent in the mid-2000s).

## Speeches and Personal Interactions

Legislators also routinely give speeches on the floor of Congress and at events in their home states and districts. These speeches vary in length and can be tailored to the audience; a member of Congress may speak on the same policy topic to different groups, for example, but focus on different things depending on the needs, sentiments, or demographics of the targeted group.[24] On the topic of national health care, a member of Congress might emphasize preserving

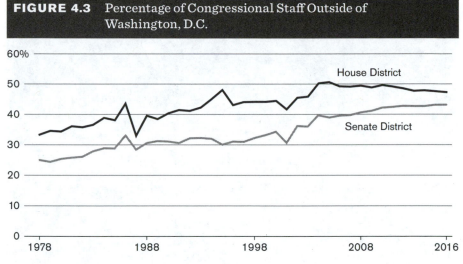

**FIGURE 4.3**  Percentage of Congressional Staff Outside of Washington, D.C.

Brookings Institution, www.brookings.edu/multi-chapter-report/vital-statistics-on-congress (accessed 5/15/18).

Medicare when speaking to a group of senior citizens but might focus instead on the importance of universal coverage when speaking to a group of young voters. Policies, and their effects, are often complex, and a successful legislator identifies how his support for or opposition to them matches the preferences of a range of his constituents.

Beyond speeches, legislators also interact with constituents on a more personal level back home. Shaking hands, kissing babies, and small talk with constituents at fundraising and campaign events are some examples. Meetings with important donors and interest groups are another. And then there are town hall meetings, which are often more policy-focused than campaign events and sometimes put members of Congress on the spot to clarify their positions on emerging policies, explain complex legislation, or defend their votes on contentious issues. The Obamacare town halls discussed at the start of this chapter—where Republicans faced hostile audiences opposed to repeal efforts—were particularly unruly. More recently, in February 2018, after 17 people were shot and killed at a high school in Parkland, Florida, Senator Marco Rubio (R-Fla.) faced grief-stricken parents and students who challenged him on his past and future positions on gun regulations.[25]

Just as lawmakers have located more of their staff in their home districts or states, they have also spent more of their own time back home. Under increased pressure to interact personally with constituents, lawmakers typically arrive in

After the shooting at Marjory Stoneman Douglas High School in February 2018, students and other constituents challenged Senator Marco Rubio (R-Fla., right) on his positions on gun control at a town hall meeting sponsored by CNN.

Washington on Tuesday, in time for evening votes, and stay through Thursday afternoon, after which they fly back to their districts or states. As a result, the modern Congress has been called the Tuesday-to-Thursday Club (or, more pejoratively, the Part-Time Congress).[26] This Tuesday–Thursday arrangement allows members of Congress maximum interactions with constituents back home, but it also affects how congressional proceedings are conducted. Leaders pack more into a tighter schedule, and less time for votes means more omnibus bills (which package together several legislative measures that might be on diverse topics), limited debate, and fewer amendments. Only one full day, Wednesday, is devoted to important legislative matters such as committee hearings and bill markups. Thus the realities of modern representative life pull members' attention toward their home activities and away from legislating.

## ORGANIZING REPRESENTATIONAL ACTIVITIES

Political scientist David Mayhew famously detailed a scheme for organizing the various representational activities of members of Congress.[27] For Mayhew, all such activities should be interpreted through the lens of legislators desiring and seeking reelection, and they fall into one of three categories.

The first category is **credit claiming**. Here a member of Congress takes credit for producing something positive for a constituent. Casework falls within this category, as a legislator can credibly make the case for providing the service: she (with the help of her staff) locates the lost Social Security check, identifies the correct forms to fill out, or writes the letter of recommendation. Claiming credit for a policy is harder. A legislator may argue that he voted for a piece of legislation, but his vote is only one of many that are needed for its passage. Instead, being on the committee responsible for crafting the legislation is a stronger signal that a legislator played a vital role in the policy-making process. And for members of both the House and Senate, tailoring committee assignments to their constituents' needs has been a standard and important way to strengthen the constituent-representative link in the modern congressional era.[28] For example, members who represent rural constituencies with significant farming interests gravitate toward the agriculture committees in both chambers, whereas members from large urban areas seek spots on the small business committees. (See also Chapter 5.)

The second category is **position taking**. This category is less about producing something tangible for constituents, such as casework or policy, and more about providing symbolic support. Position taking includes making a speech for or against a policy according to constituent preferences. A vote can also be an example of position taking. While a single vote does not usually determine whether a policy succeeds or not—few bills pass or fail by a single vote—it does place a member of Congress on the record, and she can accurately state that she supported or opposed a piece of legislation based on her constituents' preferences. Position taking is often more important for members of the minority party in Congress. Because the minority party does not control the legislative agenda and thus is rarely able to make policy, minority-party members must focus on representing constituents through speeches and votes that are often in opposition to the majority's policy initiatives. In this way, they signal that they are "fighting the good fight" for their constituents.

The third category, **advertising**, is more general. Here a member of Congress focuses on attributes rather than activities—it is more about who he is than what he has done. For example, a member may focus on his experience in office (how long he has served on important committees or what leadership positions he has held) or on personal qualities (being hardworking and responsible). A member of Congress often turns to advertising when interacting with constituents before elections. At its core, advertising is about building trust. There will be many occasions when a member of Congress must make judgments on policy matters—and thus serve as a trustee—and advertising is about making clear to constituents that he can be relied on.

## COMMUNICATING REPRESENTATIONAL ACTIVITIES

How do members communicate their representational activities to constituents? While members of Congress sometimes interact with constituents face-to-face, they typically use media as a vehicle. For much of American history, the near-exclusive media source was the U.S. mail. From the nation's inception, members of Congress have had the ability (subject to various caps) to reach constituents through the mail at no cost to themselves. This ability is known as the **franking privilege**. In lieu of a stamp, the member simply affixes his signature (the "frank") to a piece of mail, and the U.S. Postal Service delivers it. All members send a general newsletter to constituents, outlining their positions on votes, policy accomplishments, and general stances on issues of the day. These news-letters might include photos of particular benefits that a member was able to secure for her constituents, such as a new post office, bridge, or other public works project. Members also use special mailings to target particular constituencies. Sometimes the mailing includes an opinion poll inviting constituents to weigh in on important policy matters.

In recent years, members of Congress have graduated from paper communication and now have websites that provide constituents with a wealth of information, including biographical sketches, the committees on which they serve, policy positions, and key votes. Many members post videos from recent speeches or television appearances and make their newsletters available electronically. They also rely heavily on social media, as all House members and senators have Facebook and Twitter accounts, which staff—or sometimes members themselves—maintain and update on a daily basis.

Members of Congress also want their accomplishments, positions, and votes covered in the traditional newspaper and television media, and they generally hire press aides to keep local media outlets up to date. Local media typically do not have the budgets or resources to cover the activities of their members of Congress in depth, so they often welcome the information that press aides provide, even while recognizing that it is exclusively positive and self-serving. The House and Senate also provide television and radio technology for their members, with easy ways to uplink via satellite to local stations and provide informational content. These communications to local newspapers, television stations, and radio stations—expedited by technology and staff provided by congressional appropriations—are a tremendous electoral boon to members of Congress and serve as a major component of the incumbency advantage (covered in Chapter 3).

# WHO ARE A MEMBER'S CONSTITUENTS?

Who exactly are constituents? Technically speaking, a member's constituents are the citizens in the geographic unit that she represents. For a House member, this would be everyone in her congressional district. For a senator, this would be everyone in her state. However, defining a constituency by a member's geographic unit is only a starting point. The true nature of congressional representation is more complex and revealing.

## Fenno's Concentric Circles

Political scientist Richard Fenno has argued that a member of Congress "sees" different constituencies, depending on his needs and situation. Fenno conceived of these different constituencies as a set of concentric circles to indicate both size and proximity to a member on a personal level (see Figure 4.4).

The largest circle is the **geographic constituency** just discussed. Technically, a member's geographic constituency is everyone in his district or state. In more practical—or political—terms, a member of Congress might consider his geographic constituency to be the full set of voters in his district or state. Within this circle, there are three others. The next-largest circle is the **reelection constituency**, or the portion of the geographic constituency that is likely to support the member of Congress in the next election. While legislators technically represent their entire geographic unit, they rely on these subconstituencies within their districts or states for reelection.[29] In contemporary politics, for example, urban areas tend to vote Democratic, while suburban and rural areas often lean Republican. And even when legislators are of the same party and represent the same geographic constituency, as can happen with a unified party delegation in the Senate, they often build different support networks and represent different groups. As political scientist Wendy Schiller notes, same-party senators can be thought of as both partners and rivals, as they tend to assert control and represent constituencies in distinct areas of the state.[30]

The next-largest circle is the **primary constituency**, which represents that portion of the reelection constituency that actively supports a member of Congress. These voters typically identify strongly with the party. They will often contribute money to the member's campaign and advertise their allegiance with bumper stickers and yard signs, and sometimes they volunteer their time to work for the campaign itself. They also can be counted on to participate in the member's primary election. Finally, the smallest circle is the **personal constituency**, which represents a member's personal friends, closest advisors, and biggest donors. These are the people whom she trusts the most, relying on them for financial and moral support as well as critical political advice.

FIGURE 4.4    Fenno's View of Congressional Constituencies

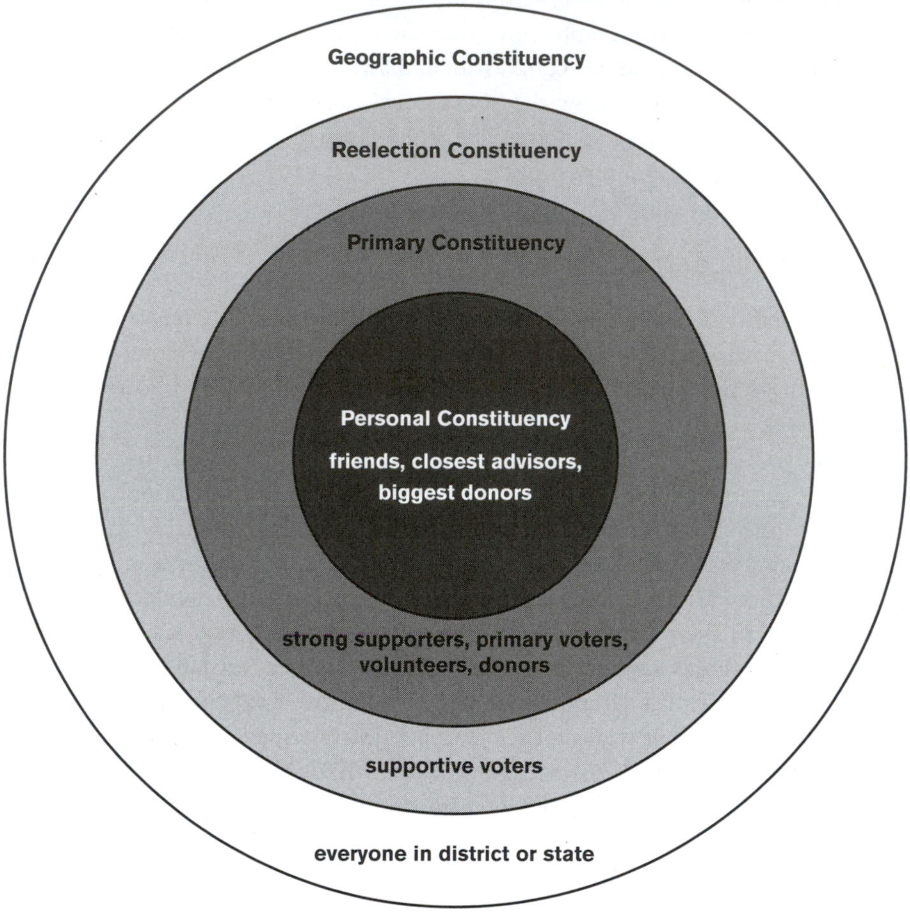

Geographic Constituency

Reelection Constituency

Primary Constituency

**Personal Constituency**

**friends, closest advisors,**
**biggest donors**

**strong supporters, primary voters,**
**volunteers, donors**

**supportive voters**

**everyone in district or state**

Based on Richard F. Fenno, *Home Style: House Members in Their Districts* (Boston, MA: Little, Brown, 1978).

Summarizing Fenno's characterization of constituencies, political scientists John Aldrich and Kenneth Shepsle write, "While a geographic constituency is *assigned* a legislator as a matter of constitutional practice, a legislator's 'constituency' is *chosen*."[31] A member of Congress focuses on different constituencies depending on the issue or problem at hand. For example, if a member faces a serious challenger within his party, he will pay special attention to his primary constituency. And if he is successful in beating back that primary challenge, he will then work on mending fences within the party and, by doing so, expand his focus to his reelection constituency. Alternatively, if a House member finds that his congressional district has been redrawn, he will focus on his geographic constituency in order to learn the range of voters that he now represents. And through it all, a member will lean on his personal constituency for advice and support.

Political scientist Kristina Miler has built on Fenno's work by delving more deeply into the representational perceptions of members of Congress.[32] Miler argues that members of Congress have limited time, resources, and capabilities, and thus (rationally) they pay attention to some subconstituencies more than others. Relying on work in psychology, she argues that members of Congress use simple cues to identify which subconstituencies to focus on. For example, those subconstituencies that are resource rich or highly active in politics shine brightly on members' radar. This creates a subsequent bias in how members of Congress vote, what types of committees they serve on, and what bills they sponsor. Ultimately, Miler's findings are somewhat depressing: members of Congress, concerned about reelection, are most likely to see and respond to money and political involvement. Poorer constituents and those without the time or desire to be active in politics are, by comparison, largely ignored.

## THEN AND NOW
## THE SHIFTING COMPOSITION OF THE GEOGRAPHIC CONSTITUENCY

In the Constitution (Article I, Section 2, Clause 3), the nature of the geographic constituency was most closely tied to representation in the House of Representatives (and the electoral college) and the allocation of House seats by state. To establish a formula for distributing said representation, the Framers wrote,

> Representatives . . . shall be apportioned among the several States . . . according to their respective Numbers, which shall be determined by adding to the whole Number of free Persons, including those bound to Service for a Term of Years, and excluding Indians not taxed, three-fifths of all other Persons.

The key provision here was the "three-fifths of all other Persons," as the South had a significant population of enslaved Africans who were considered property and not people. To account for the enslaved population, the Framers reached a compromise: they would count each of the enslaved as three-fifths of a person for the purpose of determining how many House seats each state would receive. The Three-Fifths Compromise would remain in effect until the Civil War, when it would finally be repealed by Section 2 of the Fourteenth Amendment (1868).[33]

Counting people is the simplest way to think of geographic constituency. But if we think of a member's geographic constituency not as the total population within a state or district ("their respective Numbers," per the Framers), but rather as the number of eligible voters—because this is often the view held by members themselves and is the basis of electoral accountability—we see that the concept has in fact evolved since the Founding, based on changing politics, perceptions, and values, tracking closely to the right to vote in federal elections.

Before the Revolution, voting rights were quite limited and stringently guarded. Members of the upper class ran the political system, and they were not willing to risk the social order by sharing power. Voting was the province of the independent and virtuous, which meant White Protestant men who owned property. As a result, the voting percentage of the population was quite small.

After the Revolution, the system began to open up. First to go was the property restriction, as gainful employment became the new standard for voting rights. Pressure for greater participation increased in the 1820s and 1830s as the Democratic Party, led by Andrew Jackson, sought to build a coalition that included the common (White) man. The Whigs, on the other hand, represented society's elite and thus sought to keep the voting-eligible population small. After more than a decade of conflict, Jacksonian democracy triumphed and universal suffrage for all White men became a reality.

These suffrage gains were made outside of the constitutional structure. In fact, the original Constitution (including the Bill of Rights) had nothing to say about who could vote. The closest provision was found in Article I, Section 4, wherein the power to determine the "times, places, and manner of holding elections" was granted to states, with the times and manner subject to federal regulation.

Voting rights would begin to find a home in the Constitution following the Civil War, during the Reconstruction era. Adopted in 1870, the Fifteenth Amendment stipulated, "The right of citizens of the United States to vote shall not be denied or abridged by the United States or by any State on account of race, color, or previous condition of servitude." The Fifteenth Amendment provided universal suffrage for African American men (many of whom had previously been enslaved),[34] and thus the voting-eligible population expanded to include all male citizens generally. This expansion in members' geographic constituencies had the greatest effect in the South. The Republican Party—thanks to the votes of formerly enslaved people—was able to make considerable inroads in the ex-Confederacy and thus (for a time) evolve into a true national party.

The voting rights provided in the Fifteenth Amendment were *negative* rights. That is, particular conditions for the *denial* of rights were stipulated and prohibited. This meant that other conditions (which were *not* stipulated and prohibited) could potentially be used to deny some citizens' voting rights. In time, the former slaveholding elite (represented by the Democratic Party) returned to power in the southern states and enacted legal provisions to disenfranchise African American voters. Examples included poll taxes (a dollar amount that a citizen must pay before registering to vote) and literacy tests (educational requirements that a citizen needs to meet before registering to vote). Because these initiatives were not based strictly on race but rather on wealth and education, and thus class, they sometimes also disenfranchised poor, uneducated White voters. Thus allowances were often made to keep lower-class Whites on the voting rolls—namely, grandfather clauses, which waived poll taxes and literacy tests if an individual's grandfather had possessed the right to vote.

For the first two decades of the twentieth century, a southern member of Congress considered his geographic constituency to be the adult White male population in his district or state (thus hearkening back to the pre–Civil War era)—and voted accordingly. However, in 1920, the Nineteenth Amendment was adopted, providing universal suffrage for women, and members of Congress saw their geographic constituencies effectively double in size.

With African Americans disenfranchised, the South became a one-party (Democratic) state for more than a half-century. In the 1950s, however, the civil rights movement began to gain momentum, and liberal northern Democrats in Congress began to push for change. In the 1960s, suffrage restrictions against African Americans were rolled back considerably: the Twenty-Fourth Amendment (1964) prohibited poll taxes, and the Voting Rights Act of 1965 outlawed literacy tests. As a result, by the late 1960s, African Americans in the South were beginning to register to vote in high numbers, and over the next two decades, congressional candidates in the South—some grudgingly—began viewing their geographic constituencies as including both Whites and African Americans. By the 1980s, enfranchisement of African Americans had shifted the partisan dynamics in the South, as conservative Whites found a home in the Republican Party while African Americans and liberal to moderate Whites associated with the Democratic Party.[35]

The last major change to federal voting rights occurred in 1971 with the adoption of the Twenty-Sixth Amendment, which established 18 years as the national voting age. Prior to the Twenty-Sixth Amendment, each state could set its own voting age, and many selected 21 years. With the advent of the Vietnam draft, wherein 18-year-olds were being sent to Southeast Asia to fight for their country, pressure mounted at home to give similarly aged citizens a direct say in political matters. Thus, the Twenty-Sixth Amendment further expanded the voting-eligible population and with it members' geographic constituencies.

Despite the constitutional amendments and the Voting Rights Act, states continue to restrict or expand voting rights within established federal guidelines. In recent years, some states have sought to restrict voting rights by requiring valid identification to register or vote, while other states have sought to expand voting rights by eliminating suffrage restrictions on former felons. Partisan motivations have driven these attempts, and the goal is to gain an electoral advantage. These are contemporary examples of the parties trying, in a strategic way, to expand or limit the size and composition of geographical constituencies for their own benefit.

While these recent attempts by states to restrict or expand the voting-eligible population have been controversial, they affect only small groups of voters (or potential voters). This is not to say that these changes are unimportant. Marginal changes in the size and composition of geographic constituencies can sometimes mean the difference between winning and losing an election. And in an era when both parties believe they can win majority control of Congress every election cycle, these marginal changes might have huge consequences.

### Critical Thinking

1. After disenfranchisement laws like poll taxes and literacy tests helped create a one-party Democratic state in the South, did southern Democrats in Congress still have an incentive to represent their constituents? Why or why not?
2. Do you think members of Congress changed their representational activities after the Twenty-Sixth Amendment? If so, provide some examples.
3. Do you think voting rights should ever be restricted? Why or why not? What are some concerns in pursuing such restrictions?

## Beyond Concentric Circles

Fenno's characterization of constituency as a set of concentric circles helps us understand the complex nature of congressional representation. But these circles, by themselves, do not capture everything. Political scientists often conceive of congressional representation in other ways. We discuss three such ways in the following sections: national representation, substantive representation, and descriptive representation.

**NATIONAL REPRESENTATION**   Although geographic boundaries are useful for identifying the full set of voters and establishing a clear accountability mechanism for a member of Congress, they also have their limitations. For one thing, some members of Congress think and act on a more national scale. These members often serve on the most powerful congressional committees, and they use their influence to design federal policy and compete with the president for national authority.[36]

Senators on the Armed Services Committee, for example, often vie with the president to establish policy and respond politically on matters of national security. This interbranch competition includes responding to threats made against the United States and its citizens—a governing focus that extends far beyond the needs of any one congressional district or state. From his position as Senate Armed Services chair, John McCain (R-Ariz.) pushed President Obama to take a stronger stance against worldwide threats, especially those made by proponents of what McCain called "radical Islam." He later criticized President Trump as poorly informed and impulsive and insisted that Congress would not play a subordinate role on important policy matters or refrain from checking the power of the president when necessary.[37] More recently, in June 2020, Tom Cotton (R-Ark.) used his position on the Senate Armed Services Committee to advocate for using U.S. troops to maintain order in American cities that saw large protests in response to the killing of George Floyd, an unarmed African American, by officers of the Minneapolis Police Department.[38]

Senator Tom Cotton (R-Ark.), a member of the Senate Armed Services Committee, controversially advocated for the military to intervene during the Black Lives Matter protests in 2020.

Another factor that leads certain members to think and act more on a national scale is the lure of higher office. With their eyes on the White House, some members of Congress push their way onto the national stage in order to build a reputation that extends beyond their geographic constituency. Overall, senators are more likely to be national representatives than House members because they have already built electoral coalitions on a broader (state versus district) scale. Senators who serve on powerful committees with a national focus have a further advantage. John McCain, for example, ran for president twice (in 2000 and 2008) and was the Republican nominee in 2008. Likewise, recent Democratic presidential nominees Hillary Clinton (2016), Barack Obama (2008 and 2012), and John Kerry (2004) were all sitting senators and served on the important Foreign Relations Committee. While House members have a harder time building a national constituency than senators do, some are able to accomplish that goal. One recent example is Paul Ryan (R-Wis.), who served as the chair of the House Ways and Means and Budget Committees and as Speaker of the House. Ryan has not run for president, but he was Mitt Romney's vice-presidential running mate in 2012 and is widely believed to desire the nation's top office (despite his retirement from the House).

**SUBSTANTIVE REPRESENTATION**   Another way to think about representation is to focus on the underlying substance of the representation, where "substance" reflects issue or policy content. Here the question might be, how well do a legislator's issue or policy positions correspond to what her constituents want? The term scholars often use to describe this correspondence is **policy congruence.**

Policy congruence can take various forms. One form is public statements—as in speeches made on the floor of Congress or elsewhere—and the degree to which such statements reflect the positions held by constituents. Such statements are relatively low cost, however, and thus mostly symbolic. Another more significant form is the introduction of policies, which involves actions—the crafting of legislation—rather than just statements. Congruence, in this case, can be assessed by how well the bills that a member of Congress sponsors reflect the policy preferences of her constituents.[39] Finally, perhaps the most common form is roll call votes. The House and Senate, as legislative bodies, vote on hundreds of issues each term, from the small or symbolic (on resolutions) to the large and consequential (on major policy initiatives), and members stake out positions through their individual vote choices. Constituents can track those votes to determine how closely their member of Congress is acting on their behalf.

Vote-based policy congruence can itself take various forms. For example, some constituents focus on single issues, and their decisions to support or oppose a legislator's reelection will depend on how he voted on legislation that dealt with that issue. In contemporary politics, issues that draw the exclusive attention of some constituents are often polarizing, such as reproductive rights and gun control.[40] Other constituents care about a range of issues or whether a member of Congress is voting in a suitably liberal or conservative direction. In this case, we can assess policy congruence by examining how a legislator votes on a number of roll calls, which can range from a handful of votes, to a few dozen, to perhaps all votes in a given Congress.

**DESCRIPTIVE REPRESENTATION**    Still another way to think about representation is to focus on the underlying qualities of the members of Congress themselves. We can think of descriptive representation in pure demographic terms: Does the representative "look like" his constituents? (Recall that we discussed the issue of descriptive representation for the entire Congress earlier in the chapter.) The answer might be based on background. For example, is the legislator a Catholic? Does he have a college degree? Is he a lawyer or business owner? More often, descriptive representation involves a characteristic that is immutable. Is the legislator African American? Latino? A woman?

Many scholars argue that descriptive representation leads to better substantive representation. Most of this research has focused on African Americans, investigating whether African American Democrats in Congress do a better job of representing the interests of African American constituents than do White Democrats in Congress. And most of these studies—which rely on roll call votes—find a significant relationship between descriptive and substantive representation: African American members of Congress do represent African American constituents better than White members do.[41] The literature on Latinos is less developed, but the existing work suggests that there is also a link between descriptive and substantive representation: Latino members of Congress represent Latino constituents better than White members do.[42]

When we dig deeper, we find evidence that descriptive representation often manifests itself before votes are taken. That is, descriptive characteristics predict the kinds of bills a member introduces. For example, African American Democrats in Congress are more likely to introduce legislation that is important to African American constituents than are White Democrats.[43] And the pre-floor stage is where clear differences occur by gender, as a number of studies find that female members of Congress are significantly more likely to sponsor legislation on "women's issues," such as gender equity, child care, abortion, and employee flex time, than are male members of Congress.[44]

A related literature delves into the theoretical connection between descriptive and substantive representation. Some of this research suggests that low-cost (or symbolic) substantive representation by African American members of Congress provides a crucial benefit for their African American constituents. While awarding Rosa Parks a congressional medal or ensuring that Dr. Martin Luther King, Jr.'s birthday becomes a national holiday may not be commensurate with generating new policy, such symbolic initiatives are important. As political scientist Katherine Tate argues, they provide "voice and recognition" for African Americans, which is a "vital currency" in the "marketplace of ideas and ideologies."[45]

Other research suggests that "shared fate," or common experiences related to a descriptive characteristic, leads members of Congress to better understand what their descriptive group needs and craft legislation to meet those needs.[46] For instance, growing up Black in America creates a personal experience vis-à-vis discrimination in its many forms. An African American member of Congress, therefore, possesses an advantage in crafting legislation to combat discrimination because he may have faced such discrimination in the past and, as an elected representative, he desires to pursue antidiscrimination legislation. And the intersection of race and gender creates an important descriptive subcategory, as women of color share distinct experiences which may manifest in Congress as well. For example, Black and Latina congresswomen were especially active in representing the interests of battered immigrant women in the 2013 Violence Against Women Act (VAWA) Reauthorization.[47]

Two recent studies have explored common experiences among members of Congress in great detail. First, economist Ebonya Washington examined how male legislators voted on women's health issues before and after they became fathers to baby girls. Her expectation was that if shared fate mattered, male members of Congress with new daughters would be more likely to vote in support of women's issues as compared to all other male members of Congress. And this, in fact, is what she found, particularly on issues involving reproductive rights.[48] Second, political scientists Kenneth Lowande, Melinda Ritchie, and Erinn Lauterbach collected 88,000 records of communication between members of Congress and federal agencies over a dozen years to examine the nature of constituency service. They found that women, racial and ethnic minorities, and veterans were more likely to work on behalf of constituents who "looked like them." From this, they conclude that "shared experiences operate as a critical mechanism for representation" in Congress.[49]

## HOW WE STUDY
## MEASURING REPRESENTATION

Theoretically, congressional representation is straightforward: members of Congress will, sometimes and to varying degrees, act in accordance with their constituents' wishes, either broadly or narrowly defined. Elections provide the

The number of African American and Latina women in Congress has increased significantly in recent years, especially after the 2018 midterm elections. Here, (from left) Representatives Bonnie Watson Coleman (D-N.J.), Ilhan Omar (D-Minn.), and Ayanna Pressley (D-Mass.) hold a press conference introducing legislation to end discriminatory school discipline.

accountability mechanism; if legislators deviate from representative behavior, they risk being voted out of office and replaced by someone constituents believe will do a better job of acting on their behalf.

Determining if members of Congress are in fact acting in accordance with constituents' wishes has been more challenging for political scientists. The most common attempt to measure representation has occurred at the geographic level. Studies have examined whether members of Congress vote in ways that are congruent with broad interests in their districts or states. Often, such attempts have taken the form of statistical analyses. Researchers collect data across members and across time, then assess whether a significant correlation exists between members' roll call votes and constituents' interests (measured with economic, demographic, or survey data).[50] If a significant correlation exists, then we can argue that policy congruence exists. One difficulty is establishing that the correlation is actually capturing a causal relationship.[51] Members could be voting for what constituents want in order to maximize their chances of reelection. That would be a causal relationship. However, it could also be that members of Congress simply share the preferences of their constituencies. In that case, legislators are just voting for what they personally believe to be the best policies.

Policy congruence would thus be accidental and not driven by concerns about reelection. Recent research has focused on tackling this thorny problem, and establishing policy congruence as a true causal relationship.[52]

Measuring representation more narrowly than at the geographic level has been challenging because variables used to measure constituent interests are collected according to geographic boundaries. If census data are used, for example, the underlying geographic unit will be the county. And county-level data can then be aggregated up to district and state levels. The other concentric circles at the heart of Fenno's conception of representation do not follow geographic boundaries neatly. Reelection and primary constituencies, for example, are embedded within geographic units, but so are those voters who are not part of either constituency and will not be supporting the member in his reelection efforts. Determining whether a member of Congress accurately represents such subgeographic constituencies does not naturally lend itself to the same broad statistical approach.

Fenno approached the study of the subgeographic constituencies in a wholly different way. Instead of analyzing quantitative data, Fenno embedded himself in the reelection campaigns of various members of Congress, following them to different events with different constituents and talking with them about their motivations and strategies. He referred to this qualitative approach as "soaking and poking."[53] Such a case-by-case approach yields inherently anecdotal evidence; however, Fenno argued that it could also generate evidence of individual causal relationships. In particular, he believed that legislators were "goal seeking [but also] . . . situation interpreting."[54] That is, members of Congress developed "home styles," or strategic ways of presenting themselves and their accomplishments to constituents. For example, a member wants to get reelected, so she assesses how a key set of constituents would react to certain policy positions, and then she offers such policy positions in their presence while at a fundraiser or in a speech.[55] This logical chain would provide some evidence that electoral accountability is driving a member of Congress to adopt certain policy positions. While this sort of evidence, based on intensive participant observation, might not satisfy scholars doing statistical research on large data sets, Fenno believed it might be the best that scholars could achieve in the study of subgeographic constituencies.

Fenno's work on congressional home styles began in the late 1970s, and the soaking-and-poking approach was considered the gold standard for the scholarly investigation of subgeographic constituencies for almost four decades. Recently, political scientist Justin Grimmer leveraged data and statistical advances to study in a more systematic way how members of Congress present themselves to constituents.[56] Grimmer focused on the Senate and examined more than 64,000 press releases issued from senators' offices between 2005 and 2007. Applying computational techniques to the text of these press releases, Grimmer studied which issues senators emphasized, why they focused on these issues, and how their choices mattered for representation. He concluded that senators pursue two basic styles of presentation. The first is an issue-oriented style in which they engage in debates on national issues. This style is most often used by senators who are ideologically well aligned with constituents. The second is an appropriator style in which they focus on claiming credit for projects that benefit their states. This style is most often used by senators who are not ideologically well aligned with constituents. Many senators pursue a mixed style, focusing sometimes on issues and sometimes on their particular accomplishments.

Moving beyond Fenno's concentric circles, policy congruence connected to the concerns of particular groups is also a topic of considerable study. Interest groups often select a set of roll call votes from the congressional agenda to assess how well members of Congress support the issues and policies that they care about. Two well-known interest groups are the Americans for Democratic Action (ADA) and the Leadership Council on Civil Rights (LCCR). The ADA selects votes related to the broad topic of "political liberalism," while the LCCR chooses a narrower set of votes related to "civil rights." With these votes in hand, the ADA and LCCR identify how a member of Congress should vote (either "yea" or "nay" by roll call) and construct a "support score" based on this set of votes.

As we discussed in Chapter 2, political scientists routinely use these scores as measures of members' preferences in statistical analyses. For example, ADA scores measure members' preferences on a general liberalism spectrum, ranging from not at all liberal (or perfectly conservative) to perfectly liberal.[57] LCCR scores also measure members' preferences on a liberalism spectrum, but a more specific one related to the concerns of racial and ethnic minorities.[58] LCCR scores range from strongly anti-minority to strongly pro-minority.

ADA scores and LCCR scores for the 115th Congress (2017–19) appear in Table 4.2, broken down by party and chamber. The ADA scores are based on 40 roll calls in each chamber, while the LCCR scores are based on 32 roll calls in the House and 42 in the Senate. Each set of scores reflects averages. So, for instance, the average ADA support score in the entire Senate was 45 percent. Stated another way, the average Senate member voted for—that is, supported— the ADA's position 45 percent of the time.

When we consider the two sets of support scores by party, we find huge differences. Democrats voted much more in keeping with basic policy liberalism (as measured by the ADA) and pro–civil rights positions (as measured by the LCCR). The average Democratic score was nearly 80 percent in the House and nearly 90 percent in the Senate on ADA and more than 90 percent in both

| **TABLE 4.2** Legislative Support Scores, 115th Congress (2017–19) | | | | |
|---|---|---|---|---|
| | ADA Scores | | LCCR Scores | |
| | House | Senate | House | Senate |
| All members | 36% | 45% | 43% | 46% |
| Democrats | 77% | 89% | 92% | 96% |
| Republicans | 4% | 4% | 5% | 2% |

0% = perfectly conservative; 100% = perfectly liberal.

"The Leadership Conference on Civil and Human Rights Voting Record: 115th Congress, October 2018." http://civilrightsdocs.info/pdf/voting-record/FINAL-2018-Voting-Record-10222018.pdf; Americans for Democratic Action, https://adaction.org/wp-content/uploads/2019/09/2017.pdf; and Americans for Democratic Action, https://adaction.org/wp-content/uploads/2019/10/2018.pdf (accessed 2/15/20).

chambers on LCCR. The average Republican score was below 10 percent (on both ADA and LCCR) in both chambers.

Although these scores can illuminate the differences between the parties, we need to be mindful of artificial extremism (see Chapter 2). While interest groups choose roll calls that relate to their governing mission and values, the roll calls themselves are often on controversial, high-profile issues that typically divide the parties on their own core beliefs. Thus the scores help identify "heroes" (members who vote *for* the group's position on every roll call) and "zeroes" (members who vote *against* the group's position on every roll call).[59] Identifying these extreme legislators is one way that groups lobby legislators indirectly—using both rewards (showcasing their names on a heroes list) and punishments (showcasing their names on a zeroes list).[60]

Thus while interest-group scores can be useful in studying representation, they should also be used with caution. The limitations of interest-group scores explain why scholars have increasingly turned to measures that incorporate all (or nearly all) roll call votes, such as Poole and Rosenthal's NOMINATE scores, to estimate ideology for members of Congress (see "How We Study," Chapter 2). However, while measures such as NOMINATE better differentiate members within party and limit the artificial extremism problem, they incorporate votes on all kinds of things—procedures, amendments, and policies—and thus do not neatly measure specific issue areas.

### Critical Thinking

1. We have noted some of the methodological difficulties in establishing policy congruence between members of Congress and their constituents. How might redistricting—in which a House member's district is redrawn, with

some new areas (usually counties) added and some old areas dropped—provide an opportunity to assess policy congruence? Speculate.

2. Might a member of Congress's home style change over time? Or does she establish such a home style when she first arrives in Congress and stick with it throughout her career? Explain.

3. Sometimes a member of Congress will switch parties—from Democrat to Republican or vice versa. When this happens, will his ADA and LCCR scores change? Why or why not?

---

# COLLECTIVE REPRESENTATION

Our discussion of representation to this point has focused on the connection between individual members of Congress and their constituents. But there is another kind of representation that is also important. **Collective representation** is the connection between Congress as a whole and the American public. Stated differently, assessing collective representation means determining whether, and how well, Congress as an institution represents the preferences of the nation.

Does Congress reflect the wishes of the American public? A useful place to start is citizens' perceptions of how well Congress is doing its job versus how well they believe their individual member of Congress is doing his job. This macro versus micro distinction is, in fact, quite telling.

To make this collective versus individual comparison, we use congressional job approval data collected across time by Gallup, a long-standing U.S. polling firm. Gallup asks a random sample of Americans at regular intervals two questions: (1) Do you approve of the way Congress is handling its job? and (2) do you approve or disapprove of the way the representative from your congressional district is handling his or her job? From these responses, we can assess whether citizens view the collective performance of Congress differently from how they view the individual performance of their particular House member.

Figure 4.5 presents congressional job approval data from the mid-1970s to the present. Until the early 1990s, around 35 to 40 percent of Americans approved of the way Congress was doing its job. This figure dipped to 25 to 30 percent through the mid-1990s and then gradually crept up through the mid-2000s to the 50 to 55 percent level, with a huge spike (84 percent) right after the 9/11 terrorist attacks. Congressional approval numbers declined significantly during George W. Bush's second term in office (as war efforts in Afghanistan and Iraq stagnated), bounced back during Barack Obama's first term in office (when Obamacare was adopted), then sank again and stayed mostly in the teens

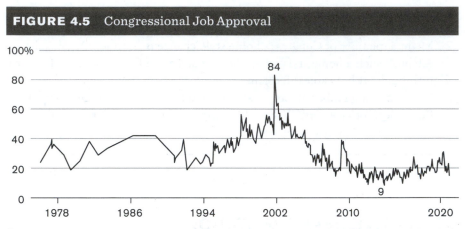

**FIGURE 4.5** Congressional Job Approval

Gallup, http://news.gallup.com/poll/1600/congress-public.aspx (accessed 12/7/20).

through the summer of 2019 before creeping up into the 20s and eventually cracking the 30s in April 2020. However, in advance of the November 2020 election and amidst the struggle Congress had in passing a supplementary COVID-19 relief bill both before and after the election, congressional approval dropped again—and by December 2020, it was at 15 percent.

These data suggest that few Americans in recent years approve of the job that Congress as an institution is doing. But how does this assessment compare to how Americans evaluate the job performance of their individual member of Congress? While Gallup has asked about individual member job approval more sporadically over time, the data in Figure 4.6 are still illuminating: Americans view their individual House member's performance quite differently from how they view Congress as a whole.[61] Even as congressional job approval bottomed out at 9 percent in late 2013, around 44 percent of Americans judged their individual member of Congress favorably. And by late 2014, while congressional job approval was still only 14 percent, around 54 percent of Americans felt that their individual member of Congress was performing well. When Gallup next asked about individual job approval in January 2019, the result was essentially the same: 53 percent of Americans approved of the way their individual House member was handling his or her job.

Thus while Americans in recent years have taken a negative view of Congress's job performance, they are considerably more positive in how they view their individual House member. In fact, a majority of Americans believe their individual member of Congress is doing a good job.[62]

There are many reasons why few Americans view congressional job performance in a positive light. Some scholars have suggested that Americans use different criteria to judge Congress as a whole as opposed to individual members: Congress is evaluated based on domestic and foreign policy

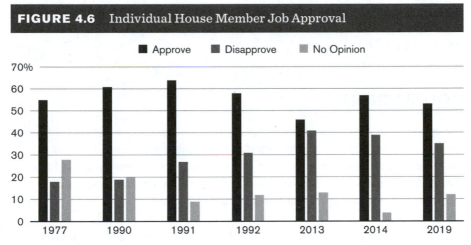

**FIGURE 4.6**   Individual House Member Job Approval

Gallup, http://news.gallup.com (accessed 1/12/21).

produced, while individual members are evaluated on constituency service (or casework).[63] And, in recent years, it has become common to view Congress as dysfunctional, or the "broken branch," because of its high degree of partisan rancor and polarization, which has led to gridlock even on traditionally simple governing responsibilities (see Chapter 8).[64] At the same time, individual members have maintained or increased their constituency service efforts, which has kept them in the good graces of a majority of voters back home.

More fundamentally, the question is, does Congress as a whole respond to what Americans say they want? In fact, according to political scientists who study collective representation, the answer is mostly "yes." The work of political scientist James Stimson and his coauthors is the gold standard for research on collective representation.[65] Stimson constructs an aggregate measure of public opinion over time, which he characterizes as "public mood," or Americans' desire for liberal or conservative policy. He then examines whether policy decisions in the House and Senate (using interest-group ratings and roll call votes) track the public mood. In this way, he asks whether congressional decisions reflect what the public wants and whether Congress changes in response to changes in public mood. Stimson finds that both the House and Senate are responsive to changes in public mood, with the House responding more quickly to short-term changes and the Senate responding a bit more slowly. Some of this responsiveness is due to sitting members of Congress rationally anticipating trends in public opinion and adjusting their voting behavior accordingly, but much of it is a function of membership turnover in Congress. That is, newly elected members of Congress will often reflect the most recent trends in public opinion better than the members they replace, and they help move Congress as a whole in the direction of that opinion. This latter finding highlights the power of elections and the significant degree to which representatives remain accountable to the public.

## CONCLUSION

We opened this chapter with a description of how Republican members of Congress faced constituent anger over their party's goal of repealing Obamacare. This example is important for a couple of reasons. First, representing and governing do not always go easily hand in hand. Major policy change will make some constituents unhappy—or benefit some more than others—and members of Congress will face the ire of those on the losing end. Second, the definition of a constituent is somewhat fluid. Most of the citizens who attended the GOP town halls in the spring and summer of 2017 were residents of the members' districts or states, so they were in fact geographic constituents. But many—and likely most—of them were not Republican voters, and thus they were not considered part of the members' reelection constituencies. For Republican lawmakers, representing the interests of constituents who did not vote for them, and probably would not vote for them in the future, was not a winning strategy. In the short term, a hostile audience meant that they had to accept being yelled at in town halls. But in the long term, they hoped that their supporters—members of their reelection constituencies—would approve of their actions in Congress, turn out to vote, and reelect them. Most were successful in this regard, but some were not—as the Republicans lost 40 seats and majority control of the House.

Members of Congress can never make everyone in their districts or states happy, but most political science research finds that democratic accountability underlies representative government. That is, regular elections force lawmakers to serve at least a majority of their geographic constituents through roll call voting, bill introduction, and casework. If a member of Congress shirks these representational activities, he risks being voted out of office. And, on a macro level, the evidence suggests that aggregate decision making in Congress follows aggregate public opinion in the nation. As the public's policy mood shifts left or right, House and Senate decisions follow.

This is not to say that our representational system is perfect. Women and people of color are underrepresented in both the House and Senate relative to the U.S. population. Congressional job approval figures are embarrassingly low. And while the trend has been toward more equitable descriptive representation in Congress, as the percentages of women and people of color have increased substantially in the last quarter century, there is less hope that Congress's job approval numbers will change for the better. Why?

The answer lies in how representation and governing play out in contemporary American politics. Congress today is so highly polarized that representation and governing are nearly incompatible. Republicans and Democrats remain deeply divided on most policy issues, reflecting similar trends in American society. Members of Congress can serve their constituents' needs even as the stark differences between the parties leave little chance of finding compromise policy positions that can produce congressional majorities. And passing legislation with only majority-party votes is not easy. As a result, Congress underperforms, other institutions—the presidency, bureaucracy, and courts—step in to fill the policy void, and the public rates Congress's job performance as dismal.

Can this situation change? Can we reach a point where the public approves of the performance of their member of Congress *and* the performance of Congress as a whole? Unless polarization decreases, creating more opportunities for compromise, this seems unlikely, at least in the short term. Rather, more of the same looms on the horizon.

## Discussion Questions

1. If a member of Congress believes an issue that most of his constituents support is actually bad for them—or inconsistent with their interests—what should he do? In this case, what does representing them entail?
2. If a House member from New York City is elected to the Senate from New York State, will her reelection constituency change? Why or why not? Will her personal constituency change?
3. How has the Internet changed the way members of Congress represent their constituents? Are constituents today—compared to constituents in the pre-Internet era—more or less able to hold members of Congress accountable? Explain.
4. Should the percentages of women, African Americans, and other people of color in Congress mirror their respective percentages in the U.S. population? Why or why not? If all structural barriers to election that these groups face are eliminated, will we see the percentages converge in time?
5. Americans do not like Congress, but they generally like their representatives (their House member and senators). Does this disconnect indicate that citizens are irrational? Why or why not?

# 5

## Committees

As the 2014 elections approached, nine House and Senate committee chairs announced their retirement from Congress. First among them was Carl Levin (D-Mich.), who gave up his powerful perch as chair of the Senate Armed Services Committee. Shortly thereafter, Max Baucus (D-Mont.) stepped down from his chairmanship of the Senate Finance Committee to become ambassador to China. Only a few months later, Dave Camp (R-Mich.), chair of the influential House Ways and Means Committee, announced his retirement. Many other influential committee chairs followed suit. Just a few short years later, when Republicans controlled both chambers of Congress and the presidency, another slew of powerful chairs announced their retirement, including Bill Shuster (R-Pa.) of the House Transportation Committee, Bob Goodlatte (R-Va.) of the House Judiciary Committee, Jeb Hensarling (R-Tex.) of the House Financial Services Committee, Bob Corker (R-Tenn.) of the Senate Foreign Relations Committee, and Orrin Hatch (R-Utah) of the Senate Finance Committee. Some of these announcements came more than a year before the November 2018 elections.

Why would so many members of Congress voluntarily leave positions long considered among the most influential on Capitol Hill? One can point to

Senator Orrin Hatch (R-Utah), chair of the Senate Finance Committee, announced his retirement in January 2018, after more than 40 years in the Senate.

idiosyncratic reasons for each retirement, including age (Levin was 79 years old), bleak reelection outlook (Corker faced the real possibility of losing in the GOP primary), and dim prospects for the party retaining its majority after the next election (House Republicans in 2017–18). However, far more sitting chairs are stepping down from their posts than in the past.[1] The position is just less attractive and powerful than it once was. For Republicans, committee chairs are term-limited (although the party leadership occasionally waives those limits), and they have less say over policy than they used to. Mike Rogers's (R-Ala.) departure from his perch atop the House Intelligence Committee for a spot as a talk-radio host in 2014 epitomizes this shift. Rogers, a very influential and hardworking insider in national security policy, was telling anyone who would listen that he believed he would have a greater influence over the direction of his party's agenda and government on the airwaves than chairing a House committee.[2]

Tom Cole (R-Okla.), chair of the House Appropriations Transportation subcommittee, summarized the effect of this shift in policy-making authority from committees to party leaders. Speaking about compromise legislation that the House and Senate Appropriations Committees had drafted earlier in the year to fund government agencies, which was rejected by Speaker John Boehner

(R-Ohio) and his leadership team because of pushback from conservatives in their own caucus, Cole said, "You just see your work product thrown away. . . . [Republican leaders are] more and more disconnected from the life of an average member, and a lot of them got there without having done much at the committee level."[3] The exodus of committee chairs from Congress continues even today. In the Senate four veteran Republican committee chairs retired before the 2020 election, and the very small number of Democratic retirements in the House included the powerful chair of the Appropriations Committee.

Committees were once the center of the policy world. As the modern Congress was taking shape in the latter part of the nineteenth century, contemporaneous legislative scholars recognized how central committees were to the House and Senate's operations. As Woodrow Wilson famously noted in 1885, "Congress in session is Congress on public exhibition, whilst Congress in its committee-rooms is Congress at work."[4]

Wilson's statement was no less true four generations later when the nation finally moved in a meaningful way to ensure African American civil rights. While popular accounts often credit President Lyndon Johnson, who certainly advocated for what became the Civil Rights Act of 1964, in reality, much of the policy-based heavy lifting was handled in congressional committees, notably the House Judiciary Committee chaired by Emanuel Celler (D-N.Y.).[5] Other committees, like the House Rules Committee chaired by Howard W. Smith (D-Va.) and the Senate Judiciary Committee chaired by James Eastland (D-Miss.), played a significant role in the process—by attempting to torpedo the bill. Put simply, the major civil rights legislation produced from the late 1950s through the late 1960s was the product of committee politics. And the most prominent congressional figures in the legislative narratives were often committee chairs.

But with the wave of recent chair departures, the vaunted role of committees in the lawmaking process appears to be diminishing. Is it true that committees are no longer able to represent and govern as they once did? Do members no longer see committees as places from which they can wield influence to benefit their constituents? Have party leaders replaced committee chairs as the legislative actors responsible for crafting new policy proposals? In essence, how powerful are congressional committees today?

## THE BASIC STRUCTURE OF COMMITTEE GOVERNMENT

Congress has many responsibilities, and the committee system is designed to make the complex policy world easier to manage. Committees are smaller structural units within the larger body that help manage the workload in Congress and provide specialized expertise by concentrating responsibilities and lawmaking authority within particular policy areas.

## Types of Committees

Congress is home to many types of committees: standing committees, subcommittees, select or special committees, joint committees, conference committees, and the Committee of the Whole.

**Standing committees** do the bulk of the legislative work in Congress. They are the only committees that exist from one congressional term to the next, and they receive and report bills to the wider chamber.[6]

Standing committees are almost always further divided into **subcommittees**, whose responsibilities encompass a portion of the committee's overall issue area (or jurisdiction—see below). For example, the Foreign Affairs Committee in the House has regularly divided its subcommittees by regions of the world (for example, Asia and the Pacific, Middle East and North Africa, Western Hemisphere) along with a few topics of contemporary interest (including Terrorism, Nonproliferation, and Trade). A few standing committees in the House are not broken into subcommittees; these panels have narrower or more specific jurisdictions, such as the Ethics Committee, the Committee on House Administration, and the House Budget Committee. In the Senate, four committees operate without subcommittees: Budget, Rules and Administration, Small Business and Entrepreneurship, and Veterans' Affairs.

**Select** or **special committees** (such as the House Select Committee on the Climate Crisis and the House Select Committee on Benghazi) are generally temporary, without the authority to consider or report legislative proposals to their respective chambers. For example, the House committee investigating the 2012 attacks on the U.S. diplomatic compound in Benghazi was charged only with examining the circumstances surrounding the events and creating a report with policy recommendations. (The House and Senate Select Committees on Intelligence are the major exceptions in recent history; they are granted a certain degree of legislative authority and possess permanent status through respective chamber rules.) Similarly, most **joint committees**—those composed of members from both the House and Senate—do not usually have legislative authority. These committees oversee relatively minor matters such as the Government Printing Office or the Library of Congress.

Conference committees and the Committee of the Whole, while not permanent, do possess legislative authority. The main purpose of **conference committees** is to reconcile differences in legislation passed by the two chambers on the same topic before that legislation moves on to the president for consideration. Like joint committees, conference committees are composed of members from both chambers, and they are commonly dominated by the members of the original committees of jurisdiction in the House and Senate. Conference committees exist only for consideration of a single piece of legislation and are dissolved when the job is done. The **Committee of the Whole (COW)** operates in the House and makes conducting legislative business easier. The COW is mostly a procedural device that allows the House to organize itself more easily (the COW's quorum requirement is 100 members, instead of a majority of the House) and handle bill amendments more quickly (by limiting debate). The COW became an important mechanism of majority party control in the late nineteenth century, when the minority would try to shut down House business by not responding to quorum calls. Amendments approved in the COW must be dealt with again in the whole House, but amendments defeated in the COW are killed for good.

## Committee Jurisdictions

**Jurisdictions** refer to the issue boundaries within which a committee is allowed to legislate. Senate and House rules allocate control over specific issues and determine standing committee jurisdictions. The rules also clarify how bills are referred to committees. Sometimes the text defining a committee jurisdiction is vague; other times it is precise. For example, the House Committee on Energy and Commerce is given the very specific jurisdiction of "generation and marketing of power (except by federally chartered or Federal regional power marketing authorities); reliability and interstate transmission of, and ratemaking for, all power; and siting of generation facilities (except the installation of interconnections between Government waterpower projects)." At the same time, it also has authority over the wide-ranging and vague concept of "interstate and foreign commerce generally." Longtime Energy and Commerce chair John Dingell (D-Mich.) hung a photo of Earth taken from outer space on his Capitol Hill office wall; he would point to it as the jurisdiction of the panel he chaired and say, "If it moves, it's energy, and if it doesn't, it's commerce."[7]

Committee jurisdictions are not always obvious. Consider the House Agriculture Committee. While the vast majority of its jurisdiction covers agricultural policy, the committee also controls the federal Supplemental Nutrition Assistance Program (SNAP, commonly referred to as food stamps), which is a food assistance program for low-income people.

Why are committee jurisdictions important? Jurisdictions regulate which committees receive bills, so they effectively determine who has legislative authority for specific issue areas. The textbook view of congressional lawmaking holds that a bill, once introduced, must be referred to an appropriate committee in the same chamber, per the relevant chamber rule(s). The House Speaker and

Select committees are convened to consider or report specific legislative proposals. In 2019, the Democratic majority in the House established the House Select Committee on the Climate Crisis, chaired by Representative Kathy Castor (D-Fla.).

Senate majority leader handle bill referral.[8] For example, when a bill is introduced directing that unclaimed money recovered at airport security checkpoints go to nonprofit organizations that help members of the armed forces and their families, the bill would be referred to the Homeland Security Committee because of its stated jurisdiction over the Transportation Security Administration. Internal committee rules govern the additional referral of a bill to the appropriate subcommittee, in this case the Subcommittee on Transportation and Maritime Security.

For the most part, the referral of bills to committees is routine, thanks to detailed jurisdictional language and long-standing, referral-based precedent. Nevertheless, vagaries in jurisdictions and bill subject matter provide openings for lawmakers to manipulate the bill referral process so that legislation is directed toward a more desirable venue for deliberation. In 2005, shortly after a controversial Supreme Court decision affirmed the right of state and local governments to seize property from landowners for private development deemed to be in the community interest (*Kelo v. City of New London*), Representative Henry Bonilla (R-Tex.) introduced legislation that would deny federal funding to any state or local government that engaged in this form of eminent domain. While the subject of eminent domain fell largely under the jurisdiction of the Judiciary Committee, Bonilla knew that Judiciary chair James Sensenbrenner (R-Wis.) would not be receptive to the bill's heavy-handed approach. Bonilla, therefore, wrote his bill in such a way that placed it under the control of the House Agriculture Committee and its more receptive chair, Bob Goodlatte (R-Va.).[9]

In an effort to avoid these strategic moves, and to leverage the expertise of multiple committees in legislative matters that span jurisdictions, the House adopted a rules change in 1974 that allowed bills to be referred to more than one committee—either jointly, split into pieces, or sequentially. (Multiple referral also exists in the Senate, but because it is easier to tack one bill on to another in the Senate—see the discussion of germaneness later in this chapter—it is rarely used.) Between the mid-1970s and mid-2000s, about 15 to 20 percent of House bills were referred to multiple committees, but that percentage was even higher for important legislation, and by the mid-2010s well over half of major legislation was referred to multiple committees in the House.[10] Committee members are usually eager to handle meaningful legislation that has a high likelihood of floor consideration and eventual adoption, because it provides an opportunity for members to claim credit for legislative success. However, multiple referrals deteriorate committee power, and chamber leaders move legislation forward without the actions of any particular committee. Leaders also use multiple referrals to skirt the influence of uncooperative committees.[11] In addition, more committees involved in the crafting of legislation mean more opportunities to obstruct legislation.[12]

We saw the multiple referral process in action during the Obama administration's initiative to overhaul health insurance in the United States, which resulted in the Affordable Care Act. The bill was considered by five different committees in the House and Senate, according to the provisions in the legislation that matched their jurisdictions. For example, the House Ways and Means Committee considered the taxation and Medicare portions of the bill, and the House Education and Labor Committee considered aspects of the law that affected worker issues and eligibility for subsidies related to employment.[13]

Congressional researchers have taken a keen interest in the topic of jurisdictions as a way to understand how committees interact and how this interaction influences policy deliberations. One study finds that jurisdictional change is part of a concerted effort by committees to extend their reach through the bill referral process. According to the study, members (and sometimes committees or committee members) craft legislative language to increase the likelihood that a bill on a topic of interest will be referred to a specific committee. Often, committees will then try to codify their jurisdictional control over an issue area acquired through bill referrals in a more formal way by having that jurisdiction written into the chamber rules.[14]

In recent years, cybersecurity matters have generated jurisdictional competition between committees. After the digital theft of consumer data from companies such as Target, Home Depot, and Walmart, several House committees introduced legislation that would require the private sector and government agencies to share cyber threat information (House Intelligence Committee), create federal information security programs (House Oversight and Government Reform Committee), and require government agencies to develop cybersecurity research and development plans and expand advanced computer networking and security (House Science Committee).[15] In the Senate, during the 113th Congress (2013–14), the Commerce, Intelligence, Banking, and Homeland Security Committees all introduced legislation or held hearings on the issue of cybersecurity.[16] With seven committees vying for the spotlight, it's not surprising that none was able to hold it, and in the end, none of these proposals were enacted into law. Senator Jay Rockefeller (D-W.Va.), chair of the Senate Commerce Committee, laid the blame for inaction squarely on the jurisdictional turf battles between committees.[17]

But the process of granting one committee jurisdictional authority over a policy area isn't always about power. Research has shown that when lawmakers make jurisdictional changes, those changes are usually intended to promote efficiency and clarify responsibility.[18] For instance, in 1999, Congress reconfigured regulation of the financial services industry by eliminating the barriers between banks and securities and insurance companies. The new law expanded market opportunities for banks in the United States, but it also made it more difficult for government regulators to monitor the banks' behavior. Two years later, as a way of rationalizing committee jurisdictions and improving oversight of the financial services industry (as well as solving a nasty turf battle between two Republicans vying for the chairmanship of the House Energy and Commerce Committee), the Republican leadership consolidated the jurisdictions of securities and insurance industry regulation with the committee that already controlled bank regulation. The result was the newly reconfigured House Financial Services Committee.[19]

## THEN AND NOW
## THE EVOLUTION OF COMMITTEES

The notion of a subgroup of lawmakers crafting legislative proposals for consideration by the entire House or Senate took some time to develop (see the related discussion in Chapter 2). Committees in both the House and Senate grew out of the system that existed in the first Continental Congress. Legislation was first considered by the entire membership of each chamber before being sent to a select committee appointed specifically to iron out the details of a given bill. To handle recurring business and to build expertise, lawmakers in the House quickly turned to standing committees. The standing committee system began with a committee on elections (1789), followed by more policy-oriented committees such as the Interstate and Foreign Commerce Committee (1795) and the Ways and Means Committee (1802), both of which still exist in roughly the same form today. As the new century progressed, Congress created more committees: Public Lands (1805), Post Offices and Postal Roads (1808), Judiciary (1813), Agriculture (1820), Indian Affairs (1821), and Military Affairs (1822). The Senate was slower to transition from select committees to standing committees, finally making a wholesale shift in the early 1820s.[20] Ultimately, standing committees made Congress more autonomous in the larger political system. With its own structures for policy knowledge and governing expertise, Congress could craft legislation without direction from the president or input from executive branch agencies.

After the Civil War, Congress and its committee system changed dramatically. Instead of moving back and forth between state and national office within the prevailing party structure, lawmakers increasingly saw service in Congress as a long-term career choice. Around the turn of the century, Progressive Era reforms such as the Australian ballot and the direct primary eroded the parties' control over elections and connected members more directly to the citizens they represented. As a result, members felt increasing pressure to service the needs of voters back home. Because committees regulated and promoted policies that were important to particular districts or states, members came to view seats on committees as a way to claim credit for generating policy benefits, thereby satisfying both their constituents' demands and their own career aspirations.[21] Thus a variety of committees oriented toward constituency service were created during this time: Mines and Mining and Pacific Railroads (both created in 1865), Levees and Improvements of the Mississippi River (1875), Rivers and Harbors (1883), Merchant Marine and Fisheries (1887), Irrigation and Reclamation and Civil Service (both created in 1893), Roads (1913), and Flood Control (1916). These were among the most popular committees with lawmakers, with Rivers and Harbors ranking as one of the most attractive destinations between 1889 and 1947.[22]

During this same period, the number of seats on committees grew dramatically. The largest growth took place on panels with appropriating authority over the federal budget. Many of these committees, such as Agriculture and Post Office, were able to funnel benefits directly to constituents. Moreover, the concept of a **property right** to one's committee assignment (that is, a norm entitling a lawmaker to maintain his seat on a committee from one congressional term to the next) was solidified during this period.[23] While this right was never set down in chamber or party rules, the norm that returning members could retain their previous committee assignments (if desired) was rarely violated.

The textbook, committee-oriented Congress came about through the adoption of legislative reforms just after World War II. Both chambers consolidated committees and constructed formal committee jurisdiction. Along with these rearrangements came provisions for greater staff resources and a clear directive that committees stand watch over executive branch agencies. Equally notable, lawmakers rejected measures that would have shifted some control over the legislative agenda to party and chamber leaders, such as party caucus–based policy committees.

At the end of the mid-twentieth-century reform period, congressional committee chairs dominated policy matters under their control. But, as we see in this chapter, this era of authoritarian committee chairs and committee domination of the policy-making process has given way to one that is controlled more tightly by party leadership.

### Critical Thinking

1. How does the role of committees in the formulation of policy proposals in the modern era differ from their role in the earliest days of Congress?
2. What fueled the expansion in the number of congressional committees from the late nineteenth century through the mid-twentieth century?
3. What new committee would you create to address an under-served policy area?

## COMMITTEE SEAT ASSIGNMENTS AND COMMITTEE CHAIRS

Seats on certain committees are particularly attractive because they confer power and influence. Before we unpack that, however, we must first understand how the assignment process works.

In both the House and Senate, parties assign members to committees. The majority party in both chambers determines the number of committee slots for itself and the minority party. As a result, the majority party nearly always grants itself more slots on each committee, sometimes based on the ratio of majority to minority party members in the chamber and sometimes in far greater proportion

**TABLE 5.1**  House of Representatives Standing Committees, 117th Congress (2021–23)

| Committee (# of members) | Majority Seats | Minority Seats | Chairperson |
|---|---|---|---|
| Agriculture (51) | 53% | 47% | David Scott (D-Ga.) |
| Appropriations (59) | 56 | 44 | Rosa DeLauro (D-Conn.) |
| Armed Services (59) | 53 | 47 | Adam Smith (D-Wash.) |
| Budget (37) | 57 | 43 | John Yarmuth (D-Ky.) |
| Education and Labor (53) | 55 | 45 | Robert Scott (D-Va.) |
| Energy and Commerce (58) | 55 | 45 | Frank Pallone, Jr. (D-N.J.) |
| Ethics (10) | 50 | 50 | Ted Deutch (D-Fla.) |
| Financial Services (54) | 56 | 44 | Maxine Waters (D-Calif.) |
| Foreign Affairs (51) | 53 | 47 | Gregory Meeks (D-N.Y.) |
| Homeland Security (35) | 54 | 46 | Bennie Thompson (D-Miss.) |
| House Administration (9) | 67 | 33 | Zoe Lofgren (D-Calif.) |
| Judiciary (44) | 57 | 43 | Jerrold Nadler (D-N.Y.) |
| Natural Resources (48) | 54 | 46 | Raúl M. Grijalva (D-Ariz.) |
| Oversight and Reform (45) | 56 | 44 | Carolyn Maloney (D-N.Y.) |
| Rules (13) | 69 | 31 | Jim McGovern (D-Mass.) |
| Science, Space, and Technology (42) | 55 | 45 | Eddie Johnson (D-Tex.) |
| Small Business (27) | 56 | 44 | Nydia M. Velázquez (D-N.Y.) |
| Transportation and Infrastructure (69) | 54 | 46 | Peter A. DeFazio (D-Ore.) |
| Veterans' Affairs (31) | 55 | 45 | Mark Takano (D-Calif.) |
| Ways and Means (43) | 56 | 44 | Richard Neal (D-Mass.) |
| **Total House Seats (435)** | **51** | **49** | |

U.S. House, http://clerk.house.gov/committee_info/index.aspx (accessed 2/8/21).

(see Tables 5.1 and 5.2). The particular ratio often reflects the majority party's desire to influence a committee's agenda. Compare, for example, the majority-minority ratios on the House Veterans' Affairs Committee and the House Rules Committee. The Veterans' Affairs panel rarely deals with matters that are vital to either party's political agenda, but it is responsible for issues important to veterans, who comprise a key cross-partisan population. As a result, it has a ratio of

**TABLE 5.2   Senate Standing Committees, 117th Congress (2021–23)**

| Committee (# of members) | Majority Seats | Minority Seats | Chairperson |
|---|---|---|---|
| Agriculture (22) | 50% | 50% | Debbie Stabenow (D-Mich.) |
| Appropriations (30) | 50 | 50 | Patrick Leahy (D-Vt.) |
| Armed Services (26) | 50 | 50 | Jack Reed (D-R.I.) |
| Banking, Housing, and Urban Affairs (24) | 50 | 50 | Sherrod Brown (D-Ohio) |
| Commerce, Science, and Transportation (28) | 50 | 50 | Maria Cantwell (D-Wa.) |
| Energy and Natural Resources (20) | 50 | 50 | Joe Manchin (D-W. Va.) |
| Environment and Public Works (20) | 50 | 50 | Thomas Carper (D-Del.) |
| Finance (28) | 50 | 50 | Ron Wyden (D-Ore.) |
| Foreign Relations (22) | 50 | 50 | Bob Menendez (D-N.J.) |
| Health, Education, Labor, and Pensions (22) | 50 | 50 | Patty Murray (D-Wa.) |
| Homeland Security and Governmental Affairs (14) | 50 | 50 | Gary Peters (D-Mich.) |
| Indian Affairs (12) | 50 | 50 | Brain Schatz (D-Hawaii) |
| Rules and Administration (18) | 50 | 50 | Amy Klobuchar (D-Minn.) |
| Small Business and Entrepreneurship (20) | 50 | 50 | Benjamin Cardin (D-Md.) |
| Budget (22) | 50 | 50 | Bernie Sanders (D-Vt.) |
| Judiciary (22) | 50 | 50 | Dick Durbin (D-Ill.) |
| Veterans' Affairs (18) | 50 | 50 | Jon Tester (D-Mt.) |
| Select Intelligence (20) | 50 | 50 | Mark Warner (D-Va.) |
| **Total Senate Seats (100)** | **48** (2 Independents caucus with the Democrats) | **50** | |

U.S. Senate, www.senate.gov/general/committee_membership/committee_memberships_SLIN.htm (accessed 2/8/21).

Democrats to Republicans (17:14) that approximates the overall chamber composition. The Rules Committee, in contrast, determines whether and how bills are considered on the House floor. As a result, Rules is considered to be an "arm of the party leadership,"[24] and thus is controlled by a supermajority (usually 2:1 or greater).

In the House, members cannot serve on more than two standing committees (although exceptions to this rule are common when a member has a less desirable assignment, such as the Small Business Committee). In the Senate, however, because of the much smaller membership, lawmakers may serve on up to four standing committees. In addition, parties in both chambers group committees based on their importance, influence, and workload, further restricting committee membership. For example, both Democrats and Republicans in the House consider Appropriations, Rules, Ways and Means, Energy and Commerce, and Financial Services to be exclusive committees, whose members generally do not serve on any other committees.

Senate committees also have varying levels of power and desirability and thus different sets of guidelines regarding committee seat assignment. When Lyndon Johnson became Senate majority leader in 1953, he established a method for allocating committee assignments known as the Johnson Rule, which both parties now use. Committees are separated into tiered categories: major (or exclusive) committees in category A, mid-level committees in category B, and minor committees in category C. Every senator must be assigned to a major (category A) committee before any senator can be assigned to a second major committee. (Like their House counterparts, Democrats and Republicans in the Senate have a few very exclusive committees—Appropriations, Armed Services, and Finance for the Democrats; Republicans add Foreign Relations to this list). After that, each senator can select one mid-level (category B) committee and then one minor (category C) committee.

As noted earlier, lawmakers usually have a property right to their existing seat from one term to the next. That is, assuming the majority party in one Congress doesn't lose its majority during election to the next Congress, incumbent lawmakers wishing to return to their previous term's committee assignments normally can do so.

Committee vacancies do occur, of course, because of committee expansion, retirements, and members transferring from one committee to another. Filling those vacancies is an important task fraught with political complications and wider implications for representation and governance. To fill open committee seats, Democrats and Republicans in both chambers have **steering committees** that consider rank-ordered requests from incoming freshmen and incumbents seeking transfers from one panel to another. These committees are typically composed of party leaders, important committee chairs and ranking members, and regional representatives. (The minority party member of a committee who possesses the most seniority is called the **ranking minority member** and serves as the leader of the minority on the committee.)

Many factors determine whether an initial assignment or transfer is granted, including the member's ideology and party loyalty. Unquestionably, lawmakers' constituency needs are critical in determining their best fit on committees. Accordingly, the Agriculture Committee is filled with lawmakers from districts heavily reliant on farming, the Natural Resources panel is usually chock full of members from the West, and the Financial Services Committee usually has a disproportionate number of representatives hailing from the Northeast. In recent years, both Democrats and Republicans have used vacant spots on powerful committees as a way to boost the reelection prospects of vulnerable lawmakers.[25] House Democratic leaders have also sought greater diversity in committee composition, allocating seats as a way to broaden a committee's regional, racial, ethnic, gender, and generational makeup. When Republicans controlled the House they usually distributed seats to maintain ideological control of the party, granting plum assignments to members in the conservative mainstream rather than to uncooperative Freedom Caucus members; however, as the party lost its majority following the 2018 election and the caucus defended President Trump during his impeachment, members of the Freedom Caucus emerged as leaders and received more prominent committee positions.[26]

Once each party's steering committee names the members of the various committees, the slate goes before the entire caucus for a vote. It is then subject to ratification (majority vote) by the entire chamber, where it is usually approved without controversy.

## Committee Assignments and Attractiveness

The movement of representatives and senators between committees can signal the attractiveness of committee assignments and how that attractiveness changes over time. Tim Groseclose and Charles Stewart's study of committee value is based on the observation that members of Congress will seek a transfer only if they can "trade up"—that is, if the committee assignment they get is more attractive than the one they have.[27] Based on this assumption, they have generated scores and a ranking for all committees across time. Table 5.3 shows the change in committee seat value from the late 1970s to the early 2010s, with the period divided at 1995 (when Republicans regained majority control of Congress after many years in the minority party; under Republican leadership, control of the legislative agenda and committee system tightened considerably).

The Groseclose-Stewart measure of committee value shows few dramatic shake-ups among the top committees in either chamber. In the House, Ways and Means, Energy and Commerce, Appropriations, and Rules remain the four most highly valued committees. However, the Rules Committee suffered a

**TABLE 5.3**   Relative Value of Congressional Committees, 96th–112th Congresses (1979–2013)

**House**

| | 96th–103rd Congresses (1979–95) | 104th–112th Congresses (1995–2013) |
|---|---|---|
| **More Sought After** | Rules | Ways and Means |
| | Ways and Means | Energy and Commerce |
| | Appropriations | Appropriations |
| | Energy and Commerce | Rules |
| | Armed Services | Foreign Affairs |
| | House Administration | Financial Services |
| | Foreign Affairs | Armed Services |
| | Post Office and Civil Service | Judiciary |
| | Judiciary | Ethics |
| | Budget | House Administration |
| | Natural Resources | Budget |
| **Less Sought After** | Ethics | Transportation and Infrastructure |
| | Merchant Marine and Fisheries | Natural Resources |
| | D.C. | Oversight and Government Reform |
| | Financial Services | Education and the Workforce |
| | Education and the Workforce | Agriculture |
| | Veterans' Affairs | Veterans' Affairs |
| | Transportation and Infrastructure | Science, Space, and Technology |
| | Science, Space, and Technology | Homeland Security |
| | Small Business | Small Business |
| | Oversight and Government Reform | |
| | Agriculture | |

**Senate**

| | 96th–103rd Congresses (1979–95) | 104th–112th Congresses (1995–2013) |
|---|---|---|
| **More Sought After** ↑ | Finance | Finance |
| | Rules and Administration | Appropriations |
| | Appropriations | Rules and Administration |
| | Foreign Relations | Armed Services |
| | Veterans' Affairs | Commerce, Science, and Transportation |
| | Armed Services | Judiciary |
| | Energy and Natural Resources | Homeland Security and Governmental Affairs |
| | Budget | Budget |
| | Small Business | Veterans' Affairs |
| | Homeland Security and Governmental Affairs | Foreign Relations |
| | Banking, Housing, and Urban Affairs | Environment and Public Works |
| | Agriculture, Nutrition, and Forestry | Agriculture, Nutrition, and Forestry |
| | Judiciary | Energy and Natural Resources |
| | Environment and Public Works | Banking, Housing, and Urban Affairs |
| **Less Sought After** ↓ | Commerce, Science, and Transportation | Small Business |

From Charles Stewart III. April 6, 2012. "The Value of Committee Assignments in Congress since 1994." Midwest Political Science Association, MIT Political Science Department Research Paper 2012–07. SSRN. https://ssrn.com/abstract=2035632 (accessed 6/1/18).

moderate drop in its relative value after the Republican takeover, likely because GOP leaders sought to centralize control of the chamber agenda, eroding the Rules Committee's autonomy in moving bills from committee deliberations to chamber consideration.

On the Senate side, there has been almost no movement among the top three committees: Finance, Appropriations, and Rules and Administration. However, Foreign Relations, which used to be a very popular policy committee, fell dramatically, from the fourth slot to the tenth. Other broad policy-focused panels fared better during this period, notably the Judiciary Committee and the reformed Governmental Affairs Committee with its expanded jurisdiction to include Homeland Security matters.

One of Congress's key functions is controlling the federal purse strings, so it's not surprising that the money committees, which dole out funds from the federal Treasury (Appropriations in both chambers) and control tax policy (Ways and Means in the House, Finance in the Senate), are always among the most popular with lawmakers. A seat on these committees means increased opportunities to provide programs, services, and financial benefits to constituents. In addition, three more narrow, constituency-focused committees have become more attractive: Agriculture and Transportation in the House and Commerce, Science, and Transportation in the Senate.

Finally, the House Financial Services Committee has become more attractive over time because of factors related to its expanded governing role (recall the jurisdictional rearrangement that resulted from legislative changes in the financial industry in the early 2000s discussed earlier in this chapter). In 2008, as the financial industry was facing near-calamity amid the Great Recession, the committee was again at the center of key governing decisions and a new set of sweeping financial regulations known as the Dodd-Frank Wall Street Reform and Consumer Protection Act, enacted in 2010. Financial Services became more powerful and expanded its authority over a very deep-pocketed constituency (the financial industry). When it comes to campaign contributions, Financial Services is often second only to the tax committee (Ways and Means) for its members' haul.

## The Evolution of Committee Chair Appointments

Over the decades, the rules governing the selection and retention of **committee chairs** have evolved dramatically, transforming what used to be considered a seniority property right into an intraparty electoral competition. Throughout much of the twentieth century, committee chairs in the House were held by the majority party member with the longest continuous service on the committee. This norm, known as the seniority system, governed committee hierarchy and put southern Democrats in many of the top spots.[28] As a result, the most conservative subset of Democratic lawmakers controlled key policy-making areas during this time. While important in the Senate, committee chair positions were not nearly as coveted as they were in the House, because the Senate agenda is much more open.

As the Democratic Caucus became more liberal in the 1960s, a backlash occurred against the domineering control by conservative chairs. Over the next decade, the Democratic Caucus and the House as a whole adopted a series of democratizing reforms, one of which partially undermined the seniority system by implementing rules regarding selection and retention of committee chairs. Democrats eventually required committee chair candidates to stand for a secret ballot vote by the entire party caucus. In 1975, the Democratic Caucus, bolstered by a sizable freshman class of liberal lawmakers (the Watergate Babies), unseated three long-standing committee chairs whose conservative and heavy-handed decisions had rankled the emboldened liberals.[29]

This unseating of a senior majority-party member from a committee chair is known as a seniority violation. Such violations increased from 1975 to 2010. The high number of seniority violations in the 94th Congress supports the post-Watergate narrative of liberals flexing their muscles. Seniority violations also rose following the 1994 elections when Republicans took control of the House and instituted a number of changes that upended the power of committee chairs. As part of this Republican Revolution, Speaker Newt Gingrich hand-picked most of the committee chairs, and though he did not entirely ignore committee seniority, he bypassed high-ranking members on several key committees and instead selected individuals who were more ideologically reliable, politically skilled, and energetic.[30]

Perhaps just as important, Republicans of the 104th Congress instituted chair term limits, which would significantly affect long-term committee operations in the House and seniority violations. Specifically, the GOP changed its caucus rules, limiting lawmakers to three congressional terms as committee chair before they were rotated out of the position. Seniority violations, particularly involving chairs, ticked up again in the 107th Congress, three terms after the Republicans took control of the House. When the Democrats regained control of the House in the 110th Congress, seniority violations for committee chairs tapered off, although there have been several seniority violations for the position of ranking minority member on the GOP side.

One result of the new chair term limits is lawmakers now actively campaign among their colleagues for chair positions.[31] For example, Jerry Lewis, a long-serving Republican from California, along with two rivals, engaged in an extensive campaign in 2004 to become the chair of the House Appropriations

Committee following the six-year term of C. W. Bill Young of Florida. Lewis not only had to impress the GOP leadership with his management skills on one of the House's most powerful committees, but he also needed to demonstrate his commitment to national party principles of limited government. Most of all, Lewis had long outperformed his rivals in his fundraising efforts to increase the Republicans' House majority. In the election cycle immediately prior to his selection as Appropriations chair, Lewis brought in more than $1.35 million to the campaigns of GOP House candidates.[32] In the new world of chair term limits, leadership ambition goes hand in hand with fundraising ability.

# THE TEXTBOOK COMMITTEE SYSTEM

Committees are deeply embedded in the textbook view of how a bill becomes law and how Congress operates. This perception of the regular order of congressional operations has existed for many decades, and it assumes a variety of duties for committees at several critical stages of the governing process: policy formulation and deliberation, reconciliation of differences between the two chambers, and oversight of the executive branch's implementation of the laws. Here we review the textbook notion of committee duties and provide an updated perspective on the status of each.

## Policy Formulation and Committee Deliberation

Policy formulation and deliberation is generally considered the core role of committees. As described earlier, governing is one of Congress's fundamental responsibilities, and the committee system has long been the structure for achieving it.

**PROPOSING POLICY**   Committees formulate policy in both positive and negative ways. **Positive** or **proposal authority** occurs when committees introduce legislation, with the hope of getting legislation onto the agenda and to the final passage stage. Positive authority is important, but it does not guarantee legislative success. Indeed, legislation will face a series of roadblocks along the way.

Once a member of Congress introduces legislation it is referred to a committee according to its topic. Lawmakers will often introduce legislation aimed at their own committee's jurisdiction. After referral, further action is not guaranteed. In fact, most bills die in the committee stage. In the last two decades, only 10 to 20 percent of bills introduced in Congress have navigated the legislative gauntlet to become law.[33] For example, in the 115th Congress (2017–19), there were 7,542 bills introduced in the House, and only 1,162 passed the chamber. Similarly, of the 3,874 Senate bills introduced, only 583 passed the entire Senate. In the end, a total of 442 public laws were enacted that term—passed by both chambers and signed into law.[34] On top of that, a fairly sizable proportion of laws in any term (about 45 percent) are either commemorative or of minor importance.[35]

At the committee level, and in accordance with the substance of the bill, action typically begins with a referral to a subcommittee, where consideration usually takes the form of hearings and then a markup session. Hearings, in which members of Congress and other interested parties meet to discuss the legislation, are the most public way that committees engage in lawmaking and governance. While hearings are sometimes held to address a specific piece of legislation, they can also revolve around a general issue of government concern or oversight of an executive branch agency (as discussed below).

Members of Congress use hearings for three primary purposes: (1) to generate information and opinions about the merits or pitfalls of a legislative proposal, (2) to oversee the actions of an executive branch agency or program (see Chapter 10), or (3, specific to the Senate) to provide advice and consent with regard to treaties and presidential appointments (see Chapter 9). Within these broad purposes, hearings may also be used to satisfy a number of other aims. Hearings may help with the practical functions of lawmaking, such as determining if a new law is warranted in the first place, garnering publicity for a policy matter (or a particular perspective on that issue), assessing congressional support for a bill or amendment, or protecting jurisdictional boundaries (or asserting the committee's jurisdictional reach)—that is, informally, but publicly, establishing what issues the committee will tackle in the future. Hearings may also address members' political concerns by providing a platform for external actors to make their case, establishing a public record of scrutiny on an issue and thus building the committee members' reputations, or simply providing a venue for partisan attacks.

Various chamber rules govern the format and procedures of committee hearings. Nevertheless, committee and subcommittee chairs exercise a great deal of discretion in deciding what bills get hearings, when those hearings occur, and how they are to be carried out, particularly concerning the privileges of the minority party. In particularly partisan hearings, chairs have been known to prevent particular witnesses from testifying, to schedule hearings when most lawmakers are out of town, and to end hearings abruptly. For example, in 2014, during a heated and partisan House Committee on Oversight and Government Reform hearing on Internal Revenue Service scrutiny of Tea Party groups, Chair

Committees spend much of their time in bill markup sessions. Here, the House Ways and Means Committee meets to mark up the Tax Cuts and Jobs Act in November 2017.

Darrell Issa (R-Calif.) cut off the microphone and ended the meeting before the ranking minority member, Representative Elijah Cummings (D-Md.), had a chance to speak.[36] In recent years, exhibitions of partisanship during hearings have become somewhat common, with questioning of witnesses devolving into shouting matches[37] and walkouts by members.[38]

Another crucial part of a committee's responsibility in advancing legislation is the markup of bills. Markup sessions occur after hearings and other information gathering and involve the more formal debate and amending of legislation. At this point, committee members, usually led by the chair, choose the bill that will move the policy matter forward to the entire chamber. In almost all cases, the chosen bill is one offered by a committee member, and by far the most common bill at this stage is the **chair's mark**, a bill introduced by the chair (sometimes just before markup) that contains her perspective on what should be included in the legislation.

During the markup, members synthesize the input they receive from hearings, leadership, interest groups, and other experts and hash out a bill's details. Markup sessions are generally less formal than hearings or floor debate, where members negotiate the details of legislation, trade support for key amendments, and eventually build coalitions necessary for success when the bill is considered on the chamber floor. During markup, opponents of the bill attempt to tack on amendments to complicate legislation or make the language unacceptable to a majority of the wider chamber. Because it can be very difficult to remove language from a reported bill, committee members have been known to delay or obstruct to prevent bills they oppose from moving on to the chamber for further consideration.

During the public period of hearings and markup, committees are also heavily engaged in activities behind closed doors, including gathering information from stakeholders (affected constituents, lobbyists, and governmental or bureaucratic actors), interviewing potential witnesses, composing questions for hearings, following up with witnesses regarding matters that arose during testimony, securing legislative cosponsors, and building consensus among key decision makers (including other committee members, critical leaders in the chamber or across the Capitol, outside groups, and perhaps White House officials), to craft a viable bill.

While lawmakers are the public face of working committees, the professional committee staff carries out much of the behind-the-scenes activity. Committees can have sizable staff operations, with the number varying with the policy scope and culture of a particular panel. Staff size ranges from 20 to 30 on the House Small Business or Veterans' Affairs Committee to 150 to 200 on the House Appropriations Committee. Committee staff members are generally older, more experienced, and better paid than the staff who serve in individual lawmakers' offices. They are the eyes, ears, and, in some cases, the brain trust for the committee and its chair. They possess much of the historical policy knowledge, often having been involved in many prior rounds of policy formulation and legislative battles. Committee staff members hold both formal and informal discussions with rank-and-file committee members and minority party lawmakers (and their staff) to discern priorities and the committee's latitude regarding the content of legislative proposals. They examine lawmakers' preferences on particular aspects of policy, warning of potential problems as bills develop and move through committee consideration and on to floor consideration. Ultimately, the committee staff translates lawmakers' policy preferences and priorities into workable bill language.[39]

Finally, once the committee has completed its work on a bill, it votes to report it to the wider chamber. Accompanying the bill is an official committee report, which provides background information and justification for the legislative language used. In some cases, a committee report later serves as an important part of the legislative history, particularly when courts are trying to discern lawmakers' intent (see Chapter 11).

**UPDATING POLICY**  For many decades, committees have been charged with renewing or reauthorizing legislation for specific government departments, which ultimately makes committees quite powerful. This broad power is perhaps best exemplified by the annual defense reauthorization, controlled by the House and Senate Armed Services Committees. Usually, these two panels wrap nearly all defense-related legislative activity into one annual bill. The defense authorization often includes matters ranging from funding for new weapons systems to policy regarding how the military deals with sexual assault to whether or not detainees remain at Guantánamo Bay, Cuba.

Policy reauthorization allows committees' members, particularly committee leaders, to bring their legislative ideas to the floor with the designation of "must pass." Why the sense of urgency? Failure to extend an existing authorizing statute can shut down popular and vital programs and agencies. For example, in the summer of 2011, amid partisan wrangling over a deficit-reduction package, the House and Senate Transportation Committees were unable to agree on the specifics of a short-term extension of the authorization for the Federal Aviation Administration (FAA). While such stopgap measures normally do not include any new legislative language and usually extend existing funding levels until a longer-term reauthorization can be completed, House Transportation chair John Mica (R-Fla.) included language to cut subsidies for small airports, and Democrats in the House and Senate balked. The partial shutdown of the agency, which lasted two weeks, resulted in the furlough of several thousand nonessential FAA employees (not air traffic controllers) and halted much-needed construction projects at airports across the country.[40] A temporary authorization was eventually passed to bring the agency back to full force, and Congress approved a long-term authorization, including the small airport funding, in February of 2012.

**BLOCKING POLICY**  Committees also possess **negative** or **gatekeeping authority**, which they use to limit or prevent unwanted legislative proposals from gaining traction. Negative authority is derived from several organizational rules: (1) adherence to committee jurisdictions and their exclusivity with respect to policy property rights, (2) requirements that bills be referred to committees once introduced, and (3) a germaneness clause (in the House) preventing unrelated measures from being attached to bills. Committees thus can serve as a choke point in the movement of legislative proposals. Committee members, particularly committee leaders, can kill legislation simply by failing to act on bills or amendments (beyond what is required in chamber rules). This is the fate of the vast majority of bills introduced in Congress each term. One of the more infamous examples of this conscious neglect occurred in the late 1950s and early 1960s, when the House Rules Committee, led by avowed segregationist

Howard W. Smith of Virginia, refused to permit early versions of the Civil Rights Act to go to the floor.

This ability to kill legislative proposals is often used as a raw expression of representational power. For instance, the House and Senate Agriculture Committees have used their exclusive control over the Farm Bill to prevent any elimination or serious restructuring of the rules regarding federal government subsidies to farmers. (As we discuss elsewhere in this chapter, lawmakers from constituencies that depend on farm economies dominate the agriculture committees.)

While Senate committees also propose legislation authorizing government programs and agencies, they do not have the House committees' ability to block unwanted legislation from receiving floor consideration. Because of the germaneness clause in the House—"no motion or proposition on a subject different from that under consideration shall be admitted under color of amendment"—a House committee retains exclusive control over policy that falls within its jurisdiction. In the Senate, no such germaneness rule exists, and members can compete with committees on policy by proposing legislation via a nongermane amendment. For example, in 2009, a federal court banned guns in national parks. House Republicans attempted to reverse this ruling by placing new language in that year's omnibus public lands bill. Their goal was to codify the rights of individuals to carry concealed weapons on federal lands. The amendment was rejected by the House Natural Resources Committee and then turned back by the House Rules Committee during its crafting of a rule for floor debate.[41] However, later that year, Senator Tom Coburn (R-Okla.) successfully attached similar language to a measure imposing new restrictions on credit card companies. The credit card bill was strongly supported by the Obama administration, which very much wanted it to be completed before the impending Memorial Day break, and the gun amendment was passed and signed into law.[42]

In addition, once a House committee's bill reaches the floor, it can be protected by a **special rule** granted by the Rules Committee. Special rules typically limit or restrict amendments that can be offered, with the **closed rule** (no amendments) being the most prohibitive. No such similar ability to protect bills exists in the Senate.

## House–Senate Reconciliation: Conference Committees

Committee members often play another key role: negotiating differences between House and Senate versions of legislation. Traditionally, when the House and Senate pass differing bills on the same legislative matter, a conference committee—a joint House–Senate Committee—negotiates the differences.

Conferees, the House and Senate members assigned to the conference committee, come mostly from the original committees of jurisdiction. Members of a conference committee have a great deal of authority over the final legislation, as their compromise almost always comes back to their respective chambers for a take-it-or-leave-it vote (no amendments allowed). Thus any changes made on the chamber floors after initial committee consideration and report of the bill can be reversed later in the conference negotiations. This ability to undo floor decisions after the fact effectively gives conference committees a final veto over legislation, which can be a tremendous source of power.[43]

For instance, in the winter of 2013–14, a conference committee composed mostly of members from the House and Senate Agriculture Committees negotiated a compromise on a five-year deal to reauthorize farm programs (the previously mentioned Farm Bill). In what turned out to be a surprisingly contentious fight, conferees, in conjunction with some chamber leaders, were able to stop attempts to end all farm subsidy programs. A halt to government farm subsidies would have had severe consequences for committee members' constituencies and their supportive interest groups. Instead, chamber leaders negotiated deep cuts in food stamp programs that were part of the House legislation.

## Oversight of the Executive Branch

Beyond legislation, Congressional committees play a role in the separation of powers by overseeing executive branch agencies. Such oversight takes the form of monitoring, adjusting, and updating the actions and administrative duties of federal agencies. Former House Committee on Oversight and Government Reform chair Henry Waxman (D-Calif.) contended that congressional oversight of the executive branch may be "just as important, if not more important, than legislation."[44]

Committees oversee in a number of ways, most visibly in public hearings. In the spring of 2014, after revelations of mismanagement at the Department of Veterans Affairs (the VA), the House and Senate Veterans' Affairs Committees held a set of hearings focused on delays in the provision of health care to veterans and the falsification of associated documents. As a result, Secretary of Veterans Affairs Eric Shinseki was fired (along with a number of other top department officials) and new legislation intended to fix some of the more glaring problems in an underfunded, understaffed, and mismanaged agency was passed.[45] In recent decades, oversight hearings have become more frequent in the House. From the end of World War II through the late 1960s, the House averaged about 120 days of oversight hearings per year across all its committees; since then, the average has increased dramatically to about 550 oversight hearing days, in some years reaching close to 1,000.

Despite the media attention garnered by high-profile investigations, the bulk of federal agency oversight by committees occurs through normal hearings and other legislative efforts as part of the regularly scheduled reauthorization of agencies and programs. Committees also often require agencies, through language in authorizing or appropriating statutes, to report details about their activities for approval or consideration. For example, the VA must submit any new lease that amounts to more than $1 million annually to the two Appropriations Committees in Congress for approval prior to the allocation of funds.

While standing committees perform most of Congress's oversight and investigation functions, lawmakers sometimes create special committees for a high-profile investigation of the president (the Special Whitewater Committee to investigate the Clintons' private investments) or a specific federal department or agency (House Select Committee on Benghazi to investigate the State Department's handling of the attack on the U.S. Consulate in Libya in 2012).[46] Oversight can also take the form of investigating illegal or problematic activities within and outside of government, such as the prominent anticommunist investigations in 1953 led by Senator Joseph McCarthy (R-Wis.) in his position as chair of the Senate Committee on Government Operations. More recently, in 2008 the House Committee on Oversight and Government Reform investigated steroid use in Major League Baseball, landing superstar pitcher Roger Clemens in court facing perjury charges after telling Congress he had not used banned substances.

## ARE COMMITTEES STILL RELEVANT?

The committee system was once relatively autonomous, and partisanship and ideology were just a part of the mix of influences on members, along with constituency needs, policy expertise, and political ambition. Today, however, the dominance of partisan agendas pervades nearly all committee activities and has changed the nature of committee work. These changes have limited committees' governance and representation functions while highlighting their oversight and lawmaking role. The changes have also diminished committees' role in the legislative process. Has the vaunted position of committees been lost? Are committees no longer central to governance?

The shift away from the textbook functioning of committees has been more tectonic than tidal-wave. It began in the late 1960s, as the Democratic Caucus became increasingly populated by liberals who were unhappy with the iron-fisted control of committees by more conservative and senior members. As noted earlier, the committee reforms of the early 1970s shifted control of committee agendas and operations away from committee chairs and toward both party leadership (giving party leaders more influence over committee assignments) and junior members (through an expansion of the subcommittee system). At the same time, Republican and Democratic caucuses in both chambers were beginning their ideological sorting, resulting in greater policy polarization and increasing partisan battles over matters of governance. Eventually, in the 1980s, major legislation that had previously been the domain of committees came to be handled more often through negotiations between party leadership and the White House. This legislation included the crafting of Social Security reforms in 1983 and the Gramm-Rudman-Hollings deficit-reduction package in 1985.[47]

Committee power continued to decline into the early 1990s, particularly at the beginning of the Clinton presidency as the administration overplayed its hand in its efforts to overhaul health care policy. The White House's insistence on a costly and wholesale reorganization of national health coverage was politically unworkable, and it cost the many House and Senate committees who had devoted considerable time and resources to the effort some credibility. In the end, the initiative's failure contributed significantly to the Democrats' losing majority control in both chambers in the 1994 elections.

Leading the Republican sweep that year was House Speaker-to-be Newt Gingrich (R-Ga.), whose ambitious legislative agenda, the Contract with America, included ten policy proposals planned for consideration during the first 100 days of the term. Gingrich's unorthodox policy agenda was defined and developed outside the regular channels of committee authority, jurisdictional boundaries, and expertise. Political scientist Barbara Sinclair believes that this approach ushered in a new era of weakened congressional committee power and greater reliance on entities outside the normal power arrangements in Congress.[48]

Over the succeeding years, both Republican and Democratic leaders employed mechanisms outside the traditional committee system for policy making and governance. In particular, Gingrich was fond of using task forces (small groups of handpicked GOP lawmakers assembled on an ad hoc basis to consider and propose one specific piece of legislation) to legislate in a manner that was more tightly controlled by the Speaker and his small inner circle of trusted party leaders.[49] More than a dozen such task forces were created at the start of 1995. Several were run by majority leader Dick Armey (Tex.) and focused on items in the Contract, such as regulatory reform, term limits, and welfare. Others were structured around Gingrich's personal priorities, including health care, gun rights, outreach to people of color, and immigration, and were intended to be more permanent.[50]

While task forces fell out of favor following Gingrich's departure as Speaker,[51] the use of other mechanisms to formulate and shepherd policy proposals through the legislative process, and thus circumvent the traditional authority and expertise of committees, persists. A recent study by Sinclair finds that committees in the last few decades have become less involved in basic policy formulation and deliberation. Sinclair's data on major legislation reveal that normal committee procedures were bypassed less than 10 percent of the time in the 1960s and 1970s House and Senate, but that over the past two decades, regular committees of jurisdiction have been bypassed a third and sometimes half the time (Figure 5.1). Similarly, post-committee adjustment of bills (for example, floor amendments) was rare in the 1960s and 1970s, but the practice has increased dramatically, occurring in at least 40 percent of cases in the last few congressional terms.[52]

Some observers have suggested that the work of the House and Senate Appropriations Committees exemplifies the dysfunction of current Washington politics. Textbook budget procedure tells us that these committees (or, more accurately, the various Appropriations subcommittees) must produce annual appropriations bills for the 13 different categories of discretionary spending in the federal budget (including agriculture, commerce/justice/science, energy and

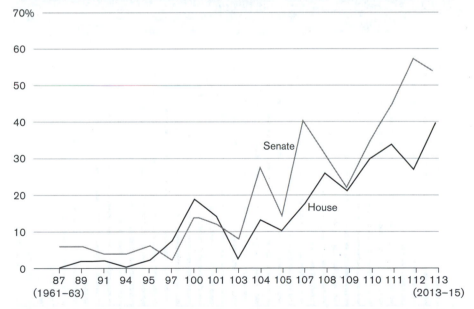

**FIGURE 5.1** Percentage of Major Legislation That Bypassed Committee of Jurisdiction, 87th–113th Congresses (1961–2015)

Barbara Sinclair. 2017. *Unorthodox Lawmaking: New Legislative Processes in the U.S. Congress*, 5th ed. Washington, D.C.: CQ Press.

water, and others). Otherwise, the associated government agencies and programs cannot spend any money. And it does seem that standard budgetary procedures are increasingly ignored, as more federal agencies are funded through omnibus appropriations (in which numerous appropriations bills are lumped together and adopted as a package) or simply maintained through continuing resolutions that extend the previous year's funding for another period (sometimes a year, sometimes less). These practices do not allow for adjustments to either keep up with inflation or reflect new circumstances or events.

The story of reduced committee influence in governance is not as simple as Sinclair's data, or the use of omnibus appropriations, might suggest, however. Recent research by Nolan McCarty indicates that the growth in omnibus appropriations does not necessarily reflect a lack of participation by the Appropriations Committees in budgetary lawmaking. In fact, McCarty shows that while there have been periods over the last four decades in which the Appropriations subcommittees have struggled to complete their required spending bills (in the early 1980s and from 2011 to 2013), for the most part, they have fulfilled their legislative responsibilities (see Figure 5.2).[53] The trouble has arisen in either passing these measures on the chamber floors or in coming to a cross-

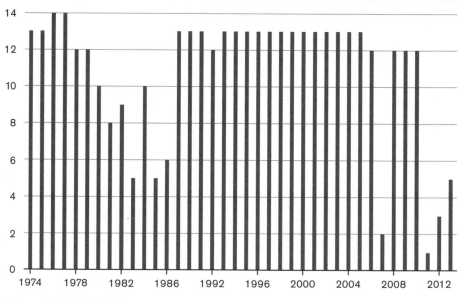

**FIGURE 5.2**  Number of Appropriations Bills Completed by Committee (1974–2013)

Data provided by Nolan McCarty.

chamber agreement for specific bills. Nevertheless, the details of the Appropriations subcommittees' work have been included in the omnibus measures that are eventually adopted to keep government running.

On occasion, the contemporary Congress resorts to ad hoc committee structures to fulfill governing responsibilities when normal committee procedures are inadequate. For example, in 2011, with Congress facing a critical deadline to increase the federal debt limit (the statutory cap on the amount of financial debt the U.S. government can hold)—which, if missed, would mean defaulting on federal debt obligations and potentially setting off economic chaos—lawmakers hurriedly created the Joint Select Committee on Deficit Reduction, informally known at the time as the "Supercommittee." This bipartisan panel of House and Senate members was charged with accomplishing something no other committee would have been capable of doing: negotiating a meaningful agreement to reduce the federal budget by $1.2 trillion by cutting budgets (normally under the purview of the Appropriations Committees) and increasing federal taxes (normally controlled by the House Ways and Means and the Senate Finance Committees). Ultimately, the Supercommittee was unsuccessful in reaching an agreement by the deadline, and budget sequestration (deep cuts across the entire federal budget) resulted.

## The Declining Influence of Conference Committees

As committee influence has waned at the policy-development stage, so has it waned in negotiations between chambers. In the early 1970s, the House and Senate relied on conference committees over 40 percent of the time to resolve their legislative differences and move bills on to final passage. Today, conference committees are rarely used (see also Chapter 7). This change is related to two phenomena. First, as already described, party leaders in both chambers have taken more control over the policy-making agenda from standing committees. Second, lawmakers have often prevented the formation of conference committees on legislation they oppose. Prior to the mid-1990s, senators had never blocked a motion to form a conference committee. The first blocked motion came in 1994, when Republicans filibustered a conference motion on a campaign finance measure. Such tactics became commonplace over the next two decades,[54] and the government shutdown in 2013 occurred largely because lawmakers in both chambers refused to appoint members to a conference committee to negotiate differences between House and Senate budget bills.[55] Conservative lawmakers were particularly concerned that conferees would produce a take-it-or-leave-it compromise that would lead to more spending than they preferred.

In place of conference committees, the two chambers initially turned to **ping-ponging**: offering amendments to legislation being considered in each chamber until the two chamber bills align. However, in recent years, all interchamber bargaining has declined dramatically, with less than a quarter of legislation involving any type of negotiations and conference committees engaged in less than 5 percent of all completed legislation.

Today, the chambers often simply accept the language offered to them by their counterparts across the Capitol. This form of reconciliation accounts for 80 percent or more of legislation passed on to the president for signature.[56] Occasionally, a chamber is backed into a corner and forced to accept the language of the other chamber due to lack of time. A good example is the 2009 extension of funds in the Cash for Clunkers program, a very popular economic stimulus measure that allowed owners of older inefficient automobiles to trade them in for a voucher toward the purchase of a more fuel-efficient vehicle. Cash for Clunkers passed because the House had already adjourned for their August recess, and the Senate had little choice but to adopt the House's language.[57]

## The New Realities of Committee Oversight

While the influence of committees has seemingly waned with regard to legislation, most evidence points to an increase in committee influence in overseeing executive branch activities. The post-1994 Republican takeover of Congress brought a series of rules changes in both chambers that expanded committees' oversight functions and responsibilities. The changes included the creation of subcommittees devoted to oversight and requirements that committee reports include regulatory impact statements. As a result, oversight hearings today consume a larger proportion of committee time than in the past.[58] Tom Mann, congressional expert at the Brookings Institution, has argued that the rise of oversight "has been the most important change since the 2006 election in terms of relations between the Congress and the administration."[59]

When scholars began to study committee oversight in the post–World War II era, they initially found that the frequency of investigations of presidential administrations did not depend on whether government was divided or unified.[60] For example, the Senate Foreign Relations Committee, under the control of Senator William Fulbright (D-Ark.), for several years conducted hearings into both the Johnson and Nixon administrations' Southeast Asia policy and the conduct of the war in Vietnam. Likewise, missteps by the U.S. Secret Service, including lapses in security around the White House, prompted a largely bipartisan investigation by the House Committee on Oversight and Government

Congressional committee oversight activity is a crucial check on the executive branch and has increased recently, especially during periods of divided government. From 2011–12, Darrell Issa (R-Calif.) spearheaded an investigation into the executive branch's mishandling of efforts to track the movement of guns into Mexico. Attorney General Eric Holder, pictured here, testified in front of the committee and was issued a "contempt of Congress" citation for refusing to hand over certain documents.

Reform in 2014, including hearings just prior to the resignation of Julia Pierson, director of the Secret Service.

However, more recent and sophisticated statistical analyses have uncovered a surge in investigations into the executive branch when Congress is controlled by a party different from the president's.[61] Moreover, as congressional majorities have become more ideologically homogeneous (see Chapter 6), such committee oversight has become more intense.[62] For example, from 2011 to 2012, Representative Darrell Issa, chair of the House Oversight and Government Reform Committee, held a series of hearings investigating a botched operation by the Bureau of Alcohol, Tobacco, Firearms, and Explosives to track guns moving across the border to Mexico (which came to be known as Operation Fast and Furious). The hearings culminated in the first contempt of Congress citation for a standing attorney general when the administration refused to comply with the committee's subpoena for documents related to the operation.

# HOW WE STUDY
## COMMITTEES: THEORY AND EVIDENCE

Many scholars believe that the only way to truly understand how Congress functions is to grasp the role that committees play. Accordingly, scholars have developed different theories of how members of Congress perceive committees and what committees can do for members as representatives and lawmakers. We present three theories of congressional committees: the distributive, informational, and partisan theories.

## Distributive Theory

The distributive theory of legislative organization goes hand in hand with the textbook view of committee functioning. Its proponents see Congress as an institutional means to satisfy constituent interests (and thus lawmakers' reelection needs).[63] That is, committees are the structures that allow for a meaningful constituency-representative linkage. Distributive theory holds that because constituents' interests are geographically based, members must find a way to claim credit for policy achievements intended to satisfy those needs, and the committee system is designed to fulfill this role. Members with a clear constituency stake in a particular realm of federal policy receive a seat on the committee with jurisdictional control of that issue, and, under the distributive theory, they are allowed to serve on that committee indefinitely. As a result, when enacting **pork-barrel policies**—legislation that directs federal spending to projects and programs in a particular lawmaker's constituency—committee members can legitimately claim to constituents that they had a hand in writing and producing the legislation. Similarly, they can make clear that they blocked any legislative efforts that might have harmed district interests.

Senator Mary Landrieu (D-La.) illustrated this dynamic during her hotly contested 2014 reelection campaign when she said, speaking about her newly acquired position as chair of the Senate Energy and Natural Resources Committee, "Now that I am the chair, and have this clout for the people of Louisiana, I'm running for reelection to use that on behalf of creating jobs, and hope, and opportunity here. Why would we want to throw this clout away when that committee is so important, so essential to economic growth of our state?"[64]

Distributive theory predicts that committee composition should follow constituency interests. That is, membership on committees should be based on the underlying economic demographics of legislators' constituencies. Committees should thus be composed of members who come from high-demand districts. For example, the Agriculture Committee should be composed of members from rural farm areas that have strong views on agricultural issues (subsidies, crop insurance, and so on). Indeed, lawmakers gravitate to committees that control issues of heightened interest to their districts and constituents.

A distributive approach to committee composition is predicated on "gains from trade," meaning, in this case, that members of Congress benefit from the ability to negotiate with other members of Congress. Issue jurisdictions are turf to be divided and allocated to committees based on geographic (economic) need. Committee members have agenda power to control policy making within their jurisdictions, and they use that power to benefit their constituents. The committee system, then, is an institutionalized logroll in which members trade rights and influence across committee areas and members of each committee get what they need for reelection purposes. The result is a committee system that is efficiently constructed for specific payouts in narrow policy areas, but it is not a system that generates a broader collective good.

## Informational Theory

In the late 1980s, a theory based on the informational role of committees emerged as an alternative to the distributive theory. Informational scholars consider congressional policy making to be more complex than the mere distribution of geographically-based benefits. They believe that effective policy making requires a more nuanced understanding of policies and their consequences. Specifically, there may be general agreement on broad societal goals among lawmakers—a clean environment, a good economy, a healthy citizenry—but what policies best achieve those goals is far from clear or consensual. Detailed information and policy expertise among members of Congress improves lawmaking and offers some clarity on the most effective policies, but obtaining that expertise is costly. How can Congress be organized such that policy expertise—a collective good for the entire chamber—is achieved? Informational scholars answer this question by arguing that committees not be composed of lawmakers from high-demand districts, as in distributive theory, but rather should be constructed as smaller versions (microcosms) of the overall chamber. Thus committees represent the array of preferences of the entire membership, and members can be induced to (1) invest in expertise and (2) share that expertise with the rest of the chamber.

Thus, while informational scholars agree that members of Congress care deeply about reelection and thus seek to provide distributive benefits to constituents, they also believe that members organize the committee system to meet the informational needs of the overall membership. If committees can represent the chamber's overall policy preferences, rather than being ideologically extreme, they can produce a public good—information regarding the connection between policies and outcomes—that is both widely shared and necessary for the production of good policy.

## Partisan Theory

As Congress became increasingly partisan and polarized at the end of the twentieth century, scholars came to view committees as subordinate to parties. Partisan theory holds that Congress is organized primarily for the benefit of the majority party. Committees play a role in partisan theory only insofar as leaders can use committees to achieve partisan goals, with majority party members on committees using their gatekeeping power and proposal authority to promote majority party interests.

Partisan theories consider committee chairs to be agents of the majority party rather than autonomous actors (as in distributive theory) or operatives of the wider chamber (as in informational theory). Members are appointed to committee chairs as rewards for party loyalty. Partisan theories hold that committee seniority, which in distributive theory is the primary criterion for chair appointments, can be bypassed if a member has not been sufficiently loyal to party leadership.

For some committees, nearly all major legislative activities are highly partisan. For example, evidence suggests that majority party leaders have taken greater control of the House Appropriations Committee over the last two decades. That is, while majority party members on the committee have preferences similar to those of their party in general, the actions of the committee are more in keeping with the wishes of the majority party leadership in particular—and more likely to be opposed by the minority party. One of the first actions of the Gingrich Congress in 1995 was to have Republican Appropriations Committee members sign a "letter of fidelity" to Gingrich and his agenda of budget cutting.[65] In recent years, floor amendments to appropriations bills have largely come from the minority party, but they are far less likely to pass than those from the majority party.[66]

A stark example of how party leaders recently have asserted more control over committees occurred in December 2012, just prior to the start of the 113th Congress. As the Republican Steering Committee was making its list of House GOP committee assignments, Speaker Boehner and his leadership team stripped four incumbent members from their assignments on the Financial Services, Budget, and Agriculture Committees. All four lawmakers had opposed the GOP leadership's positions on important legislation, including critical budget votes, and one ousted lawmaker was told that his removal occurred because his "votes were not in lockstep with leadership."[67]

## The Theories in Practice

As these theories emerged, scholars searched for data that would allow them to test theoretical predictions. Proponents of each perspective had an underlying structural argument for why committee composition would conform to their theoretical view. Distributive theorists thought that reelection-seeking, constituency-oriented lawmakers would self-select with committee assignment requests such that over time, many committees would be composed of a dispro- portionate number of members who hailed from districts with excessive or con- centrated need in the policy area under the panel's control. So, for example, the Agriculture Committee would be composed of many members from farming districts, the Armed Services Committee would be populated with lawmakers whose districts had·large military installations, and so on.

Alternatively, informational and partisan theories are more concerned with lawmakers' overall ideological orientations than with their direct constituency interests. But the theories focus on different memberships: informational theory is concerned with the orientation of the entire committee relative to the cham- ber as whole, whereas partisan theory focuses only on the ideology of majority party members of the committee relative to the orientation of the chamber's majority caucus as a whole. Both theories, however, predict that (most) commit- tees will be representative of the larger underlying body.

To analyze the ideological orientation of committees, we examine lawmakers' NOMINATE scores (as described in Chapter 2). To test the informational hypothesis, we compare the median NOMINATE score of each committee's membership against the chamber's entire membership to see if the scores are significantly different.[68] To evaluate the partisan theory, we compare the median NOMINATE score of the majority party members on each committee to that of the entire majority party caucus in the chamber.

In Table 5.4, we show the results of these tests for all standing committees in the House between the 106th Congress (1999–2001) and the 112th Congress (2011–13). The columns show the results of the informational theory tests (entire committee versus entire chamber) and the partisan theory tests (majority party committee members versus entire majority caucus) for each Congress. A cell with the letter C indicates that the committee or majority party members are significantly more conservative than the chamber or majority party caucus and are therefore not representative. The letter L indicates instead that there is a significant liberal bias. A blank cell indicates that the committee or majority party members are representative of the relevant, larger body.

Examining the committees' ideological orientations, we see very little evidence of unrepresentative committees, with the ideological outliers occur- ring repeatedly in just a few instances. In Republican-controlled Houses, the

**TABLE 5.4** House Committee Outlier Tests Using Ideology Scores for Members of Congress

Info = Informational theory tests
Partisan = Partisan theory tests
C = Committee is significantly more conservative than the chamber
L = Committee is significantly more liberal than the chamber
Blank = Committee is representative of the larger body

| Committee | 106th Congress (1999–2001) Republican | | 107th Congress (2001–03) Republican | | 108th Congress (2003–05) Republican | |
|---|---|---|---|---|---|---|
| **Majority** | Info | Partisan | Info | Partisan | Info | Partisan |
| Agriculture | | | | | | |
| Appropriations | | | | L | | L |
| Armed Services | | | | | | |
| Financial Services | | | | | | |
| Budget | | C | | | | |
| Education and Workforce | | | | C | | |
| Energy and Commerce | | | | | | |
| Foreign Affairs | | | | | | |
| Government Operations | | C | | | | |
| Homeland Security* | N/A | N/A | | | | |
| House Administration | | | | | | |
| Judiciary | C | | C | C | C | C |
| Natural Resources | | | C | | | |
| Transportation | | L | | | | |
| Rules | C | | C | | C | |
| Space, Science, and Technology | | C | | | | |
| Small Business | | | | | C | |
| Ethics | | | | | | |
| Veterans' Affairs | | | | | | |
| Ways and Means | C | | | | | |
| Select Intelligence | | L | | | | |

Data compiled by authors with Adam Cayton.
* The Department of Homeland Security didn't exist in the 106th Congress.

| 109th Congress (2005–07) | | 110th Congress (2007–09) | | 111th Congress (2009–11) | | 112th Congress (2011–13) | |
|---|---|---|---|---|---|---|---|
| Republican | | Democrat | | Democrat | | Republican | |
| **Info** | **Partisan** | **Info** | **Partisan** | **Info** | **Partisan** | **Info** | **Partisan** |
|  |  |  | C |  | C |  |  |
|  | L |  |  |  |  |  | L |
|  |  |  | C |  | C |  |  |
|  |  |  |  |  |  |  |  |
|  |  |  |  |  |  |  | C |
|  |  |  |  | C |  |  |  |
|  |  |  |  |  |  |  |  |
|  |  |  |  |  |  |  |  |
|  |  |  |  |  |  |  |  |
|  |  |  |  |  |  |  |  |
|  |  |  |  |  |  |  |  |
| C | C | L | L | L | L | C | C |
|  |  |  |  |  |  |  |  |
| C |  | L |  | L | L | C |  |
|  |  |  | C |  |  |  |  |
|  |  |  |  |  | C |  |  |
|  |  |  |  |  |  |  |  |
|  |  |  | C |  | C |  |  |
|  |  |  |  |  |  |  |  |
|  |  |  |  |  |  |  |  |

Judiciary Committee always appears to be a conservative outlier. In Democratic-controlled Houses, it is a liberal outlier. We see similar results for the informational tests when examining the Rules Committee. In Republican Houses, the Rules Committee is more conservative than the chamber; in Democratic Houses, it is more liberal than the chamber.

Beyond these two examples, there are only a few instances where the committee is more extreme in the informational tests. Ways and Means, Natural Resources, Small Business, and Education and Workforce are all more conservative than the chamber in just one congressional term. There are, however, several instances where the analysis of the partisan makeup of committees offers other interesting findings. For instance, during nearly all Republican-controlled Congresses, the Republican contingent on Appropriations is significantly more liberal than the Republican Caucus. Similarly, during Democratic-controlled Houses, the majority party contingents on the Agriculture, Armed Services, and Veterans' Affairs Committees are considerably more conservative than the Democratic Caucus as a whole. All told, the tests indicate that between 1999 and 2012, there is some evidence of outlier committees, but for the most part, there have been only a few.

Finally, in testing the distributive orientation of committees, we employ various measures of constituency characteristics that are relevant to each committee's jurisdiction. We are trying to discern if committees are composed of lawmakers whose district needs are systematically higher than that of the overall chamber—and, therefore, if the committee preferences are not likely to represent the chamber preferences. Because many committee jurisdictions are broad, and it is hard to pinpoint a single indicator of constituency need for each committee's policy jurisdiction, we conduct these tests on only six committees, with the relevant constituency measure listed below the committee name (Table 5.5).

Four committees stand out as being consistently composed of lawmakers from high-demand districts. Agriculture is always dominated by members from farming districts (measured by the percent of the population employed in agriculture); the Armed Services Committee is dominated by members from districts with a heavy concentration of people employed in the military; Financial Services is almost always composed largely of lawmakers from districts with high employment in the financial and banking sectors; Veterans' Affairs is mostly made up of members with large numbers of veterans in their districts. The Transportation Committee showed only occasional instances in the later years where its membership was dominated by high-demand outliers as measured by employment in transportation and construction.

Looking at all the evidence presented in these tests, it is not possible to say that one theory best explains all the committees.[69] Clearly, some, but not all, committees seem to attract a disproportionate number of lawmakers whose dis-

**TABLE 5.5** House Committee Outlier Tests: Constituency Characteristics

| | 106th (1999– 2001) | 107th (2001– 03) | 108th (2003– 05) | 109th (2005– 07) | 110th (2007– 09) | 111th (2009– 11) | 112th (2011– 13) |
|---|---|---|---|---|---|---|---|
| Agriculture | High percentage of constituents employed in agriculture | | | | | | |
| | ✓ | ✓ | ✓ | ✓ | ✓ | ✓ | ✓ |
| Armed Services | Large military workforce in district | | | | | | |
| | ✓ | ✓ | ✓ | ✓ | ✓ | ✓ | ✓ |
| Financial Services | High percentage employed in banking, finance, or real estate in district | | | | | | |
| | | ✓ | ✓ | ✓ | ✓ | ✓ | ✓ |
| Government Operations | High percentage of civilians employed by federal government in district | | | | | | |
| | | | | | | | |
| Transportation | High percentage of constituents employed in transportation and construction in district | | | | | | |
| | | | | | ✓ | ✓ | ✓ |
| Veterans' Affairs | High percentage of military veterans in district | | | | | | |
| | ✓ | ✓ | ✓ | ✓ | ✓ | ✓ | |

Data compiled by authors with the help of Adam Cayton.

tricts are heavily invested in a committee's jurisdiction. Parties encourage this because it helps bolster the reelection prospects of many of their members. Alternatively, there are some committees whose collective policy preferences, or those of the majority party contingents, frequently, but not always, align closely with those of the parent body. Again, it is not entirely surprising that the majority party caucus feels the need to load certain committees handling ideologically sensitive policies with members who come from the extreme ends of their party. Though they might not explain all committee behavior in Congress, the theories help us understand what is happening in various instances or at various times. They also offer a framework by which to measure lawmaker behavior and organization.

### Critical Thinking

1. Which theory do you find most persuasive? Why?
2. If you asked a member of Congress which of these theories best describes their work on committees, what do you think she would say? Why?

3. Can the theories presented here be complementary and together help build our understanding of committee organization? If so, how?

## CONCLUSION

During the middle of the twentieth century, committees dominated policy making in Congress. The textbook view of the legislative process then held that governing power resided in committees, and parties did little more than assist committee chairs in coordinating policy outcomes. Today's view is much different. Parties reemerged in the 1980s and 1990s as a driving force of congressional activity, usurping much of committees' independent power. A new view of the legislative process would place committees in a supporting role, no longer the lead actors in the congressional drama.

Yet to conclude that modern congressional committees are a shell of what they once were would paint an incomplete and perhaps misleading picture. In terms of governing, while parties do set the legislative agenda in today's Congress, committees are not cut out of the process entirely.

The intense partisan conflict that is so frequently the centerpiece of contemporary congressional activity has in some ways enhanced the role of committees in legislative operations. Modern government is frequently divided, and partisan conflict has often amounted to conflict between branches. Because of their responsibility for executive branch oversight, committees are central in the political tussle of today's separation-of-powers system.

Similarly, intense partisan gridlock has stymied historic legislation.[70] As a result, congressional lawmaking has defaulted to maintaining the governing status quo and renewing expiring programs and laws. Thus legislative committees and their leaders have for the most part been able to keep the machinery of government functioning by reauthorizing existing programs and agencies.

Moreover, some genuine bipartisanship remains on a variety of committees. Partisan consensus still permeates governing on constituency service committees, and partisan conflict is only slightly higher on policy committees.[71] In 2015, after years of struggle to renew the expired No Child Left Behind Act (legislation governing a wide variety of Department of Education programs), the Republican chair of the Senate Committee on Health, Education, Labor, and Pensions, Senator Lamar Alexander (Tenn.), and his Democratic counterpart on the committee, ranking minority member Senator Patty Murray (Wash.), shepherded through Congress a compromise reauthorization that gave states and school districts more autonomy in using controversial math and reading assessments. The bipartisan agreement passed both chambers with overwhelming majorities of both parties. Stated simply, considerable policy work is still done in committee, and even in a strongly partisan era, that work often reveals bipartisan compromise.

## Discussion Questions

1. Why are committee jurisdictional boundaries so important?
2. Why do committee members often see committee seat assignments as critical to their influence in Congress and their reelection strategies?
3. What does it mean for a lawmaker to have property rights to a committee seat? Do you think strong property rights should exist or do you think members should cycle in and out of committees more often?
4. How do committee seat assignments, and transfers between committees, indicate the value of specific committees?
5. In what ways has committee involvement in congressional lawmaking changed in the last few decades? What role has hyperpartisanship and the increased power of party leaders played in these changes?

# 6

## Parties

As 2017 was coming to an end, President Donald Trump and Republican majorities in Congress needed a policy victory. The first year of the Trump administration had not met important policy goals, despite Republicans' unified control of government. The major policy initiative to that point—the repeal of the Affordable Care Act—had failed, and GOP leaders believed a significant policy success was important for the party as the end of the year neared. They settled on tax reform, a shared policy goal of the White House and congressional Republicans.

The bill was first introduced in the House in early November 2017. By early December, both chambers had passed separate bills. After some differences in the House and Senate bills were ironed out, the Tax Cuts and Jobs Act of 2017 was passed and signed by President Trump in late December 2017. The legislation reduced tax rates for individuals and businesses, reduced the alternative minimum tax for individuals and eliminated it for corporations, and repealed the Affordable Care Act's individual mandate. While 12 Republicans in the House opposed the final bill, largely because it limited deductions for state and local taxes and mortgage interest, nearly all GOP lawmakers hung together to pass the legislation.[1] Perhaps more telling, not a single Democrat in the House or

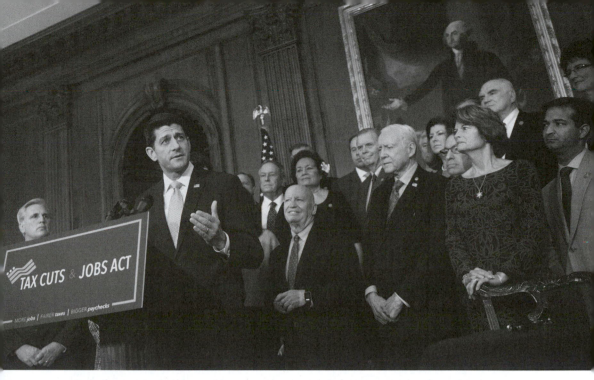

Paul Ryan (R-Wis.), then Speaker of the House, and other Republican members of Congress celebrate the passage of the Tax Cuts and Jobs Act. Despite months of debate, discussion, and political posturing, the Tax Cuts and Jobs Act passed without a single Democratic vote, reflecting the continuing partisan divide in today's Congress.

Senate supported the bill. The Tax Cuts and Jobs Act of 2017 was a wholly Republican policy initiative.[2]

The story of the GOP's tax reform is consistent with how policy has been made in Washington in recent years. Major policy change is often the product of partisan effort and initiative rather than bipartisan coordination. This is especially true when one party enjoys unified control of government. When the Democrats controlled the House, Senate, and presidency in 2010, the Affordable Care Act, the signature legislative achievement of the Obama administration, followed the same pattern as the Tax Cuts and Jobs Act, passing into law without a single minority party (Republican) member in the House or Senate voting for the measure.

Moreover, there is considerable evidence that congressional actions today embody larger partisan conflicts. Partisan polarization, or the ideological distance between the parties, distinguishes the contemporary Congress. Presidents rail against congressional gridlock and partisan conflict, members of Congress run for reelection touting their political skills in navigating the partisanship on Capitol Hill, and political commentators and newspaper editorialists blame party leaders and their unwavering agendas for everything that ails Washington.

We live in a time in which partisan polarization in Congress is greater than at any time in modern history—and perhaps ever. In 2014 the *National Journal* reported that the ideological overlap between Democrats and Republicans in the Senate was nonexistent. That is, no Senate Democrat was more conservative than any Senate Republican, and no Senate Republican was more liberal than any Senate Democrat. In the House, the story was much the same.[3] In 2016, political scientist Keith Poole arrived at the same general conclusion, describing the 114th Congress (2015–17) as "the most polarized Congress since the early 20th century."[4] Finally, we find that in both the House and Senate, the percentage of **party-unity votes**—votes in which a majority of one party opposes a majority of the other party—in the 114th Congress was the highest of any Congress since World War II (and that percentage has dropped off only slightly since then).[5]

This picture of Congress riven by partisan disagreement and gridlock, however, is incomplete. Over the last few years, bipartisan majorities have produced major legislative accomplishments. Early in 2013, Congress ended the tax cuts on the wealthiest Americans enacted by President George W. Bush, provided a massive aid package for communities in the Northeast damaged by Hurricane Sandy, and renewed the Violence Against Women Act. All were passed with at least some support from both parties. In 2015 and 2016, Congress made sweeping changes to the formula for Medicare payments to physicians that had been lingering for years (the so-called doc fix), replaced President Bush's No Child Left Behind education reform bill with a law that returned teacher-evaluation power to the states, and overhauled regulations on toxic chemicals. All these laws were adopted with the overwhelming support of both parties in the House and Senate. And, more recently, large majorities of Democrats and Republicans joined forces in 2020 to pass a series of stimulus packages to relieve economic hardship for Americans in the wake of the COVID-19 (coronavirus) pandemic.[6]

All in all, parties' influence in Congress is more complicated than we might assume. There are certainly plenty of activities on Capitol Hill that are fraught with partisan rancor and finger-pointing. And considerable evidence suggests that the congressional parties are more deeply divided than at any time since the Civil War. That said, circumstances and leadership efforts can bring lawmakers on either side of the partisan aisle together to pass important legislation. This is true not only on high-profile matters but also on issues that typically divide Democrats and Republicans.

Partisanship structures how individual members of Congress behave, how collective decisions are made (or not) within a chamber, and how the branches of government are organized and relate to one another. Parties focus the legislative agenda, establish a hierarchy of leadership, and provide tools to construct majority coalitions to get things done. Yet facilitating governing can come at a cost. For party members, conforming to a strict party agenda and toeing the line on roll call votes can mean compromising on constituent preferences. This important tension between governing and representation has defined much of Congress as it has evolved over time.

We begin this chapter by describing how parties arrange Congress's structures and organizational activities both for the entire membership (for example, by writing and adopting the rules and organizing committees) and for their own members (for example, by electing their leadership and providing electoral assistance to party candidates). We also note several informal party duties, such as coming up with a unified agenda, negotiating with an opposing party president, and overcoming collective-action problems. We then examine the different theories of why parties would structure institutional arrangements in Congress, exploring when, and to what degree, the majority party controls the legislative agenda. Next, we explore the polarization of the two parties, describing what polarization means, its historical development, and its causes. Finally, we discuss the changes in parties over the last few years—particularly fractionalization in the Republican Party—and how these changes have altered governing and representation in Congress.

# PARTIES AND THE ORGANIZATION OF CONGRESS

Although political parties are not mentioned in the U.S. Constitution, their history as an organizing force in Congress, as discussed in Chapter 2, dates back nearly to the Founding.[7] Since then, the role that parties play in the organization of Congress has been codified both in the rules of each chamber and in the rules that the party caucus approves at the start of each congressional term.[8]

## Electing Chamber Leaders

Selecting chamber leadership is the parties' most important formal duty. Chamber leaders are essentially party positions, meaning that, with the exception of the Speaker of the House and the president of the Senate, none of these positions is mentioned in the Constitution. Nevertheless, occupants of formal party positions, such as majority leader and minority leader, have a set of official duties as defined by the chamber rules. These chamber and party officers are critically important for organizing House and Senate business, as they decide who is permitted to speak on the floor, how the legislative agenda is structured, and how information is disseminated and controlled.

**ELECTING THE SPEAKER**   The election of the Speaker of the House occurs on the first day of each two-year congressional term. It is the first order of business once the House clerk calls the roll of members-elect. Prior to the formal opening of the legislative term, the majority caucus convenes, usually between the November elections and the end of the calendar year, to select its speakership nominee. After a quorum is established, the Speaker is elected in the first recorded roll call taken by the whole chamber, which typically breaks down perfectly along party lines—with minority party members voting for the individual who will become minority leader.[9]

The Speaker is the only House leadership position that is elected by the entire chamber, and the vote is open (not by secret ballot) so that all lawmakers— in particular the Speaker himself or herself—know if there are defections.[10] Consequently, multiple ballots (required when no candidate wins a majority) for Speaker are rare. In fact, the last time a speakership race extended beyond a single ballot was in 1923, when eight ballots were necessary to produce a majority winner. Since 1923, majority party defections on speakership votes have been quite uncommon—that is, until the last few years. In 2013, nine Republicans voted for someone other than the party nominee, John Boehner (Ohio); in 2015, that number increased to 25, the greatest number of party defections in a speakership election in nearly a century. While Boehner was elected Speaker each time, his constant and contentious battles with his party's most conservative wing eventually led him to resign in late 2015.[11] His replacement, Paul Ryan (Wis.), was more popular with conservative Republicans, but he still faced 10 party defections in 2017.[12] And in 2019, when the Democrats were back in the majority, Nancy Pelosi (Calif.) was elected with 15 party defections, many of whom were first-term members.[13] More generally, these intraparty battles perhaps foreshadow significant and lasting changes in the way Speakers are elected in the contemporary Congress and in the operations of the body more generally.

**ELECTING OTHER PARTY LEADERS**   The remaining party leadership structure in the House and Senate is determined in party caucus elections that traditionally occur in the weeks following the November general election. Table 6.1 provides an overview of the Republican and Democratic leadership in the 117th Congress.

In the House, the majority leader and majority whip—which have existed as formal leadership positions since the late nineteenth century—operate just below the Speaker in the party hierarchy. The members who hold these three positions, generally speaking, are the faces and voices of the majority party in the House. Below them are secondary leadership positions in the broader majority party organization.

**TABLE 6.1**   Party Leadership, 117th Congress (2021–23)

HOUSE

| Democratic Majority | |
|---|---|
| Speaker of the House | Nancy Pelosi (Calif.) |
| Majority Leader | Steny Hoyer (Md.) |
| Majority Whip | James Clyburn (S.C.) |
| Assistant Speaker | Katherine Clark (Mass.) |
| Caucus Chair | Hakeem Jeffries (N.Y.) |
| Caucus Vice Chair | Pete Aguilar (Calif.) |
| Campaign Committee Chair | Sean Maloney (N.Y.) |

| Republican Minority | |
|---|---|
| Minority Leader | Kevin McCarthy (Calif.) |
| Minority Whip | Steve Scalise (La.) |
| Conference Chair | Liz Cheney (Wyo.) |
| Campaign Committee Chair | Tom Emmer (Minn.) |
| Policy Committee Chair | Gary Palmer (Ala.) |
| Conference Vice Chair | Mike Johnson (La.) |
| Conference Secretary | Richard Hudson (N.C.) |

SENATE

| Democratic Majority | |
|---|---|
| Majority Leader and Caucus Chair | Chuck Schumer (N.Y.) |
| Majority Whip | Dick Durbin (Ill.) |
| Assistant Majority Leader | Patty Murray (Wash.) |
| Policy and Communications Committee Chair | Debbie Stabenow (Mich.) |
| Caucus Vice Chairs | Mark Warner (Va.), Elizabeth Warren (Mass.) |
| Steering Committee Chair | Amy Klobuchar (Minn.) |
| Outreach Chair | Bernie Sanders (Vt.) |
| Policy and Communications Committees | Joe Manchin (W.Va.), Cory Booker (N.J.) |
| Vice Chairs | Tammy Baldwin (Wisc.) |
| Caucus Secretary | Catherine Cortez-Masto (Nev.) |
| Campaign Committee Chair | |

| Republican Minority | |
|---|---|
| Minority Leader | Mitch McConnell (Ky.) |
| Minority Whip | John Thune (S.D.) |
| Conference Chair | John Barrasso (Wyo.) |
| Policy Committee Chair | Roy Blunt (Mo.) |
| Conference Vice Chair | Joni Ernst (Iowa) |
| Campaign Committee Chair | Rick Scott (Fla.) |

In the Senate, there is no exact equivalent of the Speaker. The president of the Senate, per the Constitution, is the vice president of the United States. While the president of the Senate technically presides over the chamber's proceedings, the rules of the Senate give the holder of this position little authority—with the most important power being the ability to cast a tie-breaking vote when the chamber is deadlocked. However, in the 117th Congress, with the Democrats and Republicans both controlling 50 Senate seats, Vice President Kamala Harris played a key role in giving majority control of the chamber to the Democrats, along with being the tie-breaking vote on bills that divided perfectly by party. In the vice president's absence, the Senate chooses a president pro tempore to preside who, like the president of the Senate, has little authority.

The majority leader is actually the most powerful Senate leader. As the name suggests, the majority leader of the Senate is a partisan position. While powerful, partisan Senate leaders have operated since the antebellum era, formal majority (and minority) leadership positions emerged only in the early twentieth century.[14] Below the majority leader in the party hierarchy are the majority whip (or assistant majority leader) and a set of other leadership positions.

Occasionally, these leadership positions are actively contested. For example, in 1984, five senators initially sought to become majority leader. After four ballots, Bob Dole (R-Kan.) was elected majority leader by just three votes over Ted Stevens (R-Alas.).[15] Dole's election would shuffle lower-level positions in the Senate and reestablish moderate leadership within the governing Republican Party. And in February 2006, after Tom DeLay (R-Tex.) stepped down as House majority leader after his indictment on charges of conspiracy to violate election law, John Boehner (R-Ohio) scored an upset victory over Roy Blunt (R-Mo.) on the second ballot (after Boehner, Blunt, and two others split the vote on the first ballot). Boehner had trailed Blunt, the acting majority leader (after DeLay's departure) and former majority whip, by 31 votes on the first ballot, and was able to successfully coordinate all the non-Blunt votes on the second ballot, after the other two contestants dropped out.[16] Boehner would go on to become the leader of the House Republican Party in 2011 with his election as Speaker.

Leaders elected via intraparty vote generally reflect the central tendency in the party. A study by political scientists Stephen Jessee and Neil Malhotra explored the ideological position of chamber leaders (speakers, majority and minority leaders, whips, and lower elected party officials). They found that Democratic leaders tend to be slightly more liberal than the median of the Democratic Caucus in their chamber, and Republican leaders are slightly more conservative than the median of the GOP Conference in the chamber.[17]

The choice of recent House leaders largely supports these findings. Nancy Pelosi has been the Democratic leader since she was elected minority leader in

Following the 2020 elections, the Democratic majority nominated Nancy Pelosi (D-Calif., left) again to be Speaker of the House. Republicans renominated Kevin McCarthy (R-Calif., right) to be House Minority Leader.

2003; she became Speaker in 2007, transitioned back to minority leader after the Democrats lost majority control in the 2010 elections, and was elected Speaker again in 2019, after the Democrats returned to power. For much of that time, she has been slightly more liberal than the median of the Democratic Caucus. A similar story has been true on the Republican side of the aisle: John Boehner, who served as minority leader from 2007 to 2011 and Speaker from 2011 to 2015, largely reflected the median of the Republican Conference. Boehner was replaced as Speaker by Paul Ryan in 2015. Ryan was somewhat more conservative than Boehner, though not as far right as the most conservative House Republicans.

In recent decades, campaign contributions have increasingly been used to garner support in leadership elections.[18] Lawmakers pursuing a leadership position often direct contributions from specially created political action committees (PACs) to potential supporters, with the hope of obtaining their support in a future intraparty campaign. For example, in the 2010 election cycle, Eric Cantor (R-Va.), the minority whip in the House, was positioning himself to become majority leader should the Republicans win a majority of seats in that year's elections—which they did. The $1.7 million in contributions that Cantor distributed from his "Every Republican Is Crucial" (ERIC) PAC to GOP candidates helped him secure the majority leader position after the election.[19] More recently, Nancy Pelosi, through her "Nancy Pelosi Victory Fund," raised and distributed $3.3 million to Democratic candidates in the 2018 election cycle. Those contributions helped her maintain majority support in the Democratic Caucus—despite opposition from younger, more progressive members—and be elected Speaker in 2019.[20]

## Writing and Adopting the Chamber Rules

Prior to the start of each congressional term, the majority party in each chamber reviews the existing rules in the House and Senate. It then considers revisions, which span from the trivial (such as increasing the number of Congressional Gold Medals that can be awarded each year) to the consequential (such as changes to committee jurisdictions). The majority party's authority to propose and (at least in the House) adopt changes to the rules derives mainly from its ability to control the agenda and keep its members aligned on key procedural votes at the opening of the term.[21]

As we saw in Chapter 5, one recent change in House rules is the adoption of term limits for committee chairs. Originally adopted by the new Republican majority in the 104th Congress (1995–97), the change restricted committee and subcommittee chairs to three consecutive terms before they had to step aside. Two years after Democrats regained control of the House, at the start of the 111th Congress (2009–11), they eliminated this rule. Since then, Republicans have maintained term limits for committee chairs while in the majority, and Democrats have rejected them. And this party difference has consequences. Political scientist Molly Reynolds finds that Republican chairs, once their terms are up, have retired from the House at a significantly higher rate than other members—because they typically become less-effective legislators without the authority that comes from holding a chair.[22]

Rules changes in the Senate are slightly more complicated, as the chamber operates as a continuous body from one term to the next. (Recall that only one-third of Senate seats are up for election every two years, which means that a majority of senators remain in office during any election cycle.) Thus chamber rules in the Senate do not have to be readopted at the start of each Congress, as they do in the House. And because senators can filibuster—or refuse to end debate—changing the rules has generally required a supermajority of support.[23] As a result, the Senate is less susceptible to external forces, such as majority party influence, that in the House might lead to rules changes.

Nonetheless, change does occur occasionally in the Senate. For example, November 2013 witnessed a major revision to the cloture rule. Frustrated by persistent Republican efforts to block votes on President Obama's judicial

In order to avoid a Democratic filibuster of Neil Gorsuch (right), Senate Majority Leader Mitch McConnell (R-Ky., left) and the Senate Republicans reinterpreted the rule to invoke cloture on Supreme Court nominees. Instead of 60 votes, only a simple majority would be necessary to confirm nominees, allowing Gorsuch to join the Supreme Court.

nominees, Democrats, led by Majority Leader Harry Reid (D-Nev.), reinterpreted the chamber's cloture rule as applied to executive branch and judicial appointments below the Supreme Court level. Dubbed the nuclear option, this declaration by Democrats—on a 52-to-48 vote—required only a simple majority, rather than a supermajority of 60 senators, to end debate and bring a nomination to a vote.[24] Upon retaking majority control of the Senate following the 2014 elections, the Republicans did not reverse this change,[25] and evidence suggests that it improved the number of President Obama's judicial nominees that were confirmed by the Senate.[26] However, after Republican Donald Trump was elected president in 2016, Majority Leader Mitch McConnell (R-Ky.), who had spent most of that year refusing to consider Obama's nomination of Merrick Garland to Antonin Scalia's Supreme Court seat (Scalia died in February 2016), decided to up the ante. In April 2017, Senate Republicans, on a 52-to-48 vote, extended the nuclear option to Supreme Court nominees.[27] As a result, the Senate was able to advance President Trump's nomination of Neil Gorsuch to the Supreme Court by a simple majority vote.[28]

Ultimately, parties change the rules in order to win more often. Sometimes, as in the GOP's adoption of committee term limits, this means fulfilling a promise to Republican voters in an effort to win elections. More often, however, rules changes are intended to increase the majority party's ability to win on its agenda—whether by the Senate confirming more federal judges or Congress as a whole passing more policy. And even when a rules change is made ostensibly to adapt to changing circumstances—like in May 2020, when the House passed a rules change to allow remote voting and remote committee meetings during the COVID-19 pandemic—partisan divisions occur, as all but three Democrats supported the change and all Republicans opposed it. Republicans argued that Democrats could use remote voting for partisan advantage, calling it "the most significant power grab in the history of the Congress."[29]

## Organizing Committees

As discussed in Chapter 5, parties have a great deal of responsibility in organizing committees, from the majority party determining the overall size of each committee and the proportion of seats allocated to the minority party, to deciding which of their own members will serve on which committees. Party leaders view certain committees as more critical for pursuing party priorities and therefore maintain tighter control over their memberships.

Party leaders typically reward loyal members with committee assignments and chairs, particularly on committees that are critical to the fulfillment of the party agenda. For example, in 2013, when several Appropriations subcommittee chairs opened up in the middle of the term because of unforeseen circumstances (a death and two resignations from the House), Republican leaders awarded these coveted positions to moderates with long histories of demonstrated loyalty to the leadership. Earlier in 2013, in a controversial vote to raise the debt limit and avoid a government default, each of these lawmakers had bucked the GOP majority and voted with the leadership and, out of necessity, House Democrats to pass the legislation.[30]

Party leaders have also punished rogue lawmakers through their control over committee seats. The influential Rules Committee in the House is responsible for carrying out the Speaker's agenda on important items as they pertain to floor activities. Consequently, the committee's membership is tightly restricted to those party members most trusted by the Speaker. When Rules Committee members have been disloyal, they have lost their seats. In January 2015, when Speaker Boehner faced 25 Republican defection votes in his speakership election that year (not enough to derail his reelection, but enough to reveal serious cracks in Republican Party discipline), two of the dissenting GOP votes came from Rules Committee members: Daniel Webster and Rich Nugent, both of Florida. They were soon thereafter relieved of their seats on the Rules Committee and replaced by more reliable supporters.[31] Webster and Nugent also lost campaign support from the GOP establishment and were unable to move legislation forward.[32]

Punishment for disloyal behavior is not only a Republican strategy. After her election as Speaker in 2019, Nancy Pelosi punished her chief Democratic critic, Kathleen Rice (N.Y.), who actively sought to build and coordinate opposition to Pelosi on the speakership vote. When Rice sought a spot on the influential Judiciary Committee shortly after the speakership vote, Pelosi denied the request. As Representative John Garamendi (D-Calif.) said afterward, "We are a team. . . . If you don't want to be on the team, you can sit on the bench."[33]

# PARTIES AND CONGRESSIONAL OPERATIONS

Once the House and Senate are organized after a new Congress convenes, parties continue to play a major role by structuring how each chamber operates. Much of this work concerns how chamber business is conducted, which includes bill scheduling and coordinating (or whipping) party members' votes. But it also involves supporting party members in advance of their next election cycle.

## Bill Scheduling

Party leaders control **bill scheduling**, or floor consideration of legislation that has successfully navigated its way through the committee process. In the House, the Speaker, working with the party's leadership team, chooses the date that a bill will undergo debate (more on the stages of floor debate in Chapter 7). And the Rules Committee determines how the bill will be considered, in terms of both the time allocated for debate and the types and number of amendments allowed. In the Senate, the process is a little more complicated, but power still largely resides with the majority party, specifically with the majority leader, who is recognized on the Senate floor before all other lawmakers. The majority leader also takes the lead in constructing unanimous consent agreements, which are negotiated with the minority leader and act much like special rules in the House by structuring the terms of debate (more in Chapter 7).

## Whipping Votes

**Whipping** refers to the act of keeping members informed as well as persuading them to vote in a certain way. Whips emerged in Congress in the late nineteenth century. As the chambers increased in size, consistent and timely information flow between leaders and the rank and file became more important. The structure and duties of the parties' whip systems in each chamber have evolved over time. The chief whip of each party now has a complicated network of assistant whips: chief deputy whips, deputy whips, at-large whips, and regional whips.[34]

Today, whips are normally responsible for ensuring that sufficient numbers of party members are present when important business occurs, conducting informal polls or counts of votes prior to the consideration of major legislation on the floor, providing information on the details and timing of pending activities, tabulating summary information on current votes for busy lawmakers, and convincing members to stay loyal to party positions when such positions are declared.

In the mid-2000s, whip operations in the House, which were spearheaded by Tom DeLay (R-Tex.) and later Roy Blunt (R-Mo.), were at perhaps their most efficient. DeLay, known as the Hammer, was especially forceful at getting Republican members to support issues important to the party leadership, and Blunt followed in DeLay's footsteps. This effectiveness was on display in the summer of 2005 during the final-passage vote on the Central American Free Trade Agreement (CAFTA), a GOP priority that year. With many Republican House members concerned that CAFTA could cost jobs in their districts, Blunt (majority whip at the time) and DeLay (majority leader) built a majority coalition. Over the course of nearly six months, they oversaw a wide-ranging whip operation that secured nearly 70 Republican votes. The whip network included corporate and trade association lobbyists, as well as former Bush administration officials, and it brokered side deals with individual lawmakers to secure votes. On the day of the final roll call, with the Republican majority seemingly short of votes, Blunt and DeLay pulled out all the stops. President Bush, Vice President Dick Cheney, and other high-ranking administration officials met with the GOP conference, and Republican leaders even postponed the final vote on a major transportation measure until after the CAFTA vote—a signal to members that their individual highway projects could be threatened if CAFTA failed. Thanks to this extensive whipping, the measure passed just after midnight by a bare majority, 217–215.[35]

## Electoral Support

Each chamber's party caucus has its own campaign operation, or **Hill committee**, responsible for electing and reelecting party members. In the House, they are the Democratic Congressional Campaign Committee (DCCC) and the National Republican Congressional Committee (NRCC). Their Senate counterparts are the Democratic Senatorial Campaign Committee (DSCC) and the National Republican Senatorial Committee (NRSC). These Hill committees recruit candidates, court donors, and distribute funds and resources.

Resources are sometimes provided directly to campaign organizations, but more often than not, support takes the form of uncoordinated activities on behalf of a candidate's campaign, which allows candidates to avoid violating campaign finance laws.

Hill committees often raise and spend considerable funds on television advertising in highly competitive races. For instance, in 2020 both the NRCC an DCCC ran dueling television ads in Florida 26th Congressional District, accusing the other party's candidate—Democratic incumbent Debbie Mucarsel-Powell and Republican challenger Carlos Giménez, respectively—of corruption. A DCCC ad claimed: "Clouds of suspicion growing darker, moving over Debbie Mucarsel-Powell." A NRCC ad charged: "For 'Corrupt Carlos' Giménez, taking care of family means shady deals and government contracts." In the end, Giménez won a close race (51.7 percent to 48.3 percent) and flipped the seat for the Republicans.[36]

Conversely, as the election season progresses and the likely outcome of a given race crystallizes, the campaign committees withdraw their resources from hopeless campaigns. For example, in mid-October 2018 the DCCC canceled extensive television ad buys in the Sarasota area, which was intended for Florida's 16th Congressional District to defeat Republican incumbent Vern Buchanan.[37] But independent polling suggested that Buchanan's support was too strong, so the DCCC pulled out. Buchanan ended up winning by more than nine percentage points. Similarly, in mid-September 2020, the NRCC canceled $2 million in advertising—intended to cover the last two weeks of the election—that it had reserved for the Houston television market.[38] This money was intended for the 7th Congressional District, to help unseat Democratic incumbent Lizzie Pannill Fletcher. Republican operatives had decided that Fletcher was likely to retain her seat and moved the $2 million to other areas of Texas. Fletcher was indeed reelected by three percentage points.

During the 2006 election cycle, Representative Rahm Emanuel (D-Ill.) headed up the DCCC, and he made recruiting top-notch candidates a priority. Emanuel's efforts helped the Democrats retake majority control of the House with a 31-seat pickup for his party. Among his many recruits were two high-profile candidates: (1) Tammy Duckworth, a disabled Iraq War veteran, and (2) Heath Shuler, a former NFL quarterback.[39] Duckworth narrowly lost an open-seat election in an Illinois district long held by Republicans; however, after serving in various appointed government positions, she went on to win election to the House in 2012. Four years later, she ran for and won election to the Senate. Shuler handily defeated an eight-term incumbent Republican in a reliably conservative North Carolina district; he eventually retired in 2012 after Republicans in the state legislature redrew the district to remove many Democratic voters.

Funding for these Hill committees comes in part from dues from current party members. That is, lawmakers are responsible for raising money on behalf of the campaign committees, which then use these funds to support the election (and reelection) efforts of other party members. The amount of these dues varies by the seniority, status, and electoral security of the lawmaker, but it is routinely in the hundreds of thousands of dollars.[40] Raising large amounts of money for the campaign committees is one way that members show their loyalty to the party and position themselves for advancement within the party hierarchy. At the same time, some members have bucked the party and refused to pay their dues. The most high-profile example is Representative Alexandria Ocasio-Cortez (N.Y.), who owed $250,000 in dues to the DCCC in 2020. Instead of paying, Ocasio-Cortez created her own political action committee to counter the Democratic establishment in key races—by backing an all-female slate of progressive candidates.[41]

# PARTIES AND THE CONGRESSIONAL AGENDA

Aside from their role in structuring congressional organization and operations, parties also help articulate and expedite Congress's governing agenda. These efforts encompass a wide range of less-formal activities that seek to translate policy ideas into legislative outcomes.

## Presenting the Party Agenda

When the president's party controls the majority in Congress, the president usually sets the legislative agenda (with some input from majority party leaders; see Chapter 9). The minority party leadership often presents a legislative vision—sometimes quite bold—to counter the party in power, attract voters in a coming election, and unify partisan lawmakers around particular policy objectives.[42] When the president and Congress are from opposing parties, majority party leaders sometimes espouse a broad legislative vision, often national in scope, in contrast to the president's agenda.

Perhaps the best-known statement of legislative vision is the Republican Contract with America, which was formulated in 1994 (during the first midterm election of the Clinton presidency) by then-minority whip Newt Gingrich (R-Ga.) and then-conference chair Dick Armey (R-Tex.). Rolled out in late September, the Contract was signed by 350 GOP House members and candidates who pledged to support its provisions during the first 100 days of the coming congressional term—should they become the majority party. Provisions of the Contract included welfare and Social Security reform, tax cuts, crime prevention, and a constitutional amendment mandating a balanced federal budget. In truth, many voters were unaware of the Contract at the time of the election,[43] but it nonetheless became the primary agenda for lawmaking in the following term after the GOP's historic (and stunning) electoral victory. Ultimately, the Republican House leadership struggled to enact many of the Contract's provisions, with President Bill Clinton, the Republican-controlled Senate, and even some members of the GOP House majority acting as road-blocks. At the end of the 100 days, only relatively minor Contract provisions—applying federal labor laws to Congress and curbing unfunded federal mandates—had been signed into law.[44]

In the 2006 election, House and Senate Democrats sought to match the Republicans' 1994 success by crafting a New Direction for America.[45] The Democrats planned to enact a number of agenda items in the first 100 hours of congressional deliberations, including a minimum wage hike, student loan reform, and strengthened national security. Democrats gained control of both chambers in the 2006 election, but they struggled to legislate on the New Direction for America. Lawmakers did succeed in raising the minimum wage and implementing many of the recommendations of the 9/11 Commission, but President Bush vetoed changes to stem-cell policy, and other items (like fixing the Medicare prescription-drug program) were never completed.

When government is divided, and minority party lawmakers have a co-partisan in the White House, they are expected to support the president's policy priorities and positions. They deviate from supporting the president, however, when it suits their electoral needs and when it will not influence the outcome of a vote. When government is unified, and a congressional party is both in the minority in Congress and without presidential leadership, the minority's agenda is often simply to oppose the majority and the president. For instance, after Obama's election victory in 2008, which unified the House, Senate, and presidency under the Democrats, GOP leaders constructed an agenda of united and unyielding opposition.[46] During the first two years of the Obama administration, Republicans voted as a bloc against all major Democratic initiatives, including the economic recovery package to counter the Great Recession, Obamacare, and the overhaul of Wall Street regulations. And following the 2016 election, during the first two years of the Trump administration, in which the president enjoyed Republican majorities in both the House and Senate, the minority Democrats actively opposed his policy initiatives, chiefly any and all attempts to repeal Obamacare.

## Negotiating with the President

Party leaders also work with the president on legislation. Because the Constitution provides the president with veto power, the lawmaking process involves more than just the House and Senate. For a measure to become law, the president must support it, or two-thirds of the membership of both chambers must be willing to override the president's veto. Policy making by veto override has happened in the past—most notably in the aftermath of the Civil War, when the Republican Congress repeatedly overrode President Andrew Johnson on Reconstruction policy—but it is much rarer today. An override is easier to achieve when a party has two-thirds majorities in both the House and Senate, but that has been rare in the post–World War II era.

As a result, majority party leaders often need to negotiate with the president on important legislation. They could try to challenge the president, forcing him to accede to a policy measure by courting public opinion, but such pressure tactics are not always effective.[47] Finding common ground with the president is often the safer and more efficient strategy, especially because the majority has many policy goals and limited time to accomplish them.

Two examples of majority party leaders negotiating with the president highlight the benefits and costs of the separation-of-powers arrangement. The first (welfare reform in 1996) was successful, while the second (the "grand bargain" in budget negotiations in 2012) was not. The difference between these cases lay in the key congressional leader's ability to negotiate a settlement that both the president and his co-partisans in Congress could accept.

In the 104th Congress (1995–97), Republicans controlled both the House and Senate for the first time in more than 40 years, and they sought to enact a key provision of their Contract with America: an overhaul of the nation's welfare system. There appeared to be room to work with President Clinton, who made welfare reform a key element of his election campaign in 1992. But the GOP's initial attempts to force a conservative policy change met with resistance. Clinton issued two vetoes, and Republicans did not have the votes to override them. As the 1996 election season neared, both congressional Republicans and Clinton sought to pass a welfare reform bill. Speaker Gingrich worked behind the scenes with Clinton and his policy advisers to share information and adjust the legislation enough to keep congressional Republicans on board and get the president's signature.[48] Eventually, the Personal Responsibility and Work Opportunity Reconciliation Act of 1996 was adopted. It overhauled the existing welfare system by establishing welfare-to-work provisions (limiting lifetime benefits to five years and requiring able-bodied adults to enter the workforce two years after receiving benefits), providing states with considerably more discretion over policy, and tightening eligibility requirements for the federal food stamp program.

In the 112th Congress (2011–13), Republicans controlled the House, Democrats controlled the Senate, and all struggled to govern. In July 2011, Tea Party–affiliated Republicans in the House balked at raising the nation's debt limit by $2.4 trillion (which came with an August deadline). As worries about the United States defaulting on its debt obligations grew, Speaker Boehner and

President Obama met privately in an attempt to negotiate a wide-ranging solution to the federal government's fiscal problems. Put simply, Boehner and Obama set out to craft a "grand bargain" that would "rewrite the tax code, roll back the cost of entitlements, and slash deficits."[49] Such an agreement would tentatively yield around $800 billion in revenue and significantly reduce various entitlement programs, such as Medicare, Medicaid, and Social Security.[50] Unlike the Gingrich–Clinton partnership in 1994, the Boehner–Obama pact in 2011 fell apart. In the end, while Gingrich was able to keep his Republican colleagues together on welfare reform, Boehner was not able to sell the economic deal to his co-partisans. Conservative Republicans in the House opposed the deal, and Boehner's second in command, Majority Leader Eric Cantor, would not support him. In many ways, Boehner was a victim of the ever-growing polarization in Congress, and without enough members of his own party, he could not successfully negotiate a historic agreement with the president.

## Overcoming Collective-Action Problems

Since their emergence not long after the Founding of the republic, parties have helped like-minded lawmakers bring together all the necessary actors to overcome various obstacles in our complicated system of governing. In other words, lawmakers use parties to coordinate behavior and overcome problems in acting collectively.

**BUILDING COALITIONS**   One of the most important duties of congressional parties is building majority coalitions to support the party's agenda and pass legislation. Coalition building can include promises of campaign support and resources, side deals on legislation, and pressure tactics to corral lawmakers.

Coalition building is most difficult when it involves high-profile and controversial legislation. During the Obama administration, no legislation required more deft coalition building than the Affordable Care Act. President Obama had repeatedly stated that he wanted major health care legislation to be a bipartisan effort, and he sought to incorporate Republicans' input and perspective in the final package; however, as the months wore on, it became increasingly clear that President Obama and his party members would have to go it alone. This strategy was possible because Democrats had large majorities in both chambers of Congress—nearly an 80-seat majority in the House and 20 seats in the Senate. Perhaps most important, Senate Democrats had a filibuster-proof majority of 60 lawmakers until Senator Ted Kennedy (D-Mass.) died in late 2009 (and was replaced, in a surprising special election, by Republican Scott Brown).

With so much on the line, Democratic leaders needed to help wavering co-partisans who were facing resistance from their constituents. Building a supportive coalition required delicate negotiations and, in some cases, side deals with individual members to mollify constituent concerns. For example, two of the more moderate Democratic senators, Ben Nelson (Neb.) and Mary Landrieu (La.), both from Republican-leaning states, were granted federal funding intended to subsidize health care programs under Medicare (Nebraska) and Medicaid (Louisiana). Both Nelson and Landrieu claimed that they were not solely responsible for the increased funding and that it did not influence their votes. Nelson's "Cornhusker Kickback" was eventually removed from the version of the bill that passed in the House, but Landrieu's "Louisiana Purchase" was kept in.[51] In addition, a small but sizable group of antiabortion lawmakers in the House, led by Bart Stupak (D-Mich.), threatened to oppose the legislation unless it contained language that precluded federal funding for abortion. To win the support of these dissidents, President Obama issued an executive order clarifying that existing limits on the federal funding of abortion would remain in place under the new health care law.[52]

**DEVELOPING A PARTY BRAND**   Over the last several decades, as the parties have polarized, politics has nationalized. (See Chapter 3 for more on nationalization.) The result is that parties have developed brands—or reputations—that voters use when deciding how to vote. These **party brands** can include the policies the parties advocate, the values they stand for, and the degree to which they have fulfilled campaign promises, appear well organized, and govern effectively.[53]

In an era of greater and greater polarization, as voters make decisions based on party brands, Democrats and Republicans increasingly win or lose elections together. A party with a unified message and a coherent party brand sends a strong signal to voters. Consequently, another way that party leaders build coalitions in the modern Congress is by keeping individual party members on message—that is, ensuring that members buy into the party leadership's legislative strategy and support the party agenda on key roll call votes. If party members defect from the agenda that party leaders put together, the party brand will weaken (what the party stands for will be less clear to voters) and all members of the party will suffer in elections. Thus, party leaders will actively enforce party discipline, especially on highly visible issues and key parts of the party agenda.

**ENFORCING PARTY DISCIPLINE**   Party leaders have a variety of means to punish members who do not toe the line on important party matters and reward members who do. These means are often called carrots and sticks. A carrot is an incentive to support the party leadership. Carrots may be the promise of a good committee assignment or of bringing a bill important to a member's constituency to the floor. A stick is just the opposite: the threat of something unpleasant. For example, an important committee assignment might be withheld, or a bill important to a member's constituency will not be pursued. Leaders recognize that such carrots and sticks are not limitless, and thus they use them sparingly and strategically, where they might have the greatest effect for the party.

Recently, majority party leaders have used sticks on litmus-test votes (such as a vote to support the party's speakership nominee) as well as less-visible actions. For instance, lawmakers who are part of their caucus's whip system have traditionally been required to support the party's position on important procedural votes. In June 2015, as GOP leaders sought a major international trade deal involving many Pacific Rim nations, a small band of Republicans in the House defected on a vote that would grant President Obama fast-track authority to negotiate the deal. Such authority would have prohibited Congress from amending the deal, leaving lawmakers to either approve or reject it in its entirety. Among the defectors on this procedural vote were three members of the Republican whip system. Days later, Speaker Boehner relieved all three members of their positions.[54]

Sticks also extend into the realm of direct electoral support. Recently, Representative David Jolly (R-Fla.) drew the ire of Republican leaders, especially the NRCC. In 2014, Jolly won a special election in his Florida congressional district, thanks in part to $2.5 million raised on his behalf by the NRCC. Once reelected to his first full term in office, Jolly criticized the NRCC for requiring him (and other GOP lawmakers) to spend considerable time each day fundraising, and he sought to introduce legislation that would prevent members from directly soliciting campaign donations. In addition, Jolly went on CBS's *60 Minutes*, sneaking a hidden camera into the party's call center near the Capitol where members "dial for dollars."[55] The NRCC felt that Jolly, by attempting to position himself as a reformer in order to run for a Senate seat, was being actively disloyal to the party. As a result, when Jolly later reconsidered his Senate run and decided instead to seek reelection to the House, the NRCC struck back, refusing to pledge any further financial support and thus leaving him to twist in the wind.[56] Jolly would go on to lose a close election in 2016 to Democratic candidate (and former Florida governor) Charlie Crist.

**BENDING OR BREAKING RULES**   Parties also occasionally bend or break legislative rules to win votes and enact policy. A high-profile example occurred in 2003, when the Republican leadership used its powers over the agenda to reform Medicare. Such a reform had been promised to senior citizens for years, and neither President Bush nor the Republican Congress wanted to face voters empty-handed in 2004. But when GOP leaders proposed adding prescription-drug benefits to the established Medicare program, House Republicans were divided over the reform, with more conservative members troubled by the significant cost of the drug-benefit provision. This conservative opposition jeopardized the passage of the bill.

Republican leaders responded by using several tactics to push the measure forward. National GOP leaders, including Vice President Cheney, intervened and lobbied for the bill. And congressional leaders tacked on provisions that were popular among some Republicans, including one to expand medical savings accounts and another to permit the importation of some less-expensive drugs from Canada. Nevertheless, arm-twisting and favor trading would not be enough by themselves.

During the roll call on final passage, the Republican leadership knew that they were short of votes. After the initial electronic vote tally suggested they would lose 214–218, GOP leaders kept the roll call open an additional 50 minutes (a typical roll call takes only 15 minutes to complete) until they could round up enough votes to secure passage. Eventually, one Republican was convinced to switch his "nay" vote to "present," while two others were pressured to switch their votes from "nay" to "yea." As a result, the Republicans eked out a 216–215 victory.[57] The Democrats cried foul, but the Republicans were the majority party and thus dictated how the rules would—or would not—be followed.[58]

In November 2013, Senate Democrats too would manipulate the rules—this time, to get more of President Obama's judicial nominees confirmed. Senate Republicans had been filibustering these nominations, and the rules of the Senate stipulated that a three-fifths majority (or 60 senators) was required to invoke cloture and overcome the filibusters. But the Senate Democrats, behind Majority Leader Harry Reid, decided to "go nuclear" and lower the threshold to a simple majority to cut off debate on all executive nominations below the Supreme Court level. As political scientist Sarah Binder notes: "Democrats thus reinterpreted 'three-fifths' to mean 'simple majority' when applied to nominations." Mitch McConnell, the GOP minority leader in the Senate, was outraged "that Democrats had broken the rules to change the rules," but could do nothing about it.[59] McConnell would later extend the majority-rule threshold to Supreme Court nominees and use it to benefit the Republican Party by adding Neil Gorsuch to the Court in 2017.

# WHEN DO PARTIES WIELD INFLUENCE?

We have seen that parties can wield influence in Congress through organization, operations, and overcoming collective-action problems. But when do they wield influence? Always or sometimes? And what approaches do they follow?

There are two major political science theories that focus on party influence: conditional party government theory (CPG) and party cartel theory. These theories differ on when parties wield influence and the approaches they follow. In addition, an alternative theory questions whether parties ever really wield influence.

## Conditional Party Government Theory

**Conditional party government (CPG) theory**, most closely linked to the research of political scientists John Aldrich and David Rohde, holds that party power waxes and wanes based on certain conditions.[60] That is, the majority party does not always wield influence in Congress, but it is more likely to do so when (1) the majority party is unified ideologically, and (2) there is a wide ideological gulf between the majority party and the minority party.

When these two conditions are met, members of the majority party will entrust their leadership with greater organizational authority and agenda-setting powers to help overcome the coordination problems inherent in a large and complex legislature. Under CPG, the goal is to exercise **positive agenda control**— that is, to get a bill onto the agenda, through the legislative process, and enacted into law.

The 111th Congress (2009–11), which was President Obama's first Congress after his initial election in 2008, is a good example of CPG in operation. The Democrats controlled both chambers of Congress and the presidency, congressional Democrats were quite unified in their policy preferences, and the Democrats controlled 60 seats in the Senate (until Senator Kennedy's death in August 2009), which provided them—if they voted as a bloc—with the ability to overcome any Republican filibusters. These factors enabled the Democrats to design an ambitious policy agenda and enact an assortment of landmark laws, such as the American Recovery and Reinvestment Act (an important economic stimulus package in the wake of the Great Recession), the Credit Card Accountability and Responsibility Disclosure Act (which provided consumers with a credit card bill of rights), the Matthew Shepard and James Byrd Jr. Hate Crimes Prevention Act (which expanded the definition of federal hate crimes to include attacks based on gender, sexual orientation, and disability), and the Affordable Care Act.

The 96th Congress (1979–81), which was President Jimmy Carter's second Congress, represents the other side of the CPG coin. Despite factors that were similar to President Obama's situation in the 111th Congress (Democrats controlled the presidency and enjoyed large majorities in both chambers of Congress), the Democrats in the 96th Congress were not very ideologically unified, as conservative and liberal factions often disagreed on policy. And President Carter did not have a good working relationship with congressional leaders. Thus considerably fewer landmark laws were enacted.

## Party Cartel Theory

**Party cartel theory**, which was developed by political scientists Gary Cox and Mathew McCubbins, offers a view of parties that differs from CPG in two ways.[61] First, party cartel theory assumes the majority party, no matter its size or composition, can control the agenda. That is, there are no conditions on the majority party's power. Party cartel theory is based on the premise that majority party leaders in the House—that is, the Speaker, the committee chairs, and the Rules Committee—act as a procedural team. Like a cartel in economics (a collection of businesses or countries that act together to influence the price of certain goods and services by controlling production and marketing), the majority party cartel in the House sets the legislative agenda exclusively for the benefit of majority party members. Setting the agenda, in this case, means screening out legislation that would adversely affect the majority party. That is, cartel leaders block bills from reaching the floor of the chamber that would, if passed, be opposed by a majority of majority party members. This **negative agenda control** represents the second way that party cartel theory differs from CPG: where CPG is about enhancing the party brand by pushing majority-preferred bills onto the agenda and enacting them into law, party cartel theory is about protecting the party brand by weeding out bills that divide the majority and thus keeping existing laws in place.

How might the screening process in party cartel theory work? There are several possibilities. The Speaker, for example, might use her power of recognition to avoid calling on members who she believes would offer motions or amendments that would divide the majority. Committee chairs could use their scheduling powers to bury legislation that would harm the majority. The Rules Committee could refuse to provide a rule on a bill that would run counter to the majority's interests. If these party actors are working in concert, they enact multiple barriers to protect the majority. If one barrier fails, other barriers stem the tide.

In the contemporary era, this screening process has been embodied in the **Hastert Rule**, a principle of behavior named after former speaker Dennis Hastert (R-Ill.). In 2003, Hastert remarked, "The job of the Speaker is not to expedite legislation that runs counter to the wishes of the majority of his majority. . . . I do not feel comfortable scheduling any controversial legislation unless I know we have the votes on our side first." There is considerable evidence that Gingrich, Hastert's predecessor in the Speaker's chair, held fast to the same rule.[62]

From the perspective of party leaders, negative agenda control is critical for party success. If legislation that divides the party gets to the floor and passes, the majority's ability to govern suffers, and voters become confused about what the party stands for. And both of these effects will damage the overall party brand.

# HOW WE STUDY
## NEGATIVE AGENDA CONTROL

What evidence can we find to assess whether the majority party exercises negative agenda control by removing items from the agenda that would pass over the opposition of a majority of the majority? In other words, can we use party cartel theory to measure how successful the majority party is at setting the legislative agenda?

Cox and McCubbins have argued that if the majority party effectively exercises negative agenda control by controlling positions of power, then we should rarely observe instances in which the majority party is "rolled"—that is, where a majority of the majority party opposes a bill on the floor but the bill nonetheless passes. In addition, we should regularly observe instances in which the minority party is rolled—when a majority of the *minority* party opposes a bill on the floor but the bill nonetheless passes. This is because the minority party does not control positions of power (the speakership, the Rules Committee, and committee chairs) that can be used to block items from getting onto the agenda. Thus the minority party should be rolled considerably more often than the majority party.

To gather evidence to test their conjectures, Cox and McCubbins examined final-passage votes in the House of Representatives across time. For each Congress, they calculated roll rates for the majority and minority parties. A **roll rate** is a percentage that answers the question, How often did a majority of a given party vote to oppose a bill that ultimately went on to pass, relative to all final-passage votes? So, for example, if there were 125 final-passage votes in a given Congress, and in 25 of those cases, a majority of the party opposed the bill, but it passed anyway, then the party's roll rate would be 20 percent.

Do the data support party cartel theory? Does the majority party really have a negative agenda control advantage? Figure 6.1 plots majority and minority party roll rates from the 45th through 112th Congresses. The evidence is striking, and it validates Cox and McCubbins's conjectures. Over the entire data series, the majority party was rolled on only 2.3 percent of final-passage votes, but the minority party was rolled 32 percent of the time. Examined from a different perspective, the majority party is rolled, on average, once every 43 votes, but the minority party is rolled, on average, once every three votes. Thus the incidence of final-passage votes that pass over the objections of the two parties is not random; the majority party is clearly in a superior position when it comes to being rolled. These results are consistent with the majority party operating like a cartel and setting the agenda to benefit the majority at the expense of the minority.

What about the Senate? While Cox and McCubbins developed party cartel theory with the U.S. House in mind, we can also analyze roll rates on final-passage votes in the Senate (Figure 6.2). We would expect majority party influence to be weaker in

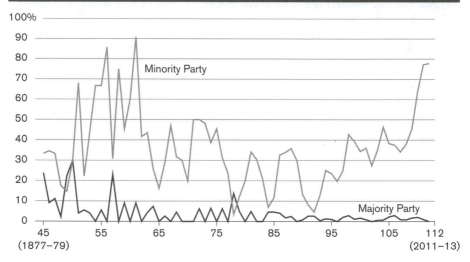

**FIGURE 6.1**  Party Roll Rates in the House of Representatives, 45th–112th Congresses (1877–2013)

Data until 2005 from Gary W. Cox and Mathew D. McCubbins. 2005. *Setting the Agenda: Responsible Party Government in the U.S. House of Representatives*. Cambridge: Cambridge University Press. Data after 2005 were compiled by the authors.

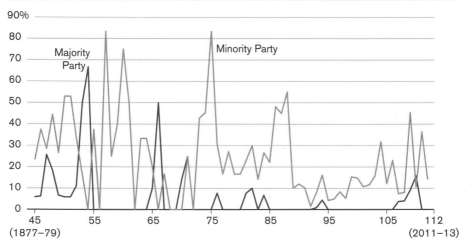

**FIGURE 6.2**  Party Roll Rates in the Senate, 45th–112th Congresses (1877–2013)

Data until 2005 from Gary W. Cox and Mathew D. McCubbins. 2005. *Setting the Agenda: Responsible Party Government in the U.S. House of Representatives*. Cambridge: Cambridge University Press. Data after 2005 were compiled by the authors.

the Senate because the Senate doesn't have the House's institutional mechanisms for exercising negative agenda control. Specifically, the Senate has no Speaker, there is a much less powerful Rules Committee, and committee chairs have less authority to prevent bills from receiving floor consideration. As a result, the minority party in the Senate should be less disadvantaged than the minority party in the House. Figure 6.2 confirms these expectations. The majority party roll rate in the Senate for the same set of Congresses is 3.6 percent. That number is still low, but it is also more than 56 percent larger than in the House. Similarly, the minority party roll rate is lower in the Senate, at 19.5 percent, or 39 percent lower than in the House. Together, these results suggest that the majority party's negative-agenda-setting advantage is weaker in the Senate than it is in the House. How the majority party in the Senate exercises such an advantage without the benefit of obvious institutional mechanisms to screen out bills is the subject of ongoing research.

## Critical Thinking

1. Are roll rates a good measure for empirically validating party cartel theory? Why or why not?
2. While majority party roll rates in the House show little variation across time (they are always quite low), minority party roll rates fluctuate considerably. What factors might explain these fluctuations? Why would minority party roll rates sometimes be higher or lower?
3. Majority party roll rates are higher in the Senate than in the House, but they are still quite low overall—and much lower than minority party roll rates in the Senate. And yet the Senate lacks the institutional mechanisms that scholars believe are important for controlling the legislative agenda and protecting majority party interests. What, then, explains the low majority party roll rates in the Senate?

---

## Preference Theory

While political scientists and pundits often point to the critical role that parties play in contemporary congressional politics, not everyone believes that parties significantly affect legislative organization and decision making. One critic of the party theories is political scientist Keith Krehbiel, who holds that lawmakers today make choices based solely on their ideological preferences.[63] Krehbiel argues that when we observe unified voting among Democrats or Republicans in Congress, their votes may not be the result of party leaders pressuring them to toe the party line. Rather, lawmakers, like voters, could simply have, over time, sorted themselves better along ideological lines, with conservatives taking on the Republican label and liberals taking on the Democratic label. Thus when we observe Republicans and Democrats dividing neatly into "yea" and "nay" groups on a roll call vote, it could be that their ideological preferences are determining their vote choices, with party (specifically, party leaders) playing no independent role.

History provides some context. From the middle of the twentieth century through the 1970s, there was considerable overlap in the preferences of the two parties. While the Democrats were mostly a liberal party and the Republicans were mostly a conservative party, members from the opposite ideological persuasion were also present in each party. Southern Democrats were very conservative—and made up a sizable portion of the caucus—and many northeastern Republicans were liberal. Beginning in the 1980s, this ideological overlap started to disappear as voters began to elect only Republicans from the conservative end of the spectrum and Democrats from the liberal end. And as partisan voting in Congress increased, so did gridlock on some important issues. Partisan voting and gridlock ramped up considerably in the mid-1990s with the GOP's return to majority status in Congress, and it reached even greater heights in the twenty-first century, first with the George W. Bush administration, then with the Obama administration and with the Trump administration.

As Democrats and Republicans self-sort into unified liberal and conservative groups, it becomes difficult to determine the source of the polarized voting behavior that we observe in Congress. Is it being driven mostly by party leaders' influence and organizational decisions? Or is it occurring naturally because members simply have very divergent policy preferences? Either view could be correct, according to Krehbiel, and simply examining how Democrats and Republicans vote will not provide an answer.[64] And while there is anecdotal evidence of party being influential in Congress—like when party leaders hold open votes until they can pressure enough members to achieve the outcome that they want, as for example the Republicans did to pass the 2003 Medicare reforms, mentioned above—more systematic evidence of party influence is considerably harder to come by.

The "parties or preferences" conundrum created a research agenda that spanned a generation. Political scientists designed creative analyses to separate party-based influence from preference-based influence. Examples included finding separate ways to measure members' preferences that did not rely on roll call votes, comparing how members voted in legislatures with and without parties, and looking for party influence on votes where one would expect pressure to be applied (votes with close outcomes) versus votes where one wouldn't (votes with lopsided outcomes).[65] None of these examples by themselves proved the existence of party influence, but together they built an empirical case for party playing an independent role in structuring voting and organization in Congress.

In short, scholars today believe that preferences definitely matter in how law-makers behave in Congress. But most scholars also believe, based on a wide array of evidence, that party also matters.

# WHEN PARTY INFLUENCE BREAKS DOWN

While scholars debate whether party influence is conditional (CPG) or uncondi-tional (cartel), and how much influence parties actually have (Krehbiel and his critics), we can point to two cases in congressional history where party influence clearly broke down. The first occurred when the cross-party conservative coali-tion emerged on ideological grounds to compete with the majority party for influence. The second occurred when unity within the governing Republican Party disintegrated.

## The Conservative Coalition

A good historical example of ideologically-driven (as opposed to party-driven) influence is the conservative coalition, which was a significant force in Congress from the late 1930s through the early 1980s. The conservative coalition was an alliance of Republicans and southern Democrats that formed in reaction to Franklin Roosevelt's (and northern Democrats') attempt to expand New Deal policies, especially in the area of labor. After World War II, the coalition expanded its purview to resist federal social-welfare programs more generally. By the 1950s, the conservative coalition crept into matters of foreign policy and civil liberties.[66] By the early 1960s, the conservative coalition was a major influence in congressional lawmaking. In terms of measurement, a **conservative coalition vote** was one in which a majority of Republicans and a majority of southern Democrats opposed a majority of northern Democrats. As Figure 6.3 indicates, in some Congresses during the 1960s and into the 1970s, the conser-vative coalition was active on around a third of all roll call votes.[67]

Scholars disagree whether the conservative coalition simply acted as a voting bloc on the floor or was organized around a procedural agenda and thus operated as a different kind of cartel.[68] Regardless, the conservative coalition was power-ful at midcentury and put its stamp on congressional policy making. Its ultimate influence was more negative than positive, blocking policy change that liberal northern Democrats sought rather than enacting new conservative policy.[69]

With the passage of the Voting Rights Act of 1965, the conservative coali-tion's reign began to crumble. As African Americans in the South secured voting rights and protections, party politics began to change. Liberal Democrats began winning elections in the South. To survive in the new political environment,

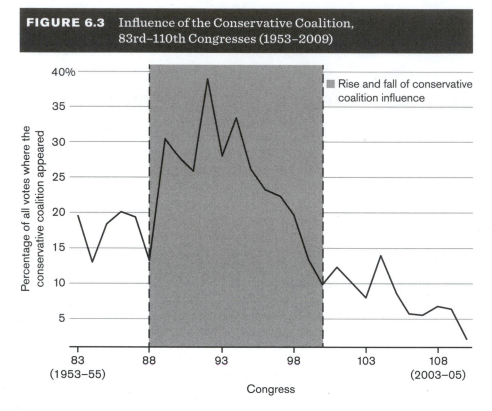

**FIGURE 6.3**   Influence of the Conservative Coalition, 83rd–110th Congresses (1953–2009)

John Wilkerson and Barry Pump. 2011. "The Ties That Bind: Coalitions in Congress," in *The Oxford Handbook of the American Congress*, ed. by Eric Schickler and Frances Lee, 625. Oxford: Oxford University Press.

conservative White Democrats either moderated their behavior or joined the emerging Republican Party in the South. By the mid-1980s, the South had realigned: southern Democrats voted more like northern Democrats and a conservative Republican Party was now a force to be reckoned with. As a result, the ideological split in the Democratic Party, brought about by the rise of the conservative coalition, had effectively ended.

## Divisions within the Republican Party: The Rise of the Tea Party

The contemporary Republican Party in Congress has experienced its own internal divisions over the last decade. In the late 2000s, as the financial crisis resulted in bailout programs for Wall Street, the housing market, and the auto industry

(General Motors and Chrysler), a segment of the Republican Party grew particularly hostile toward government intervention in the economy. This new wing of the Republican Party—voters and subsequently lawmakers—eventually coalesced into the Tea Party movement in 2009, in reaction first to the Obama administration's stimulus package during the recession and then to Obamacare.[70]

The 2010 through 2014 election cycles saw the most ideologically driven primary challenges of any election cycle since the early 1970s, and all these challenges were in the Republican Party.[71] Many of these primary challenges captured voters' attention because they occurred during the slow-news summer months, and some included high-profile candidates. The most prominent of these challenges led to the 2014 ouster of House Majority Leader Eric Cantor (R-Va.), who lost his primary reelection to David Brat, a little-known and underfunded college professor who was backed by Tea Party organizations.[72]

After the 2010 election, about 40 lawmakers elected with the support of various Tea Party–affiliated groups organized into a caucus in the House under the leadership of Michele Bachmann (R-Minn.). They opposed what they viewed as a bloated federal budget and were unwilling to increase statutory limits on the federal debt.[73] Their intransigence, along with a growing fear among more mainstream Republicans that they could face their own Tea Party challenge at home, resulted in several near misses on government shutdowns and federal government defaults.

Following the 2014 election, in which the Republicans won majority control of the Senate, a new Tea Party–inspired caucus in the House formed: the Freedom Caucus. Its goal was to coordinate lawmaking activities and pressure leadership to enact a more conservative agenda. The Freedom Caucus led a serious, but ultimately unsuccessful, insurgency against John Boehner's speakership election at the start of the term. In response, Boehner immediately removed two of the rebel leaders from their plum positions on the Rules Committee. Later in 2015, Boehner pressured House Government Reform Chair Jason Chaffetz (R-Utah) to remove Mark Meadows (a Freedom Caucus member) as a subcommittee chair after Meadows refused to support Boehner on an important procedural vote. Chaffetz, however, faced fierce opposition from Freedom Caucus members on the committee and ultimately allowed Meadows to keep his leadership post.[74] Later, emboldened by his victory, Meadows filed a petition to vacate the speakership—a direct affront to Boehner's leadership. As a key budget deadline loomed in the fall of 2015—regarding funding to prevent another federal government shutdown, with Freedom Caucus members refusing to accede without a cut in funding to Planned Parenthood—Speaker Boehner decided that he'd had enough and announced his resignation.

Freedom Caucus relations with the new speaker Paul Ryan (R-Wis.) were better, though ideological tensions within the Republican Party still ran high. After

Attempts to unseat a sitting Speaker—like Mark Meadows's (R-N.C.) effort to replace John Boehner (R-Ohio)—are rare and always unsuccessful, but they reflect often intense disagreements between factions within a party.

the Republicans lost control of the House in the 2018 midterms, the rift within the party abated—in part, because the GOP no longer controlled the agenda—and members of the Freedom Caucus assumed new roles as President Trump's strongest supporters. The president would prove to be an ally on policies they cared about, and he would appoint Representative Mick Mulvaney (R-S.C.), a Freedom Caucus cofounder, as his budget director and then later as his acting chief of staff.[75] And in late 2019, members of the Freedom Caucus would play a key role in defending President Trump during his impeachment.[76]

## THEN AND NOW
## PARTISAN POLARIZATION

In any discussion of the contemporary Congress, the term "polarization"—or the degree of ideological division between the parties—immediately comes to mind. Perhaps the best way to conceive of polarization is to think of Democratic and

Republican lawmakers distributed from left to right along a line, in keeping with the spatial model that we introduced in Chapter 2. Party polarization occurs when (1) parties are more internally cohesive on policy matters, and (2) each party's preferred policies are far apart.[77]

To measure polarization we must first measure the policy preferences of members of Congress so that we can compare the preferences of Democrats to those of Republicans. Where can we obtain such preference measures both across chambers and across time?

One option would be to collect survey responses from members of Congress on a battery of questions, which could then be transformed into measures of preference. The problem is that such surveys exist only for the most recent Congresses, and even within such surveys, the number and types of questions to which members respond vary considerably.

Another option—the one that most scholars of Congress adopt—is to use NOMINATE scores, which we introduced in Chapter 2.[78] Developed by political scientists Keith Poole and Howard Rosenthal, NOMINATE scores measure revealed preference because they are created from members' votes on roll calls. NOMINATE scores exist across chambers and across time (because roll calls are used in both the House and Senate and have been used in every Congress back to the first federal Congress), and thanks to innovations in the NOMINATE estimation procedure, scores can be compared by chamber across time. However, NOMINATE scores rely on the agenda items underlying the roll calls, which may not represent the issues that are important at a given point in time. For example, the majority party might set the agenda in such a way—by blocking some issues while allowing others—as to make divisions between the parties appear to be more extreme than they really are. Nonetheless, NOMINATE scores represent the best method scholars have devised (so far) to compare the ideological positions of lawmakers across chambers and across time.

To assess the positions of Democrats and Republicans in each chamber, Poole and Rosenthal calculate the mean (average) NOMINATE score for the total membership of each party. The mean score measures the central tendency of each party. Figure 6.4 shows House and Senate Democratic and Republican means on the NOMINATE scale from the 46th Congress (1879–81) through the 116th Congress (2019–21). While there has certainly been some variation in the average ideological positions of House Democrats and Republicans, the distance between the two parties is what stands out. In recent years, there has been a wide gap between the average Democrat and Republican. That gap is similar to the division that existed between the parties in the late nineteenth and early twentieth centuries.

Interestingly, if we examine the middle of the twentieth century, from about the mid-1930s to the late 1960s, we see that the distance between the parties

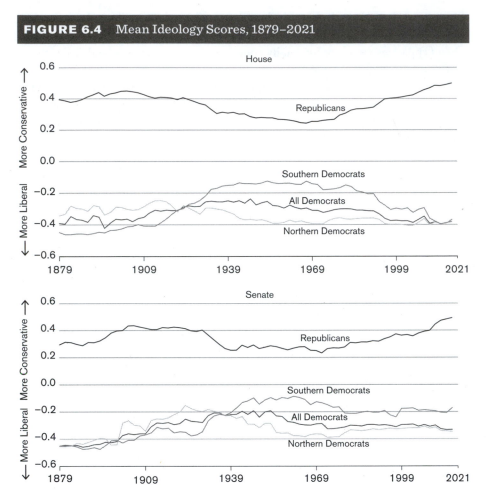

**FIGURE 6.4**   Mean Ideology Scores, 1879–2021

Jeff Lewis, "Party Means on the Liberal-Conservative dimensions over Time by Chamber," June 4, 2020, Voteview, voteview.com/articles/party_polarization (accessed 1/12/21).

narrows considerably. To better understand this narrowing, note that the Democrats who most closely align with Republicans in this period are from the South. This was a period of deep division within the Democratic Party, when southern Democrats often voted with Republicans as a conservative coalition to limit liberal initiatives.[79] In the years following the re-enfranchisement of African American voters in the South via the Voting Rights Act of 1965, the policy positions of the two groups diverged again. Over time, as the NOMINATE scores demonstrate, the ideological position of southern Democrats began to look more like the rest of the Democratic Party.

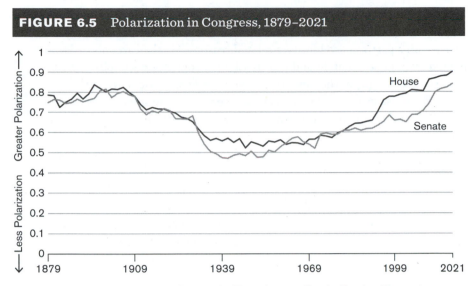

**FIGURE 6.5**  Polarization in Congress, 1879–2021

Jeff Lewis, "Party Means on the Liberal-Conservative Dimensions over Time by Chamber, Distance between Party Means," June 4, 2020; Voteview, voteview.com/articles/party_polarization (accessed 1/12/21).

Poole and Rosenthal provide a direct measure of polarization by calculating the distance between the average Democrat and the average Republican. Figure 6.5 plots this distance for the 46th Congress (1879–81) through the 116th Congress (2019–21), illustrating that polarization in both the House and Senate is greater now than it has been at any point in the last century and a half.

What explains this increasing polarization?[80] Rather than identifying a single cause, scholars have suggested many contributing factors, both external (electoral-driven) and internal (agenda-related). Externally, in the decades following the passage of the Voting Rights Act in 1965, partisan realignment in the South meant that areas that had traditionally elected conservative Democrats were increasingly electing Republicans. Similarly, voters in the South and elsewhere were sorting themselves ideologically into more consistent party affiliations. Today, more than ever before, conservatives are likely to identify as Republicans and liberals as Democrats. The result is that lawmakers more often represent homogeneous constituencies, with little pressure to vote or behave in a bipartisan way.

Two changes in the internal workings of Congress have also highlighted differences between Democrats and Republicans. The first is a shift in the types of policies that Congress addresses. Specifically, Congress has focused more on economic issues than in the past, and these issues are more divided along partisan lines than many other issues (including more traditional moral issues). The second internal factor involves process. Congress must take votes on matters of organization and procedure to move legislation forward, and the number of such votes has increased substantially in recent decades. Procedural votes are more divisive on a partisan level for two related reasons: (1) they are more disconnected from policy content and thus harder for constituents to observe and understand, and (2) at the same time, party leaders, particularly in the majority party, see these procedural votes as vital to ensuring the smooth operation of the chamber and thus hold their members to vote the party line. Defections are often not tolerated.

Finally, it is worth noting that some scholars attribute increased partisanship to the choices made by party leadership. For example, political scientist Laurel Harbridge finds that leaders from both parties choose to highlight (and vote on) issues that are particularly divisive. Focusing on roll call votes emphasizes these divisions. When Harbridge looks at the cosponsorship of bills, which takes place before party leaders set the agenda, she finds much less evidence of polarization.[81]

## Critical Thinking

1. What are the pros and cons associated with using NOMINATE scores to measure polarization in Congress?
2. It has been suggested that polarization in Congress is increasingly driven by Republicans becoming more conservative. Do you think this trend will continue? Will Democrats become increasingly more liberal in the future? Why or why not?
3. During the 1980s and into the 1990s, based on NOMINATE scores, the House and Senate were about equally polarized. Over the last 25 years, the House has become considerably more polarized than the Senate. Why do you think this is so?

# THE REPUBLICAN PARTY'S ROLE IN CONTEMPORARY POLARIZATION

Longtime observers of congressional affairs, Thomas Mann (of the left-of-center Brookings Institution) and Norman Ornstein (of the right-of-center American Enterprise Institute) assert that the Republican Party has driven partisanship and growing polarization in recent years. As moderate members in each party began to disappear in the 1970s and 1980s, the Republicans became more extreme. (Recall Figure 6.4, which shows that the ideological shift as measured by NOMINATE scores is twice as large among Republicans as it is among Democrats.) This disproportionate shift by the Republicans was not due solely to changing policy preferences; it also involved changing tactics. Mann and Ornstein contend that the GOP has based its platform on ideology and that it has become scornful of compromise and the political opposition.[82]

From the perspective of representation, the most conservative Republicans, like those affiliated with the House Freedom Caucus, believe they are acting as faithful agents. They feel that their constituents want something different than the traditional notion of what it means to govern—they want government to do less, be smaller, and refrain from intervening in many aspects of their lives. Freedom Caucus members are thus working to represent those smaller-government interests by opposing the governing activities that scholars typically associate with legislative effectiveness.

This less traditional philosophy of representation has changed the Republican Party as a governing coalition. The Freedom Caucus's independence has made it difficult for the Republican majority to ensure that budgets are completed on time and that expiring programs are reauthorized. House Speaker Boehner, for example, found it difficult to build the necessary coalition for such critical votes as raising the debt ceiling and providing aid for victims of Hurricane Sandy. He had to build a coalition with Democrats on many of these high-profile votes to ensure their passage. These moves were strategic compromises during a period of divided government, but they incensed those Republicans who refused to work with the Democratic Obama administration. Eventually, Boehner's decisions to govern—in the traditional sense—led members of the Freedom Caucus to attempt to remove him from the speakership. Rather than allow a civil war to break out in the party, Boehner resigned as Speaker.

On the Senate side, Majority Leader McConnell (R-Ky.) presided over a more fluid and open lawmaking environment, but he too was compelled to collaborate with the Democrats to enact several important measures. His efforts in this regard exposed him to attacks from his right flank, led by Senator Ted Cruz (R-Tex.) and others. As a result, McConnell sometimes had to give in to their demands and schedule votes on conservative priorities (such as defunding Planned Parenthood), rather than continue to risk the far right's ire.

Despite being elected on the promise of never compromising on conservative values, ultraconservatives have found that constituents don't like it when they prioritize independence over governing responsibilities. In 2016, for example, Freedom Caucus leader Tim Huelskamp (R-Kan.) lost in the GOP primary mainly because he rejected traditional governing obligations, which prevented him from adequately representing the farming interests of his rural Kansas district (he voted against reauthorizing the massive package of farm programs through the USDA, and his Freedom Caucus activities cost him his seat on the Agriculture Committee).[83] Ultimately, we do not know yet whether Huelskamp is the rule or the exception. As we move into the Biden era, it is still an open question whether traditional notions of partisan governing will reestablish themselves or not.

# CONCLUSION

Scholarship on how Congress operates has long placed parties in a highly privileged position. For the last several decades, political scientists have considered parties to be the chief analytic units for understanding how the legislative agenda is structured and policy change is produced in Congress. Whereas committees were once seen as the key lawmaking institution in Congress, parties have since commandeered that role. In recent decades, majority party priorities have largely defined the legislative agenda, and party leadership, for the most part, has designed the laws that are produced.

While much of this remains true today—the majority party clearly still dominates the legislative agenda, policy change still disproportionately benefits members of the majority, and partisan polarization remains at an all-time high—we believe change is in the air. A growing number of lawmakers are less attached to traditional notions of what a party in Congress means and the majority's responsibility to ensure that the institution fulfills its traditional governing duties. The revolt by Freedom Caucus members in the Republican Party is one example. More recently, a set of progressives in the Democratic Party, known as "The Squad" and led by Representative Alexandria Ocasio-Cortez (N.Y.), has made political life difficult for Speaker Nancy Pelosi and the party establishment. Will such internal strife become the norm and thus complicate governing for both parties in the coming years? We shall see.

## Discussion Questions

1. As more major legislation is being developed largely (or wholly) by one political party because of the intense polarization in Washington, what are some of the possible consequences? What are the pros and cons of this approach to lawmaking?
2. Many commentators bemoan the high degree of partisan polarization in Congress. But is polarization necessarily a bad thing? Can polarization be viewed in a positive light? Why or why not?
3. For a member of Congress, to what extent does being a good party member potentially conflict with being a good representative of one's district or

state? Why and when will a member of Congress sometimes be torn between her constituency and her party? Explain.

4. Scholars often talk about party leaders in Congress using carrots and sticks to keep party members in line. But when Republican John Boehner was Speaker of the House, he had a difficult time controlling members of the Freedom Caucus. Why? What factors allowed Freedom Caucus members to actively, and often successfully, oppose Boehner?

5. Recently, the filibuster has been weakened in the Senate; executive appointments are now entirely governed by simple majority vote. If the filibuster is eventually eliminated on policy measures, what do you think will be the impact? How will the kinds of policies that Congress produces change, if at all?

# 7

# Policy Making in the House and Senate

Immigration is one of the most complicated and thorny issues that Congress has faced in recent years. A surge of refugees at our southern border, a ban on migrant travel from a number of foreign countries, and funding for a border wall are among the many dimensions of our immigration policy that have confronted members of Congress. One of the most challenging aspects of immigration policy is what to do about the DREAMers (individuals who were brought to the United States as children yet have no legal status to reside here). Though these young people can obtain a free public education through high school, the federal government (as a result of a 1996 statute) actively discourages states from granting such individuals postsecondary education benefits, and undocumented immigrants are unable to work legally in the United States. In June 2020 the Supreme Court rejected the Trump administration's attempt to dismantle Deferred Action on Childhood Arrivals (DACA), an Obama-era policy that instructed the Department of Homeland Security to defer action on any deportation of qualified individuals, including many who had been brought to the United States as children. With Chief Justice John Roberts

In 2010, the unique processes of the House of Representatives and the Senate stymied significant immigration reform. While immigration is a particularly divisive issue nationwide, the differences between how the House and Senate make policy ultimately led to the bill's demise.

casting the pivotal swing vote along with the Court's liberal wing, the 5–4 ruling found that while the Trump administration is legally permitted to rescind DACA, it did not follow the proper procedure in offering a reasoned explanation for its action. In particular, the Court's majority stated that the Department of Homeland Security must consider the potential hardships to DACA recipients, their families, and their employers. Within a day, President Trump stated that the Department of Homeland Security would again attempt to rescind the DACA program.

While the Supreme Court decision affected President Trump's actions, it was Congress's inability to enact legislation over the course of many years that resulted in President Obama taking unilateral action beyond the legislative process. Congressional stalemate on protections for DREAMers is an outstanding example of how the differences in the House and Senate can stymie legislation even when members of Congress seem to agree on the desired policy outcome. Our journey to the 2020 Supreme Court decision really begins a decade earlier in 2010, when Congress came close to changing the DREAMers' legal status. As that year wound down, lawmakers were in a frenzy to complete legislative work on Capitol Hill. The November election had dealt the Democrats a harsh blow; they had lost their majority control of the House, and they were facing significant seat losses in the Senate. Consequently, the Democrats worked hard to pass important legislation in the lame-duck session, before the new Congress started in January. Over a quarter of the total laws enacted during that two-year congressional term were passed during the brief lame-duck session.

The Development, Relief, and Education for Alien Minors (DREAM) Act was one important piece of legislation up for consideration during the lame-duck session. For many years, versions of the DREAM Act had been introduced, but none of them had progressed very far, and Congress had failed to overhaul immigration prior to the November election. Now, proponents of the DREAM Act wanted to capitalize on the friendly conditions in the lame-duck session (while the Democrats still held power) and get a law passed.

With the clock ticking in mid-December, Democratic leadership in the House took up the legislation in an extraordinary and unexpected manner. Rather than advancing an existing House bill, the Democrats used a number of long-held practices and powers of the majority party to advance a new Senate version of the legislation that had been written to please moderate lawmakers in both parties. First, the House Rules Committee offered a resolution to replace an existing unrelated bill that was moving through both chambers with the text of the Senate's DREAM Act. The resolution, which restricted the length of debate and prohibited floor amendments, passed 211–208, with no Republican support. In opposing the legislation, Robert Goodlatte (R-Va.) complained that the bill had been brought to the chamber floor with only a single day's notice and no opportunity for committee consideration or floor changes.[1] Just a few hours after the resolution was adopted, the bill passed 216–198, with Democrats attracting the support of only eight Republicans.

In the Senate, the Democrats had a 58-to-42 majority, and several Republicans had previously introduced or voiced support for similar legislation. However, in recent decades, the Senate had come to require a supermajority—three-fifths of the chamber, or 60 votes—to end debate and move to enact any legislation of note. Even though Democratic leaders had made changes to the legislation to attract GOP support—such as a surcharge to apply for legal status, significant background checks, and a lengthy (10-year) waiting period to qualify for a green card—in the end, the bill fell victim to Senate rules. On December 18, when Majority Leader Harry Reid (D-Nev.) sought to end debate and move to a final vote on the bill, the measure failed, 55–41. While Democratic leaders were able to get the support of moderate Republicans Richard Lugar (Ind.) and Lisa Murkowski (Alas.), they lost the votes of some Democrats, including Max Baucus (Mont.), Kay Hagan (N.C.), Ben Nelson

(Neb.), Mark Pryor (Ark.), and Jon Tester (Mont.). The DREAM Act died in that final effort to close off debate because the majority fell short of the 60-vote standard.

A year and a half later, in June 2012, with no prospect of Congress adopting new immigration legislation, President Barack Obama enacted DACA through executive order, setting up the Trump administration's Supreme Court battle eight years later. Later in this chapter, we discuss how DACA recurred as a major agenda item in 2018 as moderate House Republicans employed a rarely used legislative maneuver to press the issue forward.

These recent actions on immigration illustrate the many challenges facing members of Congress as they try to move legislation forward (or attempt to block it). In this chapter we look more closely at how the legislative process works and how differences in House and Senate procedures affect the behavior and outcomes of the two chambers.

## THE HOUSE AND SENATE: TWO VERY DIFFERENT ANIMALS

There is perhaps no part of the legislative process where the House and Senate differ more than in their lawmaking practices (or floor procedures) after committees have considered bills. The House is a majoritarian body whose large membership reflects the populace that it represents. With such a diversity of interests, achieving a reasonable consensus in the House is often like herding cats and requires a tight set of rules. On the other side of the Capitol, the Senate is the more deliberative body. Its emphasis on open debate makes outcomes less certain.

In explaining how floor procedure works, we will highlight the differences between the two chambers. Some of these factors seem straightforward but nonetheless have an enormous impact on how the House and Senate operate. For example, we will examine how the different constituencies of the House and Senate, the size of each chamber, the length of terms of representatives and senators, and the minimum age of representatives and senators all affect how policy making differs in the two chambers.

We will also discuss how the House and Senate have operated in past eras and how those operations have changed in recent years. For example, what is sometimes called **regular order**—what the House and Senate rules prescribe for the procedures of legislative deliberation and enactment—barely exists, if it exists at all, in the contemporary Congress. Consequently, Congress today is less able to govern and participate equally with the president in the oversight of executive agencies.

## The Roots of House and Senate Floor Procedure

In Article I, Section 5, of the Constitution, the Framers gave each chamber responsibility for designing its own internal rules: "Each House may determine the Rules of its Proceedings." The members of each chamber were left to decide how they would represent their various constituencies and govern the rapidly growing nation. Each chamber's ability to create its own set of rules might have resulted in two different groups of representatives developing quite different procedures. But the Framers did far more than just give the two chambers free rein over their internal organization. Through the structure of Congress as written into the Constitution, the Framers shaped and influenced the differences in the chambers' operations. We focus here on four main design aspects of the two chambers that fundamentally affect and differentiate their operations: constituencies, size, length of service, and age. (See Chapters 1 and 2 for more detailed discussion of the origins of congressional design.)

**CONSTITUENCIES** The Constitution reflects a key compromise among the Framers over the scheme of representation in the legislature: the number of legislators in one body—the House—would be determined by the size of the populace in the various states, while the other body—the Senate—would provide for equal representation of the states themselves. Popular election of representatives in the House meant close ties to the changing political winds within home constituencies. At the same time, the Framers gave state legislatures the power to select senators, thereby making senators beholden to another political body. (The Framers understood that the states would have to ratify the newly written Constitution, and it was likely that state legislators would be influential in, and perhaps even critical to, that process.)

The Framers' goal was to remove popular pressure from the Senate's day-to-day operations and allow it to focus on lawmaking. While selection by state legislatures seemed like a good way to ensure state representation, a variety of problems emerged. Over the course of the nineteenth century, a number of state legislatures deadlocked in their selection process, resulting in no senator being sent to Washington. In fact, at one point, Delaware had so much trouble settling on a senator that it had no representation in the Senate for two years. Bribery and political corruption also found their way into the selection process, so that by the early part of the twentieth century, many states had already moved to a state referendum for selection of senators.

Even with the change to popular election of senators with the Seventeenth Amendment (added to the Constitution in 1913), the constituencies of the two chambers remained quite different. While senators no longer directly represented state legislatures, their constituencies (states) were typically more diverse than those of House members (districts).

**SIZE**  The starkest difference between the House and Senate is the size of each chamber's membership, a consequence of the unique representational arrangements envisioned by the Framers. The Framers decided that the House of Representatives—the "people's house"—would expand with population growth. Starting with the first Congress (1789–90), the House had 65 members, but that number rapidly grew. Just two terms later (1793–94), the House had 105 members, and by 1823, it had over 200. By the turn of the twentieth century, the House included 357 lawmakers, and it reached its current size—435, capped by law[2]—in 1913.

Given that the Framers intended the Senate to represent the states, it would be smaller, but exactly how small was unclear. During constitutional debates, some delegates argued that one senator was too few because the state might go unrepresented in the case of the senator's absence or illness. Alternatively, too many senators would eliminate the Senate's distinctiveness and might allow senators to avoid taking responsibility for their decisions and actions.[3] Small states feared that some variation on proportional representation would result in their being swamped in a majority-rule institution. Ultimately the delegates chose two senators per state. Even as the nation grew, this choice meant that the Senate would remain a significantly smaller body than the House. The Senate started with 26 members in 1789, and it took until 1835 to grow to over 50 senators. By the turn of the century, the Senate was at 90 lawmakers, and it was not until Hawaii and Alaska joined the union in 1959 that the Senate achieved its current size of 100 members.

**LENGTH OF SERVICE**  The Framers also differentiated the two chambers in terms of the members' length of service. In keeping with the notion that representatives should be closely tied to their home districts, delegate Roger Sherman stated during the Constitutional Convention, "Representatives ought to return home and mix with the people."[4] Delegates were concerned that lawmakers who did not face regular elections would become detached from their constituents' needs. Although some delegates suggested a one-year election cycle—a relatively common period of tenure in state legislatures at the time—it was ultimately determined that two years between elections would allow House members to familiarize themselves with their districts; it was also acknowledged that frequent travel home would be time-consuming.

Moreover, the Framers saw the Senate as the body that would provide leadership, stability, and a measure of independence from popular opinion. Consequently, delegates supported both longer terms and staggered elections (separating senators into three distinct election classes). In emulation of the upper houses of several state legislatures, many of which had five-year or longer terms, delegates chose six-year terms for senators. These longer terms would further allow for a continuous body split evenly among the classes. That continuity of the Senate over time, the Framers believed, could provide for leadership in times of crisis.[5]

**AGE** Finally, the Framers considered the matter of age. The median age at that time was 16 years old, and over 65 percent of people in the United States were under the age of 25. Initially, 21 years old was proposed for members of the House, but delegates raised it to 25 in response to George Mason's assertion that persons in the position of representing a sizable number of others should have gone beyond managing their own affairs to managing the "affairs of a great nation." At the time, Britain's prime minister was William Pitt. He was 24 years old.[6] The "senatorial trust," in contrast, was thought to require a "greater extent of information and stability of character," and as a result justified a minimum age of 30.[7]

## Two Chambers, Two Governing Philosophies

The structural differences of the two chambers were intended to assuage the demands of different interests—particularly small versus big states, North versus South, and supporters of stronger versus weaker central government. But those differences were also intended to provide two approaches to governing.

In the words of Madison, the Framers saw the House of Representatives as "the grand repository of the democratic principle of the government."[8] Madison felt that the House should be the locus of the new governing structure that "will derive its powers from the people of America."[9] Because of their direct representation of smaller constituencies amid shorter election cycles, House members would have "common interest . . . immediate dependence on, and an intimate sympathy with the people."[10] As the lower—or people's—chamber, the House was intended to translate constituents' interests at their most basic level into a relatively direct form of governance.

For this reason, the House of Representatives was the primary manager of the federal Treasury. Massachusetts's Elbridge Gerry stated that the House "was more immediately the representatives of the people, and it was a maxim that the people ought to hold the purse-strings."[11] As directed by the Constitution, all tax bills originate in the House. The Framers considered doing the same with spending (appropriations) bills, potentially going as far as barring any amendments by the Senate.[12] In the end, the Constitution did not grant the House the sole power to introduce appropriations bills, but the House by tradition retains agenda-setting power over appropriations, usually offering its bill first.

While the House was intended to be responsive to the changing winds of the populace, the Senate was intended to counter the excesses of democracy. An often-recounted exchange between Thomas Jefferson and George Washington illuminates the relationship between the House and Senate. Jefferson asked Washington why he had consented to the creation of a second chamber, the Senate. Washington replied, "Why did you pour that coffee into your saucer?" "To cool it," said Jefferson. "Even so," said Washington, "we pour legislation into the senatorial saucer to cool it."[13] The Framers envisioned the House yielding to the "impulse of sudden and violent passions" of the populace and thus created a counterpart that would be free of these influences and possess greater firmness.[14] Thus the vast majority of legislation in the first decades of the republic originated with the House, with it then going to the Senate for review and revision. During the first year of the new Congress, the House originated and passed 26 bills. The Senate modified or rejected nearly all of them. The Senate originated only five bills that year.

In addition, the Framers gave the Senate a greater say in the national interest via a set of quasi-executive functions. Specifically, they granted the Senate authority to confirm executive branch and judicial appointments, ratify treaties with foreign allies, and adjudicate impeachment charges against the president brought by the House of Representatives. As one observer noted, it was expected that the "Senate would serve as an advisory council to the President, but natural friction between the two, aggravated by the rise of the party system, made such a relationship impracticable. As time passed, the Senate was far more likely to try to manage the President than to advise him."[15] The vice president nominally presides over the chamber, although some delegates to the Constitutional Convention saw this role as a way of giving the vice president's position some purpose.

A perhaps less explicitly intended—but equally important—result of the design of the two lawmaking bodies was the *form* of their eventual decision making. The House, with its representation of diverse, populace-based interests, was intended to be the chamber for decisive action. However, its size and inevitable growth meant that it would need to grant substantial powers to an agenda-setting entity. Consequently, a highly structured lawmaking body with strong partisan leaders would mean diminished power for individual lawmakers.[16] In short, it was evident that action in the House was going to involve majoritarianism. And, for much of its existence, particularly in the nineteenth century, that majority coalition was going to be partisan.

Within a few decades of its inception, the House saw its first powerful Speaker, Henry Clay (Ky.). Clay pushed the body to tackle more national policy issues. He also addressed the chamber's coordination problems by introducing more partisanship. Speaker Thomas Bracket Reed (R-Maine), who served at the end of the nineteenth century, expanded the legislative authority of the majority party by reducing the minority's ability to use delaying tactics. Speaker Joseph Cannon (R-Ill.) followed soon after Reed and exerted the same iron control over the chamber. But, in doing so, he faced a revolt from lawmakers. A bipartisan House coalition, led by progressive Republicans, dismantled the party-oriented control that Reed and Cannon had constructed and ushered in committee-based governing that typified the House for the better part of the twentieth century. The majoritarian coalition for much of the second half of the twentieth century, interestingly, was not always partisan. Sometimes, for example, a "conservative coalition" of southern Democrats and Republicans emerged on labor and union issues. It was not until the very end of the twentieth century that Speakers, particularly Newt Gingrich, began acting on behalf of more unified parties and reasserting centralized control of internal organization and the legislative agenda.

Meanwhile, the Senate built a reputation as the world's greatest deliberative body.[17] The essence of that deliberation lies in the powers granted to individual lawmakers. Since the inception of the Senate, senators have often viewed themselves almost as ambassadors of sovereign states. As such, senators have felt entitled to unlimited debate and the inherent right to consent (or not) to the major actions taken by the body. In addition, the Framers purposely gave senators long terms of service to breed familiarity within the body. Over time, the power of individual senators and the custom of deliberation became the most cherished traditions of the upper chamber.[18] As long-serving senator Lamar Alexander (R-Tenn.) reflected, "The Senate, by its nature, is a place where consensus reigns and personal relationships are paramount. . . . And that's not changed."[19]

## Insecure Majorities

Given the inherent differences in the design of the House and Senate, it is not surprising that they developed in distinctive ways. Several factors have contributed to how the two chambers operate today.

First and foremost, partisan polarization has grown significantly in recent decades. Various factors have contributed to this growth. One factor has been the rise of "insecure majorities" in Congress. A generation ago, maintaining a majority in either chamber of Congress was not difficult. For years after World War II, controlling majorities (mostly Democratic Party majorities) had a sizable advantage, averaging around 81 seats in the House. Maintaining a majority is much less certain today.[20] The 1994 election was a turning point. Since then, control of the House has switched parties four times. More important, the majority seat advantage has shrunk considerably to an average of 32 seats, and party leaders today are concerned that they could lose control of the chamber with each coming election.

The modern Congress is characterized by deep partisan divides, and parties are more likely to be unified when creating policies. The support for and opposition to the Tax Cuts and Jobs Act, passed in December 2017, fell squarely along party lines, epitomized by the support of Senate Majority Leader Mitch McConnell (R-Ky.) and opposition of House Minority Leader Nancy Pelosi (D-Calif.).

These partisan electoral fears have caused lawmakers, party officials, and voters to treat elections differently than they did in the past. Congressional districts have become less competitive in the general election because (1) the U.S. population has "sorted" itself into politically homogeneous regions, and (2) state-level parties have gerrymandered aggressively to draw congressional district lines that produce solid partisan majorities. As a result, in a very large number of districts, there is little chance of party turnover from election to election. Thus many incumbents hail from districts where they fear defeat more at the primary stage than in the general election. In addition, voters are more reluctant to split their tickets because they are increasingly aligned with a single party. All of these changes have increased the degree to which House and Senate elections have become nationalized (see also Chapter 4).

These circumstances encourage more ideologically driven behavior by members of Congress. In considering bills on the floor of the House and Senate, lawmakers today dig more deeply into their ideological trenches than they have at any point in modern history. As a result, they find it more difficult to build coalitions to enact legislation. Members of Congress are less likely to compromise, which is evident in the amendments they offer and their roll call votes on the floor. If lawmakers fail to stand by ideological principles, they face the wrath of their partisan base back home.

In short, behavior in the two chambers promotes the party agenda, not necessarily good governing. In the House, which is already a staunchly majoritarian institution, the minority party has little opportunity to shape legislation on the floor. In the Senate, traditionally a more egalitarian body, the majority party uses its power to prevent undesirable legislation from moving forward while its leadership shapes the chamber agenda to avoid unwanted and potentially embarrassing votes.

# STAGES OF FLOOR CONSIDERATION

The stages of legislative consideration in the House and Senate reveal the differences in functioning between the two chambers. These stages also help explain the fate of much legislation in the contemporary Congress.

## Moving Bills from Committee to the Floor

The process of moving bills from committee to chamber deliberations can occur in different ways. One might assume that legislation handled by committees would proceed to the floor in an orderly, chronological fashion. Indeed, this **calendar system** is one way that bills can move. We discuss this system first, and then move to a discussion of the less formal paths taken by consensual or privileged legislation and more controversial or higher-profile legislation.

**CALENDARS**   Each chamber has calendars on which bills are placed for consideration. The Senate has a Calendar of Business for most legislation reported by committees, and it has the Executive Calendar for executive branch nominations and treaties. Some of these calendars specify that discussion of particular legislative matters should occur on particular days of the week. The House has the Union Calendar for tax, authorization, and appropriations measures; the House Calendar for other public bills and resolutions; and the Private Calendar for measures affecting specific individuals. In 2019 the House adopted a new Consensus Calendar to move legislation with broad support to the top of the floor agenda even if it has not been reported by a committee. Lawmakers in the House, with the help and publicity of comedian Jon Stewart, used the new Consensus Calendar later that year to move forward stalled legislation to replenish the compensation fund for 9/11 first responders.[21]

Though calendars are important, if the chambers were to stick to a strict procession of bills as they trickle in from committees, most of the critical lawmaking that takes the longest to formulate—spending (appropriations), reauthorizations of major programs and agencies, new and transformative legislation—would fall to the back of the line and likely not get completed before the end of the congressional term. For that reason, both chambers have devised alternative means for scheduling legislation for wider floor consideration.

**CONSENSUAL OR PRIVILEGED LEGISLATION**  The House of Representatives grants the Speaker significant authority over scheduling legislation. This authority, along with the power to refer legislation to particular committees, is central to the modern powers of the Speaker. After consulting with the relevant committee(s), the Speaker may permit a member to make a motion that a bill pass under **suspension of the rules**. This expedited procedure, meant for less controversial matters, limits debate to 40 minutes and prohibits the consideration of any amendments to the bill. The trade-off is that expedited bills require a two-thirds majority for adoption, thereby limiting this option to legislation with high levels of support and needing no further alteration. While such legislation is often minor (for example, the naming of post offices), the procedure can be used for more substantive legislation. In fact, recent years have seen an increase in legislation moving through the House under suspension of the rules, with nearly 800 bills using this process in the 115th Congress (2019–21). In the past, bills passed under suspension of the rules include fairly substantial measures such as the Food and Drug Administration Reauthorization Act and legislation meant to curb the spread of the feared Zika virus.[22]

In the Senate, the majority leader's privilege to decide the Senate's schedule or agenda is effectively derived from his or her right of first recognition to make a motion on the Senate floor. Interestingly, this privilege does not appear in the Constitution, any statute, or even the chamber rules. Rather, it exists through long-held precedent. (By one count, the Senate has more than 1 million precedents that govern its operations.[23])

The Senate does not have a suspension process, so it passes more trivial and consensual legislation by simple **unanimous consent agreements (UCAs)**. This means that the majority leader can dispose of many bills and executive nominations with a simple motion asking for unanimous consent to adopt. The majority leader does this with the cooperation of the other members (mainly the minority leader). Simple UCAs are often reserved for issues of relatively little importance and give tremendous latitude to the senators, permitting them to pass a package of noncontroversial bills all at once.

Finally, some legislative matters are considered privileged and may be called up for consideration on the floor of either chamber at almost any time without special permission, agreements, or calendars. These matters include budget resolutions and appropriations legislation, ethics resolutions, veto messages from the president, reports from conference committees, and special rules regarding the consideration of bills in the House (discussed later in this chapter).

**COMPLICATED OR MAJOR LEGISLATION**  The House and Senate use different procedures to consider controversial and complicated bills, and these procedures reflect the inherent differences in how the chambers function.

The House is guided by a clear set of majoritarian procedures. Because a good portion of the chamber floor time would be otherwise occupied by bills considered in accordance with the House's various calendars, Speakers in the 1880s developed the concept of the **special rule** (see Chapter 5). Speaker Reed made heavy use of the special rule as a means of deliberating important and pressing matters on the chamber floor in a timely fashion and within fairly restrictive limits on debate and amendment. In the modern era, the House Rules Committee has the power to draft special rules.

A special rule defines the terms and conditions of floor debate on a bill. It takes the form of a resolution and falls along a spectrum of restrictiveness that ranges from "open," permitting any germane amendment to be offered and debated on the House floor; to "modified" or "structured," limiting the specific amendments to be considered; to "closed," permitting no amendments to be offered on the reported bill. Open rules were more or less the norm until recently (more on this later in the chapter), but they came with the cost of potentially allowing lengthy floor consideration of a wide variety of amendments. Closed rules were traditionally common for tax bills; it was argued that such measures were too complex for the details to be formulated (and amended) beyond the expertise of the Ways and Means Committee members and staff.

Special rules are likely to include another set of exceptions that are necessary to keep the chamber functioning: waivers on points of order to chamber rules. It is somewhat common for the procedures being employed or the actual bill language to violate existing House rules. For example, a waiver might speed consideration of a bill or resolution that would otherwise have a one-day waiting period.

---

## HOW WE STUDY
## CONGRESSIONAL ORGANIZATION AND RESTRICTIVE RULES IN THE HOUSE

Restrictive rules began to increase in the second half of the twentieth century. Scholars of Congress became interested in what this trend revealed about the role of committees in the House as well as the power of the majority to control outcomes in the chamber. How leadership and the House chamber treat such bills—as protected or unprotected—reveals who they think should have the final say on legislation.

As experts in a particular realm of federal policy, committee members work hard on shaping legislation so that Congress adopts what they believe to be the best policies. One way party leaders encourage that effort is by assuring committees that their investment in gaining expertise and expending time and resources on new policy proposals will not be picked apart and undone by others, especially nonspecialists, on the chamber floor. To assure committees and protect their work, the Rules Committee grants them restrictive rules that limit amendments. Use of restrictive rules, particularly for bills coming from committees seen as information specialists, signals the importance of these committees' informational roles and the House's trust in the committees' expertise.

Political scientist Keith Krehbiel studied the frequency of restrictive rules in the House of Representatives in the mid-1980s and found that they were often used to protect bills coming out of committees comprised of issue specialists and not for bills from committees that were excessively partisan or ideologically extreme.[24] However, a follow-up study by political scientist Bryan Marshall, which examined many of the same factors but also included bills from a decade later (through the mid-1990s) did not find evidence to support the notion of protection for legislative proposals coming from informational or specialist committees. In fact, there was much more evidence that the Rules Committee was providing restrictive rules to protect the bills from the most partisan committees.[25]

What changed? As noted in Chapter 6, the 1980s were the beginning of our current era of excessive partisanship and polarization. Electoral changes and institutional reforms in the 1970s diminished the autonomy of committees, particularly their chairs. These changes placed committees more under the control of the party leadership and its pursuit of a partisan agenda. Consequently, the work of the Rules Committee became just a part of the grander strategy for an increasingly homogeneous majority party focused on achieving its legislative agenda.

As the political and electoral environment became increasingly partisan, legislators felt greater pressure from constituents and fellow party members alike to conform to the party line. As a result, they grew more uncomfortable with holding votes on the chamber floor that they would inevitably struggle to explain to these stakeholders. To ensure that only the most partisan matters—bills where the majority and minority party profoundly disagree—came up for a vote on the House floor, successive Speakers were under pressure from their majority-party colleagues to expand the use of restrictive rules. Figure 7.1 displays the increase in the use of restrictive rules from around 15 percent in the mid-1970s, to 50 percent in the mid-1990s, to 100 percent by the late 2010s. Ironically, these increases have occurred despite the fact that each party declares its opposition to such restrictions when it is in the minority but perpetuates the trend when it becomes the majority.[26]

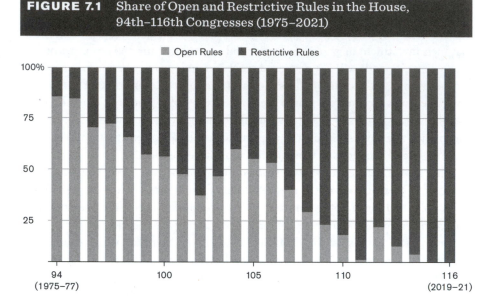

**FIGURE 7.1**  Share of Open and Restrictive Rules in the House, 94th–116th Congresses (1975–2021)

Vox, www.vox.com/polyarchy/2015/10/20/9570747/house-freedom-caucus-process-demands; Bipartisan Policy Center, https://bipartisanpolicy.org/wp-content/uploads/2020/09/116th-Full-House-Rules-Data.pdf (accessed 1/14/21).

## Critical Thinking

1. Restrictive rules in the House are often used to protect bills produced by committees from amendments on the floor. Is this limitation on chamber influence warranted, or should the entire membership of the House have a fair chance to amend all legislation?
2. Restrictive rules are one of the primary sources of control over the flow of legislation granted to the majority party in the House. Does the majority party have too much influence today (in contrast to a generation or two ago), or is it best to have a strongly majoritarian lawmaking body?
3. If polarization were to decrease in the future, would you expect the number of restrictive rules to decrease as well? Why or why not?

## Skirting Committees in the House

In general, there is considerable deference to committee jurisdictional authority. Lawmakers are hesitant to force a committee to relinquish a policy proposal that it has not fully considered and crafted into its desired form (that is, a fully reported bill). However, a committee will occasionally refuse to report out a bill even though there is sufficient support in the chamber to consider the matter. In the House, the membership can force the committee to act via a **discharge petition**, a procedure that extracts a bill from an unwilling committee and allows it to be considered by the chamber. A successful discharge petition requires the signature of an absolute majority of House members (218).

Filing a discharge petition is typically seen as hostile to the jurisdictional authority of a committee and its chair, and therefore lawmakers are hesitant to do so. More often than not, representatives will take such action only when they consider the measure of the highest importance and believe that they have the support to gain the required signatures. Occasionally, discharge petitions are used in a largely futile effort by the minority party to call out majority obstruction. For example, in 2018, as the work of Special Counsel Robert Mueller investigating Russian collusion in the 2016 election generated speculation that President Trump might fire him, House Democrats introduced more than one discharge petition aimed at extracting legislation from the Judiciary Committee to provide for judicial review of any such firing. The effort did not generate much support among the majority Republicans in the House.[27]

It is rare for the entire discharge process to play itself out. Often, filing a petition or even the threat of filing a petition is enough to induce the committee to act. Committees would rather keep control of the process by reporting out a bill on their own terms than relinquish control of the legislation to others. A recent study by political scientists Kathryn Pearson and Eric Schickler found that, in the modern era, legislators who have less of a stake in the committee system (less seniority with fewer good committee assignments) and minority-party members are more likely to sign discharge petitions.[28]

In the summer of 2018, DACA reemerged as a very public battle within the House Republican majority. With election season heating up, moderate Republicans, particularly those facing reelection in districts where Democrat Hillary Clinton performed well during the 2016 presidential election, feared that their opponents would capitalize on the lack of progress on immigration. They were most concerned about the perception of DACA recipients losing their legal status. Knowing that they would receive widespread support among chamber Democrats, a group of Republican lawmakers rolled out a petition to discharge a bill from the Rules Committee that would provide legal protections for DACA recipients along with a number of border security measures. As the petition racked up signatures (including those of nearly every Democrat) and looked like it would gain a chamber majority, House GOP leaders began intense negotiations that also folded in the policy preferences of the more conservative Freedom Caucus. At around the same time, the Trump administration was cracking down on the flow of unauthorized migrants crossing the southern border, many of whom were seeking asylum, based on a zero-tolerance policy issued by the Department of Justice. The administration's practice of separating minor children entering the United States from their family members became national news. Thanks to this attention, Republican moderates were able to leverage a floor vote for their immigration bill. However, their moderate bill (along with a more hardline Republican bill) failed to gain majority support in a full House vote.[29]

## Debate and Amendments in the House

The first stage of considering consequential legislation on the House floor is the adoption of the rule that the Rules Committee has crafted. To begin, the Speaker normally recognizes a majority-party member of the Rules Committee who then explains the special rule defining the potential limitations on debate and amendments. After no more than an hour's debate, the House votes to either adopt the rule and proceed to consideration of the bill or reject it and thus kill the bill before the chamber even gets started. It is uncommon for majority-party members to vote against a special rule; such an action would be seen as a rejection of the leadership's agenda.

Members of the majority party rarely defect from the leadership on procedural votes,[30] and in the modern era, it is uncommon for Speakers to bring forward legislation that would not garner the support of the majority (usually the vast majority) of their own party—a practice commonly referred to as the Hastert Rule. However, in recent years, defections have increased with the rise of the Tea Party and the Freedom Caucus in the Republican conference. Leaders frown on such defections, and a history of defections can be problematic for offending lawmakers seeking favors from the leadership.

After adopting the rule, the House proceeds to debate. Under its regular rules of procedure, sometimes called the one-hour rule, the House restricts the length of debate, the order of votes, and the opportunity for amendments. However, this may not provide sufficient time for the House to consider many important and controversial bills. Thus, the House much more frequently uses the **Committee of the Whole (COW)**, where the entire chamber acts as a committee for consideration of the bill. The rules under the COW allow for a smaller quorum size, or number of members that must be present to do business—100 members versus the typical 218 members—and greater flexibility in debate and amending. Although the particulars are often specified in the special rule (that is, the resolution coming out of the Rules Committee), the COW procedure generally provides each member with five minutes of debate time on amendments. Debate is controlled by floor managers, who are often the leaders on the bill's committee of jurisdiction (its chair or subcommittee chair and the associated ranking minority member).

Amendments are considered one at a time. **Germaneness**, the criterion used to limit debate and changes to only those items directly related to the bill at hand, is a much more severe restriction in the House than in the Senate. Usually the COW will consider amendments from the original committee of jurisdiction first and then others' recommendations—again, it all depends on the terms of the special rule. Ultimately, the House will likely vote on the amendments, but those adopted in the COW are simply recommendations for inclusion in the bill's final draft.

At the end of a bill's consideration, the COW will "rise and report," effectively no longer operating under the COW rules and returning to the formal House rules. It then proceeds to a formal vote. Often the House will officially include the recommended amendments, usually by simple voice vote, and then move to the final stages of passage. The final stages often entail an initial "motion to recommit" the bill to the originating committee, usually from a member of the minority party. This motion, if passed, would effectively kill the bill, although sometimes it includes a list of the changes the chamber would like to see. More often than not, bills that make it to this stage do not get recommitted, and thus the House proceeds to vote on adopting the bill.

## SENATE FLOOR AND UNANIMITY: A DIFFERENT KIND OF PLACE

When it comes to consequential legislation, the Senate, thanks to its standing rules, is more permissive than the House. Whereas the House relies on majoritarian procedures, much of the power to determine the fate of bills in the Senate, in theory at least, resides in the hands of its individual members. The Senate is built on the collective experience and knowledge of its members and their autonomy to deliberate, compromise, and reach agreements without depending on party or coalition leadership for direction and coordination. Today, Senate procedure is organized through a combination of rules and precedents built over time around the rights and privileges of its individual members, who are all positioned to play a role in policy making.

There is much for the Senate to do—from meeting constitutional and statutory obligations to responding to the demands of the public, interest groups, agencies, and the president—and relatively scarce time to complete the work. As a practical matter, the Senate could not effectively function if it had to give in to the whims of every individual on every issue up for debate. For this reason, delaying tactics are likely to be most effective at the end of a session, when there is a pressing need to complete tasks.

However, the need to complete important tasks can also serve as a motivator not to employ delaying tactics. As one long-time observer of the Senate noted,

"The legislative process on the Senate floor reflects a balance between the rights guaranteed to Senators under the standing rules and the willingness of Senators to forego exercising some of these rights in order to expedite the conduct of business."[31] Ultimately, the success or failure of the Senate as a governing body depends on its members not exercising their prerogative powers in every instance or with every disagreement. To a much greater degree than the House, the Senate is built on compromise. Therefore, its functioning in many ways relies on its members' willingness to be accommodating.

## Unanimous Consent Agreements in the Senate

Like the House, the Senate has developed a set of practices for its most important legislation so that it is not beholden to its prescribed calendar system. But because of its permissive rules of engagement and prerogative powers, the Senate has for most of its existence honored one critical difference: all senators must at least tacitly acquiesce in proceeding to consideration of any matter at hand. This is the notion of unanimous consent (explained above).

A unanimous consent agreement (UCA) for consequential legislation allows the Senate to avoid chamber rules that would otherwise bog it down. UCAs are usually the result of a negotiation between the majority and minority leaders, often with input from the partisan leadership of the relevant committee(s). In many ways, UCAs are the Senate's version of special rules, defining the terms of debate on a bill. However, unlike the House, the Senate faces few rules that limit the prerogative powers of individual senators. There are no effective limits on debate in the Senate (and while there is a limit of two speeches per senator per question per legislative day, this rule is rarely enforced). Therefore, the UCA can structure the time of debate, the necessary amendments, and the timing of a vote.

In short, the UCA is a necessary informal modification that helps the chamber complete needed legislation and provides senators with a rough sense of the chamber's schedule, which helps them plan their own time. The critical difference from floor procedures in the House is the unanimity required in the Senate. Any senator can object (refuse to grant consent), in which case the body lacks an agreement regarding how it will proceed with consideration of a bill. Thus individual senators have substantial power to hold up consideration of legislation. For example, Senator Rand Paul (R-Ky.) forced a very brief government shutdown in February 2018 when he initially refused to agree to a UCA on a spending bill, citing the bill's lack of fiscal restraint.[32] However, it is rare for the Senate majority leader to offer a UCA until all senators concerned have had an opportunity to inform their leaders that they find it acceptable.

These prerogative powers mean that any senator can bring almost anything in the chamber to a halt. And the threat of such a stoppage is often enough to spur some accommodation. Bill sponsors who meet resistance usually try to resolve it in one of two ways: (1) they negotiate with the aggrieved lawmakers to accommodate their demands, or (2) they accept that the chamber is at an impasse and move on to other important legislation that the Senate needs to consider.

In the mid-1970s the Senate, under Majority Leader Mike Mansfield (D-Mont.), developed the **two-track system** for considering legislation, in which two or more pieces of legislation may be considered at the same time. Thus the Senate, most often through agreement between the majority and minority leaders (although also possible through UCAs), can continue considering important legislation even during a filibuster. The two-track system permits the chamber to address critical or time-sensitive bills without grinding to a complete standstill over opposition to a single bill. However, with the chamber able to continue lawmaking by diverting around the legislative blockage, the obstruction tactic becomes less costly and more likely to occur and succeed.

## Germaneness in the Senate

The Senate does not have the same restrictions on germaneness that exist in the House, meaning that senators may offer practically any amendment to a bill being considered on the chamber floor (to the extent allowed by the relevant consent agreement).[33] As a practical matter, amendments can help to move forward a piece of legislation that has stalled at the committee stage or is otherwise difficult to advance. While the Senate may get around reluctant committees by using methods similar to the House's discharge petition, the far more common practice is to attach a bill as a nongermane amendment (otherwise known as a **rider**) to an existing bill.

## Withholding Consent: Filibusters and Holds

In recent years, lawmakers have been increasingly disinclined to agree to unanimous consent agreements, thus implicitly threatening to extend debate on a bill. This withholding of consent may result from something related to the bill itself, or it may be driven by a different matter entirely. Senators have two general ways to withhold consent: filibusters and holds.

By definition, a **filibuster** is any tactic that blocks a measure on the Senate floor from coming to a vote. It often takes the form of a single lawmaker's refusal to end debate by making a long, uninterrupted speech. The filibuster is possible for two reasons: (1) chamber rules require the presiding officer to

In 2013, Senator Ted Cruz (R-Tex.) spoke for 21 hours on the Senate floor, urging his colleagues to vote against funding the Affordable Care Act. While this filibuster did not change the outcome of the vote, it was a symbolic gesture in defiance of the bill.

recognize all senators wishing to speak, and (2) the Senate lacks any formal provision regarding time limits on debate.

Once recognized, the senator may speak at length, without yielding the floor, but must remain standing and speak continuously. Senate precedent prohibits members from yielding the floor to each other, and while the Senate does not always observe this restriction during the normal conduct of business, it is more likely to be insisted upon during the extended debate of a filibuster. In most cases, senators are not required to keep the debate germane to the topic at hand, so filibustering speeches may be very wide ranging, including the occasional reading of the phonebook or Dr. Seuss's *Green Eggs and Ham*.[34] Senate rules do permit other senators to ask questions during a filibuster. Of course, the Senate being the Senate, questions can take quite a bit of time to formulate and thus a friendly colleague may be able to provide a filibustering senator some relief with the articulation of a very long question.

Filibusters are often scheduled to reduce disruptions to the Senate's normal functioning and to increase the cost of conducting the obstruction. However, scheduling can work to the filibustering senator's advantage. It is not unusual for filibusters to continue into the night or even overnight, often requiring cots to be brought to the Senate for members. Proponents of the measure must be able to maintain a quorum at any time. If there is no quorum, then the Senate must adjourn, providing some relief to those filibustering. The longest actual filibuster to date occurred in 1957 in Senator Strom Thurmond's (D-S.C.) 24-hour speech attempting to thwart the Civil Rights Act of 1957.

A more informal version of the filibuster—informal in that it is not specifically ensconced in chamber rules—is the **hold**. By requesting a hold on a bill, senators express their opposition to the bill's proceeding to chamber consideration.[35] A hold registers a senator's intention to object to any unanimous consent request for consideration of the measure. As a matter of practice, this maneuver, sometimes called the "silent filibuster," is recognized by the majority leader. The hold is derived from a very old courtesy extended to senators in the days of horse travel, when senators often needed time to return to Washington to cast their votes.[36]

The hold usually occurs on less salient legislation and may be intended only to ensure that the senator requesting the hold is informed that a matter will be coming up for debate. An unusual aspect of this obstruction tactic is that the holder's name is kept secret. Party leaders keep "hold lists" and never release them to the public. It is not unheard of for a senator to hold up Senate business—sometimes quite important action—in order to accomplish a completely different goal.[37] For example, Senator Richard Shelby (R-Ala.) put a hold on the confirmation process of at least 70 of President Obama's nominees in a dispute over defense earmarks for his state. When his obstruction made the news, Shelby relented on all but a few of the nominations.[38]

In 2007, the Senate passed a bill banning secret holds that last longer than six days. However, that new law did not put an end to the practice. To get around the ban, two or more senators can pass the hold back and forth in a "rolling hold" that keeps their names secret.

## Cloture

The Senate is not always held hostage to the preferences and desires of one or two uncooperative lawmakers. Rather, a supermajoritarian threshold allows the chamber to move beyond most blockages. For regular legislation, the threshold to limit debate (or invoke **cloture**) is three-fifths of the members, or 60 senators. A cloture petition can be filed with the signature of 16 members. On the second calendar day after the petition is filed a roll call vote on the cloture motion is triggered, and the motion is not debatable. If invoked, cloture does not completely terminate consideration of the matter, but it limits additional debate to 30 hours. Under cloture, only germane amendments are in order.

This limit on debate in the Senate was established in 1917. Initially, the threshold to invoke cloture was two-thirds (67 votes). In 1975, the Senate lowered the threshold to three-fifths (60 votes). This supermajority threshold reinforces compromise and accommodation in the Senate. In most instances, ending a filibuster means conceding to the preferences of at least some of the more centrist members of the minority party. Only twice in the modern cloture era has a party had a large enough majority by itself to break a filibuster. Both times it was the Democrats, who had a supermajority of 61 members from 1975 to 1978 and 60 members for a few months in 2009 (the Affordable Care Act was passed during this period).

Recently, the threshold to invoke cloture was lowered again—by precedent, not by a change to chamber rules. In 2013, the Democrats sought a change to address the Senate's unwillingness to approve President Obama's lower-court judicial nominees. Majority Leader Harry Reid (D-Nev.) thus lowered the necessary votes for cloture to a simple majority on votes for executive branch nominations and federal court nominations below the Supreme Court. This change was termed the "nuclear option" because it upended many years of Senate precedent. Just a few years later, the tables turned, and a Democratic-controlled Senate with a Democratic president (Obama) became a Republican-controlled Senate with a Republican president (Trump). The GOP played its "nuclear" card in 2017 when it extended the simple-majority threshold to Supreme Court nominations. The Republicans used this change to confirm President Trump's Supreme Court nominee Neil Gorsuch and subsequent nominations of Brett Kavanaugh and Amy Coney Barrett.

As of now, the three-fifths threshold still stands on most legislation and changes to the chamber's rules, upholding the Senate's long-held notions of deliberation and compromise. But one person's standard for accommodation is another's undemocratic decree. Senators who take advantage of the supermajoritarianism of the Senate when in the minority often complain when the tables have turned and they are in the majority—and a small group of legislators from the other party are thwarting their will.

---

## THEN AND NOW
## FILIBUSTERS AND CLOTURE

The use of the filibuster dates back to 1806, when the Senate eliminated the rule that allowed the "previous question" to be called to a vote. Without this rule, the chamber had no majoritarian means of closing debate and therefore relied on unanimous consent to bring a matter to a final vote. Over time, the use of the filibuster has evolved considerably. Because filibusters (and other delaying tactics) come in different forms, identifying what is or is not a filibuster is not easy. Recall that a filibuster is effectively the extension of normal Senate practices, in this case debate, to prevent legislation from moving forward. Senators may engage in such obstructionist tactics without specifically identifying the action as a filibuster. Therefore, until recently, there was no single list of Senate filibusters. Moreover, the intent to filibuster without actually engaging in it—the hold—can create the same outcome. Understanding the use of filibusters and trends over time requires some novel data-collection efforts.

**FIGURE 7.2**   Number of Filibusters, 57th–112th Congresses (1901–2013)

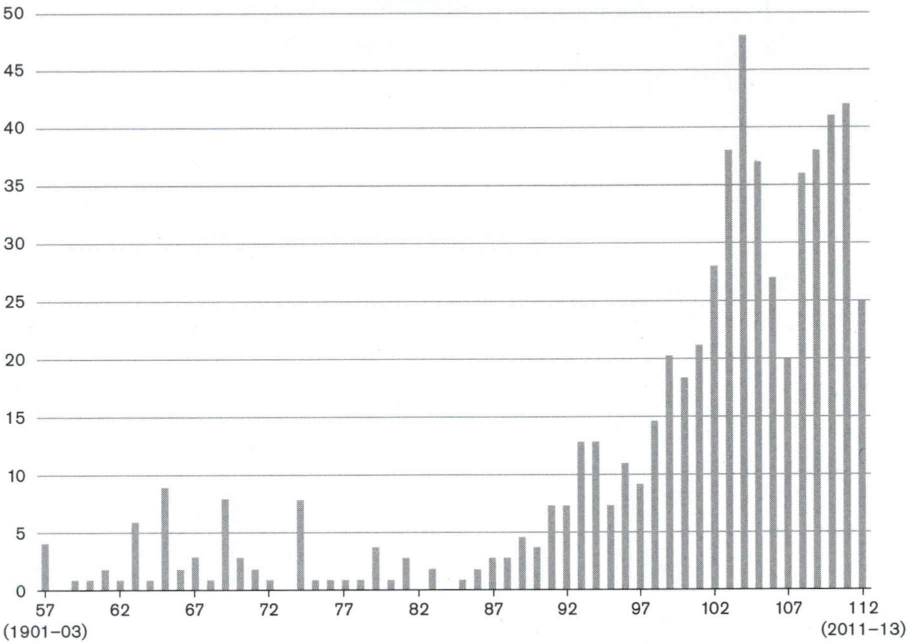

Gregory Koger. 2010. *Filibustering: A Political History of Obstruction in the House and Senate.* Chicago: IL: University of Chicago Press. 107, with updates by Gregory Koger through the 112th Congress.

The best-known catalog of filibuster activity, compiled by political scientist Gregory Koger, resulted from an extensive search through public mentions of filibusters, mostly in the media.[39] Koger found that filibusters were relatively unheard of in the Senate in its early years. By the 1870s, about 20 bills in total had faced a filibuster in the Senate, many related to Reconstruction or civil rights issues. By the turn of the nineteenth century, the practice had tapered off considerably under increased public scrutiny of Washington lawmakers.

The use of filibusters remained rather low through the 1960s, with only a handful of measures facing this obstruction each congressional term. But within these low numbers were some intense legislative fights, particularly with respect to anti-lynching and civil rights legislation. Perhaps the most controversial fili-buster of that era was attempted against what eventually became the Civil Rights Act of 1964. In the politically charged public debate over this landmark policy achievement, many feared the consequences if southern segregationist senators used a filibuster to kill the bill.

Filibusters have become much more common in the last few decades (Figure 7.2). Senate historian Donald Ritchie dates the increasing use of the filibuster to the Democrats in the late 1980s, when Majority Leader Robert Byrd (D-W.Va.) used it to reassert the Democratic Party's agenda after it regained a chamber majority in 1987 and faced a Republican president, Ronald Reagan, with a very different set of priorities.[40]

Cloture motions provide another view of obstructionist tactics in the Senate. Scholars debate what a count of cloture motions tells us. Multiple cloture motions can be filed on the same obstructed bill, and the majority can file cloture motions in anticipation of an obstruction that has not yet occurred. Nevertheless, because Senate leaders unquestionably prefer the certainty and structure of a UCA, the cloture motion becomes a necessity when a UCA is not possible. Thus, while not synonymous with obstruction, cloture motions indicate the degree to which the majority sees the need to move bills forward absent a UCA.[41]

Figure 7.3 shows the trend in cloture motions filed over the past several decades. The rapid increase is obvious through the 1980s and 1990s, but one of the most severe spikes in cloture motions occurred in the last two years of the Bush presidency (2007–08), after the Democrats took control of the Senate. According to congressional expert Norman Ornstein, all the legislative initiatives considered in the Senate at that point were coming from Democrats, and the Republicans were trying to slow down or kill them. Republican filibuster threats were "like throwing molasses in the road."[42] Democrats doubled the number of cloture motions, with one in five roll call votes that term aimed simply at cutting off debate. (Note a second uptick after the Democrats exercised the nuclear option in 2013.)

What explains the increase in continuous debate/filibustering as a delaying tactic? First, the Senate has far more on its agenda today than it has ever had before. These time pressures mean that delaying tactics can be very effective. Because a supermajority is so difficult to achieve, filibustering members will likely be granted concessions, otherwise the legislative proposal will be killed. Second, through the accepted use of holds and the multiple track system, Senate leaders have simplified the process of engaging in these delaying tactics, severely reducing their cost to the perpetrating lawmakers. Finally, in an era of strong public opinion, senators have discovered that they can gain considerable attention by engaging in a filibuster on an important issue.[43] Senator Ted Cruz (R-Tex.) in 2013 engaged in a 21-hour filibuster of a critical appropriations bill as a stunt to highlight opposition to Obamacare. His obstruction resulted in a several-day government shutdown, which many of his conservative colleagues felt was unnecessary and futile. A year and a half later, Cruz announced his candidacy for the presidency.

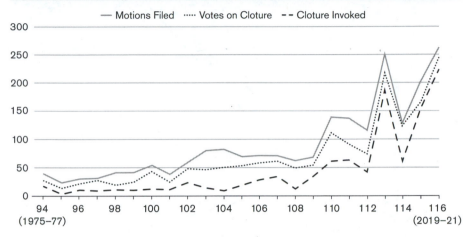

**FIGURE 7.3**   Cloture Motions, 94th–116th Congresses (1975–2021)

U.S. Senate, www.senate.gov/pagelayout/reference/cloture_motions/clotureCounts.htm (accessed 10/15/20).

## Critical Thinking

1.  Do opportunities for obstruction in the Senate, such as the filibuster or hold, provide senators with too much power to impede the progress of legislation? Or is it sufficient that a supermajority of senators can invoke cloture to overrule a small group of obstructionists?
2.  We have seen many more cloture motions in the Senate in recent years. Is it best that the majority party now almost always seeks some degree of agreement from a small group of senators from the minority party?
3.  What effect does a 60-vote threshold have on the quality and content of legislation? How would the content of laws be different if the filibuster on policy proposals were eliminated?

## Amendments in the Senate

Once a bill reaches the Senate floor, it is open to amendments at any time, but the boundaries of the amending process are largely defined by UCAs (or potentially the germaneness provisions of a cloture motion). A bill can be amended in a variety of ways: (1) changing the text of the bill (first-degree amendment), (2) changing the text of an amendment (second-degree

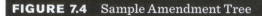

**FIGURE 7.4**   Sample Amendment Tree

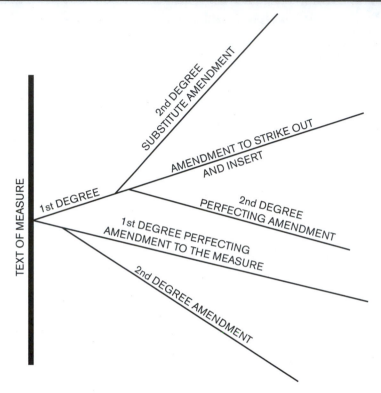

Christopher Davis. September 16, 2015. "The Amending Process in the Senate." *CRS Report for Congress.* Washington, DC: Congressional Research Service.

amendment), (3) striking language from a bill, (4) inserting new language into a bill, or (5) replacing the entire text of a bill with new language. Recall that Senate amendments are not required to be germane to the bill (germaneness applies only to appropriations or budget measures, or bills under cloture or a restrictive UCA), so amendments in the Senate can change the legislation significantly or tack on unrelated riders.

The Senate relies on diagrams (like the one shown in Figure 7.4) that define the order in which amendments are offered and voted on. These diagrams, called amendment trees, vary with the type of amendments being considered. This process has developed over time into a set of precedents that often severely limit the number of amendments to a bill that is up for consideration (the cap is usually 11).

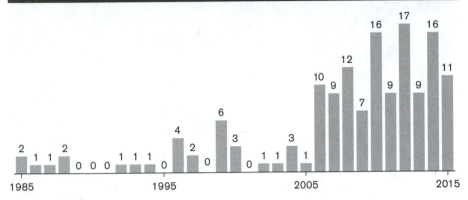

**FIGURE 7.5**   Instances of Filling the Amendment Tree in the Senate, 1985–2015

Congressional Research Service, www.crs.gov (accessed 7/16/18).

In the process of amending legislation, the Senate has begun to look much like the House, with majority leadership limiting the minority's involvement by restricting their amendments or precluding them altogether. Because the Senate majority leader has the right to be recognized before any other senator and can offer as many amendments as he or she wishes, it is possible for the majority leader to fill the entire amendment tree, thereby blocking anyone else from offering amendments.[44]

The majority leader might seek to control the amendment process for a number of reasons: to prevent a potentially controversial amendment from being offered, to gain bargaining leverage in pursuit of a UCA, or to move the bill along more quickly without any additions or changes. As Figure 7.5 shows, this approach to Senate agenda control gained considerable traction under Majority Leader Reid after the Democrats regained control of the chamber following the 2006 election.

In 2014, Reid filled the amendment tree on an unemployment insurance extension bill to prevent Republicans from using it as an opportunity to force votes repealing portions of the Affordable Care Act (Obamacare). Reid's amendments were simply filler, making mostly meaningless alterations to the bill, such as changing the enactment date by one day, then two days, and then three days. Mitch McConnell (R-Ky.), the majority leader after the Republicans took control of the Senate following the 2016 election, continued using this tactic to control the Senate floor agenda until Democrats took control of the chamber in 2021.[45]

Conference committees, like the one pictured here, were once essential to rendering identical legislation to pass in the House of Representatives and the Senate. Today, very few pieces of legislation are left to be decided on by conference committees.

## RECONCILING DIFFERENCES BETWEEN CHAMBERS

After the House and Senate have crafted their own versions of the same bill, they must reconcile those differences. Recall that the presentation clause of the U.S. Constitution includes the phrase "every Bill which shall have passed the House of Representatives and the Senate," which is interpreted to mean a bill passed *in identical form*. Reconciling the two versions of the bill can be a daunting task. Nonetheless, the two chambers usually are able to bridge their divide and come up with mutually agreed upon language. About 97 percent of bills that pass both the House and Senate in one form or another eventually get enacted into law.

The textbook process for reconciling House and Senate differences has traditionally been the **conference committee** (see Chapter 5). This committee, usually composed of members of the originating House and Senate panels,

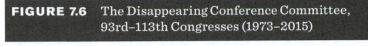

**FIGURE 7.6** The Disappearing Conference Committee, 93rd–113th Congresses (1973–2015)

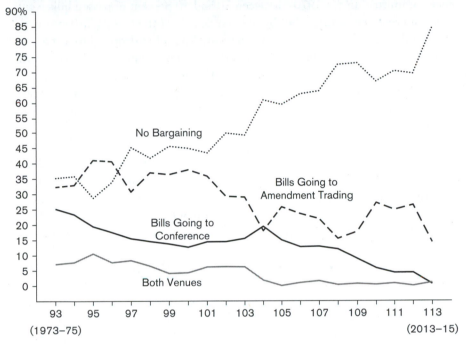

Josh Ryan. 2018. *The Congressional Endgame: Interchamber Bargaining and Compromise.* Chicago: University of Chicago Press.

negotiates the differences in the two chambers' versions of the same legislation after they have been passed. The committee's goal is to come up with a compromise. The negotiations are meant to be constrained to the "scope of differences," with the committee bargaining only on those aspects where the House and Senate bills differ. But determining where that scope ends is often a difficult matter, and if conferees must interpret this boundary broadly to reach an agreement, then so be it. Once an agreement is struck, the conferees bring the bill back to their respective chambers as a conference report. They offer the conference report to their chamber as a take-it-or-leave-it proposal, with no amendments or changes allowed.

For many years, it was generally believed that the higher the profile of the legislation, the more likely that House and Senate differences would be ironed out in a conference committee. However, recent decades have seen a disruption in this process. Political scientist Josh Ryan examined all the possible avenues that the two chambers used, going back to the mid-1970s, to iron out their differences on legislation that was enacted (Figure 7.6). First and foremost, he found a severe drop-off in the percentage of successful bills that go to a conference committee. In the 1970s, between 30 and 40 percent of passed bills went to a conference committee, but by the first decade of the twenty-first century, this number was down to less than 5 percent. And it has dropped to just a handful (fewer than five bills) in each of the last four congressional terms.[46] In short, congressional leaders no longer leave the process of negotiating agreements across the two bodies to some other entity (committee members). Now, even with the most important legislation, conference committees are not part of the post-passage bargaining.

Moreover, all forms of bargaining between the chambers have decreased. Occasionally, the two chambers engage in more informal negotiations, trading amendments back and forth until the two versions of the bill look identical. The majority leadership often does this horse-trading, but sometimes prominent committee members are also involved. The use of this tactic has decreased, too, however, with only about 20 percent of successful bills using amendment trading.

Perhaps the most important part of Figure 7.6 is the upward trend of bill adoption in Congress with no bargaining whatsoever. Now, for the most part, one chamber simply adopts the other chamber's version of the bill with no conference and no horse-trading, just simple capitulation. Why? As lawmaking in both chambers has become more fraught—with more partisan polarization and fewer lawmakers willing to give way on any ideological ground—extending deliberation and bargaining makes reconciling differences more precarious. If a bill is going to make it through the legislative gauntlet, the chamber with the greatest challenges will often have to adopt the other chamber's bill simply to get something done.

## CONCLUSION

This chapter has highlighted some of the major features of the postcommittee policy-making practices in the House and Senate. The two chambers differ not only in terms of the intent of the Framers, who purposely equipped them differently, but also because of how the two bodies have evolved over more than two centuries. The House, with its more orderly structure, grants greater control to the majority party to direct the flow of legislation and advance its agenda. The Senate, in contrast, is more egalitarian in its design, providing more privileges to its members, who can influence Senate operations by obstructing legislation.

Recent political developments, particularly increased partisan polarization and more intense competition for majority control of both chambers, have created a new era of procedural politics in the House and Senate. In the House, the increase in partisanship tracks almost directly with the increase in restrictive rules for consideration of bills on the chamber floor. The majority-party leadership is keeping a tighter and tighter grip on what legislation looks like and what kinds of amendments the chamber can consider. The Senate has also changed. While Senate majority leaders have slightly tightened their grip on floor amendments, the Senate has also experienced a very sharp increase in member independence through the use of obstructionist maneuvers. Although the Senate has always been a body governed by its members' privileges, the perpetual threat of a filibuster means that almost everything that goes through the Senate must now surpass the three-fifths threshold of support.

The evolution of the two chambers over the nation's history suggests that Congress's operations will continue to change with the times. Indeed, nearly every election in recent years has brought about significant surprises, with implications for Congress's composition and its members' incentives. We should expect further changes and continued evolution in the way policy is made in Congress.

## Discussion Questions

1. The Framers intentionally constructed the membership of the House and Senate differently. What were those differences? Did they result in law-making bodies with contrasting perspectives? Do the House and Senate today reflect the distinctions that the Framers intended?
2. The propriety and utility of the Senate filibuster became a subject of debate during the 2020 presidential election. Should the Senate eliminate the ability to filibuster entirely?
3. Does the Senate majority leader's ability to restrict floor amendments (by filling the amendment tree) make the Senate operate too much like the House in terms of majority-party control? Should this power be restricted?
4. What does the almost total disappearance of conference committees mean—if anything—for the quality and content of legislation?
5. Congressional policy making has always been hard, given the separation of powers and checks and balances, and with greater polarization in recent years it seems to be getting only harder. Is this a cause for concern? Why or why not?

# 8

## The Legislative Effectiveness of Congress and Its Members: Governing, Policy Making, and the Budget

During his reelection campaign in 1948, President Harry Truman railed against the "do-nothing" Republican Congress. He was determined to win reelection by campaigning against a Congress that he characterized as uncooperative and wary of supporting his policy agenda. The strategy worked. Truman won reelection, and the Democrats recaptured a majority in the House and the Senate. The moniker stuck, and the lawmakers who served that term would forever be known as members of the "Do-Nothing 80th Congress." Yet a close examination of the accomplishments of those two years reveals a different picture. The achievements of that Congress included statutes that authorized the Marshall Plan for reconstructing Europe after World War II, the Taft-Hartley Labor Management Relations Act to rein in trade unions, legislation to unify the armed services into the

In recent years, we have seen multiple government shutdowns and seemingly intractable partisanship in Congress. Does this mean that Congress, as a whole, is not doing its job effectively? What about its individual members?

Department of Defense and create the Central Intelligence Agency, and adoption of critical economic and military aid to countries (such as Greece and Turkey) threatened by the Soviet Union. The 80th Congress (1947–49) also produced a constitutional amendment limiting presidents to two terms.

Unsurprisingly, many presidents as well as members of Congress themselves have used the perception of an unproductive and obstinate legislature to justify their own necessity in Washington—often saying, "Elect me, because I'll go to Washington to get things done!" (Interestingly, years later, many of the same lawmakers cite lack of progress in Washington as their reason for retiring.) Recently, the phrase "Do-Nothing Congress" was resurrected to describe Congress during President Barack Obama's last term.[1] It had also been used to describe the prior 113th Congress (2013–15),[2] and in the term immediately preceding that, longtime Congress observer and scholar Norman Ornstein declared the 112th Congress (2011–13) the "Worst. Congress. Ever."[3] Even by December 2017—only halfway through the 115th Congress and a full ten months before the 2018 midterm elections—Democrats had already signaled that they were planning to use the donothing label against the Republican majority.[4] You get the picture. For a long time, journalists, commentators, scholars, and even lawmakers themselves have noted Congress's incapacity for fulfilling its role as the nation's central governing body.

But is Congress really that dysfunctional? How do we measure whether Congress is doing its job? Certainly, it is easy to see how many bills Congress enacts, but does this measure effectiveness? It could be the case that lawmakers are filling their time with a great deal of legislative fluff—for example, commemorative and symbolic legislation—that does little to advance and adapt federal policy to evolving circumstances. Likewise, how do we know if individual lawmakers are effective at their jobs? And what does it even mean to be effective? Simply being in Washington does not necessarily mean representatives are making a difference serving their constituents or the nation as a whole. How can we measure congressional accomplishment at the individual level?

To tackle these questions, we divide this chapter into two sections: institutional effectiveness and individual effectiveness in Congress. First, we focus on the macro view of Congress's governing responsibility. Accordingly, we conceive of "effectiveness" as the collective success of Congress as a lawmaking body. Reflecting on the definition of governing presented in Chapter 1—the ability of Congress to keep the country and its government functioning in a competent manner—we ask, Is Congress meeting this obligation? The second part of the chapter explores the effectiveness of individual senators and representatives in terms of participating in the lawmaking process and representing their constituents.

In most of the other chapters in this book, we have asked you to think about *how* Congress works. Here we ask, *Does* Congress work?

## INSTITUTIONAL EFFECTIVENESS

To explore the effectiveness of Congress as a lawmaking and governing institution, we essentially examine its performance over time. Interest in studying this aspect of Congress goes back for decades, and "performance" has mainly been defined as an analysis of the branch's institutional operations, where its output or productivity is considered in terms of categories such as lawmaking, oversight, and constituent service.[5] We analyze constituent service and congressional oversight elsewhere in this book (Chapters 4 and 10, respectively), so here we focus on lawmaking and governing performance. We concentrate on the range of activities Congress must perform to keep government operating and to meet its own fiscal and statutory obligations. These activities include authorizations, annual budgets and appropriations, monitoring of the federal debt, and the wider matter of enacting major legislation to meet broader concerns of government and citizens. The primary question guiding our examination of congressional effectiveness is, How well does Congress meet its responsibilities in each of these categories?

## Authorizations

Authorizing legislation is one of the most important responsibilities of Congress. **Authorizations** establish or renew federal programs, agencies, policies, and other various projects, or they adjust the purpose or mission of an existing program or agency. In most instances, the authorization alone does not provide funding for the programs or agencies it authorizes. Rather, **appropriations** legislation specifies the exact funding level of programs and agencies previously authorized, granting agencies the authority to incur obligations and make payments out of the federal treasury. The goal of separating these two decisions is to ensure that policy disagreements do not interfere with a program or agency's funding.

Authorizations can be either short-term (a matter of a few months or years) or permanent (no statutory expiration date). In most cases, Congress enacts authorizations for a limited period—usually three to six years—but the authorization can be as long as a quarter-century or more. According to congressional rules, when an authorization expires, funds are not to be appropriated and agencies responsible for implementing the expired program should cease their operations (though Congress can make exceptions, which we discuss later in this chapter).

The use of short-term authorizations goes back to the Framers. Alexander Hamilton argued in the *Federalist Papers* that such short-term legislation serves as a safeguard, allowing groups to sound alarms on policies they deem unfit. While these short-term measures were used in the nation's early days, they became commonplace only in the 1960s and 1970s.

Beyond the loftier goals of providing a periodic safeguard against problematic statutes and allowing Congress to update existing programs and legislation according to changing circumstances, short-term authorizations were also attractive for more practical political reasons. Forcing Congress to renew the authorization of many programs gives members of the authorizing committees some control over the agencies within their purview. Without the requirement to renew legislation that enables agencies and programs to exist, Congress's year-to-year influence over executive branch departments would reside with the Appropriations Committee members and their annual appropriations legislation.[6]

In addition, as Congress's governing responsibilities ballooned in the post–World War II period, multiyear authorizations with staggered expiration dates made the agendas of House and Senate committees more manageable and predictable. Thus, except in cases of crisis, lawmakers could put off stakeholders' persistent demands and proposals for policy changes until committees and their staff were prepared to consider the various aspects of the relevant policies.[7] Some scholars have even argued that by forcing the reconsideration of laws important to key corporate stakeholders (who often have deep pockets and extensive government-relations operations), lawmakers are simply "extracting rent" or ensuring a flow of campaign contributions from these stakeholders, who wish to influence legislative decisions.[8] For example, the Gallo family, long the owners of the largest winemaking company in the world, became top contributors to the campaign committee of Senator Bob Dole (and two of his sponsored foundations) in the 1980s and 1990s. The family's goal was to protect a deferment in federal estate tax written specifically for them. This tax carve-out was continually up for review, and Dole had been the chair of the Senate Finance Committee (which is responsible for reviewing tax legislation) and Senate minority leader.[9]

Placing so many government programs on short-term authorizations requires future Congresses to update and renew them with some degree of regularity. In some instances, the laws contain a small number of expirations or a singular expiration that is critical to the existence of a program, such as the tax on the chemical and petroleum industries contained in the Comprehensive Environmental Response, Compensation, and Liability Act of 1980 (also known as Superfund), which provides federal authority over and funding for hazardous-waste cleanup. The massive Department of Defense authorization bill wraps up all the major matters regarding the department into one piece of legislation that needs to be authorized annually. In other instances, sizable laws contain dozens or even hundreds of expiring provisions that fund a wide variety of programs (such as the Farm Bill or the Highway Bill) that have to be reauthorized every four to five years.

By one estimate, nearly a quarter of federal policy must undergo periodic reauthorization, making up an enormous proportion of the legislative work Congress performs.[10] With hundreds of important expiring laws in need of review each legislative term, the rate at which these laws are successfully renewed on time can serve as a good measurement of legislative productivity and accomplishment. It bears mentioning that expired programs and agencies that do not get reauthorized don't just simply go away; they can continue to exist through annual appropriations (more on this below). If Congress is not reauthorizing the plethora of federal programs, authorizing committees are abdicating their responsibility and putting governing on autopilot while new national and world issues, events, and circumstances emerge.

When Congress is on autopilot, problematic programs can linger for years, wasting money and not fulfilling their original mission. One of the clearest examples of this problem is the Endangered Species Act. Originally enacted in 1973 to prevent the extinction and help in the recovery of endangered and threatened species, the law was last reauthorized in 1988, and its spending authority expired in 1992. Since then, difficulties and concerns with the law have racked up. Congress has been able to enact only very minor amendments to the law (mainly having to do with the Department of Defense), with no real substantive updates.

Why doesn't Congress reauthorize programs on time? The reasons can vary. Sometimes lawmakers are trying to avoid the controversy of the program or agency itself. For example, the Federal Election Commission—which oversees the always-controversial laws governing campaign finance—has not seen its authorizing legislation renewed since 1980. The Endangered Species Act has made nearly no progress toward renewal in decades because lawmakers in the two parties have opposing goals (Republicans want to roll back the government's authority to restrict the actions of private citizens and landowners, while Democrats want to update the law's language and protections to better account for new scientific findings regarding climate change).

For other agencies and programs, Congress might not act on a reauthorization simply because the agency is doing its job well. The Civil Rights Commission, with its duties of promoting understanding and enforcement of U.S. civil rights laws, has been cited as an example of "if it ain't broke, don't fix it."[11] And in other instances programs or laws are permitted to expire because they are no longer considered necessary. For example, in 2011 Congress permitted the expiration of decades-old federal subsidies to ethanol producers because, as a spokesperson for the industry stated, "the marketplace had evolved. The tax incentive is less necessary now."[12]

Sometimes, reauthorization is a victim of the broader political environment on Capitol Hill. For example, in the midst of the debt-ceiling crisis that gripped Washington in the summer of 2011, the Federal Aviation Administration's (FAA) authorization expired. While the expiration went largely unnoticed, mainly because suspension of this relatively uncontroversial agency did not ultimately halt air travel, it did disrupt FAA operations not directly related to air travel, such as the work of its construction contractors. Lawmakers were more interested in scoring political points over the debt-ceiling crisis and taking their summer recess in July than keeping FAA operations up and running.

Figure 8.1 illustrates Congress's growing problem with unauthorized programs and agencies. This figure accounts for the percentage of total discretionary spending that Congress has had to appropriate without proper authorization. As the figure shows, the percentage of federal spending that is unauthorized has increased significantly since the early 1990s.

What happens when Congress is unable to reauthorize a program or law? Government does not completely grind to a halt when one agency's authorization expires. If it is inclined to keep a program going, Congress can use a waiver in the appropriations to fund the program, even if it lacks an active authorization. Congress can also offer guidance to administrators through oversight hearings. This is what Congress has done for decades with the U.S. Fish and Wildlife Service and its administration of the Endangered Species Act. But funding a program is not the same as Congress governing responsibly. That short lapse in the FAA authorization (mentioned earlier) resulted in the temporary layoff of 4,000 FAA employees and halted construction across the country, affecting $2.5 billion in airport projects and 24,000 construction workers.[13]

**FIGURE 8.1** Percentage of Unauthorized Discretionary Spending, 1987–2019

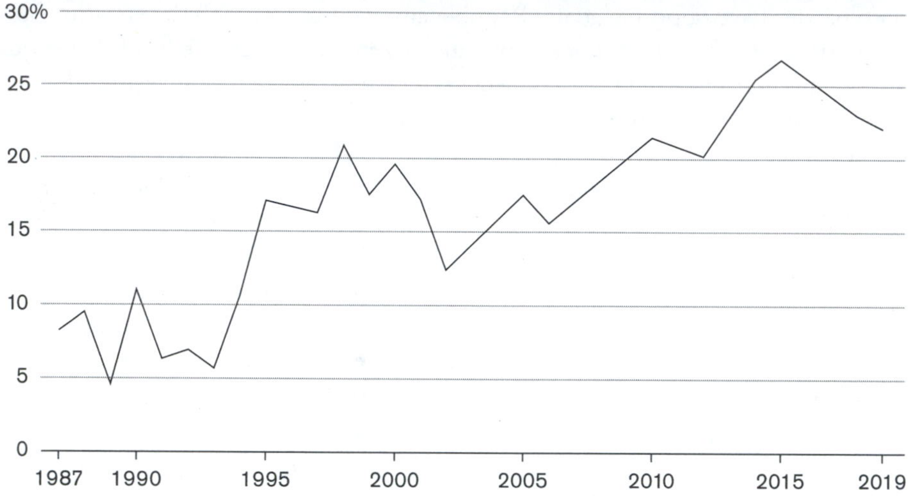

Note: Data for years in which appropriations or defense authorization bills were not passed promptly are excluded from the graph.

Politico, www.politico.com/agenda/story/2016/02/government-agencies-programs-unauthorized-000036 -000037 (accessed 6/19/18) and author's updates.

## Keeping the Lights On: The Congressional Budget and Appropriations Process

Among the most basic functions of Congress is its responsibility to approve spending for existing federal programs. It does so through a two-step process: budgeting (deciding the overall blueprint on spending) and appropriations (determining how much each individual program or agency can spend).

**STEP 1: THE BUDGET** The word "budget" is often bandied about loosely when referring to how Congress spends money. To be exact, there are really three elements of the budget process: authorizing legislation (already discussed), the budget resolution, and appropriations legislation. Since authorizations generally entail multiyear planning, the annual budget process mostly involves passing a budget resolution and appropriations bills.

For nearly a century, the president has started the budget process every February with a proposal for the entire federal budget, incorporating the administration's estimates for revenues and expenditures in the coming year, its projections for several years going forward, and the president's budget request for each agency. You

**TABLE 8.1**  Budget and Appropriations Timeline

| Date | Action |
|------|--------|
| First Monday in February | President submits budget to Congress. |
| February 15 | Congressional Budget Office submits economic and budget outlook report to budget committees. |
| Six weeks after president submits budget | Committees submit views and estimates to budget committees. |
| April 1 | Senate Budget Committee reports budget resolution. |
| April 15 | Congress completes action on budget resolution. |
| May 15 | Annual appropriations bills may be considered in the House, even if action on budget resolution has not been completed. |
| June 10 | House Appropriations Committee reports last annual appropriations bill. |
| June 15 | Congress completes reconciliation legislation (if required by budget resolution). |
| June 30 | House completes annual appropriations bills. |
| July 15 | President submits mid-session review of budget to Congress. |
| October 1 | Fiscal year begins. |

Bill Heniff Jr. March 20, 2008. "The Congressional Budget Process Timetable." *CRS Report for Congress.* Washington, DC: Congressional Research Service.

can think of this budget as the president's opening bid. Federal agencies offer additional information to committees in the form of a budget justification. (Table 8.1 shows a complete timeline of the budget and appropriations process.)

Congress's response over the course of the next several weeks includes hearings by the budget committees in both the House and Senate, reports on the proposed budget issued by the authorizing committees, and an important report from the Congressional Budget Office assessing the economy, along with revenue and expenditure projections.

By mid-April, the House and Senate are required to produce their **concurrent budget resolution** on the budget for the coming year. (Because it is a resolution and not a public law, it does not require the president's signature.) Think of the concurrent resolution as a target cap on overall spending meant to constrain Congress when it completes the appropriations bills. While the budget resolution is usually about a month late, some are considerably later, and in many recent years, Congress has not been able to pass a budget resolution at all (as in fiscal years 1999, 2003, 2005, 2007, 2011–15, 2019, and 2020). There are no

| TABLE 8.2 | Dates of Final Adoption of the Budget Resolution | | |
|---|---|---|---|
| Fiscal Year | Date Adopted | Fiscal Year | Date Adopted |
| 1976 | 05-14-1975 | 1999 | [none] |
| 1977 | 05-13-1976 | 2000 | 04-15-1999 |
| 1978 | 05-17-1977 | 2001 | 04-13-2000 |
| 1979 | 05-17-1978 | 2002 | 05-10-2001 |
| 1980 | 05-24-1979 | 2003 | [none] |
| 1981 | 06-12-1980 | 2004 | 04-11-2003 |
| 1982 | 05-21-1981 | 2005 | [none] |
| 1983 | 06-23-1982 | 2006 | 04-28-2005 |
| 1984 | 06-23-1983 | 2007 | [none] |
| 1985 | 10-01-1984 | 2008 | 05-17-2007 |
| 1986 | 08-01-1985 | 2009 | 06-05-2008 |
| 1987 | 06-27-1986 | 2010 | 04-29-2009 |
| 1988 | 06-24-1987 | 2011 | [none] |
| 1989 | 06-06-1988 | 2012 | [none] |
| 1990 | 05-18-1989 | 2013 | [none] |
| 1991 | 10-09-1990 | 2014 | [none] |
| 1992 | 05-22-1991 | 2015 | [none] |
| 1993 | 05-21-1992 | 2016 | 05-05-2015 |
| 1994 | 04-01-1993 | 2017 | 01-13-2017 |
| 1995 | 05-12-1994 | 2018 | 10-26-2017 |
| 1996 | 06-29-1995 | 2019 | [none] |
| 1997 | 06-13-1996 | 2020 | [none] |
| 1998 | 06-05-1997 | | |

real consequences for the budget being late, other than the absence of a coherent plan to guide the appropriations process. (For more details, see Table 8.2.)

**STEP 2: APPROPRIATIONS** While the budget resolution sets the context for overall spending, appropriations bills allow the Treasury to make payments for specific programs or agencies. Appropriations acts must be passed every year to fund the continued operation of federal departments, agencies, and various government activities.

The U.S. Constitution outlines the appropriations process in Article I, Section 9: "No money shall be drawn from the Treasury, but in Consequence of Appropriations made by Law." In effect, the Constitution declares that the process of spending money out of the Treasury is like any other statute enacted by the legislature. In laws passed over the years, Congress has reinforced this power of appropriation with other statutory provisions, including language stipulating that public funds may be used only for the purposes for which Congress appropriated the funds.

The appropriations process garners considerable attention because it serves as a flash point for battles between the two parties, between coalitions within Congress, and between governmental and nongovernmental stakeholders—but the appropriations process does not account for the majority of government expenses. An enormous proportion of federal spending is mandatory in that it must be incurred (it does not require annual appropriations), and the only thing that could change it would be an act of Congress. These obligatory spending responsibilities include interest on the national debt, contractual obligations, and (most prominently) entitlement spending. *Entitlement* programs—including large government programs such as Social Security, Medicare, veterans' compensation, Medicaid, and Temporary Assistance for Needy Families (TANF)—are mandatory because they rely on formulas whereby anyone who meets certain criteria receives the benefit. *Discretionary spending* is, by definition, not mandatory. It covers the costs of executive branch agencies, congressional offices, and international programs.

Figure 8.2 shows how the three major categories of federal spending have changed since the early 1960s. As these data demonstrate, the ratio of discretionary to mandatory federal spending—and thus the degree to which congressional appropriators influence how the government spends money—has changed dramatically in the last few decades. As the federal government adopted new entitlement programs in the 1960s (such as Medicare and Medicaid) and as the large baby-boom generation reached retirement age, the cost of mandatory spending programs increased from about one-third of total federal outlays to two-thirds.

How does Congress decide what to do with the remaining third of the government's money? The process of congressional appropriating effectively begins in the House of Representatives, which has constitutional authority to originate revenue bills—a privilege that has historically been extended to include appropriations bills. However, rather than wait to consider the House appropriations bills, Senate appropriators have, in recent years, frequently considered their own versions of appropriations bills simultaneously with their House counterparts. Starting in the second half of May, the various subcommittees of the House and Senate Appropriations Committees (Table 8.3) take action on the respective appropriations bills that coincide with their jurisdictions.

Members of Congress first consider appropriations bills in subcommittee. The process includes hearings, bill drafting, markup, and reporting.

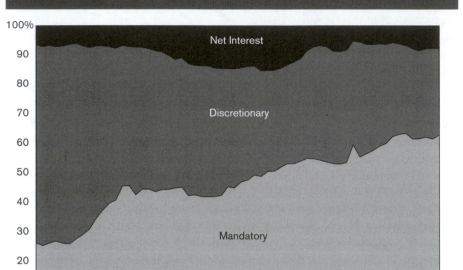

**FIGURE 8.2**  Percentage of Total Government Spending by Category, 1962–2022

Office of Management and Budget, "Historical Tables, Table 8.4: Outlays by Budget Enforcement Act Category as Percentages of GDP, 1962–2025," https://www.whitehouse.gov/omb/historical-tables/ (accessed 1/24/21).

Appropriations hearings focus on the relevant agencies' budget justifications and often include agency officials' testimonies. The subcommittee often solicits input from other members of Congress on programmatic spending levels and instructions to be tied to appropriations language. Each individual appropriations bill is then reported to the full Appropriations Committee for consideration. The Appropriations Committee's subsequent report is brought to the entire chamber. Both House and Senate Appropriations Committees are expected to have completed their consideration of these bills by July, just prior to Congress's summer recess, so that early fall can be used for chamber consideration and reconciliation of differences in House and Senate versions. However, delays in this process, driven by disputes over spending levels, have led to more frequent consolidation of the separate appropriations bills into large "omnibus" legislation.

After appropriations measures are reported by their respective chambers' committees, they are then considered on the House and Senate floors. This process, however, can be complicated by other factors. According to House and

| **TABLE 8.3** House Appropriations Subcommittees, 116th Congress (2019–21) |
| --- |
| Agriculture, Rural Development, Food and Drug Administration, and Related Agencies |
| Commerce, Justice, Science, and Related Agencies |
| Defense |
| Energy and Water Development, and Related Agencies |
| Financial Services and General Government |
| Homeland Security |
| Interior, Environment, and Related Agencies |
| Labor, Health and Human Services, Education, and Related Agencies |
| Legislative Branch |
| Military Construction, Veterans Affairs, and Related Agencies |
| State, Foreign Operations, and Related Programs |
| Transportation, Housing and Urban Development, and Related Agencies |

Senate rules, any program or agency needs an *authorization* from Congress, defining the terms of its existence and its budgetary cap, before it can receive an appropriation. But as we have seen, authorization often faces its own roadblocks, and lawmakers often cannot afford to have programs simply go away just because rules require authorization before appropriation. In these cases, Congress will pass a waiver that allows funding to be enacted even though the authorization is no longer in effect. Essentially, members of Congress are continuing a program or agency through appropriations but without a proper authorization.

Once each individual appropriations measure is debated and adopted by the respective chambers, the textbook process instructs the House and Senate to use conference committees to reconcile their differences. Recall from Chapter 7 that conferees for these panels are normally drawn from the relevant committees of jurisdiction, in this case the Appropriations subcommittees.

But as with many aspects of congressional operations, the traditional mechanisms of lawmaking and governance that reigned for years rarely apply today. Changes to the appropriations process reflect changes in congressional performance. In recent years, Congress has often failed to pass all appropriations measures separately, and in many cases, it has had to lump together all or several of the separate bills into an omnibus measure. Often, these omnibus measures include the full text of each separate appropriations measure as it was crafted by its original subcommittee. Packaging the separate bills into one omnibus bill can smooth out negotiations between the chambers (or between Congress and the president) by providing more areas on which the relevant parties may give and take.[14]

Increasing polarization over the last few decades has resulted in a more dysfunctional appropriations process, with Congress getting fewer appropriations bills done on time.[15] When Congress is unable to complete appropriations legislation by the end of the fiscal year (October 1), it must pass a stopgap measure to fund programs and agencies until regular appropriations can be finalized. This continuing appropriations act, commonly called a **continuing resolution (CR)**, provides for the uninterrupted operation of programs and agencies without current legal appropriation.

CRs are common in the modern Congress, and analyzing their use offers one indication of how successful the body is in completing its federal budgeting duties. First, though, it is important to understand the distinction between full-year and temporary CRs. Temporary CRs are intended to buy Congress a few days, weeks, or months to complete and pass the regular appropriations, and they are usually an indication that lawmakers are close to a deal and simply need a little more time. Accordingly, these acts are often "clean" in that they generally fund programs at the same rate as the previous year's appropriations and do not add new legislation or start new programs.

A full-year CR, on the other hand, indicates that Congress has decided to abandon the regular appropriations process until the next year, largely because a new deal is either a distant prospect or completely infeasible. In these circumstances, we are more likely to see changes to the funding rate of existing programs or even new legislative provisions (the equivalent of "authorizing" language). In these circumstances, the CR process supplants regular appropriations legislation. While legislative provisions are restricted in regular appropriations bills (although the restrictions are sometimes waived), these restrictions are more relaxed for CRs. As a result, meaningful legislation is sometimes included in these statutes. Because unauthorized federal programs and agencies rely on CRs to continue operating, most lawmakers usually consider this legislation to be must-pass, which makes it easier to slide new legislation into a CR. For example, the 1984 Comprehensive Crime Control Act—one of the most significant revisions of federal criminal statutes in nearly a century—was contained in a CR for fiscal year (FY) 1985. Interestingly, the CRs and omnibus appropriations—which, it bears repeating, are deviations from the textbook procedure—have little meaningful effect on the overall budget surplus, total federal spending, or even the economy as a whole. In essence, it appears that lawmakers see these operations as the new normal.[16]

What are the trends with regard to Congress's use of CRs? Since FY 1977, Congress has completed all the regular appropriations acts before the start of

**FIGURE 8.3**   Duration of Continuing Resolutions, 1998–2019

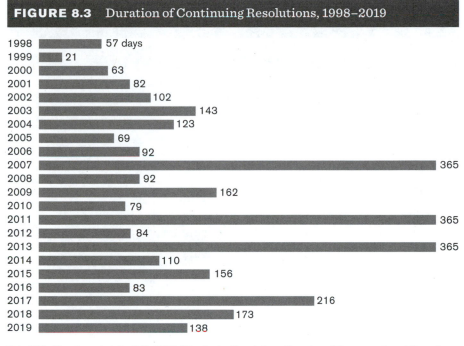

|  |  |
|------|------|
| 1998 | 57 days |
| 1999 | 21 |
| 2000 | 63 |
| 2001 | 82 |
| 2002 | 102 |
| 2003 | 143 |
| 2004 | 123 |
| 2005 | 69 |
| 2006 | 92 |
| 2007 | 365 |
| 2008 | 92 |
| 2009 | 162 |
| 2010 | 79 |
| 2011 | 365 |
| 2012 | 84 |
| 2013 | 365 |
| 2014 | 110 |
| 2015 | 156 |
| 2016 | 83 |
| 2017 | 216 |
| 2018 | 173 |
| 2019 | 138 |

Kate P. McClanahan, et al. April 19, 2019. "Continuing Resolutions: Overview of Components and Recent Practices." *CRS Report for Congress*. Washington, DC: Congressional Research Service.

the fiscal year only four times—FY 1977, FY 1989, FY 1995, and FY 1997. The number and duration of CRs have varied considerably from year to year. In every year between 1978 and 1988, Congress used full-year CRs to cover at least one, and sometimes all, of the unpassed appropriations bills. In some recent years, lawmakers have used a considerable number of temporary CRs (Figure 8.3). For instance, in 2001, Congress passed 21 CRs, averaging just under four days per act. Full-year CRs covered all or nearly all required appropriations acts in FY 2007, FY 2011, and FY 2013.

**FUNDING GAPS**   Sometimes, Congress is incapable of enacting either the required appropriations legislation or the stopgap CRs. When this funding gap occurs, federal law bars the obligation or expenditure of federal funds, thus resulting in a shutdown of federal government activities. (Exceptions are made for the continuance of activities involving "the safety of human life or the protection of property.")

Since the late 1970s, funding gaps have occurred a number of times with varying degrees of effect on the functioning of the federal government (Table 8.4). The number and length of funding gaps provide another way to

**TABLE 8.4**  Appropriations Funding Gaps since 1976

| Year | Full Day(s) of Gaps | Year | Full Day(s) of Gaps |
|------|---------------------|------|---------------------|
| 1976 | 10 | 1984 | 2 |
| 1977 | 12 |  | 1 |
|  | 8 | 1986 | 1 |
|  | 8 | 1987 | 1 |
| 1978 | 17 | 1990 | 3 |
| 1979 | 11 | 1995 | 5 |
| 1981 | 2 |  | 21 |
| 1982 | 1 | 2013 | 16 |
|  | 3 | 2018 | 2 |
| 1983 | 3 | 2019 | 34 |

James Saturno. February 4, 2019. "Federal Funding Gaps: A Brief Overview." *CRS Report for Congress.* Washington, DC: Congressional Research Service.

measure Congress's effectiveness. For example, during the four years of Jimmy Carter's administration there were several lengthy funding gaps, resulting in many government shutdowns. During a number of these funding gaps, agencies continued partial operations under expired funding.

Subsequently, in 1980 and 1981, the U.S. attorney general issued several opinions outlining more clearly the limitations of agency spending in the absence of appropriations and the procedures to be taken by agencies to shut down their activities in the event of a funding gap. The result was more pressure on lawmakers to resolve their differences before a funding gap would affect citizens. Many of the funding gaps in the following 15 years were of short duration and occurred over a weekend. Agencies were sometimes instructed not to shut down completely because a budget agreement among lawmakers seemed imminent.

Two of the longer shutdowns in recent memory included back-to-back funding gaps during the winter of 1995–96. The impasse was the result of a disagreement between President Bill Clinton and the Republican Congress over Medicare premium increases contained in the CR and a provision requiring the president to produce a balanced budget in seven years. President Clinton's veto of the CR resulted in the furlough of 800,000 federal workers. A funding gap in 2013 was caused primarily by a Democratic-controlled Senate unwilling to agree with a Republican-led House over language in the Republican CR that defunded part of the Affordable Care Act ("Obamacare"). The result was a game of

The use of continuing resolutions (CRs) to fund government activities can become controversial. In 2013, the government shut down over language Republicans wanted in the CR that would defund Obamacare. President Obama promised to veto any such resolution, leading to the stalemate.

chicken between the two chambers with funding of the U.S. government at stake. Another long shutdown occurred over the winter in 2019–20, when President Donald Trump refused to sign a temporary spending measure for several agencies because it did not include significant funding for a border wall with Mexico. The shutdown lasted 35 days and affected airline travel for millions. It ended when Trump acceded to signing a CR that included no funding for the wall. A day later, the president declared a national emergency and ordered that funding from the Pentagon budget be transferred for use in building a border wall.

**FEDERAL DEBT LIMIT**   The process of raising the federal debt limit can also shed light on congressional effectiveness. Here we must begin with an understanding of the **gross federal debt**, or the total debt held by the federal government (including money owed to the public and obligations held within the government's own trust fund accounts—Social Security, Medicare, highways, and so on). Since the early twentieth century, Congress has limited federal debt. We approach that limit when government spending increases, or when the economy lags and therefore tax revenues decrease. Given that the federal government runs annual deficits regularly—incoming receipts into the Treasury Department do not keep pace with the daily obligations of federal spending—Congress must authorize any increase in the debt limit to allow the government to continue to borrow and pay for its commitments. Without statutory approval for increasing debt, the federal government would default on its obligations, including Social Security benefits, the salaries of federal employees, and veterans' benefits.

A default is a more serious crisis than a government shutdown. In the case of a shutdown, government employees and contractors are not paid. But in a default, everyone to whom the government owes money is at risk of not being paid. The government is unable to make all mandatory payments, pay interest on its debt, or pay interest to U.S. bondholders around the world. While a default has never occurred, such an action could crush global financial markets and foreign economies with skyrocketing interest rates, a plummeting value for the U.S. dollar, and likely worldwide financial crises as foreign governments divest their U.S. Treasury holdings.

Most members of Congress believe that an increase in the debt limit is must-pass legislation. Most often, the debt limit is raised with little disagreement among lawmakers or between parties. In recent years Congress has also resorted to short-term debt limit "suspensions" (effectively ignoring breaches in the debt limit for a period of time) when an agreement on formal increases was too difficult to reach. From 2008 to 2019, the debt ceiling was raised or suspended 14 times, with four increases in 2008 and 2009 alone.[17] Nevertheless, increases in the debt limit can become a battleground for larger disagreements on Capitol Hill and between Congress and the president regarding the federal budget and **fiscal policy** (that is, policies that affect federal taxing and spending).

When federal debt approaches the existing limit, the Treasury Department can temporarily reduce debt by taking extraordinary measures to handle its cash and debt-management responsibilities, including sophisticated accounting techniques and the shifting around of federal funds. Such actions might entail suspending payments into the retirement funds of federal government and postal employees. The Treasury Department taking these steps to avoid an impending default is a sign of dysfunction in Congress.

The Treasury Department has been compelled to take extreme measures during congressional debt-limit impasses in 1985, 1995–96, 2002 (twice), 2003, 2011, 2013, 2014, and 2015. The 2011 battle occurred between President Obama—allied with his Democratic majority in the Senate—and the Republican-controlled House of Representatives. Each side had a vision for cutting the deficit, but those visions were completely different and largely incompatible. Democrats wanted to end tax cuts that were instituted under President George W. Bush and reduce defense spending, while Republicans wanted to turn Medicare into a voucher program, defund Obamacare, and cut domestic spending. As the debt limit approached with no resolution in sight, Treasury Secretary Timothy Geithner engaged in several financial maneuvers to stave off a default on the debt. In response, Standard & Poor's (a bond rating agency) lowered the U.S. credit rating from AAA to AA+ in August 2011, causing a severe dip in U.S. stock markets. The ultimate agreement between President Obama and congressional Republicans raised the debt ceiling but put off deficit reduction until after the 2012 election.[18]

As such crises become more common, it is clear that Congress is increasingly struggling to find common ground on fiscal policy. However, scholars have found that lawmakers' positions on debt-limit increases are less often driven by their ideological stance on government spending and more often driven by their party's stake in keeping the machinery of government operating. In particular, "the debt limit is generally a burden of those in power, meaning that majority parties and those controlling the presidency typically have to carry these bills. Meanwhile, the out party exploits these votes as an opportunity to denounce the performance of those responsible for governance."[19] In practice, members of Congress oppose debt-limit increases when they are in the minority but support debt-limit increases when they are in the majority or belong to the same party as the president. This phenomenon holds regardless of which party is in power, although the effect intensifies when one party has unified control of both chambers of Congress and the presidency.

By all the metrics we have examined thus far, it seems clear that Congress has had increasing difficulty in the last few decades fulfilling its governing responsibilities. From late or incomplete budgets, to appropriations bills enacted as a batch or through CRs, to continual games of chicken on the debt ceiling, to the growing number of federal programs without active authorizations, Congress has demonstrated a wide array of dysfunction in its normal duties of overseeing the federal budget and keeping programs operating. But these examples also illustrate the variety of techniques and strategies that lawmakers pursue to stave off disaster. We can conclude that as long as lawmakers have ways of getting around the difficult and controversial decisions of governing, they will likely continue to put off those decisions for as long as they can.

## HOW WE STUDY
## MAKING HISTORIC LEGISLATION

To gauge the effectiveness of Congress on a broader scale, we could look beyond how it handles the federal budget to a broader question: how well it steers the ship of government. As conditions arise and constituents' needs and opinions evolve, Congress must adjust federal policy and redefine its role in society. Thus, rather than examining the year-to-year upkeep of government functions—renewing existing programs or ensuring their funding—a broader gauge of congressional performance is the body's ability to make major shifts in policy.

Whether members of Congress favor larger or smaller government or federal authority, they know that changing the size of government, moving it in different directions, or rescinding or reassigning existing powers takes meaningful new legislation. The decision by Congress and President Lyndon B. Johnson to widen the federal government's programs providing assistance for elderly, poor, and disabled Americans required a wide array of new legislation, including the Food Stamp Act of 1964, the Social Security Amendments of 1965 (which created Medicare and Medicaid), and the Demonstration Cities and Metropolitan Development Act of 1966 (for urban renewal), among others. In 1996, President Clinton and Congress's decision to diminish the federal government's role in basic welfare programs resulted in the Personal Responsibility and Work Opportunity Reconciliation Act, which ended many direct payments from the federal government to impoverished individuals, limited eligibility for benefits, and added in a work requirement. This act is still considered one of the major legislative accomplishments of the Clinton presidency and the most profound welfare reform in a generation.

So how do we examine Congress's responsiveness to the needs of society? Simple measures might include the time members of Congress put into lawmaking. For example, if we examine days in session since World War II, we see that the House had its largest number (384 days) in the most recent term (115th, 2017–19), and its smallest number (226 days) decades earlier in the 84th Congress (1953–55).[20] However, days in session does not necessarily correspond to work accomplished, concerns of constituents addressed, or even actual hours worked. Last term's 384 *days* in session accounted for one of the lowest total number of *hours* in session (1,517) since the mid-1970s.

If we turn our gaze to a more direct measure of congressional accomplishment—total bills enacted—it would appear that the last few Congresses have demonstrated an anemic ability to respond to society's demands (see Figure 8.4). The last four congressional terms (from 2011 to 2019) have been among the four lowest in total bills enacted since World War II, averaging only about 337 public laws per term.[21] However, total enactments is not a particularly subtle measure of the substance of lawmaking. As Congress has been enacting fewer bills, those bills have become considerably longer—the average number of pages per statute has increased significantly in the last decade.

Another way we could examine the responsiveness of Congress would be exploring how and how quickly lawmakers respond to the growing or acute

**FIGURE 8.4** Number of Bills Enacted and Average Pages per Statute, 80th–115th Congresses (1947–2019)

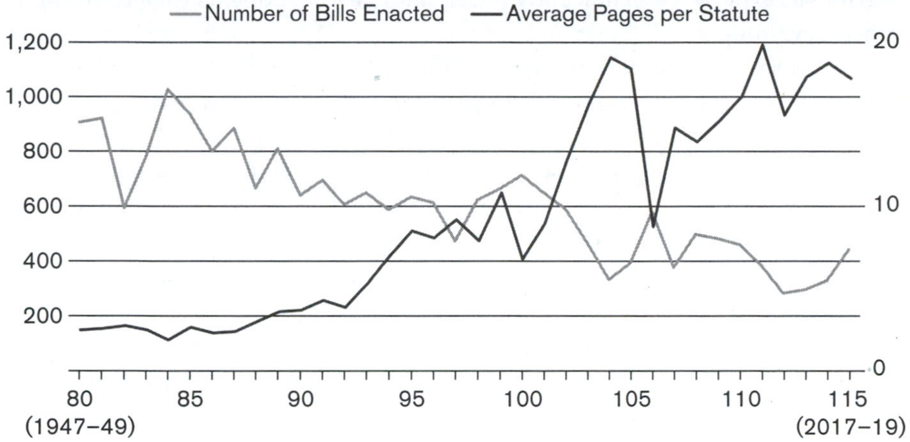

Brookings Institution, www.brookings.edu/multi-chapter-report/vital-statistics-on-congress (accessed 5/10/2019), Table 6-4.

needs of citizens within particular policy areas. It is not difficult to find instances, like immigration, where there is widespread and increasing demand for Congress to act but year after year passes without progress. As we saw in Chapter 7, Congress has missed a number of opportunities in recent years to address the plight of DREAMers, and its gridlock on this matter has abdicated responsibility for federal action to the president and the courts. Alternatively, there have also been instances in which a crisis, such as the COVID-19 pandemic (discussed in Chapter 1), motivated lawmakers to enact a number of sizable and effective statutes in just a matter of weeks.

While these examples can illuminate the various obstacles and stimuli to congressional action in specific areas of public policy, they do not provide much depth to our understanding of Congress's overall effectiveness. To that end, researchers have sought better ways to gain an aggregate view of the lawmaking body's legislative accomplishments. Many observers of Congress see the pace and extent of adoption of landmark laws as a good way to gauge the body's ability to react to changing societal conditions. Yet, even this endeavor raises some important questions: How do we identify landmark legislation? What distinguishes a run-of-the-mill law from one that should be considered historic or of landmark importance? What should be the threshold for distinguishing an effective Congress?

Perhaps the most important early work on these questions has been con-ducted by political scientist David Mayhew. Mayhew was interested in whether **divided government** (different parties controlling the presidency and one or both chambers of Congress) affects what legislation gets passed. Mayhew's simple question was: Do congressional terms characterized by divided government experience significantly fewer landmark enactments than terms of **unified government**?

Mayhew sought to answer this question by creating a list of landmark laws enacted during each two-year congressional term. He first examined annual end-of-the-congressional-session wrap-up articles in the *New York Times* and the *Washington Post*. These articles by expert observers assess the most significant legislation passed by Congress in the previous year. Mayhew then wanted to capture policy specialists' retrospective judgments on which laws should be considered historically significant. To do so, he relied on scholarly accounts of the development of a large number of specific policy areas over time.

The result of Mayhew's work was a term-by-term catalog of the landmark legislation enacted by Congress from the end of World War II until the present.[22] Aggregating the list of historic statutes by congressional term gives us a historical overview of Congress's ability to produce important legislation under different internal and external conditions (Figure 8.5).

We see a few important trends. There is clearly a "bulge" in significant legislation throughout much of the 1960s and the early 1970s. This was a period of many profound legislative changes surrounding civil rights and the expansion of federal programs that characterized President Johnson's Great Society initiative. Subsequently, there are ebbs and flows of legislation but no real sustained surges or slumps in lawmaking. Mayhew's measure shows that unified government does not contribute appreciably to the passage of landmark statutes. Other than the bulge of the Johnson/Richard Nixon era, periods of divided government (gray) do not show a significantly lower count of historic laws passed than periods of unified government (black).

In reaction to Mayhew's novel way of thinking about congressional accomplishment, other scholars undertook their own accounting of high-level lawmaking on Capitol Hill, often employing different primary-source information to denote "significant" or landmark legislation. For example, William Howell and his colleagues categorized all laws enacted in the postwar period by importance based on their coverage not just in the *New York Times* and the *Washington Post* but also in the larger and more comprehensive *Congressional Quarterly Almanac,* a 500- to 600-page yearly retrospective of all activity in Congress.[23] These researchers found that divided government *does* have a depressing effect on the output of important legislation, and the lack of activity on landmark bills is apparently offset by more symbolic legislation. Alternatively, Joshua Clinton and John S. Lapinski, who measured significant legislation back to the 1870s, relied on the ratings of a more expansive set of experts, many of them from

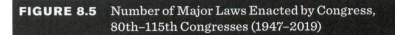

**FIGURE 8.5**  Number of Major Laws Enacted by Congress, 80th–115th Congresses (1947–2019)

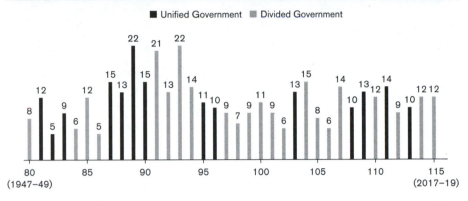

David Mayhew. "List of Important Enactments, 1947–1990," "List of Important Enactments 1991–2002," "List of Important Enactments 2003–2018." *Datasets and Materials: Divided We Govern*, http://campuspress.yale .edu/davidmayhew/datasets-divided-we-govern (accessed 11/25/20).

academia.[24] They too found that productivity is positively related to periods of unified governmental control.

While the number of historic laws passed is an important metric for evaluating legislative effectiveness, shouldn't effectiveness also be measured in terms of what the people actually want from Congress? Some scholars argue that the raw count of total important laws does not account for expectations of, or demand for, change in policy areas. Of particular note is Sarah Binder's exploration of **legislative gridlock**. For her research, she created a list of legislative agenda items by congressional term—effectively, a measure of the expectations of Congress—based on the issues discussed in editorials in the *New York Times*. She used the level of the *Times*'s attention to an issue as an indicator of its salience among the public and political elites. Binder then examined whether Congress and the president took legislative action in that two-year congressional term to address each salient issue. The resulting gridlock score captures the percentage of agenda items left in limbo at the close of the Congress (Figure 8.6).[25]

Binder's measure shows an overall increase in gridlock over time. Although the increase has not been linear, from 1947 to 2013, more and more gridlocked policies or agenda items were left in limbo, on average, at the end of each legislative term. Binder explains the trend in two ways. First, as the ideological center shrinks and the two parties become more polarized, it is harder to create policy coalitions to pass agenda items, regardless of unified or divided partisan control of Congress and the presidency. Second, even controlling for party polarization,

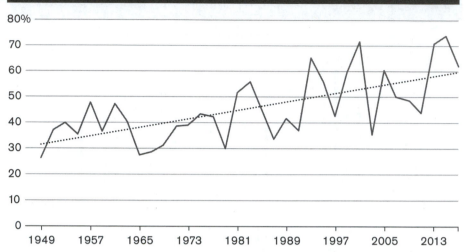

FIGURE 8.6  Percentage of Legislative Issues in Gridlock, 1949–2016

Sarah Binder, 2021, "The Struggle to Legislate in Polarized Times," in Congress Reconsidered, 12th Edition, eds. Lawrence C. Dodd, Bruce I. Oppenheimer, and C. Lawrence Evans, Sage Publications, Thousand Oaks, CA. pp. 251–274.

differences in the ideological positions of the two chambers intensify gridlock. The further apart the median ideological position of the House and Senate (even factoring in divergent partisan majorities), the lower the probability that the two chambers can agree to adopt legislation addressing policy-agenda items.

The quantitative metrics we have discussed so far do not always capture "accomplishment" or even what lawmakers are aiming to achieve. Political scientist Doug Arnold has expanded on this note of caution, asserting that there is a liberal bias in believing that successful governing or legislative performance should be judged by new laws, especially laws that redirect governance.[26] Arnold argues that many, particularly those pursuing a shrinking of government, would prefer to judge Congress by the degree to which policy goals are achieved. Perhaps such an evaluation can be conducted on the basis of a small number of laws and congressional actions that are part of the normal functioning of Congress—omnibus appropriations, budget reconciliations, and so on—or even extraordinary actions that do not result in any new legislation, such as a government shutdown or an instance of sequestration. Based on these criteria, recent Congresses could be judged as wildly successful.

Arnold's reservations notwithstanding, these broad measures of governing provide a closer look at congressional effectiveness. Lawmakers lately seem to be producing significant legislation at about the same rate that Congress has historically, although recent terms would not rank anywhere near the most productive Congresses in current memory. While there is some dispute as to whether unified or divided government makes a difference, we can draw a similar conclusion as that gained from our examination of budgets, appropriations, and authorizations: Congress increasingly struggles to govern effectively.

### Critical Thinking

1. At its most productive (in the 1960s and early 1970s), according to the work of Mayhew, Congress was producing 20 to 25 pieces of historic legislation in each two-year congressional term. In the last few decades, it rarely produces more than 10 to 15. Does its recent work seem sufficient, or would you call Congress underproductive?

2. Do you consider Binder's method of using *New York Times* editorials to construct a public agenda a good technique for creating a measure of demand for legislation? Does her gauge of gridlock conform with your perceptions of Congress's productivity?

3. Can you name historic legislation produced by Congress that you would consider liberal, conservative, neither, or both? Does Congress produce more liberal or conservative historic legislation? What effect do the conditions inside Congress and in the political climate overall have on the kind and amount of historic legislation passed?

## INDIVIDUAL EFFECTIVENESS

Understanding effectiveness at the institutional level versus the individual level is comparable to contrasting congressional governance versus representation. Governing refers to the legislature making laws and conducting oversight in an effective manner. Representation, at least in part, means making legislation on behalf of the varied interests represented by the member of Congress. Here we examine how effective individual lawmakers are at performing their job of making laws.

Evaluating individual lawmakers' legislative effectiveness involves more than simply measuring who gets what done in Washington. When lawmakers campaign in their districts, they often justify their pursuit of power and policy on Capitol Hill with an emphasis on being legislatively effective.[27] Voters often cite effectiveness as a central reason for liking or disliking incumbent representatives.[28] Given that legislative effectiveness is integral to lawmakers' "home styles" (see Chapter 4) and how voters assess them, it is not surprising that scholars have created measures of effectiveness based on a variety of indicators.

Some are relatively straightforward markers of the lawmaking process in Congress, such as a count of the total bills a representative authors or "sponsors" that are passed each term. Other measures of effectiveness construct more sophisticated metrics, ranging from the proportion of bills introduced that are enacted to a complex score that takes into account how far each of a legislator's bills has made it through the various hurdles of congressional deliberation (committee action, committee report, floor passage, and so on). While the strategies for measuring legislative accomplishment vary, they all aim to determine "the proven ability to advance a member's agenda items through the legislative process and into law."[29]

A primary goal of these analyses is to identify characteristics of individual members of Congress, or even circumstances surrounding these lawmakers, that contribute to more effective lawmaking. For decades, scholars have studied individual success—using "hit rates" or "batting averages"—to reveal the traits of lawmakers most associated with accomplishment.[30]

Scholars are interested in both inherent and acquired traits of lawmakers that are likely to lead to legislative success. Not surprisingly, a lawmaker who is a member of the majority party in either chamber—with its intrinsic control of the legislative agenda—possesses a sizable advantage when it comes to bill success. All things equal, if majority leaders need to choose between two identical bills, they will likely choose the one from a fellow majority-party member over that of a minority-party representative. In our era of hyperpartisanship and polarization, research along these lines has further discovered that loyalty to the majority-party agenda and its leaders is rewarded with a greater degree of legislative success.[31]

Ideology, while often closely associated with partisanship, does seem to have a distinct effect on lawmaking effectiveness. In a study of lawmaking in the Senate—the chamber that is institutionally designed for consensual rather than majoritarian tendencies—researchers discovered that the body is more responsive to the policy proposals of ideologically moderate lawmakers. The bills of senators who hew toward the ideological center of the chamber are the bills most likely to pass.[32]

Tenure that lawmakers build over many years of service in Congress is also frequently associated with lawmaking accomplishment.[33] The advantages associated with senior lawmakers are likely a consequence of a number of factors, including extensive experience in navigating the legislative process, a reputation of expertise in an issue area, networks of legislative partnerships, and acquired positions of institutional influence (such as party and committee leadership positions).

Specializing in an issue area confers credibility and knowledge that can be tremendously useful in propelling a lawmaker's legislative ideas forward.

Specialization has been defined in different ways, including the degree to which a member's bills are focused within a small number of issue areas. Perhaps the most common indicator of specialization is committee membership. Committee seats provide lawmakers with access to information and institutional advantages that influence the legislative process in exclusive ways. Committees have sizable and experienced staffs, and they are privy to information from agencies, external policy experts, and affected groups and stakeholders as part of the regular deliberations for authorizing legislation and oversight. And as we have already noted, committees occupy a privileged position in setting the lawmaking agenda on matters within their jurisdictions.[34]

More than anyone else, committee leaders—committee and subcommittee chairs, and to a lesser degree the ranking minority members—are responsible for ensuring that the panel's work gets done. Due to the prevalence and importance of authorizing legislation that contains expirations, it is the committee leaders who nearly always take the lead in the effort to renew and update these laws. Thus legislative "success" is an imperative of their institutional position.[35]

Finally, some legislative effectiveness is attributed to lawmakers' entrepreneurial efforts to build winning coalitions and to educate their colleagues about the advantages of proposed legislation. Scholars have discovered that bills are more likely to pass when members give speeches in support of their bills on the chamber floor and when they seek cosponsors for their legislative proposals.[36]

Perhaps the most comprehensive effort to examine legislative effectiveness at the lawmaker level was undertaken by political scientists Craig Volden and Alan Wiseman, who took a broad view in measuring bill success. Volden and Wiseman explored effectiveness holistically, taking into account more nuanced measures than just total laws attributed or statutory batting averages. They contend that the ability to propel bills forward, even when those bills are not enacted into law, demonstrates a level of legislative acumen. Moreover, it is important to differentiate among commemorative (or symbolic) bills, more substantive bills, and proposals that are the most legislatively significant (that is, similar to Mayhew's historic statutes discussed earlier). Volden and Wiseman therefore accounted for the fraction of each member's bills that (1) are introduced, (2) receive action in committee, (3) receive action beyond committee, (4) pass the House, and (5) become law. With each subsequent step worth proportionally more than the previous steps, and additionally weighting in favor of more significant legislation, a cumulative tally results in a lawmaker's **legislative effectiveness score (LES)**.

Analyzing this score confirms that several lawmaker characteristics are correlated with a representative's LES. These factors may be circumstantial, such as being a member of the majority party, being more electorally safe, or being female. Electorally precarious members of Congress are likely to focus their

Ways and Means is considered a "power committee" in the House, but a seat on the committee doesn't necessarily lead to greater legislative effectiveness. Representatives Pete Aguilar (D-Calif.) (right) and Peter Visclosky (D-Ind.) (left) are both members of the Ways and Means Committee, pictured here during a committee markup meeting, but are not considered particularly effective legislators.

efforts on activities that are more reelection-oriented, such as fundraising and constituent contact, rather than bill activity. Alternatively, Volden and Wiseman found that female legislators adopt different strategies than male legislators, and legislative success comes in different ways depending on whether they are in the majority or minority parties. They contend that female members of Congress in the minority party tend to use consensus-building and coalitions to strengthen the prospects of their legislative proposals. (Although, notably, Jennifer Lawless, Sean Theriault, and Samantha Guthrie do not find that female members of Congress are any more likely to move legislation along in a bipartisan fashion than male lawmakers.[37]) Female representatives who belong to the majority party increase the perception of their legislative effectiveness, as measured by Volden and Wiseman, by introducing more bills. The latter strategy, however, has created fewer new laws in the more contentious and polarized modern Congress.[38]

Not surprisingly, committee membership is very influential in a lawmaker's LES. For example, acquiring a position of committee leadership (committee or subcommittee chair) influences LES enormously among members of Congress, as Figure 8.7 shows. For example, in the 113th Congress (2013–15),

**FIGURE 8.7**   Average Legislative Effectiveness Score, by Seniority and Status

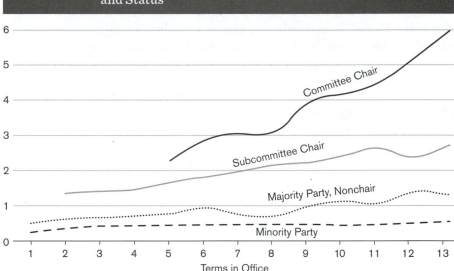

Note: Based on all lawmakers in the House from 1973 to 2014.

Craig Volden and Alan Wiseman. 2017. "Legislative Effectiveness and Representation," in *Congress Reconsidered*, 11th edition, ed. by Lawrence Dodd and Bruce Oppenheimer, 259–84. Washington, DC: Congressional Quarterly Press.

the 10 lawmakers in the House with the highest legislative effectiveness scores, and 20 of the top 25, were committee or subcommittee chairs. These included the chairs of Ways and Means (David Camp, R-Mich.), Appropriations (Hal Rogers, R-Ky.), and Judiciary (Bob Goodlatte, R-Va.), as well as the subcommittee chairs Chris Smith (R-N.J.) and Don Young (R-Alas.)—two former committee chairs and among the longest-serving members in the chamber. Somewhat surprisingly, Volden and Wiseman found that having a seat on a House "power" committee (which they identify as Appropriations, Rules, and Ways and Means) other than a leadership slot often results in a lower LES. Rank-and-file members of these committees often focus all their legislative work on the supporting duties of these panels' bill responsibilities, while committee leaders sponsor the committees' critical bills.

Finally, less tangible factors influence legislative success, including prior experience and some level of innate ability. Volden and Wiseman demonstrated that lawmakers raise their LES as they gain experience over their years in Congress and as they learn to navigate the gauntlet of policy making. Even lawmaking experience in places other than Capitol Hill can raise a member's LES. Prior elective office in "professionalized" state legislatures (those that resemble

Congress in number of staff, salary, and time in session) bolsters a member's effectiveness in Congress.[39] Finally, some lawmakers simply show more natural ability when they first arrive on Capitol Hill in executing the duties that propel their policy ideas. "Natural ability" can mean a number of intangibles, such as networking, hustle, hard work, luck, and the ability to read the political winds.

## THEN AND NOW
## INDIVIDUAL EFFECTIVENESS IN THE SENATE

Congress in the mid-twentieth century was an institution with different beliefs and norms than we see today. In no place is that difference more evident than the lawmaking activities and expectations of senators. If we compare senators' behavior with respect to policy deliberation and the formulation of new legislation in the decade just after World War II to how senators approached the institution and their role by the end of the twentieth century, we see a stark contrast in what constitutes an effective lawmaker in the Senate.

Donald Matthews's in-depth study dominates our image of the Senate in the 1940s and 1950s.[40] In particular, Matthews emphasizes that the chamber—a clubby, inward-looking body—regulated behavior through a set of "folkways" or norms required of its members. Among these were the belief that senators focused their work on a small number of issues directly related to their states' interests or their own committee assignments, that lawmakers prioritized legislating over seeking publicity, and that they sought reciprocity among the members so as to assist colleagues when feasible. Junior members were expected to serve in an apprenticeship role, gaining experience and knowledge in a small number of policy areas before they started seeking leadership roles in the Senate.

These norms had important implications for senators' participation and success in the legislative arena.[41] First-term senators in the 1950s sponsored fewer floor amendments (by half) than members who had served just one term longer, and they did the vast majority of their policy work solely within their assigned committees.[42] Ultimately, senators who adhered to institutional norms, such as deference to seniority, experienced greater legislative success.[43]

Yet there is not complete agreement that these norms entirely regulated Senate operations in the mid-twentieth century.[44] Scholars also note that the Senate had long tolerated a wide variety of institutional mavericks who frequently operated and pursued leadership roles beyond the body's behavior restrictions. These mavericks included Robert La Follette, Sr. (R-Wisc.); Estes Kefauver (D-Tenn.); and Robert Taft (R-Ohio).[45] Not the least of these institutional insurgents was Lyndon Johnson (D-Tex.), whose assent to Senate majority leader occurred quickly in the 1950s and who operated outside the body's norms of behavior on more than a few occasions.[46]

Through the 1960s and 1970s, demands on lawmakers shifted as the scope of federal government activities widened and the nature of elections changed. Accordingly, many of the norms that had previously regulated senators' behavior began to fade. The politics of the 1960s undermined the restrictions that older folkways had imposed on junior members. In particular, the decade saw liberal issues gain salience: civil rights, the women's movement, and opposition to the Vietnam War. In earlier decades, behavioral expectations within the upper chamber had limited the ability of younger, more liberal Democrats to redirect the work of committees, which had largely been under the influence of older and considerably more conservative Democrats, particularly from the South. By the 1960s, an ever-expanding national and local news media created both a demand and an opportunity for all senators to become policy leaders in a variety of issue areas beyond their committee assignments.[47] Consequently, less-senior senators began to flout the norm of apprenticeship and take an active role in agenda setting and lawmaking.

As a result, committee rules changed. The new rules expanded the number of assignments members could have to the most influential panels (thereby keeping senior lawmakers from monopolizing the power positions) and provided resources to allow junior lawmakers to hire additional staff to assist in their participation in committee legislative activities.[48]

The changes eliminated the clubbiness of the legislative body and created more individualistic lawmakers in the Senate (for more detail, see Chapter 7). In the early 1970s, senators were reporting that the expectation of apprenticeship by junior members no longer existed in any form. One junior Democratic senator interviewed at the time stated, "All the communications suggest 'get involved, offer amendments, make speeches. The Senate has changed, we're all equals, you should act accordingly.'"[49]

With larger staffs, more support from outside groups, and expanded opportunities for participation in legislative development, senators transformed the body's operations. Today, junior members tussle over controversial policies in committee and on the floor, offering a greater proportion of floor amendments than they used to. As well, with the more egalitarian nature of the Senate we see that committee leadership positions there are not as important for individual legislative effectiveness as they are in the House.[50] Finally, lawmaking has become more partisan, with members more freely choosing to filibuster or extend holds on nearly any legislation they oppose, which eventually led to a new three-fifths voting threshold for all meaningful legislation in the Senate (see Chapter 7).

For decades, seniority dominated in Congress, leading to a "clubby" atmosphere and a lack of gender and racial diversity, especially in leadership positions, as seen in this image of the Senate Foreign Relations Committee in the 1950s (top). In 1992, four new women (bottom) were elected to the Senate—(from left) Susan Collins (R-Maine), Patty Murray (D-Wash.), Olympia Snowe (R-Maine), and Carol Moseley-Braun (D-Ill.)—joining existing female senators Kay Bailey Hutchison (R-Tex.), Barbara Mikulski (D-Md.), Dianne Feinstein (D-Calif.), and Mary Landrieu (D-La.). This "Year of the Woman" signaled that Congress was undergoing rapid change.

Perhaps no group of lawmakers faced more resistance to their changing role in the modern Congress than female senators. As political scientist Michele Swers notes, until the early 1990s, there were very few female senators. A major turning point was the confirmation hearing for Supreme Court Justice Clarence Thomas in 1991, when an all-male Judiciary Committee grilled Professor Anita Hill on her allegations of sexual harassment during her time as a subordinate to Thomas. The subsequent election year, widely referred to as the "Year of the Woman," brought four new female senators to the body.

However, Swers notes that it has taken a very long time for women to break down stereotyped perceptions that female lawmakers are interested only in "women's issues." While Swers notes that female senators unquestionably bring their unique life experiences to their lawmaking, many also go out of their way to establish expertise and policy influence in a wide range of issue areas. Moreover, senior senators continued to dominate committee and party leadership selection, and it took many years for women senators to acquire positions of influence with respect to agenda formation and lawmaking.[51]

### Critical Thinking

1. Given what you have learned about the Senate in this chapter and the chapter on policy making (Chapter 7), do you prefer the Senate of the 1950s and 1960s, where newer members had to behave more like apprentices and seniority determined whose legislation advanced in the chamber?
2. As the Senate becomes more balanced from a gender perspective, does this change how the institution operates?

# CONCLUSION

By most accounts, Congress in the modern era is a lawmaking body that struggles to govern. In nearly every way we examine here, from creating budgets, to maintaining existing federal programs, to adapting government to changing world events, representatives and senators find it increasingly difficult to perform their collective duties as a lawmaking institution. We discussed, for example, how Congress has a seemingly chronic problem of not completing much needed legislation to reauthorize critical federal programs and agencies or finish its annual appropriations. This forces federal agencies to operate with outdated legislative instructions and with tremendous budgetary uncertainty for the coming year. Clearly, this is not an ideal way to run a government.

In many of its governing responsibilities, Congress accomplishes only the bare minimum to keep federal programs and agencies operating. Lawmakers have always struggled to reach consensus on major policy changes, even when there is widespread demand from voters that something be done. Importantly, we have seen recently that even with unified government, lawmakers—even those from the same party—are not unified legislatively. For example, in 2017, Republicans controlled the presidency and both chambers of Congress, and while they were able to pass massive tax reform, they were not able to repeal Obamacare—one of the party's top priorities.

All things considered, the contemporary Congress faces many challenges, and labeling it as a "do-nothing" Congress is probably unfair. Congress has avoided some of the most potentially catastrophic governing failures, such as a breach in the debt limit. Moreover, as the evolving response to the COVID-19 pandemic demonstrates, when facing a true crisis, lawmakers can find legislative solutions quickly.

A different perspective suggests that perhaps we have simply entered a new era of congressional operations and therefore we should recalibrate our expectations about legislative accomplishment and the functioning of the lawmaking body. James Curry and Frances Lee suggest that Congress has simply adapted to the era of hyperpartisanship in a way that no longer includes the traditional hallmarks of lawmaking—committees reporting bills, meeting formal budget deadlines, etc.[52] Instead, Congress governs in a more centralized manner where party leadership is the key operative institution. Committees are consulted, coalitions are built (even bipartisan coalitions), and legislation is enacted, but the most important lawmaking is done by the key party leaders in each chamber. Congress is still as effective, but not in traditional "textbook" ways.

Our exploration of congressional accomplishment and difficulties highlights areas for improvement in the institution's performance. Rather than simply demanding that members of Congress "do their job," we can specify which changes can make a difference in congressional operations. While there is certainly no unanimous agreement on reforms or institutional adjustments, there is also no lack of innovative thinking along these lines. Among the many suggested changes are linking lawmakers' pay to the adoption of budget and appropriations bills each term, increasing the number of required days members must work in Washington, limiting the number of years that appropriations can be granted to programs without an active authorization, linking automatic increases in the debt ceiling to the levels required by adopted budgets, and requiring senators to attach their names publicly to holds on legislation. None of these proposals is a panacea for all that troubles Congress, but each would provide a useful starting point for conversations about how to improve the work of Congress as a governing body. The first step, however, is for lawmakers to acknowledge Congress's deficiencies and begin the conversation about the areas of greatest need in improving the operations of lawmaking.

## Discussion Questions

1. Congress and the executive branch have used a number of workarounds to ensure the government performs even when Congress does not meet its regular obligations (including continuing resolutions, the Treasury taking extraordinary actions to avoid a default, and other measures). Do you think that these exceptions allow Congress to shirk its responsibilities too easily?

2. Some critics of Congress have argued that there should be consequences for all members, such as withheld pay, when the body fails to meet its obligations (for example, producing a budget on time, passing appropriations legislation, or raising the debt ceiling). Should we hold these lawmakers personally accountable for the actions of the collective body? If so, is this the best means of doing so? Can you think of other ways to ensure that Congress meets its legislative obligations?

3. Of the measures offered for evaluating the performance of Congress as an institution (meeting budget deadlines, not breaching the debt limit, reauthorizing expiring programs, producing important legislation, and so forth), which is the best way to gauge congressional accomplishment and why?

4. What criteria would you use to gauge whether an individual member of Congress was "effective" at performing his or her job? How does your current representative or senator rank on these metrics?

5. Would Congress be a more effective institution if it were more diverse (composed of a greater number of women, African Americans, Latinos, or other underrepresented minorities)? Why or why not?

# 9

## Congress and the President

On December 18, 2019, the House of Representatives impeached President Donald J. Trump on charges of abuse of power and obstruction of Congress. With this action, Trump became only the third president in the nation's history to be impeached, joining Andrew Johnson and Bill Clinton.

On February 5, 2020, the Senate voted to acquit Trump on both of these charges. Trump once again joined Johnson and Clinton, both of whom were also acquitted.

And then on January 13, 2021, the House impeached Trump a second time, an action unprecedented in our nation's history. This second impeachment, which received bipartisan support, charged the president with "incitement of insurrection" for his role in spurring the mob that attacked the U.S. Capitol on January 6, 2021.

What brought us to a situation where Congress came close to removing an elected president from office? Impeachment is, after all, the most dramatic and drastic component of our checks and balances system. And earlier attempts by some Democrats in Congress to pursue impeachment—often related to the question of whether members of the Trump campaign had collaborated with Russian operatives to influence the 2016 presidential election, but also on the questions of whether Trump had violated the emoluments clause of the Consti-

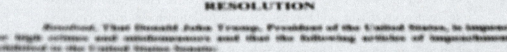

In late 2019, Democrats in the House of Representatives brought articles of impeachment against Donald Trump. He was ultimately acquitted by the Senate on February 5, 2020, with only one Republican, Mitt Romney (R-Utah), voting for conviction.

tution by profiting personally from holding office, whether he had committed campaign finance violations, and so on—had not been successful. As early as December 2017 some Democrats were able to get an impeachment resolution voted on in the House, but this resolution was soundly defeated, with most Democrats opposing it. Even after Democrats regained control of the House in the 2018 election, there was little sense that they would pursue impeachment, with Speaker Nancy Pelosi dismissing such calls by saying, "He's just not worth it."[1]

In late summer of 2019, however, Democrats who previously had opposed pursuing impeachment began to reconsider their position when a whistleblower revealed information about a recent phone call between Trump and Ukraine's president, Volodymyr Zelensky. In this conversation, according to transcripts released by the White House, Trump raised a number of issues.[2] At one point, after reminding Zelensky that "we do a lot for Ukraine . . . the United States has been very very good to Ukraine," he continued by saying, "I would like you to do us a favor though." Trump then went on to ask the Ukrainian president to investigate former vice president Joe Biden, who was widely seen at the time as Trump's most likely opponent in the 2020 election, and Biden's son Hunter, who had served on the board of Burisma, a Ukrainian natural gas company.

The whistleblower's complaint, and additional details that emerged subsequently about the phone call and other interactions with Ukraine, spurred Democrats to take action. In late September, Speaker Pelosi announced that the House would begin a formal impeachment inquiry into Trump's phone call and related activities. Over the next few months, three House committees—Intelligence, Oversight, and Foreign Affairs—took testimony from witnesses, and House leadership authorized several other committees to investigate whether Trump had used his public office for private gain (that is, to help him win the 2020 election).

Some Democrats wanted to take a broad approach and investigate several potentially impeachable actions (including but not limited to the situation with Ukraine). But in December 2019, the House leadership eventually settled on a focused approach, limiting the process to two articles of impeachment. The first article, for abuse of power, contended that Trump had used his elected office for private gain by improperly withholding aid that Congress had already appropriated for Ukraine until that country promised to investigate Biden and his son. The second article was for obstruction of justice. This article followed from the first, holding that Trump and his associates had blocked Congress from obtaining relevant information related to the phone call and associated activities.

Testimony during the impeachment hearings and investigations for this first impeachment divided members of Congress almost perfectly along party lines. Democrats looked at the transcript of the call, testimony from witnesses and participants who contended there was indeed a quid pro quo (with Trump holding back aid until his favor was granted), testimony from legal experts about whether the conduct rose to an impeachable level, and the White House's efforts to block important witnesses from testifying before Congress or cooperating in any way with the investigation, and saw evidence of impeachable conduct.

Republicans pushed back in a number of ways. Some stressed that none of the witnesses had received direct orders from Donald Trump to withhold aid in exchange for an investigation of the Bidens, and they thus concluded that there was no direct evidence of impeachable conduct. Some pointed to a different interpretation of the call: that Trump was genuinely concerned about corruption and wanted to encourage Ukraine to root out and prosecute corruption more generally. Some complained that the process Democrats had followed had been unfair and biased. Still others emphasized that the sort of discussion portrayed in the transcript of the phone call was fairly standard, with such quid pro quos happening regularly. Trump's acting chief of staff, Mick Mulvaney, voiced this most directly: "We do that all the time in foreign policy. . . . Get over it. There's going to be political influence in foreign policy" (before walking those comments back later in the day).[3] And Trump himself repeatedly described it as

**Donald J. Trump** ✔
@realDonaldTrump

## I JUST GOT IMPEACHED FOR MAKING A PERFECT PHONE CALL!

3:39 PM · Jan 16, 2020 · Twitter for iPhone

**85.2K** Retweets and comments   **330.6K** Likes

President Trump tweeted throughout his first impeachment trial asserting his innocence.

a "perfect" phone call. Other Republicans broke slightly from their fellow party members, allowing that the phone call was improper and unacceptable, but arguing that it did not rise to the level of a high crime or misdemeanor and thus was not impeachable.

In the end, nearly all Democrats in the House—along with Republican-turned-independent Justin Amash of Michigan—voted in favor of impeaching the president, while all Republicans voted against. A similar split occurred when the process moved to the Senate, with all Democrats voting to convict and nearly all Republicans—with the notable exception of Mitt Romney (R-Utah)—voting to acquit on both counts. The outcomes differed, of course, because Democrats held the majority in the House, while Republicans held the majority in the Senate. With votes falling nearly perfectly along party lines, Trump was impeached by the House but then acquitted by the Senate.

The second impeachment in 2021 played out much differently. The House moved from introducing a single article of impeachment to a vote in just a few days. The debate was much shorter, limited to a single day. And this time there were sharper divisions within the Republican party, with ten Republican representatives voting to impeach the president, and four others choosing to abstain rather than vote against impeachment. Even many staunch Trump supporters who voted against impeachment agreed that the president was indeed guilty of the charges levied against him, but they maintained either that the House process was either too rushed or flawed in some other way, or that while congressional action was indeed merited, impeachment was too drastic a step, especially with only a handful of days remaining in the president's term. The top Republican in the House, Majority Leader Kevin McCarthy (R-Calif.), made exactly these points when he stated that "[t]he President bears responsibility for Wednesday's attack on Congress by mob rioters" before adding that "[t]he President's immediate action also deserves congressional action, which is why I think a fact-finding commission and a censure resolution would be prudent."[4]

Congress and the president always interact, sometimes cooperate, and often are in conflict. The impeachments of Donald Trump illustrate this conflict at its most extreme, but they also sheds light on other features of the sometimes tense relationship between Congress and the president. They show the tools Congress has with respect to the president, such as hearings and investigations, but also exemplifies how the president can resist Congress's efforts to subdue the executive branch. They demonstrate the importance of political parties and how much the president benefits when his or her party controls at least one chamber of Congress. More generally, they show—albeit in an extreme way—how Congress and the president often conflict and what constitutional tools can be used during such conflict.

Throughout this chapter, we explore these tactics to examine how Congress and the president interact. We begin by identifying the context in which we should consider the relationship between these two branches. Specifically, we need to recognize that the separation of their powers is not nearly as clean as it might initially seem, that the balance of power between the two branches of government has fluctuated throughout the nation's history, that each branch faces different incentives in terms of how it carries out its representation and governance functions, and that as a result each branch is constantly seeking to gain the upper hand over the other.

## CONGRESS AND THE PRESIDENT IN THE CONSTITUTION

The Framers had a clear view of the relative importance of Congress, the presidency, and the courts. In the Constitution, they identified Congress as the primary branch of government, with the president serving a secondary role and the courts playing an even smaller role. Creating the position of president was a way to rectify one of the main weaknesses of the Articles of Confederation: a lack of executive power. In addition, the Framers recognized that the Constitution would need to endow the president with specific powers. Still, there is no question that they viewed Congress as the central and dominant power within the federal government (see also Chapter 2).[5]

The Framers also took care to delineate the separation of powers between the two branches: Congress would decide on and design policies, and the president (and the executive branch) would carry them out. But upon closer inspection, this separation is not so precise. The Constitution does assign the president the primary task of executing laws passed by Congress, but it also provides the president with legislative powers. The process by which a bill becomes law, for example, is not complete until the president signs the bill into law, which means that the president is the main actor in the final stage of the legislative process. The president also can choose *not* to sign a bill, which can prevent it from becoming law. As we shall see, these powers can significantly shape Congress's actions.

Just as the president plays a role in the legislative process, so too can Congress influence the activities of the executive branch. Congress can help or hinder the president's efforts to make policy, even in areas where conventional wisdom holds that the president is the main actor. Clearly, there is some separation of powers, but the system of checks and balances provides for overlap and muddies the separation. Thus the relationship between Congress and the president is best characterized as one of separate institutions that share powers.[6]

---

## THEN AND NOW
## THE RELATIVE POWER OF CONGRESS AND THE PRESIDENT

By most measures, presidents played little role in the legislative process in the country's early years, but there was a gradual increase in such activity by the end of the 1800s and then a more dramatic increase throughout the twentieth century. This level of presidential involvement in and influence over the legislative process continues today, to the point that former House Speaker Paul Ryan (R-Wis.) openly acknowledged during the first two years of the Trump administration that he would not bring bills forward unless he knew the president was already on board. None of this, however, should be taken to mean that early presidents had no power. Indeed, presidents in the early nineteenth century, including Jefferson, Madison, and Jackson, were strong and proactive leaders—for example, procuring land to expand the nation's frontiers.[7] Rather, the point is that in the contested ground between the president and Congress, the pattern has been one of growing presidential power and increasing presidential involvement in the legislative process.

One metric that illustrates this trend is the number of legislative requests that presidents from George Washington to George W. Bush have submitted to Congress—that is, the number of times the president formally asked the House and Senate to address a policy. As Figure 9.1 shows, the number of requests throughout the eighteenth and nineteenth centuries was generally low, but rising. Starting at the end of World War II (79th Congress, 1945–47), however, the rate of requests per year exploded, reaching a peak of nearly 700 during the presidency of Lyndon B. Johnson.

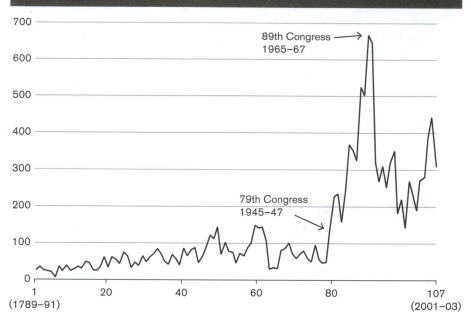

**FIGURE 9.1**    Number of Presidential Legislative Requests, 1st–107th Congresses (1789–2003)

Jeffrey Cohen. 2012. *The President's Legislative Policy Agenda, 1789–2002.* New York: Cambridge University Press, 157.

Legislative requests are not the only indicator of how the president has become much more involved in the legislative process than the Framers had envisioned. Presidential vetoes, which we explore in detail later in this chapter, were rare in the early years of the Republic, indicating that presidents almost never struck down laws passed by Congress. For perspective, presidents issued a total of 52 vetoes in the first 74 years of our nation's history, from 1787 to the start of the Civil War. Franklin Delano Roosevelt (FDR), in contrast, issued an average of 53 vetoes *per year* during his presidency.[8]

Congress bears some responsibility for this growth in presidential power, as it often has delegated broad powers to the president. When Donald Trump was unable to convince Congress to fund a wall between Mexico and the United States, he invoked the National Emergencies Act of 1976, which gives the president broad authority to declare emergencies and to take actions to address these emergencies. Trump argued that this law (along with others) gave him the power to reallocate money that Congress had designated for other purposes—in this case, funds for military construction projects like base housing and schools for family members of military personnel. With respect to funding for the wall, members of both parties criticized the president for what they believed was an unwarranted declaration of a national emergency, and bipartisan majorities in both chambers voted to cancel the emergency, although Trump successfully vetoed this action.

In other situations, however, members of Congress have actively encouraged the president to make use of the broad powers that the legislature has delegated to the executive. During the initial weeks of the coronavirus pandemic in 2020, for example, members of both parties exhorted Trump to use the National Defense Act to command companies to produce equipment, such as ventilators and face masks, that were needed to combat the virus. After hesitating for weeks—due in part to opposition from some businesses, but also because, as the president publicly stated, "We're a country not based on nationalizing our business"[9]—Trump eventually relented, invoking this act for the first time in late March to command General Motors to make ventilators and 3M to make more N95 face masks available to medical personnel in the United States.[10]

As the president's power has increased, the lines between the responsibilities of Congress and the president have further blurred. We also see the branches trying to influence each other to the point where one close observer of Congress has flipped the standard view by referring (with admitted hyperbole) to the "president as legislator and Congress as administrator."[11]

### Critical Thinking

1. We tend to take it for granted that the Framers gave Congress great powers and described them in detail, while giving presidents more limited powers and describing them more vaguely. Why wouldn't they have sought to establish a system in which the powers of Congress and the president were evenly balanced?

2. Figure 9.1 shows a dramatic increase in the number of presidential requests to Congress starting in the 1940s. What might explain this sudden increase at that time?

---

## REPRESENTATION AND CONSTITUENCIES

Blurred lines, overlapping powers, and a tug-of-war over which branch has which powers might not matter so much if the president and members of Congress always shared the same perspectives and goals. But they do not, mainly because of differences in the political foundations of the two branches, especially as they relate to representation. Separate election cycles, with the president's four-year term lying between the two-year term for representatives and the six-year term for senators, illustrate one difference. Most members of

Congress regularly seek reelection and thus are repeatedly held accountable by their constituents. The Twenty-Second Amendment, meanwhile, restricts presidents to only one reelection, which orients them to take a much longer-term view of policy, especially in their second term.

Perhaps more important are the differences in constituencies. Presidents, who are elected in a national contest, are the only elected politicians in the United States who have a nationwide constituency. To win reelection, they often need to continue catering to people in the states that supported them while trying to win over people in states that supported their opponent. Members of Congress face much different—and smaller—constituencies, with representatives elected within congressional districts and senators elected by states. An obvious difference here is size. Presidents represent all 330 million people in the United States, whereas the median state population is about 4.5 million, and the average population of a congressional district is about 750,000. Thus the president will be concerned with the interests of a much larger and more heterogeneous population. To the extent that politicians are driven by their constituents' concerns, presidents will face a very different set of incentives than members of Congress.

Overall, tensions between the two branches are at least partially baked into the political system, with the different time horizons and constituencies that affect representation producing different views. This leads to a tug-of-war between the two branches over governing and where policy-making power should reside.

## THE PRESIDENT AND THE LEGISLATIVE PROCESS

The presidential powers outlined in the Constitution deal primarily with the executive branch. As head of the executive branch, the president is charged with "faithfully executing the laws"—that is, with implementing and administering the laws that Congress passes. For example, when Congress passes laws related to agriculture, such as providing subsidies to farmers, the U.S. Department of Agriculture (USDA) makes sure that these subsidies are paid, and when Congress passes laws about tax policy, the Internal Revenue Service (IRS) ensures that the policies in these laws are implemented and followed. Similarly, Article II, Section 2, gives the president the power to ask cabinet members to submit their written opinions on "any Subject relating to the Duties of their respective Offices." It also spells out that the president "shall be Commander in Chief" of the military (which is located within the executive branch). These are purely **executive powers** that the president can carry out, largely without needing any congressional action, such as when President Truman integrated the military.[12]

As noted earlier, however, the powers of each branch do not fall neatly into separate categories, so in addition to listing the president's executive powers, the

Presidents routinely try to set the legislative agenda with Congress. In 1993–94 President Clinton pushed for major health care reform legislation conceived by his administration and advisors with little initial input from Congress. Many saw this approach as a mistake, as Congress never even voted on the legislation.

Constitution also provides the president with **legislative powers**—in other words, powers that allow the president to participate in the legislative process. Article II, Section 3, for example, gives the president the authority to "recommend to their [Congress's] Consideration such Measures as he shall judge necessary and expedient." The Constitution, however, does not explain what it means by "recommend." It could mean that presidents and their advisors may develop and write laws that friendly legislators in Congress can then introduce. This was President Bill Clinton's approach in 1993–94 when he and his administration created a health policy plan that he then sent to Congress for consideration. (As evidence of the weakness of such an approach, not only did this plan fail to become law, but Congress never even voted on it.) It is far more common for the president to exhort Congress to consider specific approaches to dealing with distinct policy areas.

In contrast to the Constitution's vagueness regarding the president's power to recommend legislation, its description of the power to veto laws is much more specific. First, it's worth taking a step back to see how the Framers constructed and conceived of the veto. For a bill to become law, the Constitution stipulates that both chambers of Congress must pass it. Next, it needs to be presented to the president. Article I, Section 7, states, "If he approve he shall sign it, but if not he shall return it" to the chamber in which it originated, with any objections spelled out. At that point, if two-thirds of the members of that chamber vote in favor of the bill, it will be sent to the other chamber, and if two-thirds of the members of that chamber approve it, then "it shall become a Law." Although the word *veto* never appears in Article I or anywhere else in the Constitution, this article describes the process by which a president can veto a bill.

The Framers undoubtedly were attempting to strike a balance. Because presidents have veto power, Congress cannot pass a law on its own. But, because of Congress's power to override presidential vetos, presidents cannot always kill bills that the House and Senate have passed. Likewise, if both chambers pass a bill and send it to the president and the president fails to sign the bill or return it to Congress with specific objections within 10 days, then the bill automatically becomes law. The Framers designed this rule to prevent presidents from ignoring bills that Congress passes and consigning them to limbo by neither signing nor vetoing them.[13]

There is some dispute about why the Framers created the veto. Some scholars argue that it was originally intended to give the president a way to block bills that would encroach on presidential prerogatives. Others identify a more expansive justification, citing Madison's and Hamilton's views that the veto would provide another layer of protection against bad or improper laws.[14] What is not in doubt is that veto power allows the president to be a part of the legislative process. In fact, it ensures this. As a result, Congress must take the president's views into account when considering any legislation.

Presidents have other powers that are primarily executive but that also involve Congress (in particular the Senate). First, as we explain in Chapters 10 and 11, presidents can make appointments to government agencies and to the judicial branch. In each case, however, the president does so "by and with the Advice and Consent of the Senate" (Article II, Section 2). Thus presidents need the Senate's approval to place political appointees in executive branch agencies and on federal courts. Second, presidents have the power to negotiate with foreign powers but can finalize treaties only if "two thirds of the Senators present concur" (Article II, Section 2).[15]

## How Do Presidents Try to Influence the Legislative Process?

The president's constitutional powers over the legislative process can seem underwhelming. Yes, presidents can suggest legislation to Congress, but there is no assurance that Congress will heed those suggestions. Having the power to veto bills may seem like a more significant power, but viewed in stark (and ultimately simplistic) terms, the veto power merely means that presidents can give either a thumbs up or a thumbs down to any law that Congress has passed. Thus the ability to veto makes the president's role seem purely reactive.

How, then, have the president's powers increasingly expanded, often at the expense of Congress, over time? One explanation is that presidents have a host of non-legislative powers that they can use. Another explanation is that presidents can use a variety of tactics and approaches to expand the reach of their legislative powers. They use some of these powers to affect what Congress pays attention to, and they can use their veto power to shape legislation by threatening to block a bill unless it meets their approval.

To explore these powers in more depth, we begin by unpacking what it means to be able to suggest or veto legislation. Next, we turn to the tactics presidents can use when attempting to influence Congress, particularly bargaining, public appeals, and unilateral action. Initially we present these tactics uncritically; these are powers that presidents have, ones they clearly can (and do) use in the hope that their actions will be effective. After identifying and discussing these tactics, we then investigate whether they are effective.

**HOW CAN PRESIDENTS USE THEIR LEGISLATIVE POWERS?**  The ability to suggest legislation might seem like a fairly weak power. However, to get Congress to pay attention, presidents take actions that lend their suggestions more power and weight.

Presidents begin by deciding which issues to prioritize. President Ronald Reagan, for example, excelled at focusing on a few core ideas he wanted to see implemented, such as his specific "four-part plan to increase economic growth and reduce deficits" outlined in his 1983 State of the Union address.[16] More recently, President Trump concentrated his energies on immigration and trade. When being interviewed, giving speeches, or interacting with the press, presidents aim to focus on their preferred issues, which in turn draws media attention to these issues. Clear statements of presidential priorities also enable other actors in the administration—cabinet secretaries, bureaucrats, the president's staff—to direct their energies accordingly. Such focus can reduce executive infighting and can better direct White House resources to where they will do the most good.[17]

Setting priorities allows presidents to direct the national policy initiative by influencing which issues Congress addresses and how it does so. In other words, by stating priorities, presidents engage in agenda-setting (see also Chapter 6). For example, several recent presidents, most notably Presidents Clinton, Obama, and Trump, placed reforming the complicated and inefficient U.S. health care system at the top of their agendas and asked Congress to address this issue (although only Obama was successful).

After presidents have convinced Congress to place an issue on the agenda, they can frame, or define, the issue in specific ways. In the area of health care, for example, presidents might emphasize reducing the number of uninsured Americans, reducing health care costs, or improving overall health outcomes. Identifying and framing issues can subsequently shape press coverage and involve the public, which in turn generates pressure on Congress to address the issues.[18]

Just as the prioritizing of some issues over others can lead to presidential influence over the congressional agenda, so too can presidents use their veto power to influence what Congress does. As Figure 9.2 shows, some presidents have used this tool often.

The power to veto can affect the legislative process in two ways. First, presidents can use it to block legislation that they dislike. Second, the possibility of a presidential veto affects *how* Congress addresses issues. Strategically, Congress should anticipate whether a president is likely to veto a bill, and if so, should act to avoid this outcome when drafting the bill.

This logic of strategic anticipation dramatically affects how Congress writes bills. Consider, for example, a bill that increases the minimum wage. Members of Congress might prefer an increase of, say, 20 percent. They could simply write a bill specifying this increase, send it to the president, and see what happens. But they could also act more strategically by paying attention to any statements the president has made about what would constitute an appropriate increase, attempting to gauge the likelihood of a veto if they exceed the target the president has set, and so on. While they may prefer an increase of 20 percent, they might be willing to settle for a 10 percent increase, and they would much prefer the 10 percent increase to no increase at all.

The president, meanwhile, has an equally strong incentive to act strategically. Suppose that, in the president's view, a 10 percent increase is ideal, but a 20 percent increase is likely to pass both chambers. The president could wait for the 20 percent increase to pass both chambers and then veto it, but then the resulting policy (absent an override) would be no change to the minimum wage rather than the president's preferred 10 percent increase. So the president instead can signal to Congress that a 20 percent increase is out of the question, but a 10 percent increase is a possibility. From the perspectives of both institutions, the current minimum wage needs to be increased, but if both the president and Congress stick to their guns, no change will be made. This result would be a lose-lose situation, with neither side getting what it wants. Thus both sides will act strategically to produce a better outcome. Which side will win? The extent to which presidents can use or threaten vetoes to shape legislation, and the extent to which they can set the legislative agenda or otherwise influence Congress, depends on their abilities to bargain and to directly reach the American public.

**CONVINCING CONGRESS: BARGAINING, GOING PUBLIC, AND UNILATERAL ACTIONS** Perhaps the most famous line ever written by a political scientist about presidents and presidential power is Richard Neustadt's dictum that

**FIGURE 9.2** Presidential Vetoes

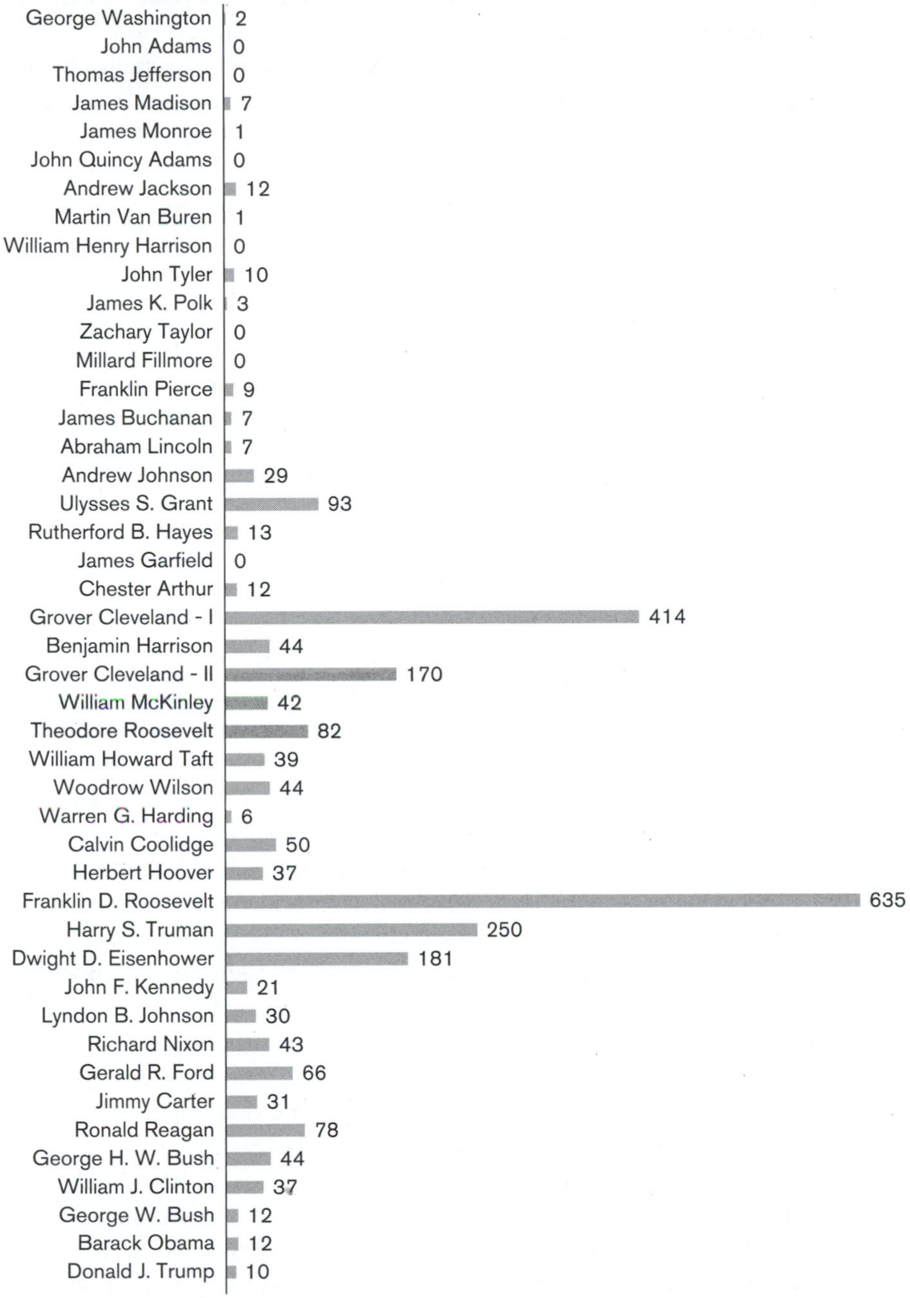

|  |  |
|---|---|
| George Washington | 2 |
| John Adams | 0 |
| Thomas Jefferson | 0 |
| James Madison | 7 |
| James Monroe | 1 |
| John Quincy Adams | 0 |
| Andrew Jackson | 12 |
| Martin Van Buren | 1 |
| William Henry Harrison | 0 |
| John Tyler | 10 |
| James K. Polk | 3 |
| Zachary Taylor | 0 |
| Millard Fillmore | 0 |
| Franklin Pierce | 9 |
| James Buchanan | 7 |
| Abraham Lincoln | 7 |
| Andrew Johnson | 29 |
| Ulysses S. Grant | 93 |
| Rutherford B. Hayes | 13 |
| James Garfield | 0 |
| Chester Arthur | 12 |
| Grover Cleveland - I | 414 |
| Benjamin Harrison | 44 |
| Grover Cleveland - II | 170 |
| William McKinley | 42 |
| Theodore Roosevelt | 82 |
| William Howard Taft | 39 |
| Woodrow Wilson | 44 |
| Warren G. Harding | 6 |
| Calvin Coolidge | 50 |
| Herbert Hoover | 37 |
| Franklin D. Roosevelt | 635 |
| Harry S. Truman | 250 |
| Dwight D. Eisenhower | 181 |
| John F. Kennedy | 21 |
| Lyndon B. Johnson | 30 |
| Richard Nixon | 43 |
| Gerald R. Ford | 66 |
| Jimmy Carter | 31 |
| Ronald Reagan | 78 |
| George H. W. Bush | 44 |
| William J. Clinton | 37 |
| George W. Bush | 12 |
| Barack Obama | 12 |
| Donald J. Trump | 10 |

U.S. House of Representatives, https://history.house.gov/Institution/Presidential-Vetoes/Presidential-Vetoes/ (accessed 1/14/21).

"[p]residential power is the power to persuade."[19] Neustadt is pointing out that presidents are not kings; they cannot command. Instead, they need to bargain with other political actors. With respect to statutes, they need to convince members of Congress to take certain actions and not others. Neustadt writes, "The essence of a President's persuasive task, with congressmen and everybody else, is to induce them to believe that what he wants of them is what their own appraisal of their own responsibilities requires them to do in their interest, not his."[20]

Of course, a president's ability to bargain effectively and successfully is not absolute. Rather, it relies on a mixture of popularity, status, authority, and interpersonal skills. When presidents are more popular with the public, for example, they can use this popularity to get lawmakers to support their programs.[21]

Presidents also seek to elevate their status and authority in the eyes of Congress by claiming an **electoral mandate**, in which they move quickly to extend the political momentum of their election campaign into the governing arena. Usually, they claim that they ran for office on certain issues and their victory indicates that the public wants these issues addressed. Most presidential scholars give little credence to the idea that mandates actually exist; still, presidents regularly claim them.[22] Lyndon B. Johnson, for example, pledged during his campaign to pursue civil rights and social welfare programs and then did so soon after taking office. Similarly, Reagan campaigned on reducing the role of government in the domestic arena and then immediately took steps in that direction upon taking office.[23] And Joe Biden followed his criticism of the Trump administration's handling of the COVID-19 pandemic in the United States by pushing for a number of actions designed to limit the spread of the disease and to facilitate vaccinations. Claims of mandates do not always produce success, however. For example, George W. Bush's misreading of his 2004 electoral victory led him to pursue policies that had little public support, such as privatization of Social Security, immigration reform, and increasing troop levels in Iraq.[24]

When presidents are seen (or see themselves) as formidable and authoritative, they are better able to persuade members of Congress to consider the issues they have prioritized. Similarly, presidents or members of their administration will bargain with Congress over the *content* of legislation, pushing for changes that help ensure that the president will sign the bill into law rather than veto it. During the presidency of George W. Bush, for example, Vice President Dick Cheney notified Congress that he planned to recommend that Bush veto a $288 billion appropriations bill for the military "unless lawmakers change it to take account of Defense Department objections."[25] More recently, the Trump administration used a "statement of administrative policy" to try to influence the content of the National Defense Authorization Act of 2018.[26] Specifically, President Trump objected to provisions that would have prevented military base closures (which the military wants, but senators do not), limited the president's ability to

Presidents often try to influence the content of legislation by directly negotiating with key members of Congress. Here, President Trump meets with lawmakers to discuss how to address the issue of young undocumented immigrants brought to the United States by their parents.

determine military pay raises, and reduced housing subsidies for dual-career military families.[27] Presidents might not be able to get Congress to do exactly what they want, but through bargaining and negotiation—such as when Trump had Treasury Secretary Steven Mnuchin work directly with House Speaker Nancy Pelosi on the Coronavirus Aid, Relief, and Economic Security (CARES) Act, as we saw in Chapter 1—they often can obtain at least some of what they want.

Presidential bargaining often includes direct attempts at persuasion, such as meetings in the Oval Office, invitations to White House dinners, and one-on-one meetings by the president. An alternative approach relies on the president's ability to speak directly to the American people in an attempt to rally their support. When presidents do this, they are **going public**, to use the term coined by Samuel Kernell.[28] They engage in this tactic with the expectation that the public will pressure members of Congress in a way that presidents cannot—that is, by threatening not to vote for a representative or senator who does not support the president's position, or promising to vote for those who do support the president.

When presidents go public, they are using what President Theodore Roosevelt famously referred to as the **bully pulpit**, where the word "bully" refers not to someone who relies on intimidation or force but rather an earlier meaning of the word that conveyed excellence. Roosevelt saw the presidency as a bully pulpit

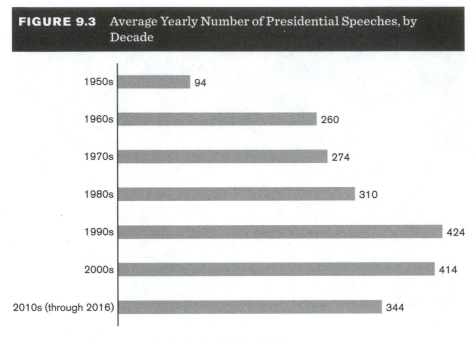

**FIGURE 9.3** Average Yearly Number of Presidential Speeches, by Decade

1950s — 94
1960s — 260
1970s — 274
1980s — 310
1990s — 424
2000s — 414
2010s (through 2016) — 344

Based on data provided to the authors by Matthew Eshbaugh-Soha.

because it was an outstanding position from which to promulgate his ideas and views.[29] Presidents can use this bully pulpit to try to prevent action, as when President Reagan, reacting to a proposed tax increase that Congress was considering, famously remarked, "I have my veto pen drawn and ready for any tax increase that Congress might even think of sending up. And I have only one thing to say to the tax increasers. Go ahead—make my day."[30] Or they can try to spur Congress to act, as President Trump did in July of 2017 when he told broadcaster Pat Robertson that he would be "very angry" with senators if they failed to pass a bill to kill Obamacare, adding that he was "sitting in the Oval Office with a pen in hand, waiting for our senators to give it to me. . . . It has to get passed. They have to do it. They have to get together and get it done."[31]

Presidents can go public in a variety of ways. Essentially, any use of travel or technology that allows presidents to reach outside of Washington, D.C., in order to stimulate pressure on members of Congress constitutes going public. Presidents can hold televised press conferences or address the nation from the Oval Office. They can give speeches, an activity that, as Figure 9.3 shows, became more frequent from the 1950s through the 2000s and still happens on a nearly daily basis. They also can tailor these speeches toward the goals of the day, whether setting the agenda, moving bills out of committee, or trying to secure votes.[32] More recently, although President Obama and his staff pioneered the

**Donald J. Trump** ✓
@realDonaldTrump

## I will be making a public statement tomorrow at 12:00pm from the @WhiteHouse to discuss our Country's VICTORY on the Impeachment Hoax!

5:07 PM · Feb 5, 2020 · Twitter for iPhone

**53.8K** Retweets   **7.4K** Quote Tweets   **274K** Likes

After his acquittal in his first impeachment trial, President Trump reiterated to his supporters that he believed the impeachment itself was a hoax.

use of social media to communicate with the public, President Trump relied on social media—especially Twitter—to a much greater extent, and in unorthodox ways, to speak directly to his supporters and opponents. Figure 9.4 indicates the topics he tweeted about most frequently during the first three years of his administration. He especially used tweets to speak directly to his supporters during the impeachment process, culminating in the triumphant tweet shown above, which followed his acquittal in the Senate.

In some respects, bargaining and going public are mutually exclusive strategies. Bargaining is generally private—that is, negotiations are conducted behind closed doors. In contrast, going public, as the name suggests, is a more visible strategy, tipping one's hand for all to see. Bargaining also tends to take place with a small handful of important members of Congress, especially those who have the power to make changes or those who will be most affected by a bill. Going public, on the other hand, is a much broader tactic, allowing the president to reach out to people across the country and thus, potentially, to influence a broader set of legislators.

For exactly these reasons, Kernell views going public as an alternative, not a complement, to bargaining, because it entails taking very public positions, which can then make bargaining and compromise harder. Although this may be true in some cases, in other cases the approaches could in fact be complementary. Presidents could, for example, go public in order to shore up their bargaining position. A Speaker of the House who might not have been receptive to a president's views on, say, Medicare reforms or tax cuts might suddenly become more receptive if members of the majority-party caucus are feeling pressure from their constituents because of the president's public appeals.

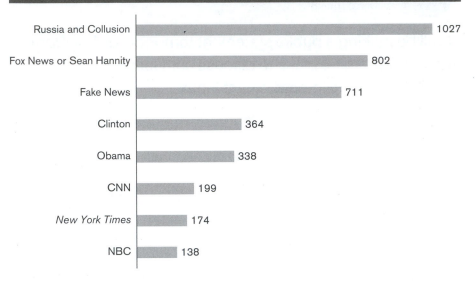

**FIGURE 9.4**  Topics President Trump Tweeted about Most Frequently

| Topic | Count |
|---|---|
| Russia and Collusion | 1027 |
| Fox News or Sean Hannity | 802 |
| Fake News | 711 |
| Clinton | 364 |
| Obama | 338 |
| CNN | 199 |
| New York Times | 174 |
| NBC | 138 |

Trump Twitter Archive, www.trumptwitterarchive.com/ (updated through June 2020).

Why have recent presidents gone public more frequently than their predecessors did? Kernell identifies three reasons why going public is a more fitting strategy for modern presidents. First, the increasingly intense and contentious nature of politics in recent decades discourages quiet and considered bargaining, rewarding more public strategies instead. Second, reforms to the presidential nomination process have produced presidents who are more inclined toward and skilled at public appeals. Third, the increased frequency of divided government, along with polarization, has made bargaining more difficult. When the two parties are ideologically distant from each other and one party controls the presidency while the other controls Congress, it is difficult for presidents to quietly compromise with members of Congress, as there may be few areas of agreement. In such cases, going public may be more effective in increasing pressure on those members of Congress.

In addition to bargaining and going public, presidents can threaten to use what have become known as **unilateral actions**, which are initiatives presidents can take on their own as the head of the executive branch. There are many forms of unilateral action. Presidents can, for example, change (or waive) some requirements that statutes have imposed on the states—for example, giving states waivers that allow them to impose more onerous requirements on Medicaid applicants than those outlined by federal statute.[33] Or they can issue signing statements, in which they explain their interpretation of a congressional statute and how they will implement it—or, in some cases, ignore it, as President George W. Bush did when he announced that he had the authority to direct officials to ignore the ban on torture that Congress had passed.[34] Another example comes from the CARES Act. When Congress passed this law in 2020, it worried that the bill's $500 billion in corporate relief might be inappropriately distributed, so it created an inspector general to oversee the executive branch's disbursement of these funds and to report any improprieties to Congress. When Donald Trump signed the law, however, he issued a signing statement saying that he would not allow the inspector general to release any information without presidential approval. Although signing statements do not have the force of law, they do indicate how presidents might try to avoid congressional stipulations.[35]

The most common and prominent unilateral action is the **executive order** (or related actions such as a presidential memorandum or proclamation), which is a presidential statement instructing agencies within the executive branch (e.g., the State Department, the Environmental Protection Agency) to take certain actions or follow specific processes. Upon taking office, for example, Trump issued Executive Order #13765, which directed the secretary of Health and Human Services, along with other agency leaders, to interpret any regulations related to the Affordable Care Act "as loosely as possible to minimize the financial burden on individuals, insurers, health care providers, and others."[36]

As Figure 9.5 shows, executive orders became much more common during Theodore Roosevelt's presidency in the early years of the twentieth century, remained at a high level through FDR's presidency, and since then have settled at a lower level (although still higher than in the 1800s). Even at this lower level, presidents in recent years have issued approximately 40 executive orders per year.[37] And in each of these cases, presidents have been able to change policy without securing congressional approval. Rather than bargaining directly with Congress, or speaking directly to voters who then pressure Congress, presidents use executive orders to circumvent Congress entirely.

Although executive orders and other unilateral actions allow presidents to act independently of Congress, there are limits on how and when these tactics can be used. Executive orders cannot be in direct conflict with existing laws, the president needs governors to agree to the terms of waivers, and recent research has shown that many constitutional signing statements are meant to reinforce proper boundaries between the president and Congress rather than suggest substantive changes to policy.[38] But each of these tactics allows presidents to act alone.

Furthermore, simply threatening to act unilaterally is a way for presidents to pressure Congress. Thus, just as the House and Senate may change a bill in order to avoid a veto and obtain the president's signature, they will attempt to anticipate whether the president is likely to issue an executive order, signing statement, or waiver. If so, representatives and senators may find it in their

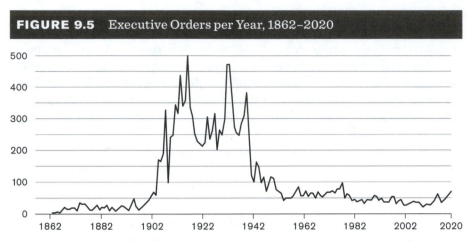

**FIGURE 9.5**   Executive Orders per Year, 1862–2020

Data obtained from Alexander Bolton and Sharece Thrower and from the *Federal Register*, https://www.federal register.gov/presidential-documents/executive-orders/ (accessed 1/14/21).

interest to compromise on the content of a bill to avoid triggering a unilateral action that would, from their perspective, produce an outcome worse than the compromise.

## Are Presidential Tactics Effective?

Do presidential pressure tactics work? That is, are presidents able to use these tactics to place their issues on the legislative agenda, to ensure that the content of bills is consistent with their preferences, and to alter policies when Congress is not compliant?

Agenda-setting is the first place to look for such evidence, and we begin by examining whether presidents are proactive in proposing agenda items. Evidence indicates that they are; however, we must keep in mind that presidents are just one of many actors (including political parties and interest groups) jostling to influence the agenda. Moreover, they are able to set the agenda across a range of issue areas, including health care, the environment, defense, crime, and the economy, and they have even greater influence in the area of international affairs.[39]

One of the most comprehensive studies of presidential attempts to influence the congressional agenda examined the *Public Papers of the Presidents* for every president from Harry Truman through Bill Clinton.[40] These papers contain all the president's public communications from each administration, including those communications in which the president specifically proposes legislation and asks Congress to consider it. Two main points emerge from Figure 9.6,

**FIGURE 9.6**   Average Number of Proposals per Year by President

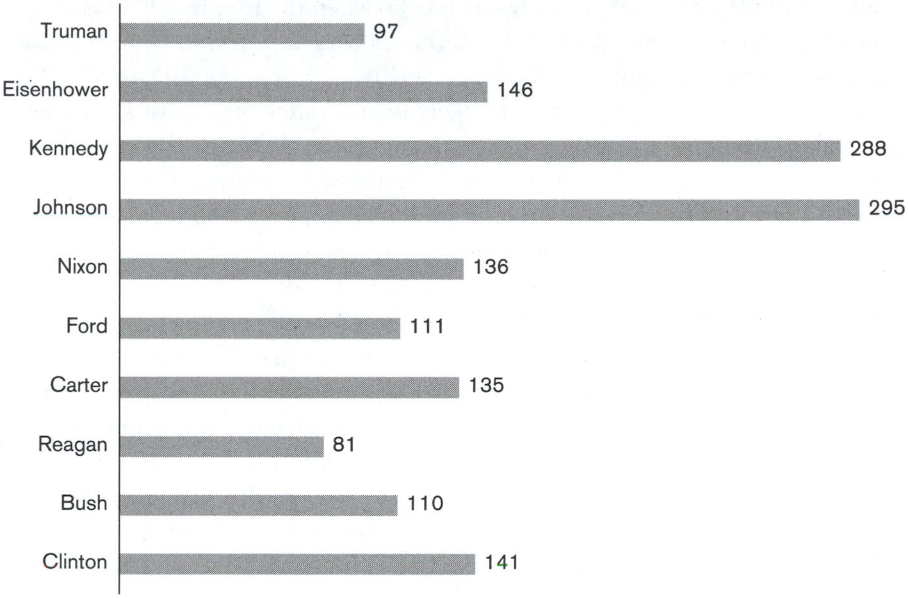

| President | Average Number of Proposals per Year |
|-----------|--------------------------------------|
| Truman | 97 |
| Eisenhower | 146 |
| Kennedy | 288 |
| Johnson | 295 |
| Nixon | 136 |
| Ford | 111 |
| Carter | 135 |
| Reagan | 81 |
| Bush | 110 |
| Clinton | 141 |

Based on data in Andrew Rudalevige. 2002. *Managing the President's Program: Presidential Leadership and Legislative Policy Formulation*, 72. Princeton, NJ: Princeton University Press.

which shows the number of proposals each president made. First, there is considerable variation across presidents, with Kennedy and Johnson far more active than the others. Second, and just as important, all of these presidents, even those who were relatively less active, asked Congress to consider a large number of proposals. The average number of proposals per year for all presidents was approximately 140 (just under three per week), but even if we exclude the two most proactive presidents, the others still submitted, on average, more than two proposals per week.

Based on our earlier discussion of how presidential power has increased over time, we might also expect that presidents of earlier eras were less likely to insert themselves into the legislative process, leaving that realm of governance to Congress. Scholar Jeffrey Cohen found precisely such a pattern. Using the *Public Papers* and a variety of other sources, he identified all legislative proposals that presidents have made over time.[41] His findings, which we saw earlier in Figure 9.1, show a steady and gradual increase in presidential involvement from the nation's birth through the end of World War I and then a dramatic increase starting immediately after World War II.

Not only do presidents make proposals, they often do so right after being inaugurated. In his book *The Strategic Presidency*, James P. Pfiffner stresses the need for presidents to move quickly and "strike when the iron is hot" to get Congress to consider their proposals.[42] Officials who have served in presidential administrations have confirmed the value of this approach, pointing to a straightforward reason: presidents are likely to encounter their most favorable political environment when they are first inaugurated.[43] During this period, presidential approval tends to be highest, which enables presidents to bargain successfully with Congress. It is also a period when opposition in Congress might not yet have solidified. And as time moves on, Congress will add its own items to the agenda. As an official in Jimmy Carter's administration put it, "It's definitely a race. The first months are the starting line. If you don't get off the blocks fast, you'll lose the race. Congress will come in first."[44]

Does Congress then take up the president's proposals? In other words, is a newly inaugurated president able to set the congressional agenda in a meaningful way? Studies find that in the second half of the twentieth century presidents proposed approximately one-third of the significant bills that Congress considered. According to political scientist Mark Peterson, most of the major proposals the White House submits to Congress receive at least some consideration. In addition, nearly half of the minor proposals receive consideration.[45] Overall, one recent analysis concluded, "If there is a clear leader in the agenda stage of the policy process, it is the president."[46]

In short, by drawing attention to an issue, presidents can induce Congress to focus on that issue, especially when the president has strong public approval ratings. When the president mentions particular issue areas in a State of the Union address, Congress becomes increasingly likely to hold hearings on those same issues. The effect is relatively short-lived, however, which further incentivizes presidents to move quickly. And the effect is weaker under divided government than unified government.[47]

The obvious next question is whether these proposals find success. Congress might, after all, just pay lip service to the president's ideas and favored policies. But it turns out that presidential proposals do fairly well once they reach Congress. Not surprisingly, presidents have trumpeted their success in this area. Lyndon Johnson boasted that in the two years after his election (1965 and 1966), he had a 91 percent success rate in Congress. Bill Clinton maintained that in his first two years in office, he worked with Congress to "substantially or partially accomplish" more than three-quarters of the issues on which he had campaigned.[48]

Of course, presidents are hardly unbiased evaluators of their own accomplishments. But independent studies confirm that once presidents place their items on the legislative agenda, these items do tend to find success.[49] In 29 percent of these cases, presidents received essentially everything they sought when they proposed a bill. In another 20 percent of proposals, presidents received the majority of what they sought, and in another 12 percent, they received some of what they sought. Taken together, presidents received some or all of what they wanted in more than 60 percent of the proposals that they suggested to Congress—not a perfect record, but a strong one. Presidents were especially likely to succeed when their ideology was similar to that of Congress, when the policy area was domestic, and when their approval ratings were high.

In many cases, presidents bargain to get their items on the congressional agenda or to get the items turned into laws. High approval ratings can increase presidential support among legislators, as legislators are more likely to respond to appeals from presidents who are popular—but not on all issues. Instead, the effect of approval is conditional: higher levels of approval help presidents achieve greater success in Congress (as measured by a majority of the House voting to support the president's position) if the issue is salient but the public has not yet formed entrenched opinions about it.[50]

Going public is another way presidents can attempt to improve their odds of legislative success, but evidence that this strategy can be successful is mainly anecdotal. For example, during Reagan's first term in office, members of Congress spoke of their offices being "inundated with phone calls" after Reagan gave a televised speech promoting his proposed tax cuts. The speech was widely viewed as having secured the necessary support for Reagan's position.[51] However, it is just as easy to find instances in which going public did not produce increased support for a president's preferred policy. A historical example is Woodrow Wilson's push for the League of Nations. More recent examples include Bill Clinton's attempt to pass health care reform, George W. Bush's goal of privatizing Social Security, Barack Obama's push for immigration reform, and Donald Trump's use of Twitter to attempt to generate support for repealing the Affordable Care Act and instituting a payroll tax cut during the coronavirus pandemic—none of which succeeded.

Systematic appraisals of the president's ability to influence public opinion have produced mixed findings. We might expect that the presidents regarded as great communicators—Reagan, Clinton, or Obama, for example—would be able to pull public opinion toward their positions. Yet a careful evaluation of public opinion prior to major presidential addresses and after those addresses reveals that public opinion rarely changes in response to a president's public appeals, and when it does, the effect tends to be very short-lived.[52]

Still, there is some evidence that presidents' public appeals sway Congress, so even if appeals do not significantly move public opinion, legislators might believe

Presidents often "go public" to influence legislation, but it's questionable if this tactic is effective. In the wake of the Sandy Hook school shootings, President Obama held several public events to press for stricter gun control. Ultimately, Congress took little action on the issue, despite legislation introduced by Ted Cruz (R-Tex.) and Chuck Grassley (R-Iowa).

that they do. Budget data provide a useful way to examine the effect of public appeals from the president on congressional actions. If public appeals do matter, then when a president makes a public appeal, we should see congruence between the budget request the president sends to Congress and the amount of spending that Congress ends up authorizing.

An examination of televised presidential addresses shows that presidents make public appeals regarding budget items about two or three times per year.[53] Looking for appropriations requests and budgetary outlays in these appeals produces a number of interesting findings. First, presidents are more likely to make public appeals on proposals that they know are popular. When the public's approval of a specific budget proposal—say, spending more money on defense—increases by 10 percent, presidents are 22 percent more likely to go public on that issue. Presidents also make public appeals more often on issues when they think such appeals are necessary. In other words, if they think they're likely to get their way anyway, they won't make an appeal, but if the only way for them to succeed is by making an appeal, they'll do so. As a consequence, presidents are strategic about when they appeal to the public. Most importantly, though, presidential appeals on budget matters do make a difference, with such appeals causing the change in appropriations from one year to the next to be 12 percent closer to what the president requested.[54]

Veto threats also can induce Congress to move policy toward the president's preferred position. In theory, Congress should have an incentive to anticipate a presidential veto and to make concessions that might avoid such a veto—and one recent study identified such an effect. Focusing on appropriations bills and explicit veto threats, it found that in 68 percent of cases where the president voiced opposition to legislation but did not threaten a veto, Congress ended up moving the content of the bill closer to the president's preferences. But when the president explicitly threatened a veto, this percentage jumped to 91 percent, indicating that such threats are far more powerful, and taken much more seriously, than milder statements of opposition.[55] Of course, presidents must be selective about issuing such threats, which would quickly lose their power if made too frequently or not backed up. But when used judiciously, veto threats provide another way for presidents to influence the content of congressional bills.

## How the Political Context Affects Presidential Success in Congress

Three features of the political environment during a president's time in office have a particularly strong effect on the president's ability to influence Congress: divided government, polarization, and war.

**DIVIDED GOVERNMENT**   Divided government is the most obvious constraint on the president. A president whose party controls Congress can rely on co-partisans within Congress in numerous ways—for example, to introduce the president's proposals and then shepherd them through the legislative process. In the case of Donald Trump's first impeachment, the Senate, which was controlled by Trump's fellow Republicans, did not convict him after the Democratic-controlled House had voted to impeach. In contrast, a president faced with a Congress controlled by the opposing party can expect to encounter regular opposition, as this party will put its own issues (rather than the president's) on the agenda, oppose the president's bills in committee and on the floor, and fail to support the president's budget requests.

As Bryan Marshall and Bruce Wolpe have explained, members of Congress from the president's party are always more supportive of the president than members of the opposition party are.[56] Figure 9.7 shows that during George W. Bush's administration between 2000 and 2008, the president received the support of about 80 percent of House Republicans on issues where he had taken a public position. Meanwhile, he received the support of only 25 to 30 percent of House Democrats on those issues. The figure also shows that the gap in support between co-partisans and the opposing party has been increasing over time, with levels of support being fairly similar in the late 1960s and then diverging thereafter. Consequently, when the president's co-partisans in Congress outnumber members of the opposing party, as during unified government, the

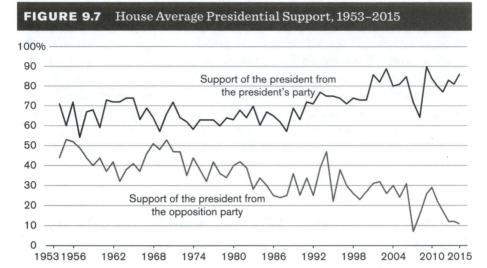

**FIGURE 9.7** House Average Presidential Support, 1953–2015

Bryan Marshall. 2012. "Congress and the Executive: Unilateralism and Legislative Bargaining," in *New Directions in Congressional Politics*, ed. by Jamie L. Carson, 184. New York: Routledge; updated with data from Bryan Marshall.

president's policy proposals are more likely to receive support. This support during unified government, and the corresponding lack of support during divided government, suggests that presidents might be more likely to use unilateral actions during divided government. Somewhat surprisingly, the evidence on this point is mixed. Although some studies find that presidents are more likely to use unilateral actions during divided government, others find that presidents use these tactics more often under unified government.[57]

**PARTY POLARIZATION**  The increase in legislative polarization—that is, the ideological distance between Republicans and Democrats in Congress—has been well documented (see Chapter 6). Polarization can combine with divided government to make life difficult for presidents who try to influence Congress. If there is little ideological distance between the two parties, then divided government might not matter all that much, because presidents would be able to find plenty of ideological common ground with members of the opposing party. But as Figure 9.7 shows, the parties have moved farther apart and such common ground is scarce, which in turn affects the strategies that presidents use when dealing with Congress. For example, the use of veto threats has increased as the parties have become more polarized, but mainly during periods of divided government.[58] At the same time, polarization might affect the president's decision to go public. For going public to have a chance of succeeding, the president must first mobilize public opinion, and the public in turn must influence their representatives. With the large and growing divide between the parties, combined with fewer moderates in Congress and strong partisan loyalty, members have become less susceptible to "political breezes the president can stir up in their constituencies."[59]

The overall effect of polarization on presidential success in Congress, measured by Congressional Quarterly as the percentage of key votes in which the president takes a position and Congress votes to support that position, is also contingent on divided government. Figure 9.8 shows that in the 1960s and 1970s, when the parties were less polarized, presidents had more success under unified government than under divided government, but the differences were not huge. More recently, however, and coinciding with increased polarization, the gap is much larger. Polarization is thus impeding presidential success in Congress under divided government.[60]

**WAR AND FOREIGN POLICY** Finally, war affects the relationship between the president and Congress. During times of war, members of Congress become more deferential to presidents on foreign and domestic policies. During World War I and World War II, as well as in the post–September 11 period, individual members of Congress tended to shift away from their standard voting patterns and cast votes more in line with the president's views.[61] Thus a liberal member of Congress faced with a conservative president will vote more conservatively during wartime than in times of peace, while a conservative member of Congress faced with a liberal president will vote more liberally.

Presidents are especially dominant in foreign policy, where they operate more independently of Congress. Serving in the role of commander in chief, they are directly in charge of the armed forces and have the authority to order troop movements. They appoint ambassadors to other countries, and they alone have the power to negotiate and initiate treaties and trade agreements with these other countries.

Though Congress can push back on some of these powers, it often has only limited success. For example, the Senate has to approve treaties, but in reality, treaties are rarely struck down; the Senate's vote in 2012 to prevent the United States from entering the United Nations Disabilities Convention (a treaty President Obama supported) offers a rare exception. The Senate can, however, block presidential treaties by simply not taking any action, which has happened with dozens of treaties (including the United Nations Law of the Sea).

Inaction provides Congress with a measure of power, but if presidents are concerned about either rejection or inaction, they can take a different tack and avoid the Senate entirely. They can take unilateral action and pursue international goals via executive agreements, which are not subject to Senate approval.[62] In fact, Obama effectively abandoned the Article II treaty process,

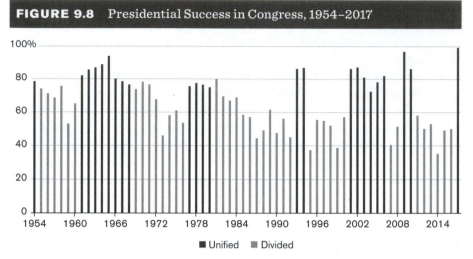

FIGURE 9.8 Presidential Success in Congress, 1954–2017

■ Unified   ■ Divided

Created by the authors based on data obtained from Michael P. Fix and from various editions of *Congressional Quarterly Almanac.*

submitting far fewer treaties to the Senate than any other modern president and winning a very low percentage of approvals when he did submit them. Instead, the Obama administration turned to executive agreements and political agreements to pursue a wide range of international policies, including the highly prominent Iran Nuclear Accord and the Paris Climate Agreement. In pursuing diplomatic goals through these means, President Obama effectively shut Congress out of the process. Obama's approach might have allowed him to avoid the Senate, but it also made it easier for his successor, Donald Trump, to withdraw from both agreements.

The push and pull between the president and Congress extends to war powers. According to the War Powers Resolution, Congress, not the president, has the power to declare war. This resolution also restricts the president's ability to take military action. Still, presidents have found a number of creative ways to work around these restrictions—for example, by entering into hostilities with another country without calling it a war (which is what happened with both Korea in the 1950s and Vietnam in the 1960s). Congress can use its power to appropriate money (the "power of the purse") to limit the president's use of the military, but Congress does not like to be seen as not supporting the troops.

Overall, presidents clearly are more powerful in foreign affairs than in domestic affairs. This power allows presidents to react more quickly to crises, but it can be seriously problematic if a president is inexperienced, uninformed, or makes bad decisions in the foreign policy arena. For example, when Congress passed sanctions on Russia to punish it for interfering with the 2016 presidential election, legislators worried about Donald Trump unilaterally lifting the sanctions, so they stipulated that Congress must approve any changes to these sanctions.[63]

## CONGRESSIONAL INFLUENCE ON THE PRESIDENT

Clearly, presidents have the power to influence Congress, they use that power in practice, and their attempts to influence Congress are often successful. None of this, however, should be taken to imply that presidents can simply toy with Congress, or that they get what they want whenever they want, or that Congress is helpless in the face of presidential power. Although it has lost power to the president over time, Congress has a variety of tools that it can use to counteract presidential activities.

Consider the president's setting of the legislative agenda. Although we have seen that Congress often does address the president's policy proposals, it often does not. In fact, in as many as 25 percent of cases, Congress simply ignores the president's proposals and takes no action on them.[64] Furthermore, Congress can and does introduce its own proposals,[65] and it can do so regardless of whether these are issues the president wants to tackle, which is why the size of the agenda tends to increase under divided government.[66] And while presidents propose budgets, Congress, with its power of the purse, needs to pass them. Although we have seen that presidents can use public appeals to move the final budget numbers closer to their own preferences, the effect is rather small, and Congress often ignores the president's requests. Senator John McCain (R-Ariz.), for example, bluntly characterized Trump's first budget proposal as "inadequate" and "dead on arrival."[67] At the same time, Senate Majority Leader Mitch McConnell (R-Ky.) reminded everyone that Congress ultimately would decide what was in the budget: "The president's budget, as we all know, is a recommendation [that] will not be determinative in every respect."[68]

Vetoes may give presidents leverage, but Congress can override vetoes, and as Figure 9.9 shows, it does so on a limited but fairly consistent basis: Congress has overridden vetoes from approximately 80 percent of presidents since the Civil War. Furthermore, Congress can try to use a president's veto threat against that president. In such cases, Congress passes a law not *despite* knowing that the president will veto it, but rather *because* members know that the president will veto it. This course of action might sound counterintuitive, but the underlying logic makes sense. For example, suppose that Congress wants to pass a bill, but the president has taken a position against the bill. If Congress has a strong sense that the public will disapprove of the president's veto, it might pass the bill and send

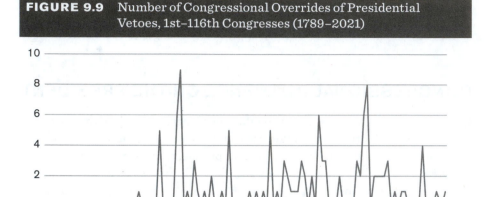

**FIGURE 9.9** Number of Congressional Overrides of Presidential Vetoes, 1st–116th Congresses (1789–2021)

U.S. House of Representatives, https://history.house.gov/Institution/Presidential-Vetoes/Presidential-Vetoes/ (accessed 1/14/21).

it to the president, knowing that the resulting disapproval will then hurt the president politically, giving Congress greater leverage in dealing with other issues.[69]

Congress played this blame game in 1992 when the Democratic leaders of the House and Senate worked together to pass a family leave bill.[70] Notably, they did so knowing that President George H. W. Bush had promised to veto the specific version of the bill they were writing. Equally notable is that many observers believed that Bush was open to a more moderate version of the bill. Yet Congress chose to go forward with its preferred version, knowing that Bush would veto it and that public opinion would turn against him, which is exactly what happened. More generally, vetoes are associated with drops in presidential approval, with the now familiar caveat that this relationship is especially likely to occur under divided government.

Congress also has tools it can use to counter the president's unilateral powers. Most basically (if not easily), it can pass new laws. For example, if Congress disapproves of a president's executive order, it can pass a new law that supersedes the order. It can do the same if it dislikes the way the president's agencies are implementing a law or if it opposes the interpretation that the president sets out in a signing statement.[71] Such laws would, of course, be subject to a veto, so Congress often will bundle instructions to the executive branch into must-pass laws in order to constrain the executive. For example, Congress regularly includes riders—provisions that place limits on what agencies can do—in appropriations bills, because these bills must be signed into law in order to keep the government running. Here Congress hopes that even if the president does not like a specific rider, that rider will not be enough to spur a veto of the entire appropriations bill. Nonetheless, when faced with the possibility that Congress will include riders to limit presidential action, presidents sometimes do threaten vetoes. These threats can be enough to force Congress to moderate the riders, bringing them closer to the president's preferred position.[72]

Congress doesn't need to pass laws to exert power.[73] If a president is directing an agency to take actions that Congress believes run counter to statutes it has passed, it can engage in more diligent and aggressive oversight in order to counter the president's actions and pressure the agency into following its intent. A recent study by Scott Ainsworth, Brian Harward, and Kenneth Moffett shows that Congress does just that. When presidents object to provisions in laws (for example, when they issue a signing statement), Congress—in particular, the congressional committees with responsibility for overseeing agencies—responds by holding more frequent oversight hearings.[74] As we will see in Chapter 10, these hearings can influence agencies and the actions they take.

## HOW WE STUDY
## CONGRESSIONAL INVESTIGATIONS

Congress has another useful arrow in its quiver: it can investigate the president. The right to conduct investigations, and more generally to oversee the president and the executive branch, is a significant congressional responsibility, one that derives from the implied powers provisions of the Constitution, which give Congress the authority to engage in activities that allow it to pursue its enumerated powers. The power to investigate is one that Congress takes seriously and engages in regularly. According to the Brookings Institution, between January 2019 and April 2020 Congress held 300 separate hearings, and issued 660 letters requesting information from the president and members of his administration, to investigate topics personally connected to Trump and his family (such as his tax returns, abuse of the White House security clearance procedure, payment of hush money connected to the election, and potential cooperation with Russian agents during and after the 2016 election) and to his administration (such as the administration's preparedness for and response to the COVID-19 outbreak).[75]

Congress can influence the actions of the president through its power to investigate executive branch activity. In 2020, Congress held public oversight hearings about the Trump administration's preparedness for the COVID-19 outbreak. Among the officials questioned was Dr. Anthony Fauci, director of the National Institute of Allergy and Infectious Diseases, who led much of the country's response to the pandemic.

Even when investigations of presidents and their teams appear mainly to be politically motivated, proponents of the investigations usually argue that they have legitimate and nonpolitical purposes. Republicans who led the many investigations of Secretary of State Hillary Clinton's actions related to the Benghazi tragedy (in which four Americans were killed in an attack on the American embassy there) undoubtedly wanted to know if Clinton had made specific mistakes and whether safeguards could be put in place in the future, just as Democrats who pushed for the investigations of Russian meddling in the 2016 presidential election and the Trump campaign's potential cooperation with the Russians wanted to know how to protect our country's elections from tampering by foreign adversaries. In the views of these proponents, when Congress investigates presidents, it is exercising its governing function.

That said, there is no doubt that investigations can be used to weaken the president, or members of the president's team, politically, and that members of Congress recognize this. In unguarded moments, members of Congress have even acknowledged the political subtext of investigations. For example, House

Majority Leader Kevin McCarthy (R-Calif.) acknowledged that the hearings about the deaths of Americans in Benghazi were part of a strategy to make Hillary Clinton easier to defeat in an election: "Everybody thought Hillary Clinton was unbeatable, right? But we put together a Benghazi special committee, a select committee. What are her numbers today? Her numbers are dropping. Why? Because she's untrustable."[76]

With so many other ways to improve its position vis-à-vis the president (passing laws, overriding vetoes, voting against nominees, holding press conferences), why does Congress sometimes turn to investigations to score political points? The most thorough and convincing analysis of investigations appears in Douglas Kriner and Eric Schickler's *Investigating the President*. To begin with, it is far easier to initiate and conduct investigations, which are entirely under Congress's control, than to pass laws, which require the president's signature. Indeed, an investigation requires only the agreement of the majority-party leaders and (usually) the chairs of the relevant committees. In addition, all Senate and House committees have subpoena power, which gives them great authority to compel witnesses to testify during investigations.

Because conducting investigations does not require the same collective action as passing laws, it is often easier for members to claim credit for investigations.[77] Furthermore, the members who lead investigations often receive favorable publicity, which means that they simultaneously benefit their party (by questioning the president) and improve their own reelection chances. Thus both individually and collectively, members of Congress have an incentive to investigate the president.

To determine the frequency of investigations and to assess their arguments, Kriner and Schickler drew upon data provided by the Congressional Information Service (and later ProQuest) to identify hearings that "involved some official or entity within the executive branch" and that investigated misconduct or scandal. Figure 9.10, drawn from their study, shows their findings. The data show that not only does Congress have an incentive to investigate the president, it also does so frequently. From 1898 through 2014, Congress conducted 4,522 hearings aimed at investigating potential misconduct by the executive branch. Because many hearings occur across multiple days, this number of hearings corresponds to more than 11,900 days that Congress spent investigating the president, an average of more than 100 days per year.

Figure 9.10 shows peaks during the scandal-ridden presidencies of Warren Harding in the 1920s and Richard Nixon in the 1970s, but the figure also makes it clear that congressional investigations of the executive branch are a regular feature of the Washington, D.C., landscape. Kriner and Schickler's findings support the conventional wisdom: investigations are more common when control of government is divided and polarization is high. Furthermore, these

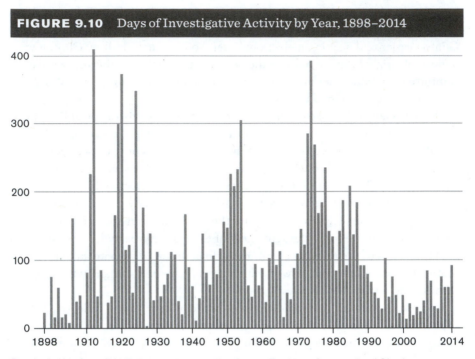

**FIGURE 9.10** Days of Investigative Activity by Year, 1898–2014

Douglas L. Kriner and Eric Schickler. 2016. *Investigating the President: Congressional Checks on Presidential Power*, 36. Princeton, NJ: Princeton University Press. In some years there are more than 365 days of hearings because multiple hearings occurred on some days.

investigations are often damaging to the president. They attract media attention to the issue or action under investigation, sometimes trigger further legislative responses, often cause the president to change the course of policy preemptively, and can lead to a drop in the president's public approval. As Kriner and Schickler conclude, "Investigations systematically impose political costs on the president by diminishing his support among the public. . . . Even when it cannot legislatively compel the president to change course, Congress can raise the political costs of certain executive actions by alleging abuses of power and battling the president in the public sphere."[78]

## Critical Thinking

1. Is there any way to distinguish congressional investigations of the president that are purely political from those that are not driven solely by political considerations?

2. We often see more congressional investigations during scandal-ridden presidencies. Still, many investigations occur during relatively scandal-free presidencies, such as the Benghazi investigations during the Obama administration. What might explain why these investigations occur?

3. Investigations are more common under divided government than under unified government. Yet investigations also occur under unified government.
Why might Congress investigate a president from its own party, knowing
that such investigations might hurt the president's approval?

## Impeachment

Congress's ultimate power over the president is the power of impeachment.
According to Article II, Section 4, of the Constitution, the president (as well as
other government officials) "shall be removed from Office on Impeachment for,
and conviction of, Treason, Bribery, or other High Crimes and Misdemeanors."
Although individual members of Congress often have raised the topic of
impeachment, and sometimes even have taken steps to introduce articles of
impeachment, no president has been impeached and then convicted. As we saw
at the start of this chapter, Donald Trump was impeached twice, joining
Andrew Johnson and Bill Clinton as the only presidents to be impeached. Like
them, he was not convicted and remained in office.[79]

A complicating factor regarding impeachment is the unclear meaning of
"other High Crimes and Misdemeanors," where "High" refers to crimes and misdemeanors committed while holding office (and is not a synonym for "severe").
Legal standards do play a role in impeachment, but ultimately impeachment is a
political decision, and each member of Congress must decide whether a president's transgressions rise to the level of being impeachable. The fact that a
president has committed a criminal offense does not mean that Congress must
impeach. A president who jaywalks may have committed a crime, but very few
people would consider this an impeachable offense. Conversely, Congress can
impeach a president even if the president did not commit a crime (although
some of Trump's supporters in Congress contended otherwise).

Given the uncertainty about the standards for impeachment, it is worth
considering the Framers' views. Although the Framers recognized the necessity for a president to head the executive branch in the new constitutional
system, they were deeply concerned about the possibility that presidents
might abuse their powers—a pattern they had seen in previous regimes around
the world and throughout time. As one political observer has written, the Framers especially "worried that the enormous powers attendant to the office could
be abused, that they could fall into the hands of an unfit incumbent, or that they
could come under the influence of foreign powers."[80] Thus the Framers viewed
impeachment as a potential remedy for cases in which presidents were unfit for
office because they were not acting in the best interests of the United States

and consequently were a threat to the Republic. Hamilton elaborated this view in *Federalist 65*, identifying impeachable offenses as those "that proceed from the misconduct of public men, or in other words from the abuse or violation of some public trust. They are of a nature which may with peculiar propriety be denominated political, as they relate chiefly to injuries done immediately to the society itself."[81] The Framers did not view impeachment as equivalent to a coup; rather, they saw it as a necessary if unfortunate option for dealing with a president who put his own interests ahead of those of the nation. They therefore viewed impeachment as a drastic remedy, one that Congress should never consider lightly, but that must be available as a potentially necessary recourse in dire situations.

## CONCLUSION

When the Framers created the presidency, they had in mind democracies and republics of antiquity, many of which were eventually undermined by single leaders who became tyrants. Thus they recognized that a president, as the head of the new American system of government, could pose a serious threat to the new Republic's survival. At the same time, they knew they needed a single person to head the executive branch. The Framers' experiences with the Articles of Confederation had made it obvious that without a president, the government would be undermined by its own potential impotence. Hence, they had a fine line to walk between giving the president too much power and not enough power.

Because the Framers created a system of checks and balances in which the president has some legislative powers and Congress is able to influence the actions of the executive branch, tensions between Congress and the president are inevitable. Indeed, these tensions are built into the relationship and have been since the nation's founding. As a result, cooperation between the branches is necessary to get things done. Cooperation does not mean that Congress and the president need to agree on everything. It simply means that they need to find ways to work together.

If tension is the primary characteristic of the relationship between the two branches, then a close second is the always-changing nature of this relationship. Each branch uses the tools at its disposal to attempt to gain an upper hand over the other branch, with the president relying on public appeals and the power of the veto, and Congress using investigations and control over its own agenda. Complete agreement over which issues to address and how to address them is unlikely to happen, even when one party controls both chambers. But each institution will react to the other's actions. Through this process of tension, change, and strategic behavior, politics plays out and policy is made.

## Discussion Questions

1. This chapter argues that the balance of power between Congress and the president has shifted steadily in favor of the president over time. Is it possible for that trend to reverse? What would it take for that to happen?

2. Why do vetoes ever occur? After all, Congress and the president are in constant communication about each other's policy views. Why don't they just work out any differences in advance?

3. Many political observers contend that when presidents fail to get Congress to pass their programs, it is because they didn't work hard enough to convince the public of the value of their policy goals. Yet as we point out in this chapter, many studies find that presidents are unable to change public opinion. Given the bully pulpit, why are presidents so limited in their ability to influence public opinion?

4. Some studies find that unilateral powers are used more commonly under divided government, but others do not. Why might presidents turn to unilateral actions when their party controls Congress (that is, under unified government)?

5. Although Donald Trump was the first president ever to have members of his own party vote to impeach and convict him, the majority of his co-partisans in Congress voted against impeachment and for acquittal. Does this imply that impeachment cannot work in a highly partisan era?

# 10

## Congress and the Bureaucracy

Government agencies rarely seek the spotlight. When an agency is doing its job, the public, interest groups, the media, and members of Congress usually have little reason to pay attention to it. Instead, such attention usually happens when an agency has done something wrong—for example, when it is being singled out for incompetence, or, worse, when it is suspected of being at the heart of a political scandal.

   This is exactly the unenviable position in which the IRS (Internal Revenue Service), already among the least popular of all government institutions, found itself in 2012 and 2013, when it was accused of targeting conservative groups for intensive and unreasonable scrutiny. The situation first came to light when a number of nonprofit conservative interest groups began to complain of unfair treatment by the IRS. These groups had applied for a specific legal status—known as 501(c)(4) status, after the relevant portion of the Internal Revenue Code—that includes several desirable features. As long as a group can certify that its primary purpose is not political (that is, it is not endorsing specific candidates for office), then it is designated as a tax-exempt organization and allowed to engage in unlimited lobbying and keep the names of its donors anonymous.

In 2012 and 2013, the IRS was accused of unfairly targeting conservative nonprofit groups for special scrutiny. In response, Congress required several IRS officials to testify at hearings about this activity. This scuffle shows the tensions that can arise between government agencies and a Congress that tries to control them.

Because the IRS needs to certify whether groups' missions are nonpolitical, it frequently asks them about their activities. That part of the process is standard, and all groups expect it. But conservative groups claimed that they were being singled out and asked to provide an excessive amount of information, while liberal groups were not.

When conservative groups raised this complaint, members of Congress began to look for a pattern of bias. The head of the IRS at the time, Douglas Shulman, a George W. Bush appointee who stayed on in President Barack Obama's administration, stated unequivocally that the agency had not targeted conservative groups. IRS officials also pointed out that the increased scrutiny of groups applying for 501(c)(4) status was a natural result of a sudden and unexpectedly large increase in the number of such applications after 2010. Still, conservative groups kept complaining, members of Congress kept inquiring, and the media kept investigating. Ultimately, these investigations revealed that the IRS had been searching for groups with names that included words or phrases such as Tea Party, Patriots, and 9/12, all of which are strongly associated with conservative organizations, and had subjected these groups to extra scrutiny.[1]

In response to this revelation, congressional committees flew into action, calling high-level IRS bureaucrats and many former employees in for thorough and aggressive questioning. In response, the agency produced 1.3 million pages of documents. Committees conducted more than 30 hearings and issued scathing reports about the agency's actions.[2] Perhaps most importantly, Congress cut the agency's budget by approximately $1 billion over the next several years, making it difficult for the agency to carry out its duties or conduct additional investigations into groups seeking 501(c)(4) status.

The aftershocks of this scandal were felt for years. The agency's attempts to write new rules for dealing with 501(c)(4) applications drew immediate further criticism from Congress. In 2016, for example, the chair of the House Oversight and Government Reform Committee introduced legislation to impeach then head of the IRS, John Koskinen, even though Koskinen had not been in charge of the IRS when the scandal occurred. Some members of Congress even supported a move that would have reduced the yearly salaries of specific bureaucrats to as little as $1.

The IRS scandal stood out for the amount of attention it generated. At the same time, the actions that Congress took in response to the scandal—hearings, investigations, subpoenas, budget cuts—are typical of how Congress deals with government agencies. In this chapter, we assess how Congress influences agencies, not just in reaction to scandals, but more generally. We begin by considering what agencies do and why Congress would even want to influence agencies. Then, after examining the factors that Congress takes into account when creating and staffing these agencies, we explain how Congress uses statutes, procedural constraints, budgets, and other means of oversight to influence agency activities.

## WHAT DO GOVERNMENT BUREAUCRACIES DO?

As the first branch of government, Congress is responsible for setting policy in the United States. Throughout this book, we have seen the many ways Congress can affect policy: through the committee system, which allows different members to specialize in different policy areas; through political parties, which choose to emphasize some policy areas and de-emphasize others when they control a chamber; and through the actions of individual representatives and senators, who focus their efforts on specific policy areas. Congress plays an active role in setting and influencing policy. However, **government bureaucracies**, or agencies, create the vast majority of policies in the United States today. Modern American government is, in many respects, bureaucratic government.

Indeed, it is hard to think of a policy area in which government agencies do *not* play a key role. After you wake up in the morning, perhaps you listen to the radio while drinking a cup of coffee and eating some cereal. Decisions from several government agencies influence all of those mundane activities. The radio station can broadcast only because it has a license issued by the Federal Communications Commission (FCC); the Food and Drug Administration (FDA) designed the nutrition label on your box of cereal; the Federal Trade Commission (FTC) makes sure that the cereal company does not put any false claims about their product on the box; the Consumer Product Safety Commission (CPSC) regulates the safety of your coffee maker. We could continue with other activities throughout the day. The car you drive or the bus you take to get to school, the wage you're paid at your job, the working conditions at that job, even the water you drink and the air you breathe—all of these involve policies set by government agencies.

Another way to consider the range of agency activity is to think about all the policies overseen by a single agency. Take, for example, the Department of Health and Human Services (HHS). Within HHS are units responsible for setting policy in key programs, including Medicare, which provides health care and prescription drug benefits to more than 50 million senior citizens and disabled people. HHS also sets policy for Medicaid and the Children's Health Insurance Program, which cover more than 70 million children and lower-income citizens. HHS units are also responsible for minimizing the public's exposure to hazardous substances; regulating food safety and drug efficacy; providing health care for Native Americans; conducting biomedical and health research, as well as research targeted toward improving the quality of health care; overseeing a host of additional programs that supervise mental health policies and address substance abuse issues; managing children's programs such as Head Start; tracking the spread of contagious diseases in the United States and abroad; and developing policies that outline how the United States should respond to outbreaks. And during the COVID-19 pandemic, HHS was responsible for distributing hundreds of millions of dollars in support to hospitals and health care providers.

This is just a partial list of the programs and activities that fall under the auspices of this single agency. If we were to dig into any specific subagency or department within HHS—say, the Centers for Medicare & Medicaid Services or the Indian Health Service—we would find a wide range of additional programs, policies, and activities. More generally, if we look across agencies, we see the incredible breadth of what we expect agencies to do—from sending out Social Security checks to eradicating poverty to building nuclear bombs.

Some numbers provide additional perspective about the size and reach of government agencies. Table 10.1 illuminates the size, in terms of budget and number of employees, of cabinet-level agencies—that is, the major agencies

| TABLE 10.1   The Size of Cabinet Departments | | |
| --- | --- | --- |
| Department | Number of Employees | Budget Authority |
| Defense | 741,955 | $704.3 million |
| Veterans Affairs | 392,287 | 217.1 |
| Homeland Security | 205,121 | 63.0 |
| Justice | 113,462 | 37.0 |
| Agriculture | 90,382 | 118.7 |
| Treasury | 88,605 | 790.2 |
| Health and Human Services | 82,518 | 1,286.2 |
| Interior | 66,750 | 13.9 |
| Transportation | 54,111 | 85.7 |
| Commerce | 46,004 | 16.6 |
| Energy | 14,382 | 31.5 |
| Labor | 14,311 | 39.4 |
| State | 11,709 | 24.8 |
| Housing and Urban Development | 7,466 | 50.2 |
| Education | 3,712 | 80.6 |

Employment for Defense is the sum of Defense, Air Force, Army, and Navy. Budget Authority is estimated for 2020. Fedscope, www.fedscope.opm.gov/ibmcognos/cgi-bin/cognosisapi.dll (accessed 10/21/19); Statista, www.statista.com/statistics/200386/budget-of-the-us-government-for-fiscal-year-2012-by-agencies/ (accessed 10/21/19).

within the executive branch that are headed by people who report directly to the president. Two of the agencies that receive the most funds are HHS (which, along with the Social Security Administration, is responsible for approximately one-quarter of all government spending, due largely to the high costs of Medicare and Social Security) and the Department of Defense (which has the most employees). But many other cabinet agencies have substantial numbers of employees, large budgets, or both. Some comparisons provide perspective in terms of agency spending. The Department of Energy and the Department of Housing and Urban Development (HUD) have budgets that roughly correspond to the budgets of the states of Georgia and Colorado respectively, while the Departments of Education and Transportation are about the same size, in terms of budget, as the states of Oregon and Minnesota. Meanwhile, the Department of Veterans Affairs has a budget roughly equal to that of Texas and New Jersey combined![3]

## Types of Agency Actions

Government agencies use a variety of approaches to carry out their responsibilities. In some instances, agencies **implement** laws that Congress and the president have created. If, for example, Congress writes a law about health care for veterans that spells out exactly who qualifies as a veteran, then the Department of Veterans Affairs would simply look at the law when determining whether people seeking health care through the department are eligible to receive it. If the applicants meet those qualifications, then they are eligible. In cases like this, Congress can prescribe exactly how policy should be applied, and agencies then carry out Congress's instructions.

Pure implementation accounts for some of what agencies do, but not a lot. In fact, much agency action involves judgments and decisions about how to carry out or interpret guidelines that Congress has set. In such cases, the law that Congress has passed is not specific or detailed enough to tell the agency precisely what to do. Rather, the law sets out general principles and ideas that Congress wants the agency to follow; the agency makes decisions about exactly what the law means and how to apply it.

Agencies can also carry out their duties through a process known as **adjudication**, in which an agency acts like a court, hearing two sides of a particular case and then deciding which side wins. Take, for example, the National Labor Relations Board (NLRB), which is charged with determining whether the rights of employees, employers, and unions have been violated. Because Congress cannot foresee every particular issue or controversy that might arise among these three groups, it instead has passed laws that set out general guidelines governing employer-employee relations and has empowered the NLRB to hear cases about whether, in a particular instance, someone has violated these guidelines. Thus an employee who believes that her employer has engaged in unfair labor practices can file charges and have her case heard in a trial-like setting, where the Board will decide whether the employer's actions were consistent with existing statutes or whether they were unlawful.[4]

**Rule making** is the most prominent and wide-ranging way in which agencies act. Unlike adjudication, in which agencies are pseudo-courts, in rule making they are pseudo-legislatures, issuing broad policies that have the force of law. Agencies make rules for a variety of reasons: because Congress has asked the agency to fill in details that the law has left out, because the underlying statute is unclear, or because the agency views the topic as falling within its jurisdiction based on earlier legislation. When an agency decides to devise a new rule, Congress may pressure the agency against creating a new rule at all or may advocate for the rule to take a specific form. In 2015, for example, the FDA proposed a rule to regulate electronic cigarettes, including a ban on flavored electronic cigarettes.

substantial progress toward completion, FDA may consider, on a case-by-case basis, whether to

defer enforcement of the premarket authorization requirements for a reasonable time period.

~~2. Flavored Tobacco Products~~

~~In accordance with the Tobacco Control Act (sections 905 and 910 of the FD&C Act), a~~

~~new tobacco product may be legally marketed only if FDA has authorized its marketing under~~

~~one of the three premarket pathways described throughout this document.~~ Given the

attractiveness of flavors, especially to youth and young adults, and the impact flavored tobacco

products may have on youth initiation, the Agency is not extending its compliance policy for

premarket review to flavored new tobacco products. Retailers of flavored tobacco products will

Congress can influence the way agencies act by pressuring them to enact or refrain from enacting certain policies. The Food and Drug Administration proposed a rule restricting the sale of flavored electronic cigarettes, but Norman Sharpless, acting commissioner of the FDA, announced in September 2019 that the agency would not be moving forward with the rule.

But due in part to pressure from Congress—spurred by strong opposition to the rule from the tobacco industry, new vaping shops, and White House—the agency omitted any regulation of flavored tobacco products from its proposed rule.[5]

The issue of water pollution provides a good example of how agencies can act to build on a law and fill in policy details. Congress passed the Clean Water Act, which is the nation's primary law protecting the country's water from pollution, in order to "to restore and maintain the chemical, physical, and biological integrity of the Nation's waters." The law's mission might seem clear, but it turns out that this phrase, especially the part about the "Nation's waters," contains ambiguity. Is the law designed to protect only navigable waters, as it seems to indicate in some places?[6] Only waters that reach the drinking water supply? All waters? In response to this ambiguity, the Environmental Protection Agency (EPA), which Congress had charged with implementing the Clean Water Act, issued the "Waters of the United States" (WOTUS) rule in 2015, defining the "Nation's waters" as including upstream waters (for example, wetlands and headstreams) that affect the cleanliness of navigable waters. Thus, in this case, the agency used its powers to clarify the meaning of legislation and expand the scope of waters covered by the law.[7]

The WOTUS rule is not a rare example of agencies engaging in policy making; this is what agencies do. To illustrate the volume of rule making and other policy-making activities, we can turn to the *Federal Register*, in which agencies are required to publish their policy-making activities, including new rules that they are proposing, their solicitation of comments about such rules, and the final rules that, if implemented, will have the force of law. Figure 10.1 shows that agencies engage in a remarkable—and steadily growing—amount of policy making, as reflected by the approximately 80,000 pages of the *Federal Register* that have been filled annually by the text of these rules and other agency activities in recent years. In contrast, the laws passed annually by Congress fill only about 7,000 pages.[8]

## The Decision to Delegate

On issue after issue, Congress writes laws and then turns the process over to agencies for implementation and interpretation. When implementation is not straightforward, Congress **delegates** policy-making responsibility to agencies, giving them discretion to determine the meaning of provisions in laws, to fill in gaps created by existing laws, and to create new policies.

Congress delegates and gives discretion to agencies for a variety of reasons. First, representatives and senators simply lack the time to deal with every policy

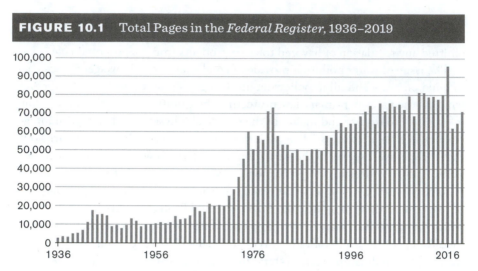

**FIGURE 10.1**   Total Pages in the *Federal Register*, 1936–2019

Regulatory Studies Center, https://regulatorystudies.columbian.gwu.edu/reg-stats (accessed 11/15/20).

issue in minute detail or anticipate every future consideration that might arise (especially considering that they are also spending time running for reelection, engaging with constituents, meeting with the press, and so on). Second, Congress might consider some issues to be too controversial. When an issue is likely to generate controversy no matter what Congress does—for example, the question of who might be exempt from complying with the Affordable Care Act—Congress may choose to hand the issue off to an agency rather than make a decision itself (which is exactly what it did in that case).

Perhaps most importantly, Congress often lacks the expertise necessary to write detailed laws, and expertise is exactly what agencies have. When it comes to laws about telecommunications, Congress knows far less about technical issues related to broadband, the Internet, satellites, and the broadcast spectrum than do the bureaucrats at the FCC who work on these issues every day. With respect to drug approvals, Congress knows much less than the scientists at the FDA. When writing laws about our nation's nuclear capacity and storage, Congress is much less knowledgeable than the professionals at the Department of Energy. As a result, members of Congress know that agencies will produce policies that are more informed, more predictable, and more flexible than Congress itself ever could write.

**THE RISKS OF DELEGATION**   In some ways, delegation sounds ideal for members of Congress—they get to hand off particularly time-consuming, controversial, or complicated issues to agencies that have both the expertise and the time to deal with them appropriately. But delegating can create a new problem: the agency's views on a policy might differ, in some cases substantially, from those of Congress. And because delegation is usually accompanied by some measure of discretion that allows agencies to use their expertise, it also gives agencies the opportunity to act in ways that Congress might not prefer. This is known as a **principal-agent problem**, which occurs in any situation where one person or institution (here Congress) gives authority to another (here an agency), but the agent then takes actions different from what the principal would like. Congress might, for example, delegate aspects of food safety to the USDA (United States Department of Agriculture), only to find that the agency creates rules that are far stricter than rules that Congress would have enacted if it had taken the time, and had the expertise, to write out detailed laws.[9]

Before considering how Congress might deal with this principal-agent problem, we first need to consider a more basic question: Does Congress even care whether agencies take actions that might differ from what legislators prefer? That is, do legislators have an incentive to monitor and then possibly influence agency action? After all, given the benefits to delegation described above, it's not implausible that many members would be happy to pass policy-making authority along to agencies. But further consideration reveals that legislators do want to keep tabs on agencies and influence their actions.

First of all, agency policies and activities affect citizens and groups within a representative's district or a senator's state. If constituents are unhappy with these policies—for example, if an agency is planning to cut funding for a nearby national park or military base—then they will hold their senators and representatives responsible for the agency's action. Relatedly, bureaucracies often provide services to citizens, such as health care for senior citizens or supplemental food to lower-income women. When a problem arises with any of these services, constituents often turn to their local representative for help. This allows the representative to fix the problem and claim credit for doing so. Monitoring agencies therefore helps members perform their representative function.

Legislators also know that agencies are responsible for distributing federal money to districts, often deciding how much and in which regions money should be distributed. For example, the Department of Justice distributes funds to support crime reduction programs, while the Department of Labor allocates money for job training and youth employment programs. Legislators know that constituents value these sorts of programs, so they have an incentive to pressure agencies to send grant money to their districts and to make sure that constituents know that they had a hand in securing these funds. Representative Stephanie Herseth Sandlin (D-S. Dak.), for example, claimed credit for obtaining $3 million for affordable housing in tribal communities, additional funds for highways in the Cheyenne River Indian Reservation, money to hire and retain

30 police officers, and financial support for a project designed to raise awareness of and provide treatment for methamphetamine addiction.[10]

In addition to fulfilling a purely representative function, members of Congress want to monitor agencies to ensure that they are implementing and enacting policies that reflect the members' own policy preferences. In other words, oversight also helps the members fulfill their governing function. Members might actually prefer to make policy themselves, especially in areas they care about, but, as we mentioned, they might lack the time or expertise. Thus, when they delegate to an agency, they are not simply washing their hands of a policy area, but rather asking the agency to make the same decisions that they would make if they had more time or expertise. That is, Congress, acting as the principal, is asking the agency to serve as a faithful agent.

Members of Congress with the strongest incentives to influence agencies are those who sit on committees relevant to those agencies, so in many ways it is the members of these committees, rather than members of Congress more generally, who act as an agency's principal. As noted in Chapter 5, committees in Congress have specific and overlapping policy jurisdictions, and members who sit on these committees specialize and gain expertise in those policy areas. Thus, if an agency is taking action on a specific policy, then members of committees with jurisdiction over that policy will pay special attention to the agency and will be in the best position to evaluate what the agency is doing. Members of the judiciary committees will have an incentive to look closely at the actions of the Department of Justice, members of the House Armed Services Committee will pay special attention to the activities of the Department of Defense, and so on.[11]

## HOW CONGRESS CREATES AND STAFFS AGENCIES

We've determined that members of Congress have an incentive to keep close tabs on government agencies. The next question is whether they have the ability to do so. In this section we focus on how Congress can influence agencies by determining how to structure and staff them; in the next section we will explore how Congress can oversee agency activities.

### Agency Location

One way Congress can influence an agency is to designate where within the government the agency will be located. Most (although not all) government agencies are created by acts of Congress. For example, Congress created the

FCC in 1934 by passing the Federal Communications Act, the Occupational Safety and Health Administration (OSHA) in 1970 via the Occupational Safety and Health Act, and the Office of the Special Inspector General for the Troubled Asset Relief Program (SIGTARP) with the Emergency Economic Stabilization Act of 2008.[12] When creating agencies like these, Congress needs to decide whether to locate them within the executive branch or to give them independent status by placing them outside the executive branch.[13] This decision can have significant implications for how an agency carries out its mission and how sensitive it is to political pressures.

Congress often places agencies within the executive branch, which fits with the Constitution's conception of that branch's duty to ensure that laws will "be faithfully executed." The main executive branch agencies are the cabinet-level departments, as shown earlier in Table 10.1: the Department of Defense, the Department of State, the Department of Energy, and so on. But Congress has placed important units within those larger cabinet agencies, such as the National Highway Traffic Safety Administration within the Department of Transportation and OSHA within the Department of Labor.[14]

Sometimes, Congress creates these executive branch agencies in response to a new problem; for example, it created the Department of Homeland Security in 2002 in response to the 9/11 terrorist attacks. Other times, Congress can take an existing agency and convert it into a cabinet-level agency in order to give it more prestige and prominence, as it did in 1989 when it elevated the formerly independent Veterans Administration (VA) by making it the Department of Veterans Affairs. Often Congress creates these agencies by reorganizing existing parts of the federal government, as it did with the Department of Energy Organization Act in 1977.[15]

Placing agencies within the executive branch provides them with additional prestige and prominence. It also allows Congress to respond to major issues (a governing role) and constituencies (a representational role), such as when it elevated the VA to appeal to veterans, or when it created the Department of Education in 1980 to signal support for public school teachers and students. But placing agencies in the executive branch does come at a potential cost: agencies in the executive branch are directly within the president's sphere of influence, and the heads of these agencies report directly to the president. This reporting structure can lead to conflict when the president's views differ from those of Congress.

Sometimes Congress chooses to place agencies outside of the executive branch, often to limit the president's ability to directly influence them. These independent agencies tend to be smaller than cabinet-level agencies and often focus on specific, rather than broad, issues or industries. The Nuclear Regulatory Commission, for instance, oversees nuclear power plants in the

United States, and the Securities and Exchange Commission regulates stock exchanges and securities.

## Agency Structure and Organization

In addition to deciding whether an agency will be located within the executive branch (and if so, where), Congress can influence agencies by structuring and organizing them in specific ways. Congress can, for example, decide that a single person will head an agency. Thus, agencies such as the EPA and HUD have one person in charge. If the agency is in the executive branch, then that person reports directly to the president and usually serves at the president's pleasure. In the case of the Consumer Finance Protection Bureau, Congress tried to protect the agency at least somewhat from presidential influence by preventing the president from firing the agency's director (except in cases of, say, illegal behavior). The Supreme Court, however, struck this down, holding that given the agency's location within the executive branch, the director "must be removable by the President at will."[16]

Alternatively, Congress can create a multimember board to head an agency. The FCC and the Federal Trade Commission are both governed by five-member boards. Furthermore, Congress can require that multimember boards have other features, such as partisan balance (for example, no more than three of five seats can be filled by members of one party) or longer terms of service (members of the Federal Reserve serve for 14 years, ensuring that they outlast any specific president and will be in place longer than most members of Congress).

An agency's leadership structure affects how independent the agency will be when making decisions. In agencies headed by a single person, Congress or the president can try to ensure that the secretary shares, and will act on, their policy views. Agencies headed by multimember boards are less susceptible to political influence because these board members will need to work together, build coalitions, and reach agreements. Congress knows that if it wants to make an agency more independent and less sensitive to political pressure, it can place a multimember board at the head of the agency, which both slows down the agency's policy-making process and increases the likelihood that decisions will incorporate political compromises. For example, when the Trump administration tried to pressure the Federal Energy Regulatory Commission to send additional subsidies to the coal and nuclear power industries in order to prop them up, the agency's five-commissioner board refused to go along.[17]

Congress also can specify the methods, or approaches, that agencies use to make decisions. If Congress wants to limit an agency's powers, it can give the agency the ability to adjudicate (that is, create policy in a manner similar to a court), but not to create rules (that is, create policy in a manner similar to a legislature). If Congress wants to increase an agency's powers, it can do the reverse. Rule making gives agencies considerably more authority to create policies that have far-ranging effects, and, once finalized, rules can be difficult to overturn.

## Appointments

In addition to determining structure and location, Congress can also use the nomination process to influence agencies. The president appoints approximately 4,000 people to serve in government agencies. Roughly 1,200 of these people fill what are known as **PAS positions**, which is short for "Presidential Appointments with Senate Confirmation."[18] Presidents are strategic about making these appointments. Because they prioritize certain policy areas, presidents want agencies that deal with those policies to be more responsive to presidential directives. Consequently, they seek to place more political appointees in those agencies.[19] However, the Constitution does not give the president sole power to make appointments; this power is shared with the Senate. For the 1,200 PAS positions, the Senate uses its constitutionally prescribed role to influence the nominee and the agency to which the nominee will, if confirmed, be appointed.

Presidents, especially those who are new to office, usually do not want to be drawn into a fight with the Senate over nominees. Thus, the Senate's first role in the appointment process usually occurs when new presidents seek the advice of Senate leaders to determine whether a potential nominee is likely to raise any red flags. Second, once the president nominates someone, senators begin to consider that nominee. Some of this consideration takes place informally and behind the scenes, with nominees visiting senators in their offices and responding to their questions. Other aspects of this stage, such as congressional hearings, are more formal and more public. Finally, the full Senate conducts a vote.

It turns out that the Senate rarely votes to reject a president's nominee. When it does so, the rejection is usually tied to a scandal having been revealed during the confirmation process. As Table 10.2 shows, over the past four decades, presidents have nominated 138 people to cabinet-level positions. Of these, the Senate confirmed 129, a success rate of 93 percent.[20] Of the nine who were not confirmed, eight withdrew. Thus even in a period in which polarization is increasing, over a span of seven presidents, the Senate rejected only 1 out of 138 nominees! Indeed, in the history of the United States, the Senate has formally rejected only nine nominees to cabinet positions. A similar pattern holds for lower-level PAS positions.[21]

Why does the Senate approve such a high percentage of the president's nominees? For starters, as we discussed, presidents often check to make sure their

**TABLE 10.2** Presidential Success in Nominating Cabinet Secretaries

| President | Confirmed | Rejected | Withdrawn |
|---|---|---|---|
| Jimmy Carter | 13 | 0 | 0 |
| Ronald Reagan | 16 | 0 | 0 |
| George H. W. Bush | 14 | 1 | 0 |
| Bill Clinton | 19 | 0 | 1 |
| George W. Bush | 16 | 0 | 1 |
| Barack Obama | 15 | 0 | 3 |
| Donald Trump | 36 | 0 | 3 |
| **Total** | **129** | **1** | **8** |

FiveThirtyEight, https://fivethirtyeight.com/features/its-really-hard-to-block-a-cabinet-nominee/ (accessed 8/6/18); *Washington Post*, www.washingtonpost.com/graphics/politics/trump-administration-appointee-tracker/database/ (accessed 1/13/21).

nominees are not likely to encounter significant opposition. If they learn that prominent senators might oppose the nominee, they may choose not to go forward with that person. In addition, senators typically give presidents a good deal of leeway in filling key positions, confirming nominees who are not caught up in a scandal or hampered by a notable lack of qualifications.[22] In part, this tradition stems from a recognition that the president won the election and thus should be afforded deference in staffing the executive branch. Even among senators who are not members of the president's party, it reflects a view that the two parties are partners in a long-running game, where the out-party knows that it will at some time control the presidency and at that time will want members from the opposing party to support its president's nominees. Senator Brian Schatz (D-Hawaii) expressed this view in 2017 when explaining why he voted for some of President Donald Trump's nominees: "The door swings both ways in Washington. . . . At some point we're going to want a Democratic president to [set] up a Cabinet. So we're trying to be reasonable when the nominees are reasonable."[23]

Finally, senators from the president's party are especially reluctant to oppose a president's nominees, particularly if their opposition would endanger the nominee's chances. In 2017, for example, during the Senate Foreign Relations Committee's hearings, three Republican senators—John McCain (R-Ariz.), Lindsey Graham (R-S.C.), and Marco Rubio (R-Fla.)—expressed strong dissatisfaction with Rex Tillerson, who was Donald Trump's first nominee to head the Department of State. Nonetheless, between the presumption that presidents

Congress provides oversight of bureaucratic agencies through its confirmation of presidential appointments. Appointments can be contentious, but presidential appointees are usually confirmed. In early 2019, the Senate held confirmation hearings for William Barr, President Trump's nominee for U.S. attorney general. While the hearings were heated, Barr was confirmed along party lines, with all Republican senators voting for confirmation and all but three Democratic senators voting against.

should be allowed to choose their nominees and the inclination not to undercut a president of their own party, all three indicated that they would support Tillerson's nomination within the committee, allowing it to go forward to the full Senate with a narrow 11–10 majority.

The lack of rejections does not necessarily mean that the Senate's role is unimportant. As noted, the president might have anticipated the Senate's reaction before submitting a nomination, which would mean that Senate influence took place early and out of the public eye. More important, the floor discussion of a nominee and especially the committee hearings provide senators with opportunities to extract promises from the nominees (for example, regarding future actions the nominee might take) and to make sure that the nominee knows committee members' views. (The latter is especially important because, as we will see, committees play a key role in overseeing agencies.) Returning to the Senate Foreign Relations Committee's hearings for Secretary of State Tillerson, all three of the skeptical Republican senators—McCain, Graham, and Rubio—stressed to Tillerson that they favored a hard line toward Russia and countries with human rights abuses such as Saudi Arabia and the Philippines. They also pushed him to agree publicly that Russia constitutes a danger to the United States and that the United States should oppose Russian attempts to expand its spheres of influence.

Senators can also take actions to delay confirmation of a president's nominee. Indeed, there has been an increase in the average amount of time it takes the Senate to confirm nominees (see Figure 10.2), leading some scholars to argue that this "malign neglect" is a central feature of nominations today.[24] A longer delay can allow for questions to be raised about a nominee's qualifications, increase the opportunity for opposition to build and coalesce, and provide for additional time to uncover and investigate any potential scandals. Not surprisingly, studies have shown that delays increase when different parties control the presidency and the Senate.

Numerous other factors can increase delays, as political scientist Ian Ostrander has demonstrated.[25] The Senate clearly acts more quickly on higher-level appointees than on lower-level appointees, as Figure 10.2 shows. It also tends to act more quickly during a president's first term—when the president likely has greater popularity and when senators are more likely to defer—than during a second term. In contrast, the Senate takes more time when considering nominees to independent agencies, because these appointees often serve longer terms than appointees to executive branch agencies and because they generally cannot be removed from office as easily. Factors internal to the Senate also affect the length of delay. Most prominently, polarization within the Senate has significantly increased delays in confirmations. Clearly, though, delays can also be attributed to increased conflict between Congress and the president.

There are no rules or even guidelines about how quickly the Senate needs to consider a president's nominees, and delays certainly can be strategic. Still, longer delays mean that agencies go longer without being fully staffed. Two seats on the important Federal Reserve Board, for example, were left vacant during the last two years of Barack Obama's second term. Obama had nominated Allan Landon, the retired CEO of the Bank of Hawaii, and Kathryn Dominguez, a highly respected economist at the University of Michigan, to fill these positions in January and July (respectively) of 2015. Yet when the 114th Congress ended in January 2017, the Senate had not acted on either of these two nominees. As the *Economist* noted, such vacancies have the effect of weakening and "addling America's central bank," with potentially severe effects on America's monetary policy.[26]

Sometimes the threat of Senate opposition or delay can cause the president to leave a position open. In extreme cases, the Senate can cripple an agency by denying it a director, which leaves the agency without strong leadership. In

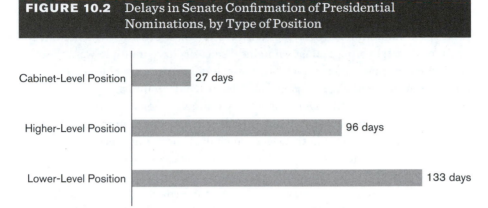

**FIGURE 10.2**  Delays in Senate Confirmation of Presidential Nominations, by Type of Position

Cabinet-Level Position — 27 days

Higher-Level Position — 96 days

Lower-Level Position — 133 days

"Cabinet-Level Position" includes Attorney General. Figure created from information presented in Ian Ostrander. 2016. "The Logic of Collective Inaction: Senatorial Delay in Executive Nominations." *American Journal of Political Science* 60(4): 1067.

2006, for example, the Senate passed a law that converted the director position of the Bureau of Alcohol, Tobacco, Firearms and Explosives (ATF)—the agency responsible for the enforcement of federal gun laws—to a PAS position, meaning that the Senate would get to weigh in on, and potentially oppose, any presidential nominee to this position, especially one who might be inclined to more tightly regulate guns. As a result, over the next thirteen years presidents generally chose to avoid conflict with the Senate by not nominating anyone to the position of director, instead relying on a series of temporary directors (who do not require confirmation).[27]

At other times the majority party in the Senate has wanted to approve a nominee, only to be stymied by the minority party's opposition—most notably in the form of a filibuster. In 2013, the majority-party Democrats in the Senate grew so frustrated with the frequency (and effectiveness) with which Senate Republicans were obstructing President Obama's nominees that they made use of a procedural maneuver, known as the nuclear option, to avoid obstruction of presidential nominees to agency positions and to the lower federal courts by allowing a majority vote to end a filibuster. It paved the way for a similar action in 2017 when the majority-party Republicans in the Senate voted to end filibusters on Supreme Court nominees in order to ensure the confirmation of Neil Gorsuch. Adoption of the nuclear option ensured a president's nominees would be voted on, assuming the nominee had majority support in the Senate, but it removed a powerful tool for the minority. Many senators lamented this change, in part because it decreased the incentive for presidents to select nominees with broad bipartisan appeal.[28]

Whether by discussing potential nominees with the president prior to an official nomination, using hearings to propound their views or to extract promises from nominees, delaying consideration of or obstructing a nominee, or (in rare cases) voting against a nominee, senators have multiple ways they can influence appointments. Notably, these appointments are not only for positions at the head of each agency but also reach deep into an agency's lower levels. For example, at the Department of Commerce, Senate confirmation is necessary for the appointment of not only the Secretary of Commerce but also for 20 other positions within the agency, including the deputy secretary; the assistant secretaries for industry and analysis, enforcement and compliance, and environmental observations and prediction; and various undersecretary positions (for example, the undersecretaries of international trade and the National Oceanic and Atmospheric Administration).[29] Consequently, the Senate can use the confirmation process to affect who sits in positions of importance throughout an agency and to make sure those people know exactly where the Senate stands on key policy issues.

**LIMITS TO CONGRESSIONAL INFLUENCE ON APPOINTMENTS** There are, of course, limits to the Senate's ability to influence who occupies agency positions of authority and how the nominees will, if confirmed, approach issues. Nothing prevents a nominee from breaking a promise after he or she is in office. Congress can threaten impeachment, as it did in the aftermath of the IRS scandal discussed at the start of this chapter, but given that only one executive branch official in the nation's history has been impeached, such a threat rings hollow.[30]

In addition, presidents can take steps to avoid the Senate. Earlier we saw that the Senate's power of confirmation can force presidents to rely on **interim appointees**. But this is also an approach that presidents can use to their advantage, as it is a way for them to place people in positions of power without having to worry about Senate approval. Furthermore, these interim, or acting, appointees, who can serve up to 210 days (and sometimes longer), often are viewed as being more responsive to the president, which Donald Trump noted when he stated, "I like acting [appointees]. It gives me more flexibility."[31] And this was not just a feature of the Trump presidency. Over the past few decades, temporary appointments throughout the bureaucracy have been common, as recent research by political scientist Christina Kinane has revealed. In fact, as Figure 10.3 demonstrates, between 10 percent and 20 percent of PAS positions in agencies commonly are filled with temporary, or interim, appointees.[32]

The president can also choose to appoint people to related positions that do not require Senate approval. In late 2016, for example, President Donald Trump

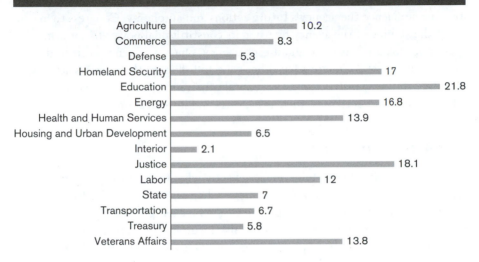

**FIGURE 10.3**   Average Percentage of Positions Filled with Interims, 1977–2015

Agriculture 10.2
Commerce 8.3
Defense 5.3
Homeland Security 17
Education 21.8
Energy 16.8
Health and Human Services 13.9
Housing and Urban Development 6.5
Interior 2.1
Justice 18.1
Labor 12
State 7
Transportation 6.7
Treasury 5.8
Veterans Affairs 13.8

Data from Christina Kinane.

announced his intention to appoint Michael Flynn as his national security advisor, a position that falls within the Executive Office of the President and therefore does not require Senate confirmation. Flynn's history of inflammatory remarks and his forced resignation as the head of the Defense Intelligence Agency (reportedly because of his ineffective and chaotic managerial skills) would have made for a hard sell in the Republican-controlled Senate if he had been nominated to lead, say, the Department of Defense.[33] Instead, President Trump nominated the widely respected James Mattis for the PAS position of Secretary of Defense while ensuring that he would continue to get the advice he wanted from Flynn in the non-PAS position of national security advisor.[34]

One additional presidential power derives directly from the Constitution: the power to make **recess appointments** to agencies. With this power, the president can wait until the Senate is in recess and then appoint someone, thereby avoiding the Senate entirely. This appointee is entitled to occupy that position until the end of the next Senate session, which can last up to one year. Concerned about recess appointments by Presidents George W. Bush and Barack Obama, Senate majority leaders from the opposition party—Harry Reid in the former case and Mitch McConnell in the latter—kept the Senate in session more or less permanently, preventing these presidents from making any such appointments.

# HOW CONGRESS INFLUENCES AGENCY ACTIONS

When Congress creates an agency, the decisions it makes about location and structure influence the agency's future actions and autonomy. Congress then can affect the staffing of the agency by using its constitutional power to confirm appointees to positions throughout each agency. Once the agency is created, located, and staffed, Congress has other ways to influence the agency's actions, including statutory instructions, procedural constraints, control of agency budgets, and oversight activities, such as hearings and investigations.

## Statutory Instructions

Congress can write laws to tell agencies exactly what to do, although usually it prefers to allow for discretion. For example, when writing the Affordable Care Act, Congress decided that some people would be exempt from the law's requirement that everyone must carry health insurance but left it to the agency to decide who could be exempt. Congress could have spelled out in detail exactly who qualified for this exemption and then tasked the agency with implementing its decision. Had Congress chosen this course of action, it would have removed any discretion from the agency, leaving it to mechanically implement what Congress told it to do. Statutory instructions move an agency closer to a pure implementation role, where Congress tells an agency what to do and the agency then follows those instructions.

In other cases, Congress can use statutes to require a specific action by an agency that has done something that Congress disliked. In February of 2013, for example, the U.S. Postal Service announced that it was going to end Saturday mail delivery, a move it predicted would save up to $2 billion per year.[35] Congress reacted swiftly by passing a law requiring the Postal Service to deliver mail six days a week.[36]

Congressional attempts to pass laws that tell agencies what to do are not always successful. But even unsuccessful attempts indicate that the threat of legislation is real and can cause agencies to think twice before taking actions Congress might not like.[37] In 2015, for example, the Consumer Financial Protection Bureau (CFPB), which Congress created in the aftermath of the financial crisis of 2007 and 2008, issued new rules that allowed it to regulate automobile loans (based on its general authority to regulate loans). The House of Representatives responded by passing legislation, the Reforming CFPB Indirect Auto Financing Guidance Act, to overturn these rules and to curtail the CFPB's ability to regulate auto loans. The bill easily passed in the House with a vote of 332–96, with nearly all Republicans and almost half of Democrats voting in favor of the bill. Because the bill was never introduced in the Senate, it never became law. Still, the House legislation acted as a shot across the bow of the agency. Not coincidentally, when the agency was asked about its fair lending priorities for 2017, it did not list auto loans.[38]

Such attempted-but-failed laws can also build momentum toward change in the future.[39] In 2013, it was revealed that the NSA had been collecting metadata from Americans' e-mails and phone calls that revealed who contacted whom, when the contact occurred, and the duration of phone calls (but did not contain information about the content of communications). The data collection was legal, authorized by Section 215 of the USA PATRIOT Act, which Congress passed and President George W. Bush signed into law in 2001. Supporters of this provision of the law argued that it helped to protect against terrorist acts, while opponents raised concerns about privacy violations and infringement on liberty.[40] In response to the 2013 revelations, a bipartisan group of legislators introduced legislation aimed at curtailing the agency's ability to collect such data. The bill eventually failed, but by a much narrower margin (217–205) than anyone expected. More important, it revealed the depth of opposition to the NSA's activities, mobilized this opposition, and indicated that future success of a similar bill, if not guaranteed, was more likely than anyone had anticipated.[41] Indeed, in 2015, Congress allowed the NSA's authority to engage in such activities to expire.[42]

In addition to passing laws that limit agencies' discretion and telling these agencies what policies to put in place, Congress has other statutory tools it can use to affect agency actions and rules. For a long time, it used **legislative vetoes**, which are provisions in laws that make it easier for Congress to stop, or veto, an agency rule from going into effect (for example, the law might stipulate that a single chamber can act on its own to veto an agency rule). In the 1983 case of *Immigration and Naturalization Service v. Chadha*, however, the Supreme Court ruled that legislative vetoes were unconstitutional because they ran afoul of the constitutionally prescribed process by which new laws needed to be passed in the same form by both chambers and then presented to (and signed by) the president.[43] Notwithstanding, Congress has continued to include legislative vetoes in new laws, even though their effectiveness is unclear.[44]

As an alternative to the legislative veto, Congress passed the **Congressional Review Act (CRA)** in 1996, which gave it the power to strike down an agency action in a way that attempted to avoid the constitutional problems the Supreme Court had identified in its *Chadha* decision. According to the CRA, once an agency announces its intention to issue a final rule, that rule will not go into effect for 60 days, during which time Congress can take action— passing a resolution of disapproval by majority vote in each chamber and then getting it signed by the president—to stop the rule from going into effect.

The CRA was little used initially. Out of more than 48,000 rules that agencies sent to Congress in the 12 years following the passage of the CRA,

Congress struck down precisely one, a workplace safety rule about ergonomics proposed by OSHA in 2000.[45] But in the weeks after Donald Trump's inauguration in 2017, Congress rediscovered the power of the CRA, using it to strike down major rules that the Departments of Interior, Education, and Labor, as well as the Securities and Exchange Commission, the Social Security Administration, and others, had finalized at the end of the Obama administration.[46] For example, in one case Congress and President Trump, citing privacy and gun rights justifications, used the CRA to strike down an Obama administration rule that made it more difficult for mentally ill people to obtain guns. In another, it overturned a rule that prevented states from withholding federal funds from family planning clinics that provide abortion services.

Why this sudden increased usage of a tactic that had essentially been dormant for 20 years? The answer is that the conditions, with unified Republican control following a Democratic presidency, were exactly those under which this tool is most useful. When a final rule is proposed at the end of a presidential administration but has not yet gone into effect when the new president takes office, that new president is more likely to sign the resolution of disapproval than the previous president, who would most likely have protected the agency action by refusing to sign the resolution. The conditions will again be ripe for the use of the CRA during the Biden administration, with unified Democratic control following a Republican presidency.

## Procedural Constraints

Many statutes tell agencies exactly what they should or should not do. But Congress can also use a subtler statutory approach to exert influence: placing constraints on agency actions. Congress does this by inserting various procedural provisions into laws. The idea is that by telling the agency which procedures to follow, Congress can influence an agency without telling it exactly what to do. This approach allows Congress to get the public policy it wants while delegating to an agency with expertise in that area.

Congress can use a variety of procedural controls to influence an agency's actions.[47] It can require an agency to issue reports about its activities and to do so within a specific time frame. It can compel an agency to hold public hearings when developing a new policy or to consult with specific groups when creating the policy. It can instruct agencies to follow certain procedures when creating new rules. And it can choose to either protect agencies from the courts or open agency actions up to judicial review.

Procedural controls operate in two ways. First, they force agencies to expose their actions, making their policies more visible to the public and interested groups, as well as to members of Congress. Public hearings attract attention and allow opponents a chance to be heard, while regular reports let senators and representatives know what agencies are up to. Second, these provisions can increase the likelihood of some policy outcomes while decreasing the likelihood of others. If, for example, a law instructs the EPA to meet with farmers when considering new policies regarding stormwater runoff from farms, it is more likely that the agency will hear about farmers' concerns and that any proposed rules will take these concerns into account. These legislative provisions do not dictate which actions agencies should take, but they can cause the agency to lean in one policy direction rather than another.

Because these provisions are enacted prior to the agency taking any action (rather than in response to specific actions), they are sometimes called *ex ante* controls, where *ex ante* is Latin for "before the event." The idea is that putting these controls in place ahead of time guides agencies to make certain types of decisions and not others—say, because the agency has to be public about what it is doing (which minimizes the dangers of powerful interest groups prevailing behind closed doors) or because it is required to take the perspectives of certain interests into account. This differs from *ex post*, or after the fact, oversight, where Congress sees what an agency has done (or is doing) and then tries to correct it. (We discuss oversight in more detail below.)

## Budgets

In addition to putting policy instructions and procedural constraints into laws, Congress can use appropriations legislation, wherein it provides an agency with its yearly budget, to affect agency actions. To understand this tactic, recall that two types of statutes affect agencies. First, authorizing statutes give agencies the authority to carry out their duties. These statutes delegate policy-making responsibility to agencies and can limit their discretion. Second, appropriations laws provide agencies with the money they need to carry out the duties and responsibilities outlined in authorizing statutes.

Suppose, for example, that an authorizing statute gives an agency power to regulate a specific industry. As part of this power, the agency can monitor the activities of the businesses that it regulates. To do that, it needs funding to hire employees to carry out the monitoring, to conduct inspections, and so on. If Congress decides that an agency is being too aggressive in carrying out these functions, it can cut the agency's budget, leaving the agency with fewer funds to hire people or to pay the costs necessary to carry out investigations. This is exactly what happened in the years following the IRS scandal discussed in the introduction to this chapter. If, on the other hand, Congress likes what the agency is doing or wants the agency to be more proactive, it can increase the agency's budget. Budgets, therefore, can act as punishments or incentives (although they are more effective as punishments).

The budget provides Congress with real power over agencies.[48] But it also comes with a limitation: the power of the budget is one that Congress shares with the president. Indeed, because the initial budget proposal comes from the president, Congress is often in reactive mode when it comes to the budget. In addition, because the president must sign off on the budget, Congress cannot unilaterally change the amount of funding an agency receives. Instead, the two institutions must work together to establish shared priorities for each agency.

Unlike regular authorizing bills, appropriations bills are must-pass bills, which means that Congress has to pass them in order to keep the government running (see Chapter 7). These important bills, along with some procedural protections that accompany them, provide members with the opportunity to attach **limitation riders**, which constrain agency actions. While Congress might not have passed the provisions in these riders on their own, they're likely to pass them when attached to an appropriations bill; the president and Congress are unlikely to hold up the entire bill—at the risk of shutting down the government—just because they oppose a relatively minor rider.

It is not unusual for Congress to include 300 or more riders in each year's appropriations bills.[49] For example, Congress continues to rely on a limitation rider known as the Hyde Amendment (after its original sponsor) to prevent federal funds from being used to pay for most abortions. More recently, in the 2013 appropriations bill Congress included a rider that prohibited the National Science Foundation from providing any funding to political science projects unless those projects were aimed at improving national security or the economy. By using these riders, Congress can prevent agencies from taking actions that members of Congress might disapprove of. Not surprisingly, Congress is especially likely to use limitation riders when the president is not from the majority party in Congress and when Appropriations Committee members have unfavorable views of the policies that likely would be produced in the absence of such riders.

## Oversight Activities

Congress keeps a close eye on agencies as they develop and implement policies. This surveillance can take the form of procedural provisions (which are activated like fire alarms to alert Congress to certain activity) or formal or informal oversight activities (in which Congress patrols agency activity in the same way police officers patrol neighborhoods or districts). In **fire alarm oversight**, Congress makes it easier for concerned constituents and groups to notify it when an agency is taking actions that might differ from what Congress wants. To draw out the fire alarm analogy, consider the differences between how fire alarms work and how police patrols work. Fire alarms are placed at various locations, and when someone sees a fire that needs to be put out, he or she can pull the alarm. Once an alarm is pulled, the fire department springs into action, sending trucks and firefighters to put out the fire. This approach is much more efficient and effective than if fire trucks just drove around on patrol, looking for fires to put out.

Procedural provisions act like fire alarms. Congress puts them in place via legislation and then waits for them to be pulled, which in this context means that some person or persons—an interest group, concerned citizens, congressional staff members—can notify members of Congress about what the agency is doing. This notification, in turn, can spur members of Congress to take actions, such as introducing new laws, holding hearings, or conducting investigations, that are designed to persuade or coerce the agency to change course. Provisions that require agencies to issue reports, conduct public hearings, meet with certain interest groups, follow certain procedures, or meet certain deadlines all provide opportunities for interested parties to observe what agencies are doing and, if necessary, turn to Congress for corrective action. And although Congress can, and does, effectively use other tactics that resemble patrols, these fire alarm procedural provisions serve as useful early warning systems. By putting them in place *ex ante*, Congress can ensure an efficient system of *ex post* oversight.

An alternative and more proactive form of influence falls under the heading of **police patrol oversight**. Just as it sounds, this approach entails members of Congress actively going out and looking for potentially problematic agency actions. When Congress goes on patrol, it keeps an eye on agencies' activities.[50] These oversight activities are sometimes called *ex post* controls because they consist of actions that Congress takes after agencies have created policies or have begun to engage in new policy-making episodes.

Sometimes oversight is informal, with members of Congress and their staff communicating directly with agency officials, either to encourage the agency's activities or to register complaints.[51] Agency officials are especially likely to take these informal contacts seriously when they come from legislators who sit on relevant oversight committees (who are both more knowledgeable about the policy area and more likely to exert pressure on an agency) or when they come from the Committee on Oversight and Reform (which has broad authority to review agencies). Thus, officials at the USDA will pay far more attention to contacts from members of the agriculture committees in Congress, or from the Oversight Committee, than from other members of Congress.

An illustrative anecdote comes from a study by political scientists Jason MacDonald and Robert McGrath. A staffer for a representative on the Oversight

Committee recounted how a constituent contacted the staffer about an FDA policy. More specifically, this constituent, who was a nurse, noticed that the FDA had approved a label for a particular drug that neglected to include a warning that the drug could have potentially deadly effects for patients who were already suffering from kidney disease. She told the staffer that people had died because of this omission. After some back and forth, the FDA agreed to change the label. This example shows both how agencies can be responsive to members of Congress (especially those who sit on oversight committees) and how members can engage in their representative function through oversight.

Many other instances of oversight are more formal. Congress can, for example, audit agencies. It can include expiration dates (known as sunset provisions) in laws, giving members of Congress a new chance to examine agency activities.[52] Congress can also issue reports that call (perhaps unwanted) attention to an agency. It can enlist the services of an agency's inspector general—a bureaucrat placed in an agency by Congress to conduct separate and independent investigations of agency actions. In early 2017, for example, a bipartisan group of chairs and ranking minority members of a range of oversight committees asked the Department of Justice's inspector general to investigate whether FBI Director James Comey acted improperly in the investigation of Hillary Clinton's e-mails.[53] Generally inspectors general are not well known, but occasionally they are thrust into the public eye, as in the case of Michael Atkinson, the inspector general for the Intelligence Community who publicly supported a whistleblower who alleged that President Trump had improperly attempted to enlist a foreign country to influence the 2020 election (see Chapter 9). Some of these formal oversight mechanisms involve a mixture of *ex ante* and *ex post* controls. For example, sunset provisions are placed in laws *ex ante*, but are included in order to increase *ex post* activities. Inspectors general are appointed before they are needed, but they can also take part in ongoing investigations.

## What about the President?

Of course, Congress is not alone in wanting to influence bureaucratic actions: the president also has the incentive and ability to do so. Thus, power over agencies is shared between the two branches. This isn't a problem when the president's views align with Congress's. However, when these preferences diverge, Congress enacts institutional reforms to prevent agencies from moving closer to the president and farther from Congress, and to counteract the innate advantage presidents have as head of the executive branch. For example, Congress gave itself more staff in the 1946 Legislative Reorganization Act in order to counter the growth in both executive agencies and the president's control over those agencies. Essentially, our separation-of-powers system incentivizes

Congress to keep track of agencies' activities and to try to prevent them from falling further into the president's orbit, and this incentive is heightened when different parties control Congress and the presidency.

Even when the same party controls Congress and the White House, members of the majority party want to watch over agencies closely. Here Congress's representative function stands out, because members of Congress will, for all of the reasons discussed earlier, want to make sure that agencies are taking actions that will help, and not hurt, their constituents. But the governing and policy functions also remain. For the former, legislators will not simply cede ground to the executive branch, preferring to maintain Congress's power. For the latter, legislators and presidents from the same party do not always agree on policies. During the 2016 presidential election, for example, Donald Trump announced his intention to triple the number of agents assigned to deportation at the U.S. Immigration and Customs Enforcement agency. When asked about Trump's plan at a town hall meeting, however, House Speaker Paul Ryan stated unequivocally that Congress would not create such a force, as he saw no need for it.[54]

## HOW WE STUDY
## THE COMPETITION FOR CONTROL OF BUREAUCRATIC AGENCIES

Bureaucracies often seem like the puck in a game of air hockey between Congress and the president, smacked back and forth with particular aggression under divided government. For example, Congress might want an agency to write rules that create more and stricter regulations, while a president might prefer deregulation. Or Congress might want an agency to engage in fewer investigations and less oversight, while the president might prefer that the agency do more of each.

Given that both Congress and the president have the incentive and ability to influence agencies, are they actually able to exert this influence? And is Congress or the president more influential? That is, do bureaucrats pay more attention to signals coming from Congress or from the president?

These are the questions that political scientists Joshua Clinton, David Lewis, and Jennifer Selin addressed in an article entitled "Influencing the Bureaucracy: The Irony of Congressional Oversight."[55] What these researchers wanted to know is how bureaucrats themselves perceive the relative influence of Congress and the president, both of whom regularly try to exert power over agency actions.

Assessing whether Congress or the president has more influence over an agency is surprisingly difficult. For example, suppose that Congress simply confirms all appointees to the agency, conducts little oversight, regularly approves increases to the agency's budget, and does not challenge an agency's rules. One might conclude that Congress has little effect on the agency, since it is engaging in none of the activities that could exert pressure. The problem with this conclusion is that these exact conditions would apply to an agency that is doing precisely what Congress wants. After all, if the agency anticipates what Congress wants it to do, and then takes these actions, Congress would have little incentive to try to change what the agency is doing.

Since we cannot learn about congressional influence—much less whether Congress is more influential that the president—by simply observing how Congress handles bureaucratic agencies, Clinton, Lewis, and Selin took a different tack: they surveyed more than 2,200 bureaucrats who worked at 128 different federal agencies and bureaus. They identified several potential sources of influence—including the majority party in Congress, congressional committees, and the White House—and asked each respondent to identify how much sway each of these sources had over their actions. They then used these responses to create a scale that captures how responsive each agency is to Congress at one end and to the president at the other.

One key finding is that bureaucrats view the White House as more influential over their activities than either congressional committees or the majority party. Beyond that, bureaucrats clearly view committees as being more influential than the majority party, and to the extent the majority party affects agencies, that influence comes through the party's influence on committees.

As part of their survey the researchers looked more closely at the influence of committees by asking each respondent to identify the number of committees that oversee their agency. They found that some agencies are subject to oversight from only one or two committees, whereas other agencies—for example, ones with a policy portfolio that overlaps with the jurisdictions of several committees, such as the Environmental Protection Agency—are overseen by a half dozen or more different committees.[56] This question allowed the researchers to derive interesting conclusions about how the organization of Congress—in particular, overlapping responsibilities for committees—influences its ability to oversee agencies. One might imagine, for example, that having more committees involved with an agency would give Congress more power over that agency relative to the White House, since more legislators are paying attention to that agency. Or perhaps having more committees oversee an agency would lead to confusion about who is in charge, which could reduce congressional influence and open the door to greater presidential influence.

As chair of the House Oversight Committee, Representative Carolyn Maloney (D-N.Y.) was highly active in congressional investigations and hearings, which she used to push reluctant agencies to take important action on issues.

Their results are clear: when few committees oversee an agency, the relative ability of Congress and the president to influence agencies is close, with the White House having a slight advantage. But as the number of committees with oversight authority increases, the White House's advantage relative to Congress also grows. This finding holds an important lesson for members of Congress: if they want to increase congressional influence over agencies, they should streamline the role of committees and have fewer committees oversee each agency. However, such a change seems unlikely, since as we have seen in earlier chapters, members have a strong incentive to sit on committees in specific issue areas and strongly prefer that those committees are individually powerful, even though this comes at the expense of the institution's overall power relative to agencies and the president.

## Critical Thinking

1. If you were a high-level appointee in an executive branch agency, would you be more worried about doing something that angers Congress or doing something that angers the president? Why?

2. Some scholars argue that when Congress and the president disagree about what an agency should do, this gives the agency more leeway to do whatever it wants. Others argue that it limits the agency, since no matter what action it takes, it is likely to bother one of those principals. Which view do you hold, and why?

3. Has the increased polarization in Congress increased or decreased its influence over agencies, relative to the president?

## Hearings and Investigations

By far the two most prominent forms of congressional oversight are hearings and investigations, which often work in tandem. Hearings provide Congress an opportunity to bring agency officials to the Capitol, where legislators can shine a bright light on agency activities. If they like an agency policy and want to promote or defend it, hearings give them the chance to do so. But hearings (and investigations) also allow them to confront agency officials—very publicly—about whether their actions are subverting laws, are inconsistent with the preferences of current members of Congress, or conflict with the Constitution. During these hearings, members can question whether agency officials have abused their powers, why agencies have prioritized some activities and policies at the expense of others, and how these agencies have spent their funding. And they can express their concerns about specific agency actions or the general direction of agency policy making.

Do agency officials really need to worry about these hearings and investigations? After all, if Congress is as dysfunctional as many critics suggest, it might not be able to follow through on threats that it makes at hearings or during investigations. Furthermore, structural changes in Congress have curtailed oversight. Indeed, two of the most respected observers of Congress, Thomas Mann and Norman Ornstein, have written that "executive agencies that once viewed Congress with at least some trepidation because of its oversight activities now tend to view Congress with contempt."[57] Furthermore, presidents and the heads of agencies can resist Congress's attempts to conduct investigations. When Congress started to ask current and former members of the State Department to testify about the potential scandal surrounding the claim that the president asked the Ukrainian government to help investigate Joe Biden, Secretary of State Mike Pompeo pushed back, saying that Congress's actions can be "understood only as an attempt to intimidate, bully, and treat improperly the distinguished professionals of the Department of State" and that these officials would not be permitted to testify.

It would be inaccurate, however, to paint all hearings as ineffective. Certainly, some hearings are simply cases of political grandstanding during which members attract publicity, take positions, and claim credit. But hearings also allow members to carry out their representative function, ensuring that agency officials are aware of how their actions will affect members' constituents. Hearings also provide members of Congress with the opportunity to carry out their policy-making duties by showing that, despite having delegated powers to agencies, they have not abdicated their responsibilities. Similarly, hearings allow members to engage in their governing function by making their policy preferences known to the executive branch, with the goal of influencing agency policy. The IRS example at the start of this chapter provides such an example: although Congress passed no new laws after conducting hearings, the agency did change some of its policies as a result.

## THEN AND NOW
## CHANGES IN CONGRESSIONAL OVERSIGHT

It might seem that Congress has little incentive to regularly, proactively engage in hearings and investigations as a form of police patrol oversight.[58] And credible arguments can be made that fire alarm forms of influence are more effective and efficient.[59] But the evidence reveals that Congress carries out a great deal of police patrol oversight. As MacDonald and McGrath have shown, for more than four decades, Congress has been quite active in conducting oversight hearings, as measured by the number of days that Congress devotes to these types of hearings (Figure 10.4).[60] Furthermore, as the figure demonstrates, the number of days spent on hearings has been on the rise. In the House, for example, there has been an increase from approximately 100 days per year in the 1950s and 1960s, to 500 in the 1970s through the 1990s, and then to an average of 700 since 2000.

Why did oversight hearings skyrocket in the 1970s? Political scientist Joel Aberbach, in one of the first systematic studies of congressional oversight, attributed the change at this time to a series of interrelated factors.[61] Some of these were external to Congress; for example, the size of government, which had been increasing, jumped even more in the 1970s, spurred in part by the creation of new agencies, including the EPA, OSHA, and CPSC. More generally, presidents had gained legislative power relative to Congress, and oversight allowed members to recapture some of that power. Internal factors also mattered: congressional reforms in the 1970s gave subcommittees more power to hold hearings, and

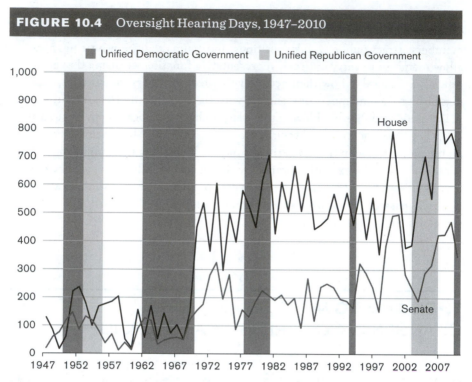

FIGURE 10.4    Oversight Hearing Days, 1947–2010

Adapted from Jason MacDonald and Robert J. McGrath. 2016. "Retrospective Congressional Oversight and the Dynamics of Legislative Influence over the Bureaucracy." *Legislative Studies Quarterly* 41(4): 899–934.

members and committees also started to hire more staff, allowing them to engage in more oversight. Finally, increasing deficits and concerns about high taxes prevented members from creating and funding new programs, so they instead turned their attention to the functioning of existing programs.[62]

Other studies using slightly different measures have confirmed that Congress regularly engages in police patrol oversight. Political scientists Steven Balla and Christopher Deering carefully distinguished between hearings that Congress held in response to fire alarms and those that represented instances of routine, ongoing police patrol oversight of agency activities.[63] They show that from the late 1970s through the 2000s, Congress regularly engaged in police patrol oversight. In fact, although there was some variation across the committees they examined, all committees were far more likely to hold hearings of the police patrol variety.

Finally, Figure 10.4 reveals not only a significant difference in oversight before and after 1970 but also significant year-to-year variation. MacDonald and McGrath provide a clever and convincing explanation for this variation. They start with the assumption that when the same party that controls Congress also holds the presidency, Congress and the president will largely agree on the direction the agency should take, but when Congress and the presidency are controlled by different parties, Congress may disagree with instructions that the president gives an agency, giving Congress a greater incentive to keep a watchful eye on the agency. Therefore, there will be more hearings under divided government because Congress is less likely to trust agencies under the control of an opposing-party president.

MacDonald and McGrath find clear evidence that hearings increase under divided government. But they also propose an explanation for why there are high levels of hearings and variation within periods of unified government, when we might reasonably expect to see fewer hearings.[64] MacDonald and McGrath argue that under unified government, congressional committees have an incentive to engage in retrospective oversight, where they look back at actions taken by the agency under the previous administration. The authors found that there are more hearings—even under unified government—when control of Congress and the presidency had been divided just before and when the opposition party had controlled the presidency for a longer period of time, giving agencies more opportunity to create new policies.

### Critical Thinking

1. Police patrol oversight requires more effort than fire alarm oversight. Why don't members rely solely on fire alarms?
2. Given the increasing conflict and polarization in American politics, would you expect oversight hearings to continue increasing?

# CONCLUSION

The Framers envisioned Congress as the primary policy-making branch of the federal government. Laws still originate in Congress, of course. But in terms of volume, there is no question that government agencies—both executive branch agencies and independent agencies—generate more policies. They do so because Congress has created these agencies and then delegated vast amounts of discretion to them. This leads to two questions. First, wouldn't it be better if Congress simply told agencies what to do, rather than giving them broad discretion to set policy? Second, given that agencies play such a significant policy-making role, has Congress lost influence?

The idea that Congress should simply tell agencies what to do certainly has some appeal. When Congress writes general laws that omit important details and then hands these laws off to agencies to fill in the missing parts, Congress could be considered derelict in its duty. This would be particularly concerning if Congress did not take other actions to ensure that agencies are acting in ways consistent with Congress's preferences. At the same time, recall why Congress delegates: it does so because it does not have time to write detailed statutes that cover every eventuality, because it does not always have the expertise necessary to write good laws, and because delegating discretion to an agency can allow a law to be more flexible and more easily adjusted to changing times. When Congress micromanages, it loses many of the benefits of delegation, most notably the time and expertise that an agency can devote to an issue.[65]

Congress does not necessarily abdicate its policy-making role when it empowers agencies to make policy. Certainly, delegation means that Congress has less power than when it makes policy itself. And some would argue that presidents exert more control over agencies than Congress does.[66] Still, Congress has numerous tools that it can use to influence agencies and to pressure agencies to act in certain ways. Congress's power starts with the creation and the staffing of agencies, both of which can increase the agencies' receptiveness toward Congress. And it continues with Congress's ability to conduct investigations, threaten legislation, cut budgets, and hold hearings. Congress can use these tools to influence agencies even without passing new laws, which we saw when the IRS changed its practices toward conservative groups in deference to Congress's views, even though Congress did not pass a new law telling the agency what to do.

Interest groups play a central role in helping Congress fulfill its policy-making and governing roles with respect to agencies. These groups let members know whether they should support or oppose a president's nominees. They pay close attention to agency activities, ready to pull fire alarms to let members of Congress know when agencies are taking actions that the groups—and that members of Congress—dislike (as occurred with the IRS). And they can testify at hearings, make suggestions about budgets, and provide information for statutes. In Chapter 12, we explore in more detail the relationship between interest groups and Congress. First, however, we turn to the connection between Congress and the third branch of government: the courts.

## Discussion Questions

1. What are the arguments in favor of Congress delegating policy-making authority to agencies? What are the arguments against delegation?
2. Why would agencies be especially responsive to members of congressional committees?
3. The number of representatives and senators has not increased for more than half a century. During that same time, however, the government bureau-

cracy has grown dramatically. Given this difference, is it possible for Congress to maintain any control over the bureaucracy? What could Congress do to increase its control?

4. If Congress is worried about the president's power over agencies, why wouldn't it just place all new agencies outside of the executive branch?

5. Should the majority party be able to ignore a president's agency nominations? Or should it be required to hold a vote?

# 11

## Congress and the Courts

In February 2016, Supreme Court Justice Antonin Scalia joined a group of friends on a quail-hunting trip to Texas. Following dinner at the Cibolo Creek Ranch, Scalia said he was tired and went to his room. When he did not come down to join the group for breakfast the next morning, workers at the resort went to check on him. They discovered that Justice Scalia, at the time the longest-serving justice on the Court, had died during the night.

Scalia's unexpected death presented President Barack Obama with the opportunity to nominate a new justice. About one month later, Obama nominated Merrick Garland, who at the time was chief judge of the U.S. Court of Appeals for the District of Columbia, generally considered the second-most-powerful court in the country. Before Obama had even selected a nominee, however, Senate Majority Leader Mitch McConnell (R-Ky.) announced that the Senate would not consider any nominee whom Obama put forth. In McConnell's view, "[t]he American people should have a voice in the selection of their next Supreme Court Justice . . . [and] this vacancy should not be filled until we have a new president."[1] Then, and only then, he said, would the Senate consider a new nominee.

McConnell's unprecedented tactic paid off when Donald Trump defeated Hillary Clinton, putting control over the nomination in the hands of the new

The ever-present tensions between Congress and the courts were on full display during Brett Kavanaugh's Supreme Court confirmation hearings. After Kavanaugh responded to accusations of sexual assault, the Senate confirmed him 50–48—one of the narrowest margins in history.

Republican president and the Republican majority in the Senate. Trump nominated Judge Neil Gorsuch for the Court, and the Senate confirmed Gorsuch—albeit by the fairly close margin of 54–45. All Republican senators voted in favor of Gorsuch, while nearly all Democrats voted against.

Just over a year later, Justice Anthony Kennedy announced his retirement from the Court. Trump's nominee, Brett Kavanaugh, proved to be even more controversial. Justice Kennedy had been the swing vote—that is, the fifth vote in many cases decided by a 5–4 majority—which meant that replacing him with a more conservative jurist like Kavanaugh would likely pull the Court significantly to the right on issues like abortion, voting rights, free speech, and civil rights. Then, just as the Senate Judiciary Committee was getting ready to vote to move the confirmation to the Senate floor, Democrats on the committee revealed the serious allegation that Kavanaugh had committed sexual assault when he was a teenager, throwing the process into turmoil.

The committee invited Dr. Christine Blasey Ford, who had made this allegation, to testify. Kavanaugh responded to her testimony with a passionate denial of the accusation and, in the eyes of some observers, a sharp partisan attack on Democrats. At this point it was unclear whether Kavanaugh had enough votes to be confirmed; the Republicans had only a narrow majority in the Senate, and several senators from both parties were undecided due to Ford's initial allegations and further allegations that followed. Just before the committee was set to vote, Jeff

Flake (R-Ariz.)—who earlier that day had been confronted in a Senate elevator by two survivors of sexual assault—announced that he would not be able to support the nominee without further investigation of the allegations by the FBI. Other undecided senators agreed. After a short, one-week investigation that failed to shed much light on the situation, the Senate confirmed Kavanaugh by the narrowest of margins—50–48, the second closest margin of any successful nominee in the history of the Court, and once again almost entirely along partisan lines.

Controversy over Supreme Court nominations then erupted yet again in September 2020, when Supreme Court Justice Ruth Bader Ginsburg died at the age of 87. In response to Ginsburg's death, within days Donald Trump nominated Judge Amy Coney Barrett to fill this seat on the Court. Senate Democrats strongly objected to Coney Barrett's nomination on two grounds. In terms of process, they pointed out that Republicans had refused to consider Garland's nomination because it was an election year, even though the election was ten months away, and now they were promising to push through a nomination with little over a month left until the election. Just as importantly, Democrats realized that replacing Ginsburg, a liberal icon who had served 27 years on the Court, with Coney Barrett, a strongly conservative judge, would swing the center of gravity on the Court dramatically to the right and almost certainly would lead to more conservative rulings on a wide range of policy issues. In the end, the Senate confirmed Coney Barrett by a vote of 52–48, with nearly all Republicans voting in favor and all Democrats voting against.

The conflicts between the president and the Senate over Scalia's seat, and within the Senate over Kavanaugh's nomination, were unusually contentious. But the unusual nature of these cases should not obscure a more general point: judicial nominations are inevitably contentious, for although courts are legal institutions, they are also political institutions. The federal courts issue tens of thousands of decisions per year, making them prominent participants in the policy-making process.[2] In Scalia's last two years as a justice, for example, the Court struck down the Environmental Protection Agency's rule requiring power plants to reduce emissions, recognized a national right to same-sex marriage, and upheld a portion of The Affordable Care Act.

Congress faces two main types of conflict involving the courts. The first type, which takes place between the Senate and the president, concerns who will serve as judges and justices on the federal courts. Because the courts are heavily involved in setting policy and because Congress cannot influence the courts' actions directly, the Senate wields its influence by determining who sits on the courts. Courts make policy when they reach decisions and issue opinions. A court might reach a decision in, say, an abortion case, based on existing laws and precedents; but in doing so, it is setting new policy—about who can get an abortion, and under what conditions.

The second type of conflict comes from policy differences between Congress and the courts. When these two institutions do not agree on public policy, is there anything Congress can do about it? After all, the courts are not subservient to Congress in the same way that executive agencies are subservient to the president (or to Congress); rather, Congress and the judicial branch are explicitly constitutional creations, each endowed with specific powers. But as we will explore, Congress has ways to influence the courts.

Separation of powers, governing, and representation are central to the relationship between Congress and the courts. When Congress interacts with the courts, or engages with the president over who can serve on the courts, we see the separation of powers at work. This separation of powers creates a conflict over who has the right to govern. Can the Senate influence presidential nominations to the courts, or does the president dominate this process? Can the House and Senate influence court actions, or do the courts act independently?

At the same time, Congress's activities surrounding the courts demonstrate its representative function. Republican senators who stated their refusal to vote for, or even meet with, Judge Garland, or who found Kavanaugh's repudiation of the allegations credible, believed that their constituents would agree with their actions.[3] Members of Congress are driven to try to influence the courts for the same reason. These themes of separation of powers, the power to govern, and representation are found in nearly every interaction between Congress and the courts.

## CONGRESS AND THE CREATION OF THE FEDERAL COURTS

Many of the Framers of the Constitution saw the lack of federal (that is, national) courts under the Articles of Confederation as a serious weakness, and one that the new Constitution would need to rectify. At the Constitutional Convention in 1787, there was general agreement about the need for federal courts, but there was disagreement about the form that these courts should take. Proponents of a stronger national government pushed for the creation of a Supreme Tribunal (or Supreme Court) and a series of inferior (or lower) courts. Meanwhile, proponents of state power, who agreed on the need for a Supreme Tribunal, argued that inferior courts at the national level would be unnecessary (since state courts already could hear most cases) and would further shift power away from states and toward the national government.[4]

As with many issues that arose at the Constitutional Convention, the result was a compromise. Article III of the Constitution explicitly creates a Supreme Court, but the Constitution does not explicitly create lower federal courts. In Section 1 of Article III, however, it does provide for the possible future creation of "such inferior Courts as the Congress may from time to time ordain and establish." In essence, the Framers kicked the can down the road, increasing Congress's power by giving it the authority to create additional courts.[5]

Article III is surprisingly vague. The entire text of this article runs to only 369 words, approximately one-third the length of Article II, which deals with the presidency, and only one-sixth the length of Article I, which outlines the legislative branch. Given this lack of detail, it did not take Congress long to accept the invitation extended in Article III, Section 1. In its first session, Congress quickly passed the Judiciary Act of 1789, creating circuit courts (also known as appellate courts) and district courts. In creating these courts—known as **Article III courts**, in recognition of the article that allows for their creation—Congress added to the Constitution's skeletal details regarding the operation of the judicial branch and set out a structure for the federal judicial system that still exists today.

## The Structure of the Federal Courts

The Supreme Court sits atop the federal judicial hierarchy, given this privilege of place by the Constitution's designation that "the judicial Power of the United States, shall be vested in one supreme Court." Directly below the Supreme Court are the federal circuit courts. Below them are the federal district courts.

District courts function as trial courts at the federal level. As a result, most cases enter the federal court system through one of the 94 federal district courts that are spread across the United States.[6] In 2015, for example, district courts held 2,912 civil trials and 1,998 criminal trials, while also helping to settle hundreds of thousands more cases.[7] In these cases, the district court, presided over by a federal judge, hears evidence from both sides to reach a verdict.

Once a case is decided by a district court, the verdict can be appealed to one of the 13 federal appellate courts. Eleven of these courts encompass specific states (for example, the Sixth Circuit Court of Appeals covers Michigan, Ohio, Kentucky, and Tennessee). The two other appellate courts are the D.C. Court of Appeals and the Court of Appeals for the Federal Circuit. Although cases can enter the federal court system directly at the level of appellate courts, the vast majority of cases that these circuit courts hear started out in the district courts.[8]

Finally, a party that loses at the appellate court level can appeal this decision to the Supreme Court. However, the Court is not obligated to hear all appeals of lower court decisions and instead gets to decide which cases it wants to hear. Congress specifically gave the Court this discretionary power in the Supreme Court Case Selections Act of 1988.[9] As a result of this discretion, most appeals are not heard, and in recent years the Court's docket (the list of cases it agrees to hear) has been getting smaller.

But also as a result of its discretion, the Court chooses to hear cases covering some of the most significant and controversial issues in American politics each year, from abortion to immigration to voting rights. Many of these cases derive directly from laws that Congress has passed. In 2007, for example, the Supreme Court heard *Gonzales v. Carhart*, which challenged an abortion law that Congress passed in 2003. That law, the Partial-Birth Abortion Ban Act, banned a specific kind of abortion procedure. Pro-choice groups challenged the constitutionality of this law, and district courts in the Northern District of California, the Southern District of New York, and the District of Nebraska found the law unconstitutional. The federal government appealed the district court rulings to several circuit courts and then to the Supreme Court. In the end, the Supreme Court upheld the law.

Another case involving a congressional statute occurred in 2013 when the Supreme Court ruled on the constitutionality of two provisions of the Voting Rights Act (VRA) in *Shelby County v. Holder*. Congress passed the VRA in 1965 to address racial discrimination in voting procedures. The law required certain states and local governments to obtain permission (or preclearance) from the federal government before changing their voting laws. The goal was to ensure that any such changes do not negatively affect minority groups. One of those local governments, Shelby County, Alabama, sought to avoid the preclearance requirement, arguing that it was no longer necessary. A district court judge ruled that the preclearance provisions were constitutional, and the Court of Appeals for the D.C. Circuit affirmed that decision. The Supreme Court then heard the case and ultimately sided with Shelby County, ruling that the parts of the VRA to which the county objected were unconstitutional. In this case, the courts influenced not only public policies but also the processes by which members are elected to Congress.

## Appointments

The Framers strove to keep the judiciary independent from the elected branches, reasoning that independence would allow judges to approach issues in a fair and impartial way.[10] One tactic the Framers adopted to increase the judiciary's independence was to give federal judges lifetime appointments. Participants at the Constitutional Convention made arguments both for and against this idea, which remains controversial.[11] The arguments on both sides were, and are, straightforward. If judges can be removed from office for making a decision that is unpopular (with citizens, members of Congress, or the president), then they will not have the independence necessary to act impartially. On the other hand, if there is no possibility of removing a judge, then there is nothing to stop him or her from behaving improperly, unethically, or illegally. To balance these competing concerns, Article III, Section 1, stipulates that federal judges "shall hold their Offices during good Behavior," which means that in the absence of misconduct, they keep their positions.

The Framers also sought to make the courts independent of the other branches by dividing the power over judicial appointments between Congress and the president.[12] Article II, Section 2, of the Constitution gives the president the power to select a nominee but requires that the Senate consent to that nominee before he or she takes a seat on a federal court. Both branches having a say in determining the appointment of judges decreases the likelihood that the courts will be subservient to either branch. Of course, it also means that conflict is endemic, as we saw in the clash between President Obama and the Senate over Garland's nomination. Sometimes the president wins these disputes, but other times, the Senate does: Mitch McConnell's successful obstruction of Garland paved the way for President Trump to nominate Neil Gorsuch, whom the Senate then confirmed.

There always has been, and always will be, conflict over judicial nominations. The situation after Scalia's death was extreme and unprecedented, but in recent decades, the level of conflict has increased, due in part to the greater prominence of the courts in policy making and in politics. This prominence, when combined with the life tenure that a judicial appointment affords, incentivizes senators and the president to make sure that the "right" people end up serving on the courts. Furthermore, when the president and members of the Senate differ ideologically and disagree about policies, they do not want to let the other institution dominate the governing process.

**THE DESIGN OF THE APPOINTMENT PROCESS**  At first glance, the Constitution appears to be quite clear about the roles that the Senate and president play in the appointment process. Article II, Section 2, states that the president "shall nominate, and, by and with the advice and consent of the Senate, shall appoint . . . judges of the Supreme Court." Three features of this provision stand out. First, the Constitution prescribes a role for both the Senate and the president. Second, the president gets to take the lead in the process; if he does not act, there is no appointment for the Senate to consider. Third, the Constitution requires the Senate to be a part of the appointment process, but it provides only vague details about the Senate's role. What does it mean when it specifies that the Senate should give "advice"? And what should senators base their consent on? Policy preferences? Qualifications? Other factors?

It will come as no surprise that the wording of Article II, Section 2, was yet another compromise at the Constitutional Convention, one that followed two weeks of intense debate. Some participants, including Alexander Hamilton and James Wilson, favored assigning the appointment power predominantly, or even solely, to the executive. Others, including James Madison and Benjamin Franklin, worried that such an approach would concentrate too much power within the executive branch.[13] The compromise ended up closer to the Madison-Franklin position, assigning the primary and first-mover role to the president but giving the Senate a powerful check on this role.

**THE APPOINTMENT PROCESS TODAY**   Currently the appointment process plays out in multiple stages. The stages are roughly the same for the lower courts as for the Supreme Court, but there are some differences. We will first discuss the process in detail as it relates to the Supreme Court, and then we will discuss additional features that apply to lower-court appointments.

The process of appointing a justice to the Supreme Court begins with an opening on the Court owing to the death, retirement, or resignation of a sitting justice. Between 1869, when the size of the Court was set at nine justices, and 2020, there have been 76 vacancies on the Court, with the most recent vacancy created by the death of Justice Ruth Bader Ginsburg. Since vacancies occur approximately every other year, a president serving a full four-year term can expect to have two opportunities on average to make an appointment. There is considerable variation, however. Some presidents, such as Jimmy Carter, never had a chance to make an appointment. At the other end of the scale, William Taft appointed five justices during his four years in office.

When a vacancy occurs, the president consults with relevant advisors and, usually, prominent senators—including senators from any potential nominee's home states—before selecting a nominee. Since 1870, presidents have submitted nominees' names to the Senate Judiciary Committee for initial consideration.[14] At this point, the Senate's formal role begins.[15] The Judiciary Committee investigates the nominee, deliberates about his or her qualifications, and then sends

In most cases, a president's nominee for the Supreme Court is considered and confirmed by the Senate. In 2016, however, Senate Majority Leader Mitch McConnell (R-Ky.) refused to consider Merrick Garland, President Obama's choice to replace Antonin Scalia.

its recommendation to the full Senate. Initially, the committee conducted its activities behind closed doors. It was only in the 1950s, with President Dwight Eisenhower's nomination of John M. Harlan, that nominees began to testify before the committee. And it was not until 1981, with President Ronald Reagan's nomination of Sandra Day O'Connor, that the committee allowed these hearings to be broadcast.

The Judiciary Committee's role in the process is primarily informational. Members of the committee question the nominee to learn about his or her views on specific policy issues, judicial philosophy, and qualifications. The hearings also give members a moment in the public eye, which in turn allows them to make their positions publicly known, to show that they are representing their constituents in this process, and to impress upon the nominee their views of specific cases and of the judiciary's role in the political process. The committee then votes on whether to report the nominee favorably to the full Senate, to report the nominee unfavorably, or to make no recommendation.[16] The hearings thus provide information about the nominee to the committee, to the full Senate, and to the public. They also provide committee members' views to the full Senate.

Once the Judiciary Committee submits its report, the full Senate begins its work. The majority leader schedules consideration of the nominee, which takes place in executive session consisting of speeches and general floor debate. Senators use this stage as an opportunity to state, for the public record, their reasons for supporting or opposing the nominee. When debate comes to a close, the Senate votes. In the past, many confirmation votes were voice votes, but since 1967, all have been roll call votes. If the vote is favorable, it is reported to the president, who signs the commission that officially seats the nominee on the Court.

**CONFIRMATION VOTES** In the vast majority of cases, this process results in the appointment of a new justice to the Supreme Court. Through President Trump's nomination of Amy Coney Barrett, presidents have made 163 nominations for positions on the Court. Of these, the Senate formally rejected only 11. In other words, in less than 7 percent of nominations did the Senate actually vote against confirming the president's nominee. Yet this figure, while striking, overstates the president's success. In 11 more cases, the president withdrew the nomination, while in another 15 cases—including Merrick Garland's nomination—the term ended before the Senate held a vote (although some of those nominees were later renominated and confirmed). Still, even taking all of these other instances into account, the Senate failed to confirm only 37 of the presidents' 163 nominations. Furthermore, nearly half of these failures were clustered during four nineteenth-century presidencies: John Tyler, Millard Fillmore, Ulysses S. Grant, and Grover Cleveland. Presidential success rates in the twentieth and twenty-first centuries have been high.

Anticipating a supportive Democratic Senate, President Obama was able to nominate liberal justices Sonia Sotomayor (left) and Elena Kagan (center), whom the Senate approved rather easily. When Republicans controlled the Senate, Obama nominated the more moderate Merrick Garland, on whom the Senate refused to hold hearings.

Why have presidents been so successful with their nominations? In part, their success derives from the sense that the Senate, in the words of Senator Orrin Hatch (R-Utah), "owes some deference to the president's qualified nominees."[17] Moreover, presidents have, by and large, chosen well-qualified nominees, especially in the past century or so. But a big part of presidents' success is due to their awareness of the Senate's power and its preferences. Presidents seek nominees whose appointments would shift the Court toward their own views. But the Constitution forces presidents to anticipate the Senate's reaction.[18]

Recall that the process consists of two stages. First, the president submits a nominee. Second, the Senate votes on that nominee. The Senate's vote might not provide much of a constraint when the Senate and president agree ideologically; however, when the Senate and president do not agree, the Senate can constrain the president. Of course, presidents are free to nominate whomever they want, but if their nominee would shift the Court in a direction that the Senate dislikes, then the Senate is more likely to vote against confirmation. A rejection would damage the president's reputation, relationship with the Senate, and future opportunities. Because presidents want to avoid these costs, they will take the Senate's view into account and choose a nominee who most closely shares their own views but whom the Senate also will confirm.

With the Senate playing this constraining role, we should expect to find two patterns. First, when the president and Senate are more distant, in terms of either partisanship or ideology, we should find that the president takes longer to make a nomination, as the president is likely to spend more time consulting with Senate leaders to find out which nominees will be acceptable. Second, we would expect presidents to choose nominees who share their views when they are unconstrained, but to select nominees who do not exactly share their views when they need to take the Senate into account. In general, these patterns have held: presidents do take longer to make nominations, and they moderate their choices, when they face a Senate that does not share their views. President Obama's nominations illustrate this latter point. The two nominations he made when Democrats controlled the Senate (Sonia Sotomayor and Elena Kagan) are to the left of the nomination he made when Republicans controlled the Senate (Garland).

---

## THEN AND NOW
## CONFIRMATION VOTES

The Senate has shown a strong tendency to confirm presidential Supreme Court nominations, but this tendency masks variation across senators. For starters, even in positive confirmation votes, there are often senators who vote against confirmation. Furthermore, the negative confirmation votes have increased markedly in recent decades. Prior to 1985, only about 9 percent of confirmation votes that senators cast were negative, but this rate has nearly tripled since then, with nearly 25 percent of votes being negative.[19]

Senators are more likely to vote for a nominee if the president is popular, if the president's party controls the Senate and the president is not in the last year of his or her term, and when the senators' constituents and interest groups support the nominee.[20] But the most important factors in a senator's vote are the nominee's qualifications and ideology. The more qualified the nominee, the greater the probability that a senator will vote to confirm him or her, hence the president's incentive to choose qualified nominees. In addition, senators are more likely to vote for nominees who share their ideologies and less likely to vote for those who are ideologically distant, which encourages the president to

**TABLE 11.1**  Frequency of Yes and No Confirmation Votes on Supreme Court Nominees by Party

|  |  | Yes | No |
|---|---|---|---|
| Pre-1985 | Opposing-party senators | 1,003 (84.1%) | 190 (15.9%) |
|  | Same-party senators | 1,557 (95.6%) | 72 (4.4%) |
| Post-1985 | Opposing-party senators | 289 (50.8%) | 280 (49.2%) |
|  | Same-party senators | 605 (98.1%) | 12 (1.9%) |

consider the Senate's ideology when selecting nominees. Finally, the combination of these factors is especially potent: while senators are likely to vote for a qualified nominee and are likely to vote for a nominee who shares their ideology, they are even more likely to vote for a nominee who is both highly qualified and who shares their ideology.

These factors have always influenced the voting calculus of senators, but the process has changed in two ways. First, ideology has become more important over time. Whether this shift began in 1987 with the Senate's high-profile rejection of Robert Bork, or in 1985 with objection to William Rehnquist's nomination for the position of chief justice, or at some earlier point, it's clear that there has been a change.

Second, party has become increasingly influential in Senate voting on Supreme Court nominations. A senator's vote is now more dependent than ever before on whether he or she is a member of the president's party,[21] as Table 11.1 makes clear. Prior to 1985, opposing-party senators were 3.6 times more likely to vote against a president's nominee than were senators from the president's party. Since 1985, opposing-party senators have been nearly 26 times more likely to do so.

## Critical Thinking

1. Should senators consider a nominee's ideology during the confirmation process? Or should their decision be based on qualifications alone?
2. As noted in this chapter, Senator Hatch has argued that there should be a presumption of deference from senators toward a president's nominees. Would the Framers agree with Senator Hatch's view? Why or why not?
3. Why have opposing-party senators become so much more likely to oppose Supreme Court nominees?

**THE LOWER COURTS** Lower-court appointments resemble Supreme Court appointments, albeit with much less salience and public attention. As with the Supreme Court, the appointment process for lower courts begins with a vacancy. The president selects a nominee, and the Senate then has the authority to advise and consent. Within these stages, however, the lower-court process differs in a few key ways.

Unlike the Supreme Court, which is a true national court whose rulings cover the entire country, district and appellate courts are located in specific areas: the District Court for Northern Illinois, for example, or the Fifth Circuit Court of Appeals, which covers Texas, Louisiana, and Mississippi. When these courts reach a decision, their rulings generally hold only for their specific geographical area. Because these courts are located in or among specific states, and because their rulings apply only to those states, those states' senators are especially inclined to provide advice about which nominees are acceptable. Furthermore, because senators want their preferences over appointments in their states to be honored by other senators, a system of reciprocity has sprung up, with **senatorial courtesy** causing senators to defer to the wishes of the nominees' home-state senators.

To formalize this system, in the early part of the twentieth century, the Senate Judiciary Committee created the blue slip procedure, in which the committee solicits the views of the home-state senators by sending them a blue slip of paper, asking for their opinion of a nominee. If these home-state senators approve of the nominee, the committee proceeds with its work. If not, the committee generally defers to the individual senators and does not consider the nominee. This system, of course, greatly empowers individual senators, with a president needing their consent before making a lower-court nomination.[22]

Until recently, a nomination to a federal court could be filibustered; however, this delaying tactic began to erode in 2005 when Senate Majority Leader Bill Frist, frustrated by the Senate Democrats blocking President George W. Bush's nominations, threatened to change Senate rules so that a filibuster for such nominations could be ended by a majority vote, rather than a three-fifths (cloture) vote.[23] At that time, Democrats vowed to shut down the Senate if Frist invoked this **nuclear option**, and the parties struck a deal to avoid filibusters in most cases. In 2013, with all the partisan roles switched—now Senate Democrats were frustrated with Senate Republicans blocking President Obama's nominations—the majority party carried through on the threat to use the nuclear option to eliminate filibusters on lower-court nominations, giving presidents a clearer path, if not necessarily an easy one, to getting their nominees through the Senate. (The tables turned yet again in 2017 when Senate Republicans, worried about potential Democratic opposition to Gorsuch, eliminated the filibuster for Supreme Court nominations.)

## Relative Power of Congress and the Courts

With the power of appointment divided between Congress and the president, the Framers provided the courts with independence while allowing the other branches to check and balance them. But in truth, the Framers did not see much of a need for checks on the courts, since they expected the courts to be, in the words of Hamilton, the "least dangerous" branch.[24]

Over time, however—particularly over the course of the nineteenth century—the courts gained power through their actions and decisions. The Supreme Court's decision in *Marbury v. Madison* (1803) was particularly conse-quential.[25] In this case Chief Justice John Marshall, writing for the Court, declared that a portion of the Judiciary Act of 1789—specifically, the portion that gave courts the power to issue writs of mandamus, which are essentially statements ordering other government institutions, including Congress and the president, to take specific actions—was inconsistent with the Constitution. Through *Marbury*, Marshall claimed the power of **judicial review** for the courts, and did so by denying the court a small power (to issue writs of mandamus) while claiming the much greater power to review the laws that Congress passed and to determine whether those statutes were constitutional.

The courts did not immediately become a significant force in the policy-making process after *Marbury*. But as the nineteenth century wore on, the courts increasingly assumed this role. In a series of landmark cases throughout the nineteenth century, the courts continued to increase their power as national policy makers.[26] By the end of the nineteenth century, the federal judiciary had traveled from its humble origins as the "least dangerous" branch to a position of power on par with—if distinct from—Congress.

These nineteenth-century judicial actions led to what is now widely accepted as the division of labor between Congress and the courts. Congress's main power, in this view, is to legislate. Fulfilling both Congress's representative func-tion and its governing function, the primary job of members of Congress is to represent their constituents during the lawmaking process and to produce laws that will govern the country. At that point, the courts can weigh in, determining whether congressionally enacted laws fall within the boundaries set by the Con-stitution. When they do fall within these bounds, the courts allow the laws to remain in effect. When they fall outside the bounds of the Constitution, the courts can exercise the power of judicial review and deem these laws unconstitutional.

But Congress was not merely a passive bystander in the judiciary's ascension, watching idly while the courts accumulated new powers or objecting to these powers but unable to halt them. Instead, Congress has often preferred that the courts play a more active role in the governing and policy-making process, and it has delegated such authority to the courts.

Congress might prefer a more active judiciary, including one that can strike down congressional laws, for a variety of reasons. In some situations, Congress might not want to take the lead in setting policy. For example, Congress might want a certain policy to be enacted but worry about potential political consequences. Such a policy might occur in an area where it would be difficult to reach an agreement within or across the two legislative chambers. Or the policy action may be likely to have negative repercussions.[27] In addition, the majority party in Congress might be happy to let the judiciary take the lead on issues that could jeopardize its majority status, especially if the majority party believes its current hold on power is tenuous.[28]

Sometimes Congress writes statutes in a way that welcomes judicial activity. In such statutes, Congress crafts laws that are deliberately ambiguous, knowing that such an approach invites judges to step in and impose order on the ambiguity.[29] Congress might choose this course of action because the policy questions are difficult, because legislators want to give the courts flexibility when considering cases, because Congress wants to provide for additional oversight of executive agencies, or because it wants to break a stalemate. Sometimes each faction in Congress thinks its best chance of policy success is to write a vague statute that the courts will interpret in a manner consistent with the faction's own views.[30] For these and other reasons, Congress often invites the courts to play a more prominent role in the policy-making process.

In short, the view that "Congress legislates, and the courts interpret" can be a useful shorthand description, but the reality is more complex. Initially, it was not clear that the courts had the power to interpret the constitutionality of laws. After the courts asserted this power, they began to play a more central role in governing and policy making—slowly at first, then more assertively as time went on. Congress both acquiesced and added to this increased judicial role. The relationship between Congress and the courts is thus a complex one that has evolved over time. And regardless of how the courts gained their power, Congress retains the ability to criticize, challenge, correct, and restrict the courts—a topic that we explore in the next section.

## HOW CONGRESS AND THE COURTS INTERACT: RESPONSE AND ANTICIPATION

Today's Congress shares the national policy-making stage with the courts (and, as we discussed in Chapter 9, the executive branch). Congress retains its role as the originator of legislation, which helps it fulfill its governing function and

Supreme Court Justice Ruth Bader Ginsburg's strong dissent in *Ledbetter v. Goodyear Tire & Rubber Co.* encouraged Congress to eventually pass a law to restore protections against gender-based pay discrimination. Here, Lilly Ledbetter speaks at a rally for equal pay, with supporters and members of Congress, including then-senator Hillary Clinton (D-N.Y., right), looking on.

allows members to pursue policies that represent their constituents' goals and desires. But the involvement of the courts in virtually every policy area means that conflict between the two branches is frequent and often unavoidable.

Has the increased judicial role weakened Congress to the point where the courts now have the final say? Conventional wisdom holds that the courts review laws when the laws are challenged and decide which ones will be allowed to stand. In fact, the courts perform two distinct but related functions when they evaluate statutes. As discussed earlier, they assess whether a statute is constitutional by considering whether it stays within the bounds created by the Constitution. They also engage in **statutory interpretation**, which means determining what a statute actually means. Statutes are often ambiguous. Sometimes this ambiguity is intentional, but it might also be the unintended result of the complicated process by which laws are passed and the inability of legislators and congressional staffers to anticipate every situation or outcome that the law might encounter.

The case of Lilly Ledbetter provides a good example of the power of the courts to interpret a statute and Congress's power to respond. Ledbetter filed suit against her employer, the Goodyear Tire and Rubber Company, arguing that she was paid less than men who held similar positions. After Ledbetter won some initial court victories, Goodyear appealed to the Eleventh Circuit. This court ruled against Ledbetter on statutory interpretation grounds: it held that, based on its reading of the Civil Rights Act of 1964, Ledbetter's complaint was filed after the window for taking such action had closed. In other words, Ledbetter had not filed her claim soon enough for it to be valid. Although she sued Goodyear soon after learning about the pay discrepancy, the court ruled that the time limit on complaints applied to when the discriminatory action took place, not to when an employee learned about it. Thus, she was not entitled to redress under the earlier statute.

A closely divided Supreme Court agreed with the appellate court's ruling. However, Justice Ruth Bader Ginsburg disagreed with the majority's interpretation. In her dissent, she noted that companies would be able to get away with discriminatory actions if they could hide that discrimination just long enough to avoid the window for filing suit. She also directly invited Congress to clarify that employees should be able to file complaints even against company actions that had not taken place recently but rather had occurred earlier in the employee's time with the company. After a couple of failed attempts, in 2009 the 111th Congress passed, and President Obama signed, the Lilly Ledbetter Fair Pay Act, which lengthened the period during which complaints of workplace discrimination can be filed.

Given the courts' powers of judicial review and statutory interpretation, it is reasonable to ask whether the courts now dominate the policy-making process. There is little doubt that the balance of power between Congress and the courts has shifted in ways that the Framers neither intended nor anticipated. The crucial question is whether Congress has the ability to respond to or shape the actions of the courts. In other words, what tools does Congress have at its disposal to deal with the more powerful courts it faces today?

## Overrides

The most straightforward action that Congress can take when it disagrees with a judicial decision is to override that decision. The exact manner in which Congress overrides a judicial decision depends on the nature of the judicial action. For example, if the Supreme Court strikes down a statute on constitutional grounds, then Congress can override this decision by passing a constitutional amendment. If, however, the Court relies on statutory interpretation, as it did in the Lilly Ledbetter case, then Congress can override the Court's decision by passing another law.

The controversial area of campaign finance provides a good example of Congress's options for overriding a Supreme Court constitutional decision. In 2002, Congress passed the Bipartisan Campaign Reform Act (BCRA), also known as McCain-Feingold. Although this law covered a number of aspects of campaign finance, one key provision prohibited corporations, unions, and other groups from broadcasting political advertisements close to an election. Specifically, the law prohibited these groups from paying for ads that were ostensibly about policy or political issues but that also named specific candidates, on the grounds that such ads were attempts to evade other limitations on campaign contributions. (See Chapter 12 for further discussion of this law and the court cases that followed.)

In *Citizens United v. Federal Election Commission*, the Supreme Court ruled in a 5–4 decision that a key part of McCain-Feingold was unconstitutional because it violated the free speech clause of the First Amendment.[31] Congress, the Court ruled, did not have the power to prevent corporations and unions from making independent expenditures and engaging in electioneering communications in the period leading up to an election.

When the Court strikes down all or part of a law as unconstitutional, what can Congress do? One option is to attempt to rewrite the law in a way that avoids the constitutional conflict or that achieves the desired effects of the law in other ways. After *Citizens United*, members of Congress introduced bills that attempted to offset the significant advantages that the decision conferred upon corporations (for example, by providing for increased public funding for elections) or that required additional public disclosure of campaign spending by corporations. As another option, Congress could introduce a constitutional amendment designed to overturn the decision. In this case, the Court decision rested on the idea that corporations should be treated like individuals; thus, some politicians proposed an amendment that would eliminate or restrict this notion of "corporate personhood." In neither case—passing new laws or constitutional amendments—was Congress successful in counteracting the Court's decision.

To characterize the possibility of any proposed constitutional amendment succeeding as a long shot would be a severe understatement. Since the founding of the country, more than 11,000 constitutional amendments have been proposed.[32] But because passage requires two-thirds of the members of each congressional chamber to agree to the amendment and then three-quarters of the states to ratify it, only 27 amendments—scarcely more than 0.2 percent of attempts—have succeeded. And only seven of these amendments have been responses to judicial decisions.[33] Congress has the theoretical power to override the Court's constitutional decisions, but in practice, its ability to do so is limited.

This is not to say that constitutional amendments as responses to Court actions never succeed. Consider the Sixteenth Amendment, which established the income tax. Congress previously had tried to shoehorn permanent income tax provisions into tariff legislation, but the courts struck down such attempts as unconstitutional. In response, Congress initiated the process of amending the Constitution to allow for such a tax, passing the amendment in 1909 and adopting it 1913.

Congress has much more power when it comes to addressing the judiciary's statutory interpretations. In cases like Lilly Ledbetter's, for example, Congress can attempt to override the court's action. Overriding a statutory decision requires only a majority vote in each chamber—a much simpler hurdle to clear than the requirements for a constitutional override. Once the president signs the bill that the two chambers have approved, the bill becomes law, and the decision is overridden.

Of course, although passing a law is easier than passing a constitutional amendment, throughout this book we have learned about all the ways a bill can be derailed on its way to passage. Given all the challenges to enacting a meaningful congressional response, do the courts, in effect, have the final word on policy making? For a long time, scholars and political observers argued that members of Congress paid little attention to judicial decisions, and when the members did pay attention, they were unable to overcome the various obstacles preventing them from overriding these decisions.[34] But then a number of political scientists and legal scholars started looking more closely at this issue and found something unexpected: Congress actually is highly aware of statutory decisions and ends up successfully overriding these decisions with surprising frequency.

A landmark study by legal scholar William Eskridge provided the first systematic evidence regarding overrides. Eskridge looked at all reports written by congressional committees between 1967 and 1990 to see if they mentioned any judicial decisions that were affected by laws that the committee was considering.[35] One of his primary findings was that the House Judiciary Committee scrutinizes between 44 and 65 judicial decisions per Congress, a surprisingly high number. He then examined whether responses to judicial decisions ended up being enacted into law. Again, the number was unexpectedly high. During the period he examined, Eskridge identified 187 laws containing provisions that overrode a total of 344 judicial decisions.

**FIGURE 11.1** Number of Overrides by Congress, 90th–112th Congresses (1967–2013)

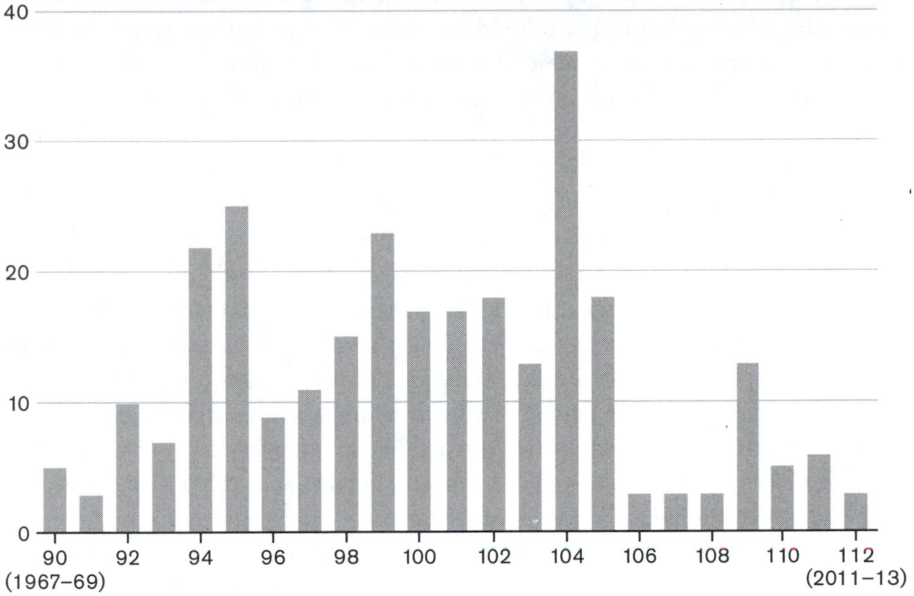

Matthew R. Christiansen and William N. Eskridge Jr. 2014. "Congressional Overrides of Supreme Court Statutory Interpretation Decisions, 1967–2011." *Texas Law Review* 92: 1317.

An important question is whether the period Eskridge examined was an outlier, with Congress more attentive to judicial actions and more successful at overriding them in those years. Indeed, one later study using Eskridge's methodology showed that after 1990, in the period following the initial study, congressional overrides dropped dramatically, with Congress overriding fewer than three judicial decisions per Congress.[36] Eskridge himself then updated his analysis using a more inclusive methodology. He found that the number of overrides actually increased in the 1990s, but then, as Figure 11.1 shows, decreased dramatically in the 2000s—most likely because increased political polarization has made the passage of any laws in Congress, and not just overrides, more difficult.[37]

Overall, the evidence indicates that Congress does indeed pay attention to judicial decisions and that it overrides the courts' statutory decisions more regularly than many observers suspected (and far more frequently than in cases involving constitutional interpretations).

## Pressure

In addition to passing laws that override judicial decisions, Congress can also pressure the courts to change their actions. The goal is not to reverse a particular judicial decision, but rather to send a warning shot signaling congressional displeasure with recent judicial actions. In so doing, Congress can both govern (by influencing the courts) and represent (thereby currying favor with constituents).

Some of these tools are informal. Members of Congress can, for example, voice their displeasure with judicial rulings. After the Court's ruling in *Burwell v. Hobby Lobby* (which held that for-profit corporations can be exempted from laws on religious grounds), Representative Nancy Pelosi (D-Calif.) tweeted that "SCOTUS [the Supreme Court] took an outrageous step against women's rights, setting a dangerous precedent that permits corporations to choose which laws to obey." In response to *United States v. Windsor* and *Hollingsworth v. Perry*, which paved the way for marriage equality by overturning existing prohibitions on same-sex marriages, Representative Michele Bachmann (R-Minn.) announced that the Court "undercut the people's representatives [and] the will of their constituencies."[38] Members of Congress can also voice displeasure with specific judges. Representative Peter DeFazio (D-Ore.), in response to the Court's *Citizens United* ruling, announced, "I'm investigating articles of impeachment against Justice Roberts for perjuring during his Senate hearings, where he said he wouldn't be a judicial activist, and he wouldn't overturn precedents."[39]

Other tactics are more formal. Although they cannot vote to decrease judges' salaries, members of Congress can choose not to increase these salaries. And they can limit funding allocations to the courts each year, thereby constraining judges' ability to hire staff to help with their work. None of these actions truly threaten judicial independence, but they do signal congressional displeasure to the courts and make the job of being a judge at least marginally less enjoyable.

## The Structure and Composition of the Judicial Branch

In addition to these formal and informal tools of pressure, Congress can influence the structure and composition of the judicial branch. Because the Constitution is silent about the number of justices who should comprise the Supreme Court, it falls to Congress to determine this number by statute. Although the current size of nine justices has been in place since just after the Civil War, the Court has not always been this size.[40] In fact, the number of seats on the Court has ranged from a low of 5 in the early 1800s to a high of 10 during the Civil War.

Changes in the size of the Supreme Court in the 1860s illustrate how Congress can use its powers to influence the Court based on political and strategic considerations. In 1863, the Republican Congress increased the size of the Court from nine justices to ten, providing President Abraham Lincoln (also a Republican) with the opportunity to select an additional justice. Then, shortly after the end of the Civil War, the Republican-controlled Congress passed the Judicial Circuits Act of 1866. Part of this act reduced the number of justices on the Court from ten to seven, with the reduction to come from not replacing departing justices. Congress's goal in making this change was evident: it was to prevent President Andrew Johnson—who acceded to the presidency after Lincoln's assassination and who was a Democrat, unlike his predecessor—from naming any new justices to the Court.

Similarly, as the Reconstruction era continued, Republicans in Congress increased the number of lower federal courts and their jurisdictions. They then worked to populate these courts with Republican-leaning judges in order to insulate the policies they had passed. Essentially, the GOP knew it would not be able to hold off the Democratic resurgence forever, so it sought to preserve its laws by stacking the courts.[41]

If the Civil War and its aftermath demonstrate how Congress can use its powers to change the size of the Court, then a well-known episode from the 1930s shows how Congress can attempt to use these powers to *block* change. During this decade, President Franklin D. Roosevelt (FDR) grew increasingly frustrated by the conservative Supreme Court as it struck down aspects of his liberal New Deal plan. In response to these rulings, and knowing that none of the conservative justices who formed a majority on the Court had any intention of stepping down anytime soon, FDR attempted to "pack" the Court by adding new justices who were more supportive of his New Deal programs. Although FDR had won a landslide victory only one year earlier, and his party (Democrats) controlled Congress, his plan died in the Senate, where the Judiciary Committee described it as "an invasion of judicial power such as has never been attempted in the country."[42]

Congress also can threaten to limit or eliminate life tenure for judges. Because the Constitution gives federal judges life tenure, members of Congress often have introduced constitutional amendments to limit the number of years a justice can serve. But members also have introduced regular statutes designed to chip away at life tenure and otherwise alter who gets to serve on the Court and for how long. Proposals have included creating a means other than impeachment for the removal of justices, prescribing specific qualifications, and adopting a mandatory retirement age.

Recall that life tenure for judges is not absolute, but rather is circumscribed. Thus Congress can also change the composition of the courts by impeaching, or threatening to impeach, federal judges. Several sections of the Constitution combine to provide guidance for how this process works. Article II, Section 4, states, "The President, Vice President and all civil Officers of the United States, shall be removed from Office on Impeachment for, and Conviction of, Treason, Bribery, or other High crimes and Misdemeanors." Article I, Section 2, says, "The House of Representatives . . . shall have the sole Power of Impeachment," while Article I, Section 3, continues, "The Senate shall have the sole Power to try all Impeachments." In addition, as noted earlier, Article III, Section 1, provides that "Judges, both of the supreme and inferior courts, shall hold their Offices during good Behaviour."

Taken together, these constitutional provisions have several implications. First, judges—like presidents and other officials—can be impeached. Second, although the word "impeachment" is sometimes used colloquially to mean "remove from office," in reality (and as discussed in Chapter 9), impeachment is the first stage of the process, and an official is removed from office only if the House votes to impeach and the Senate follows this impeachment by voting to convict. Third, the criteria for removing a judge are murky at best, as the Constitution spells out neither what constitutes "High crimes and Misdemeanors" nor what is meant by "good Behaviour." Although there is no doubt that some impeachment hearings have been based on purely political grounds, in general, impeachment proceedings against judges, particularly those cases that reach the Senate, have been reserved for instances where judges behaved unethically or illegally.

Congress has used its impeachment power infrequently. The only impeachment of a Supreme Court justice took place in 1805, when the House impeached Justice Samuel Chase for inappropriately engaging in partisan activity and allowing his partisan leanings to affect his rulings. The Senate, however, acquitted Chase of all charges.[43] The most recent removal of a federal judge took place in 2010, when the House impeached, and the Senate then convicted, Thomas Porteous Jr., a judge on the U.S. District Court for the Eastern District of Louisiana, for a wide range of improprieties.[44]

All told, the House has impeached 15 federal judges. Of these, the Senate has convicted eight. Spread out over more than 200 years and thousands of federal judges, these are obviously not large numbers. But the threat of impeachment hovers over judges. The House, after all, has conducted formal inquiries into the conduct of judges approximately every two-and-a-half years.[45] And individual members regularly raise the possibility of impeachment, such as Representative Louie Gohmert's (R-Tex.) call to consider Justice Kagan for impeachment because of her role in upholding major provisions of the Affordable Care Act.[46]

## Curbing the Courts

As we have seen, the textbook view of policy making—Congress passes a bill, the president signs it, then the courts interpret it—is incomplete, because it ignores Congress's ability to react to judicial decisions. In addition, the textbook description presumes that the courts can always act. In reality, Congress can spell out when the courts can act and which cases the courts can hear by passing **court-curbing bills**, which are laws that Congress uses to constrain and place pressure on the courts.[47]

Court curbing can take several forms. For example, bills that affect the composition of the courts are considered to be court curbing. Congress's response to Roosevelt's attempt to pack the Court provides a well-known example. Court curbing also encompasses congressional attempts to limit the policy outcomes that courts can prescribe in their decisions—for example, if a statute were to say that when the courts hear cases about segregation in the schools, they cannot turn to busing as a remedy.

The most prominent way Congress can curb the courts is by limiting their jurisdiction.[48] Members of Congress can, for example, define issues as occurring at the state level, rather than at the federal level, which would indicate that they fall outside of the federal courts' jurisdiction. Or they can be more specific. In several sessions of Congress during the 2000s, for example, members introduced the Pledge Protection Act, which aimed to strip all federal courts of their jurisdiction to hear constitutional challenges to the Pledge of Allegiance. The pledge had recently been (and continues to be) the topic of several court cases, and some courts ruled that the inclusion of the phrase "under God" was unconstitutional because it violated the First Amendment. Although Congress did not pass the Pledge Protection Act, its introduction was a way for many members to signal their displeasure with these judicial decisions and to indicate that future such decisions would likely be met with serious attempts to remove the judiciary's jurisdiction over this issue.

Members of Congress have introduced court-curbing bills regularly throughout history but more frequently in certain periods, as Figure 11.2 shows. Not surprisingly, these spikes in court-curbing bills coincide with periods when the Court tackled controversial issues that irritated members of Congress. In particular, as the Supreme Court began to consider hot-button issues like school prayer, school desegregation, and the rights of criminal defendants in the 1950s and 1960s, members of Congress started to introduce more and more bills designed to limit the Court's jurisdiction and to constrain its ability to review laws for constitutionality.[49]

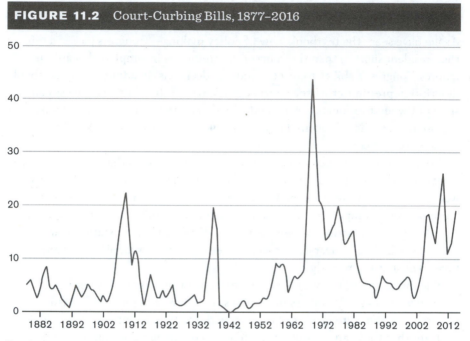

Data from 1877–2008 is from Tom S. Clark. 2011. *The Limits of Judicial Independence*, 43, Figure 2.1. New York: Cambridge University Press; data from 2009–2016 is from Alyx Mark and Michael A. Zilis 2019. "The Conditional Effectiveness of Legislative Threats: How Court Curbing Alters the Behavior of (Some) Supreme Court Justices." *Political Research Quarterly* 72(3): 570–83.

## Do Judges Care about Congressional Actions?

Members of Congress clearly can and do introduce a variety of laws that pose threats to the judicial branch. They can threaten to remove jurisdiction from the courts. They can attempt to limit the judiciary's ability to conduct judicial review. They can change the size of the courts, threaten to impeach judges, or propose actions that would limit life tenure. They can refuse to raise judges' salaries, cut the judiciary's budget, or take to the airwaves or social media to castigate judges for specific decisions or for broader trends in judicial policy making.

The question that arises is, Why should judges care about any of these congressional actions? After all, federal judges have life tenure, and threats to remove them rarely succeed. Although changes to the size of the Supreme Court are hypothetically possible, the Court has remained the same size for over 150 years. Bills to limit the federal judiciary's ability to conduct judicial review or to limit its jurisdiction are frequently introduced but infrequently passed.

There are several reasons why judges might care about these congressional actions.[50] To begin with, many (and perhaps even most) lower-court judges aspire to serve on a higher court, and they need Senate approval to achieve this goal. Avoiding controversy—or backing off when they receive signals from Congress that they are generating controversy—is a way to increase the odds of any future confirmations being successful. In addition, judges, like most other people, pay attention to what others say about them.

Perhaps more importantly, judges are concerned about the institutional legitimacy of the judiciary. Consider the members of the Supreme Court. They want to protect the Court's reputation and its prestige, and as a result they do not want to regularly cross the other branches, given the Court's need for the executive branch to carry out its decisions and the legislative branch to provide funding. Furthermore, this institutional legitimacy helps the Court (and the judiciary more generally) to remain the most trusted of American national institutions in the eyes of the public. Evidence indicates that when the judicial branch exhibits lower levels of consensus or allows itself to be pulled into political fights, its approval drops, making it more susceptible to attacks from other institutions.[51]

Given that the courts have reason to worry about threats from members of Congress, the next question is whether these threats affect the courts' behavior. That is, do judges anticipate congressional threats and actions and modify their own actions to avoid negative repercussions? Perhaps they do not need to be concerned about how Congress might react. After all, Congress often suffers from a decided lack of information about recent judicial rulings.[52] And even if Congress is aware of recent or upcoming judicial actions, it may not be able to act because of all the institutional and behavioral reasons discussed earlier (for example, the power of majority party leaders to keep issues off the agenda, the gatekeeping power of committee chairs, the multiple veto points that must be navigated to pass any law, and so on).

One way to approach this question is to investigate whether judges change their voting behavior when their own views conflict with those of Congress and the president. For example, is a conservative justice more likely to moderate his or her views when Congress and the president are more liberal? There are good theoretical reasons to expect this to be the case. Judges do not want to be overridden by Congress, because overrides can damage personal and institutional prestige and produce policies they dislike. But what does research tell us?

Social scientists disagree about whether the ideological leanings of elected officials influence the actions of judges. Some scholars find no evidence of influence. For example, one of the first and most prominent studies to examine this issue systematically found little evidence that individual justices moderate their views when faced with a Congress (or president) holding opposing views.[53] That is, conservative justices do not vote in a less conservative manner when Congress is controlled by Democrats, and liberal justices do not vote less liberally when Congress is controlled by Republicans. Other studies similarly concluded that justices do not take the views of Congress into account when voting on cases.[54]

However, some analyses have reached the opposite conclusion, showing that justices take into account the preferences of members of Congress and the president.[55] For example, one study found that the conservative Rehnquist Court was unlikely to strike down acts passed by prior Democratic Congresses while Congress remained under Democratic control. But after Republicans took control of Congress in 1994, the Court became much more likely to overturn those earlier Democratic laws. In addition, Congress influences not only how justices rule on cases but also which cases justices hear. Justices are far less likely to agree to hear constitutional cases in which their preferred outcomes differ significantly from Congress's.[56] Finally, justices tend to hear fewer cases overall when their views are out of step with those of Congress, in part because they are more likely to avoid controversial cases that might spur a strong, negative congressional reaction.[57]

Additional evidence for the influence of Congress, and whether it can exert subtle (or sometimes not-so-subtle) pressure on the courts, comes from a closer examination of the court-curbing bills discussed earlier. If the Supreme Court is concerned about institutional legitimacy, then it should be highly sensitive to signals indicating that this legitimacy is being challenged. An examination of court-curbing bills reveals that the courts are, in fact, influenced by these congressional actions. Court-curbing bills indicate congressional discontent with the Court's activity, with members of Congress more likely to introduce such measures when they and their constituents are dissatisfied with the Court's recent actions. When the Court observes these signals, it changes its ways. In particular, when it sees an increase in court-curbing bills, it becomes less likely to exercise its power of judicial review and to declare laws to be unconstitutional.[58]

When we examine congressional action and judicial response, a portrait of the relationship between Congress and the courts starts to emerge. Congress does have the power to override judicial decisions, and it does so to a greater extent than most observers realize. But even when it does not directly override judicial decisions, it is not powerless; a lack of overrides does not indicate acquiescence or surrender to the judicial branch. Much, but not all, evidence indicates that the courts consider congressional preferences when issuing decisions.

# HOW WE STUDY
# THE INTERACTION OF CONGRESS AND THE
# COURTS

Recent research has taken advantage of new statistical techniques to revisit the question of whether congressional preferences influence the votes of Supreme Court justices. One complication for political scientists who want to study the relationship between Congress and other branches has always been how to make comparisons when the political actors in these two branches cast votes on completely different sets of issues. A member of Congress might have a NOMINATE score of 0.45 (see Chapter 2), but how does that score compare to a Supreme Court justice who casts a conservative vote 65 percent of the time?

To address this problem, scholars have developed new and innovative measures of ideology that are comparable across political institutions. One measure, Judicial Common Space scores, calculates ideology scores for Supreme Court justices based on their votes and then adjusts and converts these scores (known as Martin-Quinn scores, after the scholars who developed them) to the same scale as NOMINATE scores.

Another approach, developed by political scientist Michael Bailey and colleagues, starts with the observation that although members of Congress vote on a different set of issues than do members of the Court, there are overlapping questions that can tell us what members of different institutions think about the same policy issues. For example, members of Congress often take public positions on Court cases, noting whether they agree or disagree with the Court's decisions. And sometimes they file briefs with the Court, urging the Court to vote in a certain way. Using these and other areas of overlap, Bailey has developed measures of ideology that place members of Congress and Supreme Court justices (as well as presidents) on the same ideological scale.

These scores allow us to see how the median ideology in Congress compares to the median ideology of the Court. Figure 11.3 illustrates how the ideologies of the Supreme Court, the House, and the Senate have varied over time and how they compare. In some periods, such as the 1960s, Congress was more conservative than the Court. But since the mid-1970s, the Court has, with only a few exceptions, been more conservative than the two chambers of Congress.

With these scores in hand, Bailey and his colleague Forrest Maltzman were able to test whether justices exhibit different voting patterns when the Court's ideology differs from Congress's. To do this, they controlled for the extent to which justices allow legal factors (for example, adherence to precedent) to

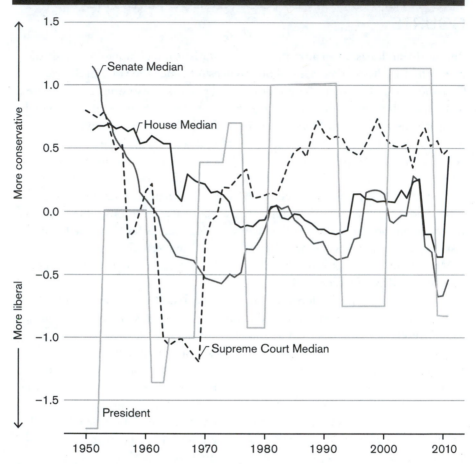

**FIGURE 11.3** Comparing the Ideology of the Supreme Court, the President, and Congress

Michael A. Bailey. 2017. "Measuring Ideology of the Courts," in *Routledge Handbook of Judicial Behavior*, ed. by Robert M. Howard and Kirk A. Randazzo, 72. New York: Routledge.

influence their votes, which is a factor that earlier studies of congressional influence had neglected. Bailey and Maltzman find that since 1950, about half of the justices were likely to vote differently when their ideological beliefs did not align with those of Congress than they would when they shared similar beliefs with Congress. That is, conservative justices voted less conservatively when Congress was liberal, while liberal justices voted less liberally when Congress was more conservative. In addition, they found that justices also changed their voting patterns after elections that moved the ideological center in Congress and the presidency. Justices tend to move in the direction of this ideological shift, voting more liberally when the shift is in a liberal direction and more conservatively when the shift is in a conservative direction.[59]

## Critical Thinking

1. Given that judges tend to view themselves as legal actors, not as political actors, does it make sense to think of them having ideology scores?
2. When members of Congress take a position on a court case, is it reasonable to treat their positions as equivalent to having voted on that case?
3. Why might justices shift their voting behavior rightward after an election that puts Republicans in control of the elected branches or leftward after an election that puts Democrats in control? Why might they not do so?

# Congressional Anticipation and Judicial Review

We have examined whether the courts anticipate congressional reactions. But anticipation can work both ways. Not only might the courts anticipate Congress's reaction, Congress also might anticipate the courts' actions once an issue reaches the judiciary.

Although legislators might not pay close attention to the nuances and details of judicial doctrines and recent rulings, they do know that the courts often play a crucial role in the policy-making process. Thus Congress has every reason to expect the courts to issue rulings that will affect laws that Congress has passed. Given this expectation, members of Congress frequently consider how the courts might interpret a law and, more importantly, how they might be able to influence that interpretation.

Sometimes, as we have discussed, laws may be intentionally ambiguous or contain contradictory language. But often Congress wants to make its intent as clear as possible, knowing that the courts may be called upon to assess and interpret laws. In these cases, there is much that Congress can do to influence how the courts view a law. For example, many judges, when trying to ascertain the meaning of a law, will turn to the law's legislative history. This history consists of materials that are not contained in the text of the law itself but that suggests what those who wrote the law and those who voted for it had in mind. Not all judges pay attention to this information, but many do.[60]

One source of legislative history is the record of discussions and debates on the floor of Congress. With future judicial interpretations of a law in mind, members can use these floor statements to signal to the courts what the law means, in much the same way that a president might use a signing statement

The makeup of the Supreme Court has profound effects on congressional action. Before finalizing legislation, members of Congress often anticipate how the Court will interpret its laws. When Ruth Bader Ginsburg was on the Court, as in the image above, the Court had five conservative members and four liberal members. With Ginsburg's death and Amy Coney Barrett's appointment, the Court now consists of six conservative members and three liberal members.

(see Chapter 9). This is a particularly effective technique if it comes from a prominent legislator, such as a party leader or a floor manager for the bill. Committee reports constitute another useful source of information about a bill. In these reports, the committees can explain, in standard English rather than the formal and legal language used in legislation, what certain provisions of the law mean, what goals the law is trying to accomplish, and the intentions of those who support the law.

Congress can take a number of other actions to communicate its intent to judges more clearly—for example, making the text of laws clearer or having the floor manager identify which statements made on the floor should be taken as especially authoritative.[61] Again, not all judges will pay attention to these materials. Justice Scalia, for example, was dismissive of the value of such materials and instead adhered to an approach known as textualism, in which judges look only at what the text of the law meant at the time it was written, not to other sources that document the law's path to creation.[62] But given that most judges rely, to some extent, on legislative history to aid in their interpretation of a law,

Congress can significantly influence this interpretation by paying attention to these details.

Congress can be strategic about future court behavior in another way: it can carefully construct laws so that they constrain what the courts may or may not do. Congress uses this approach when it writes a statute that delegates policy making and implementation authority to an executive or independent agency. When an agency acts pursuant to the passage of legislation, the courts are often called upon to assess whether the agency's action was consistent with the law, in much the same way that courts can assess whether a statute is consistent with the Constitution. This type of **administrative judicial review** can have broad implications for policy, as it can either validate an agency action (as in *Chevron U.S.A., Inc. v. Natural Resources Defense Council*[63]) or strike it down (as in *Citizens to Preserve Overton Park v. Volpe*[64]).

Congress knows that the courts are likely to hear cases that challenge agency actions, so it has an incentive to structure how the courts can proceed. Specifically, it can insert distinct types of judicial review provisions into laws that will make it either easier for the courts to review agency actions (thus opening the agency up to review) or harder to do so (thus protecting the agency from review). It can, for example, specifically say that courts either can or cannot review agency actions; it can limit the time period in which review can occur; and it can tell the courts whether they must defer to the agency's interpretation of the facts of a case.[65]

These provisions sound minor, but Congress can use them to dramatically affect how courts can review important regulatory actions. And although there has long been the perception that Congress rarely uses some of these provisions, especially the prohibition of review, it turns out that Congress uses them quite frequently. An assessment of 403 major laws passed since the mid-twentieth century (specifically, laws that delegate policy-making responsibility to agencies) found that in nearly a quarter of them, Congress included provisions that precluded review of some agency actions (and in another 15 percent it placed limits on the court's ability to review).[66]

Congress can use statutes to anticipate judicial action in another way: by increasing or decreasing the specificity of laws. If Congress wants to constrain the courts, it can write more detailed and specific laws. Congress might choose this route when it has clear policy preferences, because by spelling out in careful detail what a law is supposed to accomplish and how it should work, Congress can narrow the discretion of any court that examines the law, helping to ensure that its policy preferences survive an encounter with the courts. In contrast, legislation that is unclear or ambiguous leaves judges less constrained and affords them the opportunity to incorporate their own policy preferences into their decisions.[67]

# CONCLUSION

The relationship between Congress and the courts has been described as a "continuing colloquy," one in which the two institutions are interacting and responding to each other on a regular basis, rather than a system in which one institution is completely dominant.[68] Although in some respects, the courts might be seen as dominant (because they have the power to declare acts of Congress unconstitutional), this view ignores the myriad ways in which Congress can, and does, influence the courts.

To begin with, the Senate plays a significant role in determining who occupies seats on the federal courts. Whether it is the individual senators whose opinions the president considers when making lower-court appointments, or the broader set of senators whose votes are needed to confirm Supreme Court nominees, the Senate can influence the courts by influencing who the president nominates and who becomes a federal judge.

Once these judges and justices are in place, Congress is far from powerless. It can, and often does, override judicial statutory interpretation decisions. But it has other ways of influencing the courts. In some cases, the mere threat of legislation is enough to cause the courts to shift their positions and vote differently or to avoid hearing certain sorts of cases. And it can pressure the courts in other ways.

None of this is to say that Congress dominates the courts. Because of judicial independence, the courts often successfully take positions at odds with Congress. But it is also clear that Congress has a wide range of tools that it can use to attract the judiciary's attention. The result is a classic separation-of-powers situation in which the two branches sometimes work together and sometimes do not. In responding to and anticipating the actions of the courts, members of Congress are motivated by policy and representation concerns to influence the courts, especially with the courts now playing such a prominent policy-making role. These concerns are consistent with the constitutional view of Congress as the first branch of government, because failure to monitor and weigh in on the court's behavior would be an abdication of Congress's governing role.

## Discussion Questions

1. The Framers sought to make the courts independent by giving judges life tenure. What are the positive aspects of judges having life tenure? What are the negative aspects?
2. Should senators who oppose a president's judicial nominees be allowed to use the filibuster to prevent a vote on these nominations?

3. In what ways would the Framers be satisfied or dissatisfied with the current relationship between Congress and the courts?
4. Which factors might explain why the number of congressional overrides of judicial decisions has dropped so dramatically in the 2000s?
5. Should Congress be allowed to curb the courts? Or does court curbing violate the spirit of checks and balances by giving Congress too much power?

# 12

## Congress and Interest Groups

When Republicans won unified control over government in the 2016 elections, with majorities in the House and Senate along with Donald Trump in the White House, the party eagerly anticipated enacting many of its main legislative priorities. Among these priorities, which included strengthening national security, cutting regulations, and reducing government spending, two stood out.[1] First, Republicans planned to enact a set of significant tax cuts centering on a reduction in the corporate tax rate, which Trump had touted as a key component of his platform. Second, the party aimed to fulfill a promise it had been making for the past six years: to repeal the Affordable Care Act (ACA).

By the end of the first year of Republican control, only one of those goals had been achieved. In December 2017, Republican leaders from the House and Senate proudly watched as President Trump signed the Tax Cuts and Jobs Act into law. In contrast, multiple attempts during the year to repeal the ACA ended in failure. A dramatic moment came in July when Senator John McCain (R-Ariz.) moved to the center of the Senate chamber and gave a thumbs-down signal to express his vote against repealing some aspects of the ACA, an attempt known as "skinny repeal." Then, in September, McCain announced his opposition to a

Although Republicans were able to pass the Tax Cuts and Jobs Act in 2017, their repeated efforts to repeal and replace the ACA failed. Here, Senator John McCain (R-Ariz.) leaves the Senate chamber after dramatically voting against the skinny repeal of the ACA. Did pressure from interest groups influence the outcomes of these important bills?

repeal attempt sponsored by Representative Bill Cassidy (R-Fla.) and McCain's good friend Senator Lindsey Graham (R-S.C.). In both cases, McCain's opposition, along with that of a handful of other Republican senators, meant that the GOP would not be able to muster enough votes to repeal.

Why did one legislative goal succeed while the other failed? The answer cannot be found in differing levels of commitment, as both were among the highest priorities the Republican Party had promised to tackle and achieve immediately after winning the election. It cannot be due to a lack of support from the president; Trump's "Contract with the American Voter" listed both tax cuts and repealing the ACA among his top ten priorities. It also is unlikely that differences in public opinion mattered much. Although the tax cut had slightly more public support, neither policy was very popular, and in any case the difference was small: about 24 percent of the public favored repeal of the ACA and 30 percent favored the tax-cut bill.[2] Furthermore, it was not about procedural differences. When McCain announced his opposition to Graham's bill, he made it known that he was opposing it specifically because it had not followed standard procedures that the Senate usually uses to consider legislation: the Senate's

Republican leaders had not let the bill be developed by expert committees, held informative hearings, allowed the Congressional Budget Office to analyze the bill's effects, or allowed Democrats to participate in debating and writing the bill. Yet each of these claims also could have been made about the tax-cut bill.

There was one significant difference, however: the positions taken by interest groups. The dominant feature of the political landscape surrounding repeal of the ACA was interest-group opposition. Not all groups were opposed, but the groups that were opposed were numerous, prominent, and varied, and they included coalitions of groups that do not usually band together.

Table 12.1 lists the groups that took positions on the Graham-Cassidy attempt to repeal the ACA. A handful of conservative groups that traditionally align with Republicans did favor this repeal attempt. But most other groups opposed the repeal, including virtually every association in the country that focuses on the treatment of specific diseases (including the American Cancer Society), insurance companies (including Blue Cross Blue Shield), all major professional associations (including the American Medical Association), hospital associations, major nonprofits in the medical field (including Kaiser), and perhaps the nation's most powerful interest group, the AARP (formerly the American Association of Retired People). Even some prominent conservative groups, including Heritage Action and the Citizens Council for Health Freedom, opposed this bill (albeit for very different reasons). This resistance to the Graham-Cassidy bill mirrored the opposition to repeal of the ACA overall. According to MapLight.org, which tracks interest-group positions, a total of 76 organizations took public positions against repeal while only 13 organizations favored repeal.[3]

Meanwhile, interest-group support for the tax-cut bill was much stronger, and opposition was less intense and less coordinated. Although some groups opposed the bill, including the AARP, most major corporations and business associations favored it.[4] While most of the relevant groups affected by the ACA opposed its repeal, the major beneficiaries of the tax-cut bill—U.S. corporations—lined up in favor of enactment. The U.S. Chamber of Commerce, for example, took a strong position in favor of this law, as did the Business Roundtable.[5] The support of these groups is not surprising; after all, cutting taxes has been at the heart of the Republican Party's brand for decades, and it is perhaps the single issue that unites the disparate groups comprising the party's coalition.[6] Unlike the issue of health care, the policy area of taxes exhibits a much tighter link between party and interest groups, which identify with the Republican Party overall but especially do so on the issue of tax cuts.

Members of Congress frankly acknowledged that groups were heavily pressuring them to enact the tax-cut bill. In discussing the "flurry of lobbying from special interests" regarding this bill, Representative Chris Collins (R-N.Y.)

**TABLE 12.1**   Interest-Group Positions on the Graham-Cassidy Repeal of the Affordable Care Act

| Opposed | | In Favor |
|---|---|---|
| American Cancer Society | American Hospital Association | FreedomWorks |
| American Diabetes Association | America's Essential Hospitals | Americans for Prosperity |
| American Heart Association | American Medical Association | Tea Party Patriots |
| American Lung Association | American Psychiatric Association | Club for Growth |
| Arthritis Foundation | American Academy of Family Physicians | |
| Cystic Fibrosis Foundation | American Academy of Pediatrics | |
| ALS Foundation | American College of Physicians | |
| March of Dimes | American Congress of Obstetricians and Gynecologists | |
| Multiple Sclerosis Society | American Osteopathic Association | |
| AARP | Heritage Action | |
| National Council for Behavioral Health | Citizens Council for Health Freedom | |
| Kaiser Family Foundation | Association for Community Affiliated Plans | |
| Blue Cross Blue Shield | | |

Compiled by authors from various sources. See, in particular, *Washington Post*, www.washingtonpost.com/news /powerpost/paloma/the-health-202/2017/09/20/the-health-202-everything-you-need-to-know-about-who -stands-where-on-graham-cassidy/59c157fc30fb045176650d46/ (accessed 8/23/18); and *Forbes*, www.forbes .com/sites/brucejapsen/2017/09/12/even-conservatives-skeptical-about-cassidy-graham-trumpcare-bill (accessed 8/23/18).

acknowledged, "My donors are basically saying, 'Get it done or don't ever call me again.'"[7] Senator Graham voiced a similar concern about the likely reaction of groups and donors if the GOP failed to pass the tax-cut bill, noting that "financial contributions will stop."[8]

It is far too simplistic to ascribe the passage of the tax-cut bill and the defeat of the ACA repeal bills solely to the distribution and desires of interest groups. But we cannot ignore the stark differences in the interest-group context for these two bills. Interest groups might have affected the outcomes of these legislative attempts only marginally, but as we have seen throughout this book, margins can be all-important in politics, especially in situations where passage or defeat is determined by a handful of votes.

Many interest groups, from insurance companies to citizen groups, opposed the repeal of the Affordable Care Act proposed by Republicans in 2017. Given the strong opposition to this measure, the repeal attempt failed.

In addition to showing the power of interest groups, these cases illustrate how the relationship between interest groups and Congress connects to the key concepts of representation and governance. All interest groups represent individuals with a stake in the issues under consideration. These groups turn to legislators to represent their concerns in Congress. Furthermore, to the extent that interest groups did influence the eventual outcomes of the tax-cut bill and the ACA repeal bill, they were affecting Congress's governing function.

## INTEREST GROUPS IN THE UNITED STATES

Any discussion of interest groups in the United States must start with James Madison's observations about factions, particularly his statements in *Federalist 10*. In this document, Madison does not use the term "interest group," which had not yet come into fashion. But his definition of a faction as "a majority or a minority of the whole, who are united and actuated by some common impulse of passion, or of interest" aligns with the current definition of an interest group.[9]

*Federalist 10* is rich with insights, two of which stand out. The first is Madison's recognition that factions, or groups pursuing different interests, are inevitable in any society. Anywhere there is liberty, and anywhere people are free to form coalitions and act on their opinions, factions will form. In Madison's view, the inclination to band together with others sharing similar views to pursue common interests is "sown in the nature of man," and he warned the designers of the new nation to keep this in mind. The question then becomes how to prevent any particular group from dominating government at the expense of the remainder of the public.

Madison's second major insight concerned what he called the "mischiefs," or dangers, of factions. One option for dealing with these mischiefs would be to outlaw factions, but Madison quickly dismissed this option, noting that to prohibit factions would mean "destroying the liberty which is essential to [their] existence." Given that the notion of liberty was at the core of the new nation, this was a nonstarter. The other option was to control the effects of factions by decreasing the likelihood that any one group would be able to dominate government. Here Madison noted that a system of representation in government would provide one bulwark against domination by a particular group. The large size of the new nation would provide another. To these options he added, in *Federalist 51*, the importance of dividing and separating power across institutions as well as giving institutions the power to check each other.[10] Together, the representative form of government, the large size of the nation, the separation of powers, and checks and balances would prevent any group, or faction, from dominating and imposing its policies on others.

Later in this chapter, we explore whether Madison's vision has come to pass. That is, we examine whether interest groups in the United States are able to get what they want, or whether a well-designed representative government in a large country can prevent any one group from dominating government and policy making. First, however, we need to lay down some foundational ideas.

## WHAT ARE INTEREST GROUPS?

What makes a group an interest group? People join groups to share overlapping or common interests, but shared interests alone do not make a group an interest group. A local Little League team or a dance club certainly would qualify as a group, for example, but they are unlikely to be labeled interest groups because they do not mainly engage in political activity. However, if the Little League team were to push for public funding for a new baseball field, then it could indeed be considered an interest group. With these criteria in mind, we can define **interest groups** (or **organized interests**) as institutions (such as corporations, universities, or hospitals) or associations of individuals or companies that organize and attempt to influence policy, elections, or legislation in pursuit of a common interest.

Interest groups can engage in politics by actively seeking to influence the actions of public officials, including members of Congress, either by directly interacting with these officials or by exerting pressures on them. This tactic, which we explore in detail throughout this chapter, is known as **lobbying**, and the groups that engage in it are called lobbies. The right to lobby is enshrined in the Constitution, with the First Amendment providing people (and, by extension, groups) with the right to "petition the Government." The First Amendment therefore guarantees the public the right to make its views and preferences about policy known to its representatives in Congress.

One way to characterize interest groups is to distinguish between those that exist primarily to seek economic benefits and those that focus mainly on noneconomic benefits. These categories can be subdivided further. For example, economic interest groups include corporations such as Alphabet (Google's parent company), General Electric, Boeing, and AT&T; professional associations such as the American Medical Association and the National Association of Realtors; labor groups such as the AFL-CIO; and a variety of business groups and trade associations. Economic interest groups can range from extremely large, prominent, and well-funded groups, including the U.S. Chamber of Commerce and the National Association of Manufacturers, to more specific and obscure (although no less enthusiastic) groups, such as the Society for Protective Coatings and the Association of the Nonwoven Fabrics Industry. On the noneconomic side, some groups, such as the National Rifle Association (NRA) and the Brady Campaign to Prevent Gun Violence, focus on single issues. Others, such as Public Citizen (which is active on a wide range of consumer interests), are broader and characterize themselves as "public interest" groups (although almost all groups emphasize how their actions benefit the general public). All of these groups take political actions to further their goals, whether those goals are economic (for example, lower tax rates for corporations) or noneconomic (for example, cleaner water or air).

Naming or categorizing groups that are involved in lobbying suggests some of the variety of interests that exist. But to get a better sense of the enormous scope of lobbying, it helps to look at aggregate numbers. Figure 12.1 shows the number of lobbyists in Washington, D.C., along with the amount of money these organizations and individuals spent on lobbying between 1998 and 2019. Clearly, lobbies are omnipresent in national politics.

Despite, or perhaps because of, interest groups' omnipresence in U.S. politics, it is not difficult to find negative views of these groups and their potential effects. In general, the American people disapprove of interest groups, at least in the abstract. For example, when asked whether wealthy special interests have too much power and influence over elections, 80 percent of voters say that they do.[11] Nearly as many—69 percent—agree that Congress is too "focused on the

**FIGURE 12.1**  Total Spending on Lobbying and Number of Lobbyists in the United States, 1998–2019

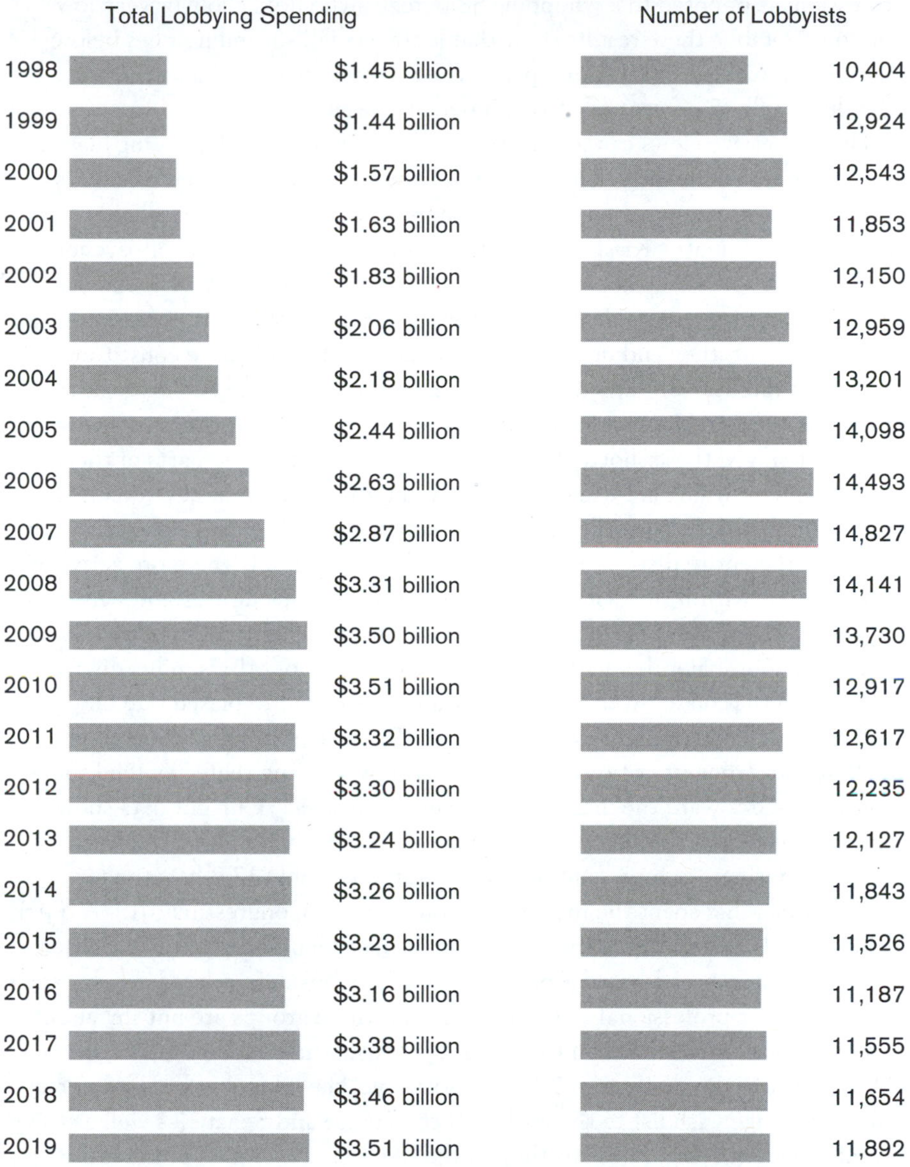

| Year | Total Lobbying Spending | Number of Lobbyists |
|---|---|---|
| 1998 | $1.45 billion | 10,404 |
| 1999 | $1.44 billion | 12,924 |
| 2000 | $1.57 billion | 12,543 |
| 2001 | $1.63 billion | 11,853 |
| 2002 | $1.83 billion | 12,150 |
| 2003 | $2.06 billion | 12,959 |
| 2004 | $2.18 billion | 13,201 |
| 2005 | $2.44 billion | 14,098 |
| 2006 | $2.63 billion | 14,493 |
| 2007 | $2.87 billion | 14,827 |
| 2008 | $3.31 billion | 14,141 |
| 2009 | $3.50 billion | 13,730 |
| 2010 | $3.51 billion | 12,917 |
| 2011 | $3.32 billion | 12,617 |
| 2012 | $3.30 billion | 12,235 |
| 2013 | $3.24 billion | 12,127 |
| 2014 | $3.26 billion | 11,843 |
| 2015 | $3.23 billion | 11,526 |
| 2016 | $3.16 billion | 11,187 |
| 2017 | $3.38 billion | 11,555 |
| 2018 | $3.46 billion | 11,654 |
| 2019 | $3.51 billion | 11,892 |

Center for Responsive Politics, www.opensecrets.org/federal-lobbying (accessed 7/23/20).

needs of special interests."[12] When Americans were asked their opinions of the honesty and ethics of a set of 22 professions, lobbyists came in dead last, with only 5 percent of the public having a high or very high opinion of people in this profession, as opposed to a whopping 58 percent who hold a low or very low opinion. Notably, these results show that lobbyists fall several notches below members of Congress (9 percent positive, 45 percent negative) and even below car salespeople (5 percent positive, 53 percent negative).[13]

These negative views cannot be attributed solely to the public being biased or uninformed. In fact, the public might not be wrong to believe that members of Congress pay more attention to special interests than to their overall constituents. Political scientist Kristina Miler has drawn on the discipline of psychology to explain people's low opinion of interest groups. She argues that even when legislators look out across the multiple constituencies in their districts to perceive what they want, they end up seeing only a biased subset of those constituents. This is not intentional; rather, because of time restrictions and other cognitive limitations, they rely on various shortcuts to determine what constituents want. Not surprisingly, these shortcuts tend to favor the most visible parts of their constituencies, which are usually groups (and individuals) that have donated money and lobbied their offices. In other words, even a legislator who sets out to represent the entire district often ends up representing only the more active and richer groups within the district. Miler's analysis helps us understand why Representative Collins (in our example earlier in this chapter) emphasized his concerns about major donors rather than the concerns of others in his district.

The idea that biases in the interest-group system lead to biased outcomes is far from new. More than five decades ago, E. E. Schattschneider issued one of the first and strongest critiques of interest groups, arguing that they tend to be heavily biased toward the interests of the upper classes.[14] Current data show that this imbalance in the interest-group system, which is weighted toward wealthier business groups, continues to exist today. Table 12.2 lists the ten organizations that spent the most money on lobbying Congress in 2019. A quick glance reveals that with the sole exception of the Open Society Policy Center (a left-of-center, broad-based group), nearly all are business-related groups, trade associations, or professional associations.[15] And these groups are not shy about making major requests. When Congress was considering a follow-up to the CARES Act in the summer of 2020, for example, the Chamber of Commerce sent an 18-page wish list to the leaders of the House and Senate (as well as the president) identifying the items they would like to see included in the bill.[16]

Identifying problems with, and complaints about, interest groups is a bit like shooting fish in a barrel: they're an easy target. Yet it's worth considering an alternative perspective. Because there are so many groups, because they spend so much money, and because the biggest spenders tend to be corporations and other econom-

**TABLE 12.2** Top Spenders on Lobbying Congress, 2019

| Lobbying Client | Total |
|---|---|
| U.S. Chamber of Commerce | $77,245,000 |
| Open Society Policy Center | $48,470,000 |
| National Association of Realtors | $41,241,006 |
| Pharmaceutical Research and Manufacturers of America | $29,301,000 |
| American Hospital Association | $26,272,680 |
| Blue Cross Blue Shield | $25,236,590 |
| American Medical Association | $20,910,000 |
| Business Roundtable | $19,990,000 |
| Amazon.com | $16,790,000 |
| Facebook Inc. | $16,710,000 |

Center for Responsive Politics, www.opensecrets.org (accessed 11/3/20).

ically motivated groups, it is tempting to assume that groups dominate the policy-making process. But this is an empirical question—that is, one that we can examine with data, a task to which we turn later in this chapter. In addition, the Framers explicitly considered whether the Bill of Rights should protect the right to petition the government (that is, to lobby), and they quickly agreed that it was essential.

Lobbying also can help members of Congress represent and govern. It can tell them what their constituents want. And lobbying can provide members of Congress with information about specific policies: the main issues and problems in the policy area, proposed solutions, the potential effects of these solutions, and so on. As Senator (and future president) John F. Kennedy (D-Mass.) said:

> Lobbyists are in many cases expert technicians and capable of explaining complex and difficult subjects in a clear, understandable fashion. They engage in personal discussions with Members of Congress in which they can explain in detail the reasons for positions they advocate. . . . Because our congressional representation is based on geographical boundaries, the lobbyists who speak for the various economic, commercial, and other functional interests of this country serve a very useful purpose and have assumed an important role in the legislative process.[17]

Furthermore, interest groups can provide a way for citizens to be heard by government when their views differ from those of their representatives and senators in Congress. Consider, for example, a gun-loving resident of San Francisco or a pro-choice Mississippian. These people are unlikely to see their views represented in Congress by their legislators, because a representative from San Francisco will almost certainly be in favor of gun control, while a senator from Mississippi will almost certainly be pro-life. By joining a pro-gun-rights group or a pro-choice group, citizens benefit from these groups' lobbying efforts and thus see their views represented before Congress.

In addition, a dominant theory in political science, known as **pluralism**, holds that good policy results from the interplay of interest groups in the political system. Like Madison, pluralists recognize that groups are simply a fact of life and will turn to the government to pursue their goals. Pluralists go on to argue that group activity will produce good policy. The idea is that with so many groups, any individual group will rarely be unopposed. Instead, groups will be countered by other groups, and policy will spring from the interplay of all groups active in an area. Furthermore, no group will be powerful on all issues; some will be more powerful on some issues, while others will be more powerful on other issues. That equilibrium, combined with the likelihood that people will belong to various groups, prevents any single group from dominating across a variety of government activities and produces good, balanced policy.

Does pluralism accurately describe the realities of U.S. policy making? Americans often rail against "special interests," a label that is almost always used pejoratively. Yet one citizen's "special interest" is another citizen's legitimate organization that works to represent his or her views to the government. For example, an advocate for gun control might view the NRA as a distasteful special interest that uses its power to produce a set of policy outcomes that the gun-control advocate finds wrong and offensive. Yet a gun-rights advocate may view the NRA as an organization that bravely stands up for the Second Amendment and pushes back against those who seek to limit gun owners' constitutional rights. Whether an interest is considered negatively as a "special interest" or positively as a beneficial force is, like beauty, in the eye of the beholder.

## INTEREST GROUPS AND CONGRESSIONAL ELECTIONS

Interest groups know that if their preferred candidates are elected, good policy outcomes are likely to follow. Supporters in Congress can help pass desirable new laws, keep favorable regulations in place, and prevent changes to existing policies that the interest group likes. To influence elections and achieve these goals, interest groups rely on three main tactics: mobilizing their members, contributing money, and providing information.

Member mobilization is perhaps the most direct way for groups to influence elections; after all, members vote. For example, AARP informs its members

AARP is one of the largest member groups in the country. It encourages senior citizens to vote for candidates who promise to support and enhance Medicare and Social Security.

which senators and representatives have been most supportive of senior citizens' issues. FreedomWorks urges its members to support candidates who favor less government involvement in the economy. These calls to action can have significant effects, motivating people to vote or to become engaged in other campaign activities.

Groups also attempt to influence elections by spending money to support some candidates and defeat others. Often, they make contributions directly to candidates and to political parties. In fact, groups have donated more than $1 billion to candidates for congressional and presidential elections in recent campaigns. Incumbents and aspiring members of Congress use these direct contributions to finance their campaigns, pay for travel, organize events, pay campaign staff, advertise in the media, and more. Given the exorbitant (and growing) cost of running for national office—in the 2018 election, candidates for the House of Representatives spent a total of $1.5 billion, while candidates for the Senate spent a total of $989 million—significant donations are necessary to run a competitive campaign.[18] Because campaigns are so costly, interest groups also can credibly use the threat of withholding funds to shape actions or take punitive action against members. After the events of January 6, 2021, when rioters attacked the Capitol and many members of Congress refused to accept the election results from some states that had voted in favor of Joe Biden, the powerful and conservative Chamber of Commerce said that it would no longer provide financial support to members of Congress who cast votes to undermine the election results.[19]

Not all campaign contributions come from interest groups; individuals can also contribute to candidates' campaigns, as can political parties and other elected officials. But rarely can an individual match a group's financial impact, and groups are extremely active in the area of campaign finance. In the 2018 election cycle, for example, fourteen different organizations—including prominent companies like AT&T, Honeywell International, and Lockheed Martin—contributed more than $2.5 million to federal campaigns.[20]

**Political action committees (PACs)** are the primary means by which interest groups contribute to campaigns and candidates. PACs raise and spend money to support or oppose political candidates. They are usually tied to interest groups, both economic and noneconomic, and they provide a way for these groups and their members to donate to campaigns. The NRA, for example, created the NRA Political Victory Fund in the 1970s to support the cause of gun rights through campaign contributions. Other PACs are associated with industries, such as the National Beer Wholesalers Association; professions, such as the National Air Traffic Controllers Association; and companies, such as Lockheed Martin.[21] Interestingly, although many people now think of PACs mainly in terms of corporations or business associations (such as those listed in Table 12.2), PACs formed in the 1930s as a way to get around bans that existed at the time on unions donating to candidates' political campaigns. It wasn't until the 1960s and 1970s, when the idea of a separate organization to provide donations became more fully accepted, that corporations started using PACs regularly in their political activity. Thus what started as a union strategy ended up becoming a part of politics that is now dominated by corporations.

PACs are not entirely unconstrained in what they can do, how they can spend their money, and how they can use their contributions. To begin with, all PACs must register with the Federal Election Commission (FEC) and provide that government agency with information about their activities. In addition, they face dollar limits. PACs can contribute only $5,000 per election per year to individual congressional candidates and only $15,000 to the national parties.[22]

The political landscape of campaign contributions shifted dramatically with the *Citizens United v. FEC* case in 2010. In this decision, the Supreme Court ruled that the government cannot regulate or limit independent spending on behalf of a candidate for public office. Corporations, unions, and other groups still face limitations on direct contributions to candidates, but they can spend unlimited amounts of money in support of candidates as long as they do not coordinate with them or their campaigns directly. As a result, a group can now spend as much money as it wants on, for example, running ads in a member's district informing constituents about a scandal the member was involved in or the member's voting record on a particular issue. Furthermore, this spending does not need to be reported to the FEC, which makes it much more difficult to

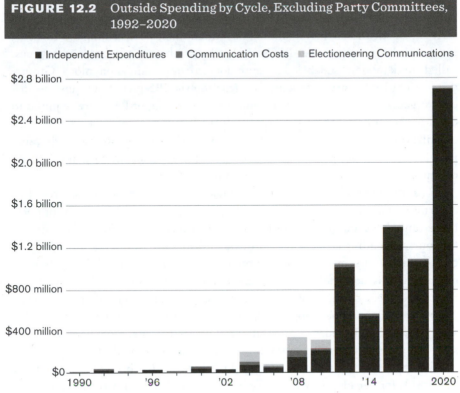

**FIGURE 12.2**    Outside Spending by Cycle, Excluding Party Committees, 1992–2020

■ Independent Expenditures    ■ Communication Costs    ■ Electioneering Communications

Center for Responsive Politics, www.opensecrets.org/outsidespending (accessed 11/3/20).

track. Nonetheless, data from the Center for Responsive Politics, a nonpartisan organization that tracks money in politics, show that independent spending has dramatically increased since *Citizens United* (Figure 12.2).

These activities have led to the creation of a new type of organization: **super PACs**. Super PACs are prohibited from giving money directly to candidates and parties, but they are largely unlimited in their ability to spend money to support or defeat a candidate, provided they do not coordinate with any candidates. Super PACs are deeply unpopular with the public, with 78 percent of survey respondents favoring legal limits on super PAC spending and only 19 percent opposing limits.[23]

Although it is less well known, a second case from 2010, *SpeechNOW.org v. Federal Elections Commission*, also had a significant effect on how money is spent in elections. In this case, the D.C. Circuit Court ruled against FEC limits on contributions from individuals to organizations, such as SpeechNOW.org, which pool these contributions and then spend them as independent expenditures. The court, using *Citizens United* as a guide, ruled that such limits on both what individuals can give to groups like SpeechNOW and what these groups can spend were unconstitutional, based on the First Amendment. This ruling has further increased the power of super PACs and has led to the rise of what is sometimes called "dark money," so labeled because donors can remain anonymous. Groups can form **501(c)(4) organizations**, a designation the IRS gives to groups specifically organized to promote social welfare. Although super PACs are required to disclose the names of their donors, 501(c)(4) organizations are not. Hence, these organizations provide a backdoor way to avoid disclosure requirements, because individuals can give unlimited amounts to 501(c)(4) organizations, and these organizations in turn can give money to super PACs.[24]

In addition to mobilizing voters and spending money on elections, either by contributing directly to candidates or by spending money indirectly to support those candidates, interest groups influence elections by providing information. Of course, spending is one way to provide information, as when a super PAC creates an advertisement to inform potential voters about a candidate's stances on particular issues. But groups also create **legislative scorecards** in which they record members' specific votes on a variety of issues and then calculate a score of how well the member supports the group's positions, usually on a 0 to 100 scale or with letter grades of A through F. The groups then publicize these scores in press conferences, on the Internet, and through mailings to supporters.

The League of Conservation Voters (LCV), which has been creating these scorecards for decades, provides a useful example.[25] In each Congress, it chooses a specific series of key votes that allow it to identify legislators who share their views and those who do not. In 2016, for example, the Senate held a vote on whether to require providers of electricity and natural gas to meet targets for energy efficiency. It also voted on an amendment to limit the president's power to designate national monuments. In the former case, a "yes" vote was considered a pro-environment vote, while in the latter, a "no" vote was categorized the same way. Based on the votes that LCV used to compute its scorecards, Senators Brian Schatz (D-Hawaii), Patty Murray (D-Wash.), and Cory Booker (D-N.J.) earned scores of 100, indicating they took a pro-environment position on each issue identified by LCV. At the other end of the scale, Senators Bob Corker (R-Tenn.), Ben Sasse (R-Neb.), Joni Ernst (R-Iowa), and Ted Cruz (R-Tex.) received scores of zero.

In what the organization calls its signature program, each year LCV draws up a list of the "Dirty Dozen," borrowing from the classic film of the same name.[26] The goal is to draw attention to candidates who, in LCV's view, "consistently side against the environment."[27] The organization then touts which of these candidates subsequently suffered electoral defeats. In 2014, for example, LCV bragged that it had helped to defeat 11 of the 12 Dirty Dozen candidates.[28]

Organizations like Planned Parenthood are powerful interest groups that can influence lawmakers and legislation. Alexis McGill Johnson, the president of Planned Parenthood, frequently advocates for her organization's priorities with members of Congress.

Groups can use strategies like scorecards not only to inform voters but also to threaten candidates. LCV makes it clear that it will publicize its scorecards, targeting specific members for defeat based in part on their scores. Likewise, in the battle over tax cuts at the end of 2017, the U.S. Chamber of Commerce, a pro-business interest group that ranks among the largest and most powerful interest groups in the United States, put senators on notice that it would be using any votes related to the tax cuts in creating its legislative scorecard. It issued a public letter in which it not only stated its views about the benefits of these cuts but also made a not-so-veiled threat against senators who might vote against the bill. The Chamber of Commerce boldfaced and underlined the relevant part so that senators would not miss it.[29]

When interest groups publicize members' voting records in their efforts to influence election outcomes, we see these activities in a new light. We know that the public considers interest groups to be overly powerful and to have too much influence in politics. But consider the actions of the U.S. Chamber of Commerce, LCV, or NRA. Gun-control activists might be furious about the purported power of the NRA, people worried about the political power of business might cite the Chamber of Commerce as a case for limiting such groups, and small-business owners might be concerned about the pro-environment policies espoused by LCV. At the same time, there is no question that the NRA represents the views of many gun owners, that the Chamber of Commerce works on behalf of the owners of large businesses as well as many of the people who work at these businesses, and that environmentalists are delighted to have the LCV highlighting which legislators do (or do not) share their views. In all of these cases, the groups are working to make sure that the people who get elected to office will represent their interests. PACs and super PACs play the same role.

# LOBBYING

In addition to their efforts to influence elections, interest groups engage in lobbying. But why do groups lobby Congress, whom do they lobby, and what forms does this lobbying take?

## Why Lobby Congress?

At the most basic level, groups lobby to pursue their goals through politics. However, this oversimplification obscures some differences in what groups are trying to do. Lobbyists certainly try to get Congress to pass policies, although the popular myth that groups can simply buy the policies they want is a dramatic overstatement of these groups' power. But groups do not limit their activities to pushing for the creation of new policies. If they are satisfied with the current policies, groups often exert considerable pressure to keep them.[30] They are not always successful at doing so, but they have a built-in advantage over groups that are trying to effect change: those seeking change need to succeed at every stage of the legislative process, while those seeking to block the change have multiple opportunities to stop a bill, and they need to succeed at only one of these stages.[31]

Even when policies do change despite a group's efforts, that group might be able to forestall such changes for long periods of time. Frank Baumgartner and Bryan Jones have characterized a system in which policy remains stable for a long time before undergoing change as one of punctuated equilibrium. Prior to a change, policy tends to be stable, due in large part to the tactics that groups use to keep policy from changing. These tactics include urging legislators to frame policies in certain ways, preventing the consideration of new issues and perspectives, and ensuring that policy is decided in a venue that favors the group's goals.[32] Indeed, policy is often difficult to change because a substantial number of powerful groups oppose such change. These groups not only lobby members to oppose changes to existing policies but also work to keep these potential changes off of the policy agenda, exercising negative agenda control (see Chapters 5 and 6).[33]

In addition, groups may lobby to change the content of a bill. Even if like-minded groups are confident that the bill will pass, often parts of the bill can be improved. Therefore, groups might lobby members to make such changes, as we saw in 2020 when groups spent a near record-setting amount of money on lobbying in an attempt to affect the contents of the stimulus bill that the government passed in response to the coronavirus pandemic.[34] They might also push members to be active in shaping the legislation instead of sitting on the sidelines. As political scientist Richard Hall has documented, participation in Congress is rarely universal and never equal. Thus groups have an incentive to lobby more favorably inclined senators and representatives to be more actively involved in shaping a bill.[35]

Groups also might set their sights on policy making outside the legislative branch, particularly in the bureaucracy. In such cases, groups might observe actions that agencies are taking or planning to take and then enlist Congress to stop the agencies from acting or to pass legislation to overturn the agencies' actions. In 2017, a small nonprofit group named Fight for the Future used exactly this tactic to oppose the Federal Communications Commission's (FCC) decision to revoke net neutrality rules.[36] The group had supporters of net neutrality file comments against repeal with the FCC. At the same time, it lobbied members of Congress to pressure the FCC. When neither of these tactics succeeded, it lobbied Congress to write a law putting net neutrality rules back into effect. Other groups joined Fight for the Future, with the president of one of these other groups, Free Press, explicitly stating the groups' shared goal of pressuring Congress to lean on, and possibly overturn, the agency: "We want to raise the political costs on this issue. . . . We want members of Congress to think of this as a third-rail issue that they have to support or else they will suffer in their elections."

## THEN AND NOW
## THE INFLUENCE OF BUSINESS INTERESTS

Businesses, like other interest groups, are heavily involved in politics. The start of this chapter showed how business groups (along with other groups) attempted to influence health care and tax policy. Additional examples of policies important to businesses are easy to identify, from agriculture to immigration to energy. But have businesses always been so proactive in attempting to change policy?

Surprisingly, the answer is no. Businesses have always been attentive to politics, but their goals and activities have changed markedly over time.[37] In the past, businesses dedicated their political efforts primarily to protecting the status quo. Their goal was to maintain existing policies that benefited them. In recent years, however, businesses have expended much more effort to change the status quo to produce more favorable policies.

This change was hidden in plain sight until recent scholarship by Lee Drutman shined a spotlight on it.[38] Drutman offers a brief case study of the Boeing Company, which, as one lobbyist pointed out to him, switched from playing defense (that is, protecting the status quo) 75 percent of the time in the 1970s and early 1980s to playing offense 75 percent of the time after 2000. Along the way, the company expanded its staff of in-house lobbyists from just a few to 26 while also contracting with 28 outside lobbying firms, all to become more involved in politics.

Boeing is just one example of what businesses and corporations were doing more generally. One lobbyist whom Drutman interviewed nicely captured this change: "I think twenty years ago, you had a Washington office to keep the government out of your business, and I think people have evolved to understand now that there are opportunities, partnerships with government. . . . We try to get out in front of issues."[39] Another put it even more succinctly: "It's gone from 'leave us alone' to 'let's work on this together.'"[40]

This change from passive to proactive took place over the course of several decades, slowly at first and then gaining momentum. In the post–World War II years, businesses were relatively passive because politics was already strongly pro-business. The public agreed on the positive effects business had on society.[41] A former president of General Motors, then serving in the Eisenhower administration, characterized this sentiment: "What was good for the country was good for General Motors and vice versa." These positive views, along with routinely impressive economic growth at the time, gave business little incentive to shake things up. Perhaps the most respected study of lobbying in the era concluded that on many prominent issues, legislators experienced almost no lobbying by business interests.[42]

The situation shifted in the 1960s and 1970s. First, social movements began to both spur and capitalize on Americans' growing distrust of all institutions, including political organizations and corporations. Second, during the Richard Nixon administration, the government began to impose major restrictions on business by passing laws (for example, the National Environmental Protection Act) and creating regulatory agencies (for example, the Consumer Protection Safety Commission and the Occupational Safety and Health Administration). These laws and agencies, which reflected a change in political attitudes toward business, constrained businesses' ability to act.

**FIGURE 12.3** The Growth of Corporate Lobbying Presence, 1981–2004

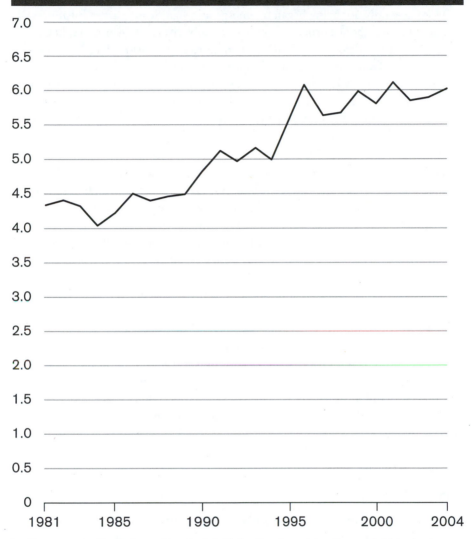

Lee Drutman. 2015. *The Business of America Is Lobbying: How Corporations Became Politicized and Politics Became More Corporate*, 67. New York: Oxford University Press.

Initially, businesses' reaction to these changes was muted—in part, as one lobbyist suggested to Drutman, because of the "general disdain for relations in Washington" among members of the business elite at the time.[43] But business leaders soon realized that the ground was shifting beneath their feet, that they lacked political skill and influence, and that they needed to act to prevent further losses. It was during this period that the U.S. Chamber of Commerce transformed from a minor political player to a major political force, and the powerful Business Roundtable was formed.

More generally, lobbying began to emerge as a significant part of business activity. The number of firms with registered lobbyists in Washington, D.C., increased fourteenfold from 175 in 1971 to more than 2,400 a decade later. PACs were created, executives spent more time on lobbying, and companies created internal units to address policy issues. Figure 12.3 shows that the average amount of "lobbying presence," which is the value on the y-axis in the figure and is measured by an index combining lobbying expenditures and increases in lobbying staff, continued to grow for the next few decades.

What started in the 1970s solidified in the 1980s. The election of Ronald Reagan, an ardently pro-business Republican, further emboldened business interest groups. Business began to use its newfound lobbying power to push for lower tax rates, less regulation, better trade arrangements, and other business-friendly policies.

Business became fully entrenched in Washington politics in the 1990s. The fight over President Bill Clinton's health care plan was perhaps the first instance in which businesses not only lobbied for policy changes but also formed coalitions to increase their influence. In fact, one study showed that the number of health care companies lobbying in Washington, D.C., almost doubled from 1992 to 1994.[44] Success on a number of issues during this decade, including the passage of the Telecommunications Act of 1996 and the Medicare Modernization Act of 2003, further spurred business lobbying.

By the 2000s, the transformation was complete. Once a minor presence in the Washington landscape, business was now heavily represented and was attempting to influence nearly all major policy issues. Even firms that initially entered politics only reluctantly, perhaps to focus on one specific issue, kept (and increased) their presence in the nation's capital. Once content mainly to protect the status quo, now businesses were initiating contacts with politicians to effect significant policy changes.

### Critical Thinking

1. Why were businesses much less likely to have a presence in Washington, D.C., in the past?
2. Was it a mistake for businesses to avoid politics for so long (in other words, would they have benefited earlier from a stronger presence)? If not, what has changed about politics to make it more attractive or even necessary for businesses to be more active lobbyists?
3. Do you think the amount of business involvement in national politics will continue to increase? What might it take for that level of involvement to flatten out or even decrease?

## Whom to Lobby?

Given that groups have a variety of reasons to engage in lobbying, the next question to ask is, Whom do they lobby? Do they aim to influence members of Congress who disagree with them? Do they lobby those who already agree with them? Or do they take the middle ground, targeting members who are on the fence, neither strongly opposed to nor supportive of the group's position?

A case can be made for each of these options. Lobbying opponents is a straightforward proposition: these opponents do not agree with your group, so you lobby them to bring them around to your point of view. Although this strategy is direct, it is also risky. Members who are opposed to your group's position might already be entrenched in their views, making it hard for them to take a different position, even if they come to see the merits of your case. Consequently, this approach has a low chance of success.

Alternatively, groups could lobby the fence-sitters. These are legislators who have not yet taken a public position on a bill or issue, who are indifferent, who have equivocated about it, or who have sometimes favored and sometimes opposed your group. As with lobbying opponents, the goal is to persuade members to join your cause, but the bar is lower in this case, as the fence-sitters have not already fully committed to an opposing position. Coming around to your position is therefore less costly for them than it is for opponents.

Lobbying fence-sitters can be characterized as a strategy of exchange, in which groups give resources (for example, campaign donations) to a member in exchange for his or her support. Another way to think about fence-sitters is that if you don't lobby them, someone else will. In **counteractive lobbying**, the goal is still persuasion, but the motivation is slightly different. A group engages in counteractive lobbying when it worries that if it does not lobby these fence-sitters, opposing groups will, and they will be easy targets.

Finally, why might groups lobby their supporters? Time and money are scarce, and lobbying legislators who already support you might seem like a waste of these resources. Decades of observations by political scientists, however, show that lobbyists often do spend time and money lobbying their friends and supporters. One potential explanation for why groups lobby friends is that ignoring them might open them to lobbying from opposing groups. In other words, lobbying your supporters could be a form of counteractive lobbying.

Several political scientists, from Raymond Bauer, Ithiel de Sola Pool, and Lewis Anthony Dexter in the 1950s to Frank Baumgartner and Beth Leech in the 1990s, have fashioned another explanation for why groups frequently lobby supporters: to urge those supporters to champion their cause.[45] More recently, Richard Hall and Alan Deardorff have constructed a strong theoretical foundation explaining why this is a smart strategy.[46] Their starting point is the idea that legislation is difficult and costly to produce. In addition, legislators have limited time and information, so even though they might care about multiple issues, they find it hard to become informed about all of them. As a result, they end up uncertain about the outcomes that different policy choices might produce. Essentially, legislators are generalists who find it difficult to become deeply informed about various policies because of the competing demands on their time.

Groups, on the other hand, are specialists. A legislator might not know exactly how changes in health policy are likely to affect doctor-patient relationships, but the American Medical Association is likely to be deeply informed about this issue. As specialists, lobbyists can provide valuable and timely information to legislators, which means that they are providing what Hall and Deardorff call a **legislative subsidy**. In providing legislators with valuable information, they subsidize legislators' knowledge and free up time they can then use to participate in a range of policy-making activities: attending hearings, contributing to committee markups, offering amendments, and so on.[47] Lobbyists also enlist the aid of these members in lobbying other members. That is, a group can provide some legislators with helpful information, which those legislators can then use to persuade other senators and representatives to join their cause.

---

## HOW WE STUDY
## WHO LOBBIES WHOM?

As we have seen, groups might lobby their opponents, fence-sitters, or their supporters. But which of these approaches do groups actually take, and under what conditions? This is the question that Marie Hojnacki and David C. Kimball explored in their perceptive article "Organized Interests and the Decision of Whom to Lobby in Congress."[48] In approaching this topic, the authors started simply: they asked interest groups whom they lobbied. In analyzing the responses, they considered two related goals of all groups. First, groups want to increase the size of the legislative coalition that supports them or, at the very least, to maintain it. Second, they want to make sure that the content of a bill under consideration reflects their preferences and that the bill is likely to pass.

Given these goals, which legislators will lobbyists approach? Hojnacki and Kimball identified a series of factors that might determine the answer to this question, but two stand out. First, groups should be more likely to lobby supportive legislators, since they can count on those legislators to invest the time and effort to shape legislation. Second, groups should be more likely to lobby legislators who occupy influential positions—namely, committee, subcommittee, and party leaders. In addition to these two main expectations, Hojnacki and Kimball also recognized that the question of whom to lobby might be affected by the group's resources, with wealthier groups potentially taking a different approach than those with fewer resources.

To examine whether groups target supporters and those in positions of power, Hojnacki and Kimball chose four policy areas—product liability, financial services, criminal justice reform, and grazing rights—and sent questionnaires to 648 groups that work on those issues.[49] Groups responded by indicating whether they had lobbied on those issues, and if so, which members of Congress they had lobbied. The researchers also identified the group's level of resources and measured whether the group had a strong presence in the member's district (for example, a large number of constituents working in that field or a business located there). Finally, the researchers identified whether each legislator held an influential institutional position—party leader, committee chair, or subcommittee chair—and whether he or she had previously indicated support for the group's positions (which the researchers determined by examining past votes in each specific policy area).

At this point Hojnacki and Kimball had all the information they needed to analyze why groups choose to lobby some legislators and not others. That is, they knew whether each lobbying organization lobbied each legislator; whether the group was resource-rich or resource-poor; whether the group had a strong presence in the legislator's district; whether the legislator held an influential position; and whether the legislator could be classified as a supporter, opponent, or fence-sitter. They then used this information to identify and explain groups' lobbying decisions.

Table 12.3 summarizes their main findings. Most importantly, they found that groups are most likely to lobby supporters and least likely to lobby opponents, with fence-sitters in between. The data confirm that groups turn to their supporters in Congress for help. The researchers also found that groups frequently target committee chairs, but not subcommittee chairs or party leaders.

Overall, these findings confirm that groups lobby legislators who agree with them and who are in a position to help further their goals. However, Hojnacki and Kimball also uncovered some nuances underlying these general conclusions. For instance, groups were more likely to lobby a member of Congress if they had a strong presence in that member's district, even if that member was an opponent.[50] In addition, groups with more resources were more likely to lobby opponents and fence-sitters than groups with fewer resources, and resource-rich groups were less likely to bias their efforts toward committee chairs. These observations make sense: if a group had unlimited resources, it would lobby all

**TABLE 12.3**  Whom to Lobby?

| Legislator's Prior Position | Likelihood of Lobbying |
|---|---|
| Has supported the group | Most likely |
| Uncertain | Less likely |
| Has opposed the group | Least likely |

Adapted from Marie Hojnacki and David C. Kimball. 1998. "Organized Interests and the Decision of Whom to Lobby in Congress." *American Political Science Review* 92(4): 775–90.

legislators. Taken together, these findings suggest that while groups are, on average, more likely to target supporters, there are also times they will choose to lobby fence-sitters and even opponents.[51]

### Critical Thinking

1. Would we expect the type of lobbying—that is, whether groups lobby their supporters, fence-sitters, or opponents—to vary by policy area? If so, what types of policies might cause groups to focus on opponents rather than fence-sitters, or fence-sitters rather than supporters?
2. If you were a member of a group with limited resources, what might cause you to focus your lobbying efforts on fence-sitters rather than friends?
3. When might you expect legislators to be willing to change their position based on lobbying from interest groups?

## What Forms Does Lobbying Take?

We have seen that groups lobby Congress for a variety of reasons: to change laws, to prevent change, to shape the content of bills, and to spur oversight of agencies. And we know that they lobby supporters most frequently, but also turn to fence-sitters and opponents when they can and when the conditions are right. What we have not addressed yet is how they actually go about lobbying legislators. That is, what forms does lobbying take?

**INSIDE LOBBYING**  Political scientists distinguish between inside lobbying and outside lobbying. **Inside (or direct) lobbying** involves groups directly approaching legislators and their staff to make requests. This type of lobbying usually occurs behind closed doors in legislators' offices rather than in a public forum. At times, though, it can take place in public, as when a committee chair invites a group to testify at a congressional hearing on behalf of a policy proposal. Inside lobbying also includes invitations to legislators to participate in various activities where the group gets a chance to make its case. In the past, these activities frequently involved travel (perhaps to warm, sunny, and enticing places like Hawaii or the Bahamas) or centered on lavish meals, but congressional reforms passed in 2007 prohibited travel-based lobbying and placed restrictions on meals. Still, groups often find loopholes in these rules and regulations.

To engage in inside lobbying, groups either use an in-house employee or hire someone outside the group to lobby on their behalf. Professional lobbyists who are not in-house often work as part of a broader lobbying firm or a legal firm with lobbying branches. Rather than representing a single client, external lobbyists might represent several groups at the same time.[52]

Some professional lobbyists are former employees of federal agencies, former legislative staff, or former members of Congress. These lobbyists are sometimes called **revolvers** because they revolve in and out of government, often using their personal connections to acquire lucrative lobbying contracts. Revolvers are not new, but they have become more common in recent decades. According to political scientists Jeffrey Lazarus, Amy McKay, and Lindsay Herbel, in the 1970s well under 10 percent of departing members of the House and Senate became lobbyists after retiring from Congress. In recent Congresses, more than 30 percent of departing legislators have become lobbyists right after leaving Congress.[53] As Figure 12.4 shows, of the members who left Congress in January of 2019 and had new employment, 50 percent took positions as lobbyists and thus can be classified as revolvers.[54] Strikingly, this is a far lower percentage than in other recent Congresses—for example, the figure for the 114th Congress is 80 percent.

Studies indicate that revolvers, who can credibly claim to have better access to politicians than other lobbyists, are paid more than their colleagues and get better results for their clients.[55] In part, these revolvers produce better results because they tend to be more actively involved with lobbying for bills that have advanced beyond the committee stage (and that therefore already have a greater chance of success). In addition, many lobbyists are policy specialists, but revolvers tend to be more informed about the political strategies that can make or break a bill: how party leaders use negative agenda tactics, how a bill manager's marks are finalized, how party leaders negotiate unanimous consent agreements, how amendment trees get filled, and so on. Knowledge of political strategies overlaps with access to legislators, of course, but revolvers are products of the system and know from experience how it works.[56] Indeed, a disproportionate

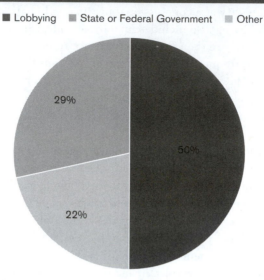

**FIGURE 12.4** New Careers for Former Members of the 115th Congress

■ Lobbying ■ State or Federal Government ▨ Other

29%

50%

22%

Numbers add up to greater than 100 percent due to rounding. Center for Responsive Politics,
www.opensecrets.org/revolving/departing.php?cong=115 (accessed 6/25/2020).

number of revolvers served as party leaders, committee chairs, or members of
the powerful Appropriations or Ways and Means Committees during their time
in Congress.

The role of revolvers in lobbying raises a host of concerns. To begin with,
because revolvers are more expensive to hire and deliver better results
(because of their political access), they can amplify representational disparities
among interest groups. If only the wealthiest groups can afford to hire revolvers, who then deliver the best results, the result is problematic for pluralism,
because it means that only those groups with the most money can benefit from
the best lobbyists. More generally, it raises the specter of current members of
Congress (and staffers) thinking about the lucrative lobbying positions they
might pursue later, rather than their constituents' needs or the broader public
interest.

Even members of Congress who don't immediately become lobbyists frequently become consultants in the lobbying world after leaving office. Former
speaker John Boehner followed this path. As reported at the time in the *Washington Post*, "Boehner will be a 'strategic adviser' at [lobbying firm Squire Patton
Boggs]—a common designation for former legislators who take K Street jobs
after leaving office but do not register to lobby. The firm said Boehner will not

lobby Congress and will instead advise corporate clients on global business development."[57] The last sentence is crucial: if a former member does not register to lobby, then he or she technically is not in violation of revolving door laws (also known as cooling-off periods). These non-registered former members can be particularly well positioned to lobby current members of Congress because they retain floor, dining, parking, and gym privileges. In fact, they may also receive commissions for lobbying even while receiving their congressional pensions.[58] To address the possibility of problems ranging from the appearance of impropriety to outright corruption, in 2007 Congress passed the Honest Leadership and Open Government Act, which lengthened the cooling-off period for former members. Although this act has helped to ameliorate some of the problems associated with former legislators lobbying current legislators, some analysis has suggested that the act has merely driven lobbyists underground because they choose not to register.[59]

**OUTSIDE LOBBYING**   In contrast to inside lobbying, interest groups use **outside (or indirect) lobbying** to increase pressure on a legislator by involving the legislator's constituents. Outside lobbying can include a variety of tactics, such as getting constituents to make phone calls, send letters, or participate in town halls. Groups spur these activities by sponsoring protests, advertising on television or radio, conducting phone campaigns, organizing meetings, and using social media. The main goal of outside lobbying is to generate grassroots activity that signals to legislators whether their constituents support or oppose a given issue.

Sometimes, this can be difficult, such as when constituent support is weak or hard to find. As a result, groups with broader bases of support (such as labor unions) are more likely to use outside lobbying than, for example, corporations. Other times, groups find it easy to send these signals. They can be especially effective, for example, when support or opposition in a district is already there and simply needs to be activated. In the case of the CARES Act that Congress passed in summer of 2020, direct access to members of Congress and their staff was more limited, so groups turned to outside lobbying via social media and the Internet in general. The restaurant industry enlisted its workers to ask for a $120 million bailout, resulting in half a million appeals to Congress. American Airlines did the same, writing directly to its workers and encouraging them to support the airline industry's request for continued aid from Congress.[60]

A classic analysis of interest groups by Ken Kollman explores when groups rely on either inside or outside lobbying. Kollman draws on a survey of interest groups to show that inside versus outside tactics tend to cluster by group type, with labor groups relying more on outside lobbying while businesses use inside lobbying. Among groups that rely on outside lobbying, labor unions and public interest groups employ a wider variety of outside tactics, and outside lobbying works better when groups have broad public support for their positions. For example, despite having only 10 employees, the leaders of Fight for the Future (the group supportive of net neutrality rules) took advantage of the widespread public support for these rules—and their technological savvy—to get the public to bombard Congress with more than 800,000 calls and 6.7 million e-mails.[61]

Groups with less popular or even more specialized goals may also engage in outside lobbying. They try to follow the same playbook as groups with more popular goals, sending signals to legislators about support in their district that may or may not actually exist. This type of activity is sometimes referred to as **astroturf lobbying** (to distinguish it from real grassroots lobbying). For example, an astroturf approach might consist of groups organizing haphazard call-ins during which constituents are ushered into a room where they can press a phone button that connects them with a member's office. At this point, they are supposed to state their support for the group's position, but staffers report that these constituents often do not know what to say once the call goes through.

Although inside and outside lobbying are different tactics, they can and do work together. The NRA provides a good example. Although the group certainly engages in inside lobbying, such as making direct contributions to legislators, this aspect of the NRA's influence is generally overstated. In the 2018 election cycle, the NRA directly contributed $879,000 to candidates for federal office (nearly all of them Republican). That sounds like a lot of money until you realize that the NRA ranks only 541st among groups in terms of contributions, and overall candidates collected a total of $880 million in direct contributions.[62] Yet the group is regarded as exceptionally powerful on Capitol Hill because it energetically engages in outside lobbying, working hard to keep its members informed and motivating them to vote and engage in other political activities, such as protests, based on their views about guns. As a result, the NRA then has more power when it engages in inside lobbying, as it can credibly point to its large and motivated membership.

## Does Lobbying Work?

What do lobbyists get in return for their efforts? Many people assume that there is some sort of quid pro quo in which groups give legislators money and legislators give groups votes. Is this how it works? The answer to this question is complicated, but the evidence points to "no." Various studies have used sophisticated statistical techniques to look for evidence of such a relationship and have not found it.[63]

This finding might be comforting to those worried about the influence of money on politics. But it is puzzling. Why wouldn't contributions lead to votes that are consistent with a group's goals? And why would a group continue to donate money to campaigns and expend significant resources to lobby members if doing so doesn't deliver votes?

One possible explanation for the lack of a relationship between money and votes lies in the realities of outside lobbying. Studies of outside lobbying, as well as studies of group activity and influence overall, suggest that gaining influence with members of Congress is a nuanced process based on more than just money. Some groups might not have as much money as others to make contributions or hire sophisticated lobbyists, but that does not mean they lack power and influence. For example, some groups achieve power by virtue of having a huge membership base. Vigorous outside lobbying can build on these groups' strength of numbers, allowing them to further their aims and counter the efforts of wealthier groups that make more donations.

Another explanation is that even if groups do not directly get votes in exchange for contributions, they do get access. Legislators are exceptionally busy, and it can be extremely difficult to get on their schedules. But given their essential need for cash to fund their campaigns, legislators make time to meet with groups that have made campaign contributions in the past and may do so again in the future. Few current or former members of Congress were as blunt about this relationship as Mick Mulvaney, a former representative from South Carolina. When later serving in the Trump administration as both director of the Office of Management and Budget and interim director of the Consumer Financial Protection Bureau, Mulvaney told a group of lobbyists, "We had a hierarchy in my office in Congress. If you're a lobbyist who never gave us money, I didn't talk to you. If you're a lobbyist who gave us money, I might talk to you."[64] These meetings are essential for groups to lobby legislators and to seek their support. In addition, as mentioned earlier, evidence suggests that revolvers (those who formerly served in Congress) are especially adept at gaining access.[65]

In short, even if money doesn't buy votes, it does buy access. Access can then give groups the opportunity to make their case about which provisions a particular bill should include, to explain why the legislator should spend time on a policy, and to provide information about the policy that the legislator can then pass along to colleagues. After all, there is more to representation than just voting. Indeed, one of the fundamental decisions that legislators make, repeatedly, is whether to be involved in an issue at all.[66] That is, legislators can engage in a variety of activities that consume their limited time, and depending on their priorities, they can choose to focus more on particular issues by spending more time and legislative resources ushering those bills through committee.

The NRA is a powerful organization not only because it is able to make campaign contributions to candidates that support gun ownership but also because it mobilizes its members to protest stricter gun control.

Along these lines, an innovative article by Richard Hall and Frank Wayman contends that to find influence, one must look at stages before the final floor outcome—that is, at stages where bills are developed, debated, and revised.[67] Given the importance of these earlier stages, which have dramatic effects on the shape and content of bills, lobbyists have an incentive to act during these periods. Thus, lobbyists do not lobby or donate only to change votes; rather, they do so to mobilize members to participate in the earlier stages, when bills are first being formed. Hall and Wayman found that PAC contributions from particular groups were associated with greater committee activity by particular members.[68]

Another way to assess whether powerful groups get what they want is to look at overall outcomes rather than individual votes. Do groups with more resources get the policy outcomes they desire? Again, the conventional wisdom is that big money buys policy, with politicians in the pocket of rich interests. Media reports feed this perception, focusing on campaign contributions and the even larger amounts spent on lobbying and confirming that groups are highly active, business interests are predominant, and large amounts of cash flow through the system.

The issue of whether more resources lead to favored outcomes is challenging to unpack, but a team of talented political scientists undertook a massive data-collection project designed to answer this question.[69] These researchers examined lobbying in the 1990s and 2000s, focusing on a set of policy issues ranging from high-salience and high-conflict (for example, the attempt in the 1990s to normalize trade relations with China) to less prominent, such as efforts to promote American production of recreational marine craft (that is, yachts).

They began by drawing a random sample of lobbyists involved in these issues. The researchers asked these lobbyists to point out the most recent federal issue on which they had been active (thereby ensuring that the results were likely to include most of the major issues during the years the researchers examined, as lobbyists were certain to have pressed their case on these issues). They then interviewed other groups and individuals active on these issues, asking them what policy goals they were seeking. Finally, they examined newspapers, political journals, and other sources to ascertain whether each group got what it wanted.

Overall, the researchers looked at 98 different issues where groups sought to change policy. In 58 of these cases, there was no change in policy; in 13 cases, there was marginal change; and in 27 cases, there was significant change. Surprisingly—at least from the perspective of the conventional wisdom—they found almost no relationship between a group's resources (measured in a variety of ways, including money spent through PACs or on lobbying, numbers of former government officials employed as lobbyists, and membership numbers) and whether the group got what it wanted. As the researchers said, their results "will disappoint those who assume that the wealthy interests can walk into the Washington offices of our elected officials and get what they demand." In other words, they found that neither money nor other resources appear to buy outcomes. As Table 12.4 shows, there is virtually no correlation between a group's resources and whether it gets the policy outcomes it wants in either the current Congress or the following one.

It may sound surprising that groups with more resources do not have a major advantage in terms of changing policy, but perhaps it shouldn't. To begin with, there usually are major groups on both sides of an issue, and only one side can win. When resource-rich groups are unopposed, they are much more likely to win. Furthermore, lobbying rarely involves creating a new policy from scratch. Instead, it attempts to change policy in one direction or another, and the preferences of the more powerful group might already be baked into the existing policy. Finally, many issues never get raised in the first place. Indeed, keeping issues off the agenda might be the greatest power that groups can exert, and this power remains largely hidden from view.[70]

**TABLE 12.4**   Correlation between Resources and Outcomes

*How likely is the group with more of each resource to get the policy it wants?*

| Resource | In the Current Congress | In the Next Congress |
|---|---|---|
| PAC spending | Not at all | Not at all |
| Lobbying spending | Not at all | Not at all |
| Covered officials | Not at all | Very slightly |
| Association assets | Not at all | Not at all |
| Business assets | Very slightly | Not at all |
| Members | Not at all | Not at all |

"Covered officials" refers to former government officials operating as lobbyists. Adapted from Frank R. Baumgartner, Jeffrey M. Berry, Marie Hojnacki, David C. Kimball, and Beth L. Leech. 2009. *Lobbying and Policy Change: Who Wins, Who Loses, and Why*, Table 10.3. Chicago, IL: University of Chicago Press.

## Limits on Lobbying

The continued presence of lobbyists, the vast sums of money spent on lobbying, the potential for influence, the perception of bias, and the possibility of corruption—all of these can be concerning. It is worth keeping in mind, however, that groups have an incentive to follow the rules and to provide accurate information to members of Congress. As one lobbyist noted, "As long as the members believe I'm honest and play straight with them, I'll have a chance to make my case."[71]

Given that both politicians and groups benefit from lobbying, and recognizing the potential for problems, it should come as no surprise that politicians and reformers have struggled to determine how to allow for lobbying and at the same time restrain it. As former senator Robert Byrd (D-W.Va.) observed in 1987, "Congress has always had, and always will have, lobbyists and lobbying. We could not adequately consider our workload without them. . . . At the same time, the history of the institution demonstrates the need for eternal vigilance to ensure that lobbyists do not abuse their role."[72]

Outright bribery has long been illegal at both the state and national levels. A series of other laws have attempted more nuanced approaches to regulate the conduct of lobbying, usually by restricting activity (limits on gift giving, limits on campaign donations, cooling-off periods for revolvers) or by requiring disclosure of activities. Such laws include the Foreign Agents Registration Act of 1938, the Federal Regulation of Lobbying Act of 1946, the Federal Election

Campaign Act of 1971, the Lobby Disclosure Act (LDA) of 1995, and the Honest Leadership and Open Government Act of 2007, among others.

Some aspects of these laws have been useful, but the courts have nullified other parts of them. For example, in *United States v. Harris* (1954), the courts overturned large portions of the original Regulation of Lobbying Act and left federal lobbying disclosure largely ineffective until the passage of the LDA in 1995. In addition, groups constantly seek and find loopholes. Some lobbyists, for example, might not register in order to avoid laws that apply only to registered lobbyists. As we saw in Figure 12.1, since peaking in 2007, the number of registered lobbyists has steadily declined, partly in response to limits that President Barack Obama placed on their involvement in the activities of federal agencies. That executive order was partially repealed in 2014. In addition, although contingent fees—in which a lobbyist is paid a bonus based on a particular outcome—are illegal in most states and are illegal for contractors bidding for federal projects, it remains legal to lobby Congress on a contingent basis.

## CONCLUSION

Interest groups were foretold in the early days of our republic. The Framers knew groups would exist; the question that they—and Madison in particular—wrestled with was how to prevent groups from dominating the legislative process. At the same time, it has long been recognized that despite this potential problem of domination, there are also potential benefits to the presence of groups.

These problems and benefits directly mirror two of the main themes of this book. The problem of undue group influence relates to the issue of governance. In an ideal version of the congressional process, Congress performs its governing role in the most efficient and unbiased way possible, with well-informed members making policy decisions based on efficiency, which policy proposals are best for their constituents, and which policy proposals are best for the nation as a whole. To the extent that groups interfere with any of these criteria, they are exerting a negative influence on Congress's governing function.

That scenario portrays groups in a negative light. But there is an alternative scenario. Groups also perform a necessary function that pluralists have long recognized: they help their individual members to be heard in Congress. On their own, these citizens might not be heard. Banding together, they are much more likely to be recognized. These groups thus represent individuals, and in doing so, they increase the likelihood that Congress will hear their voices. Thus groups can enhance Congress's representative function. Furthermore, they can do so by providing necessary information to congressional decision-makers.

Which scenario is accurate? The answer is almost certainly both. Ultimately, there is a trade-off, and the extent to which groups are either a negative force or a positive force depends on whether the observer places more emphasis on Congress's governing role or its representative role.

## Discussion Questions

1. On balance, do the benefits of interest-group lobbying of Congress outweigh the costs?

2. The *Citizens United* and *SpeechNOW.org* cases have both led to increased campaign spending, much of which cannot be traced back to individual donors. Given that the public tends to disapprove of the amount of money spent on election campaigns, but members of Congress tend to benefit from this money, can you identify any circumstances under which Congress might act to limit the amount of money in elections?

3. We have mentioned that groups such as the NRA and the LCV issue legislative scorecards, which show how members have voted on issues relevant to these groups. Because the public is generally poorly informed about politics, would we expect these scorecards to have any influence on how members of the public vote or on how members of Congress act? Might these scorecards be contributing to polarization?

4. Should Congress place stricter limits on the ability of representatives and senators to work as lobbyists after they retire? What are the strongest arguments in favor of such limits? What are the strongest arguments against them?

5. If lobbying does not tend to produce the outcomes that interest groups want, why do these groups continue to spend so much time, effort, and money on lobbying?

# Appendix

# PARTY CONTROL OF CONGRESS: 1789–2023

|  | Unified Control of Government |  | Divided Government |
|---|---|---|---|

| Congress | Years | Senate | | | House | | | President |
|---|---|---|---|---|---|---|---|---|
| | | Pro-Administration | Anti-Administration | Other | Pro-Administration | Anti-Administration | Other | |
| 1 | 1789–91 | 18 | 8 | — | 37 | 28 | — | George Washington |
| 2 | 1791–93 | 16 | 13 | — | 39 | 30 | — | Washington |
| 3 | 1793–95 | 16 | 14 | — | 51 | 54 | — | Washington |
| | | Federalists | Jeffersonian Republicans | Other | Federalists | Jeffersonian Republicans | Other | |
| 4 | 1795–97 | 21 | 11 | — | 47 | 59 | — | Washington |
| 5 | 1797–99 | 22 | 10 | — | 57 | 49 | — | John Adams |
| 6 | 1799–1801 | 22 | 10 | — | 60 | 46 | — | Adams |
| 7 | 1801–03 | 15 | 17 | — | 38 | 68 | — | Thomas Jefferson |
| 8 | 1803–05 | 9 | 25 | — | 39 | 103 | — | Jefferson |
| 9 | 1805–07 | 7 | 27 | — | 28 | 114 | — | Jefferson |
| 10 | 1807–09 | 6 | 28 | — | 26 | 116 | — | Jefferson |
| 11 | 1809–11 | 7 | 27 | — | 50 | 92 | — | James Madison |
| 12 | 1811–13 | 6 | 30 | — | 36 | 107 | — | Madison |
| 13 | 1813–15 | 8 | 28 | — | 68 | 114 | — | Madison |
| 14 | 1815–17 | 12 | 26 | — | 64 | 119 | — | Madison |
| 15 | 1817–19 | 12 | 30 | — | 39 | 146 | — | James Monroe |
| 16 | 1819–21 | 9 | 37 | — | 26 | 160 | — | Monroe |
| 17 | 1821–23 | 4 | 44 | — | 32 | 155 | — | Monroe |
| | | Adams-Clay Republicans | Jackson Republicans | Other | Adams-Clay Republicans | Jackson Republicans | Other | |
| 18 | 1823–25 | 17 | 31 | — | 72 | 64 | 77 | Monroe |
| 19 | 1825–27 | 22 | 26 | — | 109 | 104 | — | John Quincy Adams |
| 20 | 1827–29 | 21 | 27 | — | 100 | 113 | — | Quincy Adams |
| | | Anti-Jacksons | Jacksons | Other | Anti-Jacksons | Jacksons | Other | |
| 21 | 1829–31 | 23 | 25 | — | 72 | 136 | 5 | Andrew Jackson |
| 22 | 1831–33 | 22 | 24 | 2 | 66 | 126 | 21 | Jackson |

| Congress | Years | Senate | | | House | | | President |
|---|---|---|---|---|---|---|---|---|
| 23 | 1833–35 | 26 | 20 | 2 | 63 | 143 | 34 | Jackson |
| 24 | 1835–37 | 24 | 26 | 2 | 75 | 143 | 24 | Jackson |
| | | **Democrats** | **Whigs** | **Other** | **Democrats** | **Whigs** | **Other** | |
| 25 | 1837–39 | 35 | 17 | — | 128 | 100 | 12 | Martin Van Buren |
| 26 | 1839–41 | 30 | 22 | — | 125 | 109 | 8 | Van Buren |
| 27 | 1841–43 | 22 | 29 | — | 98 | 142 | 2 | William Henry Harrison/John Tyler |
| 28 | 1843–45 | 23 | 29 | — | 147 | 72 | 4 | Tyler |
| 29 | 1845–47 | 34 | 22 | — | 142 | 79 | 6 | James K. Polk |
| 30 | 1847–49 | 38 | 21 | 1 | 110 | 116 | 4 | Polk |
| 31 | 1849–51 | 35 | 25 | 2 | 113 | 108 | 11 | Zachary Taylor/Millard Fillmore |
| 32 | 1851–53 | 36 | 23 | 3 | 127 | 85 | 21 | Fillmore |
| 33 | 1853–55 | 38 | 22 | 2 | 157 | 71 | 6 | Franklin Pierce |
| | | **Democrats** | **Oppositions** | **Other** | **Democrats** | **Oppositions** | **Other** | |
| 34 | 1855–57 | 39 | 21 | 2 | 83 | 100 | 51 | Pierce |
| | | **Democrats** | **Republicans** | **Other** | **Democrats** | **Republicans** | **Other** | |
| 35 | 1857–59 | 41 | 20 | 5 | 132 | 90 | 15 | James Buchanan |
| 36 | 1859–61 | 38 | 26 | 2 | 83 | 116 | 39 | Buchanan |
| 37 | 1861–63 | 15 | 31 | 3 | 44 | 108 | 31 | Abraham Lincoln |
| 38 | 1863–65 | 10 | 33 | 9 | 72 | 85 | 27 | Lincoln |
| 39 | 1865–67 | 11 | 39 | 4 | 38 | 136 | 16 | Lincoln/Andrew Johnson |
| 40 | 1867–69 | 9 | 57 | — | 47 | 173 | 4 | Johnson |
| 41 | 1869–71 | 12 | 62 | — | 67 | 171 | 5 | Ulysses S. Grant |
| 42 | 1871–73 | 17 | 56 | 1 | 104 | 136 | 3 | Grant |
| 43 | 1873–75 | 19 | 47 | 7 | 88 | 199 | 5 | Grant |
| 44 | 1875–77 | 28 | 46 | 1 | 182 | 103 | 8 | Grant |
| 45 | 1877–79 | 35 | 40 | 1 | 155 | 136 | 2 | Rutherford B. Hayes |

(continued)

**PARTY CONTROL OF CONGRESS: 1789–2023 (continued)**

| Congress | Years | Senate | | | House | | | President |
|---|---|---|---|---|---|---|---|---|
| | | Democrats | Republicans | Other | Democrats | Republicans | Other | |
| 46 | 1879–81 | 42 | 33 | 1 | 141 | 132 | 21 | Hayes |
| 47 | 1881–83 | 37 | 37 | 2 | 128 | 151 | 14 | James A. Garfield/ Chester A. Arthur |
| 48 | 1883–85 | 36 | 38 | 2 | 196 | 117 | 12 | Arthur |
| 49 | 1885–87 | 34 | 42 | — | 182 | 141 | 2 | Grover Cleveland |
| 50 | 1887–89 | 37 | 39 | — | 167 | 152 | 6 | Cleveland |
| 51 | 1889–91 | 37 | 51 | — | 152 | 179 | 1 | Benjamin Harrison |
| 52 | 1891–93 | 39 | 47 | — | 238 | 86 | 8 | Harrison |
| 53 | 1893–95 | 44 | 40 | 4 | 218 | 124 | 14 | Cleveland |
| 54 | 1895–97 | 40 | 44 | 6 | 93 | 254 | 10 | Cleveland |
| 55 | 1897–99 | 34 | 44 | 12 | 124 | 206 | 27 | William McKinley |
| 56 | 1899–1901 | 26 | 53 | 10 | 161 | 187 | 9 | McKinley |
| 57 | 1901–03 | 31 | 55 | 4 | 151 | 197 | 9 | McKinley/ Theodore Roosevelt |
| 58 | 1903–05 | 33 | 57 | — | 178 | 208 | — | T. Roosevelt |
| 59 | 1905–07 | 33 | 57 | — | 136 | 250 | — | T. Roosevelt |
| 60 | 1907–09 | 31 | 61 | — | 164 | 222 | — | T. Roosevelt |
| 61 | 1909–11 | 32 | 61 | — | 172 | 219 | — | William Howard Taft |
| 62 | 1911–13 | 41 | 51 | — | 228 | 161 | 1 | Taft |
| 63 | 1913–15 | 51 | 44 | 1 | 291 | 127 | 17 | Woodrow Wilson |
| 64 | 1915–17 | 56 | 40 | — | 230 | 196 | 9 | Wilson |
| 65 | 1917–19 | 53 | 42 | — | 216 | 210 | 6 | Wilson |
| 66 | 1919–21 | 47 | 49 | — | 190 | 240 | 3 | Wilson |
| 67 | 1921–23 | 37 | 59 | — | 131 | 301 | 1 | Warren G. Harding |
| 68 | 1923–25 | 43 | 51 | 2 | 205 | 225 | 5 | Calvin Coolidge |
| 69 | 1925–27 | 39 | 56 | 1 | 183 | 247 | 4 | Coolidge |
| 70 | 1927–29 | 46 | 49 | 1 | 195 | 237 | 3 | Coolidge |
| 71 | 1929–31 | 39 | 56 | 1 | 167 | 267 | 1 | Herbert Hoover |

| Congress | Years | Senate | | | House | | | President |
|---|---|---|---|---|---|---|---|---|
| | | Democrats | Republicans | Other | Democrats | Republicans | Other | |
| 72 | 1931–33 | 47 | 48 | 1 | 220 | 214 | 1 | Hoover |
| 73 | 1933–35 | 60 | 35 | 1 | 313 | 117 | 5 | Franklin D. Roosevelt |
| 74 | 1935–37 | 69 | 25 | 2 | 319 | 103 | 10 | F.D. Roosevelt |
| 75 | 1937–39 | 76 | 16 | 4 | 331 | 89 | 13 | F.D. Roosevelt |
| 76 | 1939–41 | 69 | 23 | 4 | 261 | 164 | 4 | F.D. Roosevelt |
| 77 | 1941–43 | 66 | 28 | 2 | 268 | 162 | 5 | F.D. Roosevelt |
| 78 | 1943–45 | 58 | 37 | 1 | 218 | 208 | 4 | F.D. Roosevelt |
| 79 | 1945–47 | 56 | 38 | 1 | 242 | 190 | 2 | Harry S. Truman |
| 80 | 1947–49 | 45 | 51 | — | 188 | 245 | 1 | Truman |
| 81 | 1949–51 | 54 | 42 | — | 263 | 171 | 1 | Truman |
| 82 | 1951–53 | 49 | 47 | — | 234 | 199 | 1 | Truman |
| 83 | 1953–55 | 47 | 48 | 1 | 211 | 221 | 1 | Dwight D. Eisenhower |
| 84 | 1955–57 | 48 | 47 | 1 | 232 | 203 | — | Eisenhower |
| 85 | 1957–59 | 49 | 47 | — | 233 | 200 | — | Eisenhower |
| 86 | 1959–61 | 65 | 35 | — | 284 | 153 | — | Eisenhower |
| 87 | 1961–63 | 65 | 35 | — | 263 | 174 | — | John F. Kennedy |
| 88 | 1963–65 | 67 | 35 | — | 258 | 177 | — | Kennedy/ Lyndon B. Johnson |
| 89 | 1965–67 | 68 | 32 | — | 295 | 140 | — | Johnson |
| 90 | 1967–69 | 64 | 36 | — | 247 | 187 | — | Johnson |
| 91 | 1969–71 | 57 | 43 | — | 243 | 192 | — | Richard M. Nixon |
| 92 | 1971–73 | 54 | 44 | 2 | 254 | 180 | — | Nixon |
| 93 | 1973–75 | 56 | 42 | 2 | 239 | 192 | 1 | Nixon/ Gerald R. Ford |
| 94 | 1975–77 | 60 | 37 | 2 | 291 | 144 | — | Ford |
| 95 | 1977–79 | 61 | 38 | 1 | 292 | 143 | — | Jimmy Carter |
| 96 | 1979–81 | 58 | 41 | 1 | 276 | 157 | — | Carter |
| 97 | 1981–83 | 46 | 53 | 1 | 243 | 192 | — | Ronald Reagan |

(continued)

## PARTY CONTROL OF CONGRESS: 1789–2023 *(continued)*

| Congress | Years | Senate | | | House | | | President |
|---|---|---|---|---|---|---|---|---|
| | | Democrats | Republicans | Other | Democrats | Republicans | Other | |
| 98 | 1983–85 | 45 | 55 | — | 267 | 168 | — | Reagan |
| 99 | 1985–87 | 47 | 53 | — | 252 | 183 | — | Reagan |
| 100 | 1987–89 | 55 | 45 | — | 258 | 177 | — | Reagan |
| 101 | 1989–91 | 55 | 45 | — | 260 | 175 | — | George H.W. Bush |
| 102 | 1991–93 | 57 | 43 | — | 268 | 166 | 1 | Bush |
| 103 | 1993–95 | 56 | 44 | — | 258 | 176 | 1 | Bill Clinton |
| 104 | 1995–97 | 47 | 53 | — | 204 | 230 | 1 | Clinton |
| 105 | 1997–99 | 45 | 55 | — | 207 | 227 | 1 | Clinton |
| 106 | 1999–2001 | 45 | 55 | — | 211 | 223 | 1 | Clinton |
| *107 | 2001–03 | 50 | 49 | 1 | 210 | 222 | 3 | George W. Bush |
| 108 | 2003–05 | 48 | 51 | 1 | 205 | 229 | 1 | Bush |
| 109 | 2005–07 | 44 | 55 | 1 | 202 | 232 | 1 | Bush |
| 110 | 2007–09 | 49 | 49 | 2 | 233 | 202 | — | Bush |
| 111 | 2009–11 | 58 | 40 | 2 | 257 | 178 | — | Barack Obama |
| 112 | 2011–13 | 51 | 47 | 2 | 193 | 242 | — | Obama |
| 113 | 2013–15 | 53 | 45 | 2 | 200 | 233 | — | Obama |
| 114 | 2015–17 | 44 | 54 | 2 | 188 | 247 | — | Obama |
| 115 | 2017–19 | 47 | 51 | 2 | 193 | 236 | — | Donald Trump |
| 116 | 2019–21 | 45 | 53 | 2 | 235 | 199 | 1 | Trump |
| 117 | 2021–23 | 48 | 50 | 2 | 222 | 212 | — | Joseph R. Biden |

*The Republicans controlled the Senate in the 107th Congress, and thus had unified majority control of government until May 24, 2001, when Senator Jim Jeffords (VT) left the Republican Party to become an Independent and caucus with the Democrats. The Jeffords switch gave the Democrats organizational control of the Senate for the remainder of the Congress.

# Endnotes

## Chapter 1: Representation and Governing in a Separated System

1. Hanna F. Pitkin. 1967. *The Concept of Representation*. Berkeley, CA: University of California Press.
2. Alexander Hamilton, James Madison, and John Jay. 2012. *The Federalist Papers*. Edited by Richard Beeman. New York: Penguin Books. Hamilton wrote 51 essays, Madison 29, and Jay 5.
3. Hamilton, Madison, and Jay, *The Federalist Papers*, no. 10.
4. Robert A. Dahl. 2006. *A Preface to Democratic Theory, Expanded Edition*. Chicago, IL: University of Chicago Press; Christopher H. Achen and Larry M. Bartels. 2017. *Democracy for Realists: Why Elections Do Not Produce Responsive Government*. Princeton, NJ: Princeton University Press.
5. As Madison declared in *Federalist 51*, "The accumulation of all powers, legislative, executive and judicia[l] in the same hands, whether of one, a few, or many, and whether hereditary, self-appointed, or elective, may justly be pronounced the very definition of tyranny." Hamilton, Madison, and Jay, *The Federalist Papers*, no. 51.
6. Hamilton, Madison, and Jay, *The Federalist Papers*, no. 51.
7. Among the historic New Deal legislation originating in Congress were the Federal Emergency Relief Act (1933), the Banking Act (1933; also known as the Glass-Steagall Act), the Tennessee Valley Authority Act (1933), and the National Labor Relations Act (also known as the Wagner Act, 1935). See Patrick J. Maney. 1998. *The Roosevelt Presence: The Life and Legacy of FDR*. Berkeley, CA: University of California Press.
8. Over the course of a century, Congress extended voting rights to black men (Fifteenth Amendment in 1870), to women (Nineteenth Amendment in 1920), and to teenage voters (Twenty-Sixth Amendment in 1971).
9. For black voters (Twenty-Fourth Amendment in 1964 and Voting Rights Act in 1965), handicapped voters (Voting Accessibility for the Elderly and Handicapped Act of 1984 and the Americans with Disabilities Act of 1990), and the military (Uniformed and Overseas Citizens Absentee Voting Act of 1986).
10. The Hatch Act (1939), the National Voter Registration Act or Motor Voter Act (1993), and the Help Americans Vote Act (2002).
11. The Federal Election Campaign Act (1971; amended in 1974) and the Bipartisan Campaign Reform Act (2002), which led to the Supreme Court's *Citizens United* decision.

12. Thomas Kaplan and Alan Rappeport. December 19, 2017. "Republican Tax Bill Passes Senate in 51–48 Vote." *New York Times*, www.nytimes.com/2017/12/19/us/politics/tax-bill-vote-congress.html (accessed 5/29/18).

13. Woodrow Wilson. [1885], 1981. *Congressional Government: A Study in American Politics*. Baltimore, MD: Johns Hopkins University Press.

14. In a roll call vote, each member of Congress votes "yea" or "nay" when her name is called, so that the names of those voting on each side are recorded. The earliest statistical study of congressional roll call voting was Abbott Lawrence Lowell. 1902. *The Influence of Party upon Legislation in England and America*. Washington, DC: American Historical Association.

15. Stuart Rice. 1928. *Quantitative Methods in Politics*. New York: Alfred A. Knopf.

16. Warren Miller and Donald Stokes. 1963. "Constituency Influence in Congress." *American Political Science Review* 57(1): 45–56.

17. Roger Davidson, David Kovenock, and Michael O'Leary. 1966. *Congress in Crisis: Politics and Congressional Reform*. Belmont, CA: Wadsworth Publishing.

18. Edward Tufte. 1975. "Determinants of the Outcomes of Midterm Congressional Elections." *American Political Science Review* 69(3): 812–26; Robert S. Erikson. 1971. "The Advantage of Incumbency in Congressional Elections." *Polity* 3(3): 395–405; Alan I. Abramowitz. 1980. "A Comparison of Voting for U.S. Senator and Representative in 1978." *American Political Science Review* 74(3): 633–40.

19. See such prominent works as: David Truman. 1959. *The Congressional Party*. New York: John Wiley; Barbara Sinclair. 1995. *Legislators, Leaders, and Lawmaking: The U.S. House of Representatives in the Postreform Era*. Baltimore, MD: Johns Hopkins University Press; Barbara Sinclair. 2006. *Party Wars: Polarization and the Politics of National Policy Making*. Norman, OK: University of Oklahoma Press.

20. L. S. Shapley and Martin Shubik. 1954. "A Method for Evaluating the Distribution of Power in a Committee System." *American Political Science Review* 48(3): 787–92.

21. Duncan Black. 1958. *The Theory of Committees and Elections*. London: Cambridge University Press; Kenneth Shepsle and Barry Weingast. 1987. "The Institutional Foundations of Committee Power." *American Political Science Review* 81: 85–104; Barry Weingast and William Marshall. 1988. "The Industrial Organization of Congress; or, Why Legislatures, Like Firms, Are Not Organized as Markets." *Journal of Political Economy* 96(1): 132–63; Keith Krehbiel. 1987. "Why Are Congressional Committees Powerful?" *American Political Science Review* 81(3): 929–35; Keith Krehbiel. 1991. *Information and Legislative Organization*. Ann Arbor, MI: University of Michigan Press; Gary Cox and Mathew McCubbins. 1993. *Legislative Leviathan: Party Government in the House*. Berkeley, CA: University of California Press; David Rohde. 1991. *Parties and Leaders in the Postreform House*. Chicago, IL: University of Chicago Press; Sarah Binder. 1997. *Minority Rights, Majority Rule: Partisanship and the Development of Congress*. New York: Cambridge University Press.

22. Keith Poole and Howard Rosenthal. 1997. *Congress: A Political-Economic History of Roll Call Voting*. New York: Oxford University Press.

23. Andrew Martin and Kevin Quinn. 2002. "Dynamic Ideal Point Estimation via Markov Chain Monte Carlo for the U.S. Supreme Court, 1953–1999." *Policy Analysis* 10(2): 134–53; Boris Shor and Nolan McCarty. 2011. "The Ideological Mapping of American Legislatures." *American Political Science Review* 105(3): 530–51; Michael Bailey and Kelly H. Chang. 2001. "Comparing Presidents, Senators, and Justices: Interinstitutional Preference Estimation." *Journal of Law, Economics, and Organization* 17(2): 477–506; Erik Voeten. 2000. "Clashes in the Assembly." *International Organization* 54(2): 185–215; Simon Hix, Abdul G. Noury, and Gérard Roland. 2007. *Democratic Politics in the European Parliament*. New York: Cambridge University Press; John B. Londregan. 2000. *Legislative Institutions and Ideology in Chile*. New York: Cambridge University Press.

24. Charles Clapp. 1963. *The Congressman: His Work as He Sees It.* Garden City, NY: Doubleday; Lewis Froman. 1963. *Congressmen and Their Constituencies.* Chicago, IL: Rand McNally; David Mayhew. 1974. *Congress: The Electoral Connection.* New Haven, CT: Yale University Press.

25. Among the most prominent names are David Mayhew, David Rohde, Ada Finifter, Bruce Oppenheimer, Barbara Sinclair, Steven Smith, Hanes Walton Jr., Rick Hall, Larry Evans, Forrest Maltzman, Frances Lee, and Jennifer Victor.

26. Richard Fenno. 1978. *Home Style: House Members in Their Districts.* Glenview, IL: Scott Foresman & Co.

27. Robert Peabody. 1976. *Leadership in Congress: Stability, Succession, and Change.* Boston, MA: Little, Brown; Randall Ripley. 1969. *Majority Party Leadership in Congress.* Boston, MA: Little, Brown; John Manley. 1970. *The Politics of Finance: The House Committee on Ways and Means.* Boston, MA: Little, Brown; Richard Fenno. 1996. *The Power of the Purse: Appropriations Politics in Congress.* Boston, MA: Little, Brown; Richard Fenno. 1973. *Congressmen in Committees.* Boston, MA: Little, Brown.

28. For example, Roger Davidson, Walter Oleszek, Larry Evans, Norman Ornstein, and Thomas Mann.

29. Frances Lee. 2009. *Beyond Ideology: Politics, Principles, and Partisanship in the U.S. Senate.* Chicago, IL: University of Chicago Press.

30. Justin Grimmer. 2013. *Representational Style in Congress: What Legislators Say and Why It Matters.* New York: Cambridge University Press.

31. Nils Ringe, Jennifer Nicoll Victor, and Wendy K. Tam Cho. 2018. "Legislative Networks," in *The Oxford Handbook of Political Networks*, ed. by Jennifer Nicoll Victor, Alexander H. Montgomery, and Mark Lubell, 471–90. New York: Oxford University Press.

32. Adam Bonica. 2014. "Mapping the Ideological Marketplace." *American Journal of Political Science* 58: 367–86.

33. Solomon Messing, Patrick van Kessel, and Adam Hughes. December 18, 2017. "Sharing the News in a Polarized Congress." Washington, DC: Pew Research Center, www.people-press.org/2017/12/18/sharing-the-news-in-a-polarized-congress (accessed 6/8/18).

34. Scholars and individuals trained in advanced social science have become more active in the public debate and supply of research-based insights on contemporary politics through such websites as the Monkey Cage (www.washingtonpost.com/news/monkey-cage/), the Upshot (www.nytimes.com/section/upshot), FiveThirtyEight (http://fivethirtyeight.com/), and Mischiefs of Faction (www.vox.com/mischiefs-of-faction).

## Chapter 2: The Historical Development of Congress

1. On the problems of governing under the Articles, see Calvin Jillson and Rick K. Wilson. 1994. *Congressional Dynamics: Structure, Coordination, and Choice in the First American Congress, 1774–1789.* Stanford, CA: Stanford University Press; George William Van Cleve. 2017. *We Have Not a Government: The Articles of Confederation and the Road to the Constitution.* Chicago, IL: University of Chicago Press.

2. The literature on the Philadelphia Convention, and the events leading up to it, are voluminous. For a recent account, see Michael J. Klarman. 2016. *The Framers' Coup: The Making of the United States Constitution.* Oxford: Oxford University Press.

3. Joseph Cooper. 1970. *The Origins of the Standing Committees and the Development of the Modern House.* Houston, TX: Rice University Studies.

4. See John H. Aldrich. 1995. *Why Parties? The Origin and Transformation of Party Politics in America.* Chicago, IL: University of Chicago Press.

5. Henry Clay's leadership as Speaker of the House is explored in Gerald Gamm and Kenneth A. Shepsle. 1989. "Emergence of Legislative Institutions: Standing Committees

in the House and Senate, 1810–1825." *Legislative Studies Quarterly* 14: 39–56; Jeffery A. Jenkins. 1998. "Property Rights and the Emergence of Standing Committee Dominance in the Nineteenth-Century House." *Legislative Studies Quarterly* 23: 493–519; Jeffery A. Jenkins and Charles H. Stewart III. 2002. "Order from Chaos: The Transformation of the Committee System in the House, 1816–1822," in *Party, Process, and Political Change in Congress: New Perspectives on the History of Congress*, ed. by David W. Brady and Mathew D. McCubbins, 195–236. Stanford, CA: Stanford University Press.

6. Slavery did exist in the North in the 1700s, although it was never widespread, and it was outlawed by 1804.

7. David Potter. 1976. *The Impending Crisis, 1848–1861*. New York: Harper.

8. Southern Whigs—without a serious alternative available—would eventually join the Democratic Party.

9. The best account of the emergence of the Republican Party is William E. Gienapp. 1987. *The Origins of the Republican Party, 1852–1856*. Oxford: Oxford University Press.

10. Secession occurred in two waves: the seven states of the Lower South went first (and they founded the Confederacy), and the four states of the Upper South followed later.

11. The politics of the proposed Thirteenth Amendment are documented in Daniel W. Crofts. 2016. *Lincoln and the Politics of Slavery: The Other Thirteenth Amendment and the Struggle to Save the Union*. Chapel Hill, NC: University of North Carolina Press.

12. Ironically, the actual Thirteenth Amendment to the Constitution, which was adopted and ratified in 1865, abolished slavery.

13. A good, short history of Lincoln's interactions and relationship with the Republican-led Congress during the Civil War is William C. Harris. 2017. *Lincoln and Congress*. Carbondale, IL: Southern Illinois University Press.

14. Bruce Tap. 1998. *Over Lincoln's Shoulder: The Committee on the Conduct of the War*. Lawrence, KS: University Press of Kansas.

15. The Radicals' justification for the impeachment was based on Johnson's attempt to remove Attorney General Edwin Stanton (a fellow Radical) from office in opposition to the Tenure of Office Act (which the Radicals passed over Johnson's veto the previous year).

16. Michael Les Benedict. 1973. *The Impeachment and Trial of Andrew Johnson*. New York: W. W. Norton.

17. Eric Foner. 1988. *Reconstruction: America's Unfinished Revolution, 1863–1877*. New York: Harper & Row, 354–55.

18. The Compromise of 1877, as it became known, was an informal deal. The true elements of the compromise, and how much was explicitly agreed to by the parties involved, has been debated at length by historians. See C. Vann Woodward. 1951. *Reunion and Reaction: The Compromise of 1877 and the End of Reconstruction*. Boston, MA: Little, Brown; Allan Peskin. 1973. "Was There a Compromise of 1877?" *Journal of American History* 60: 63–75; Michael Les Benedict. 1980. "Southern Democrats in the Crisis of 1876–77: A Reconsideration of Reunion and Reaction." *Journal of Southern History* 46: 489–524.

19. In addition to disenfranchisement measures, Jim Crow laws also included measures to segregate the races in all public facilities.

20. See J. Morgan Kousser. 1974. *The Shaping of Southern Politics: Suffrage Restriction and the Establishment of the One-Party South, 1880–1910*. New Haven, CT: Yale University Press; Michael Perman. 2001. *Struggle for Mastery: Disfranchisement in the South, 1888–1908*. Chapel Hill, NC: University of North Carolina Press.

21. To combat Jim Crow, Republican members of Congress in the late nineteenth and early twentieth centuries occasionally offered bills to restrict southern representation in the House, per the "democratic form of government" guidelines of the Fourteenth Amendment. But these attempts were sporadic and, ultimately, unsuccessful.

22. Margaret Susan Thompson. 1985. *The Spider Web: Congress and Lobbying in the Age of Grant*. Ithaca, NY: Cornell University Press.

23. For example, several prominent members of Congress were implicated in the Crédit Mobilier scandal for taking bribes during the construction of the Union Pacific Railroad.

24. For more on the rise of congressional careerism, see Samuel Kernell. 1977. "Toward Understanding Nineteenth-Century Congressional Careers: Ambition, Competition, and Rotation." *American Journal of Political Science* 21: 669–93; David Brady, Kara Buckley, and Douglas Rivers. 1999. "The Roots of Careerism in the U. S. House of Representatives." *Legislative Studies Quarterly* 24: 489–510.

25. The secret ballot was often referred to as the Australian ballot based on its earlier—and successful—implementation in that country. For more on the Australian ballot in the United States, see Jerrold G. Rusk. 1970. "The Effect of the Australian Ballot Reform on Split Ticket Voting: 1876–1908." *American Political Science Review* 64: 1220–38.

26. Jonathan N. Katz and Brian R. Sala. 1996. "Careerism, Committee Assignments, and the Electoral Connection." *American Political Science Review* 90: 21–33.

27. See Alan Ware. 2002. *The American Direct Primary: Party Institutionalization and Transformation in the North*. Cambridge: Cambridge University Press.

28. See Gary W. Cox and Mathew D. McCubbins. 2005. *Setting the Agenda: Responsible Party Government in the U.S. House of Representatives*. Cambridge: Cambridge University Press. For the best biography of Reed, see William A. Robinson. 1930. *Thomas B. Reed: Parliamentarian*. New York: Dodd, Mead.

29. See Lewis L. Gould. 2005. *The Most Exclusive Club: A History of the Modern United States Senate*. New York: Basic Books.

30. For a description of intra-Republican battles during the Theodore Roosevelt administration, see Michael Wolraich. 2014. *Unreasonable Men: Theodore Roosevelt and the Republican Rebels Who Created Progressive Politics*. New York: Palgrave Macmillan.

31. See Eric Schickler. 2001. *Disjointed Pluralism: Institutional Innovation and the Development of the U.S. Congress*. Princeton, NJ: Princeton University Press.

32. See Eric Schickler. 2001. *Disjointed Pluralism: Institutional Innovation and the Development of the U.S. Congress*. Princeton, NJ: Princeton University Press.

33. Matthew N. Green. 2002. "Institutional Change, Party Discipline, and the House Democratic Caucus, 1911–19." *Legislative Studies Quarterly* 27: 601–33.

34. The relevant legislation included the Federal Reserve Act (1913), the Federal Trade Commission Act (1914), the Clayton Antitrust Act (1914), and the Keating-Owen Child Labor Act (1916).

35. Prior to the Sixteenth Amendment, the federal government got most of its revenue from the tariff. Regular revision of the tariff—lowering or raising rates on various raw materials and products—was contentious in Congress, with regions and parties dividing and wrangling, sometimes for months, as other important issues were pushed off the legislative agenda.

36. Sean Gailmard and Jeffery A. Jenkins. 2009. "Agency Problems, the 17th Amendment, and Representation in the Senate." *American Journal of Political Science* 53: 324–42.

37. Jeffery A. Jenkins and Charles Stewart III. 2013. *Fighting for the Speakership: The House and the Rise of Party Government*. Princeton, NJ: Princeton University Press.

38. Schickler, *Disjointed Pluralism*.

39. The one exception occurred for a brief period in the late 1950s and early 1960s when the House membership was increased to 437 after Hawaii and Alaska joined the Union.

40. As the first Congress held its initial meeting on March 4, 1789, March 4 (every two years thereafter) became the date that demarcated a new Congress in which new representatives and senators took office.

41. This was especially true after the passage of the Apportionment Act of 1872, which stipulated that all federal elections be held on the same day: the first Tuesday after the first Monday in November.

42. For more on the politics of lame-duck sessions, see Jeffery A. Jenkins and Timothy P. Nokken. 2008. "Partisanship, the Electoral Connection, and Lame-Duck Sessions of Congress, 1877–2006." *Journal of Politics* 70: 450–65; Jeffery A. Jenkins and Timothy P. Nokken. 2008. "Legislative Shirking in the Pre-Twentieth Amendment Era: Presidential Influence, Party Power, and Lame-Duck Sessions of Congress, 1877–1933." *Studies in American Political Development* 22: 111–40.

43. Craig Goodman and Timothy P. Nokken. 2004. "Lame-Duck Legislators and Consideration of the Ship Subsidy Bill of 1922." *American Politics Research* 32: 465–89.

44. The Twentieth Amendment also changed the presidential inauguration date from March to January.

45. For more on Congress's activities during World War II, see Nancy Beck Young. 2013. *Why We Fight: Congress and the Politics of World War II.* Lawrence, KS: University Press of Kansas.

46. Recent studies of these two landmark laws include Clay Risen. 2014. *The Bill of the Century: The Epic Battle for the Civil Rights Act.* New York: Bloomsbury; Gary May. 2013. *Bending toward Justice: The Voting Rights Act and the Transformation of American Democracy.* New York: Basic Books.

47. For more on LBJ's policy initiatives, and his relationship with Congress in achieving them, see Julian E. Zelizer. 2015. *The Fierce Urgency of Now: Lyndon Johnson, Congress, and the Battle for the Great Society.* New York: Penguin.

48. Important environmental legislation included the Water Quality Act, the Environmental Quality Act, and amendments to the Clean Air Act. Important transportation legislation included the Urban Mass Transit Assistance Act and the Rail Passenger Service Act (which created Amtrak). Important nuclear arms limitation legislation included the US–USSR Anti-Ballistic Missile Treaty and the US–USSR Strategic Arms Limitation Act.

49. Examples include *Gideon v. Wainwright* (1963), which held that criminal defendants have a right to an attorney even if they cannot afford one; *Miranda v. Arizona* (1966), which held that prisoners must be advised of their rights—such as the right to remain silent—before being questioned by the police; and *Loving v. Virginia* (1967), which struck down state laws that prohibited interracial marriages.

50. Relevant legislation included the Economic Recovery Tax Act of 1981, the Fiscal 1984 Department of Defense Authorization, the Gramm-Rudman-Hollings Act (1985), and the Tax Reform Act of 1986.

51. See David W. Rohde. 1991. *Parties and Leaders in the Postreform House.* Chicago, IL: University of Chicago Press.

52. See Barbara Sinclair. 2006. *Party Wars: Polarization and the Politics of National Policy Making.* Norman, OK: University of Oklahoma Press, 190–91.

53. Relevant legislation included the Omnibus Budget Reconciliation Act of 1993, the Brady Handgun Violence Prevention Act (1993), the Violent Crime Control and Law Enforcement Act of 1994, the North American Free Trade Act (passed with Republican help and enacted in 1994), and modifications to the the General Agreement on Tariff and Trade Act in 1994.

54. For a description of the specific reforms in the Contract with America, see John Micklethwait and Adrian Wooldridge. 2004. *The Right Nation: Conservative Power in America.* New York: Penguin.

55. Relevant legislation included the Personal Responsibility and Work Opportunity Reconciliation Act of 1996, the Balanced Budget Act of 1997, and the State Children's Health Insurance Program (SCHIP, 1997).

56. The relationship between the Republican Congress and President Clinton is explored in Steven M. Gillon. 2008. *The Pact: Bill Clinton, Newt Gingrich, and the Rivalry that Defined a Generation*. New York: Oxford University Press.
57. The House voted 228–206 on perjury and 221–212 on obstruction of justice. The Senate voted 45–55 on perjury and 50–50 on obstruction of justice.
58. For a readable account of the 2000 election recount, see Jeffrey Toobin. 2001. *Too Close to Call: The Thirty-Six Day Battle to Decide the 2000 Election*. New York: Random House.
59. A caveat is that the 107th Senate flipped from Republican to Democrat after Senator Jim Jeffords (Vt.) switched from Republican to Independent and began caucusing with the Democrats in June of 2001.
60. Note that the authorizations of military force are still in effect, and they continue to be used to justify military actions.
61. This legislation, the Economic Growth and Tax Relief Reconciliation Act of 2001, in combination with legislation two years later, the Jobs and Growth Tax Relief Reconciliation Act of 2003, are together informally referred to as the Bush tax cuts.
62. Relevant legislation included the Partial-Birth Abortion Ban Act of 2003 and the Medical Prescription Drug, Improvement, and Modernization Act of 2003.
63. Brookings Institution. 2017. "Table 6-7. Attempted and Successful Cloture Votes, 66th–114th Congress, 1919–2016," www.brookings.edu/wp-content/uploads/2017/01/vitalstats_ch6_tbl7.pdf (accessed 5/7/18).
64. The 60-seat Democratic majority in the Senate was critical to passing a comprehensive health care bill. The Clinton-era Democrats did not enjoy this advantage.
65. Relevant legislation included the American Recovery and Reinvestment Act of 2009, the Dodd–Frank Wall Street Reform and Consumer Protection Act (2010), and the Don't Ask, Don't Tell Repeal Act of 2010. Only the first of these three acts was adopted while the Democrats held 60 Senate seats.
66. Robert Draper. 2012. *Do Not Ask What Good We Do: Inside the U.S. House of Representatives*. New York: Free Press.
67. Brookings Institution, "Table 6-7. Attempted and Successful Cloture Votes, 66th–114th Congress, 1919–2016." (accessed 5/7/18). We discuss this attempt in more detail in Chapter 12.
68. Republicans in the House passed the American Health Care Act by a 217–213 vote, which would have repealed and replaced the Affordable Care Act. Republicans in the Senate sought to use the budget reconciliation process—and thus sidestep a Democratic filibuster—but could not secure the votes necessary for a repeal. The closest they got was a "skinny repeal"—a bare-bones bill that would have repealed the individual mandate in Obamacare—but it fell one vote short, 49–51 (a 50–50 tie would have made Vice President Mike Pence the tiebreaker, and he would have voted for it). Three Republican senators defected: Susan Collins (Maine), Lisa Murkowski (Ala.), and John McCain (Ariz.).
69. The legislation was known as the Tax Cut and Jobs Act of 2017.
70. With the individual mandate eliminated, the requirement that individuals purchase health care is no more. As a result, the Congressional Budget Office has estimated that up to 13 million people—principally younger, healthier people—will likely opt out of insurance coverage. This would raise the premiums on the remaining (older, less healthy) pool, force further coverage drops, and potentially destabilize the insurance market. See Congressional Budget Office, www.cbo.gov/publication/53300.
71. The vote on the first count (abuse of power) was 230–197. All Democrats voted yea, except for Collin Peterson (Minn.) and Jeff Van Drew (N.J.), who voted nay. All Republicans voted nay. Independent Justin Amash (Mich.) voted nay. Democrat Tulsi Gabbard (Hawaii) voted "present." The vote on the second count (obstruction of Congress) was

229–198. All Democrats voted yea, except for Collin Peterson (Minn.), Jeff Van Drew (N.J.), and Jared Golden (Maine), who voted nay. All Republicans voted nay. Independent Justin Amash (Mich.) voted nay. Democrat Tulsi Gabbard (Hawaii) voted "present."

72. The vote on the first count (abuse of power) was 52–48. All Democrats voted yea. Two Independents, Angus King (Maine) and Bernie Sanders (Vt.), also voted yea. All Republicans voted nay, except for Mitt Romney (Utah), who voted yea. The vote on the second count (obstruction of Congress) was 53–47. All Democrats voted yea. Two Independents, Angus King (Maine) and Bernie Sanders (Vt.), also voted yea. All Republicans voted nay.

73. Emily Cochrane. December 20, 2020. "Congress Strikes Long-Sought Stimulus Deal to Provide $900 Billion in Aid." *The New York Times*, www.nytimes.com/2020/12/20/us /politics/congress-stimulus-deal.html (accessed 1/8/21).

74. Maggie Haberman. January 6, 2020. "Trump Told Crowd 'You Will Never Take Back Our Country with Weakness.'" *The New York Times*, www.nytimes.com/2021/01/06/us /politics/trump-speech-capitol.html (accessed 1/8/21).

75. David A. Graham. January 6, 2021. "This Is a Coup." *The Atlantic*, https://www .theatlantic.com/ideas/archive/2021/01/attempted-coup/617570/ (accessed 1/8/21).

76. John Wagner, Felicia Sonmez, Mike DeBonis, Karoun Demirjian, Amy B. Wang, Colby Itkowitz, and Paulina Firozi. January 7, 2020. "Pence Declares Biden Winner of the Presidential Election after Congress Finally Counts Electoral Votes." *Washington Post*, www.washingtonpost.com/politics/2021/01/06/congress-electoral-college-vote-live -updates/ (accessed 1/8/21).

77. This phenomenon is referred to as "social desirability bias," and occurs when respondents provide answers that they believe will be viewed favorably (or are socially desirable) rather than answers that reflect their true feelings.

78. James M. Snyder Jr. 1992. "Artificial Extremism in Interest Group Ratings." *Legislative Studies Quarterly* 17: 319–45.

79. The acronym NOMINATE stands for Nominal Three-Step Estimation.

80. For more on NOMINATE scores, see Keith T. Poole and Howard Rosenthal. 2007. *Ideology and Congress: Second, Revised Edition of Congress: A Political-Economic History of Roll Call Voting*. New Brunswick, NJ: Transaction Publishers.

## Chapter 3: Elections

1. Brian McGill and Julie Bykowicz. October 9, 2018. "Health Care Crowds Out Jobs, Taxes in Midterm Ads." *Wall Street Journal*, www.wsj.com/articles/health-care-crowds-out-jobs -taxes-in-midterm-ads-1539077423 (accessed 3/1/20); Ashley Park, Philip Rucker, and Josh Dawsey. October 22, 2018. "Trump and Republicans Settle on Fear—and Falsehoods—as a Midterm Strategy." *Washington Post*, www.washingtonpost.com/politics/trump-and -republicans-settle-on-fear--and-falsehoods--as-a-midterm-strategy/2018/10/22 /1ebbf222-d614-11e8-a10f-b51546b10756_story.html (accessed 3/1/20).

2. S. Erdem Aytac and Susan Stokes. November 20, 2018. "Americans Just Set a Turnout Record for the Midterms, Voting at the Highest Rate Since 1914." *Washington Post*, www .washingtonpost.com/news/monkey-cage/wp/2018/11/20/americans-just-set-a-turnout -record-for-the-midterms-voting-at-the-highest-rate-since-1914-this-explains-why/ (accessed 3/11/20).

3. Anna North. July 18, 2019. "How 4 Congresswomen Came to Be Called 'The Squad.'" *Vox*, www.vox.com/2019/7/17/20696474/squad-congresswomen-trump-pressley-aoc -omar-tlaib (accessed 3/1/20); Susan Cornwell. October 21, 2019. "Expanding 'The Squad:' U.S. Liberals Challenge Moderate Democrats to Move Party Left." *Reuters*, www .reuters.com/article/us-usa-election-democrats/expanding-the-squad-us-liberals-challenge -moderate-democrats-to-move-party-left-idUSKBN1X00ZY (accessed 3/1/20).

4. Based on data from Tables 1-6 and 1-7, "Vital Statistics on Congress." Brookings Institution, www.brookings.edu/multi-chapter-report/vital-statistics-on-congress (accessed 5/15/18). Averages calculated from the 83rd (1953–54) through 115th (2017–18) Congresses; EveryCRSReport. January 5, 2021. "Congressional Careers: Service Tenure and Patterns of Member Service, 1789–2021." www.everycrsreport.com/reports/R41545.html (accessed 2/2/21).

5. This was the "great compromise" between small and large states at the Constitutional Convention.

6. The Seventeenth Amendment also outlines a procedure for filling Senate vacancies—either via special election or by governor appointment (per the decision of the state legislature). Article I, Section 2, Clause 4, stipulates that House vacancies will be filled via a special election.

7. Wendy Schiller and Charles Stewart III. 2015. *Electing the Senate: Indirect Democracy before the Seventeenth Amendment.* Princeton, NJ: Princeton University Press.

8. Schiller and Stewart, *Electing the Senate,* 8.

9. Disputed elections are often referred to as contested elections. But the term "contested elections" is sometimes interpreted to mean "contested races"—or when two (or more) candidates campaign for a seat in Congress. Thus we use the term "disputed elections" to make clear the phenomenon being studied in this section. This section is based in part on Jeffery A. Jenkins. 2004. "Partisanship and Contested Election Cases in the House of Representatives, 1789–2002." *Studies in American Political Development* 18: 112–35. For a similar examination of the Senate, see Jeffery A. Jenkins. 2005. "Partisanship and Contested Election Cases in the Senate, 1789–2002." *Studies in American Political Development* 19: 53–74.

10. The disputed election data in this analysis span the 1st through 112th Congresses (1789–2012). Data were taken from Jenkins, "Contested Election Cases in the House of Representatives," and updated.

11. As Geoffrey Skelley, elections analyst at FiveThirtyEight, states: "It's not hard to imagine disputed elections becoming a new battlefield in Washington if the parties decide these disputes can help them shore up their governing majorities." Geoffrey Skelley. December 14, 2018. "It's Been More Than 30 Years Since the House Reversed an Election Outcome." FiveThirtyEight. fivethirtyeight.com/features/its-been-more-than-30-years-since-the-house-reversed-an-election-outcome/ (accessed 2/29/20).

12. For an excellent history of how states elect their representatives, see Jay K. Dow. 2017. *Electing the House: The Adoption and Performance of the U.S. Single-Member District Electoral System.* Lawrence, KS: University Press of Kansas.

13. Over time, the ratio of 1 representative for every 30,000 of a state's population has decreased significantly. As of the 2010 census, the current ratio is around 1 representative for every 700,000 citizens.

14. This relationship of districts being composed of sets of whole counties is still the standard today. However, as urban areas have grown denser over time, an increasing number of districts has been carved out of single counties. For example, Cook County in Illinois—which contains Chicago—has 11 congressional districts. We refer to such densely populated urban counties as multidistrict counties.

15. In the 1840s, the United States was still predominantly an agrarian society. Tuesday was chosen because Sunday was a day of prayer and rest, while Wednesday was market day. Citizens could then use all of Monday to travel to the county seat, where voting would occur.

16. The matching of election dates was supposed to take effect four years after the passage of the act in 1876.

17. For an excellent history of methods of electing representatives, especially as it relates to voting technology, see Roy G. Saltman. 2006. *The History and Politics of Voting Technology: In Quest of Integrity and Public Confidence.* New York: Palgrave Macmillan.

18. By this time, only two states—Kentucky and Oregon—were still using voice voting at a broad level.

19. This population provision has since been amended by the second section of the Fourteenth Amendment.

20. See Charles W. Eagles. 1990. *Democracy Delayed: Congressional Reapportionment and Urban-Rural Conflict in the 1920s*. Athens, GA: University of Georgia Press.

21. For an excellent history of congressional apportionment methods, and the battles over them, see Michel L. Balinski and H. Peyton Young. 2010. *Fair Representation: Meeting the Ideal of One Man, One Vote*, 2nd edition. Washington, DC: Brookings.

22. Jefferson's method drops the remainder, regardless of the size, and then awards the whole number to a state. Webster's method rounds the remainder to the nearest whole number. Hamilton's method starts with a predetermined number of representatives (or House size) and rounds up the largest fractional remainders until that number is reached. Finally, the Huntington-Hill method is a modified version of the Webster method, but it uses a slightly different rounding method.

23. See Tables 3-9 and 3-10 in "Vital Statistics on Congress." Brookings Institution, www.brookings.edu/multi-chapter-report/vital-statistics-on-congress (accessed 5/16/18).

24. Soft-money contributions to the parties were not publicly disclosed until the 1991–92 election cycle.

25. Brennan Center for Justice. May 30, 2019. "Criminal Disenfranchisement Laws across the United States." www.brennancenter.org/criminal-disenfranchisement-laws-across-united-states (accessed 3/1/20).

26. "Voter ID History." National Conference of State Legislatures, www.ncsl.org/research/elections-and-campaigns/voter-id-history.aspx (accessed 3/1/20); "Voter ID Requirements." National Conferences of State Legislatures, www.ncsl.org/research/elections-and-campaigns/voter-id.aspx (accessed 3/1/20).

27. Nate Cohn. January 26, 2017. "Illegal Voting Claims, and Why They Don't Hold Up." *New York Times*, www.nytimes.com/2017/01/26/upshot/illegal-voting-claims-and-why-they-dont-hold-up.html (accessed 5/16/18); David Cottrell, Michael C. Herron, and Sean J. Westwood. 2018. "An Exploration of Donald Trump's Allegations of Massive Voter Fraud in the 2016 General Election." *Electoral Studies* 51: 123–42.

28. National Conference of State Legislatures. August 2, 2019. "State Laws Governing Early Voting." www.ncsl.org/research/elections-and-campaigns/early-voting-in-state-elections.aspx (accessed 3/1/20).

29. BallotPedia. "Changes to absentee/mail-in voting procedures in response to the coronavirus (COVID-19) pandemic, 2020." Ballotpedia.org, https://ballotpedia.org/Changes_to_absentee/mail-in_voting_procedures_in_response_to_the_coronavirus_(COVID-19)_pandemic,_2020 (accessed 8/8/20).

30. United States Elections Project. "2020 General Election Early Vote Statistics." U.S. Elections Project, electproject.github.io/Early-Vote-2020G/index.html (accessed 2/2/21).

31. Jerrold Rusk. 1970. "The Effect of the Australian Ballot Reform on Split Ticket Voting: 1876–1908." *American Political Science Review* 64: 1220–38.

32. In January 2011, DeLay was sentenced to serve three years in prison. He appealed his conviction and was free on bail while the appeal process played out. In September 2013, the Texas Court of Appeals acquitted him, and so did the Texas Court of Criminal Appeals (after the State of Texas appealed his first acquittal) in October 2014.

33. Anthony McGann, Charles Anthony Smith, Michael Latner, and Alex Keena. 2016. *Gerrymandering in America: The House of Representatives, the Supreme Court, and the Future of Popular Sovereignty*. New York: Cambridge University Press, 78–80.

34. García was first elected in 2018. Luis Gutiérrez (D) held the seat after the initial racial gerrymander; he was first elected in 1992 and reelected twelve times.

35. Aaron Blake. July 27, 2011. "Name That District! (Gerrymandering Edition)." *Washington Post*, www.washingtonpost.com/blogs/the-fix/post/name-that-district-gerrymandering-edition/2011/07/25/gIQA17HucI_blog.html (accessed 5/16/18).

36. Gary C. Jacobson and Jamie L. Carson. 2016. *The Politics of Congressional Elections*, 9th edition. Lanham, MD: Rowman & Littlefield.

37. David Lublin. 2004. *The Republican South: Democratization and Partisan Change*. Princeton, NJ: Princeton University Press, 115.

38. The Court cases include *Shaw v. Reno* (1993), *Miller v. Johnson* (1995), *Hunt v. Cromartie* (1999), and *Easley v. Cromartie* (2001).

39. *Davis v. Bandemer* (1986).

40. "Gill v. Whitford." January 24, 2018. Brennan Center for Justice, www.brennancenter.org/legal-work/whitford-v-gill (accessed 5/16/18).

41. Vann R. Newkirk II. June 18, 2018. "Partisan Gerrymandering Stands, for Now." *The Atlantic*, www.theatlantic.com/politics/archive/2018/06/partisan-gerrymandering-stands-for-now/563063 (accessed 6/30/18).

42. Adam Liptak. June 27, 2019. "Supreme Court Bars Challenges to Partisan Gerrymandering." *New York Times*, www.nytimes.com/2019/06/27/us/politics/supreme-court-gerrymandering.html (accessed 3/1/20).

43. See Alan Ware. 2002. *The American Direct Primary: Party Institutionalization and Transformation in the North*. New York: Cambridge University Press; John F. Reynolds. 2006. *The Demise of the American Convention System, 1880–1911*. New York: Cambridge University Press.

44. Source for the data and party maps is www.fairvote.org (accessed 5/16/18).

45. These percentages have separated a bit in the last three electoral cycles.

46. Jamie L. Carson and Jeffery A. Jenkins. 2011. "Examining the Electoral Connection across Time." *Annual Review of Political Science* 14: 25–46.

47. Samuel Kernell. 1977. "Toward Understanding 19th Century Congressional Careers: Ambition, Competition, and Rotation." *American Journal of Political Science* 21: 669–93.

48. Some of these activities were illegal, and corruption increased alongside the nation's political-economic development. Major congressional scandals occurred in the 1870s (during the Grant administration) and the 1920s (during the Harding administration).

49. David Brady, Kara Buckley, and Douglas Rivers. 1999. "The Roots of Careerism in the U.S. House of Representatives." *Legislative Studies Quarterly* 24: 489–510.

50. The classic account of political ambition is Joseph Schlesinger. 1966. *Ambition and Politics: Political Careers in the United States*. Chicago, IL: Rand McNally.

51. David R. Mayhew. 1974. *Congress: The Electoral Connection*. New Haven, CT: Yale University Press.

52. Richard F. Fenno. 1973. *Congressmen in Committees*. Boston, MA: Little, Brown.

53. David T. Canon. 1990. *Actors, Athletes, and Astronauts: Political Amateurs in the United States Congress*. Chicago, IL: University of Chicago Press.

54. See Gary Jacobson and Samuel Kernell. 1981. *Strategy and Choice in Congressional Elections*. New Haven, CT: Yale University Press; Gary Jacobson. 1989. "Strategic Politicians and the Dynamics of U.S. House Elections, 1946–86." *American Political Science Review* 83: 773–93.

55. See Jennifer L. Lawless. 2011. *Becoming a Candidate: Political Ambition and the Decision to Run for Office*. New York: Cambridge University Press; Jennifer L. Lawless. 2015. "Female Candidates and Legislators." *Annual Review of Political Science* 18: 349–66; Jennifer L. Lawless and Richard L. Fox. 2017. *Women, Men & U.S. Politics: 10 Big Questions*. New York: W. W. Norton.

56. Danielle Thomsen. 2017. *Opting Out of Congress: Partisan Polarization and the Decline of Moderate Candidates*. New York: Cambridge University Press.

57. This was a time when party ties in elections were weak and split-ticket voting was high.

58. Brookings Institution, www.brookings.edu/multi-chapter-report/vital-statistics-on-congress (accessed 1/21/2021). In 2018, while mean spending by challengers was $1,302,669, the party difference was considerable. Democratic challengers spent (on average) $1,815,084 compared to $252,881 by Republican challengers.

59. For House and Senate data, see Tables 3-3 and 3-6 in "Vital Statistics on Congress." Brookings Institution, www.brookings.edu/multi-chapter-report/vital-statistics-on -congress (accessed 5/16/18).

60. Gary W. Cox and Jonathan N. Katz. 2002. *Elbridge Gerry's Salamander: The Electoral Consequences of the Reapportionment Revolution*. New York: Cambridge University Press.

61. Jamie L. Carson, Michael H. Crespin, and Ryan D. Williamson. 2014. "Reevaluating the Effects of Redistricting on Electoral Competition, 1972–2012." *State Politics & Policy Quarterly* 14: 165–77.

62. For a recent study that challenges this basic result, and finds that independent commissions "produce virtually the same degree of insulation as plans devised in legislatures or by politician commissions," see John A. Henderson, Brian T. Hamel, and Aaron M. Goldzimer. 2018. "Gerrymandering Incumbency: Does Non-Partisan Redistricting Increase Competition?" *Journal of Politics* 80: 1011–16.

63. Robert S. Erikson. 2017. "The Congressional Incumbency Advantage over Sixty Years: Measurement, Trends, and Implications," in *Governing in a Polarized Era: Elections, Parties, and Political Representation in America*, ed. by Alan S. Gerber and Eric Schickler, 65–89. New York: Cambridge University Press.

64. Erikson (2017) offers this argument for why the Retirement Slump measure remains higher during this period: "Retirees had built up electoral immunity, maintaining their incumbency previously earned. The plunge in the vote following their exit revealed the degree to which the party success during their tenure had been incumbency-induced" (81).

65. See Susan Welch and John R. Hibbing. 1997. "The Effect of Charges of Corruption on Voting Behavior in Congressional Elections, 1982–1990." *Journal of Politics* 59: 226–39; Scott J. Basinger. 2013. "Scandals and Congressional Elections in the Post-Watergate Era." *Political Research Quarterly* 66: 385–98.

66. See Rodrigo Praino, Daniel Stockermer, and Vincent Moscardelli. 2013. "The Lingering Effects of Scandals in Congressional Elections: Incumbents, Challengers, and Voters." *Social Science Quarterly* 94: 1045–61. House members tainted by ethics violations also retired at a much higher rate.

67. Pennsylvania had lost one seat in the apportionment following the 2010 U.S. Census, and the Republican Senate essentially merged Altmire's 4th District and Critz's 12th District.

68. Jonathan Weisman. April 25, 2012. "2 House Democrats Defeated after Opposing Health Law." *New York Times*, www.nytimes.com/2012/04/26/us/politics/2-house -democrats-defeated-after-opposing-health-law.html (accessed 5/16/18).

69. The effects of the Voting Rights Act took a generation to play out fully. African American registration was initially met with increased white registration. But, in time, the African American electorate altered electoral and partisan dynamics in the South.

70. Jennifer Wolak. 2007. "The Influence of Public Preferences on Voluntary Departures from Congress." *Legislative Studies Quarterly* 32: 285–308.

71. Sheryl Gay Stolberg. September 26, 2017. "Tennessee's Bob Corker Announces Retirement from Senate." *New York Times*, www.nytimes.com/2017/09/26/us/politics /tennessees-bob-corker-announces-retirement-from-senate.html (accessed 5/16/18); Ed O'Keefe and David Weigel. October 24, 2017. "Sen. Jeff Flake of Arizona Will Retire, Citing Direction of GOP under Trump." *Washington Post*, www.washingtonpost.com /powerpost/sen-jeff-flake-will-retire-citing-direction-of-gop-under-trump/2017/10/24 /f33acdfc-b8ec-11e7-9e58-e6288544af98_story.html (accessed 5/16/18).

72. "Departures Resulting in Open Seat Races by Cycle." Center for Responsive Politics, www.opensecrets.org/members-of-congress/departures-by-cycle (accessed 12/17/18).

73. See, for example, Daniel J. Hopkins. 2018. *The Increasingly United States: How and Why American Political Behavior Nationalized.* Chicago, IL: University of Chicago Press.

74. Morris P. Fiorina. 2017. *Unstable Majorities: Polarization, Party Sorting, and Political Stalemate.* Stanford, CA: Hoover Institution Press, 127. In describing this nationalization, Fiorina refers to it as "re-nationalization," believing that "contemporary elections have returned to a pattern that was common in earlier periods of American history."

75. Larry Bartels. 2000. "Partisanship and Voting Behavior, 1952–1996." *American Journal of Political Science* 44: 35–50.

76. See Matthew Levendusky. 2009. *The Partisan Sort: How Liberals Become Democrats and Conservatives Become Republican.* Chicago, IL: University of Chicago Press; Gary Jacobson. 2015. "It's Nothing Personal: The Decline of the Incumbency Advantage in US House Elections." *Journal of Politics* 77: 861–73.

77. Frances Lee. 2016. *Insecure Majorities: Congress and the Perpetual Campaign.* Chicago, IL: University of Chicago Press; Jamie L. Carson and Jason Roberts. 2017. "Congress and the Nationalization of Congressional Elections." Working Paper.

78. On the pros and cons of wave elections, see Fiorina, *Unstable Majorities*, 140.

## Chapter 4: Representation

1. David Weigel. August 11, 2017. "At Raucous Town Halls, Republicans Have Faced Another Round of Anger over Health Care." *Washington Post*, www.washingtonpost.com/powerpost/at-raucous-town-halls-republicans-have-faced-another-round-of-anger-over-health-care/2017/08/10/9d82cbbe-7de9-11e7-83c7-5bd5460f0d7e_story.html (accessed 5/14/18).

2. Elliot Smilowitz. May 6, 2017. "GOP Rep: 'Nobody Dies Because They Don't Have Access to Healthcare.'" TheHill.com, http://thehill.com/policy/healthcare/raul-labrador-town-hall-nobody-dies-access-to-healthcare-obamacare (accessed 5/14/18).

3. Zack Hirsch. May 9, 2017. "At Town Hall Meeting, Republican Lawmakers Get An Earful over Health Care." NPR.com, www.npr.org/2017/05/09/527533782/at-town-hall-meeting-republican-lawmaker-gets-an-earful (accessed 5/14/18).

4. Andrew Rafferty. July 10, 2017. "Republicans Continue to Skirt Town Halls with August Recess Looming." NBCNews.com, www.nbcnews.com/politics/politics-news/republicans-continue-skirt-town-halls-august-recess-looming-n781506 (accessed 5/14/18).

5. John Bowden. August 12, 2017. "GOP Lawmaker Holding 'Ticket Lottery' for Access to His Town Hall." TheHill.com, http://origin-nyi.thehill.com/homenews/house/346328-gop-lawmaker-holding-ticket-lottery-for-access-to-his-town-hall (accessed 5/14/18); Javier Panzar. February 24, 2017. "Rep. Steve Knight Will Ask Attendees at His Town Hall Next Week to Provide ID to Prove They Live in His District." *Los Angeles Times*, www.latimes.com/politics/essential/la-pol-ca-essential-politics-updates-rep-steve-knight-to-hold-town-hall-1487976322-htmlstory.html (accessed 5/14/18).

6. Russell Berman. July 28, 2017. "John McCain's 'No' Vote Sinks Republicans' 'Skinny Repeal' Plan." *The Atlantic*, www.theatlantic.com/politics/archive/2017/07/john-mccains-no-vote-sinks-republicans-skinny-repeal-plan/535209/ (accessed 5/14/18).

7. Dylan Scott. November 7, 2018. "Trump's Biggest Midterm Blunder: Embracing Obamacare Repeal." Vox, www.vox.com/policy-and-politics/2018/11/7/18070152/midterm-elections-2018-results-trump-obamacare-repeal (accessed 2/15/20).

8. In addition, as political scientist Nicholas Carnes notes, members of Congress are much more likely to come from white-collar (non-working-class) backgrounds. See Nicholas Carnes. 2013. *White-Collar Government: The Hidden Role of Class in Economic Policy Making.* Chicago, IL: University of Chicago Press.

9. More generally, only 1 percent of Congress does not affiliate with an organized religion, compared to 23 percent of the American public.

10. Inter-Parliamentary Union. April 1, 2018. "Women in National Parliaments." http://archive.ipu.org/wmn-e/classif.htm (accessed 5/14/18).

11. Barbara Sprunt. January 3, 2021. "Here's a Look at Congress' Incoming Freshman Class." NPR, www.npr.org/2021/01/03/951481488/heres-a-look-at-congress-incoming-freshman-class (accessed 2/11/21).

12. Stated differently, accountability is built into the system via an electoral connection.

13. The classic theoretical treatment of representation is Hanna Fenichel Pitkin. 1967. *The Concept of Representation*. Berkeley, CA: University of California Press. Our characterization overlaps with Pitkin's, but we view representation in terms of a more traditional principal-agent model.

14. R. Douglas Arnold. 1990. *The Logic of Congressional Action*. New Haven, CT: Yale University Press.

15. See John Kingdon. 1981. *Congressmen's Voting Decisions*. Revised Edition. Ann Arbor, MI: University of Michigan Press.

16. Lou Dubose and Jan Reid. 2004. *The Hammer: Tom DeLay, God, Money, and the Rise of the Republican Congress*. New York: Public Affairs.

17. See Bob Cusack, Sarah Ferris, and Peter Sullivan. February 10, 2016. "The Chaotic Fight for ObamaCare." TheHill.com, http://thehill.com/policy/healthcare/268877-the-chaotic-fight-for-obamacare (accessed 5/14/18). Obama also brought wavering members to the White House for personal meetings.

18. Kelly Swanson. July 25, 2017. "Trump Tweets that He Will Sign Literally any Health Care Bill." Vox, https://www.vox.com/policy-and-politics/2017/7/25/16025068/trump-tweets-health-care-bill-vote (accessed 2/15/20). In the end, Senator John McCain—who Trump referred to as an "American hero" in advance of the roll call—cast the deciding vote against the repeal.

19. Ryan Sit. February 22, 2018. "Here's Why the NRA Is So Powerful and Why Gun Control Advocates Have Reason for Hope." *Newsweek*, www.newsweek.com/nra-gun-control-parkland-florida-school-shooting-campaign-donations-813940 (accessed 5/14/18); OpenSecrets.org. "Outside Spending Summary, 2020." Center for Responsive Politics, www.opensecrets.org/outsidespending/detail.php?cycle=2020&cmte=National+Rifle+Assn (accessed 2/2/21).

20. Craig Volden and Alan Wiseman. 2014. *Legislative Effectiveness in Congress: The Lawmakers*. Cambridge: Cambridge University Press.

21. For more on casework, see R. Eric Petersen and Sarah J. Eckman. January 3, 2017. "Casework in a Congressional Office: Background, Rules, Laws, and Resources." Congressional Research Service, https://fas.org/sgp/crs/misc/RL33209.pdf (accessed 5/14/18).

22. Quote is taken from an interview by Craig Horowitz. April 6, 1998. "Al D'Amato: Senator Pothole, Proudly." *New York Magazine*, http://nymag.com/nymetro/news/people/features/2421/ (accessed 5/14/18).

23. See Ida A. Brudnick. September 3, 2019. "Members' Representational Allowance: History and Usage." Congressional Research Service, https://fas.org/sgp/crs/misc/R40962.pdf (accessed 2/15/20); Congressional Research Service. November 27, 2018. "Constituent Services: Overview and Resources." www.everycrsreport.com/files/20181127_R44726_19be30ab4f34392498f65ae249cbb9b3323b6d95.pdf (accessed 2/15/20); Ida A. Brudnick. December 30, 2019. "Congressional Salaries and Allowances: In Brief." www.everycrsreport.com/files/20191230_RL30064_e0c301684846c665ee7cb428984f47dac1d7a795.pdf (accessed 2/15/20).

24. See Richard F. Fenno Jr. 1977. "U.S. House Members in Their Constituencies: An Exploration." *American Political Science Review* 71: 883–917.

25. Alexander Burns and Patricia Mazzei. February 22, 2018. "Marco Rubio Finds Himself at Center of Gun Debate, Again." *New York Times*, www.nytimes.com/2018/02/22/us /marco-rubio-florida-nra.html (accessed 5/14/18).
26. Norman Ornstein. March 7, 2006. "Part-Time Congress." *Washington Post*, www .washingtonpost.com/wp-dyn/content/article/2006/03/06/AR2006030601611.html (accessed 5/14/18).
27. David R. Mayhew. 1974. *Congress: The Electoral Connection*. New Haven, CT: Yale University Press.
28. Jonathan N. Katz and Brian R. Sala. 1996. "Careerism, Committee Assignments, and the Electoral Connection." *American Political Science Review* 90: 21–3.
29. Benjamin G. Bishin. 2009. *Tyranny of the Minority: The Subconstituency Politics Theory of Representation*. Philadelphia, PA: Temple University Press.
30. Wendy J. Schiller. 2000. *Partners and Rivals: Representation in U.S. Senate Delegations*. Princeton, NJ: Princeton University Press.
31. John H. Aldrich and Kenneth A. Shepsle. 2000. "Explaining Institutional Change: Soaking, Poking, Institutional Choice in the U.S. Congress," in *Congress on Display, Congress at Work*, ed. by William T. Bianco, 30. Ann Arbor, MI: University of Michigan Press.
32. Kristina C. Miler. 2010. *Constituency Representation in Congress: The View from Capitol Hill*. Cambridge, UK: Cambridge University Press.
33. Section 2 of the Fourteenth Amendment would also repeal the provision regarding indentured servants.
34. Slavery was prohibited in the Thirteenth Amendment, and the former slaves were provided with citizenship rights in the Fourteenth Amendment.
35. The increase in African American registration was met initially by an increase in white registration, which forestalled change for almost a generation.
36. Recent work in political science has found that Congress, as a whole, can indeed play a meaningful role in checking presidential power and thereby represent the country as a whole in matters of national significance. This is most prevalent in international affairs. Scholars have found that anticipation of pushback from Congress discourages presidents from entering military conflicts abroad. See William G. Howell and Jon C. Pevehouse. 2007. *While Dangers Gather: Congressional Checks on Presidential War Powers*. Princeton, NJ: Princeton University Press. And once involved in a military conflict, the president limits the scope and length of U.S. involvement—once again, in anticipation of active resistance in Congress. See Douglas L. Kriner. 2010. *After the Rubicon: Congress, Presidents, and the Politics of Waging War*. Chicago, IL: University of Chicago Press.
37. Laurie Kellman. January 20, 2015. "McCain Wages a New National Campaign, to Define His Legacy." Military.com, www.military.com/daily-news/2015/01/20/mccain-wages-a -new-national-campaign-to-define-his-legacy.html (accessed 5/14/18); Miranda Green. September 2, 2017. "McCain: Trump 'Poorly Informed,' Congress 'Not His Subordinates." CNN.com, www.cnn.com/2017/09/02/politics/mccain-regular-order-oped/index .html (accessed 5/14/18).
38. Tom Cotton. June 3, 2020. "Tom Cotton: Send In the Troops." *New York Times*, www .nytimes.com/2020/06/03/opinion/tom-cotton-protests-military.html (accessed 6/14/20); Alexander Bolton. June 14, 2020. "Cotton Emerges as Key Figure in Base Renaming Fight." *The Hill*, https://thehill.com/homenews/senate/502551-cotton-emerges -as-key-figure-in-base-renaming-fight (accessed 6/14/20).
39. This differs from cosponsorship of legislation, which is more of a passive, symbolic act.
40. See Scott H. Ainsworth and Thad E. Hall. 2010. *Abortion Politics in Congress: Strategic Incrementalism and Policy Change*. Cambridge: Cambridge University Press; Robert J. Spitzer. 2017. *The Politics of Gun Control*, 7th ed. New York: Routledge.

41. This work is nicely summarized in John D. Griffin. 2014. "When and Why Minority Leg-islators Matter." *Annual Review of Political Science* 17: 327–36. An exception to this gen-eral result is found in Carol Swain. 1993. *Black Faces, Black Interests: The Representation of African Americans in Congress*. Cambridge, MA: Harvard University Press.

42. See, for example, John D. Griffin and Brian P. Newman. 2007. "The Unequal Representa-tion of Latinos and Whites." *Journal of Politics* 69: 1032–46.

43. David T. Canon. 1999. *Race, Redistricting, and Representation*. Chicago, IL: University of Chicago Press.

44. See Michele L. Swers. 2002. *The Difference Women Make: The Policy Impact of Women in Congress*. Chicago, IL: University of Chicago Press; Michele L. Swers. 2013. *Women in the Club: Gender and Policy Making in the Senate*. Chicago, IL: University of Chicago Press; Danielle Kurtz. August 10, 2018. "Electing More Women Would Change Congress (But Not Make It More Bipartisan." NPR, KCUR 89.3. www.kcur.org/post/electing-more -women-would-change-congress-not-make-it-more-bipartisan#stream/0 (accessed 2/15/20).

45. Katherine Tate. 2004. *Black Faces in the Mirror: African Americans and Their Representa-tives in the U.S. Congress*. Princeton, NJ: Princeton University Press.

46. See Jane Mansbridge. 1999. "Should Blacks Represent Blacks and Women Represent Women? A Contingent 'Yes'". *Journal of Politics* 61: 628–57; John D. Griffin and Brian D. Newman. 2008. *Minority Report: Evaluating Political Equality in America*. Chicago, IL: University of Chicago Press.

47. Diana Tamashiro. 2018. "Intersectionality and the Political Representation of Battered Immigrant Women in an Analysis of the 2013 Violence Against Women Act Reauthoriza-tion." Universidad Complutense de Madrid. https://politicasysociologia.ucm.es/data/cont /docs/21-2018-12-12-TFM%20TAMASHIRO.pdf (accessed 2/15/20).

48. Ebonya L. Washington. 2008. "Female Socialization: How Daughters Affect Their Legis-lator Fathers' Voting on Women's Issues." *American Economic Review* 98: 311–32.

49. Kenneth Lowande, Melinda Ritchie, and Erinn Lauterbach. 2019. "Descriptive and Sub-stantive Representation in Congress: Evidence from 88,000 Congressional Inquiries." *American Journal of Political Science* 63: 644–59.

50. The class study here is Warren E. Miller and Donald E. Stokes. 1963. "Constituency Influence in Congress." *American Political Science Review* 57: 45–56.

51. See, for example, Christopher H. Achen. 1977. "Measuring Representation: Perils of the Correlation Coefficient." *American Journal of Political Science* 21: 805–15.

52. See, for example, Joshua D. Clinton. 2006. "Representation in Congress: Constituents and Roll Calls in the 106th House." *Journal of Politics* 68: 397–409; Joseph Bafumi and Michael Herron. 2010. "Leapfrog Representation and Extremism: A Study of American Voters and Their Members in Congress." *American Political Science Review* 104: 519–42; Chris Tausanovitch and Christopher Warshaw. 2013. "Measuring Constituent Policy Preferences in Congress, State Legislatures, and Cities." *Journal of Politics* 75: 330–42.

53. This process is described in the introduction to Richard F. Fenno Jr. 1978. *Home Style: House Members in Their Districts*. Boston, MA: Little, Brown, xi–xvi. The term appears in Richard F. Fenno Jr. 1996. *Senators on the Campaign Trail: The Politics of Representation*. Norman, OK: University of Oklahoma Press, 4.

54. Richard F. Fenno Jr. 1986. "Observation, Context, and Sequence in the Study of Politics." *American Political Science Review* 80: 3–15.

55. This strategic presentation of self generates trust among constituents, which in turn pro-vides members of Congress with more leeway to act as they wish in Washington. See Fenno, *Home Style*; William T. Bianco. 1994. *Trust: Representatives and Constituents*. Ann Arbor, MI: University of Michigan Press.

56. Justin Grimmer. 2013. *Representational Style in Congress: What Legislators Say and Why It Matters*. Cambridge, UK: Cambridge University Press.

57. The ADA chooses roll calls in keeping with its advocacy of "progressive stances on civil rights and liberties, social and economic justice, sensible foreign policy, and sustainable environmental policy." This leads to a set of votes on "a wide range of social and economic issues, both domestic and international." See "What is Americans for Democratic Action?" https://adaction.org/about/ (accessed 5/15/18).

58. The LCCR chooses roll calls in keeping with their legislative priorities, which are to work "toward the goal of a more open and just society" and "to ensure the proper enforcement of civil rights laws to unite us as a nation true to its promise of equal justice, equal opportunity, and mutual respect." See the Leadership Conference on Civil and Human Rights Voting Record, 115th Congress, October 2018, 8. For more on the composition and use of LCCR scores, see Daniel Q. Gillion. 2013. *The Political Power of Protest: Minority Activism and Shifts in Public Policy*. Cambridge, UK: Cambridge University Press.

59. The heroes and zeroes categorization started with the ADA.

60. For example, the ADA's heroes list in the 115th Congress counted 24 House Democrats and 5 Senate Democrats, while the group's zeroes list tallied 140 House Republicans and 19 Senate Republicans. The LCCR's heroes list counted 15 House Democrats and 29 Senate Democrats (along with Bernie Sanders, an Independent), and the group's zeroes list tallied 86 House Republicans and 37 Senate Republicans.

61. Elizabeth Mendes. May 9, 2013. "Americans Down on Congress, OK with Own Representative." Gallup, http://news.gallup.com/poll/162362/americans-down-congress-own-representative.aspx (accessed 5/17/18).

62. This macro versus micro difference in performance evaluations is sometimes referred to as Fenno's Paradox.

63. Glenn R. Parker and Roger H. Davidson. 1979. "Why Do Americans Love Their Congressman So Much More Than Their Congress?" *Legislative Studies Quarterly* 4: 53–61; Daniel M. Butler, Christopher F. Karpowitz, and Jeremy C. Pope. 2017. "Who Gets the Credit? Legislative Responsiveness and Evaluations of Members, Parties, and the US Congress." *Political Science Research and Methods* 5: 351–66.

64. See Kenneth R. Mayer and David T. Cannon. 1999. *The Dysfunctional Congress? The Individual Roots of an Institutional Dilemma*. Boulder, CO: Westview; Thomas E. Mann and Norman J. Ornstein. 2006. The Broken Branch: How Congress Is Failing America and How to Get It Back on Track. Oxford: Oxford University Press.

65. James A. Stimson, Michael B. MacKuen, and Robert S. Erikson. 1995. "Dynamic Representation." *American Political Science Review* 89: 543–65; James A. Stimson. 1999. *Public Opinion in America: Moods, Cycles, and Swings*, 2nd ed. Boulder, CO: Westview; James A. Stimson. 2004. *Tides of Consent: How Public Opinion Shapes American Politics*. Cambridge, UK: Cambridge University Press.

## Chapter 5: Committees

1. Molly Reynolds. November 30, 2017. "Retirement from Congress may be driven by term limits on committee chairs." FIXGOV blog, Brookings Institution, www.brookings.edu/blog/fixgov/2017/11/30/committee-chair-term-limits-and-retirements (accessed 2/4/2020).

2. Chris Cillizza. April 6, 2014. "Congressional committee chairs have lost much of their prestige, allure." *Washington Post*, www.washingtonpost.com/politics/congressional-committee-chairs-have-lost-much-of-their-prestige-allure/2014/06/06/27533af6-bd93-11e3-b574-f8748871856a_story.html (accessed 2/4/2020).

3. Paul Kane. February 16, 2013. "Congress's Committee Chairmen Push to Reassert Their Power." *Washington Post*, www.washingtonpost.com/politics/congresss-committee-chairman-push-to-reassert-their-power/2013/02/16/2acb7770-6a6a-11e2-af53-7b2b2a7510a8_story.html (accessed 5/13/18).

4. Woodrow Wilson. [1885], 1981. *Congressional Government: A Study in American Politics.* Baltimore, MD: Johns Hopkins University Press.

5. Clay Risen. 2014. *The Bill of the Century: The Epic Battle for the Civil Rights Act.* New York: Bloomsbury Press; Julian Zelizer. 2015. *The Fierce Urgency of Now: Lyndon Johnson, Congress, and the Battle for the Great Society.* New York: Penguin Press.

6. Christopher Deering and Steven Smith. 1997. *Committees in Congress*, 3rd ed. Washington, DC: Congressional Quarterly.

7. Ashley Parker. June 5, 2013. "From a 'Child of the House' to Longest-Serving Member." *New York Times.*

8. The chamber's parliamentarian refers bills to the appropriate committee based on the bill's subject matter.

9. Walter Oleszek. 2014. *Congressional Procedures and the Policy Process*, 9th ed., 114. Washington, DC: CQ Press; Jeffrey Young. September 7, 2005. "Bonilla Bill Targets Eminent Domain." *The Hill*, www.lexisnexis.com.libraries.colorado.edu/lnacui2api/api/version1/getDocCui?lni=4H2M-GCF0-00BY-M1GS&csi=153182&hl=t&hv=t&hnsd=f&hns=t&hgn=t&oc=00240&perma=tru

10. Barbara Sinclair. 2017. *Unorthodox Lawmaking: New Legislative Processes in the U.S. Congress*, 5th ed., Table 6.2. Washington, DC: Congressional Quarterly Press.

11. Garry Young and Joseph Cooper. 1993. "Multiple Referral and the Transformation of House Decision Making," in *Congress Reconsidered*, 5th ed., 211–34. Washington, DC: Congressional Quarterly.

12. Garry Young. 1996. "Committee Gatekeeping and Proposal Power under Single and Multiple Referrals." *Journal of Theoretical Politics* 8: 65–78.

13. CQ Almanac. 2010. "Landmark Health Care Overhaul: A Long, Acrimonious Journey," in CQ *Almanac 2009*, ed. by Jan Austin, 65th ed. Washington, DC: CQ-Roll Call Group.

14. David King. 1997. *Turf Wars: How Congressional Committees Claim Jurisdictions.* Chicago, IL: University of Chicago Press. Somewhat surprisingly, other research has shown that when legislators avoid the committee of jurisdiction, other legislators—despite not wanting the same thing to happen to their committees—fail to support that original committee. See Charles R. Shipan. 1992. "Individual Incentives and Institutional Imperatives: Committee Jurisdiction and Long-Term Health Care." *American Journal of Political Science* 36: 877–95; and Charles R. Shipan. 1996. "Senate Committees and Turf: Do Jurisdictions Matter?" *Political Research Quarterly* 49: 177–89

15. Rob Margetta. January 6, 2014. "2013 Legislative Summary: Cybersecurity." CQ *Weekly Report*, 59.

16. Jessica Meyers and Kevin Cirilli. January 1, 2014. "Senate Panels Fight for a Piece of Target." Politico, www.politico.com/story/2014/01/congress-target-data-breach-security-senate-commerce-judiciary-banking-102179.html (accessed 7/27/18).

17. Julian Hattem. June 8, 2014. "Anti-hacking Legislation Now on the Fritz." TheHill.com, http://thehill.com/policy/technology/208557-anti-hacking-bills-on-the-fritz (accessed 7/27/18).

18. E. Scott Adler and John Wilkerson. 2012. *Congress and the Politics of Problem Solving.* New York: Cambridge University Press.

19. Karen Foerstel and Alan Ota. January 6, 2001. "Early Grief for GOP Leaders in New Committee Rules." CQ *Weekly Report*, 10–14; Alan Ota. February 3, 2001. "Chairman Tauzin Charts a Bold Course for Commerce." CQ *Weekly Report*, 258–66.

20. Gerald Gamm and Kenneth Shepsle. 1989. "Emergence of Legislative Institutions: Standing Committees in the House and Senate, 1810–1825." *Legislative Studies Quarterly* 14: 39–66.
21. Jonathan Katz and Brian Sala. 1996. "Careerism, Committee Assignments and the Electoral Connection." *American Political Science Review* 90: 21–33.
22. David Canon and Charles Stewart. 2009. "Committee Hierarchy and Assignments in the U.S. Congress: Testing Theories of Legislative Organization 1789–1946." Presented at the Conference on Bicameralism, Duke University.
23. Charles Stewart. 1992. "The Growth of the Committee System, from Randall to Gillett," in *The Atomistic Congress: An Interpretation of Congressional Change*. Armonk, NY: M.E. Sharpe, Inc.
24. Stanley Bach and Steven Smith. 1988. *Managing Uncertainty in the House of Representatives: Adaptation and Innovation in Special Rules*. Washington, DC: Brookings Institution; Bruce I. Oppenheimer. 1977. "The Rules Committee: New Arm of Leadership in a Decentralized House," in *Congress Reconsidered*, 96–116. Washington, DC: Congressional Quarterly.
25. David Hawkings. 2014. "The Opaque World of Committee Assignments." Roll Call Blog: Hawkings Here, http://blogs.rollcall.com/hawkings/house-committee-assignments/?dcz= (accessed 4/5/15).
26. Lindsay McPherson. February 11, 2020. "No longer GOP pariahs, Freedom Caucus members earn top committee slots." Roll Call, www.rollcall.com/2020/02/11/no-longer-gop -pariahs-freedom-caucus-members-earn-top-committee-slots/ (accessed 2/11/20).
27. Tim Groseclose and Charles Stewart. 1998. "The Value of Committee Seats in the House, 1947–1991." *American Journal of Political Science* 42: 453–74.
28. Nelson W. Polsby. 1968. "The Institutionalization of the US House of Representatives." *American Political Science Review* 62: 144–68.
29. John A. Lawrence. 2018. *The Class of '74: Congress after Watergate and the Roots of Partisanship*. Baltimore, MD: Johns Hopkins University Press.
30. James Gimpel. 1996. *Legislating the Revolution: The Contract with America in Its First 100 Days*. Boston, MA: Allyn and Bacon.
31. Kristin Kanthak. 2007. "Crystal Elephants and Committee Chairs Campaign Contributions and Leadership Races in the U.S. House of Representatives." *American Politics Research* 35.3: 389–406, http://dx.doi.org/10.1177/1532673X06298079 (accessed 7/20/20).
32. Joseph Schatz. January 10, 2005. "Lewis Wins Favor of GOP Leaders—and Coveted Appropriations Chair." CQ *Weekly Report*, 71–73.
33. Norman J. Ornstein and others. 2014. *Vital Statistics on Congress*. Washington, DC: Brookings Institution and the American Enterprise Institute, www.brookings.edu /research/reports/2013/07/vital-statistics-congress-mann-ornstein (accessed 4/5/15).
34. One law—P.L. 114-222, the Justice against Sponsors of Terrorism Act—was enacted over a presidential veto.
35. Adler and Wilkerson, *Congress and the Politics of Problem Solving*.
36. Gregory Korte. March 7, 2014. "Cummings Accepts Issa Apology for Dust-up at Hearing." *USA Today*, www.usatoday.com/story/news/politics/2014/03/07/cummings-accepts -issa-apology-for-microphone-incident/6159273/ (accessed 12/12/14).
37. Tim Hains. July 12, 2018. "Peter Strzok Hearing Descends Into Chaos After First Questions, Republican vs. Democrat Shouting Match." Real Clear Politics, www .realclearpolitics.com/video/2018/07/12/peter_strzok_hearing_descends_into_chaos _after_first_question.html (accessed 2/7/20).
38. James Walker. October 30, 2019. "Republicans Storm Out of Veterans' Affairs Committee, Refuse to Vote on Health Care Bill for Women Veterans." *Newsweek*, www.newsweek .com/republicans-storm-out-female-veteran-health-care-bill-1468605 (accessed 2/7/20).

39. James M. Curry. 2015. *Legislating in the Dark: Information and Power in the House of Representatives.* Chicago, IL: University of Chicago Press.

40. Ashley Halsey. July 22, 2011. "FAA Faces Partial Shutdown." *Washington Post,* www.washingtonpost.com/local/faa-faces-partial-shutdown/2011/07/22/gIQA64o3TI_story.html (accessed 4/5/15).

41. Eric Bontrager. March 24, 2009. "House Republicans to Push for Guns Amendment to Public Lands Catchall." *New York Times,* www.nytimes.com/gwire/2009/03/24/24greenwire-house-republicans-to-push-for-guns-amendment-t-10263.html (accessed 8/30/18).

42. Associated Press. May 20, 2009. "Congress Votes to Allow Guns in National Parks." MSNBC.com, www.nbcnews.com/id/30832809/ns/politics-capitol_hill/t/congress-votes-allow-guns-national-parks (accessed 7/27/18).

43. Kenneth Shepsle and Barry Weingast. 1987. "The Institutional Foundations of Committee Power." *American Political Science Review* 81: 85–104.

44. Elizabeth Williamson. April 25, 2007. "Revival of Oversight Role Sought." *Washington Post.*

45. Richard Oppel. July 27, 2014. "Lawmakers Reach Deal on a Fix for V.A.'s Health Care System." *New York Times.*

46. Shawn Zeller. May 19, 2014. "Probe to Nowhere: Partisanship Hobbles Benghazi Panel." CQ *Weekly Report,* 704–11.

47. Richard Cohen. 1999. "Crackup of the Committees." *Congressional Quarterly Weekly Report* 2210–17.

48. Sinclair, *Unorthodox Lawmaking.*

49. Walter Oleszek. December 28, 1999. *The Use of Task Forces in the House.* Washington, DC: Congressional Research Service.

50. Deborah Kalb. March 29, 1995. "The Official Gingrich Task Force List." *The Hill.*

51. Oleszek, *Congressional Procedures and the Policy Process,* 16–17.

52. Sinclair, *Unorthodox Lawmaking.*

53. Nolan McCarty. 2016. "The Decline of Regular Order in Appropriations: Does It Matter?," in *Congress and Policy Making in the 21st Century,* ed. by Jeffery Jenkins and Eric Patashnik, 162–86. New York: Cambridge University Press.

54. Oleszek, *Congressional Procedures and the Policy Process,* 345.

55. CQ Almanac. 2014. "Symbolic Budget Resolutions Set Stage for Spending Deal, Omnibus," in *Congressional Quarterly Almanac,* 2013, 410–14. Washington, DC: CQ Press.

56. Oleszek, *Congressional Procedures and the Policy Process,* Table 8.1.

57. Oleszek, *Congressional Procedures and the Policy Process,* 335.

58. Steven J. Balla and Christopher J. Deering. 2013. "Police Patrols and Fire Alarms: An Empirical Examination of the Legislative Preference for Oversight." *Congress & the Presidency* 40.1: 27–40; Keith W. Smith. 2010. "Congressional Use of Authorization and Oversight." *Congress & the Presidency* 37.1: 45–63.

59. Charles Babington. August 22, 2007. "Democrats Pursue Agenda with Inquiries." *Associated Press.*

60. David Mayhew. 2005. *Divided We Govern: Party Control, Lawmaking, and Investigations, 1946–2002,* 2nd ed. New Haven, CT: Yale University Press.

61. In Chapter 10, we consider why committees have an incentive to oversee executive agencies under unified government.

62. Douglas Kriner and Liam Schwartz. 2008. "Divided Government and Congressional Investigations." *Legislative Studies Quarterly* 33.2: 295–321; David Parker and Matthew Dull. 2009. "Divided We Quarrel: The Politics of Congressional Investigations, 1947–2004." *Legislative Studies Quarterly* 34.3: 319–4.

63. E. Scott Adler and John S. Lapinski. 1997. "Demand-Side Theory and Congressional Committee Composition: A Constituency Characteristics Approach." *American Journal of Political Science* 41: 895–918; Scott A. Frisch and Sean Q. Kelly. 2004. "Self-Selection Reconsidered: House Committee Assignment Requests and Constituency Characteristics." *Political Research Quarterly* 57.2: 325–26; Kenneth Shepsle. 1978. *The Giant Jigsaw Puzzle*. Chicago, IL: University of Chicago Press; Shepsle and Weingast, "The Institutional Foundations of Committee Power"; Barry Weingast and William Marshall. 1988. "The Industrial Organization of Congress; or, Why Legislatures, Like Firms, Are Not Organized as Markets." *Journal of Political Economy* 96: 132–63.

64. "Senate Tracker: A Close Race in Louisiana." September 18, 2014. Hereandnow, http://hereandnow.wbur.org/2014/09/18/senate-tracker-louisiana (accessed 7/27/18).

65. Newsweek Staff. 1995. "Why Newt Is No Joke." *Newsweek*, www.newsweek.com/why-newt-no-joke-181574.

66. John H. Aldrich, Brittany N. Perry, and David W. Rohde. 2012. "House Appropriations after the Republican Revolution." *Congress & the Presidency* 39.3: 229–53.

67. Jonathan Strong. December 3, 2012. "Dissidents Pushed Off Prominent Committees." *Roll Call.*

68. Specifically, we use what is referred to as a difference-in-medians test, popularized in Groseclose (1994) and Adler and Lapinski (1997). We compare the actual median NOMINATE score for a specific committee in a given congressional term to that of a pool of 10,000 committees of the same size made up of randomly drawn members of the House. (We use the median NOMINATE score, rather than an average score, as a measure of "central tendency" of each committee because it represents an actual individual lawmaker.) The committee is considered a conservative outlier if the actual median score for the panel is higher than 95 percent of the random committees. The committee is considered a liberal outlier if the actual median score for the panel is lower than 95 percent of the random committees.

69. See also Forrest Maltzman. 1997. *Competing Principals: Committees, Parties, and the Organization of Congress*. Ann Arbor, MI: University of Michigan Press.

70. Sarah Binder. May 27, 2014. *Polarized We Govern?* Washington, DC: Brookings Institution, www.brookings.edu/research/papers/2014/05/27-polarized-we-govern-congress-legislative-gridlock-polarized-binder (accessed 7/27/18).

71. Jamie Carson, Charles Finocchiaro, and David Rohde. 2010. "Consensus, Conflict, and Partisanship in House Decision Making: A Bill-Level Examination of Committee and Floor Behavior." *Congress & the Presidency* 37.3: 231–53.

## Chapter 6: Parties

1. Eleven of the 12 Republicans were from California, New Jersey, and New York—generally considered high-tax states. These Republican House members were opposed to the bill's provision that capped the deduction for state and local taxes at $10,000.

2. Thomas Kaplan and Alan Rappeport. December 19, 2017. "Republican Tax Bill Passes Senate in 51–48 Vote." *New York Times*, www.nytimes.com/2017/12/19/us/politics/tax-bill-vote-congress.html (accessed 5/21/18); Deirdre Walsh, Phil Mattingly, Ashley Killough, Lauren Fox, and Kevin Liptak. December 20, 2017. "White House, GOP Celebrate Passing Sweeping Tax Bill." CNN, www.cnn.com/2017/12/20/politics/house-senate-trump-tax-bill/index.html (accessed 5/21/18).

3. In the House, only two Democrats were more conservative than anyone in the Republican conference, and only two Republicans were more liberal than any Democratic member. See Josh Kraushaar. 2013. "The Most Divided Congress Ever, at Least Until Next

Year." *National Journal*, www.nationaljournal.com/2013-vote-ratings/the-most-divided
-congress-ever-at-least-until-next-year-20140206 (accessed 5/21/18).

4. Voteview. December 18, 2016. "The End of the 114th Congress." https://voteviewblog
.com/2016/12/18/the-end-of-the-114th-congress/ (accessed 5/21/18).

5. Vital Statistics on Congress. 2017. "Table 8-3 Party Unity Vote in Congress, 1953–2016."
Brookings Institution, www.brookings.edu/wp-content/uploads/2017/01/vitalstats_ch8
_tbl3.pdf (accessed 5/21/18).

6. Siobhan Hughes, Kate Davidson, and Andrew Duehren. March 18, 2020. "Senate Passes
Bill to Combat Pandemic as Administration Proposes Direct Payments to Americans."
*Wall Street Journal*, www.wsj.com/articles/senate-expected-to-pass-bill-offering-free
-virus-testing-paid-leave-11584537988 (accessed 3/18/20).

7. John H. Aldrich. 1995. *Why Parties? The Origin and Transformation of Party Politics in
America*. Chicago, IL: University of Chicago Press.

8. We use the generic term "caucus" to describe the collection of members of one party in a
chamber. Formally, the House and Senate Democrats refer to themselves as a "caucus,"
while House and Senate Republicans call themselves a "conference."

9. Jeffery A. Jenkins and Charles Stewart. 2013. *Fighting for the Speakership: The House and
the Rise of Party Government*. Princeton, NJ: Princeton University Press.

10. Prior to 1839, the vote for Speaker was via secret ballot. Partisan defections, which
could not be identified, eventually led the leadership to make the balloting public. See
Jeffery A. Jenkins and Charles Stewart III. 2003. "Out in the Open: The Emergence of
Viva Voce Voting in House Speakership Elections." *Legislative Studies Quarterly* 28:
481–508.

11. Jennifer Steinhauer. September 25, 2015. "John Boehner, House Speaker, Will Resign
From Congress." *New York Times*, www.nytimes.com/2015/09/26/us/john-boehner-to
-resign-from-congress.html (accessed 8/30/18).

12. The 10 GOP defections occurred in 2015, during the replacement election. Ryan was
reelected Speaker in 2017 with only one Republican defection.

13. In 2021, Pelosi was reelected Speaker with five party defections.

14. United States Senate. "Majority and Minority Leaders, United States Senate," www
.senate.gov/artandhistory/history/common/briefing/Majority_Minority_Leaders.htm
(accessed 5/21/18).

15. Steven V. Roberts. November 29, 1984. "Dole Wins Battle to Be G.O.P. Leader in the
New Senate." *New York Times*, www.nytimes.com/1984/11/29/us/dole-wins-battle-to-be
-gop-leader-in-the-new-senate.html (accessed 5/21/18).

16. Jonathan Weisman. February 3, 2006. "In an Upset, Boehner Is Elected House GOP
Leader." *Washington Post*, www.washingtonpost.com/wp-dyn/content/article/2006/02
/02/AR2006020201046.html (accessed 5/21/18).

17. Stephen Jessee and Neil Malhotra. 2010. "Are Congressional Leaders Middlepersons or
Extremists? Yes." *Legislative Studies Quarterly* 35(3): 361–92.

18. For research in this area, see Kristin Kanthak. 2007. "Crystal Elephants and Committee
Chairs: Campaign Contributions and Leadership Races in the U.S. House of Representatives." *American Politics Research* 35(3): 389–406.

19. Every Republican Is Crucial PAC, 2010 Election cycle. OpenSecrets.org, www.open
secrets.org/pacs/expenditures.php?cmte=C00384701&cycle=2010 (accessed 5/21/18).

20. Will Lennon. November 28, 2018. "Pelosi's Prowess as a Fundraiser Helps Her Secure
Speakership." OpenSecrets.org, https://www.opensecrets.org/news/2018/11/nancy-pelosi
-returns-to-speakership/ (accessed 3/18/20).

21. Scott Meinke. 2016. *Leadership Organizations in the House of Representatives: Party
Participation and Partisan Politics*. Ann Arbor, MI: University of Michigan Press.

22. Molly E. Reynolds. November 30, 2017. "Retirement from Congress May Be Driven by Term Limits on Committee Chairs." Brookings Institution, www.brookings.edu/blog /fixgov/2017/11/30/committee-chair-term-limits-and-retirements (accessed 5/21/18).
23. Moreover, two-thirds support has typically been required to change Senate rules, rather than the normal three-fifths for other legislative matters. Richard Beth. 2013. *Procedures for Considering Changes in Senate Rules.* Washington, DC: Congressional Research Service.
24. Paul Kane. November 21, 2013. "Reid, Democrats Trigger 'Nuclear' Option; Senate Eliminates Most Nominee Filibusters in Party-Line Vote." *Washington Post,* www.washingtonpost .com/politics/senate-poised-to-limit-filibusters-in-party-line-vote-that-would-alter -centuries-of-precedent/2013/11/21/d065cfe8-52b6-11e3-9fe0-fd2ca728e67c_story .html (accessed 6/1/18).
25. Niels Lesniewski. 2014. "How the Nuclear Option Changed the Judiciary." Roll Call Blog: The World's Greatest Deliberative Body, http://blogs.rollcall.com/wgdb/nuclear -option-judiciary-nominations/?dcz (accessed 6/1/18).
26. Al Kamen and Paul Kane. December 17, 2014. "Did 'Nuclear Option' Boost Obama's Judicial Appointments?" *Washington Post,* www.washingtonpost.com/blogs/in-the-loop/wp /2014/12/17/did-nuclear-option-boost-obamas-judicial-appointments (accessed 6/1/18).
27. Alexander Bolton. April 6, 2017. "GOP Triggers 'Nuclear Option,' Gutting Filibuster in Gorsuch Fight." TheHill.com, http://thehill.com/homenews/senate/327591-gop-triggers -nuclear-option-gutting-filibuster-in-gorsuch-fight (accessed 5/21/18); Matt Flegenheimer. April 6, 2017. "Senate Republicans Deploy 'Nuclear Option' to Clear Path for Gorsuch." *New York Times,* www.nytimes.com/2017/04/06/us/politics/neil-gorsuch -supreme-court-senate.html (accessed 5/21/18).
28. Flegenheimer, "Senate Republicans Deploy 'Nuclear Option' to Clear Path for Gorsuch."
29. Nicholas Fandos. May 15, 2020. "With Move to Remote Voting, House Alters What It Means for Congress to Meet." *New York Times,* www.nytimes.com/2020/05/15/us /politics/remote-voting-house-coronavirus.html (accessed 6/4/20).
30. David Hawkings. 2013. "4 Centrists Get Money Seats in Appropriations Gavel Shuffle." Roll Call Blog: Hawkings Here, http://blogs.rollcall.com/hawkings/4-centrists-get-money -seats-in-appropriations-gavel-shuffle (accessed 6/1/18).
31. Emma Dumain. 2015. "Boehner Adds 2 Rules Republicans—Not the Ones He Booted." Roll Call Blog: 218, http://blogs.rollcall.com/218/boehner-adds-2-rules-republicans-not -ones-booted (accessed 6/1/18).
32. Marin Cogan. 2015. "The Trade Vote Reignited the War Within the House GOP." *New York Magazine: Daily Intelligencer,* http://nymag.com/daily/intelligencer/2015/06 /house-gops-family-feud.html (accessed 8/31/18); Scott Wong. June 16, 2015. "Boehner Takes His Retribution." TheHill.com, http://thehill.com/homenews/house/245136 -boehner-takes-his-retribution; Matt Fuller. 2015. "House Conservatives Emboldened, Despite Crackdown Attempt (Video)." Roll Call Blog: 218, http://blogs.rollcall.com/218 /house-conservatives-emboldened-despite-crackdown/?dcz (accessed 6/1/18).
33. Scott Wong. January 16, 2019. "How Pelosi Is Punishing Some Critics While Rewarding Others." *The Hill,* https://thehill.com/homenews/house/425744-how-pelosi-is-punishing -some-critics-while-rewarding-others (accessed 3/18/20).
34. C. Lawrence Evans and Claire Grandy. 2009. "The Whip Systems of Congress," in *Congress Reconsidered,* ed. by Lawrence Dodd and Bruce Oppenheimer, 189–215. Washington, DC: Congressional Quarterly Press.
35. Evans and Grandy, "The Whip Systems of Congress," 203–4; see also Edmund L. Andrews. July 29, 2005. "How Cafta Passed House by 2 Votes." *New York Times,* www.nytimes .com/2005/07/29/politics/how-cafta-passed-house-by-2-votes.html (accessed 5/21/18).

36. Ryan Nicol. September 22, 2020. "DCCC, NRCC Release Dueling Ads Alleging Corruption in Carlos Gimenez-Debbie Mucarsel-Powell Race." *Florida Politics*, www.florida politics.com/archives/368949-dccc-nrcc-corruption-gimenez-mucarsel-powell (accessed 2/2/21).

37. Jacob Ogles. October 15, 2018. "DCCC Cancels Ad Buy in CD 16, All But Writing Off David Shapiro." *Florida Politics*, www.floridapolitics.com/archives/277752-dccc-dumps -ad-buys-in-vern-buchanan-district (accessed 2/2/21).

38. Abby Livingston. September 18, 2020. "Republican U.S. House Campaign Arm Cancels $2 Million in Houston-area Advertising." *The Texas Tribune*, www.texastribune.org/2020 /09/18/NRCC-Houston-ads/ (accessed 2/2/21).

39. Naftali Bendavid. November 12, 2006. "The House Rahm Built." *Chicago Tribune*, www .chicagotribune.com/news/local/politics/chi-0611120215nov12-story.html#page=4 (accessed 6/1/18).

40. Kate Nocera. March 10, 2014. "House Democrats Try to Shake Down Members for Dues Payments." BuzzFeed, www.buzzfeed.com/katenocera/house-democrats-try-to-shake -down-members-for-dues-payments (accessed 8/31/18); Eric Black. April 18, 2017. "Congressional 'Dues' Help Garner Good Committee Assignments." MinnPost, www .minnpost.com/eric-black-ink/2017/04/congressional-dues-help-garner-good-committee -assignments (accessed 6/1/18).

41. Jeanine Santucci. January 10, 2020. "Alexandria Ocasio-Cortez Defends Decision Not to Pay House Democratic Campaign 'Dues.'" *USA Today*, www.usatoday.com/story/news /politics/2020/01/10/alexandria-ocasio-cortez-defends-her-decision-not-pay-dccc-dues /4435201002/ (accessed 3/18/20); Catie Edmondson. February 21, 2020. "Ocasio-Cortez Builds Progressive Campaign Arm to Challenge Democrats." *New York Times*, www .nytimes.com/2020/02/21/us/politics/aoc-democrats.html (accessed 3/18/20).

42. For more on minority party strategy, see Matthew N. Green. 2013. *Underdog Politics: The Minority Party in the U.S. House of Representatives*. New Haven, CT: Yale University Press.

43. Ron Elving. 2010. "GOP's 'Pledge' Echoes 'Contract'; But Much Myth Surrounds '94 Plan," NPR.org, www.npr.org/sections/itsallpolitics/2010/09/23/130068500/watching -washington-gop-pledge (accessed 6/1/18).

44. CQ Almanac. 1996. "104th Congress Ushers in New Era of GOP Rule," in *Congressional Quarterly Almanac 1995*. Washington, DC: CQ Press, http://0-library.cqpress.com .libraries.colorado.edu/cqalmanac/cqal95-1099419 (accessed 6/1/18).

45. A summary of the New Direction for America can be found here: www.washingtonpost .com/wp-srv/special/politics/political-rallying-cry/new-direction-for-america.pdf (accessed 3/18/20).

46. Robert Draper. 2012. *Do Not Ask What Good We Do: Inside the U.S. House of Representatives*, xix. New York: Free Press.

47. Tim Groseclose and Nolan McCarty. 2001. "The Politics of Blame: Bargaining before an Audience." *American Journal of Political Science* 45: 100–19.

48. Steven M. Gillon. 2008. *The Pact: Bill Clinton, Newt Gingrich, and the Rivalry That Defined a Generation*. New York: Oxford University Press.

49. Matt Bai. March 28, 2012. "Obama vs. Boehner: Who Killed the Debt Deal?" *New York Times*, www.nytimes.com/2012/04/01/magazine/obama-vs-boehner-who-killed-the-debt -deal.html (accessed 5/21/18).

50. David Corn. 2012. *Showdown: The Inside Story of How Obama Fought Back against Boehner, Cantor, and the Tea Party*. New York: William Morrow.

51. Megan McArdle. March 6, 2012. "The New Louisiana Purchase: Obamacare's $4.3 Billion Boondoggle," *The Atlantic*, www.theatlantic.com/business/archive/2012/03/the-new -louisiana-purchase-obamacares-43-billion-boondoggle/254003/ (accessed 6/1/18); Jordan Fabian. February 22, 2010. "Obama Healthcare Plan Nixes Ben Nelson's 'Cornhusker

Kickback' deal." TheHill.com, http://thehill.com/blogs/blog-briefing-room/news/82621 -obama-healthcare-plan-nixes-ben-nelsons-cornhusker-kickback-deal (accessed 6/1/18).

52. "President Obama Signs Executive Order on Abortion." March 24, 2010. PBS News Hour, www.pbs.org/newshour/health/president-obama-to-sign-executive-order-on -abortion (accessed 5/21/18).

53. For more on party brands, see Gary W. Cox and Mathew D. McCubbins. 2005. *Setting the Agenda: Responsible Party Government in the U.S. House of Representatives.* Cambridge, UK: Cambridge University Press; Jeffrey D. Grynaviski. 2010. *Partisan Bonds: Political Reputations and Legislative Accountability.* New York: Cambridge University Press.

54. Billy House. 2015. "Three House Republicans Said to Be Punished over Trade Vote." Bloomberg Politics, www.bloomberg.com/politics/articles/2015-06-16/three-house -republicans-said-to-be-punished-over-trade-rule-vote (accessed 8/30/18); Matt Fuller. June 17, 2015. "GOP Leadership Metes Out Retribution for Rules Votes (Updated)." Roll Call, www.rollcall.com/news/home/gop-leadership-metes-retribution-rules-votes (accessed 6/1/18).

55. "U.S. Rep. Says Calling Donors for Money Is a Shameful Distraction." April 22, 2016. CBS News, www.cbsnews.com/news/preview-dialing-for-dollars (accessed 5/21/18).

56. Heather Caygle. August 17, 2016. "How the GOP Abandoned One of Its Own." Politico, www.politico.com/story/2016/08/david-jolly-florida-party-fundraising-227020 (accessed 6/1/18).

57. Several months later, the final conference report on the legislation played out similarly. The Republicans did not have the necessary votes, and leaders held open the roll call— this time for nearly three hours—until they could obtain a majority.

58. Congressional Quarterly. 2004. "Medicare Revamp Cuts It Close," in CQ *Almanac 2003.* Washington, DC: Congressional Quarterly Press, https://library.cqpress.com/cqalmanac /document.php?id=cqal03-835-24327-1083636&type=toc&num=5 (accessed 6/1/18).

59. Sarah Binder. 2018. "Dodging the Rules in Trump's Republican Congress." *Journal of Politics* 80: 1454–63.

60. See David W. Rohde. 1991. *Parties and Leaders in the Postreform House.* Chicago, IL: University of Chicago Press; Aldrich, *Why Parties?*

61. See Gary W. Cox and Mathew D. McCubbins. 1993. *Legislative Leviathan: Party Government in the House.* Berkeley, CA: University of California Press; Cox and McCubbins, *Setting the Agenda.*

62. John Feehery. 2011. "Majority of the Majority." TheHill.com, http://thehill.com/opinion /columnists/john-feehery/174849-majority-of-the-majority (accessed 6/1/18).

63. Keith Krehbiel. 1998. *Pivotal Politics: A Theory of U.S. Lawmaking.* Chicago, IL: University of Chicago Press.

64. Keith Krehbiel. 1993. "Where's the Party?" *British Journal of Political Science* 23: 235–66.

65. Stephen Ansolabehere, James Snyder, and Charles Stewart. 2001. "The Effects of Party and Preferences on Congressional Roll-Call Voting." *Legislative Studies Quarterly* 26: 533–72; Jeffery A. Jenkins. 1999. "Examining the Bonding Effects of Party: A Compara- tive Analysis of Roll-Call Voting in the U.S. and Confederate Houses." *American Journal of Political Science* 43: 1144–65; James Snyder and Tim Groseclose. 2000. "Estimating Party Influence in Congressional Roll-Call Voting." *American Journal of Political Science* 44: 193–211; Nolan McCarty, Keith T. Poole, and Howard Rosenthal. 2001. "The Hunt for Party Discipline in Congress." *American Political Science Review* 95: 673–8.

66. Stanley P. Berard. 2012. "Southern Influence in Congress," in *Oxford Handbook of Southern Politics,* ed. by Charles Bullock and Mark Rozell. New York: Oxford University Press, 484–506; David Brady and Charles Bullock. 1980. "Is There a Conservative Coali- tion in the House?" *Journal of Politics* 42: 549–59.

67. John Wilkerson and Barry Pump. 2011. "The Ties That Bind: Coalitions in Congress," in *The Oxford Handbook of the American Congress*, ed. by Eric Schickler and Frances Lee, 618–40. Oxford: Oxford University Press.

68. Brady and Bullock, "Is There a Conservative Coalition in the House?"; Jeffery A. Jenkins and Nathan W. Monroe. 2014. "Negative Agenda Control and the Conservative Coalition in the U.S. House." *Journal of Politics* 76: 1116–27.

69. Cox and McCubbins, *Setting the Agenda*; Ira Katznelson, Kim Geiger, and Daniel Kryder. 1993. "Limiting Liberalism: The Southern Veto in Congress, 1933–1950." *Political Science Quarterly* 108: 283–306.

70. Rebecca Ballhaus. 2014. "A Short History of the Tea Party Movement," WSJ Blogs— Washington Wire, http://blogs.wsj.com/washwire/2014/02/27/a-short-history-of-the-tea -party-movement (accessed 6/1/18).

71. Robert Boatright. 2014. "The 2014 Congressional Primaries in Context" (Presented at the What the 2014 Primaries Foretell About the Future of American Politics). Washington, DC: Brookings Institution.

72. Jonathan Martin. June 10, 2014. "Eric Cantor Defeated by David Brat, Tea Party Challenger, in G.O.P. Primary Upset." *New York Times*, www.nytimes.com/2014/06/11/us /politics/eric-cantor-loses-gop-primary.html (accessed 6/1/18).

73. Michael A. Bailey, Jonathan Mummolo, and Hans Noel. 2012. "Tea Party Influence: A Story of Activists and Elites." *American Politics Research* 40: 769–809.

74. Fuller, "House Conservatives Emboldened, Despite Crackdown Attempt (Video)."

75. Matthew Green. April 16, 2019. "How the House Freedom Caucus Found an Unlikely Ally: Donald Trump." *Washington Post*, www.washingtonpost.com/politics/2019/04/15 /trump-is-heavily-influenced-by-house-freedom-caucus-minority-within-republican -minority/ (accessed 3/22/20); Peter Baker. March 6, 2020. "Trump Names Mark Meadows Chief of Staff, Ousting Mick Mulvaney." The New York Times, www.nytimes. com/2020/03/06/us/politics/trump-mark-meadows-mick-mulvaney.html (accessed 2/2/21).

76. Natalie Andrew and Lindsay Wise. November 8, 2019. "House Freedom Caucus Emerges as Trump's Main Defenders." *Wall Street Journal*, www.wsj.com/articles/house-freedom -caucus-emerges-as-trumps-main-defender-11573214400 (accessed 3/22/20).

77. Frances E. Lee. 2016. "How Party Polarization Affects Governance." *Annual Review of Political Science* 18: 261–82. In effect, these are the two primary conditions of conditional party government.

78. See Keith T. Poole and Howard Rosenthal. 2007. *Ideology and Congress*. New Brunswick, NJ: Transaction Publishers.

79. Katznelson, Geiger, and Kryder, "Limiting Liberalism."

80. Brian Schaffner. 2011. "Party Polarization," in *The Oxford Handbook of the American Congress*, ed. by Eric Schickler and Frances Lee, 527–49. Oxford: Oxford University Press.

81. Laurel Harbridge. 2015. *Is Bipartisanship Dead?: Policy Agreement and Agenda-Setting in the House of Representatives*. New York: Cambridge University Press.

82. Thomas E. Mann and Norman J. Ornstein. 2012. *It's Even Worse Than It Looks: How the American Constitutional System Collided with the New Politics of Extremism*. New York: Basic Books.

83. Elena Schneider. August 2, 2016. "Huelskamp Loses GOP Primary after Ideological Battle." Politico, www.politico.com/story/2016/08/huelskamp-defeated-in-kansas -primary-226603 (accessed 6/1/18).

# Chapter 7: Policy Making in the House and Senate

1. Kent Allen. January 3, 2011. "2010 Key House Vote: Immigration Policy." CQ *Weekly* 72.
2. The Reapportionment Act of 1929.
3. Joseph Story. 1891. *Commentaries on the Constitution of the United States*, two volumes, 5th ed., ed. by Melville Bigelow. Boston, MA: Little, Brown.
4. "Biennial Elections." n.d. *US House of Representatives: History, Art & Archives*, http://history .house.gov/Institution/Origins-Development/Biennial-Elections (accessed 7/14/18).
5. U.S. Senate. n.d. "U.S. Senate: The Senate and the United States Constitution." www.senate .gov/artandhistory/history/common/briefing/Constitution_Senate.htm (accessed 7/5/18).
6. "Constitutional Qualifications." n.d. *US House of Representatives: History, Art & Archives*, http://history.house.gov/Institution/Origins-Development/Constitutional-Qualifications (accessed 7/5/18).
7. Alexander Hamilton, James Madison, and John Jay. 2012. *The Federalist Papers*, no. 62, 1st ed., ed. by Richard Beeman. New York: Penguin Books.
8. James Madison and Adrienne Koch. 1985. *Notes of Debates in the Federal Convention of 1787*, 2nd ed. Athens, OH: Ohio University Press.
9. Hamilton, Madison, and Jay, *The Federalist Papers*, no. 39.
10. Hamilton, Madison, and Jay, *The Federalist Papers*, no. 52.
11. "Power of the Purse." n.d. *US House of Representatives: History, Art & Archives*, http:// history.house.gov/Institution/Origins-Development/Power-of-the-Purse (accessed 7/5/18).
12. Diamond, *Origins and Development of Congress*, 53–54.
13. Richard F. Fenno. 1982. *The United States Senate: A Bicameral Perspective*, 5. Washington, DC: AEI Press.
14. Hamilton, Madison, and Jay, *The Federalist Papers*, no. 62.
15. Diamond, *Origins and Development of Congress*, 175.
16. Diamond, *Origins and Development of Congress*, 3.
17. This description of the Senate is often attributed to President James Buchanan.
18. Diamond, *Origins and Development of Congress*, 175.
19. George Packer. August 2, 2010. "The Empty Chamber." *New Yorker*, 38–51.
20. Frances E. Lee. 2016. *Insecure Majorities: Congress and the Perpetual Campaign*. Chicago, IL: University of Chicago Press.
21. Ryan Clancy. June 28, 2019. "Unglamorous rules change helps a big bill pass." *The Hill*, https://thehill.com/blogs/congress-blog/politics/450714-unglamorous-rules-change-helps -a-big-bill-pass (accessed 2/9/2020).
22. Jane A. Hudiburg. 2020. "Suspension of the Rules: House Practice in the 115th Congress (2017–2018)." *CRS Report for Congress*. Washington, DC: Congressional Research Service.
23. James Wallner. 2017. "A Beginner's Guide to the Senate's Rules." *R Street Policy Study*. Washington, DC: R Street Institute. For an explanation of precedents, see Alan Frumin. 1992. *Riddick's Senate Procedure: Precedents and Practices*. Washington, DC: U.S. Govern-ment Printing Office.
24. Keith Krehbiel. 1991. *Information and Legislative Organization*. Ann Arbor, MI: University of Michigan
25. Bryan Marshall. 2002. "Explaining the Role of Restrictive Rules in the Postreform House." *Legislative Studies Quarterly* 27: 61–86.
26. Oleszek, *Congressional Procedures and the Policy Process*, 181–82.
27. Molly Reynolds. April 16, 2018. "Procedural Hurdles for the Mueller Protection Bills." *Lawfare* (blog), www.lawfareblog.com/procedural-hurdles-mueller-protection-bills (accessed 7/5/18).
28. Kathryn Pearson and Eric Schickler. 2009. "Discharge Petitions, Agenda Control, and the Congressional Committee System, 1929–76." *Journal of Politics* 71: 1238–56.

29. Catherine Lucey, Kevin Freking, and Matthew Daly. June 27, 2018. "House Rejects Republican Immigration Bill, Ignoring Trump." *Associated Press*, https://wtop.com /government/2018/06/gop-immigration-bill-faces-likely-defeat-in-showdown-vote/ (accessed 7/5/18).

30. Stephen A. Jessee and Sean M. Theriault. 2014. "The Two Faces of Congressional Roll Call Voting." *Party Politics* 20(6): 836–48.

31. Valerie Heitshusen. 2017. "The Legislative Process on the Senate Floor: An Introduction." *CRS Report for Congress*. Washington, DC: Congressional Research Service.

32. CNN, Tal Kopan, Phil Mattingly, and Deirdre Walsh. February 9, 2018. "Trump Signs Massive Budget Deal." CNN Politics, www.cnn.com/2018/02/08/politics/budget-vote -congress-shutdown/index.html (accessed 7/5/18).

33. There are some exceptions where germaneness is required, including on appropriations bills and budget measures, and after cloture has been invoked.

34. "Most Memorable Filibusters in Modern American History." March 6, 2013. *Fox News*, www .foxnews.com/politics/2013/03/06/most-memorable-filibusters-in-modern-american -history.html; Emily Keeler. September 25, 2013. "Ted Cruz Reads Dr. Seuss and Ayn Rand to Stall Senate." *Los Angeles Times*, http://articles.latimes.com/2013/sep/25/entertainment /la-et-jc-ted-cruz-dr-seuss-ayn-rand-to-stall-senate-20130925 (accessed 9/14/18).

35. Valerie Heitshusen. 2017. "The Legislative Process on the Senate Floor: An Introduction." *CRS Report for Congress*, 5. Washington, DC: Congressional Research Service.

36. Packer, "The Empty Chamber."

37. Oleszek, *Congressional Procedures and the Policy Process*, 255–57.

38. Evan McMorris-Santoro. February 4, 2010. "Report: Shelby Blocks All Obama Nominations in the Senate over AL Earmarks." *Talking Points Memo* (blog), https://talkingpointsmemo .com/dc/report-shelby-blocks-all-obama-nominations-in-the-senate-over-al-earmarks (accessed 7/5/18).

39. Gregory Koger. 2010. *Filibustering: A Political History of Obstruction in the House and Senate*. Chicago, IL: University of Chicago Press. Note that Koger has a broad list of obstruction tactics that he includes in his count of filibusters. See also the work of Gregory Wawro and Eric Schickler. 2006. *Filibuster: Obstruction and Lawmaking in the U.S. Senate*. Princeton, NJ: Princeton University Press.

40. David Lightman. February 12, 2010. "Senate Republicans: Filibuster Everything to Win in November?" *McClatchy Newspapers*, www.mcclatchydc.com/news/politics-government /article24573448.html (accessed 7/5/18).

41. Sarah Binder. November 12, 2013. "What Senate Cloture Votes Tell Us about Obstruction." Monkey Cage, *Washington Post* (blog), www.washingtonpost.com/news/monkey-cage/wp /2013/11/12/what-senate-cloture-votes-tell-us-about-obstruction (accessed 7/5/18).

42. Talking Points Memo. January 27, 2010. "The Rise Of Cloture: How GOP Filibuster Threats Have Changed the Senate." *Talking Points Memo* (blog), https://talkingpointsmemo .com/dc/the-rise-of-cloture-how-gop-filibuster-threats-have-changed-the-senate (accessed 7/5/18).

43. Sarah A. Binder and Steven Smith. 1996. *Politics or Principle? Filibustering in the United States Senate*. Washington, DC: Brookings Institution Press.

44. See Lee, *Insecure Majorities: Congress and the Perpetual Campaign*, Chapter 6, for a discussion of majority- and minority-party use of floor votes in the Senate on amendments for purposes of partisan communications.

45. Lisa Mascaro. February 12, 2018. "Senators Begin Freewheeling Immigration Debate, and It's Anyone's Guess Where It Will End Up." *Los Angeles Times* (online), www.latimes.com /politics/la-na-pol-immigration-senate-20180212-story.html (accessed 7/5/18).

46. "Healthy Congress Index." *Bipartisan Policy Center*, https://bipartisanpolicy.org/congress (accessed 05/28/18).

# Chapter 8: The Legislative Effectiveness of Congress and Its Members: Governing, Policy Making, and the Budget

1. Lauren French. March 12, 2016. "Congress Setting New Bar for Doing Nothing." Politico, www.politico.com/story/2016/03/congress-supreme-court-budget-do-nothing-221057 (accessed 9/14/18); Aaron Blake. December 20, 2016. "The 'Do-Nothing Congress' Graduates to the 'Do-Nothing-Much Congress.'" The Fix, *Washington Post* (blog), www.washingtonpost.com/news/the-fix/wp/2016/12/20/the-do-nothing-congress-graduates-to-the-do-nothing-much-congress (accessed 9/14/18).

2. Cristina Marcos. July 13, 2014. "A 'Do-Nothing Congress'?" TheHill.com, http://thehill.com/blogs/floor-action/212041-a-do-nothing-congress (accessed 9/14/18); Derek Willis. May 28, 2014. "A Do-Nothing Congress? Well, Pretty Close." *New York Times*, www.nytimes.com/2014/05/28/upshot/a-do-nothing-congress-well-pretty-close.html (accessed 9/14/18).

3. Norman Ornstein. July 19, 2011. "Worst. Congress. Ever." *Foreign Policy*, https://foreignpolicy.com/2011/07/19/worst-congress-ever/ (accessed 9/26/20).

4. Steny Hoyer. December 22, 2017. "Do-Nothing 115th GOP Congress." (press release) www.majorityleader.gov/content/do-nothing-115th-gop-congress (accessed 4/26/2020).

5. Joseph Cooper and David Brady. 1981. "Toward a Diachronic Analysis of Congress." *American Political Science Review* 75: 988–1012

6. Thad Hall. 2004. *Authorizing Policy.* Columbus, OH: Ohio State University Press.

7. John Kingdon. 1995. *Agendas, Alternatives, and Public Policies,* 2nd ed. New York: HarperCollins; E. Scott Adler and John Wilkerson. 2012. *Congress and the Politics of Problem Solving.* New York: Cambridge University Press.

8. Rebecca M. Kysar. 2006. "The Sun Also Rises: The Political Economy of Sunset Provisions in the Tax Code." *Georgia Law Review* 40: 335–405.

9. Kysar, "The Sun Also Rises: The Political Economy of Sunset Provisions in the Tax Code."

10. E. Scott Adler, Stefani R. Langehennig, and Ryan W. Bell. 2020. "Congressional Capacity and Reauthorizations," in *Congress Overwhelmed: The Decline in Congressional Capacity and Prospects for Reform,* ed. by Timothy M. LaPira, Lee Drutman and Kevin R. Kosar. Chicago, IL: University of Chicago Press.

11. Danny Vinik. February 3, 2016. "Meet Your Unauthorized Federal Government." Politico, www.politico.com/agenda/story/2016/02/government-agencies-programs-unauthorized-000036-000037 (accessed 6/19/18).

12. Robert Pear. January 1, 2012. "After Three Decades, Federal Tax Credit for Ethanol Expires." *New York Times*.

13. "Causes and Effects of the July–August 2011 Partial Shutdown of the Federal Aviation Administration." March 19, 2012. *The Center for the Study of the Presidency & Congress—Presidential Fellows Blog*, https://presidentialfellows.wordpress.com/2012/03/19/causes-and-effects-of-the-july-august-2011-partial-shutdown-of-the-federal-aviation-administration/ (accessed 6/19/18).

14. Glen Krutz. 2001. *Hitching a Ride: Omnibus Legislating in the U.S. Congress.* Columbus, OH: Ohio State University Press.

15. Nolan McCarty. 2016. "The Decline of Regular Order in Appropriations: Does It Matter?," in *Congress and Policy Making in the 21st Century,* ed. by Jeffery Jenkins and Eric Patashnik, 162–86. New York: Cambridge University Press.

16. McCarty, "The Decline of Regular Order in Appropriations: Does It Matter?"

17. D. Andrew Austin. August 29, 2019. "The Debt Limit Since 2011," *CRS Report for Congress.* Washington, DC: Congressional Research Service.

18. In his agreement with Congress, President Obama signed legislation (the Budget Control Act of 2011) creating the Joint Select Committee on Deficit Reduction, commonly called the "supercommittee." Its charge was to propose and have Congress enact a reduction in federal spending by $1.2 trillion over 10 years. If it failed in this responsibility, there would be across-the-board cuts in discretionary and defense spending of the same amount. After a flurry of negotiations, a deal was never reached, and the cuts were made.

19. Frances Lee and Timothy Cordova. 2015. "The 'Ins' vs. the 'Outs': The Congressional Politics of the Debt Limit, 1953–2014." Paper given at the History of Congress Conference, Vanderbilt University.

20. Molly Reynolds. 2019. *Vital Statistics on Congress.* Washington, DC: Brookings Institution Report. www.brookings.edu/multi-chapter-report/vital-statistics-on-congress (accessed 5/10/2019). Table 6-2.

21. Molly Reynolds. 2019. *Vital Statistics on Congress.* Washington, DC: Brookings Institution Report, www.brookings.edu/multi-chapter-report/vital-statistics-on-congress/ (accessed 5/10/2019). Table 6-4.

22. Mayhew initially ended the series in 1990, but he has subsequently updated the list at the end of each congressional term.

23. William Howell, Scott Adler, Charles Cameron, and Charles Riemann. 2000. "Divided Government and the Legislative Productivity of Congress, 1945–94." *Legislative Studies Quarterly* 25: 285–312.

24. Joshua Clinton and John S. Lapinski. 2006. "Measuring Legislative Accomplishment, 1877–1994." *American Journal of Political Science* 50: 232–49.

25. Sarah Binder. 2003. *Stalemate: Causes and Consequences of Legislative Gridlock.* Washington, DC: Brookings Institution Press.

26. R. Douglas Arnold. 2016. "Explaining Legislative Achievement," in *Congress and Policy Making in the 21st Century,* ed. by Jeffery A. Jenkins and Eric M. Patashnik, 301–23. New York: Cambridge University Press.

27. Richard Fenno. 1978. *Home Style: House Members in Their Districts.* Glenview, IL: Scott Foresman & Co.

28. Gary Jacobson. 2012. *The Politics of Congressional Elections,* 8th ed. Boston, MA: Pearson.

29. Craig Volden and Alan E. Wiseman. 2014. *Legislative Effectiveness in the United States Congress: The Lawmakers,* 18. New York: Cambridge University Press.

30. A second and related line of research is to examine the progress of individual bills, which allows us to also examine which characteristics of the bills themselves make them more likely to pass.

31. Edward B. Hasecke and Jason D. Mycoff. December 1, 2007. "Party Loyalty and Legislative Success: Are Loyal Majority Party Members More Successful in the U.S. House of Representatives?" *Political Research Quarterly* 60(4): 607–17; William D. Anderson, Janet M. Box-Steffensmeier, and Valeria Sinclair-Chapman. August 2003. "The Keys to Legislative Success in the U.S. House of Representatives." *Legislative Studies Quarterly* 28(3): 357–86; Gary Cox and William Terry. November 2008. "Legislative Productivity in the 93d–105th Congresses." *Legislative Studies Quarterly* 33: 603–18.

32. Gregory Koger and James Fowler. 2006. "Parties and Agenda-Setting in the Senate, 1973–1998." Manuscript, University of California, San Diego.

33. Cox and Terry, "Legislative Productivity in the 93d–105th Congresses."

34. Adler and Wilkerson, *Congress and the Politics of Problem Solving.*

35. Stephen Frantzich. August 1979. "Who Makes Our Laws? The Legislative Effectiveness of Members of the U. S. Congress." *Legislative Studies Quarterly* 4(3): 409–28; Cox and

Terry, "Legislative Productivity in the 93d–105th Congresses"; Adler and Wilkerson, *Congress and the Politics of Problem Solving.*

36. Koger and Fowler, "Parties and Agenda-Setting in the Senate, 1973–1998." Anderson, Box-Steffensmeier, and Sinclair-Chapman. "The Keys to Legislative Success in the U.S. House of Representatives"; Glen Krutz. 2005. "Issues and Institutions: 'Winnowing' in the U.S. Congress." *American Journal of Political Science* 49: 313–26.

37. Jennifer L. Lawless, Sean M. Theriault, and Samantha Guthrie. 2018. "Nice Girls? Sex, Collegiality, and Bipartisan Cooperation in the US Congress." *Journal of Politics* 80: 1268–82.

38. Craig Volden, Alan E. Wiseman, and Dana E. Wittmer. 2013. "When Are Women More Effective Lawmakers Than Men?" *American Journal of Political Science* 57: 326–41.

39. Peverill Squire. 1992. "Legislative Professionalization and Membership Diversity in State Legislatures." *Legislative Studies Quarterly* 17: 69–79.

40. Donald Matthews. 1960. *U.S. Senators and Their World.* New York: Vintage Books.

41. Norman Ornstein, Robert Peabody, and David Rohde. 1977. "The Changing Senate: From the 1950s to the 1970s," in *Congress Reconsidered*, 1st ed., ed. by Lawrence Dodd and Bruce Oppenheimer, 3–20. New York: Praeger Publishers; David Rohde, Norman Ornstein, and Robert Peabody. 1985. "Political Change and Legislative Norms in the U.S. Senate, 1957–1974," in *Studies of Congress*, 147–88. Washington, DC: Congressional Quarterly Press.

42. Steven Smith. 1989. *Call to Order: Floor Politics in the House and Senate*, illustrated edition. Washington, DC: Brookings Institution Press.

43. Matthews, *U.S. Senators and Their World.*

44. Richard L. Hall. 1996. *Participation in Congress.* New Haven, CT: Yale University Press.

45. Ralph K. Huitt. 1961. "The Outsider in the Senate: An Alternative Role." *American Political Science Review* 55: 566–75; Eric Schickler. 2012. "The U.S. Senate in the Mid-Twentieth Century," in *The U.S. Senate: From Deliberation to Dysfunction*, ed. by Burdett Loomis, 27–48. Washington, DC: CQ Press.

46. Robert A. Caro. 2002. *Master of the Senate: The Years of Lyndon Johnson III*, 1st ed. New York: Knopf.

47. Barbara Sinclair. 1989. *The Transformation of the U.S. Senate.* Baltimore, MD: Johns Hopkins University Press.

48. Sinclair, *The Transformation of the U.S. Senate*; Smith, *Call to Order: Floor Politics in the House and Senate.*

49. Ornstein, Peabody, and Rohde, "The Changing Senate: From the 1950s to the 1970s."

50. Craig Volden and Alan Wiseman. 2018. "Legislative Effectiveness in the United States Senate," *The Journal of Politics*, 80(2): 731–5.

51. Michele L. Swers. 2013. *Women in the Club: Gender and Policy Making in the Senate.* Chicago, IL: University of Chicago Press.

52. James M. Curry and Frances E. Lee. 2019. "Congress at Work: Legislative Capacity and Entrepreneurship in the Contemporary Congress," in *Can America Govern Itself?* 181–219. New York: Cambridge University Press.

## Chapter 9: Congress and the President

1. Joe Heim. March 11, 2019. *Washington Post*, www.washingtonpost.com/news/magazine/wp/2019/03/11/feature/nancy-pelosi-on-impeaching-president-trump-hes-just-not-worth-it/ (accessed 6/14/2020).

2. The transcript can be read at www.cnn.com/2019/09/25/politics/donald-trump-ukraine-transcript-call/index.html.

3. October 17, 2019. "Mick Mulvaney Briefing Transcript: 'Get Over It' Regarding Ukraine Quid Pro Quo." www.rev.com/blog/transcripts/mick-mulvaney-briefing-transcript-get-over-it-regarding-ukraine-quid-pro-quo (accessed 8/13/20).

4. Rev.com. January 13, 2021. "Kevin McCarthy Speech Transcript as House Debates 2nd Trump Impeachment." www.rev.com/blog/transcripts/kevin-mccarthy-speech-transcript-as-house-debates-2nd-trump-impeachment (accessed 1/21/21).

5. As with nearly every other issue, the Framers disagreed about how much power the president should have. Alexander Hamilton, true to his federalist leanings, preferred a strong executive (see Alexander Hamilton, 1788, *The Federalist Papers*, no. 70), while Thomas Jefferson predictably viewed the position with suspicion.

6. See Richard Neustadt. 1960. *Presidential Power: The Politics of Leadership*. New York: Wiley (as well as the foundations of this view in James Madison, 1787, *The Federalist Papers*, no. 51).

7. See Brian Balogh. 2009. *A Government Out of Sight*. New York: Cambridge University Press; and Paul Frymer. 2017. *Building an American Empire*. Princeton, NJ: Princeton University Press.

8. Data drawn from John Woolley and Gerhard Peters. 1999–2018. "Presidential Vetoes." *The American Presidency Project*. Santa Barbara, CA: University of California. www.presidency.ucsb.edu/data/vetoes.php (accessed 7/25/18).

9. Alex Ward. March 23, 2020. "Trump's excuses for not using the Defense Production Act are wrong—and dangerous." Vox, www.vox.com/2020/3/23/21191003/coronavirus-trump-defense-production-act-venezuela (accessed 6/14/20).

10. According to press reports, this command caught the leaders of General Motors by surprise, because they had already announced that they were already planning to manufacture ventilators. David E. Sanger, Maggie Haberman, and Annie Karni. "Under Intense Criticism, Trump Says Government Will Buy More Ventilators." *New York Times*, www.nytimes.com/2020/03/27/us/politics/coronavirus-trump-ventilators-gm-ventec.html (accessed 6/14/20).

11. Fisher, *The Politics of Shared Power: Congress and the Executive*, 16.

12. Of course, Congress has the power of the purse, which means that it controls spending. It can constrain the president's authority to execute laws by limiting funding to agencies, and it can manage the president's control of the military by choosing whether to appropriate funds. In addition, the War Powers Act gives Congress, and not the president, the power to declare war.

13. A variant of the veto is the pocket veto, where the president can effectively veto a bill that Congress sends to him during the final ten days of a congressional session by taking no action on it.

14. See the discussion in Louis Fisher. 2007. *Constitutional Conflicts between Congress and the President*, 5th ed., 116–19. Lawrence, KS: University of Kansas Press.

15. In addition, there are other powers that presidents use that do not appear in the Constitution, some of which Congress gave to them (for example, that the president starts the budget process by formally submitting a budget) and others that they claimed on their own (such as signing statements, which we discuss later in this chapter).

16. Ronald Reagan. January 25, 1983. "Address before a Joint Session of the Congress on the State of the Union." *The American Presidency Project*, www.presidency.ucsb.edu/ws/index.php?pid=41698 (accessed 6/13/18).

17. Paul C. Light. 1982. *The President's Agenda: Domestic Policy Choice from Kennedy to Carter (with Notes on Ronald Reagan)*, 158. Baltimore, MD: Johns Hopkins University Press.

18. See, for example, Andrew Rudalevige. 2002. *Managing the President's Program: Presidential Leadership and Legislative Policy Formulation*. Princeton, NJ: Princeton University

Press; and Jeffrey Cohen. 2012. *The President's Legislative Policy Agenda, 1789–2002.* New York: Cambridge University Press.

19. Neustadt, *Presidential Power: The Politics of Leadership*, 11.

20. Neustadt, *Presidential Power: The Politics of Leadership*, 40.

21. George Edwards. 2009. "Presidential Approval as a Source of Influence in Congress," in *The Oxford Handbook of the American Presidency*, ed. by George C. Edwards and William Howell, 339–61. New York: Oxford University Press.

22. See Andrew Rudalevige. May 13, 2005. "The Structure of Leadership: Presidents, Hierarchies, and Information Flow." *Presidential Studies Quarterly* 35(2): 434–6.

23. Patricia H. Conley. 2001. *Presidential Mandates: How Elections Shape the National Agenda*, 86–115. Chicago, IL: University of Chicago Press.

24. Stephen J. Wayne. 2009. "Legislative Skills," in *The Oxford Handbook of the American Presidency*, ed. by George C. Edwards and William Howell, 311–37. New York: Oxford University Press.

25. Michael R. Gordon. October 20, 1990. "The Budget Battle; Cheney May Seek Veto Unless Pentagon Is Heeded on Arms Budget." *New York Times*, www.nytimes.com/1990 /10/20/us/the-budget-battle-cheney-may-seek-veto-unless-pentagon-is-heeded-on-arms -budget.html (accessed 6/13/18).

26. See Laurie L. Rice. 2010. "Statements of Power: Presidential Use of Statements of Administration Policy and Signing Statements in the Legislative Process." *Presidential Studies Quarterly* 40: 686–707, for a more detailed discussion of statements of administrative policy.

27. Leo Shane III. September 8, 2017. "White House Objects to Military Pay, Housing Changes in Senate Budget Bill." *Military Times*, www.militarytimes.com/pay-benefits /2017/09/08/white-house-objects-to-military-pay-housing-changes-in-senate-budget -bill/ (accessed 6/13/18).

28. Samuel Kernell. 2007. *Going Public: New Strategies of Presidential Leadership.* Washington, DC: CQ Press.

29. The president has such a bully pulpit by virtue of being the single politician in the United States who is elected by the entire country, which, combined with the increasing power of the presidency over time, means that the media pay enormous attention to whatever presidents say or do.

30. George Skelton. March 14, 1985. "'Make My Day': Reagan Assails Congress, Vows Tax Hike Veto." *LA Times*, www.articles.latimes.com/1985-03-14/news/mn-26514_1 _spending-cuts (accessed 6/13/18).

31. Sean Sullivan, John Wagner, and Kelsey Snell. June 12, 2017. "Trump: 'I Will Be Very Angry' If GOP Senators Don't Pass a Health-Care Bill." *Washington Post*, www .washingtonpost.com/politics/trump-i-will-be-very-angry-if-gop-senators-dont-pass-a -health-care-bill/2017/07/12/cad615ae-673b-11e7-a1d7-9a32c91c6f40_story.html (accessed 6/13/18).

32. Matthew Eshbaugh-Soha and Thomas Miles. 2011. "Presidential Speeches and the Stages of the Legislative Process." *Congress & the Presidency* 38(3): 301–21.

33. Elizabeth Mann Levesque. 2019. "Waiving Goodbye to Congressional Constraints: Presidents and Subnational Policy Making." *Presidential Studies Quarterly* 49(2) (2019): 358–93.

34. Ian Ostrander and Joel Sievert. 2013. "What's So Sinister about Presidential Signing Statements?" *Presidential Studies Quarterly* 43: 58–80.

35. To counter Trump's announcement, Speaker Pelosi announced that she would create a bipartisan select committee that would have subpoena power to oversee the administration's distribution of the funds. Trump also fired the inspector general and the head of a

panel Congress set up to oversee the administration's management of the stimulus package.

36. "Minimizing the Economic Burden of the Patient Protection and Affordable Care Act Pending Repeal," Executive Order 13765. January 20, 2017, www.federalregister.gov /documents/2017/01/24/2017-01799/minimizing-the-economic-burden-of-the-patient -protection-and-affordable-care-act-pending-repeal (accessed 7/25/18).

37. For example, Barack Obama issued 34.6 executive orders per year, the fewest among recent presidents, slightly fewer than George W. Bush's 36.4, Bill Clinton's 45.5, George H. W. Bush's 41.5, and Ronald Reagan's 47.6. In the first three years of his term, Donald Trump issued an average of 46 executive orders per year. For perspective, FDR issued an average of 307 executive orders per year! For data on executive orders, see Amrita Khalid. June 3, 2016. "The Number of Executive Orders by Every U.S. President." *The Daily Dot*, www.dailydot.com/layer8/number-of-executive-orders-per -president (accessed 7/25/18); and www.federalregister.gov/presidential-documents /executive-orders (accessed 3/31/20).

38. Regarding the limits of signing statements, see Ostrander and Sievert, "The Logic of Presidential Signing Statements;" and Ian Ostrander and Joel Sievert. 2014. "Presidential Signing Statements and the Durability of the Law." *Congress & the Presidency* 41(3): 141–53. For a discussion of the ways in which waivers are not a pure unilateral strategy, see Mann, "Presidential Policymaking at the State Level: Revision through Waivers."

39. Paul E. Rutledge and Heather A. Larsen-Price. 2014. "The President as Agenda Setter-in-Chief: The Dynamics of Congressional and Presidential Agenda Setting." *Policy Studies Journal* 42(3): 443–64.

40. Rudalevige, *Managing the President's Program*.

41. Cohen, *The President's Legislative Policy Agenda, 1789–2002*, 157.

42. James P. Pfiffner. 1996. *The Strategic Presidency: Hitting the Ground Running*, 112. Lawrence, KS: University of Kansas Press.

43. Consistent with this view, scholars have found that presidents propose more policy initiatives to the first Congress they work with than to the second. See George C. Edwards III and Andrew Barrett. 2000. "Presidential Agenda Setting in Congress," in *Polarized Politics: Congress and the President in a Partisan Era*, ed. by Jon Bond and Richard Fleisher, 126. Washington, DC: Congressional Quarterly Press.

44. Quoted in Paul C. Light. 1999. *The President's Agenda: Domestic Policy Choice from Kennedy to Clinton*, 3rd edition, 43. Baltimore, MD: Johns Hopkins University Press. Light also notes that "presidents set their domestic agendas early and repeat them often," p. 41 (italics in original).

45. Mark A. Peterson. 1990. *Legislating Together: The White House and Capitol Hill from Eisenhower to Reagan*, 95–6, 152–7. Cambridge, MA: Harvard University Press.

46. Heather A. Larsen-Price and Paul Rutledge. 2013. "Follow the Leader: Issue-Dependent Representation in American Political Institutions." *Congress & the Presidency* 40(1): 1.

47. John Lovett, Shaun Bevan, and Frank R. Baumgartner. 2015. "Popular Presidents Can Affect Congressional Attention, for a Little While." *Policy Studies Journal* 43(1): 22–43. Presidents influence congressional attention under unified government when they have approval ratings in the upper 50s or higher. Under divided government, these ratings need to be in the 80s or above to produce a significant change in congressional attention. Roger T. Larocca also finds that the effect fades rather quickly over time (2006. *The Presidential Agenda: Sources of Executive Influence in Congress*. Columbus, OH: Ohio State Press).

48. The quote, as well as the more general claims, come from Rudalevige, *Managing the President's Program*, 63.

49. Rudalevige, *Managing the President's Program*.

50. See Brandice Canes-Wrone and Scott de Marchi. 2002. "Presidential Approval and Legislative Success." *Journal of Politics* 64(2): 491–509

51. Tom Raum. July 28, 1981. "Hill Flooded with Phone Calls, Telegrams." *Associated Press.*

52. See George C. Edwards III. 2003. *On Deaf Ears: The Limits of the Bully Pulpit.* New Haven, CT: Yale University Press; and George C. Edwards III. 2015. *Overreach: Leadership in the Obama Presidency.* Princeton, NJ: Princeton University Press.

53. This section draws on Brandice Canes-Wrone. 2001. "The President's Legislative Influence from Public Appeals." *American Journal of Political Science* 45(2): 313–29.

54. Interestingly, the effectuality of public appeals is not limited to popular presidents. Presidents with lower levels of popularity can also increase their chances of legislative success by appealing to the public, although the effect is smaller. See Brandice Canes-Wrone. 2004. "The Public Presidency, Personal Approval Ratings, and Policy Making." *Presidential Studies Quarterly* 34(3): 477–92.

55. Bryan Marshall. 2012. "Congress and the Executive: Unilateralism and Legislative Bargaining," in *New Directions in Congressional Politics*, ed. by Jamie L. Carson, 183–201. New York: Routledge. See D. Roderick Kiewiet and Matthew D. McCubbins. 1988. "Presidential Influence on Congressional Appropriations Decisions." *American Journal of Political Science* 32(30): 713–36 for an argument that veto threats are more effective at getting Congress to do less (e.g., to cut spending) than to do more (e.g., to increase spending).

56. Brian W. Marshall and Bruce C. Wolpe. 2018. *The Committee: A Study of Policy, Power, Politics and Obama's Historic Legislative Agenda on Capitol Hill.* Ann Arbor, MI: University of Michigan Press.

57. Howell shows that executive orders increase under divided government, while Kenneth Mayer. 2002. *With the Stroke of a Pen: Executive Orders and Presidential Power.* Princeton, NJ: Princeton University Press, does not. Alexander Bolton and Sharece Thrower. 2016. "Legislative Capacity and Executive Unilateralism." *American Journal of Political Science* 60(3): 649–63 (doi:10.1111/ajps.12190), suggest a middle ground: in the past, divided government led to more executive orders, but this has been less true in recent decades, because Congress now has a greater capacity to constrain the president.

58. See Barbara Sinclair. 2006. *Party Wars: Polarization and the Politics of National Policymaking*, 247. Norman, OK: University of Oklahoma Press.

59. Kernell, *Going Public: New Strategies of Presidential Leadership*, 216. Jeff Cummins. 2010. "The Partisan Considerations of the President's Agenda." *Polity* 42(3): 398–422, shows that the State of the Union increases the president's chance of success regarding the domestic agenda, but only during unified government and if polarization is average or low.

60. See Daniel Paul Franklin and Michael P. Fix. 2016. "The Best of Times and the Worst of Times: Polarization and Presidential Success in Congress." *Congress & the Presidency* 43(3): 377–94.

61. See William G. Howell and Jon C. Rogowski. 2013. "War, the Presidency, and Legislative Voting Behavior." *American Journal of Political Science* 57: 150–66. Interestingly, they do not find evidence of such an effect during the Korean or Vietnam Wars. William G. Howell, Saul P. Jackman, and Jon C. Rogowski. 2012. "The Wartime President: Insights, Lessons, and Opportunities for Continued Investigation." *Presidential Studies Quarterly* 42(4): 791–810, argue that this effect occurs because national, as opposed to local, considerations are heightened during war, and the president has clear information advantages.

62. For a more nuanced view of these agreements, see Glen S. Krutz and Jeffrey S. Peake. 2009. *Treaty Politics and the Rise of Executive Agreements.* Ann Arbor, MI: University of Michigan Press, who point out that while executive agreements give presidents a

bargaining advantage, many of them either are based on statutes or require at least some congressional action.

63. The Trump administration, however, chose not to implement any sanctions, and Congress did not act to force it to do so.
64. Peterson, *Legislating Together.*
65. See John R. Johannes. July 1974. "The President Proposes and Congress Disposes—But Not Always: Legislative Initiative on Capitol Hill," *Review of Politics* 36.
66. Charles R. Shipan. 2006. "Does Divided Government Increase the Size of the Legislative Agenda?" in *The Macro-Politics of Congress*, eds. Scott Adler and John Lapinski.
67. Jordan Carney. May 23, 2017. "McCain: Trump's Budget 'Dead on Arrival.'" TheHill .com, http://thehill.com/blogs/floor-action/senate/334731-mccain-trumps-budget-dead -on-arrival (accessed 6/13/18).
68. Carney, "McCain: Trump's Budget 'Dead on Arrival.'"
69. This logic, and the following example, is spelled out in Tim Groseclose and Nolan McCarty. 2001. "The Politics of Blame: Bargaining before an Audience." *American Journal of Political Science* 45(1): 100–19.
70. A more recent example occurred in 2015 when Congress was working on an infrastructure bill that included the controversial Keystone Pipeline. After a spokesperson for President Obama indicated that the president was unlikely to sign the legislation, Senate Majority Leader Mitch McConnell (R-Ky.) publicly rebuked the president: "The president threatening to veto the first bipartisan infrastructure bill of the new Congress must come as a shock to the American people who spoke loudly in November in favor of bipartisan accomplishments" (Coral Davenport. January 6, 2015. "With Veto Threat, Obama and Congress Head for Collision over Keystone Pipeline." *New York Times*, www.nytimes.com /2015/01/07/us/politics/with-veto-threat-obama-and-congress-head-for-collision-over -keystone-pipeline.html [accessed 7/25/18]). Congress did pass the bill, which Obama then vetoed.
71. Ostrander and Sievert, in "Presidential Signing Statements and the Durability of the Law," show that Congress is much more likely to revise laws for which presidents have issued signing statements.
72. See Hans J. G. Hassell and Samuel Kernell. 2015. "Veto Rhetoric and Legislative Riders." *American Journal of Political Science* 60(4): 845–59 (doi:10.1111/ajps.12217). These threats mainly hold out the promise that the president's co-partisans in Congress will disrupt the normal legislative process (for example, by filibustering) unless the rider is softened.
73. For a theoretical foundation for this point, see John Ferejohn and Charles Shipan. 1990. "Congressional Influence on Bureaucracy." *Journal of Law, Economics, and Organization* 6: 1–20.
74. Scott H. Ainsworth, Brian M. Harward, and Kenneth W. Moffett. 2012. "Congressional Response to Presidential Signing Statements." *American Politics Research* 40(6): 1067–91.
75. Molly E. Reynolds and Jackson Gode. June 2020. "Tracking House Oversight in the Trump Era." Brookings Institution. https://www.brookings.edu/interactives/tracking -house-oversight-in-the-trump-era/ (accessed 8/13/20). These numbers do not include the separate investigations conducted by federal criminal prosecutors and state officials.
76. David Weigel. September 30, 2015. "Boehner's Likely Successor Credits Benghazi Committee for Lowering Hillary Clinton's Poll Numbers." *Washington Post*, www .washingtonpost.com/news/post-politics/wp/2015/09/30/boehners-likely-successor -credits-benghazi-committee-for-lowering-hillary-clintons-poll-numbers (accessed 6/13/18).
77. Douglas L. Kriner and Eric Schickler. 2016. *Investigating the President: Congressional Checks on Presidential Power*, 6. Princeton, NJ: Princeton University Press

78. Kriner and Schickler, *Investigating the President*, 113.
79. The House had drawn up articles of impeachment for Richard Nixon, but he resigned in order to avoid his almost certain impeachment and conviction.
80. Andrew McCarty. July 12, 2017. "Trump, Russia, and the Misconduct of Public Men." *National Review*, www.nationalreview.com/article/449401/trump-jr-emails-high -crimes-misdemeanors (accessed 7/25/18). The Framers generally agreed that policy and politics are different, and that what Madison referred to as "maladministration" was not legitimate grounds for impeachment. But several Framers pointed to corruption, public misconduct, and illicit entanglements with foreign powers as impeachable offenses under the "High Crimes and Misdemeanors" standard. See Cass R. Sunstein. February 15, 2017. "What Impeachment Meant to the Founders." Bloomberg, www.bloomberg .com/view/articles/2017-02-15/what-impeachment-meant-to-the-founders (accessed 7/25/18).
81. Alexander Hamilton. 1788. *The Federalist Papers*, no. 65. Benjamin Franklin supported adding impeachment provisions to the Constitution because he worried that otherwise citizens' only recourse might be assassination. Franklin viewed impeachment of an official who had "rendered himself obnoxious" as far preferable to assassination. See Kat Eschner. December 19, 2016. "Presidents Can Be Impeached Because Benjamin Franklin Thought It Was Better Than Assassination." *Smart News*, www.smithsonianmag.com /smart-news/american-presidents-can-be-impeached-because-benjamin-franklin-thought -it-was-better-assassination-180961500/ (accessed 7/25/18).

## Chapter 10: Congress and the Bureaucracy

1. In the end, no groups that applied were denied 501(c)(4) status. But of the 300 groups that were targeted for extra scrutiny, 75 received this treatment after having been identified by their names, and one-third of those withdrew their applications, which could indicate either that the increased scrutiny had a chilling effect or that it worked to weed out those organizations that did not qualify. See Zachary A. Goldfarb and Karen Tumulty. May 20, 2013. "IRS Admits Targeting Conservatives for Tax Scrutiny in 2012 Election." *Washington Post*, www.washingtonpost.com/business/economy/irs-admits-targeting -conservatives-for-tax-scrutiny-in-2012-election/2013/05/10/3b6a0ada-b987-11e2-92f3 -f291801936b8_story.html (accessed 7/19/18). Although the discussion of the scandal at the time focused on the IRS's treatment of conservative interest groups, the Treasury Department's Inspector General under Donald Trump later concluded that the agency also had been subjecting groups with *liberal*-sounding names to heightened scrutiny during this period.
2. See Kelsey Snell. August 5, 2015. "Two Years after Scandal, the IRS Still Struggling." *Washington Post*, www.washingtonpost.com/news/powerpost/wp/2015/08/05/two-years -after-scandal-the-irs-still-struggling (accessed 7/19/18).
3. State budget and expenditure data are available at www.nasbo.org/mainsite/reports-data /state-expenditure-report (accessed 10/24/19).
4. In most cases, these grievances are initially heard by administrative law judges, who are bureaucrats empowered to make decisions about, or adjudicate, disputes in specific cases. Ultimately these grievances can be appealed to the five-member board at the head of the agency. The findings of the board are then final, subject in most cases to judicial review by appellate courts.
5. According to a former health official, the White House was especially worried that if the agency banned flavored products, the Republican-controlled Congress might retaliate by reducing the FDA's ability to regulate tobacco products more generally. Katie Thomas

and Sheila Kaplan. October 14, 2019. "E-cigarettes Went Unchecked in 10 Years of FDA Inaction." *New York Times*.

6. The agency's rule, which can be found at "Guidance to Identify Waters Protected by the Clean Water Act," Environmental Protection Agency, www.epa.gov/cwa-404/guidance -identify-waters-protected-clean-water-act (accessed 8/6/18), identifies the parts of the law that refer to "navigable waters."

7. The 115th Congress and President Trump joined forces to strike down this rule using the Congressional Review Act, which we discuss later in this chapter.

8. The estimate of the number of pages of laws passed by Congress comes from Christopher Beam. August 20, 2009. "Paper Weight." *Slate*, www.slate.com/articles/news_and _politics/explainer/2009/08/paper_weight.html (accessed 8/6/18). See also Pages in the *Federal Register* (1936–2015), *Regulatory Studies*, https://regulatorystudies.columbian .gwu.edu/sites/regulatorystudies.columbian.gwu.edu/files/downloads/Pages.JPG (accessed 8/6/18). It is worth noting, however, that the number of what are called "signifi-cant rules" (based on their predicted effects or costs) has dropped in recent years and was much lower under Obama than under his two predecessors.

9. In some instances, Congress tries to sidestep the potential problems associated with del-egating power to federal agencies by instead handing devolving policy-making authority to the states. See Pamela J. Clouser McCann. 2016. *The Federal Design Dilemma: Congress and Intergovernmental Delegation*. New York: Cambridge University Press.

10. Justin Grimmer, Sean J. Westwood, and Solomon Messing. 2014. *The Impression of Influ-ence*. Princeton, NJ: Princeton University Press.

11. The House Oversight and Government Reform Committee has broader responsibility for oversight but is less powerful in any given policy area.

12. See Renae Merle. October 26, 2016. "This Obscure Government Agency Has a Plan to put Wall Street CEOs in Prison." *Washington Post*, www.washingtonpost.com/news /business/wp/2016/10/26/this-obscure-government-agency-has-a-plan-to-put-wall-street -ceos-in-prison (accessed 8/6/18) for a discussion of SIGTARP.

13. As Anne Joseph O'Connell has pointed out, this dichotomy between executive-branch and independent agencies is an oversimplification (see 2013–14. "Bureaucracy at the Boundary." *University of Pennsylvania Law Review* 162: 841–927). Many well-known agencies, including the Postal Service, the National Guard, and the U.S. Anti-Doping Agency, fit into neither category. Still, most of the largest and most prominent agencies fall into one of these two classifications.

14. Meanwhile, there are other agencies within the executive branch that do not fall within one of the main cabinet agencies, such as NASA.

15. In some cases, the president can create these agencies by bringing existing departments together into a single agency. Richard Nixon took such an approach when he consolidated existing units within the Department of the Interior, the FDA, and the Council on Envi-ronmental Quality to create the EPA in 1970. Even in that case, however, Congress played a role: Government Operations subcommittees in each chamber held hearings and produced reports endorsing the president's idea.

16. *Seila Law v. Consumer Financial Protection Bureau*. 591 U.S. ___ (2020).

17. Robinson Meyer. January 9, 2018. "Trump's Coal Bailout Is Dead." *The Atlantic*. www .theatlantic.com/science/archive/2018/01/trumps-coal-bailout-is-dead/550037/ (accessed 8/13/20).

18. Data on the number of appointees comes from "United States Government Policy and Supporting Positions (Plum Book)." Government Publishing Office, https://m.gpo.gov /plumbook (accessed 8/6/18). The Senate's authority to confirm presidential nominees derives from Article II, Section 2, of the Constitution. Notably, this section also gives

Congress the power to create positions that do not require Senate approval, stating that "Congress may by Law vest the Appointment of such inferior Officers, as they think proper, in the President alone, in the Courts of Law, or in the Heads of Departments."

19. Perhaps most interestingly, presidents value this responsiveness even if it comes at the expense of competence. See David E. Lewis. *The Politics of Presidential Appointments.* Princeton, NJ: Princeton University Press, 2010.

20. Figures for Donald Trump come from www.washingtonpost.com/graphics/politics/trump -administration-appointee-tracker/database/ and are current through October 16, 2019. The number of nominees for Trump is much higher than for other presidents, especially given that they are for a partial term rather than for one or two full terms, due to an unusually high number of resignations from these positions that are followed by renominations. Figures for previous presidents come from Nathaniel Rakich. January 10, 2017. "It's Really Hard to Block a Cabinet Nominee." FiveThirtyEight, https://fivethirtyeight .com/features/its-really-hard-to-block-a-cabinet-nominee/ (accessed 8/6/18).

21. See Glen S. Krutz, Richard Fleisher, and Jon R. Bond. 1998. "From Abe Fortas to Zoë Baird: Why Some Presidential Nominations Fail in the Senate." *American Political Science Review* 92(4): 871–81.

22. See Krutz, Fleisher, and Bond, "From Abe Fortas to Zoë Baird: Why Some Presidential Nominations Fail in the Senate." The percentage of nominations that were rejected or withdrawn has increased recently, from just over 1 percent between 1945 and 2000 to just under 8 percent between 2001 and 2012. See James D. King and James W. Riddlesperger Jr. 2013. "Senate Confirmation of Cabinet Appointments: Congress-Centered, Presidency-Centered, and Nominee-Centered Explanations." *Social Science Journal* 50: 177–8.

23. Osita Nwanevu. January 27, 2017. "What the Hell Is Wrong with Senate Democrats?" *Slate,* www.slate.com/blogs/the_slatest/2017/01/27/what_the_hell_is_wrong_with _senate_democrats.html (accessed 7/19/18).

24. See also Jon R. Bond, Richard Fleisher, and Glen S. Krutz. 2009. "Malign Neglect: Evidence That Delay Has Become the Primary Method of Defeating Presidential Appointments." *Congress & the Presidency* 36: 226–43. In effect, the process of appointments is not fixed, but rather changes over time, often dramatically.

25. See Ian Ostrander. 2016. "The Logic of Collective Inaction: Senatorial Delay in Executive Nominations." *American Journal of Political Science* 60(4): 1063–76.

26. "How Vacancies are Changing the Federal Reserve." April 26, 2016. *Economist,* www .economist.com/news/business-and-finance/21697594-two-empty-board-seats-are -addling-americas-central-bank-how-vacancies-are-changing (accessed 7/19/18).

27. Only from 2011–15 did the ATF have a permanent, Senate-confirmed director.

28. Russell Berman. January 20, 2017. "How Democrats Paved the Way for the Confirmation of Trump's Cabinet." *The Atlantic,* www.theatlantic.com/politics/archive/2017/01 /democrats-trump-cabinet-senate/513782 (accessed 7/19/18).

29. The number of PAS appointees varies by agency. As of January 2017, some, such as HHS, with 18 PAS appointees, have roughly the same number as the Department of Commerce. Others have far more. The Department of State, for example, has 265, including one position formally known as "the Representative of the United States of America to the United Nations, with the rank and status of Ambassador Extraordinary and Plenipotentiary, and Representative of the United States of America in the Security Council of the United Nations."

30. In 1876, the House impeached Secretary of War William Belknap on the grounds of corruption. Belknap then resigned rather than face a Senate trial. The Senate went ahead and voted on whether to convict him anyway, and although a majority voted in favor of conviction, the margin (35–25) fell short of the required two-thirds majority, so he was

acquitted. Many of those who voted to acquit did so because they argued that the Senate no longer had jurisdiction to convict Belknap, given his resignation.

31. January 6, 2019. "Trump says acting cabinet members give him 'more flexibility.'" *The Guardian*, www.theguardian.com/us-news/2019/jan/06/trump-acting-cabinet-members -give-him-more-flexibility (accessed 8/13/20).

32. Notably, this is a power that Congress gave to presidents with the Vacancies Reform Act.

33. Matthew Rosenberg. December 12, 2016. "Michael Flynn Is Harsh Judge of C.I.A.'s Role." *New York Times*, www.nytimes.com/2016/12/12/us/politics/donald-trump-cia -michael-flynn.html (accessed 7/19/18).

34. Flynn ended up serving only 24 days in the role, the shortest stint of anyone in this position in history. He resigned over allegations of improper contacts with Russia during the presidential campaign and for having lied to the FBI about these contacts.

35. Emily Stephenson and Elvina Nawaguna. February 6, 2013. "Postal Service Will End Saturday Mail Delivery." Reuters, www.reuters.com/article/usa-postal -idUSL1N0B63K720130206 (accessed 7/19/18).

36. Elvina Nawaguna. March 21, 2013. "Congress to Force Postal Service to Keep Saturday Delivery." Reuters, www.reuters.com/article/us-usa-postal-delivery -idUSBRE92K0OL20130321 (accessed 7/19/18).

37. Charles R. Shipan. 2004. "Regulatory Regimes, Agency Actions, and the Conditional Nature of Congressional Influence." *American Political Science Review* 98(3): 467–80.

38. See Hannah Lutz. April 12, 2017. "Criticism Lingers over CFPB's Handling of Auto Lending." *Automotive News*, www.autonews.com/article/20170412/BLOG13/304129985 /criticism-lingers-over-cfpbs-handling-of-auto-lending (accessed 8/6/18).

39. See Jeremy Gelman. 2017. "Rewarding Dysfunction: Interest Groups and Intended Legislative Failure." *Legislative Studies Quarterly* 42(4): 661–92.

40. Interestingly, neither side can point to such things actually occurring—investigations revealed no instances of terrorist plots being revealed or thwarted, or of any violations of privacy or other misuse of the collected data. See Jeff Stone. June 2, 2015. "What Is 'Metadata'? NSA Loses Surveillance Power on American Phone Calls, But 'Data about Data' Remains Hazy." *International Business Times*, www.ibtimes.com/what-metadata-nsa-loses -surveillance-power-american-phone-calls-data-about-data-1947196 (accessed 8/6/18).

41. Greg Sargent. July 25, 2013. "Reform of NSA Surveillance Is Probably Inevitable." *Washington Post*, www.washingtonpost.com/blogs/plum-line/wp/2013/07/25/reform-of-nsa -surveillance-is-probably-inevitable/ (accessed 8/6/18); and David Weigel. July 25, 2013. "Killing the NSA Softly." *Slate*, www.slate.com/articles/news_and_politics/politics/2013 /07/justin_amash_s_nsa_amendment_almost_passed_congressional_critics_think_they .html (accessed 7/19/18).

42. Stone, "What Is 'Metadata'?"

43. *Immigration and Naturalization Service v. Chadha*, 462 U.S. 919 (1983).

44. Indeed, some bills have contained dozens of different legislative veto provisions. The courts have generally continued to find these post-*Chadha* legislative vetoes to be unconstitutional, but the ease of writing legislative veto provisions into a law, the ease of enacting a veto (compared to a standard law), the low likelihood that a court will strike down a particular provision, and the effect that the possibility of a veto might have on an agency (for example, by indicating that Congress will be watching the agency closely) all indicate that we will likely continue to see legislative veto provisions in laws for the foreseeable future. See Michael J. Berry. 2016. *The Modern Legislative Veto: Macropolitical Conflict and the Legacy of Chadha.* Ann Arbor, MI: University of Michigan Press.

45. Martin Rosenberg. 2008. "Congressional Review of Agency Rulemaking: An Update and Assessment of the Congressional Review Act after a Decade." Washington, DC: Congressional Review Service.

46. Furthermore, in 2018 Republicans in Congress began to explore using the CRA to over-turn a different type of agency action known as guidance documents. Although these documents are statements of agency policy, they do not need to be passed via a formal process (as rules do). Still, the Government Accountability Office informed Congress that it could treat guidance documents as equivalent to rules, which meant that they could be overturned through the CRA.

47. See David Epstein and Sharon O'Halloran. 1999. *Delegating Powers*. New York: Cambridge University Press.

48. Daniel P. Carpenter. 1996. "Adaptive Signal Processing, Hierarchy, and Budgetary Control in Federal Regulation." *American Political Science Review* 90(2): 283–302.

49. Jason A. MacDonald. 2010. "Limitation Riders and Congressional Influence over Bureaucratic Policy Decisions." *American Political Science Review* 104(04): 766–82.

50. Joel D. Aberbach. 1990. *Keeping a Watchful Eye: The Politics of Congressional Oversight*. Washington, DC: Brookings Institution Press.

51. For an insightful analysis of how Congress influences agencies informally, see Kenneth Lowande. January 2019. "Politicization and Responsiveness in Executive Agencies." *Journal of Politics*. 81(1): 33–48.

52. E. Scott Adler and John D. Wilkerson. 2013. *Congress and the Politics of Problem Solving*. New York: Cambridge University Press.

53. Michael Bromwich. January 14, 2017. "The Investigation of James Comey Is Exactly What the Country Needs." *Washington Post*, www.washingtonpost.com/opinions/the-investigation-of-james-comey-is-exactly-what-the-country-needs/2017/01/14/83a558b0-da97-11e6-b8b2-cb5164beba6b_story.html (accessed 7/19/18).

54. Stephen Dinan. January 12, 2017. "Paul Ryan Rules Out Donald Trump's 'Deportation Force.'" *Washington Post*, www.washingtontimes.com/news/2017/jan/12/paul-ryan-rules-out-donald-trumps-deportation-forc (accessed 7/19/18).

55. Joshua Clinton, David Lewis, and Jennifer Selin. 2014. "Influencing the Bureaucracy: The Irony of Congressional Oversight." *American Journal of Political Science* 58(2): 387–401.

56. The authors also note the extreme case of the Department of Homeland Security, which is overseen by 108 different committees and subcommittees!

57. Thomas E. Mann and Norman J. Ornstein. 2006. *The Broken Branch: How Congress Is Failing America and How to Get It Back on Track*, 155. Washington, DC: Brookings Institution Press.

58. Morris P. Fiorina. 1981. "Congressional Control of the Bureaucracy: A Mismatch of Incentives and Capabilities," in *Congress Reconsidered*, 2nd ed., ed. by Lawrence C. Dodd and Bruce J. Oppenheimer, 332–48. Washington, DC: CQ Press. See also Elaine Kamarck. 2016. "A Congressional Oversight Office: A Proposed Early Warning System for the United States Congress." Center for Effective Public Management, Brookings, www.brookings.edu/wp-content/uploads/2016/07/congressional/oversight.pdf (accessed 10/22/18).

59. Matthew D. McCubbins and Thomas Schwartz. 1984. "Congressional Oversight Overlooked: Police Patrols versus Fire Alarms." *American Journal of Political Science* 28(1): 165–79.

60. The figure originally comes from Jason MacDonald and Robert J. McGrath. 2016. "Retrospective Congressional Oversight and the Dynamics of Legislative Influence over the Bureaucracy." *Legislative Studies Quarterly* 41(4): 899–934. This version of their figure comes from Kamarck, "A Congressional Oversight Office."

61. See Aberbach, *Keeping a Watchful Eye: The Politics of Congressional Oversight*.

62. In a follow-up study, Aberbach distinguishes between two types of oversight. One type is primary-purpose oversight, which he finds that Congress continued to deploy at high levels in the 1990s. On the other hand, he also found a decline in the 1990s for hearings

dealing with authorizations and reauthorizations. See Joel D. Aberbach. 2002. "What's Happened to the Watchful Eye?" *Congress & the Presidency* 29:1, 3–23.

63. Steven J. Balla and Christopher J. Deering. 2013. "Police Patrols and Fire Alarms: An Empirical Examination of the Legislative Preference for Oversight." *Congress & the Presidency*, 40(1), 27–40.

64. See, for example, John D. Huber and Charles R. Shipan. 2002. *Deliberate Discretion? The Institutional Foundations of Bureaucratic Autonomy.* New York: Cambridge University Press.

65. See Joshua D. Clinton, Anthony Bertelli, Christian R. Grose, David E. Lewis, and David C. Nixon. 2012. "Separated Powers in the United States: The Ideology of Agencies, Presidents, and Congress." *American Journal of Political Science* 56(2): 341–54.

66. See Joshua D. Clinton, David E. Lewis, and Jennifer L. Selin. 2014. "Influencing the Bureaucracy: The Irony of Congressional Oversight." *American Journal of Political Science* 58(2): 387–401.

## Chapter 11: Congress and the Courts

1. Burgess Everett and Glenn Thrush. February 13, 2016. "McConnell Throws Down the Gauntlet." Politico, www.politico.com/story/2016/02/mitch-mcconnell-antonin-scalia-supreme-court-nomination-219248 (accessed 8/9/18).

2. For example, the Courts of Appeals affirmed or reversed more than 25,000 cases in 2014. United States Courts, "Table B-5—U.S. Courts of Appeals Federal Judicial Caseload Statistics," www.uscourts.gov/statistics/table/b-5/federal-judicial-caseload-statistics/2014/03/31 (accessed 8/10/18). Meanwhile, the district courts issued decisions in approximately 3,000 cases but addressed another 216,000 that were terminated as a result of some court action before trial (such as precedential opinions on summary judgment). United States Courts, "Table C-4—U.S. District Courts–Civil Statistical Tables For The Federal Judiciary," www.uscourts.gov/statistics/table/c-4/statistical-tables-federal-judiciary/2015/12/31 (accessed 7/9/20).

3. See Siobhan Hughes. April 19, 2016. "Why Republican Resistance to Vote on Supreme Court Nominee Remains Strong." *Wall Street Journal*, http://blogs.wsj.com/washwire/2016/04/19/why-republican-resistance-to-vote-on-supreme-court-nominee-remains-strong/ (accessed 8/10/18).

4. See Thomas G. Walker and Lee Epstein. 1993. *The Supreme Court of the United States: An Introduction.* New York: St. Martin's Press.

5. Supporters of lower federal courts believed that although they had enough votes to create these courts, forcing this issue might have imperiled ratification of the Constitution. Thus they were content to empower Congress to create such courts later, knowing that they would likely be successful in the first Congress. See Walker and Epstein, *The Supreme Court of the United States: An Introduction.*

6. District courts are located entirely within state boundaries. The number of district courts within a state ranges from one (as in Maine and Colorado) to four (as in California and Texas).

7. U.S. District Courts, "Table C-4, Civil Cases Terminated, by Nature of Suit and Action Taken, during the 12-Month Period Ending December 31, 2015." www.uscourts.gov/sites/default/files/data_tables/stfj_c4_1231.2015.pdf; "Table D-4, Criminal Defendants Disposed of, by Type of Disposition and Offense, during the 12-Month Period Ending December 31, 2015." www.uscourts.gov/sites/default/files/data_tables/stfj_d4_1231.2015.pdf (both accessed 9/21/18).

8. Exceptions include cases where the decisions of government agencies are appealed directly to the D.C. Court of Appeals.

9. In rare cases, the Supreme Court hears cases through what the Constitution identifies as original jurisdiction, meaning that it hears the case not on appeal, but rather as the original trial court. This occurs when there are disagreements between two states or cases involving ambassadors.

10. In Hamilton's words in *Federalist 78*, "The independence of the judges may be an essential safeguard against the effects of occasional ill humors in the society."

11. Arguing in favor, Hamilton, in *Federalist 78*, wrote, "Nothing can contribute so much to its firmness and independence as permanency in office, this quality may therefore be justly regarded as an indispensable ingredient in its constitution, and, in a great measure, as the citadel of the public justice and the public security." Thomas Jefferson, in a letter to William T. Barry (July 2, 1822), took the opposing view: "Let the future appointments of judges be for four or six years, and renewable by the President and Senate. This will bring their conduct, at regular periods, under revision and probation, and may keep them in equipoise between the general and special governments." Thomas Jefferson. "Letter CLXIV.—To William T. Barry, July 2, 1822," in *Memoir, Correspondence, and Miscellanies, from the Papers of Thomas Jefferson*. Project Gutenberg, www.gutenberg.org/files /16784/16784-h/16784-h.htm (accessed 8/20/18).

12. An additional measure of independence comes from the constitutional provision (Article III, Section 1) that prevents Congress from cutting judges' salaries.

13. See Henry J. Abraham. 1999. *Justices, Presidents, and Senators: A History of U.S. Supreme Court Appointments from Washington to Bush II*. Lanham, MD: Rowman & Littlefield.

14. For details on the role of the Judiciary Committee, see Denis Steven Rutkus. July 6, 2005. "Supreme Court Appointment Process." *Congressional Research Service Report for Congress*, http://fpc.state.gov/documents/organization/50146.pdf (accessed 8/13/18).

15. For a detailed discussion of the Senate's role in the appointment process, see Denis Steven Rutkus. February 19, 2010. "Supreme Court Appointment Process." Congressional Research Service, www.fas.org/sgp/crs/misc/RL31989.pdf (accessed 8/13/18). Much of this section draws upon this report.

16. The committee traditionally reports the nomination to the full Senate regardless of whether it has a favorable view of the nominee, allowing the Senate to always weigh in on the nomination. Indeed, there have been only six cases over the past 140 years in which the committee did not issue a favorable recommendation but sent the nomination forward anyway, most recently with the nominations of Robert Bork (who received an unfavorable report) and Clarence Thomas (whose nomination was reported without recommendation).

17. Transcript: Sen. Orrin Hatch (R-Utah) Opening Statement. July 13, 2009. *Washington Post*: CQ Transcriptions, www.washingtonpost.com/wp-srv/politics/documents/hatch _openingstatement_sotomayor.html (accessed 8/13/18).

18. See Bryon J. Moraski and Charles R. Shipan. 1999. "The Politics of Supreme Court Nominations: A Theory of Institutional Constraints and Choices." *American Journal of Political Science* 43: 1069–95. Moraski and Shipan argue and show that presidents make appointments with the goal of shifting the median of the Supreme Court, taking the preferences of the Senate into account.

19. James B. Cottrill and Terri J. Peretti. 2013. "The Partisan Dynamics of Supreme Court Confirmation Voting." *Justice System Journal* 34: 1, 15–37.

20. See Charles M. Cameron, Albert D. Cover, and Jeffrey A. Segal. 1990. "Senate Voting on Supreme Court Nominees: A Neoinstitutional Model." *American Political Science Review* 84: 525–34; Jonathan P. Kastellec, Jeffrey R. Lax, and Justin H. Phillips. 2010. "Public Opinion and Senate Confirmation of Supreme Court Nominees." *Journal of Politics* 72: 767–84.

21. See Charles R. Shipan. 2008. "Partisanship, Ideology, and Senate Voting on Supreme Court Nominees." *Journal of Empirical Legal Studies* 5: 55–76.

22. See Sarah A. Binder and Forrest Maltzman. 2009. *Advice and Dissent: The Struggle to Shape the Federal Judiciary*. Washington, DC: Brookings Institution. Although this system largely remains in place—in particular, if a home-state senator opposes a nominee, that nominee is very unlikely to be confirmed—in recent years, it has become much more common for senators to try to block the appointment of judicial nominees to federal courts in other states.

23. See Barbara Sinclair. 2006. *Party Wars*. Norman, OK: University of Oklahoma Press.

24. Alexander Hamilton, *The Federalist Papers*, no. 78.

25. See, for example, Cliff Sloan and David McKean. 2009. *The Great Decision: Jefferson, Adams, Marshall, and the Battle for the Supreme Court*. New York: Public Affairs. For a provocative and contrary view that the changes attributed to *Marbury* have been exaggerated and that the decision itself has been greatly misunderstood, see Robert Lowry Clinton. 1989. Marbury v. Madison *and Judicial Review*. Lawrence, KS: University of Kansas Press.

26. For example, in *Texas v. White*, 74 U.S. 700 (1869), which held that a state cannot unilaterally secede from the United States, meaning the Confederacy states never left the Union during the Civil War.

27. Mark A. Graber. 1993. "The Nonmajoritarian Difficulty: Legislative Deference to the Judiciary." *Studies in American Political Development* 7: 35–73. For example, Graber argues that the main intention of the Sherman Act was to enable Congress to defer to whatever antitrust policy the courts decided to employ. This allowed politicians to ignore demands for federal economic policy, which helped them avoid disrupting existing political alignments.

28. See Keith E. Whittington. 2007. *Political Foundations of Judicial Supremacy: The Presidency, the Supreme Court, and Constitutional Leadership in U.S. History*. Princeton, NJ: Princeton University Press. Even a case as well known (and infamous) as the Court's *Dred Scott* decision can be seen as an example of the Court carrying out the wishes of members of Congress who preferred not to act themselves.

29. See George Lovell. 2010. *Legislative Deferrals*. New York: Cambridge University Press, for an explication of the conditions under which Congress will prefer to defer to the courts.

30. The Sherman Antitrust Act is perhaps the most prominent law that illustrates many of these goals. In this law, Congress handed the courts the responsibility to determine what constituted an antitrust violation, rather than trying to write legislation that identified such violations. It did so for reasons outlined in the text: to avoid controversy over a difficult issue, to give the courts flexibility, and to allow for passage of the law. See Graber, "The Nonmajoritarian Difficulty: Legislative Deference to the Judiciary."

31. 558 U.S. 310 (2010).

32. "Measures Proposed to Amend the Constitution," United States Senate, www.senate.gov /pagelayout/reference/three_column_table/measures_proposed_to_amend_constitution .htm (accessed 8/13/18).

33. See John Nichols. September 11, 2014. "The Senate Tried to Overturn 'Citizens United' Today. Guess What Stopped Them?" *The Nation*, www.thenation.com/article/senate -tried-overturn-citizens-united-today-guess-what-stopped-them/ (accessed 8/13/18).

34. For a discussion of this conventional wisdom, see Virginia A. Hettinger and Christopher Zorn. 2005. "Explaining the Incidence and Timing of Congressional Responses to the U.S. Supreme Court." *Legislative Studies Quarterly* 30: 5–28.

35. William N. Eskridge Jr. 1991. "Overriding Supreme Court Statutory Interpretation Decisions." *Yale Law Journal* 101: 331–455.

36. See Richard L. Hasen. 2013. "End of the Dialogue? Political Polarization, the Supreme Court, and Congress." *Southern California Law Review* 86: 205–61.

37. See Matthew R. Christiansen and William N. Eskridge Jr. 2014. "Congressional Over-rides of Supreme Court Statutory Interpretation Decisions, 1967–2011." *Texas Law Review* 92: 1317. For a discussion of these two studies, see Amanda Frost. May 30, 2014. "Academic Highlight: Congressional Overrides of Supreme Court Decisions." SCOTUS-blog, www.scotusblog.com/2014/05/academic-highlight-congressional-overrides-of-supreme-court-decisions/ (accessed 8/13/18).

38. William Saletan. June 26, 2013. "Anti-Gay Is Yesterday." *Slate*, www.slate.com/articles/news_and_politics/frame_game/2013/06/gay_marriage_polls_and_public_opinion_the_supreme_court_s_rulings_upheld.html (accessed 8/13/18); Josh Gerstein. June 25, 2015. "Conservatives Steamed at Chief Justice John Roberts' Betrayal." Politico, www.politico.com/story/2015/06/gop-conservatives-angry-supreme-court-chief-john-roberts-obamacare-119431.

39. See John Nichols. October 25, 2010. "Congressman Considers Move to Impeach Chief Justice John Roberts." *The Nation*, www.thenation.com/article/congressman-considers-move-impeach-chief-justice-john-roberts (accessed 8/20/18).

40. Congress set the size of the Court at nine in the Judiciary Act of 1869.

41. Howard Gillman. 2002. "How Political Parties Can Use the Courts to Advance Their Agendas: Federal Courts in the United States, 1875–1891." *American Political Science Review* 96(03): 511–2

42. See Reorganization of the Federal Judiciary, 75th Cong., 1st sess., 1937, S. Rep. 711. In part, the plan died because it lacked support from key members of the Senate, such as Senator Henry Ashurst, chair of the Senate Judiciary Committee. It certainly did not help that when the bill was read in the Senate, FDR's vice president, John Garner, "stood in the well of the Senate and, as the plan was read aloud to the senators, Garner held his nose and gestured thumbs down," according to Jeff Shesol. 2010. *Supreme Power: Franklin Roosevelt vs. The Supreme Court*. New York: W. W. Norton. Finally, there is a widespread belief that when Justice Owen Roberts, who previously had voted with the conservative justices to strike down New Deal actions, switched and sided with the lib-eral faction on a minimum wage case, it relieved pressure on Congress to address the obstruction of the Court. In this view, FDR's pressure had the intended effect of producing a more amenable Court. Recent accounts, such as Shesol's, have cast doubt on this story.

43. Chase, who at the time was a Federalist, drew the ire of the Jeffersonian Democratic-Republicans who controlled the House.

44. Porteous was convicted based on a series of activities that Congress found to be corrupt and impeachable, including lying during his confirmation hearings, financial impropri-eties, failing to recuse himself from a case involving a former law partner, and accepting cash and other favors from lawyers in cases he presided over. See Jennifer Steinhauer. December 8, 2010. "Senate, for Just the 8th Time, Votes to Oust a Federal Judge." *New York Times*, www.nytimes.com/2010/12/09/us/politics/09judge.html (accessed 8/13/18). More recently, Judge Mark Fuller announced his resignation from the Middle District of Alabama in 2015 after being informed that the House Judiciary Committee was going to impeach him over charges of domestic abuse.

45. Charles Gardner Geyh. 2008. When Congress and Courts Collide, 116. Ann Arbor: Uni-versity of Michigan Press.

46. Scott Keyes. June 28, 2012. "Republican Congressman Suggests 'Impeachment' for Jus-tice over Obamacare Ruling." ThinkProgress, http://thinkprogress.org/justice/2012/06/28/508137/louie-gohmert-impeach-kagan (accessed 8/20/18). See also threats to impeach Justices John Roberts, Sotomayor, and Thomas discussed in Robert Barnes. October 31, 2010. "Impeachment Calls Part of Life for a Supreme Court Justice, but Few

Get Very Far." *Washington Post*, www.washingtonpost.com/wp-dyn/content/article/2010/10/31/AR2010103103379.html (accessed 8/13/18).

47. The most thorough and insightful consideration of court-curbing bills can be found in Tom S. Clark. 2011. *The Limits of Judicial Independence*. New York: Cambridge University Press.

48. Clark, *The Limits of Judicial Independence*, 37–8, for example, notes that "jurisdiction-stripping is generally regarded as the main mechanism by which Congress attacks the Court."

49. Other bills focused on impeachment. For example, Representative Gerald R. Ford pushed for the impeachment of Justice William O. Douglas because of Douglas's liberal rulings, on the grounds that an "impeachable offense" means "whatever a majority of the House of Representatives considers [it] to be at a given moment in history." Quoted in Geyh, *When Congress and Courts Collide*, 109.

50. Lawrence Baum. 1997. *The Puzzle of Judicial Behavior*. Ann Arbor, MI: University of Michigan Press.

51. James R. Zink, James F. Spriggs II, and John T. Scott. 2009. "Courting the Public: The Influence of Decision Attributes on Individuals' Views of Court Opinions." *Journal of Politics* 71(3): 909–25.

52. See Robert A. Katzmann. 1997. *Courts and Congress*. Washington, DC: Brookings Institution.

53. Jeffrey A. Segal. 1997. "Separation-of-Powers Games in the Positive Theory of Congress and Courts." *American Political Science Review* 91: 28–44

54. James F. Spriggs and Thomas G. Hansford. 2001. "Explaining the Overruling of U.S. Supreme Court Precedent." *Journal of Politics* 63: 1091–1111 and Brian Sala and James F. Spriggs. 2004. "Designing Tests of the Supreme Court and the Separation of Powers." *Political Research Quarterly* 57: 197–208.

55. Lee Epstein and Jack Knight. 1997. *The Choices Justices Make*. Washington, DC: CQ Press; Forrest Maltzman, James F. Spriggs, and Paul J. Wahlbeck. 2000. *Crafting Law on the Supreme Court*. New York: Cambridge University Press; Lee Epstein, Jack Knight, and Andrew D. Martin. 2001. "The Supreme Court as a Strategic National Policy Maker." *Emory Law Journal* 50(2): 583–611 (Symposium); and Pablo T. Spiller and Rafael Gely. 1992. "Congressional Control or Judicial Independence: The Determinants of US Supreme Court Labor-Relations Decisions, 1949–1988." *RAND Journal of Economics*: 463–92.

56. Anna Harvey and Barry Friedman. 2009. "Ducking Trouble: Congressionally Induced Selection Bias in the Supreme Court's Agenda." *Journal of Politics* 71: 574–92. But see also Ryan J. Owens. 2010. "The Separation of Powers, Judicial Independence, and Strategic Agenda Setting." *American Journal of Political Science* 54(2): 412–27, who finds no evidence that justices' votes are affected by the ideological distance between Congress and the Court.

57. This finding helps to explain why the size of the Court's docket (that is, the number of cases it agrees to hear each year) has been decreasing over the past few decades. See Kenneth W. Moffett, Forrest Maltzman, Karen Miranda, and Charles R. Shipan. 2016. "Strategic Behavior and Variation in the Supreme Court's Caseload over Time." *Justice System Journal* 37(1): 20–38. See also Anna Harvey. 2014. *A Mere Machine: The Supreme Court, Congress, and American Democracy*. New Haven, CT: Yale University Press.

58. See Clark, *The Limits of Judicial Independence*. Jeffrey L. Segal, Chad Westerland, and Stefanie Lindquist. 2011. "Congress, the Supreme Court, and Judicial Review: Testing a Constitutional Separation of Powers Model." *American Journal of Political Science* 55: 89–104 also find support for an institutional legitimacy argument, showing that the

Court is less likely to find laws to be unconstitutional when it is faced with a Congress that is ideologically distant.

59. Michael A. Bailey and Forrest Maltzman. 2010. *The Constrained Court: Law, Politics, and the Decisions Justices Make*. Princeton, NJ: Princeton University Press.

60. Robert A. Katzmann. 2016. *Judging Statutes*. New York: Oxford University Press.

61. See Katzmann, *Courts and Congress*.

62. In an interview, Scalia said, "You will see recited in opinions all the way back that the object of interpretation is to determine the intent of the drafter. I don't believe that. We're not governed by the drafter's intent. We're governed by laws." Pete Williams. August 22, 2012. NBC News, http://dailynightly.nbcnews.com/_news/2012/08/22 /13416169-scalia-judges-should-interpret-words-not-intent?lite (accessed 8/13/18).

63. 467 U.S. 837 (1984). The Supreme Court ruled that the EPA's definition of the word "source" in the Clean Air Act was a reasonable interpretation of the statute.

64. 401 U.S. 402 (1971). The Department of Transportation (DOT) approved the use of federal funds to construct Interstate 40 through Overton Park in Memphis, Tennessee. A group called Citizens to Preserve Overton Park filed suit to block this action, which the Supreme Court ultimately upheld, stating that the DOT violated a statute requiring the government to demonstrate that there were no "feasible and prudent" alternatives to building through public lands.

65. For a discussion of these sorts of provisions and how Congress deployed them in the area of communications policy, see Charles R. Shipan. 1997. *Designing Judicial Review: Interest Groups, Congress, and Communications Policy*. Ann Arbor, MI: University of Michigan Press.

66. In addition, between 25 and 30 percent of these laws also specify which courts can conduct reviews, who has standing, whether there are time limits, and the scope of reviews. See Pamela J. Clouser McCann, Charles R. Shipan, and Yuhua Wang. 2018. "Congress and Judicial Review of Agency Actions." Manuscript, University of Michigan.

67. Evidence from a recent study shows that Congress writes more specific laws when members want to constrain the courts (for example, because of ideological disagreements). See Kirk A. Randazzo, Richard W. Waterman, and Jeffrey A. Fine. 2006. "Checking the Federal Courts: The Impact of Congressional Statutes on Judicial Behavior." *Journal of Politics* 68: 1006–17. Quote on p. 1006.

68. Richard A. Paschal. 1991. "The Continuing Colloquy: Congress and the Finality of the Supreme Court." *Journal of Law & Politics* 8: 143.

## Chapter 12: Congress and Interest Groups

1. For a list of Republican priorities in the House of Representatives, see Speaker Paul Ryan's "A Better Way" document, https://abetterway.speaker.gov/ (accessed 8/23/18).

2. John Sides. November 18, 2017. "Here's the Incredibly Unpopular GOP Tax Reform Plan—In One Graph." *Washington Post*, www.washingtonpost.com/news/monkey-cage /wp/2017/11/18/heres-the-incredibly-unpopular-gop-tax-reform-plan-in-one-graph (accessed 8/7/18).

3. H.R. 1628 - American Health Care Act of 2017, Maplight, http://maplight.org/data /passthrough/#legacyurl=http://classic.maplight.org/us-congress/bill/115-hr-1628 /12273735/contributions-by-vote (accessed 8/7/18).

4. Gary Strauss. November 30, 2017. "AARP Opposes Senate Tax Bill." AARP, www.aarp.org/politics-society/advocacy/info-2017/senate-letter-tax-fd.html (accessed 8/7/18).

5. See Suzanne P. Clark. November 20, 2017. "Key Vote Letter: Senate 'Tax Cuts and Jobs Act.'" U.S. Chamber of Commerce, www.uschamber.com/letter/key-vote-letter-senate

-tax-cuts-and-jobs-act (accessed 8/7/18); and Joshua Bolten. November 29, 2017. "Business Roundtable Letter to Senate in Support of the Tax Cuts and Jobs Act." Business Roundtable, http://businessroundtable.org/resources/business-roundtable-letter-senate -support-the-tax-cuts-and-jobs-act (accessed 8/7/18).

6. A related point is that lobbying has become increasingly partisan in recent years. That is, the proportion of lobbying firms that work for both Democrats and Republicans has decreased over time, while the proportion that specialize in one party has increased. See Kevin Bogardus. February 11, 2014. "K Street's Holdouts Are Partisan, Proud." *The Hill*, http://thehill.com/business-a-lobbying/business-a-lobbying/198012-showing-their-colors -k-streets-holdouts-are-partisan (accessed 8/7/18).

7. Cristina Marcos. November 7, 2017. "GOP Lawmaker: Donors Are Pushing Me to Get Tax Reform Done." *The Hill*, http://thehill.com/homenews/house/359110-gop-lawmaker -donors-are-pushing-me-to-get-tax-reform-done (accessed 8/7/18).

8. Rebecca Savransky. November 9, 2017. "Graham: 'Financial Contributions Will Stop' If GOP Doesn't Pass Tax Reform." *The Hill*. http://thehill.com/policy/finance/359606 -graham-financial-contributions-will-stop-if-gop-doesnt-pass-tax-reform (accessed 8/7/18).

9. James Madison, *The Federalist Papers*, no. 10.

10. James Madison, *The Federalist Papers*, no. 51.

11. Rasmussen Reports. February 16, 2016. "Voters Say Money, Media Have Too Much Political Clout." Rasmussen Reports, www.rasmussenreports.com/public_content /politics/general_politics/february_2016/voters_say_money_media_have_too_much _political_clout (accessed 8/7/18).

12. Andrew Dugan. September 28, 2015. "Majority of Americans See Congresses as Out of Touch, Corrupt." Gallup, http://news.gallup.com/poll/185918/majority-americans -congress-touch-corrupt.aspx (accessed 8/7/18).

13. Jeffrey M. Jones. December 10, 2007. "Lobbyists Debut at Bottom of Honesty and Ethics List." Gallup, http://news.gallup.com/poll/103123/lobbyists-debut-bottom-honesty -ethics-list.aspx (accessed 8/7/18).

14. However, an exciting new study suggests that the interest group system might not be as biased toward richer interests as is commonly assumed. Jesse Crosson, Alexander Furnas, and Geoffrey Lorenz. "Polarized Pluralism: Organizational Preferences and Biases in the American Pressure System." *American Political Science Review*.

15. OpenSecrets.org. 2018. "Top Spenders." Center for Responsive Politics, www.opensecrets .org/lobby/top.php?indexType=s&showYear=2018 (accessed 8/7/18). The next 10 on the list fall into the same categories: National Association of Broadcasters, Comcast, Lockheed Martin, National Retail Federation, Business Roundtable, Southern Co., Amazon, Oracle, Verizon, and Northrop Grumman.

16. See https://int.nyt.com/data/documenttools/200716-us-chamber-of-commerce -phase4package-coronavirus-congress/9fde8dee094944ad/full.pdf (accessed 8/16/20). As the chief lobbyist for the Chamber of Commerce noted, when asked why his organization moved so quickly to make requests, "I am scrambling to make sure I am not the third monkey headed into Noah's Ark. . . . You got to hustle like hell before the flood hits." Eric Lipton. July 19, 2020. "Special Interests Mobilize to Get Piece of Next Virus Relief Package." *New York Times*, https://www.nytimes.com/2020/07/19/us/politics /coronavirus-relief-lobbyists-special-interests.html (accessed 8/16/20).

17. John F. Kennedy. February 19, 1956. "To Keep the Lobbyist within Bounds." *New York Times Magazine*, reported in *Congressional Record* (March 2, 1956), vol. 102, p. 3802–3.

18. OpenSecrets.org. February 6, 2019. "Most expensive midterm ever: Cost of 2018 election surpasses 5.7 billion." Center for Responsive Politics, https://www.opensecrets.org/news /2019/02/cost-of-2018-election-5pnt7bil/ (accessed 11/18/19).

19. Ben Brody. January 12, 2021. "Chamber of Commerce Head Blasts Trump for 'Completely Inexcusable' Conduct." Bloomberg, www.bloomberg.com/amp/news/articles /2021-01-12/chamber-head-blasts-trump-for-completely-inexcusable-conduct (accessed 1/21/21).

20. "Top PACs." Center for Responsive Politics, www.opensecrets.org/pacs/toppacs.php ?Type=C&pac=A&cycle=2018 (accessed 7/23/20).

21. For a list of PACs contributing the most money in each election cycle, see OpenSecrets .org. 2020. "Top PACs." Center for Responsive Politics, www.opensecrets.org/pacs /toppacs.php (accessed 7/23/20).

22. More precisely, multicandidate PACs can give a limit of $5,000 per election to a candidate, while PACs that are non-multicandidate (because they have fewer than 50 contributors or have been registered for less than six months) are limited to $2,700. Overall, members of the House are more reliant on PAC contributions than are senators and Senate candidates. But PAC money has been declining overall as a significant source of funds for all candidates, as we discuss in the following sections.

23. New York Times and CBS News. June 2, 2015. "Americans' View on Money in Politics." *New York Times*, www.nytimes.com/interactive/2015/06/02/us/politics/money-in -politics-poll.html (accessed 8/7/18).

24. As the Sunlight Foundation reported, for example, in the 2016 presidential primaries, a 501(c)(4) called Conservative Solutions spent millions of dollars to promote Senator Marco Rubio's candidacy, and was able to do so without revealing the names of individuals who contributed donations. See Libby Watson. January 21, 2016. "6 Years Later, the Impact of Citizens United Still Looms Large." Sunlight Foundation, https:// sunlightfoundation.com/2016/01/21/6-years-later-the-impact-of-citizens-united-still -looms-large/ (accessed 8/7/18).

25. See Charles R. Shipan and William R. Lowry. 2001. "Environmental Policy and Party Divergence in Congress." *Political Research Quarterly* 54(2): 245–63.

26. Gene Karpinski. November 3, 2014. "LCV's Dirty Dozen: The Names Are In." The Blog, www.huffingtonpost.com/gene-karpinski/lcvs-dirty-dozen-the-names-are-in_b _6095568.html (accessed 8/7/18).

27. League of Conservative Voters. 2018. "2018 Dirty Dozen." League of Conservation Voters, www.lcv.org/dirty-dozen/ (accessed 8/7/18).

28. Karpinski, "LCV's Dirty Dozen."

29. See Suzanne P. Clark. November 20, 2017. "Key Vote Letter: Senate 'Tax Cuts and Jobs Act.'" U.S. Chamber of Commerce, www.uschamber.com/letter/key-vote-letter-senate -tax-cuts-and-jobs-act (accessed 8/7/18); and Suzanne P. Clark. November 20, 2017. "Key Vote Alert." U.S. Chamber of Commerce, www.uschamber.com/sites/default/files /171120_kv_tax_reform_senate.pdf (accessed 8/7/18).

30. Of course, groups that do want change first must lobby to get their issue on the agenda. Geoffrey Lorenz has convincingly shown that groups are more successful at getting committees to put their issues on the agenda when they can form coalitions of groups that are diverse. Geoffrey Lorenz. January 2020. "Prioritized Interests: Diverse Lobbying Coalitions and Congressional Committee Agenda Setting." *The Journal of Politics* 82(1): 225–40.

31. John R. Wright. 1996. *Interest Groups and Congress: Lobbying, Contributions, and Influence*. Chicago: University of Chicago Press.

32. Frank R. Baumgartner and Bryan D. Jones. 1993. *Agenda and Instability in American Politics*. Chicago: University of Chicago Press.

33. Frank R. Baumgartner, Jeffrey M. Berry, Marie Hojnacki, David C. Kimball, and Beth L. Leech. 2009. *Lobbying and Policy Change: Who Wins, Who Loses, and Why*. Chicago, IL: University of Chicago Press.

34. Karl Evers-Hillstrom. April 24, 2020. "Coronavirus Stimulus Spurs Near-Record First-Quarter Lobbying Spending." Center for Responsive Politics, www.opensecrets.org/news/2020/04/coronavirus-stimulus-spurs-lobbying/ (accessed 1/21/21).

35. Richard L. Hall. 1996. *Participation in Congress*. New Haven, CT: Yale University Press.

36. Cecilia Kang. November 7, 2017. "Inside the Opposition to a Net Neutrality Repeal." *New York Times*, www.nytimes.com/2017/12/07/technology/net-neutrality-protests-opposition.html (accessed 8/7/18).

37. In this section, we focus on the nature and extent of business involvement in politics. Another change worth noting is that in the past, businesses generally got involved in politics through one key trade association (for example, the American Petroleum Institute) that represented a well-defined industry and market. Nowadays, businesses tend to be involved with multiple associations. These associations have proliferated as the economy has grown more complex.

38. This section draws heavily on Drutman's rich and insightful book, Lee Drutman. 2015. *The Business of America Is Lobbying: How Corporations Became Politicized and Politics Became More Corporate*. New York: Oxford University Press, particularly Chapter 3.

39. Drutman, *The Business of America Is Lobbying*, 48.

40. Drutman, *The Business of America Is Lobbying*, 49.

41. See David Vogel. 1989. *Fluctuating Fortunes: The Political Power of Business in America*, 33. New York: Basic Books.

42. Raymond A. Bauer, Ithiel de Sola Pool, and Lewis Anthony Dexter. 1972. *American Business and Public Policy*, 2nd ed. Chicago, IL: Aldine-Atherton.

43. Drutman, *The Business of America Is Lobbying*, 56.

44. Timothy LaPira. 2012. "The Allure of Reform: The Increasing Demand for Health Care Lobbying from Clinton's Task Force to Obama's Big [Expletive] Deal," in *Interest Group Politics*, 8th ed., ed. by Allan Cigler and Burdett Loomis, 345–74. Washington, DC: CQ Press.

45. See, for example, Bauer, Pool, and Dexter, *American Business and Public Policy*.

46. Richard L. Hall and Alan V. Deardorff. 2006. "Lobbying as Legislative Subsidy." *American Political Science Review* 100(91): 69–84.

47. Groups also can provide legislators with valuable information about the likelihood that a bill will pass and about how support for or opposition to a bill might affect a legislator's electoral prospects. See Wright, *Interest Groups and Congress*.

48. Marie Hojnacki and David C. Kimball. 1998. "Organized Interests and the Decision of Whom to Lobby in Congress." *American Political Science Review* 92(4): 775–90.

49. To identify the relevant groups, they drew on multiple sources, including *Congressional Quarterly*'s Washington Information Directory, articles in the *National Journal*, and lists of groups that testified at congressional hearings. One-third of groups responded to the survey. The data thus created 435 group-legislator pairs for each group, since each group is in a pair with each of the 435 representatives. Based on the answers to the questionnaire, the researchers identified whether lobbying took place within each pair.

50. This finding is consistent with other studies that argue that the composition of a district can help determine which issues a member acts on (Hall, *Participation in Congress*; Tracy Sulkin. 2005. *Issue Politics in Congress*. New York: Cambridge University Press).

51. Interestingly, the results also showed no effect for counteractive lobbying. That is, a group's decision about whether to lobby a legislator was unaffected by the number of opposing groups lobbying that legislator. They also showed more lobbying overall on the two issues—grazing and financial reform—that were narrower and less salient to the broader public.

52. See Drutman, *The Business of America Is Lobbying*, for a more detailed description of these types of lobbyists.

53. See Jeffrey L. Lazarus, Amy McKay, and Lindsey Herbel. 2016. "Who Walks through the Revolving Door? Examining the Lobbying Activity of Former Members of Congress." *Interest Groups and Advocacy* 5(1): 82–100. This increase has occurred despite laws meant to deter revolvers. As the authors write: "For example, members and staff must report outside job negotiations to the House or Senate Ethics Committee, former members of Congress who register to lobby lose their access to the chamber floor and other areas of the Capitol, staff are restricted from lobbying their former offices for 1 year, and registered lobbyists must disclose their former employment by Congress" (p. 84).

54. Center for Responsive Politics. "Revolving Door: Former Members of the 115th Congress." https://www.opensecrets.org/revolving/departing.php?cong=115 (accessed 6/25/2020).

55. See Jordi Blanes i Vidal, Mirko Draca, and Christian Fons-Rosen. 2012. "Revolving Door Lobbyists." *American Economic Review* 102(7): 3731–48 and Baumgartner et al., *Lobbying and Policy Change*, p. 208.

56. See Timothy M. LaPira and Herschel F. Thomas III. 2017. *Revolving Door Lobbying: Public Service, Private Influence, and the Unequal Representation of Interests*. Lawrence, KS: University Press of Kansas.

57. Catherine Ho. September 20, 2016. "Former Speaker John Boehner Heads to K Street." *Washington Post*, www.washingtonpost.com/news/powerpost/wp/2016/09/20/fomer-speaker-john-boehner-heads-to-k-street (accessed 8/7/18).

58. There are numerous reports of former members being paid thousands or millions of dollars by institutionalized interest groups to lobby. Former members have also registered as foreign agents. For example, at least four former members of Congress were hired by Saudi Arabia to lobby against a bill that would allow families to sue the Saudi government for its involvement in the September 2001 terrorist attacks. See H.R. 1628 - American Health Care Act of 2017. Maplight, http://classic.maplight.org/us-congress/bill/115-hr-1628/12273735/contributions-by-vote (accessed 8/7/18).

59. See, especially, Timothy M. LaPira and Herschel F. Thomas III. 2014. "Revolving Door Lobbyists and Interest Representation." *Interest Groups and Advocacy* 3(1): 4–29.

60. Lipton, "Special Interests Mobilize to Get Piece of Next Virus Relief Package."

61. Kang, "Inside the Opposition to a Net Neutrality Repeal."

62. See "National Rifle Assn." Center for Responsive Politics, https://www.opensecrets.org/orgs//summary?id=d000000082&cycle=2018 and Federal Election Commission. "Statistical Summary of 12-Month Campaign Activity of the 2017-2018 Election Cycle." Federal Election Commission, https://www.fec.gov/updates/statistical-summary-12-month-campaign-activity-2017-2018-election-cycle/ (both accessed 7/23/20). The NRA ranks much higher in terms of overall lobbying expenditures (85th) and outside spending (21st).

63. For example, Gregory Wawro. 2001. *Legislative Entrepreneurship in the U.S. House of Representatives*. Ann Arbor, MI: University of Michigan Press, investigated the relationship between campaign contributions and roll call votes on business and labor issues. He found that contributions are not a significant predictor of voting.

64. Glenn Thrush. April 24, 2018. "Mulvaney, Watchdog Bureau's Leader, Advises Bankers on Ways to Curtail Agency." *New York Times*, www.nytimes.com/2018/04/24/us/mulvaney-consumer-financial-protection-bureau.html (accessed 8/7/18). Notably, Mulvaney also emphasized that his staff always made time to meet with constituents.

65. See LaPira and Thomas, "Revolving Door Lobbyists and Interest Representation."

66. See Hall, *Participation in Congress*.

67. Richard L. Hall and Frank Wayman. September 1990. "Buying Time: Moneyed Interests and the Mobilization of Bias in Congressional Committees." *APSR* 84(3): 797–820.

68. They also ensure that their results show that contributions influence participation, rather than the other way around.

69. See Baumgartner et al., *Lobbying and Policy Change*. For an excellent summary and extension of these findings, see Frank R. Baumgartner, Jeffrey M. Berry, Marie Hojnacki, David C. Kimball, and Beth L. Leech. 2014. "Money, Priorities, and Stalemate: How Lobbying Affects Public Policy." *Election Law Journal* 13(1): 194–209.

70. Some studies of specific policy areas do show that groups are sometimes able to get the changes they seek, even if those changes are small. See the review article by John M. de Figueiredo and Brian Kelleher Richter. 2014. "Advancing the Empirical Research on Lobbying." *Annual Review of Political Science* 17: 163–85.

71. Norman J. Ornstein and Shirley Elder. 1978. *Interest Groups, Lobbying, and Policymaking*, 77. Washington, DC: CQ Press.

72. Peter Grier. September 28, 2009. "The Lobbyist through History: Villainy and Virtue." *Christian Science Monitor*, www.csmonitor.com/USA/Politics/2009/0928/the-lobbyist -through-history-villainy-and-virtue (accessed 8/7/18).

# Credits

## PHOTOS

### Chapter 1

p. **3:** AP Photo/Andrew Harnik;
p. **7:** Bettmann/Getty Images;
p. **12:** Lev Radin/Pacific Press/LightRocket via Getty Images;
p. **15:** Richard F. Fenno Jr. Papers D.359 Rare Books Special Collections and Preservation River Campus Libraries University of Rochester.

### Chapter 2

p. **19:** The Miriam and Ira D. Wallach Division of Art Prints and Photographs: Print Collection The New York Public Library;
p. **41:** Granger-All Rights Reserved;
p. **43:** AP Photo;
p. **47:** Richard Ellis/AFP/Getty Images;
p. **51:** US Senate/ZUMA Press/Newscom.

### Chapter 3

p. **61:** Mark Peterson/Redux;
p. **76:** Archive PL/Alamy Stock Photo;
p. **78:** nationalmap.gov/USGS;
p. **86 top:** Keystone Pictures USA/Alamy Stock Photo; **bottom:** Craig Lassig/Reuters/Newscom.

### Chapter 4

p. **103:** Andrew Lichtenstein/Corbis via Getty Images;
p. **111:** Everett Collection/Newscom;
p. **114:** Michael Laughlin/South Florida Sun-Sentinel via AP;
p. **124:** Andrew Harnik/Pool via Reuters/Alamy Stock Photo;
p. **125:** Alex Wong/Getty Images.

### Chapter 5

p. **137:** Andrew Harrer/Bloomberg via Getty Images;
p. **139:** Lenin Nolly/Sipa USA/Alamy Live News;
p. **156:** Kevin Dietsch/UPI/Alamy Stock Photo;
p. **167:** Mark Wilson/Getty Images.

### Chapter 6

p. **179:** Kevin Dietsch/UPI/Newscom;
p. **185 left:** Tom Williams/CQ Roll Call/Getty Images; **right:** Melina Mara/The Washington Post via Getty Images;
p. **187:** Alex Wong/Getty Images
p. **207:** ©20016 FreedomWorks, (Meadows photo): AP Photo/J.Scott Applewhite.

## Chapter 7

p. 217: Bill Clark/CQ Roll Call via AP
Images;
p. 225 left: Bill Clark/CQ Roll Call/Getty
Images; right: Reuters/Aaron Page
Bernstein/Alamy Stock Photo;
p. 236: AP Photo/Senate TV;
p. 244: Pete Marovich/ZUMApress.com
/Alamy Stock Photo.

## Chapter 8

p. 249: Bill Clark/CQ Roll Call via AP
Images;
p. 263: Kevin Dietsch/UPI/Newscom;
p. 274: Tom Williams/CQ Roll Call/
Newscom;
p. 278 top: Gordon Parks/The LIFE Picture
Collection/Getty Images; bottom: AP
Photo/Joe Marquette.

## Chapter 9

p. 283: Chip Somodevilla/Getty Images;
p. 285: Twitter;
p. 291: AP Photo/Ron Edmonds;
p. 297: Alex Wong/UPI/Alamy Stock Photo;
p. 299: Twitter;
p. 306 left: Rick Friedman/Corbis via Getty
Images; right: Bill Clark/CQ Roll Call/
Getty Images;
p. 314: AP Photo/Patrick Semansky.

## Chapter 10

p. 321: Douglas Graham/CQ Roll Call via
AP Images;
p. 326 top: Alex Edelman/Bloomberg via
Getty Images; bottom: Food and Drug
Administration;
p. 335: Xinhua/Alamy Live News;
p. 349: Tom Williams/CQ Roll Call/
Newscom.

## Chapter 11

p. 357: Tom Williams-Pool/Getty Images;
p. 363: Olivier Douliery/Sipa USA via AP
Images;
p. 365: Melina Mara/The Washington Post
via Getty Images;
p. 371: Clarissa Peterson The Leadership
Conference on Civil and Human Rights;
p. 386: Dana Verkouteren via AP.

## Chapter 12

p. 391: Drew Angerer/Getty Images;
p. 394: Saul Loeb/AFP via Getty Images;
p. 401: Andy Abeyta/Quad-City Times/
ZUMA Wire/Alamy Live News;
p. 405: Marlena Sloss/The Washington Post
via Getty Images;
p. 420: AP Photo/Jim Cole.

## TEXT

Figure 2.1: Appendix 1 from Jeffrey A.
Jenkins and Timothy Nokken, "Legisla-
tive Shirking in the Pre-Twentieth
Amendment Era: Presidential Influence,
Party Power, and Lame-Duck Sessions
of Congress, 1877–1933," *Studies in
American Development* 22(1), 111-140
(2008), reproduced with permission of
Cambridge University Press.
Figure 3.3: "Voter ID Enactments
2000–2016," Voter ID History (May 31,
2017), http://www.ncsl.org. Reprinted
by permission of the National Confer-
ence of State Legislatures.
Figures 4.1 and 4.2: From "The Changing
Face of Congress in 5 Charts." Pew
Research Center, Washington, D. C.
(February 2, 2017) http://www
.pewresearch.org/fact-tank/2017/02/02
/the-changing-face-of-congress-in-5
-charts/
Figure 4.5: Republished with permission of
Gallup, Inc. from "Congress and the
Public," Gallup.com, 2020; permission
conveyed through Copyright Clearance
Center, Inc.
Figure 5.1: Republished with permission of
SAGE College, from Barbara Sinclair,
*Unorthodox Lawmaking: New Legislative
Processes in the U.S. Congress*, 5th Ed.
(CQ Press, 2017); permission conveyed
through Copyright Clearance Center,
Inc.
Figure 6.3: From John Wilkerson and Barry
Pump, "The Ties That Bind: Coalitions
in Congress," in Eric Schickler and
Frances Lee, *The Oxford Handbook of
the American Congress* (Oxford Univer-
sity Press, 2011). Reproduced with
permission of the Licensor through
PLSclear.
Figure 6.4: "Party Means on The Liberal-
Conservative Dimensions Over Time by
Chamber" from "Polarization in

Congress," VoteView.com, accessed March 11, 2018. Reprinted with permission.

**Figure 6.5:** "Liberal-Conservative Partisan Polarization by Chamber" from "Polarization in Congress," VoteView.com, accessed March 11, 2018. Reprinted with permission.

**Figure 7.1:** From Lee Drutman, "The House Freedom Caucus Has Some Good Ideas on how the US House Should Operate," Vox.com, October 20, 2015. Reprinted with permission of Vox Media, LLC. https://www.vox.com/polyarchy/2015/10/20/9570747/house-freedom-caucus-process-demands

**Figure 7.6:** Republished with permission of University of Chicago Press, from Josh Ryan, *The Congressional Endgame: Interchamber Bargaining and Compromise* (University of Chicago Press, 2018); permission conveyed through Copyright Clearance Center, Inc.

**Figure 8.1:** From "Meet Your Unauthorized Federal Government," Politico.com, February 3, 2016. Copyright 2016 POLITICO LLC. Reprinted by permission of POLITICO LLC.

**Figure 8.6:** Figure 3 from Binder, Sarah, "Polarized We Govern?", May 2014, Center for Effective Public Management at Brookings. Reprinted by permission of The Brookings Institution.

**Figure 8.7:** Republished with permission of SAGE College, from Craig Volden and Alan Wiseman, "Legislative Effectiveness and Representation," *Congress Reconsidered*, 11th Ed., 2017; permission conveyed through Copyright Clearance Center, Inc.

**Figure 9.1:** From Jeffrey E. Cohen, *The President's Legislative Policy Agenda, 1789-2002* (Cambridge University Press, 2012). Reproduced with permission of the Licensor through PLSclear.

**Figure 9.5:** Republished with permission of John Wiley & Sons, from Alexander Bolton and Sharece Thrower, "Legislative Capacity and Executive Unilateralism," *American Journal of Political Science* 60(3): 649–663, 2015; permission conveyed through Copyright Clearance Center, Inc.

**Figure 9.7:** From "Congress and the Executive: Unilateralism and Legislative Bargaining," Bryan W. Marshall in *New Directions in Congressional Politics*, ed. Jamie L. Carson, Copyright 2012, Routledge. Reproduced by permission of Taylor & Francis Group.

**Figure 9.8:** From Daniel Paul Franklin and Michael P. Fix, "The Best of Times and the Worst of Times: Polarization and Presidential Success in Congress," *Congress & the Presidency 43*(33): 377–394, 2006, reprinted by permission of American University, Center for Congressional & Presidential Studies, https://www.american.edu/spa/ccps/journal.cfm

**Figure 9.10:** Republished with permission of Princeton University Press from Douglas L. Kriner and Eric Schickler, *Investigating the President: Congressional Checks on Presidential Power* (Princeton University Press, 2016); permission conveyed through Copyright Clearance Center, Inc.

**Figure 10.1:** From Reg Stats, https://regulatorystudies.columbian.gwu.edu/reg-stats. Used by permission of the Regulatory Studies Center.

**Figure 10.2:** Republished with permission of John Wiley & Sons, from Ian Ostrander, "The Logic of Collective Inaction: Senatorial Delay in Executive Nominations," *American Journal of Political Science* 60(4): 1063–1076, 2016; permission conveyed through Copyright Clearance Center, Inc.

**Figure 10.4:** Republished with permission of John Wiley & Sons, from Robert J. McGrath and Jason A. MacDonald, "Retrospective Congressional Oversight and the Dynamics of Legislative Influence over the Bureaucracy," *Legislative Studies Quarterly 41*(4): 899–934, 2016; permission conveyed through Copyright Clearance Center, Inc.

**Figure 11.1:** From Matthew R. Christiansen & William N. Eskridge, Jr., *Congressional Overrides of Supreme Court Statutory Interpretation Decisions, 1967–2011*, 92 Texas L. Rev. 1317, 1317–1541 (2014). Copyright Texas Law Review Association. Reprinted with permission.

**Figure 11.2:** From Tom S. Clark, *The Limits of Judicial Independence* (New York, Cambridge University Press, 2011).

Reproduced with permission of the Licensor through PLSclear.

**Figure 11.3:** From *Routledge Handbook of Judicial Behavior,* Robert M. Howard and Kirk A. Randazzo, Copyright 2017 Routledge.

**Figure 12.1:** "Total Spending on Lobbying and Number of Lobbyists in the United States, 1998–2017," from OpenSecrets .org. Reprinted with permission of Center for Responsive Politics.

**Figure 12.2:** "Outside Spending by Cycle, Excluding Party Committees," from OpenSecrets.org. Reprinted with permission of Center for Responsive Politics.

**Figure 12.3:** From Lee Drutman, *The Business of America Is Lobbying: How Corporations Became Politicized and Politics Became More Corporate* (Oxford University Press, 2015). Reproduced with permission of the Licensor through PLSclear.

# Index/Glossary

Page numbers in *italics* refer to figures or tables.